Praise for
Iowa: The Definitive Collection

"Really a fascinating read, whether you read only one or two of
the 90-plus entries or study them all."
—Cedar Rapids *Gazette*

"The table of contents alone is breath-taking—six pages of selections
ranging from Black Hawk and the Iowa Constitution to contemporary
poets laureate Ted Kooser and Mary Swander."
—*Annals of Iowa*, publication of the
State Historical Society of Iowa

"Ice Cube Press has another winner with its Iowa reader, edited by
Zachary Michael Jack. The omnibus contains 93 selections covering a
wide range of subjects written by (who else!) Iowans."
—*Wapsipinicon Almanac*

IOWA

The Definitive Collection

CLASSIC & CONTEMPORARY READINGS
BY IOWANS, ABOUT IOWA

Edited by Zachary Michael Jack

Black Hawk	Glenn Miller
Buffalo Bill	Frank Luther Mott
Carrie Chapman Catt	Herbert Quick
Paul Engle	Jay Sigmund
Bob Feller	Wallace Stegner
John T. Frederick	Phil Stong
Hamlin Garland	Ruth Suckow
Susan Glaspell	Billy Sunday
James Hearst	Mary Swander
Herbert Hoover	Henry A. Wallace
Emerson Hough	"Uncle Henry" Wallace
Ted Kooser	Grant Wood
Aldo Leopold	& more Iowa greats

TALL CORN BOOKS
NORTH LIBERTY, IOWA

Iowa The Definitive Collection
Classic and Contemporary Readings by Iowans, about Iowa

Copyright © 2009 by Zachary Michael Jack
3rd printing, 2011

ISBN 9781888160383

Library of Congress Control Number: 2008943259

Tall Corn Books, a place studies imprint of the
Ice Cube Books & Press, LLC (est. 1993)
205 North Front Street
North Liberty, Iowa 52317-9302
www.icecubepress.com
steve@icecubepress.com

No portion of this book may be reproduced in any way without permission, except for brief quotations for review, or educational work, in which case the publisher shall be provided two copies. Contact: steve@icecubepress.com

Manufactured and home spun in the USA

The paper used in this publication meets the minimum requirements of the American National Standard for Information Sciences—Permanence of Paper for Printed Library Materials, ANSI Z39.48-1992

Remembering Laughter by Wallace Stegner. Copyright © 1937 by Wallace Stegner. Copyright renewed © 1965 by Wallace Stegner. Reprinted by permission of Brandt and Hochman Literary Agents, Inc.

Featuring the history and the history-makers of the following Iowa counties and towns.

A GEOGRAPHIC INDEX

Lake Mills
LeClaire
Lee County
Le Mars
Lewis
Linn County
Lisbon
Long Grove
Louisa County
Low Moor
Lucas County
Madison County
Mahaska County
Manchester
Marion
Marion County
Marshall County
Marshalltown
Mason City
McGregor
Mechanicsville
Mediapolis
Melrose
Mills County
Mitchell County
Monona County
Monroe County
Montgomery County
Morning Sun
Mount Ayr
Mount Pleasant
Mount Vernon

Muscatine
Napoleon
Nashua
New Hampton
New London
Newton
O'Brien County
Okoboji
Oldebolt
Orient
Osage
Oskaloosa
Ottumwa
Page County
Palo Alto County
Paola
Pella
Peosta
Pittsburg
Polk County
Prairie City
Prescott
Protivin
Red Oak
Rochester
Ringgold County
Sac City
Sac County
Saint Ansgar
Salem
Scott County
Shelby County

Sigourney
Sioux County
Smithland
Spillville
Spirit Lake
Springdale
State Center
Steamboat Rock
Stone City
Story County
Tabor
Tama
Tipton
Union County
Urbandale
Van Buren County
Van Meter
Villisca
Wapello County
Warren County
Waterloo
Waubeek
Waverly
West Branch
West Des Moines
West Liberty
Winnebago County
Winneshiek County
Woodbury County
Yarmouth

Contents

To you, Iowa, you beautiful old Building and Loan

Introducing Iowa: An Appreciation, a Memoir, a Love Story, an Explanation, a Conspiracy Theory

Zachary Michael Jack

Iowa gets under your skin.

In 1854, the selfsame year my ancestors, the Pickerts, arrived from New York to settle what is now our Iowa Heritage Farm in Cedar County, another New Yorker, Mrs. Frances D. Gage, set out by rail across our newly birthed state. Her mission was to lecture our babe-in-the-woods, wet-behind-the-ears commonwealth on the importance of temperance and of women's rights. Iowa, however, had something else in store for the ambitious Mrs. Gage: an absolute, angels-singing conversion. In a hasty, almost giddy dispatch sent to the *New York Tribune*, she reported the following telltale exchange as overheard on the train to Oskaloosa:

> "Look, is not that splendid? Rolling prairie, just enough to drain it; vale, hill, woodland, park, lawn, grove, meadow, field, shrubbery, and garden, and all in luxuriant bloom and beauty from Nature's own hand; brooks, running over pebbly beds, gushing springs, or wells easily made, of clear and sparkling water. Is it not beautiful?"
>
> "Beautiful, beautiful, beautiful!" echo the ladies.
>
> "Beau-ti-ful!" answers the quail from the topmost rail of that stake-and-rider fence around that magnificent field of rye.
>
> "Beau-t-iful, beautiful!" whistles the whippoorwill at midday, in the dark grove of elms and oaks by the wayside. He had only changed his dolorous note to suit the sunshine.
>
> "Iowa for me!' says the young wife.
>
> "Bright and beautiful as a fairy dream!" says the merry maiden.

An appreciation

Fortunately for me, Iowa turned out to be for the Pickerts, too. And if you're reading this book, I imagine Iowa is—has been—for you as well.

Here then is a book—a big book—of readings by Iowans, about Iowa, for Iowa. From the beginning, the goal has been to capture this great state by going both genre-wide (campaign platforms, creeds, diaries, editorials, ethnographic studies, fictions, government documents, history, humor, journalism, legal opinions, letters, memoirs, pamphlets, speeches, travel narratives, and more) and history-deep (from Black Hawk's speech on being ordered to move west to Iowa in 1831 to Iowa writer-anthropologist Robert Leonard's 2007 roll call of the many Iowans he has known). The idea is to let Iowans—those who are world-famous (among those featured herein are Carrie Chapman Catt, Bob Feller, Susan Glaspell, Herbert Hoover, Ted Kooser, Aldo Leopold, Glenn Miller, Wallace Stegner, Henry Wallace, Grant Wood, and others) those known only to us, and those known hardly at all—to relay the history of their state in lieu of leaving it to the voiceless hacks penning many of today's sanitized texts.

Iowa has always been a land of writers. Its most conspicuous gift, among so many, is its voice, whether issued from songbird, tall corn, or typewriter.

A MEMOIR

My first real dose of Tall Corn history came in fifth grade—the same year a cadre of guest speakers first tickled our young ears with talk of birds and bees. Despite a perfectly platonic crush on the blonde-haired, blue-eyed, beautifully bespectacled Anya McMurray, I hadn't an inkling, at least that I can recall, of what might be called lust. I'm sure I didn't know how babies were made, and I didn't much care. In a classic bit of educational mistiming masquerading as preventative do-gooding, the sex talk arrived well before I knew what to do with it.

By contrast, I waited primed and pumped for our fifth-grade Iowa history lessons. Who could forget the enthusiasm with which Mrs. Bidlack, our over-the-hill, history-loving school marm—the one everybody else was too cool to like—unveiled Iowa's comical "war" with Missouri over a slim stretch of borderland and some particularly productive honey trees. For some strange reason, the Honey Wars captured me. I didn't know what a bee-tree was back then, so I imagined gnarled hardwoods oozing gold and a few hundred poorly trained, poorly equipped, poorly dressed conscripts on both sides of the border pretending they wouldn't rather be home farming. History reveals my whimsical imaginings weren't so far from the truth.

And then, just as soon as the muse of Iowa history cooed, she disappeared—poof—just like our sex speakers. Surely, our unit on Iowa lore must have lasted several weeks, but if it did, I don't remember any of it beyond some passing mention of Iowa's first territorial governor, Robert Lucas, whose one-time retirement home, Plum Grove, lurked behind a weed-tangled, wrought-iron fence not far from Henry Wadsworth Longfellow Elementary, where I dreamed of honey, and Anya.

Fifth grade ended, Anya flew the coop, and even Mrs. Bidlack was history but for a postcard I received, out of the blue, later that summer penned from some Civil War battlefield in Georgia. She must have known the Iowa history bee had stung me.

Sadly, I would never again be the beneficiary of a unit devoted exclusively to Iowa history—not in junior high, not in high school, not even at Iowa State University, where I suppose we had better things to do in honors history classes then study a ragtag Iowa militia or Iowa's stretch of Underground Railroad. But it wasn't just Iowa history that had gone missing. I majored in literature at Iowa State, and I don't remember studying a single Iowa writer in depth—not one—unless you count California's Jane Smiley. But I did learn the difference between a diphthong and a glottal, by golly.

The point is not that my education proved inferior—or that I was deprived in any way—quite the contrary. It's simply that the lessons taught me about my homeplace, the place that had shaped me, the place whose history would be mine to have and to hold, for better and for worse till death do us part, turned out to be patently incomplete, or altogether absent.

And so I cooked up this book as much for myself as for the Mrs. Bidlacks of our state and their young, soak-it-up-like-a-sponge acolytes. While an early middle age such as mine brings the horrors of love handles, it also sometimes comes bearing the gift of productive impatience—with one's own ignorance, with the "options" as they are. Thankfully, it sometimes piques the "Iowa stubborn" necessary to make for yourself and for others what does not otherwise exist—to write the book you wish you would have been taught from.

Happily, the movement to share with Iowans the rich lessons of Iowa history is well underway. In 2007 the state legislature passed the Iowa Studies Bill, SF 2320, directing the Department of Cultural Affairs to assist Iowa teachers in finding ways to incorporate Iowa studies into their classrooms.

It's an auspicious if not belated start.

A LOVE STORY

My good friend Tom Dean, who writes speeches for the president of the University of Iowa, wrote recently to a young Iowan advocating a return home: "I would encourage you to think about what you're willing to do for love. When you love another person, you get creative about making things work."

The notion of loving a state as one cherishes a beloved is at once self-evident and unexpectedly profound. All of us understand love of country, *amor patriae*, but what about love of state, love of county, love of township, town, farm, section? It seems somehow a lesser love to embrace a state, a parochial or even small-minded affection—so nineteenth century. And yet what if love rightly, and richly, begins in the smallest units, with that with which we are most intimate and most near? And how can one love a person without loving the place that birthed them—it would be, to use an Iowa simile, like drinking the milk without hugging the cow.

And so when I think about love, as I do these moonlit nights, I think about Iowa. And the kind of love I feel isn't all yellow corn and yellow school buses, red roses and red skies at sunset. It's also four-foot-high, damn-it-all-to-hell snowdrift-love. It's how-could-my-neighbors-sell-out-and-build-a-hog-confinement indignant-love. Apropos to the spiritual gifts of such a love-hate relationship, Monroe County writer Leo Ward recalls his Irish-Iowan neighbor, Muck, saying, "God means that every man should have something to suffer."

And, yes, I have suffered for Iowa—suffered in my career, in my family, in my relationships—but it has, prodigally, given back. This, then, is how I know it's real. And, beyond the love of my clan, I know of no purer, more illustrative, more edifying love than the love I have for this, my home state, my cross to bear.

My hope is that this collection might embody that affecton, or at least gesture at it.

An explanation

Over the course of a year and countless hours spent researching, interlibrary loaning, typing and, finally, editing and introducing, this collection grew...and grew...and grew to over ninety historic readings—like the man-eating plant, Audrey II, in *Little Shop of Horrors*. When I wasn't researching or editing, I took to doing odd jobs around the farm—fence-pulling, hole-filling, weed-hoeing, summer seeding. By night, I paced my long, lonely lane by moonlight when restlessness overtook me, contemplating the corn as it lifted its spiked, uniform leaves toward starshine like some strange race of lunar supplicant. The platooning of grunt work and brain work somehow sustained me. What could be a more quintessential Iowa tonic?

As a native Iowan and a scholar of its history and literature, I mostly followed my nose in deciding what and what not to include. For recommendations I turned to peers at the Iowa State Historical Library, especially Mary Bennett. Always, I endeavored to choose prose that would speak to Iowans young and old, and especially to younger Iowans, for whom history is often an awkward fit. Thus, I looked for pieces that were Iowa-wise but young at heart; pieces that explored need-to-know state landmarks and legends, and especially passages concerning Iowa young adulthoods and attendant rites of passage. I clapped my hands when idealism and its brother, pragmatism, showed up in the same reading together, and celebrated selections that conjured our peculiar Iowa inheritance of agrarianism, spiritualism, and patriotism. In short, I searched for works that distilled an Iowa quintessence across the years, decades, centuries. I eagerly reached for readings that, when quilted, might serve as an Iowa primer or secular, Tall Corn catechism.

What information, I asked myself over and over, should an Iowan not be without? Who among our own must they hear from? These questions led me to include the best-known figures in this anthology, folks like Carrie Chapman Catt, Bob Feller, Susan Glaspell, Herbert Hoover, Ted Kooser, Aldo Leopold, Glenn Miller, Wallace Stegner, Henry Wallace, Grant Wood, and others. A corollary question was: what must they hear about? And this query, in turn, pointed me in the direction of, for example, the Cherry Sisters, the Villisca Murders, the Honey Wars, the Spirit Lake Massacre, the Underground Railroad, John Brown in Iowa, the Civil War, Iowa prohibition, the Cow Wars, the Farm Crisis, the Iowa State Fair, the Little Brown Church in the Vale, and all the other Iowa fixtures fit to print.

Of course, all this is predicated on a clear definition of who "qualifies" as an Iowan. That question vexed, as one would expect in a state, where, as the *WPA Guide to Iowa* put it in 1930, "An Iowan is as likely to be found in any other of the forty-eight states as in his native one, if the term be taken simply to mean a person who was born in Iowa." Citing a 1935 survey by the National Resources Board, the guide reveals that more than one-third of all the children of Iowa were living elsewhere—1,084,000 of them. Echoing that sentiment, Iowa's Pulitzer Prize-winning author, Wallace Stegner, who himself left the Hawkeye State for the West in general and California in particular, writes in his 1937 article "The Trail of the Hawkeye": "Glenway Wescott has described the Middle West as, among other things, a 'state of mind of people born where they do not like to live.'" More recently, Iowa's John Gjerde, a history professor in—where else—California, shows how the number of Iowans living outside Iowa's borders reached a whopping 37% by the early 1970s, many of them settling in southern California, the so-called "seacoast of Iowa."

So, to be an Iowan, is, by the numbers anyway, to be a gypsy, an itinerant preaching the Iowa gospel to the Beautiful People elsewhere. In a collection such as this, some begrudging allowance must be made for our reputation as a net exporter of leaders and luminaries. Still, I set a somewhat higher bar than my editorial predecessors in Hawkeye lore. After all, Jacob Swisher and Carl Herbe, in their intriguing book *Iowa History as Told in Biography* (1932) write of Mark Twain as an "Iowa boy" for no other reason than his older brother Orion co-owned the Muscatine *Journal* for a brief period in the early 1850s. By the logic of such annexation, Iowa might as well claim Abraham Lincoln, for, as popular midwestern nonfictionist Homer Croy tells us in his book *Corn Country*, the Great Emancipator once owned a farm between our borders. For me, Twain and Lincoln don't earn their Iowa keep, and neither, for that matter, does the great W. P. Kinsella, who, while writing what is arguably the ultimate contemporary Iowa classic, *Shoeless Joe* (1982) stayed in Iowa only long enough to matriculate in the Iowa Writers' Workshop, and maybe, just maybe, husk an ear of corn or two.

To be "in" in my book, an author had either to be born or raised in Iowa or devote their adult life to working in, and writing about, the home state. Of course, given what we know about Iowans' absconding ways, more folks cleared the bar by virtue of the former criterion (birthright or rearing) than by the latter. Logical exceptions to these "membership requirements" were made for early pioneers, for whom it was neither possible to be born in "Iowa" per se or to devote one's adult life to what was then an infant among states.

Beyond the aforementioned considerations, the following criteria, listed in no particular order, helped keep me honest as a gatekeeper:

• Historical relevance of selections

• Gender, racial, and ethnic diversity of authors and subjects

• Timeliness and timelessness (I looked for readings spread evenly across the years of Iowa's existence, especially in the first one hundred years after statehood (1846–1946). Post-World War II, the years between selections increase, as the bar for "classic" becomes necessarily harder to clear as one reaches the present day. For timelessness, I sought topics of heft and lastingness, not the kind of flash-in-the pan headline, trend, or fad that dominates much newspaper copy.)

• Iowa setting or subject (I steered clear of work set in a place that might be Iowa, insisting on material confirmed to be set in our state or, in the case of fiction, based on a real-life town or place in Iowa.)

• Ample length (I resisted the urge to trim the volume by running 300 words where 1500 were needed. I like my helpings large.)

• Readability for scholar, student, and historian. (I chose work aimed, in the first place, at a general readership, hence the absence of merely academic prose or copious footnotes.)

• Genre diversity. (In making selections, I gave all relevant genres equal opportunity. I was open to the sentiment Bradford Burns expresses in *Kinship with the Land*, namely that "Iowa's novelists have been far superior to historians in re-creating the past and investing it with significance." Because I view prose as the most familiar genre to the reading public and, therefore, the most small "d" democratic, and because there have been several collections of Iowa poetry and lyric published in the last thirty-odd years, including Gary and Judith Gildner's fine anthology *Out of This World: Poems from the Hawkeye State* (1975), I excluded poetry.)

• Primacy. (As I aimed for a documentary history and one palpably different than conventional Iowa history texts, I opted, whenever possible, for firsthand accounts of historic events, either as reported on the ground in the community or as later recalled by those who lived them. For example, in choosing a reading to represent the Great Depression in the Hawkeye State, I preferred James Hearst's "We All Worked Together: A Memory of Drought and Depression" over the many secondhand and scholarly accounts of the Iowa Dust Bowl years.)

• Geographic diversity within Iowa. (An anthology claiming to represent the Land Between Two Rivers should do its level best to reach north and south, east and west, Missouri to Mississippi. While settlement patterns and population demographics, then as now, mean many of the writers featured herein hail from the earliest settled towns and counties in more populous eastern Iowa, efforts have been made at balance.)

• Objectivity, with advocacy. (So that this cross-section of quintessentially Iowa readings transcends mere boosterism and greeting card sentimentality to achieve a more robust sense of statehood, of self.)

A CONSPIRACY THEORY

The program for cultural extermination is as ancient as it is obvious, and even as I conclude this introduction with great joy and gratitude for our state as it is and as it shall be, this project itself, it's worth recalling, arises from a conspicuous cultural deficit—the collective forgetting of the best our homeland has produced. As Iowan Carl Van Vechten wryly noted in his 1920 send-up, "The Folk Songs of Iowa": "There is indeed more of the Rome of the Empire in the Rome of today than there is of the Iowa of 1870 in the Iowa City of today." And no less a luminary than Grant Wood cautioned his fellow Iowans in his 1931 manifesto "Revolt Against the City," that, given the slow cultural extinction even then underway, that a true regionalist must be something more than "a mere eulogist; he may have even be a severe critic." So, tipping our cap to Master Wood for a moment, let's consider how such staggering loss of heritage happens, where and with whom it originates, and what it all means to us, the regrettably dispossessed. And after, and ever, let us also make a case for the pulsing, groundbreaking, seed-bearing life of Iowa, instead of lingering over its alleged and epic death.

Work backwards. Reverse the psychology. Turn back the clock. Imagine yourself, for one fabulously nefarious, completely irrational moment, hell-bent on destroying or at least disabling folkways in a state like Iowa…initiating a program of cultural unmaking. Perhaps fancy yourself as some archvillian orchestrating a campaign of cultural sabotage for some huge, protean, vaguely unsettling pseudo-entity…I don't know, something like the WTO or Darth Vader's Empire. The playbook would already be well-known to you.

Step One: convince the target population of its native inferiority. Step Two: educate its young elsewhere, away from parents and grandparents. Step Three: disable or capitalize, at a profit, its native industries. Step Four: turn its farmers and factory workers into net consumers; turn sacred calling into mere "business." Step Five: convince the citizenry that what it needs for a good life may be bought at any price, without consequence. Step Six: persuade its indigenous writers, historians, pastors, philosophers, newspaper editors, and filmmakers—anyone with a redemptive or critical vision—that the real story is elsewhere. If that fails, buy them out. Step Seven: sanitize its language, purifying the dialect of it its homespun colloquialisms, homely pidgins, and original idioms. Claim its best scribes as your own.

I've never been much of a conspiracy theorist, and doubtless you, fair reader, are still more reasonable than me. And yet together we must admit the steps above sound awfully familiar in a state that yearly loses its family-owned newspapers and farms, recruits a smaller percentage of its indigenous students for enrollment in its state universities, and retains an ever smaller percentage, by comparison with neighboring states, of students who do complete a four-year degree within our borders. Meanwhile, name me one contemporary, Iowa-born writer, one who has lived in the state their whole life with the possible exception of a stint in graduate school, the military, or a study-abroad, and who has "made it big." Pulitzer Prize-winner Jane Smiley? Born in California; lives there now. University of Iowa Pulitzer Prize-winner Marilyn Robinson…born in Idaho. These are phenomenally gifted writers, don't get me wrong—the best of the best—and Iowa has been blessed to have them, but they are not Iowans in the strictest sense. They know our values, perhaps understand them better and more objectively than we ever will, but they are not *of* our values. So, yes, to be a truly Iowa writer still comes at an unnecessarily heavy price.

All of which is to say that if even a part of us—a whit, a frog's hair, an iota— allows that the aforementioned steps of cultural extermination might be operant, then we have serious work to do, and that work quite simply involves supporting what's quintessentially Iowan. The task before us asks that we let the state speak for itself with something akin to its native voice, even as that voice evolves, changes, and diversifies. And when hard times arrive, as they inevitably do, perhaps they arrive, in part, to remind us of the urgency of adding our voice to that homegrown chorus. Thus Grant Wood's words to Iowans from 1935, penned from the throes of the last Great Depression, offer abiding hope. "The talented youths," he writes, "who, in the expansive era of unlimited prosperity, were carried away on waves of enthusiasm...wanting nothing so much as to get away from the old things of home, now, when it all collapses, come back solidly to the good earth."

And so a project as modest as this, which merely offers a sort of hymnal which may be sung from when the singing mood strikes, which might be used by an Iowa teacher at such time as that teacher deems the history of his or her own people worth teaching, and by students seeking an answer to the fair and reasonable questions: Who else has come before me? What did they say or do that's worth caring about?

My favorite writer as a teen and young adult, the poet W. B. Yeats, once wrote this of cultural inheritance in his classic poem "Sailing to Byzantium":

> Nor is there singing school but studying
>
> Monuments of its own magnificence;

It took me years to get those lines—in fact I'm still not sure I cotton to their meaning completely—but what I think they say is this: there is no more important song to be sung than the song of noble deeds; there is no simpler, purer, or more democratic education than studying the best a state or a people have done or said—monuments of its own magnificence. It makes sense that a poet from Ireland—a small, green, agrarian place like our own, a place dismissed, disparaged, and nearly destroyed, and just now re-possessing itself—would learn such a lesson, and share it with the world.

My greatest pangs of indignation and regret strike me in my idlest moments. I do not think I am alone in this. Sometimes, staring out across the cornfields, I regret we've yet to shape our lives the way we buy our wine—with a firm, old-fashioned devotion to place. So, though a French nose points higher in the air than is good for it, lord knows, and much higher than a Hawkeye's, the French have a word for something we Anglophones—we Iowaphones—have missed. They call it *terrior*, that *je ne sais quoi* signifying something vital, and indivisible: the smallest patch of earth from which a crop, be it vine, branch, or person, grows. It's that peculiar hillside, hillock, and humus that ripens the grape which makes the wine that tastes like no other. It's that singular milieu which feeds and quenches the writer who fleshes and sweetens the native soil.

And so I give you this inadequate but well-meaning book of Iowa, with the hope it is worthy of song, and, if not song, then wine, and if not wine, at least occasional recitation.

And if none of these will do, dear pragmatic Iowa reader, and the kindling runs short some winter, do us all proud; do what comes naturally to you.

All material in this historic collection has been previously published. Unless otherwise noted, readings are arranged chronologically by the date of the earliest known publication of the source material. Where two or more readings bear the same date-stamp, selections have been ordered alphabetically by last name of author, with one exception—the handful of readings from the anthology *Prairie Gold* (1917), whose original order of presentation is herein preserved. For the vast majority of readings, source acknowledgement is made using the formulation *from* (indicating an excerpt from a larger work), the title of the source, and the earliest known copyright date. Where a title appears set in quotation marks in lieu of italics, the assumption may be made, unless noted to the contrary, that the piece is a stand-alone article or short story and that its source will be named in the introduction. Where multiple works with titles set in quotation marks appear from an anthology or from a journal—for example the *Midland Monthly*—note of that fact has been made in the introduction for the first reading in the grouping. Where the word *from* does not precede the source reference, the assumption may generally be made that the work appears in full. Where appropriate, acknowledgement for previously published material under copyright and known to require reprint permissions is made in the acknowledgements section. For the sake of brevity and the most dynamic distillation possible, material in some readings has been omitted between the first and last paragraphs. In such cases, an asterisk has been inserted and an extra line-space added to show where the piece deviates from the paragraph order of the material as originally published; in what is intended to be an accessible, highly readable collection, footnotes have been avoided. In the small minority of cases where footnotes appeared in the original, they have either been removed as noted in the introduction to the relevant piece, or the basic information cited in the original footnote, if deemed necessary, has been inserted in brackets. Other information judged by the editor as crucial to an understanding of the texts has been added in brackets at the point of need, in-text. As the intent here is historical veracity, the original language of the articles has been preserved, even where obsolete, anachronistic, or biased language was employed. With the exception of the above, the writings have been edited to conform to standards of contemporary usage.

Work in *Iowa, the Definitive Collection* not otherwise identified in the acknowledgments section is believed to be in the public domain by virtue of a pre-1923 publication date or by lack of copyright renewal in the case of material published between 1923 and 1963.

"Speech of Black Hawk" (1831)

Chief Black Hawk

The earliest reading in the collection comes from a reluctant Iowan, the great Sauk warrior and autobiographer, Black Hawk, whose people were forcibly removed to Iowa from their ancestral home at Saukenuk, where Rock Island is today. In the speech below, reprinted from Galland's Iowa Emigrant (1840), Black Hawk speaks to the Sauk and Fox after having received orders to remove to the west bank of the Mississippi—Iowa—where Black Hawk spent the rest of his life as both celebrity and literary sensation. In the speech that follows from 1831, the great chief speaks of a fraudulent treaty of "sixteen winters ago"—the treaty of 1816—by which his people ceded more than 50 million acres to the U.S. government. Blawk Hawk refused to acknowledge the treaty, and, resisting Chief Keokuk and other moderates among his people, engaged in the war that would bear his name, the Black Hawk War of 1832. Eventually, Black Hawk was caught, paraded before President Andrew Jackson, and placed in the custody of his rival Chief Keokuk for a short time before living out the rest of his famous life as an Iowan.

Warriors, sixty summers or more have passed away, since our fathers sat down here, while our mothers erected their lodges on this delightful spot. Upon these pastures, our horses have fattened for many successive summers these fields, cultivated by the hands of our wives and daughters, have always yielded up a plentiful supply of corn, beans, squashes, melons, etc. and from the shoals of these rivers, whose limpid waters here unite, our young men have always obtained the wanted abundance of excellent fish. Here too, you are protected by the broad current of the majestic river, [Mis-se-Se-po], from the assaults of your old and inveterate enemy, the Shaw-hawk [Sioux]. Thus supplied with food and protected from harm, our summers have passed away in mirth and gladness. With what reluctance many of you have quitted these scenes of joy and pastime, even for one winter, our patrol can testify, who have been charged with bringing up the rear of our encampment, when leaving this place in the fall for our wintering ground. And yet another, and still stronger tie binds us to this residence of our fathers. In these little enclosures, some of wood and others of stone, which we see scattered all over these plains, now rest, in undisturbed repose, the bones of our dearest relatives, our bravest warriors and many of our greatest chiefs and orators. But alas! Warriors, what do I hear? The birds which have long gladdened these groves, which the sweet melody of their notes, are now singing a melancholy song! They say, "The read man must forsake his home, to make room for the white man." The Long-knives desire it, and must have a new field opened for the exercise of their speculation and avarice. To accomplish which, the red man's wife and daughter now surrender the little piece of ground which they had marked as their own, by many days of labor and severe toil. Widows, you must forsake forever the graves of your husbands! Mothers, you shall no more see the sacred spot where the bones of your children rest! These, all these, you must forsake forever! And for what reasons, are we told that we must leave forever, our houses and our homes—the land of our nativity and the graves of our fathers! Because the Long-knives want to live in our houses, plant corn in our fields and plow up our graves! Yes, they wish to plant corn in these graves! And can you refuse a request at once so modest, and so reasonable? They want to fatten their hogs on the bodies of our dead, who are not yet moldered in their graves! Will you refuse? We are ordered to remove to the west bank of the Majestic River; there to erect other houses and open new fields, of which we shall soon again be robbed by these pale faces! They tell us that our great father, the Chief of the Long-knives, has commanded us, his red children, to give this, our greatest town, our greatest graveyard and our best home, to his white children! Do you believe this story? I do not. It cannot be true. We have vagabonds among us, and so have the Long-knives also—we have even liars of our own nation, and the Long-knives, no doubt, abound with such. The truth therefore, must be this; that a few base and avaricious of the Long-knife tribe, who, in visiting the lead mines, or exploring the country, have passed by this place, and seeing this delightful spot, have become enamored with it; have thought this to be the most probable stratagem which would promise them success in driving us from our homes; that they may seize upon our town and cornfields. But I repeat it again, it cannot be true—it is impossible that so great a Chief, as the Chief of the Long-knives is said to be, should act so unjustly, as to drive six thousand of those, whom he is pleased to call his "red children," from their native homes, from the graves of their ancestors, and from the scenes of the most tender and sacred associations. Compelling them to seek new homes, to build other houses, and to prepare new cornfields; and that, too, in a country where our women and children will be in the continual danger of being murdered by our enemies: and all this injustice is to be done, and this distress inflicted, merely to gratify the greedy avarice of twenty or thirty persons of his "white children!" No! No! Our great father, the Chief of the Long-knives, will never do this thing! Shall we therefore leave this home of our fathers, on account of such silly and unreasonable tales. No! I have heard these same fables every spring, for the last seven winters, that we were to be driven from this place. You know we have offered the Long-knives a large tract of country on the west side of the Majestic River, abounding with lead, if they would relinquish their unjust claim to this little spot. We will therefore repair our houses, which these place-faced vagabonds have torn down and burnt through the past winter, and we will plant our corn as usual; and if these white intruders annoy us we will them to depart. We will offer them no violence, except in self-defense, and even then, we will only protect ourselves and our families from their dog-like assaults. We will not kill their cattle or destroy any of their property, but their *scutah wapo*, (whiskey) we will search for and destroy, by throwing it out upon the earth, wherever we find it. We know that when men are filled with that liquor, they think that they are very rich; perhaps if their liquor was destroyed, and they should become sober, they may not then think that they are owners of all the earth! We have asked permission of these intruders to cultivate our own fields, around which they have erected wooden walls. They have refused, and have even forbid us the privilege of climbing over. We will, therefore, throw down these walls which keep us from our fields. And as these pale faces seem unwillingly to live in the same community with us, let them, and not us, depart. It was them, not us, that sought the connection, and when they become tired of the society, let them seek such as they like better. This land is ours and not theirs; we have inherited it from our forefathers—we have never parted from it—we have never sold it—we have never forfeited it—it is therefore ours! If some drunken dogs of our own people, assuming to be our chiefs, have sold lands to the Long-knives, which they did not own, our rights remain unimpaired! We have no chiefs, no agents, no delegates who are authorized to sell our cornfields, our houses, the bones of our dead! I say we have none—we cannot have such a Chief; because the very act itself proves him a traitor, and would strip him of all official authority! Many of the old braves who now hear me, remember well the cruel advantages which the Commissioners of the Long-knives took of our distressed condition, at Portage de Sioux, at the close of the war about sixteen winters ago, how they there compelled us to recognize a treaty which they themselves knew to be a fraud, and by which they still assume to claim even this little tract, though we have given up to them all the other immense countries on both sides of this great river, without a murmur, and as I have said before, we have also proposed to pay them for this. The great Chief of the Long-knives, I believe, is too wise and too good to approve of such acts of robbery and injustice; though I confess, I have found true the statement of my British friends in Canada, "that the Long-knives will always claim the land, as far as they are permitted to make a track with their foot, or mark a tree." I will not, however believe that the great Chief, who is pleased to call himself our "Father," will send an army of his warriors against his children, for no other cause than for contending to cultivate the fields which their own labor has provided, and for occupying the houses which their own hands have erected! No, I will not believe it, until I see his army! And then, and not until then, will I forsake these graves of my ancestors, and his home of my youth!

FROM NOTES ON THE WISCONSIN TERRITORY PARTICULARLY WITH REFERENCE TO THE IOWA DISTRICT OR BLACK HAWK PURCHASE (1836)

ALBERT M. LEA

Lieutenant Albert M. Lea self-published his book in 1836 after traveling through Iowa country with the First United States Dragoons in 1835. While similar to other travelogues of its day, Lea's fifty-three page volume is considered "the book that gave Iowa its name"—the title appended to a reprint published by the State Historical Society in 1935. True to its genre and its time, the lieutenant's book occasionally crosses the line from documentary to settler-minded propaganda, such as where Lea makes the dubious claim, "There is never so much snow…as to interrupt the traveling."

The climate is such as would be naturally expected in this latitude. The thermometer does not range more widely here than in similar latitudes east of the Allegheny Mountains; nor perhaps as much so, as in those districts beyond the influence of the sea breeze; for here, we have every day a breeze, from some quarter of our broad prairies almost as refreshing as that from the ocean. We are exempt, too, from the efforts of the easterly winds, so chilling and so annoying along the Atlantic seaboard; but in lieu of them, we have frequently cold blasts from the prairies, sufficiently annoying to the traveler, when the mercury is at zero. The prevailing winds are from the southwest. I have known the wind at Rock Island to remain constant in that quarter for three weeks successively, and it is said to have so remained during six weeks at Prairie du Chien.

The salubriousness of this climate varies according to locality. Along the Mississippi, where there are marshy grounds, especially from the Des Moines [River] to the vicinity of Rock Island, there will of course be much bilious disease. But even what we call much here is little compared with that on the river below the Des Moines rapids. As we ascend the river, in fact, the causes of disease diminish, and the atmosphere becomes purer; and when we arrive at the rapids at Rock Island, we enter upon a country as healthy as the Allegheny Mountains. There are some diseases, common in other parts of the United States not known here; and pulmonary consumption is one of them. But whether above or below the upper rapids, the country at a distance from the swamps of the Mississippi, is elevated, and is a healthy as any can be, where there is a free circulation of air, good water, and rolling grounds; but where there is also much vegetable matter to decay. This evil is incident to all new countries; and the richer the country in point of soil, the greater is the evil; but it is one that is continually diminishing with the progress of cultivation.

The winter is generally dry, cold, and bracing; the waters are all bridged with ice; the snow is frequently deep enough to afford good sleighing, and it is considered the best season for traveling, by those who are able to bear exposure to a cold atmosphere. The winter usually commences about the first of December, and ends early in March; though in the southern part of the district, we often have fine pleasant weather in midwinter. There is never so much snow, even as far north as Prairie du Chien, as to interrupt the traveling; as every prairie is a high road, we scarcely feel the obclusion of the icy season.

The spring is anything but what we have been taught to expect from that usually delightful season. It is a succession of rains, blows, and chills: and if the sun happen to shine, it does so gloomily, as if boding a coming storm. The whole country becomes saturated with water; the lowlands are overflowed; the streams are swollen: and locomotion is rendered difficult except by water. But as this means of traveling is greatly facilitated and extended by the floods, we even contrive to pass comfortably enough the six weeks of rain, and fog, and wind that changes the freezing winter into the warm and genial summer. We have no gradual gliding from cold to warm; it is snowy—then stormy—then balmy and delightful. There is great difficulty in planting and sowing the grains of the spring; and sometimes even after the seeds are in the earth, the rains are too great to admit of proper culture. But with experience in the climate, the agriculturalists will learn to adapt themselves to its requirements, and be able to assure themselves of crops worthy of the soil they have to cultivate.

The summer is generally of sufficient warmth to produce rapid vegetation; and yet it is seldom oppressively hot. I have, in fact, ridden through grass six feet high, in the month of July, when, for weeks together, I scarcely experienced the sensation of excessive heat. During this season, the appearance of the country is gay and beautiful, being clothed in grass, foliage, and flowers.

Of all the seasons in the year, the autumn is the most delightful. The heat of the summer is over by the middle of August; and from that time till December, we have almost one continuous succession of bright, clear, delightful, sunny days. Nothing can exceed the beauty of summer and autumn in this country, where, on one hand, we have the expansive prairie strewed with the flowers still growing; and on the other hand; the forests which skirt it, presenting all the varieties of color incident to the fading foliage of a thousand different trees.

The soil is generally about two feet deep, and is composed of clay, sand, and vegetable mould. Much of it is too tenacious of water for the most convenient production of such grains as are planted in the spring. It is of a dark brown color near the surface, and gradually becomes lighter and lighter in descending, till it imperceptibly passes into a yellowish clay, which, in turn, is based upon a blue marl, containing pebbles, and which always affords good water when penetrated. This latter stratum is found from fifteen to thirty feet below the surface in the upland prairies, so that it is only necessary to sink a well to that depth to obtain excellent water wherever it may be wanted. This is the general character of the soil of the higher prairies.

In the bottomlands along the rivers, the soil is more sandy, and is little affected by excessive rains, except such portion as are liable to be overflowed. The low grounds are peculiarly adapted to the growth of Indian corn, and the elevated lands to the growth of small grain; though the yellow maize of the North succeeds remarkably well on the coldest soils of our dry prairies.

The general appearance of the country is one of great beauty. It may be represented as one grand rolling prairie, along one side of which flows the mightiest river in the world, and through which numerous navigable streams pursue their devious way towards the ocean. In every part of his whole district, beautiful rivers and creeks are to be found, whose transparent waters are perpetually renewed by the springs from which they flow. Many of these streams are connected with lakes; and hence their supply of water is remarkably uniform throughout the seasons. All these rivers, creeks, and lakes are skirted by woods, often several miles in width, affording shelter from intense cold or heat to the animals that may there take refuge from the contiguous prairies. These woods also afford the timber necessary for building houses, fences, and boats. Though probably three-fourths of the district is without trees, yet so conveniently and admirably are the water and the woods distributed throughout, that nature appears to have made an effort to arrange them in the most desirable manner possible. Where there is no water, isolated groves are frequently found to break the monotony of the prairie, or to afford the necessary timber for the enclosure of the farmer. No part of the district is probably more than three miles from good timber; and hence it is scarcely anywhere necessary to build beyond the limits of the woods to be convenient to farming lands the most distant from them, as the trouble of hauling the timber necessary for farming purposes, a distance of one, two, three miles, is trifling. Taking this district all in all, for convenience of navigation, water, fuel, and timber; for richness of soil; for beauty or appearance; and for pleasantness of climate, it surpasses any portion of the United States with which I am acquainted.

Could I present to the mind of the reader that view of this country that is now before my eyes, he would not deem my assertion unfounded. He would see the broad Mississippi with its ten thousand islands, flowing gently and lingeringly along one entire side of this district, as if in regret at leaving so delightful a region; he would see half a dozen navigable rivers taking their sources in distant regions, and gradually accumulating their waters as they glide steadily along through this favored region to pay their tribute to the great "Father of Waters;" he would see innumerable creeks and rivulets meandering through rich pasturages, where now the domestic ox has taken the place of the untamed bison; he would see here and there the place of the untamed bison; he would see here and there neat groves of oak, and elm, and walnut, half shading, half concealing beautiful little lakes, that mirror back their waiving branches; he would see neat looking prairies of two or three miles in extent, and apparently enclosed by woods on all sides, and along the borders of which are ranged the neat, hewed long cabins of the emigrants with their fields stretching far into the prairies, where their herds are luxuriating on the native grass; he would see villages springing up, as by magic, along the banks of the rivers, and even far in the interior; and he would see the swift moving steamboats, as they ply up and down the Mississippi, to supply the wants of the settlers, to take away their surplus produce, or to bring an accession to this growing population, anxious to participate in the enjoyment of nature's bounties, here so liberally dispensed.

From **Galland's Iowa Immigrant: Containing a Map, and General Descriptions of Iowa Territory (1840)**

Isaac Galland

Credited with platting the city of Keokuk, establishing Iowa's first schoolhouse in Lee County, printing Iowa's second newspaper (The Western Adventurer and Herald of the Upper Mississippi) and nursing to health many of patients up and down the Mississippi as far north as Fort Madison, Isaac Galland was revered in Iowa and loathed in Illinois, where he was considered a scoundrel for abandoning three successive wives, horse thieving, and counterfeiting. Galland's quote "Yes, Siree, I've been found guilty of most everything except hog stealing—and I never owned a hog" was recalled in an April 13, 1960 article "A Man of Conflicting Aspects" published in Keokuk's Daily Gate City. Dr. Jekyll and Mr. Hyde behavior aside, Galland's Iowa Immigrant reveals its college-educated author's literary bent, and serves as an invaluable, bittersweet record of the wildlife—wolves, panthers, prairie hens—Iowa was then losing and has now lost.

Beasts

The buffalo is found in abundance on Red Pipe Stone, Jacques or James, St. Peters and Red Rivers; they continually recede before the white population, and are now only occasionally found on the headwaters of the river Des Moines and Lower Iowa.

Elk are frequently found much nearer the white settlements, and, occasionally, even in the limits of the present settlements.

Deer are not very abundant, being hunted out by the natives; still, however, there are many hundreds of them killed yearly.

Bears are scarce, but the Indians succeed every winter in obtaining more or less of these animals, as appears from the skins which they bring to the traders.

Raccoons are in great abundance in every district of timbered country, and more especially along the watercourses. They constitute the pork of the Indian.

Squirrels. The common grey squirrels are found plentifully in the woods, with a few scattering fox squirrels, but no black ones, however, during fourteen years residence and rambling in that country, I have not seen one, neither have I discovered the singular phenomenon of migration and emigration, profusion and scarcity, of these little animals, which are so remarkable in the early settlement of the Ohio Valley.

The panther is rarely seen in this country; their skins are to be bound sometimes among the Indians, but I have not seen the animal alive in this country. Wildcats are more frequently seen, but they are not by any means numerous.

The wolf. There are a few of the large black wolves, and some grey, but the most numerous of this class of animals are the prairie wolf, which is something above the size of the fox. These animals have not yet proved troublesome to any extent to the farmers; and probably never can, as the country is not adapted to their security, against the search of the hunter—having to burrow in the earth, in certain elevations of the prairie, they are readily found and easily destroyed. Many of those animals which have been so industriously destroyed for their skins, as the beaver, the otter, the muskrat, the mink, etc., are becoming scarce; the beaver may be said to be almost extinct, while but few of the otter remain. It is true that the muskrat abounds in great plenty in some places, and they are said to be found in the greatest abundance about the sources of the Raccoon River.

Rabbits are found in the settled parts of the country; and rats are continually arriving, with almost every accession to our white population, though it is clear that they are not natives of the country. The opossum, the polecat or skunk, the hedgehog or porcupine, and the groundhog, are severally to be found in this country.

Serpents

These reptiles are not numerous in this country, but there are a few of the large yellow-pied rattlesnakes, and still more frequently the little venomous prairie rattlesnake is heard, whizzing about the traveler's feet in passing through the prairies. There are also the bull snake, the black snake, the moccasin snake, the garter snake and a variety of water snakes, which are occasionally met with in the different sections of this country, none of which are poisonous except the moccasin.

Birds

The groves in all this vast region of country are enlivened with the morning matins and evening vespers of a great variety of singing birds.

The wild turkey, which was so abundant on the Ohio in early times, is but rarely found in Iowa; I have, however, seen large flocks of them on the river Des Moines, more frequently than in any other part of the country.

The prairie hen obtains in the greatest abundance, and more especially in the vicinity of the white population. Quails are also numerous, but the pheasant is rarely seen. Swans, geese, brants, and an almost endless variety of ducks are in the greatest abundance along the rivers, upon the lakes, and not infrequently upon the prairies.

Pelicans. These singular fowls, in the early part of autumn, often whiten the sandbars of the rivers and lakes—hundreds of them, on their passage to a southern latitude, alight together on a sandbar or an island, and give it the appearance of a bank of snow.

The crow and the blackbird are sufficiently numerous to be at times troublesome to the farmers.

Bald eagles are quite common, while the grey eagle is scarcely ever seen. Buzzards and ravens are also frequently seen.

Doves and pigeons, a great variety of woodpeckers, and a few of the real woodcock genus of a large size are found in the country.

The little hummingbird is likewise often seen, examining the flowers for his food.

The honey bee is doubtless a native of this region; they are found in the greatest abundance, as we advance beyond the white population.

Article I, the Bill of Rights, from The Iowa Constitution (1846)

The document that officially made Iowa a state, as adapted in convention May 18, 1846 and reprinted here from Nathan Howe Parker's Iowa As It Is (1855) is especially notable for its rejection of slavery and its protection of the rights of foreigners. Progressive as the framing document may have been, it should be noted that Article II restricted rights of suffrage to white male citizens twenty-one years old or older and did not grant rights of suffrage to "idiot[s] or insane persons" or those convicted of an "infamous" crime.

Preamble and Boundaries—We, People of the Territory of Iowa, grateful to the Supreme Being for the blessings hitherto enjoyed, and feeling our dependence on Him for a continuation of those blessings, do ordain and establish a free and independent government, by the name of the State of Iowa, the boundaries whereof shall be as follows:

Beginning in the middle of the main channel of the Mississippi River, at a point due east of the middle of the mouth of the main channel of the Des Moines River, thence up the middle of the main channel of the said Des Moines River, to a point on said river where the northern boundary line of the State of Missouri, as established by the Constitution of that State, adopted June 12th, 1820, crosses the said middle of the main channel of the said Des Moines River; thence westwardly, along the said northern boundary line of the State of Missouri, as established at the time aforesaid, until an extension of said line intersect the middle of the main channel of the Missouri River; thence up the middle of the main channel of the said Missouri River, to a point opposite the middle of the main channel of the Big Sioux River, according to Nicolleitt's map; thence up the main channel of the said Big Sioux River, according to said map, until it is intersected by the parallel of forty-three degrees and thirty minutes north latitude) thence east, along said parallel of forty-three degrees and thirty minutes, until said parallel intersect the middle of the main channel of the Mississippi River; thence down the middle of the main channel of said Mississippi River, to the place of beginning.

Article I.

Bill of Rights—1. All men are, by nature, free and independent, and have certain inalienable rights, among which are those of enjoying and defending life and liberty, acquiring, possessing, and protecting property, and pursuing and obtaining safety and happiness.

2. All political power is inherent in the people. Government is instituted for the protection, security, and benefit of the people; and they have the right at all times to alter or reform the same, whenever the public good may require it.

3. The General Assembly shall make no law respecting an establishment of religion, or prohibiting the free exercise thereof, nor shall any person be compelled to attend any place of worship, pay tithes, taxes, or other rates, for building or repairing places of worship, or for the maintenance of any minister or ministry.

4. No religious test shall be required as a qualification for any office or public trust, and no person shall be deprived of any of his rights, privileges or capacities, or disqualified from the performance of any of his public or private duties, or rendered incompetent to give evidence in any court of law or equity, in consequence of his opinions on the subject of religion.

5. Any citizen of this State, who may hereafter be engaged, either directly or indirectly, in a duel, either as principal or accessory before the fact, shall forever be disqualified from holding any office under the Constitution and laws of this State.

6. All laws of a general nature shall have a uniform operation.

7. Every person may speak, write, and publish his sentiments on all subjects, being responsible for the abuse of that right. No law shall be passed to restrain or abridge the liberty of speech or of the press. In all prosecutions or indictments for libel, the truth may be given in evidence to the jury, and if it appear to the jury that the matter charged as libelous was true, and was published with good motives, and for justifiable ends, the party shall be acquitted.

8. The right of the people to be secure in their persons, houses, papers and effects, against unreasonable seizures and searches, shall not be violated; and no warrant shall issue, but on probable cause, supported by oath or affirmation, particularly describing the place to be searched, and the papers and things to be seized.

9. The right of trial by jury shall remain inviolate; but the General Assembly may authorize trial by a jury of a less number than twelve men in inferior courts.

10. In all criminal prosecutions, the accused shall have a right to a speedy trial, by au impartial jury; to be informed of the accusation against him; to be confronted with the witnesses against him; to have compulsory process for own witnesses, and to have the assistance of counsel.

11. No person shall be held to answer for a criminal offence, unless on presentment or indictment by a grand jury, except in cases cognizable by justices of the peace, or arising in the army and navy, or in the militia when in actual service, in time of war, or public danger.

12. No person shall, after acquittal, be tried for the same offense. All persons shall, before conviction, be bailable, by sufficient sureties, except for capital offences, where the proof is evident, or the presumption great.

13. The writ of Habeas Corpus shall not be suspended, unless, in case of rebellion or invasion, the public safety requires it.

14. The military shall be subordinate to the civil power. No standing army shall be kept up by the State in time of peace, and in time of war no appropriation for a standing army shall be for a longer time than two years.

15. No soldier shall, in time of peace, be quartered in any house, without the consent of the owner, nor in time of war, except in the manner prescribed by law.

16. Treason against the State shall consist only in levying war against it, adhering to its enemies, or giving them aid and comfort. No person shall be convicted of treason unless on evidence of two witnesses to the same overt act, or confession in open court.

17. Excessive bail shall not be required. Excessive fines shall not be imposed; and cruel and unusual punishments shall not be inflicted.

18. Private property shall not be taken for public use with out just compensation.

19. No person shall be imprisoned for debt in any civil action on mesne, or final process, unless in cases of fraud; and no person shall be imprisoned for a militia fine in time of peace.

20. The people have the right freely to assemble together to consult for the common good, to make known their opinions to their representatives, and to petition for redress of grievances.

21. No bin of attainder, ex post facto law, or law impairing the obligation of contracts, shall ever be passed.

22. Foreigners who are, or who shall hereafter become residents of this State, shall enjoy the same rights, in respect to the possession, enjoyment, and descent of property, as native-born citizens.

23. Neither slavery, nor involuntary servitude, unless for the punishment of crimes, shall ever be tolerated in this State.

24. This enumeration of rights shall not be construed to impair or deny others, retained by the people.

FROM A GLIMPSE OF IOWA IN 1846 OR AN EMIGRANT'S GUIDE (1846)

J. B. NEWHALL

A resident of Burlington, J. B. Newhall earned distinction as "the most influential promoter of Iowa prior to 1850" by the State Historical Society of Iowa on the occasion of its reprinting of his classic work. The author of three books on Iowa, of which A Glimpse *is the most notable, Newhall made singing Iowa's praises his life's work, lecturing on the state's virtues in the U.S., England, and Europe as well as sending his heavenly testimonials to newspaper editors across the country. A favorite of Iowa territorial governor Robert Lucas, Newhall hastened to assure others that his glowing comments about Iowa could be believed, writing in his 1846 preface, "This is no fiction—I write not from books, or with the pen of romance.... I have witnessed the great work of civilization in all its various stages, from the lone cabin of the frontier settler to a happy and intelligent population of 100,000 [Iowa] souls." Of special note in the following passage is Newhall's advocacy for the prairie, and his unusually deep understanding of both its utility and its vulnerability.*

FACE OF THE COUNTRY

The predominant features in the landscape of Iowa are prairie and timber; the face of the country is beautiful in the extreme. It is what may be termed moderately undulating, no part of the territory being traversed by mountains, or even high hills (if we except the northern or mineral regions, where the hills are of considerable magnitude); on the margin of the rivers there are frequent ranges of "bluffs," or calcareous strata of lime rock, intersected with ravines. The southern portion of the territory may be termed the most picturesque, abounding with grassy lawns and verdant vales, interspersed with groves and meandering rivulets. The northern part presents more bold and rugged features in its scenery. It is a rare and singular feature in the mineral region of Iowa, that the country abounding in the richest ore is frequently in the neighborhood of the most fertile fields of grain. This territory is remarkably well watered by beautiful rivers and creeks, the margins of which are skirted with woodlands and groves. A striking characteristic of Iowa and Wisconsin over many prairie countries is the admirable distribution of prairie and woodland to the wants and convenience of the husbandman.

Although probably nearly three fourths of the territory is without trees, yet so happily and conveniently are the waters and timber arranged throughout, that nature appears to have made an effort to arrange them in the most desirable manner possible.*

Prairies

Undoubtedly, one of the most captivating features in the landscape scenery of a great portion of the upper Mississippi Valley is the unique and beautifully diversified prairies, or unwooded tracts. They are, in fact, the gardens of nature. And who that has been an eyewitness can ever forget the impressions made upon his feelings when, for the first time, he gazed with rapturous delight upon the boundless prairie? The characteristic peculiarity of the prairies is the entire absence of timber; in other respects they represent all of the varieties of soil and surface that are found elsewhere. Sometimes they are spread out in boundless plains; at other times, they are gently rolling, like the swell of the sea after a subsiding storm. A diversity of opinion exits as to the origin of prairies. Their undulating and finished surface, crowned with the richest alluvial mould, bears ample proof, (in the writer's mind) of their having been, at some anterior period, submerged beneath the waters of vast lakes, or inland seas; and these, subsequently receding, have formed the natural channels through which our vast and numerous rivers flow. Hence the rich alluvial deposit and fossil remains that so frequently occur; also, the laminae formation of secondary lime rock; and successive strata of soil, are all evidences of a once submerged country.

These meadows of nature are covered with a rich coat of natural grass, forming excellent grazing for cattle; and, in the season of flowers, present the most captivating and lovely appearance. The traveler now beholds these boundless plains, untouched by the hand of man, clothed with the deepest verdure, interspersed here and there with beautiful groves, which appear like islands in the ocean. The writer has often traveled amidst these enchanting scenes, on horseback, for hundreds of miles, long before civilization commenced; sometimes threading a narrow defile made by the "red man," through the tall grass, and again suddenly emerging to a broad expanse of thousands of acres covered with ever variegated flowers.

It has been urged by some that, however our prairies may have added to the beauty of the landscape, they are impediments to the settlements of a country. Ten years ago this objection was urged much more strenuously than at present. For in that length of time many prairies, both in Illinois and Iowa, have been converted into highly cultivated farms, upon which "croakers" of early times predicted that no settler would ever venture; and in ten years more, that such an objection ever did exist will be a matter of wonder. A little calculation would convince the most skeptical that it is cheaper, in the proportion of four to one, to haul fencing (rail) timber two or three miles (which is about the extent that any Iowa or Wisconsin farmer need to go) than to expend eight or ten years of toil and labor in clearing the heavily timbered lands of Ohio, Indiana, Kentucky, and Canada.

I have often inquired of those individuals who reason against the settlement of the prairies, if they ever knew a man to leave the prairie for the timber? I have always inquired in vain. But we do know that tens of thousands annually leave the timbered countries to settle upon the prairies.

The association of the New Englander, and most of the inhabitants of the Atlantic States, (respecting a new country) are woods—interminable woods. The English, the French, and the Belgians, have a better simile of comparison with their own landscape. I well remember my first impressions, some three years ago, the first hour I set my foot upon the shores of old England, landing upon the shore of a beautiful bay on the coast of Sussex. I voluntarily exclaimed (casting my eyes over the bright and verdant landscape) how much the scenery of Britain reminds me of the prairie scenery of America. Subsequently, I was often forcibly reminded of the striking similarity of scenery. For instance, the vale of Worcestershire and Herefordshire; likewise the scenery of the Thames above London, affords a striking resemblance of many beautiful spots upon the banks of the Des Moines. And that charming panoramic view from Richmond Hill may justly be compared to the scene which the traveler beholds from the grave of Julien Dubuque, or from the Cornice Rocks above Prairie Du Chien.

The American tourist who has or ever may travel over that pleasant road, from Brussels to the Field of Waterloo, along the forest Soignoine, will have an admirable standard of comparison for much of the scenery of Iowa, Illinois, and Wisconsin. Performing a pedestrian tour through that picturesque and highly cultivated country, in the summer of 1844, I often stopped by the roadside to contemplate the scene before me. It required no stretch of the imagination to shadow forth many of the identical spots that I was wont to look upon in my native land.

CLIMATE

Perhaps, among all the long catalogue of benefits and privations respecting emigration, none is more worthy of consideration than climate, and I doubt if upon any one topic there has been more conflicting testimony. The salubriousness of climate, in all the new states, depends much upon locality. The thermometer does not range more widely here, if as wide, than in similar latitudes east of the Alleghenies. We are exempt, too, from those easterly winds, so searching and blasting in their effects to the invalid or pulmonary complaints, upon the seaboard. Along the low "bottomlands," which are occasionally subject to inundation, there will be more liability and predisposition to bilious diseases, fever, ague, etc. But upon the uplands and broad rolling prairies, the atmosphere becomes salubrious and free from "miasma." In short, there is, almost every day, in the elevated portions of the country, a breeze from some quarter as refreshing as that from the ocean. It would be presumption on the part of the writer to advance the opinion that any new country is entirely exempt from disease. Neither can I endorse the "sweeping" assertion often ascribed to the new States "that it is impossible for people to enjoy good health." One year of general sickness, or of some prevailing epidemic, is not a criterion of the general health of the country. That our new states are not unfavorable to human life, may be inferred from the unprecedented increase of their population. The number of inhabitants in Ohio, Kentucky, Tennessee, Indiana, Missouri, Illinois, Iowa, and Wisconsin cannot be less than six or seven millions! Had they been unhealthy, it is quite incredible so great a number could have congregated within their borders since the brief period of their first settlements.

From the Letters of William Fischer to Christoph Heinrich Ficke (1851)

William Fischer

In the two letters that follow, appearing here from Charles August Ficke's Memories of Four Score Years *(1930), German immigrant William Fischer writes to his patron and sponsor in the old country. Though Charles Ficke allows that the letters contained some fanciful and secondhand notions, what impresses is their immediacy and practicality. True to his German nature, Fischer hones in on the essentials in making recommendations—suggesting ways to smuggle necessary goods such as ropes and seeds into the United States by way of dirty laundry, as well as, for example, advising as to the number of shotguns requisite for each arriving male. Fischer's "alluring" narratives, as Ficke calls them, establish Iowa as an ethnic and religious melting pot, where, despite bias and bigotry, people of different faiths managed to neighbor.*

Prairie, Near Davenport,
August 27, 1851

It is high time for me to redeem my promise to write you. You probably thought I had forgotten my promise. But that would have been rank ingratitude in return for the great help which you have rendered me. I waited thus long purposefully before writing, because what would it have profited to write you about matters concerning which I was uninformed. I have now been in the country ten weeks, and have explored it in all directions, so that I am better informed.*

In Illinois there is much prairie but also some forests. Iowa, judging by all that I have seen so far, is entitled to preference. The Mississippi forms its eastern boundary. Larger and smaller towns lie in its beautiful and romantic valley.

Davenport, which was founded fifteen years ago, is a wonderfully located city and now contains approximately 4000 inhabitants. Four or five years ago it was an unimportant place with hardly one hundred houses. This year alone one hundred houses were built and land as far out as from twelve to sixteen miles has already been sold, and I fully believe that in ten years Davenport will equal the first cities of Germany, inasmuch as the immigration largely has it for its goal. One-third of the people are Germans, and in the country perhaps one-half of the people are Germans. One hardly realizes that he is in America because everywhere you hear German spoken. A German Evangelical Lutheran Church is to be built now. There is a Catholic Church already.

Along the Mississippi there are fine bluffs which are covered with forests. Six miles from Davenport there are rich coalmines. With the exception of a narrow strip along the river there is but little forest. It is a beautiful rolling prairie, mostly rich, black, productive ground suitable for crops of every kind. It is particularly suitable for wheat, maize, barley, and oats. It produces potatoes and especially large cucumbers, onions, beans, and lettuce as well as all other vegetables. Furthermore, speculators have not made many purchases, and one can still obtain land at the price fixed by Congress, namely $1.25 an acre. Annually many families come to this district from St. Louis and the South because the climate in Davenport in the summer is excellent and in the South the contrary.

When Mr. Friedrich and I reached Davenport on our tour of inspection, we made several trips into the surrounding country and found it to be fully to our taste. After four days I returned to Peru [Illinois] alone and on foot. The two who went to Wisconsin had also returned but they brought no good news because they found nothing but dense forests, and a person in a lifetime could not place more than forty acres under cultivation. Money also was very scarce there. It was, therefore, decided to go to Iowa. Mr. Friedrich bought a horse and wagon and we took along half of the baggage, weighing about half a ton. It had rained all summer and the roads as a result were miserable. Nevertheless, we arrived safely in Davenport. We rented a house and started out on a search for land. After a few days we found a suitable tract approximately twelve miles from Davenport near a small grove. Friedrich took a claim on half a section, 320 acres. Four officers who had served in the Schleswig-Holstein army arrived here at the same time and took eighty acres adjoining this tract. At once we raised a tent, dug a well, made a fireplace with sod, and cooked and fried what we had. We also began to make hay, but I had great difficulty with my pupils because none of them stuck to it very long. The oldest Friedrich still lived in the city with the two ladies. The other four of us and the officers lived in the tent. Sundays some of us only went to town in order to once more live comfortably.*

There are no Indians here, but in winter they come here to hunt and to exchange their furs for goods in Davenport. Deer is still plentiful, as well on the prairies as in the woods along the river, and especially in winter one sees herds of these of considerable size. One sees rabbits very seldom, and these are not very large. Prairie chickens, which are very abundant, equal a German duck in size. Songbirds are absent, but in the woods there are birds of wonderful colors. Mosquitoes, gnats, and flies are not wanting, nor many kinds of snakes, of which the rattlesnake is the worst. Most of these are poisonous, but not so dangerous if one applies a quick remedy. I have already killed approximately thirty rattlesnakes and these are usually from three to four feet in length and from one to two inches in diameter.

The summer months are very hot, especially June and July, and these this year were frequently accompanied by heavy thunderstorms. The month of August, however, is a little more moderate. The nights begin to be cool, and the days more pleasant. In summer the days are not as long as in Germany, and in winter they are not as short as in that country. Soon after sunset it gets dark and twilight does not last as long as in Germany.

I have not seen sugar maple. In Iowa this tree seldom occurs. Many farmers on the prairies plant trees, usually locusts, which grow rapidly, so that in eight years one has good fenceposts and in ten years lumber. Besides, it is very hard and solid, and suitable for building wagons, and consequently one already sees many pretty locust groves in the middle of the prairie, and near these a pretty white farmhouse, and all of this surrounded by wonderful fields of grain. Orchards have also been planted, and the oldest of these already bear fruit.

A survey for a railroad from Davenport to Iowa City, and from there further into the interior has been completed. The intention is to build a railroad from here to California, and this will be of the greatest importance for Iowa. Highways have been laid out everywhere. Between every section there is a highway, so that every section is surrounded by four highways. It is but natural that the roads in such a country cannot at once be converted into "Chausseen." Temporary bridges, however, have been built over streams, and one can go almost anywhere on foot or by vehicle.

The Yankees, or native-born Americans, in many cities are most peculiar people. In the best of society the men put their feet on the table, or place a chair near a window, and let their legs stick out of the window. In New York I have seen both of these done. If an American farmer has a barn in which there is much manure, he pulls down the barn, and rebuilds it in another place, and thereby makes it unnecessary to remove the manure. When surveyor Friedrich surveyed his farm, we had to cross a wide slough in which there was much water so that our boots and shoes were filled with water. We all took off our boots and poured out the water, but the surveyor, an old Yankee, took a knife and cut a hole in his almost new boots so that the water could run out. But they are the very best of people, and to be preferred to some of the Germans.

Clothes are a little more expensive than in Germany. Girls marry even at fifteen, but men also marry much younger than in Germany. Marriage in America is not as difficult as one might think. Women there are in plenty, but those coming from Germany are given the preference for the reason that those who live here are somewhat spoiled and not as hard workers. It is not necessary to have a minister perform the marriage. One goes to a justice of the peace, who ties the knot, enters the date in his book, and the marriage is legal.

Persons who are willing to work, even if their means are insufficient to pay more than their transportation to New York or New Orleans, may safely venture to come to America, because at the ports work is easy to be obtained, and they often succeed better than those who bring a few hundred dollars and who either cannot work or are unwilling to work. For the latter class things are bad. Before they are aware of it their few dollars are gone, and unless they are willing to starve, they will be compelled to work. These will then write letters of lamentation, and concoct the rankest lies, but the people should not allow themselves to be scared by these. Whoever is willing to work, even if he is poor, can safely come to free America and no one will be disappointed. He won't have to be afraid of tyrants here who would take from him his wages in the way of high taxes.

It is quite possible that those who come with families will meet with some difficulties, but these they will soon overcome, and then they will feel free and happy. People of means, who, in addition to the cost of transportation, have a few thousand dollars can, if they purchase a well developed farm near the city, lead a life free of trouble if they hire a hand by the year who understands the work; they can hire such a person for from $150 to $200 a year. Such a person, except during harvest time, alone can do all the work. A well arranged farm of from 200 to 300 acres, with good fences, a good house and with livestock and machinery, can be bought for from $3,000 to $4,000. In my next letter I will send you an estimate of the income and outlay of such a farm. At the present, on account of the harvest, this is impossible, because the farmer, who has promised to assist me in making this estimate, is too busy at present.

—Wilhelm Fischer, Davenport, Scott County, Iowa

Long Grove, January, 1852

Dear Mr. Ficke:

I will now answer your questions to the best of my ability, and according to the best information that I have been able to obtain from old and new farmers. Farms can always be purchased. An American farmer seldom keeps his farm longer than three or four years because he thinks its producing capacity has then been exhausted. He is unwilling to fertilize his land. He again purchases prairie and opens a new farm. Here at Long Grove several farms are for sale: one with 200 acres prairie, 100 acres of which are under cultivation, with 40 acres timber, and a fairly good house, but the price of this I cannot yet give you because the owner, a Scotchman, has not made up his mind as yet what price he wants to ask. A good, well-arranged farm in Allens Grove, seven miles from here, and fifteen miles from Davenport, is for sale. Two hundred acres are in cultivation and fenced; 30 acres of good timber, a good frame dwelling and a good store, and the district is well settled. There are from thirty to forty farms in the neighborhood. Within three miles are a blacksmith shop and a school. This land lies two miles from the Wapsipinicon, which river, if the trees which are lodged in it are ever removed, will be navigable for larger vessels. The owner asks $2,600.

One can always buy larger or smaller farms. The usual size of these are 80, 160 to 200 acres. A farm of 80 acres is sufficiently large to support a large family, and for from $1,000 to $1,500, it is possible to purchase a good farm. It is not necessary to pay cash. It is always better to do so, if this is possible, and yet it is not best to divest oneself of all his cash. On a purchase of $2,000 it is enough to pay one-half; and if one keeps from $400 to $500 this will not be too much to buy horses, machinery, and stock. The best time to make a purchase is before harvest. It is true, nobody sells a farm with a crop, but one has the advantage that one can familiarize himself with the harvest work and can then start in right after harvest to plow the land. In making a purchase one should not forget to have included approximately 100 bushels of maize, some wheat, oats, barley, and potatoes. Then, too, in regard to making hay, it is best not to purchase too late because prairie grass is dry in the fall and not good, and it would cost too much to buy hay.

The schools are, as yet, not of the best. The summer term is three months, and the winter term also three months, but only reading, writing, and arithmetic are being taught. Consequently it is best for Germans if several families combine in hiring a private teacher, who can be found at smaller wages than is paid a farm hand. Here in Long Grove there are already two German families who have decided to do this if they can get a third family to join them.

The usual rate of interest here is from ten to fifteen percent, but even a rate running from twenty percent to forty percent is sometimes paid.

The winters here are changeable. When we have no northwest wind, the weather is mild and pleasant. The northwest wind is cuttingly cold, but a cold spell usually lasts only three or four days. Snow also does not remain long. We have mostly sunny and pleasant days. All in all, a mild climate. Hunting and parties are the pleasures of winter. A great many deer and wolves have made their appearance, and these shorten the farmer's time if he has any to spare. The wolves are not dangerous and easily frightened. I know of no annoyance except, that during a few days when the northwest wind is blowing, one has to remain behind the stove; or when a wolf steals a goose or a chicken, which, however, seldom happens.

Most of the settlers here at Long Grove are Scotch. It is very pleasant to meet them as most of them are well-educated.

The average farmhouse is very simple. The smallest of these contain two rooms without hall. Such a house costs $100. There are also nice larger houses with from four to eight rooms, and a good cellar, and such a house will cost from $400 to $500. There are also a number of brick houses and stone houses, inasmuch as there is good clay and near the Wapsipinicon; four miles from here, there is a quarry.

As to seeds bring everything that you care to because everything in this line one has in Germany will also grow here. In the way of weapons, if you bring a shotgun for each male, this will be enough, because hunting becomes less from year to year. Dirks or pistols you do not need. You can make use of a lot of good rope. Rope is expensive here. These and other things, which in New York are subject to duty, you can put in with the soiled clothes, and you will not be bothered about the matter. Bring a supply of empty sacks, as linen is expensive here. Bring plenty of boots and shoes, of the best of quality, because prairie grass is hard on leather. Of other clothes bring coat and trousers of heavy, coarse material for the weekday, and heavy winter clothes; and don't forget featherbeds, for, although these are unnecessary in summer, they are indispensable in winter. Don't bring any tools. These are equally cheap here and more practical. Only saws are better in Germany. Bring one if you have room for it. Don't be too particular about the size of the boxes. There is no harm in their being large.*

The stepfather of Mr. Holland, with whom I am staying, has some fine rice barley. If you can obtain from him half a barrel of this bring it along. He lives near Doemitz. He himself has but lately imported this, but if you suggest that his son in America would doubtless be pleased to get some of this he may let you have it. I am as well and happy as it is possible to be. There is little worry and want in America. Last November I hired out for a year for $120. I expect to purchase land this year, but I will wait until you arrive, and perhaps we can become neighbors. Then a few prosperous years until I can earn a few hundred dollars, and I would not swap with anyone over there. Please write me soon and give me some news. Come soon.

—William Fischer

From "Sketches on Iowa" (1854)

(Mrs.) Frances D. Gage

In this book about Iowa through the eyes of Iowans, Frances D. Gage's travelogue makes for a fascinating exception, as it offers impressions of a New York temperance and women's rights advocate as she travels through the southern half of the state in 1854 and writes about it for the New York Tribune. Gage's impressions appear here from Nathan Howe Parker's Iowa As It Is In 1855. Praising Iowa as the most beautiful state she has ever seen, Mrs. Gage transcends superlatives when she surmises, "They must have been more just than common men, or they would not at first have secured the property rights of the wife, and made her the joint guardian, with her husband, of her children."

Trip from Burlington to Oskaloosa, Impressions upon, and Expressions by, Explorers of Iowa

I have just risen from the perusal of a long and interesting letter from "Our Own Reporter," to *The Tribune*, dated St. Paul, June 8th, 1854, and have responded "True" to all the glowing descriptions of the beauty, fertility, and magnitude of the country bordering upon the Upper Mississippi; and feeling that the beauty, fertility, and excellence of the interior, are fully equal, if not superior, to the borders, I am impelled to give you a few jottings by the way of a journey just ended, from Burlington to Oskaloosa, and thence back to Keokuk. We had no great party to give éclat to our goings or comings; no music nor dancing, no celebrations, no festivals nor feasting, to gild with rainbow hues the surrounding landscape; but of speechmaking we had plenty, and an endless variety; as good and sensible, too, perhaps, as if spoken by lips quivering with the excitement of pride, ambition, or sparkling Catawba, and falling upon ears as capable of appreciation, as those dulled by hurry, sensuality, bustle, and fatigue. My business was to lecture on Temperance and "Woman's Rights" to the people, and of course I had time, in my few days of leisure at the towns by the way, to learn somewhat of the country; and changing my traveling companions every few miles of my journey brought me in contact with all classes and kinds of people, from the immovable Dutchman to the cute Yankee speculator; and from stagecoach speeches we will draw our ideas of the impression made upon the explorers by this interesting country. "Well, this is e'en-a-jest the garden of Eden, anyhow!" broke out an old man from Maine, who had been studying the landscape for some hours in silence. He was "hunting homes for his boys."

"Bless my stars, mother, look at that!" exclaimed a loquacious New Yorker to his better half, who seemed looking back, like Lot's wife, to the worn-out lands of Oswego. "Don't that make your mouth water? These cornfields look as if fifty years old; not a stump nor a stone. Look at that fellow plowing. His horse walks as if he had nothing behind him. What a furrow he rolls up, soft as a garden-plat, rich as a stable yard!"

"I'll give it up," says a stately Canadian. "I have been looking all the way from Paris, in Canada, through Ohio, Illinois, and Wisconsin for something better, and it has grown better all the way; but better than this is no use: I'll give it up. Come, wife, let's get out and go back. You wanted clear streams, and here they are. I wanted timber, stone, and prairie, and I've found them all. Let's go back, gather up the chicks, and come to Iowa."

"They tell'd us this wus little the puttyest place this side o' sundown, but I thought it half gas; but by shucks they didn't tell half on't. Uncle Nate told us we'd never want to go back to Monroe."

"I reckon we won't neither," says a stout young man to his cherry-cheeked wife; putting his hand, at the same time, near a side pocket, where, probably, the treasure was secreted that was to purchase a new home."

"Magnificent—grand—beautiful!" ejaculated the gentleman in gloves, with the linen coat over his broadcloth; "these lands will be worth ten dollars an acre in five years, every rood of them. Ten years will make this country equal to the most favored sections of New York, Pennsylvania, or Ohio. Look, is not that splendid? Rolling prairie, just enough to drain it; vale, hill, woodland, park, lawn, grove, meadow, field, shrubbery, and garden, and all in luxuriant bloom and beauty from Nature's own hand; brooks, running over pebbly beds, gushing springs, or wells easily made, of clear and sparkling water. Is it not beautiful?"

"Beautiful, beautiful, beautiful!" echo the ladies.

"Beau-ti-ful!" answers the quail from the topmost rail of that stake-and-rider fence around that magnificent field of rye.

"Beau-t-iful, beautiful!" whistles the whippoorwill at midday, in the dark grove of elms and oaks by the wayside. He had only changed his dolorous note to suit the sunshine.

"Iowa for me!' says the young wife.

"Bright and beautiful as a fairy dream!" says the merry maiden.

"Now, ladies and gentlemen," says an old stranger—old—he had been ten years in Iowa—if you are so taken with this, just hold on. Don't cry out till you get up about Oskaloosa, and round about there; up into Mahaska, Marion, Warren, Lucas, Monroe, Madison, and so on, clear out to Council Bluffs; such land for farming is not anywhere else on this Continent—not even in California—I have seen it all."

"Can't beat Clark, Union, Adams, Montgomery, and Mills," replies another voice.

"Well, gentlemen, it is all good; and it is pretty hard to tell which is best."

"Such is the tone of conversation among the explorers of this new country on the steamers, which at this season navigate the Des Moines River, and in the coaches. On roads where, three years ago, a coach twice a week was ample, now, two lines a day are required, and six or seven coaches, frequently, to carry the passengers.

Mount Pleasant, Fairfield, Ottumwa, Oskaloosa, Knoxville, and Pella—Groves and Fruit and Vegetables—Timber—Geology

Mount Pleasant is a flourishing town, twenty-five miles from Burlington (reached by a plank road), contains 1200 inhabitants, and will have a railroad through it in less than a year—good churches and good people.

Fairfield, the seat of justice of Jefferson County, is twenty-five miles from Mount Pleasant. Here are 1500 people, and everything active, vigorous, and progressive. Twenty-five miles further on is Ottumwa, built upon a fine slope on the Des Moines. It has been a little stagnant for a year or two, on account of the suspension of the Des Moines improvement, which is now about to be renewed by an eastern company, and will be speedily completed; for when any country demands a work that will pay as well as this will, there will always be found men and capital to do it. Oskaloosa, the county seat of Mahaska, is on the prairie; the Des Moines is four miles distant, upon one side, and the south fork of Skunk River two miles, on the other. It is thus bordered on either side by living streams and heavy timber. Ten years since, it was made the seat of justice; then a place where a few settlers had reared their cabins, seeing, with prophetic eye, what must follow. Now, it has from 2000 to 2500 inhabitants, and 100 buildings, it is said, will be erected this season. Every house and room is full, and every day brings new accessions to their numbers. The railroad will pass through this beautiful town in less than two years. Knoxville, the county seat of Marion, is a village of 1500 inhabitants. Pella, where a colony of Hollanders located six or eight years ago, near the border of Marion, has now its 600 people. A convention was there held the last week in May, and arrangements made for erecting a college under the patronage of the Baptist denomination. At Oskaloosa, they have now a Normal [Teacher's] school. At Fairfield and Mount Pleasant, female seminaries and colleges are in process of erection. The dwellers in the East have, as yet, no conception of this beautiful state, its present improvements, its progress, or its resources.

The prairies are high and rolling, and bordered with timber. In many places Nature seems to have laid out the farm expressly for man's use, and cleared the meadow, cornfield, and orchard, leaving no stump, tree, or bush to interfere with the plow, covering it with deep and matted roots of grass to preserve the soil and enrich it for future use. Groves and parks surround it; running streams and brooks, rippling merrily over pebbles and sand, refresh it; shrubbery and underbrush supply the new beginners with rich fruits—plums of fine quality, resembling the apricot, wild cherries, gooseberries, smooth and large, blackberries, raspberries, strawberries, grapes; all of superior quality to those growing wild in the middle states, and in quantities inexhaustible. Potatoes, both sweet and Irish, are very fine; corn, magnificent; and all agree in one thing—that one-half of the labor will produce a better crop than in the farming lands of Ohio.

Here, then, by the side or under the cover of one of those rare old groves, the farmer may make his home, break up his prairie land, and in three years have his farm under better cultivation than in hilly woodland countries in fifteen. Apple and peach trees come to maturity very soon, and good nurseries are now to be found in many places. At Pella there is a very fine one, as well as a garden, owned by the learned and gentlemanly Mr. Scottel, who takes great pleasure in giving information to travelers. Timber, such as oak, walnut, hickory, maple, elm, and ash, is abundant. There are few large prairies—five or six miles is the widest, oftener one or two, and still oftener less. Limestone, freestone, and stone-coal, without stint, and here and there quarries of a species of beautiful marble, made of marine deposits and shells, are found. Every necessary or comfort of life is here produced, or may be produced without difficulty or expense.

The Des Moines River Improvement—Napoleon, Farmington, Keosauqua—The People of Iowa—Her Laws—The Most Progressive and Best Improved State in the Union—Advice to Eastern People—Iowa the Eden of America

The Des Moines River improvement offers great facilities for mills and manufactories, and the towns already started, where dams have been erected, give evidence of a prosperous future. At Napoleon may be found a woolen factory, with men and women busily engaged in doing good work. Their machinery is very good, but they have but just begun. A flour mill, too, gives out its cheerful hum. Farmington is a pleasant town, twenty-five miles from Keokuk. Here a fine bridge spans the Des Moines; leading the way to Keosauqua, the seat of justice of Van Buren County, also a flourishing village. But I might fill columns, and yet not get to the end of these flourishing new towns, springing up, as it were, by magic, between night and morning.

But the people—what of the people?" exclaim your readers; "what are they?" Shall I say what I think? The people are the strong, earnest, energetic, right-thinking and right-feeling people of the land. Its founders must have been wiser than most men, or they would not in the beginning have recognized all grog-shops as nuisances, and have made the vender of ardent spirits liable for his own transgressions. They must have been more just than common men, or they would not at first have secured the property rights of the wife, and made her the joint guardian, with her husband, of her children. They must have been men more humane than common, or they would not have secured the homestead to the family. These good laws have led those of other States who wish to be wise, just, and humane, to become the dwellers of this fair land. Hence I hesitate not to say that it is the most moral and progressive, as well as the best-improved state, of its age, in all our country. The people of the East must cease to think of Iowa as "way out West." It is but half past one out here—not yet fashionable dinner time; and the people who last year, or last week, or even day before yesterday, left New England, New York, Pennsylvania, or Ohio, with the last Harper or Putnam in their pocket, the last Tribune in their hand, the last fashion on their heads and shoulders, and the last reform in their hearts, are very much the same people in Iowa that their neighbors found them at home, only that a new country, log cabins, and little deprivations call out all their latent powers, cultivate the fallow grounds of heart and feelings, make them more free, more earnest, more charitable; in fact, expand, enlarge, and fit them all the better for life and its duties. Why will people live pent up in cities, amid the dust, and smoke, and din, while there is here so much of beauty, freshness, and utility unappropriated. There are millions of hands wanting acres, and millions of acres wanting hands. True, Iowa may be said to be yet in its log cabinage, but what of that? Ten years ago, the farmer of Marion went sixty miles to mill. What now? Steam mills are at their very doors. Then, as my sister said, for weeks I saw not a woman's face. Now, from my door, I count the friendly, cheerful smoke of twenty home-fires. We ate and slept in these cabins. There was peace, plenty, and cheerfulness.

Not one—not one desponding wife or mother did we find; not one willing to go back and live in the old states. "Look," they would exclaim, "at our corn, our young orchard; our cows are so fine, our chickens are almost Shanghais, our gardens astonish us; we can afford to live cramped ourselves for house-room when everything else expands so fast. We shall build in a year or two, when we get our plans laid." Fourth-rate lawyers, doctors, and ministers will do well to remember that the people of Iowa have not yet forgotten the sound of the voices of the good and great they have left behind. Merchants need not take old goods to Iowa, nor faded belles flatter themselves that last year's fashions will answer. "Anything" won't do "out West" any more. I went, with other ladies, to a political meeting at Oskaloosa to hear the free-soil Whig nominee for governor talk to the dear people. The men looked just like men elsewhere, only they were a little more civil and genteel, and did not make quite so general a spittoon of the courthouse; and I did not see one that leaned towards drunkenness, though the house was full. I went to church; fine astrals, polished walnut, and crimson velvet made the pulpit look like home; ladies rustled rich brocades, or flitted in lawns as natural as life. The only point of difference that struck me was, that their bonnets, with a few exceptions, did not hang so exactly upon nothing as at the East; probably because there was less of nothing to hang on. Then rosy cheeks, sparkling eyes, and free, vigorous steps, were everyday affairs. Altogether, the women were very healthy; and the children, poor little vulgar things—taking after their mothers, as children always will—looked as though they had all the air and sunshine they needed, and would positively be so unfashionable as to live (nine-tenths of them) through the second summer, and be men and women, despite teething, chin-coughs, mumps, and measles.

Burlington and Keokuk are important towns, but too well known and understood in their infant prosperity to need comment. It would require a chapter to give them their due. I hope your reporter, who was at Keokuk while we were there, will do them justice.

To sum up all, this is the most beautiful country that I have ever seen; and when the hand of active industry and energy has overcome the difficulties necessarily attendant upon a new country, and art and wealth have embellished what nature has made so grand, it will be, as the old man said, "almost the garden of America."

From **Iowa As It Is In 1855 (1855)**

Nathan Howe Parker

An important early documenter of many midwestern states, Nathan Howe Parker was especially fond of Iowa, of which he wrote, "Iowa holds out to the emigrant inducements such as no other state in our union can boast." Howe's interpretations, more poetic and sensationalized than those of his contemporaries, are also a bit more patriotic and prejudiced, as elsewhere in Iowa As It Is In 1855, he declares, "Iowa—once the freehold of the tawny savage—is now a civilized and settled state."

Still, fresh in the memories of a few of her citizens, is the time when Iowa was one vast wilderness. Her land untilled, her groves unpeopled, and her mighty rivers flowing unimpeded—unadmired, by art or eye of man, she donned her verdant robes, and decked her fields with flowers on each returning spring, as if to woo the distant husbandman, and when chill autumn came, she shrank again into the sere and withered, waiting, patient still, and still with hope. She heard the Indian hunter's shot resound amid her solitude; she held the imprint of his step upon the yielding surface of her soil; she watched him crawl to his wigwam home, and lay him down to slothful rest, to dream of the ravage or the hunt. She saw him wake from sleep, and gird about his loins the savage tomahawk and scalping knife, while piercing war-whoops rang from dell to dell, and whistling balls and rolling thunders shook the air above, and bathed the blazing fields in gore. She heard the red man's cry of death—the white man's shout of victory. And then her streams and fields—her hills and waving woodlands—joined in one vast choral hymn, when banners were furled; and arms were lain to rest, and Peace snatched the scepter from the wearied God of War.

Then, soon, throughout the land, a lamentation rose. The red man stretched his form upon the earth, and bathed the sod with tears. He bade a long farewell to hunting-ground and riverbank—to bluff and valley, where transcendent beauty held her court, or uttered a parting wail beside the graves of his fathers—the mounds of his nation's slumbering chiefs. Here, from year to year, had successive generations learned to kneel—here had their voices risen annually, in strains of mourning and of homage, for the loved or the illustrious dead—here had been their refuge in times of sorrow or of trouble—and here had they found a retreat, sequestered from the world, and hedged round with a sacred—an unprofaned reverence. But although he lingered still—although to leave these solemn scenes occasioned him most poignant grief—called forth the wildest throes of anguish—yet, inexorable fate impelled the red man onward. Civilization required his departure; the destiny of his outcast race bade him fly from before the coming white man's face, and take another step towards that extinction which yawns before the savage tribe. He raised his voice, once more, in cries of anguish, then joined the mighty Ishmaelitish host, and, taking up the line of march, he pressed his farewell footprint on his native soil, and left behind him on the spreading plains, the last Indian trail of Iowa.

E'en yet the heavy tramp of the banished nation sounds along the western horizon—e'en yet that horizon is blackened by the forms of the retreating multitude—when lo! upon the east a long white line comes gleaming up, seemingly rising out of the distant ground. One by one, like sails at sea, the white-tented wagons of the immigrant well up into sight, and soon we shall see their occupants encamped near yonder grove, their tents gleaming in the moonlight, and the smoke of their campfires spreading like a protecting shelter, above their deep, untroubled slumbers. These hardy men, with their aged parents and adolescent families, moving onward in the wake of the expatriated Indian, are the pioneers of Iowan civilization—the vanguard of the mighty phalanx that is yet to come.

The immigration to Iowa reminds one of the legendary days of the Crusaders. As did the venturous knights of old, the emigrants resign the endearments and luxuries of home, to build up for themselves a glorious destiny, amid the wilds of a strange land. They go to rescue from the desolation entailed upon it by savage hordes, a region stored with Nature's lavish gifts; and, as those misled champions of the cross, they sally forth in banded numbers, from every point of a civilized world, to meet in the brotherhood of a great cause, on the fertile plains where tower their mutual hopes. But here the resemblance ends. The valiant knight of old went forth arrayed in all the paraphernalia of war, to conquer—to subdue—to win, by fire and sword, a land rich in historic lore—a land whose interest mainly lay in the hereditary annals of the past. But the modern emigrant wends his way to territories, whose history is yet unknown, whose annals are yet unwritten, whose value and grandeur lie in the promises of the future. The plowshare and the pruning hook are his weapons, his companions are the loved ones of either sex. The Crusader went to tear down—to demolish—a dynasty; the emigrant, to build up a state. The former had history for his guide—the latter had a history to frame and write.

And nobly has he written it. In the unexcelled prosperity of the land of his adoption—in the magic growth of her cities—upon her boundless prairies, as on a vast sheet—has he traced the records of Iowa's liberation from the darkness of the Indian ages. And these are records that posterity will read with pride, when the crumbling monument and moldering legend of battle and of victory will be as "a tale of days forgotten."

Iowa—once the freehold of the tawny savage—is now a civilized and settled state. Where once the wolf went bounding, now waves the yellow corn; and where the owlet hooted to the solitude, the cabin smoke is floating on the air. Wherever the highway winds, the ever-recurring marks of cheerful industry—of progress—of prosperity—greet the traveler's eye, till one is disposed to rank this state as cotemporary with many of her elder sisters. The immigrant is no longer called on to endure the vicissitudes, the hardships, and the dangers of a frontier life. At every step he meets civilization—in many places, finds improvements in the art of farming, such as he dreamed not of in his Eastern home; and often an old familiar face—a friend who had been a neighbor in years gone by—greets his arrival. Yet, be it not supposed that Iowa is full. Far from it; still within her vast domain lie millions of untilled acres—unentered—untouched—unreclaimed from primeval wildness. They await the immigrant—they call to him and bid him come. Shall it be asked what inducements they hold forth to tempt him, or what resources they possess to repay his labor? We ask, on the other hand, what do they not hold forth? The fertility of the soil in Iowa is unsurpassed—not merely by that of her kindred states—not merely in our union—but throughout the world! The black loam that overlies her prairies, and which varies in depth from eighteen to forty-eight inches, forms an inexhaustible storehouse of fecundity and agricultural wealth. It rests upon a deep subsoil of clay, well fitted to retain moisture; and, during the driest portions of the year, this moisture re-ascends through the surface muck—thus, by a constant reaction, weakening, if not annulling the effects of the severest drought. This was fully proved during the excessive aridity of 1854, Iowa having suffered less from its effects than any other state in the union, and having, since then, been the granary of that union, and supplied from her own stores the exhausted markets of the East and South. This may sound incredible—fabulous; and yet, Iowa, the youngest of the states, has actually accomplished it!

Such are the inducements Iowa holds out to the farmer, coupled with a promise to return him, for immeasurably less labor than would be required in the East, an unsurpassable abundance of any and every article which the zone we live in is capable of producing.

But again: to the manufacturer she also cries come! She invites him to behold for himself her immense coal regions, and examine the qualities of the coal; to roam, hand in hand with the farmer, over the vast mineral tracts; and while he admires the richness of the mines, to let the farmer wonder at the phenomenon of an exceedingly fertile soil, spread out upon the immense beds of lead. Nor is this all. The abundance of first-rate waterpower, and the amount of building-stone everywhere to be found, offer such advantages to the energetic manufacturer as he may elsewhere seek in vain.

These facts have but recently reached the East—and see with what avidity men of capital are hastening to test these boasted resources. And still the field is open—still the coffers of the earth are full, and he may help himself who will.

The poor and the lowly came a few years since, but now the rich and the lofty flock to Iowa, as well as they. And, thanks to the enterprise of these, the colossal wheel of manufacture has already been set in motion in Iowa. It revolves as yet but slowly, and its reverberating strokes do but send forth, as yet, prophetic echoes throughout the state, that tell what may—what can and will be done. When the Giant Spirit of Human Art shall have chained the flow of Iowa's great central artery, and assumed the directing of its course—when the Mississippi's waves shall foam and lash in their impeded progress—when the Missouri's waters shall be darkened by the shadows and the smoke of mammoth factories—and when the tributary streams of this great trio shall be made to join in this work of grandeur and of usefulness—then will that Giant Spirit, as he listens to the ponderous humming of that colossal wheel, whose accelerated revolutions will then keep time with the pulsations of Iowa's ambitious heart, find a genial home in the young, and promising, and vigorous state. There is in this picture no fiction—no visionary anticipation: all that we have hinted at, and more, will be realized. It requires no gift of prophecy to trace out the future path of Iowa. An observing eye—aided by a spirit of discrimination—need but take the past for a precedent—the present for an earnest—to draw a vast panorama of prosperity, such as our union has perhaps never witnessed, heretofore, and yet, which Iowa will not fail to excel.

To the law-loving and the temperate—to the enterprising, the vigorous, the ambitious—she offers a home and a field worthy of their noblest efforts. Already has she placed the early adventurer on a throne of fortune, thus amply rewarding his courage. At this day she points to still loftier thrones and richer diadems, held in reserve as the prizes of fearless energy—or better still, throws open to the world her exhaustless stores of wealth, and seems to say, "Behold your reward!" And as the multitudinous throngs hasten toward these goals of promise—as they crowd with eager steps, and work with tiring hands—they find that far from becoming drained, her resources deepen and increase in proportion as they take from them—not merely keeping pace with their accumulating wants, but ever exceeding them; it is even as the province of mind—the realms of intellect—whose boundaries still widen, and whose sphere continues to expand, the further they are explored.

There is an emigration that thins the old and crowded states on the Atlantic seaboard; there is an immigration that peoples a new world, and darkens the mountain slope of fortune; there is a journeying from the old into the new, of the Pilgrims of Industry and of Hope. But there is a mightier emigration—a vaster pilgrimage—than these. It is the march, onward and upward into the Future, of Iowa herself. As the immigrant mother leads her sons and daughters into the undeveloped paths of wealth—as civilization elevates a race out of the sloughs of semi-barbarism—as national prosperity exalts a land—or as science raises the human intellect from darkness into dazzling light—thus Iowa, with rapid strides, ascends the precipitous sides of prosperity's mountain range, bearing her sons and daughters to loftier, and still loftier peaks, and revealing to their gaze still wider and richer vistas. And the summit of this range she will never reach; for her onward progress cannot be stayed, until her arterial streams are dry—until the agricultural lifeblood in her veins has ceased to flow, until her great metallic heart has been emptied. Upon the topmost summit, then, Iowa will never stand, for through countless ages yet to come, her progress—that must be forever onward—must be upward also.*

Iowa scenery—the bluffs, etc.

Respecting the scenery of Iowa, Owen, in his *Geological Report to Congress*, pages 64, 65, 66, says:

The scenery on the Rhine, with its castellated heights, has furnished many of the most favorite subjects for the artist's pencil, and been the admiration of European travelers for centuries. Yet it is doubtful whether, in actual beauty of landscape, it is not equaled by that of some of the streams that water this region of the Far West. It is certain that, though the rock formations essentially differ, Nature has here fashioned, on an extensive scale, and in advance of all civilization, remarkable and curious counterparts to the artificial landscape which has given celebrity to that part of the European continent.

The features of the scenery are not, indeed, of the loftiest and most impressive character—such as one might expect to witness on approaching the source of one of the two largest rivers on the globe. There are no elevated peaks, rising in majestic grandeur; no mountain torrents, shrouded in foam, and chafing in their rocky channels; no deep and narrow valleys, hemmed in on every side, and forming, as it were, a little world of their own; no narrow and precipitous passes, winding through circuitous defiles; no cavernous gorges, giving exit to pent-up waters; no contorted and twisted strata, affording evidence of gigantic and violent throes. But the features of the scene, though less grave and bold than those of mountainous regions, are yet impressive and strongly marked. We find the luxuriant sward, clothing the hill slope even down to the water's edge. We have the steep cliff, shooting up through its mural escarpments. We have the stream, clear as crystal, now quiet, and smooth, and glassy, then ruffled by a temporary rapid; or, when a terrace of rock abruptly crosses it, broken up into a small, romantic cascade. We have clumps of trees, disposed with an effect that might baffle the landscape gardener; now crowning the grassy height, now dotting the green slope with partial and isolated shade. From the hilltops, the intervening valleys wear the aspect of cultivated meadows and rich pasture grounds, irrigated by frequent rivulets, that wend their way through fields of wild hay fringed with flourishing willows. Here and there, occupying its nook on the bank of the stream, at some favorable spot, occurs the solitary wigwam, with its scanty appurtenances. On the summit level spreads the wide prairie, decked with flowers of the gayest hue; its long, undulating waves, stretching away till sky and meadow mingle in the distant horizon. The whole combination suggests the idea, not of an aboriginal wilderness (so recently), inhabited by savage tribes, but of a country lately under a high state of cultivation, and suddenly deserted by its inhabitants—their dwellings, indeed, gone, but the castle homes of their chieftains only partially destroyed, and showing, in ruins, on the rocky summits around. This latter feature, especially, aids the delusion; for the peculiar aspect of the exposed limestone, and its manner of weathering, cause it to assume a semblance somewhat fantastic, indeed, but yet wonderfully close and faithful to the dilapidated wall, with its crowning parapet, and its projecting buttresses, and its flanking towers, and even the lesser details that mark the fortress of the olden time.

The rural beauty of this portion of Iowa can hardly be surpassed. Undulating prairies, interspersed with open groves of timber, and watered with pebbly or rocky-bedded streams, pure and transparent; hills of moderate height and gentle slope; here and there, especially towards the heads of streams, small lakes, as clear as the rivers, some skirted with timber, some with banks formed by the greensward of the open prairie. These are the ordinary features of the pastoral landscape.

In a few instances, the hills or bluffs along the Mississippi rise boldly from the water's edge, or push out their steep promontories, so as to change the direction of the river; but more generally, on either bank of the river, we see a series of graceful slopes, swelling and sinking as far as the eye can reach. The prairie, for the most part extending to the water's edge, renders the scenery truly beautiful. Imagine a stream a mile in width, whose waters are as transparent as those of the mountain spring, flowing over beds of rock and gravel; fancy the prairie commencing at the water's edge—a natural meadow of deep green grass and beautiful and fragrant flowers, rising with a gentle slope for miles, so that, in the vast panorama, thousands of acres are exposed to the eye. The prospect is bounded by a range of low hills, which sometimes approach the river, and again, recede, and whose summits, which are seen gently waving along the horizon, form the level of the adjacent country. Sometimes the woodland extends along this river for miles continuously; again, it stretches in a wide belt far off into the country, marking the course of some tributary streams; and sometimes, in vast groves, several miles in extent, standing alone, like islands in this wilderness of grass and flowers.

From **Downing's Civil War Dairy (1861-1865)**

Sergeant Alexander G. Downing

As Edgar R. Harlan, Curator of the Historical Department of Iowa, wrote upon the publication of the diaries in 1916, what better way to learn of the Civil War and Iowa's role in it than by a diary, with its "hearthstone phrase" and "secret and sacred appeal to the ordinary mind." The author, Cedar County native Alexander G. Downing, Company E., Eleventh Regiment, Iowa Volunteer, was still living in 1916 when he was asked to revise his invaluable journal for ultimate publication by editor Olynthus B. Clark of Drake University in Des Moines. Worth noting is the complete circle made by the understated entries below; the first finds a young Alexander Downing at work in his father's fields contemplating war and enlistment; the last rejoining his father for harvest after four years of battle and deprivation. "I am at home this time," the author reminds himself, "never to go to war again. It was a fine day for a ride in Iowa."

During the months of July and August, 1861, the country was greatly aroused over the prospects of war. Excitement rose high when the news of the battle of Bull Run, July 21st, was flashed over the wires. I was then almost 19 and living at home on a farm near Inland, Cedar County, Iowa. Naturally I was deeply stirred over the question of war. Some of our neighbors and friends had earlier opposed the use of force in preventing secession, but I distinctly remember that my father and many neighbors and friends entertained no doubt as to the righteousness of such a course.

During these days we were at work in the harvest field. We had finished cutting our wheat and oats and during the first two weeks of August were engaged in stacking the grain. Everyone had some part in the work. Father did the stacking, while John was on the stack with him, placing the sheaves at his right hand. Albert and George drove the teams to and from the fields, while Paul and Andrew attended to watering the stock during the day. [Original editor's note read: "The five boys, John, Albert, George, Paul, and Andrew, are Mr. Downing's half-brothers. They are all living at this time (March, 1916) and all reside in Iowa—Ed.] Tom Toly, as strong Irishman, who had worked for us three or four summers, pitched the sheaves to father from the wagon, and Dave Cole pitched the sheaves from the shocks in the field to me on the wagon, while I arranged them on the load.

There has been some talk of raising a company of troops at Inland, but nothing had come of it. At Tipton, the county seat, a company of one hundred men was raised when the first call for volunteers was made. But as they were not then needed, they went out under the call of July 23, 1861, and became Company A of the Fifth Iowa Infantry.

I had been pondering in my mind the matter of going to join the army. On the evening of Saturday, August 10, news came of the battle of Wilson's Creek, and that General Lyon had been killed. The First Iowa Infantry was in that battle and made glorious history for itself and for Iowa. That fact, with the excitement over the battle itself, stirred us boys in the neighborhood, and I practically reached a decision as to what I should do.

The next day was Sunday, and everybody was talking about the battle of Wilson's Creek. Ministers spoke of it in their sermons and prayers. It was the all-important topic of the day, and for the next three days—the 12th, 13th and 14th of August, it was the topic of conversation while we were finishing our work in the harvest field. On the next day, my birthday, I began my dairy and shall now let it speak.

The Diary, Chapter 1, Enlisting in the United States Service [August 1861]

Thursday, 15th—We capped our grain stacks against the rain and windstorms, and then commenced mowing wild grass for hay. This is my birthday; am nineteen years old.

Friday, 16th—I, with Tom Toly, mowed the grass all day. Swinging the scythe was hard work for me and I did not cut as wide a swath as Tom did. Father went to Tipton in the afternoon and upon his return told us the war news. I am thinking some of enlisting and going to war.

Saturday, 17th—I mowed grass all forenoon and in the afternoon went to a Sunday school celebration down at Posten's Grove. I made up my mind to enlist and go and fight our Southern brethren. In the evening I went to Mr. Willey's to stay all night with Ward. Later in the evening we attended a peace meeting at Inland.

Sunday, 18th—This morning attended the Methodist church and Sunday school at Posten's Grove. Several Methodist brethren were received into the church. In the afternoon, Mr. Wharton, the minister, delivered a patriotic speech and spoke of the war. He then called for volunteers and I put my name down to go for three years or during the war. About fifty-five boys enlisted and we are to go in Company E of the Eighth Iowa.

Monday, 19th—I helped haul and stack hay this forenoon, and in the afternoon went to Inland with the other boys who enlisted yesterday, to see about going to Camp McClellan, at Davenport.

Tuesday, 20th—I went early this morning to Inland, where all who enlisted were to meet and go to Davenport. Several of the friends came in to see us off. There were forty-five of us and at 9 o'clock we left in wagons for Davenport. After a hot, dusty ride we arrived at Davenport at 4 o'clock in the afternoon, and marched out to Camp McClellan, where they received us very kindly. We had very fine barracks to go into and the boys of the Eighth Iowa had a good supper for us. It was our first meal in the army and consisted of boiled potatoes, fried bacon and baked bean. We have lots of straw to sleep on at night. We were to meet a part of a company from Le Claire under command of Captain Foster and together form one company in the Eighth Iowa Infantry. But Captain Foster did not come, and since there are only eight Le Clarie boys here we have not enough to make a company.*

THE MOBILIZATION AT BENTON BARRACKS,
NOVEMBER 16–DECEMBER 7 [1861]

Saturday, 16th—Reveille sounded at 2 a.m., and packing our knapsacks, we started at 8 o'clock for the boat down at the levee. Here we stacked our arms and waited until the quartermaster with his detail got the commissariat loaded, putting it upon our boat and the two barges, one on either side. By noon all was ready and we marched on board, some going upon the boat and some upon the barges, at 2 P.M. left Davenport, bound for St. Louis.

We reached Muscatine about sundown and because there are so many Muscatine people in the regiment, we landed and marched uptown to Main Street. Here we had dress parade for the benefit of the citizens, who turned out in large numbers. Companies A and H are made up of Muscatine boys, while our colonel and quartermaster reside here; besides, Company I is from Louisa County just west of this place. After the parade we marched back to the boats and left at once for Keokuk. Our boat is the *Jennie Whipple*, and Company E is stationed on the hurricane deck.

Sunday, 17th—We had a pretty stiff introduction to our first night on a riverboat, for it snowed in the night. My bunkmate, James Fossett, and I lay down on the deck with our heads to the smokestack instead of our feet, in order to avoid lying with our heads downhill. By morning we were covered with snow, about two inches deep. At 8 A.M. we landed at Montrose, where two of our companies were transferred from our boat to another boat in order to lighten our boat for the purpose of passing through the rapids just above Keokuk. We reached Keokuk in safety about noon and went on shore to cook some provisions. At dusk we returned to the boats, our company being transferred to another boat which lay at Keokuk all night while the *Jennie Whipple* proceeded down the river.*

The Mustering Out, July 1865

Saturday, 22nd—Weather quite pleasant today. Our regiment was paid off this afternoon, and we received our discharge. This makes us free men again and we at once left Camp McClellan for town. I went to the Davis House and stopped for the night. Mr. Hatch came to Davenport for a load of us.

I brought some clothing this afternoon, the first citizen's suit which I was permitted to wear in four long years. I also bought a good watch for $50.00, which with my clothing, $41.50, amounted to $91.50.

The Sixteenth Iowa arrived this morning from Louisville, Kentucky. The men of our brigade, on being discharged, seem to be scattering to the four ends of the earth; even the boys of Company E after bidding one another farewell, are going in all directions.

Sunday, 23rd—I started for home, thirty miles distant, with Abner Hatch, who had come down from our neighborhood with a team for the purpose of taking a load of the boys home. We left Davenport at 7:30 o' clock this morning and I reached home at 5 P.M. I found my folks all well. I am at home this time never to go to war again. It was a fine day for a ride in Iowa; it had rained yesterday, and though it was somewhat cloudy, the prairies never looked so nice and green as they did today.

Monday, 24th—It rained all day. I remained at home and brought my dairy up to date.

Tuesday, 25th—I went into the harvest field and worked all day at binding wheat.

Wednesday, 26th—Working in the harvest field is making me quiet sore, as it is the first of the kind I have done in the last four years.

Thursday, 27th—It is the same thing and nothing of importance.

Friday, 28th—I went to Tipton today, and in the evening had a fine visit with Miss _____.

Saturday, 29th—Home again from my visits. I have worked three full days now in the harvest field.

Sunday, 30th—I went to church this morning and in the evening went to visit friends, old and new.

Monday, 31st—Today I again went out into the harvest field.

Anonymous Letter to the Editor Appearing in the *Delaware County Union* (June 1, 1866): "Farmer's Wife"

The rightful pride of Iowa farmers' wives, then as now, shapes Iowa's image. The following anonymous letter, penned a year after the conclusion of the Civil War, serves as a timeless recitation and defense of the pleasures of the farm for women in particular. Maggie May's piece, referenced below, appeared in Manchester's Delaware County Union *on May 4, 1866; it took "Farmer's Wife" less than a month to have her say-so.*

Mr. Editor: Having seen a communication from Maggie May in your paper depicting the happiness of farmers' wives (as she calls it) in glowing colors, I think it is the duty of someone of that class to say a word in favor of themselves and their calling. I have no desire to change my position, and would say to all young ladies they may do far worse than to marry a farmer. I know they do not all have mud puddles before their doors, in fact I do not know of one that has, and Maggie May might sit down anywhere in my hard and not soil her nice dress or new cloak. Neither do we go over the chips or wood to get into the house. We have nice white bread and graham bread, pickles, and as yellow butter as one can ask, a very good garden, lots of currants, rhubarb, strawberries, and live in hopes to have all kinds of fruit in time. I have plenty of eggs, and chickens to kill when I want them, and among the farmer's families of my acquaintance they are all as comfortable, and more so in some respects. Most of them are getting started now, and in time they will have larger houses and ride in their carriages.

I have any amount of flowers, and it yields me many hours enjoyment taking care of them; and my husband is always ready and willing to assist me in any way that I ask him, and to spare a little money now and then to buy a choice flower or shrub for me. I have another source of pleasure on a farm I could not have in town—the livestock, from the tiny chickens to the great horse. I love to go out after sunset and smooth the sleek slides of the cows and speak to them; and have the sheep come and put up their pretty faces for a pat and pleasant words; and watching the cunning little lambs frolic, which the finest town lady could not help laughing at and enjoying. Take it all in all, there many things worse in life than living on a farm. I do not think because one lives in the country they need to know everything. I enjoy reading as much as anyone could, and nice dressing also. Town people are, many of them, like a young man in the city of Manchester, who made the remark about one of our neighbors in his hearing, "Oh, he don't known anything—he lives in the country." Now, my private opinion is that gentleman knows more than that young man will ever know.

From Iowa: The Home for Immigrants, Being A Treatise on the Resources of Iowa and Giving Useful Information with Regard to the State, For the Benefit of Immigrants and Others (1870)

The Iowa Board of Immigration

Compelled by the occasion of the 1869 census, the General Assembly of Iowa sanctioned a Board of Immigration to prepare a pamphlet, as the preface states, "setting forth the briefly the resources of the state, and containing such information as might prove useful the immigrant." As many immigration handbooks theretofore had been produced by free-lancers and fly-by-nighters, Iowa: Home for Immigrants represented an effort by the legislature at quality control through what it hoped would be "plain statement of facts." At the time, the Iowa Board of Immigration consisted of Governor Samuel Merrill and S. F. Spofford from Des Moines, Edward Mum from Keokuk, C. L. Clausen from St. Ansgar, C. Rhynsburger from Pella and Marcus Tuttle from Clear Lake. The census data cited by the Board affirms Iowa's boom years, registering a jump in population from just over 20,000 in 1838 to well over one million in 1869. The pamphlet also treats Native Americans far more objectively than most immigration handbooks of its time, though it does perpetuate the myth that the appellation Iowa signifies "beautiful land." Current scholarship suggests that Iowa actually means "those who were separated"—a reference to the division and displacement suffered by the Ioway people at the hands of white settlers.

Historical Sketch of Iowa

Prior to the year 1763, the entire continent of North America was divided between France, England, Spain, and Russia. France held all that portion of what now constitutes our national domain west of the Mississippi River, except Texas and the territory which we have obtained from Mexico and Russia. This vast region, while under the jurisdiction of France, was known as the "Province of Louisiana," and embraced the present state of Iowa. At the close of the "Old French War" in 1763, France give up her share of the continent, and Spain came into possession of the territory west of the Mississippi River, while Great Britain retained Canada and the regions northward, having obtained that territory by conquest in the war with France. For thirty-seven years that territory now embraced within the limits of Iowa remained as a part of the possessions of Spain, and then went back to France by the treaty of St. Idlefonso, October 1, 1800. On the 30th of April, 1803, France ceded to the United States in consideration of receiving $11, 250,000, and the liquidation of certain claims held by the citizens of the United States against France, which amounted to the further sum of $3,750,000, and making a total of $15,000,000. It will thus be seen that France has twice, and Spain once, held sovereignty over the territory embracing Iowa, but the financial needs of Napoleon afforded our government an opportunity to add another empire to its domain.

On the 31st of October, 1803, an act of Congress was approved authorizing the President to take possession of the newly acquired territory and provide for it a temporary government, and another act approved March 26, 1804, authorized the division of the "Louisiana Purchase," as it was then called, into two separate territories. All that portion south of the 33rd parallel of the north latitude, was called the "Territory of Orleans," and that north of the said parallel was known as the "District of Louisiana," and was placed under the jurisdiction of what was then known as the "Indiana Territory."

By virtue of an act of Congress, approved March 3, 1805, the "District of Louisiana" was organized as the "Territory of Louisiana," with a territorial government of its own, which went into operation July 4th of the same year, and it has remained until 1812. In this year the "Territory of Orleans" became the state of Louisiana, and the "Territory of Louisiana" was organized as the "Territory of the Missouri." This change took place under an act of Congress approved June 4, 1812. In 1819, a portion of this territory was organized as "Arkansaw Territory," and in 1821 the State of Missouri was admitted, being a part of the former "Territory of Missouri." This left a vast domain still to the north, including the present state of Iowa and Minnesota, which was in 1834, made a part of the "Territory of Michigan." In July, 1836, the territory embracing the present States of Iowa, Minnesota, and Wisconsin was detached from Michigan, and organized with a separate territorial government under the name of "Wisconsin Territory."

By virtue of an act of Congress, approved June 12, 1838, on the 3rd of July of the same year, the "Territory of Iowa" was constituted. It embraced the present state of Iowa, and the greater portion of what is now the state of Minnesota. Robert Lucas, who had been one of the early governors of Ohio, was appointed the first territorial governor, and William B. Conway, secretary. The latter died during his term of office, in November, 1839, and James Clarke was appointed to the vacancy. The first Legislative Assembly convened at Burlington, November 12, 1838. That place continued as the seat of the territorial government until the Fourth Legislative Assembly, which convened at Iowa City, December 6, 1841. The latter place continued as the capital of the territory and state, until the permanent location at Des Moines, in 1857.

To say nothing of the title to the soil of Iowa that may once have vested in the natives who claimed and occupied it, it is a matter of some interest to glance at the various changes of ownership and jurisdiction through which it passed within the time of our historical period:

1. It belonged to France, with other territory now belonging to our national domain.

2. In 1763, with other territory, it was ceded to Spain

3. October 1, 1800, it was ceded with other territory from Spain back to France.

4. April 30, 1803, it was ceded with other territory by France to the United States.

5. October 31, 1803, a temporary government was authorized by Congress for the newly acquired territory.

6. October 1, 1804, it was included in the "District of Louisiana," and placed under the jurisdiction of the territorial government of Indiana.

7. July 4, 1805, it was included as a part of the "Territory of Louisiana," then organized with a separate territorial government.

8. June 4, 1812, it was embraced in what was then made the "Territory of Missouri."

9. June 28, 1834, it became part of the "Territory of Michigan."

10. July 3, 1836, it was included as a part of the newly organized "Territory of Wisconsin."

11. July 12, 1838, it was included in, and constituted a part of the newly organized "Territory of Iowa."

12. December 28, 1846, it was admitted into the union as a state.

The word *Iowa* is said to mean in the language of the Indian tribes, "The Beautiful Land." A band of Indians journeying toward the setting sun, reached the bank of the Great River that washes our eastern border, and looking across the broad water, beheld for the first time the green slopes of our beautiful prairies stretching away in the distance. Their exclamation was "Iowa!"—The Beautiful Land! It is a well attested fact that these sons of the prairie and the forest, rude and uncultivated as they are, have a vivid appreciation of the grand and beautiful in nature, and it is not unreasonable to presume that such was the original of the name, although it comes down to us as a tradition. The name itself is a beautiful one, as most Indian names are, and it is a fitting appellation for the richest and loveliest portion of the North American continent.

The greater portion of the country embraced within the limits of Iowa, was once occupied by a tribe, or a nation of Indians, known in history as the Iowas, (or Ioways), who for many years maintained an almost constant warfare with the Sioux, a powerful rival who lived to the north of them. The Iowas were originally the Pau-hoo-chee tribe and lived in the region of the lakes to the northeast, but nearly one hundred and eight years ago, they followed their chief, Mau-haw-gaw, to the banks of the Mississippi, and crossing over, settled on the west bank of Iowa River, near its mouth, and there built a village. They called the river on which they established their seat of empire Ne-o-ho-nee, or the "Master of Rivers." For some years they prospered and multiplied, but the Sioux began to envy them the prosperity which they enjoyed, and with no good intentions came down to visit them. Sending to Mau-haw-gaw the pipe of peace, with an invitation to join them in a dog-feast, they made great professions of friendship. The Iowa chief, having confidence in their protestations of good feeling, accepted the invitation. In the midst of the feast the perfidious Sioux suddenly attacked and killed him. This outrage was never forgiven by the Iowas.*

The Iowas, next to the Sioux, were once the most numerous and powerful of all the tribes between the Mississippi and Missouri Rivers. But before leaving the "Beautiful Land" to join their fortunes with other remnants of their race beyond the Missouri, they were reduced by wars, whisky, and smallpox, to about 1,300 souls.

It must have been about the year 1824 when the Sac and the Foxes, who had previously inhabited the country on the Rock River, in the present state of Illinois, began to make encroachments upon the Iowas, under the renowned chief, Blackhawk. In a great battle fought on the east bank of the Des Moines River, near the present village of Iowaville, in Davis County, the Iowas were vanquished, and the Sacs and Foxes took possession of their hunting grounds. Then the Iowas sullenly moved toward the west, and finally passed beyond the Missouri. When civilization began to dawn along our eastern border, the Sac and Foxes were the occupants of the soil in all the eastern and southern portion of the Territory, while the warlike Sioux held undisputed possession of the northern portion, about the headwaters of the Des Moines and the lakes. After the close of the Blackhawk War in 1833, the power of Blackhawk waned, and his rival, Keokuk, who had favored peace with the whites, was recognized as the chief of his nation. Many of the pioneer settles of Iowa still remember him and his subordinates, Wapello,

Appanoose, Kishkekosh, Pashepahaw and Hard Fish. Blackhawk died in October, 1838, on the Des Moines River, near the scene of his conquest over the Iowas.

Perhaps the first white man who ever had the pleasure of beholding this "Beautiful Land," was Father Louis Hennepin, a Franciscan priest, who as early as 1680, with two fur traders, ascended to the Mississippi as far as the Falls of St. Anthony, which he so named. We have, however, less authentic accounts of one or two other voyageurs prior to this date. Soon after this the French government took formal possession of all this undefined and unknown region, and established trading posts at several points. But, for one hundred and fifty years after this, the country remained in the hands of the natives, and almost unknown to our Anglo-Saxon ancestors, who were laying in the foundations of an empire along the Atlantic seaboard. On the 22nd of September, 1788, a Frenchman named Julian Dubuque, who had an Indian wife, made a purchase from the Indians, and engaged in mining and trading at the place where the important city that bears his name is now located. Others afterward engaged in mining lead at the same place, forming the nucleus of the first white settlement within the limits of Iowa. On the 30th of March, 1799, Louis Honori obtained permission from the Spanish government to establish himself at the head of the "rapids of the river Des Moines," for the purpose of trading with the Indians. This place was subsequently known as Montrose, and is situated a short distance above Keokuk. Honori built houses, planted an orchard, and cultivated a tract of land. This was the next white settlement in Iowa, if indeed that can be called a settlement, which was only a grant for the purpose of trading with the Indians.

In 1832, immediately after what is known as the "Blackhawk Purchase," being the first purchase of land from the Indians in Iowa, a few white persons began to settle on the west side of the Mississippi. A military post was established at Montrose, and the place was called Fort Des Moines. It remained a military post until 1837, when the troops were removed to Forth Leavenworth. Traces of the primitive occupancy of Iowa soil at this point by the white man are still visible, and there are those who remember the old apple trees at Montrose planted by Honori seventy years ago!

Iowa remained from 1836 to 1846 a separate territory, during which time the office of governor was held by Robert Lucas, John Chambers, and James Clarke. Congress made provision by an act, approved March 3, 1845, for its admission into the union as a state, with boundaries quite at variance with those finally established. By this law the state was to extend north to the parallel of latitude passing through the Mankato, or Blue Earth River, in the present state of Minnesota, and west to the Meridian of 17° 30´ west from Washington. This western boundary would very nearly correspond to the line between the present counties of Ringgold and Taylor, and its adoption would have deprived our state of all that fertile portion denominated the "Missouri Slope." In October, 1844, a constitutional convention had been held at Iowa City, and a constitution framed which embraced boundaries far more extensive than those of the present state, taking in much of the southern portion of the present state of Minnesota. The people of the territory disapproved of the reduction of these boundaries by Congress, and at the election held August 4, 1845, rejected the constitution—the vote being 7,235 for, and 7,656 against it. In 1846, Congress proposed the present boundary lines, and another constitutional convention convened at Iowa City on the 4th of May of this year. A session of fifteen days resulted in the framing of the constitution which was sanctioned by the people at an election held August 3, 1846—the popular vote this time being 9,492 for, and 9,036 against the constitution. This constitution was agreed to by Congress, and on the 28th of Demember of the same year, Iowa was admitted into the union as a sovereign state. On the 26th of October preceding, however, the first election had been held for state offices, when Ansel Briggs was elected governor; Elisha Cutler, Jr., secretary of state; Joseph T. Fales, auditor, and Morgan Reno, treasurer. A third constitutional convention convened at Iowa City in January, 1857, and framed the present state constitution, which was sanctioned by the people at an election held August 3, 1857—the popular vote being 40,311 for, and 38,681 against the constitution.

At the time of the organization of the territory of Wisconsin in 1836, the entire white population of that portion of said territory which now constitutes the state of Iowa, was 10,531. The following is an exhibit of the population, as shown by the different census reports: In 1838, 22,859; in 1840, 43,114; in 1844, 75,152; in 1846, 97,588; in 1847, 116,651; in 1849, 152,988; in 1850, 191,982; in 1851, 204,774; in 1852, 230,713; in 1854, 326,013; in 1856, 519,055; in 1859, 638,775; in 1860, 674, 913; in 1863, 701,732; in 1865, 754,699; in 1867, 902,040; in 1869, 1,040,819.

The permanent settlement of Iowa by the whites can hardly be said to have commenced before the year 1833, and it was then for a number of years confined to the counties along the Mississippi, the central and western portions remaining still in the possession of the Indians. The steady growth and development of the state in all that constitutes a great and prosperous commonwealth, so far as may be consistent with the purposes of this pamphlet, will be shown in subsequent pages.

From **The Rise and Fall of the Mustache and other "Hawk-eyetems" (1878)**

Robert J. Burdette

Dubbed "the Burlington Hawk-eye" after the Iowa newspaper he made a household name, Robert Jones Burdette achieved national fame as a humorist and lecturer, selling over one million copies of his seven books. Burdette also hobnobbed with some of the great writers of his era, including James Whitcomb Riley and Henry Ward Beecher, who he met on the lecture circuit. Following are two comedic treatments of classic Iowa themes—first, the inanity of living in a literal "cow town" and, second, the dangers of putting on airs while courting a savvy Iowa girl. No doubt the toxic weed that adds punch to the punch line of Burdette's "The Language of Flowers" is the fever-producing, vision-blurring jimson weed.

Voices of the Night

Mr. Joskins is not an old settler in Burlington. He came to the city of magnificent hills from Keokuk, and after looking around, selected a residence out on West Hill, because it was in such a quiet locality, and Mr. Joskins loves peace and seclusion. It is a rural kind of a neighborhood, and all of Mr. Joskins' neighbors keep cows. And every cow wears a bell. And with an instinct worthy of the Peak family, each neighbor had selected a cow bell of a different key and tone from any of the others, in order that he might know the cow of his heart from the other kind of the district. So that Mr. Joskins's nights are filled with music, of a rather wild, barbaric type; and the lone, starry hours talking nothing but cow to him, and he has learned so exactly the tones of every bell and the habits of each corresponding cow, that the voices of the night are full of intelligence, and he understands them. It makes it much easier for Mr. Joskins, who is a very nervous man, than if he had to listen and conjecture and wonder until he was fairly wild, as the rest of us would have to do. As it is, when the first sweet moments of his slumber are broken by a solemn, ponderous, resonant *Ka-lum, ka-lum, ka-lum!*, Mr. Joskins knows that the widow Barbery's old crumple horn is going down the street looking for an open front gate, and his knowledge is confirmed by a doleful *Ka-lum-pu-lum* that occurs at regular intervals as old crumple pauses to try each gate as she passes it, for she knows that appearances are deceitful, and that a boy can shut a front gate in such a way as to thoroughly deceive his father and yet leave every catch unfastened. Then when Mr. Joskins is called up from his second doze by a lively serenade of *T-link, to-lank, lank, lankle-inkle, lankle-inkel-tekinleinkletelink, kink, kink!,* he knows that Mr. Throop's young brindle is in Thorstlewaite's garden and that Throstlewaite is sailing around after her in a pair of slippers and a few clothes. And by sitting up in bed Mr. Joskins can hear the things that Mr. Thorstelwaite is throwing strike against the side of the house and the woodshed, *thud, spat, bang,* and the character of the noises tells him whether the missile was a clod, a piece of board, or a brick. And when the wind down the street is fair, it brings with it faint echoes of Mr. Thorstlewaite's remarks, which bring into Mr. Joskins's bedroom the odor of bad grammatical construction and wicked wishes and very ill-applied epithets. Then when the final crash and tinkle announce that the cow has bulged through the front fence and got away, and Mr. Joskins turns over to try and get a little sleep, he is not surprised, although he is annoyed, to be aroused by a sepulchral *Klank, klank, klank!* like the chains on the old-fashioned ghost of a murdered man, for he knows it is Throstlewaite's old duck-legged brown cow, going down to the vacant lot on the corner to fight anything that gives milk. And he waits and listens to the *klank, klank, klank* until it reaches the corner and a terrific din and medley of all the cow bells on the street tell him the skirmishers have been driven in and the action has become general. And from that on till morning, Mr. Joskins hears the *tinkle-tankle* of the little red cow going down the alley to prospect among the garbage heaps, and the *rankle-tankle, rankle-tankle* of the short-tailed black and white cow skirmishing down the street ahead of an escort of badly assorted dogs, and the *tringle-de-ding, tringle-de-ding, ding, ding* of the muley cow that goes along the sidewalk, browsing on the lower limbs of the shade trees, and the *klank, klank, klank* of the fighting cow, whose bell is cracked in three places and incessant *moo-o-oo-ah-ha* of the big black cow that has lost the clapper out of her bell and has ever since kept up an intermittent bellowing to supply its loss. And Mr. Joskins knows all these cows by their bells, and he knows what they are doing and where they are going. And although it has murdered his dreams of a quiet home, yet it has given him an opportunity to cultivate habits of intelligent observation, and it has induced him to register a vow that if he is ever rich enough he will keep nine cows, trained to sleep all day so as to be ready for duty at night, and he will live in the heart of the city with them and make them wear four bells apiece just for the pleasure of his neighbors.

The Language of Flowers

It was a Mt. Pleasant girl. No other human divinity could play such heartless trick on an admiring, nay, an adoring and adorable young man. He was always praised the flowers she wore, and talked so learnedly about flowers in general, that this incredulous young angel "put up a job" on him—if one may be so sacrilegious as to write slang in connection with so much beauty and grace. She filled the bay window with freshly potted weeds which she had laboriously gathered from the sidewalk and in the hollow under the bridge, and when he came round that evening she led the conversation to flowers, and her admirer to the bay window. "Such lovely plants she had," she told him, and he just clasped his hands and looked around him in silly ecstasy, trying to think of their names.

"That is *Patagonia influnenses*, Mr. Bogundus," she said, pointing to the miserable cheat of a young ragweed; "did you ever see anything so delicate?"

"Oh!" he ejaculated, regarding it reverentially; "beautiful, beautiful; what delicately serrated leaves!"

"And," she went on, with a face as angelic as though she was only saying *Now I lay me down to sleep*, "it breaks out in the summer in such curious green blossoms, clinging to long, slender stems. Only think of that—green blossoms." And she gazed pensively on the young man as though she saw something green what probably would never blossom.

"Wonderful, wonderful indeed," he said, "we can never tire of botany. It continually opens to us new worlds of wonders with every awakening flower and unfolded leaf."

"And here," she said, indicating with her snowy finger a villainous sprout of that little bur the boys call "beggar's lice," "this *Mendicantis parasitatis*, what…"

"Oh!" he exclaimed, rapturously, "where did you get it? Why, do you know how rare it is? I have not see one in Burlington since Mrs. O'Gheminie went to Chicago. She had such beautiful species of them; such a charming variety. She used to wear them in her hair so often."

"No doubt," the angel said dryly; and the young man feared he had done wrong in praising Mrs. O'Gheminie's plants so highly. But the dear one went on, and pointing to a young jimson weed, said:

"This is my pet, this *Jimsonata filiofensis*."

The young man gasped with the pleasure of a true lover of flowers, as he bent over it in admiration and inhaled its nauseous odor. Then he rose up and said:

"This plant has some medicinal properties."

"Ah!" she said.

"Yes," he replied, stiffly, "it has. I have smelt that plant in my boyhood days. Wilted on the kitchen stove, then bruised and applied to the eruption, the leaves are excellent remedial agents for the poison of the ivy." He strode past the smiling company that gathered in the parlor, and said sternly, "We meet no more! And, seizing his father's best hat from the rack, he extinguished himself in it, and went banging along the lien of tree-boxes which lined his darkened way.

FROM THE LIFE OF HON. WILLIAM F. CODY, KNOWN AS BUFFALO BILL, THE FAMOUS HUNTER, SCOUT, AND GUIDE. AN AUTOBIOGRAPHY (1879)

BUFFALO BILL

Said by many to be the most famous American in the world at the beginning of the twentieth century, William F. Cody, better known as Buffalo Bill, was an Iowan by birth. As he intimates in the autobiographical excerpt that follows, the Mississippi River itself and its then-plentiful wildlife well-prepared Cody for the more wild West where he would earn fame as a scout, guide, hunter, horseman, and creator of the world-famous Buffalo Bill's Wild West Show, *which ran for an unbelievable thirty years.*

My debut upon the world's state occurred on February 26, 1845. The scene of this first important event in my adventurous career, being in Scott County, in the state of Iowa. My parents, Isaac and Mary Ann Cody, who were numbered among the pioneers of Iowa, gave me the name of William Frederick. I was the fourth child in the family. Martha and Julia my sisters, and Samuel my brother, had preceded me, and the children who came after me were Eliza, Nellie, Mary, Charles, born in the order named.

At the time of my birth the family resided on a farm which they called "Napsinekee Place"—an Indian name—and here the first six or seven years of my childhood were spent. When I was about seven years old my father moved the family to the little town of LeClair, located on the bank of the Mississippi, fifteen miles above the city of Davenport. Even at that early age my adventurous spirit led me into all sorts of mischief and danger, and when I look back upon my childhood's days, I often wonder that I did not get drowned while swimming or sailing, or my neck broken while I was stealing apples in the neighboring orchards.

I well remember the day that I went sailing with two other boys; in a few minutes we found ourselves in the middle of the Mississippi; becoming frightened at the situation we lost our presence of mind as well as our oars. We at once set up a chorus of pitiful yells, when a man, who fortunately heard us, came to our rescue with a canoe and towed us ashore. We had stolen the boat, and our trouble did not end until we had each received a merited whipping which impressed the incident vividly upon my mind. I recollect several occasions when I was nearly eaten up by a large and savage dog, which acted as custodian of an orchard and also of a melon patch, which I frequently visited. Once, as I was climbing over the fence with a hatful of apples, this dog, which had started for me, caught me by the seat of the pantaloons, and while I clung to the top of the fence he literally tore my flesh. I got away with the apples, however, by tumbling over the opposite side of the fence with them.

It was at LeClair that I acquired my first experience as an equestrian. Somehow or other I had managed to corner a horse near a fence, and had climbed upon his back. The next moment the horse got his back up and hoisted me into the air, I fell violently to the ground, striking upon my side in such a way as to severely wrench and strain my arm, from the effects of which I did not recover for some time. I abandoned the art of horsemanship for a while, and was induced after considerable persuasion to turn my attention to letters—my A,B,C's—which were taught me at the village school.

My father at this time was running a stage line between Chicago and Davenport, no railroads then having been built west of Chicago. In 1849 he got the California fever and made up his mind to cross the Great Plains—which were then and for years afterwards called the American Desert—to the Pacific Coast. He got ready a complete outfit and started with quite a party. After proceeding a few miles, all but my father, and greatly to his disappointment, changed their minds for some reason and abandoned the enterprise. They all returned home, and soon afterwards father moved his family out to Walnut Grove Farm, in Scott County.

While living there I was sent to school, more for the purpose of being kept out of mischief than to learn anything. Much of my time was spent in trapping quails, which were very plentiful. I greatly enjoyed studying the habits of the little birds, and in devising traps to take them in. I was most successful with the common figure "4" trap which I could build myself. Thus I think it was that I acquired my love for hunting. I visited the quail traps twice a day, morning and evening, and as I had now become quite a good rider I was allowed to have one of the farm horses to carry me over my route. Many a jolly ride I had and many a boyish prank was perpetrated after getting well away from and out of the sight of home with the horse.

There was one event which occurred in my childhood, which I cannot recall without a feeling of sadness. It was the death of my brother Samuel, who was accidentally killed in his twelfth year.

My father at the time, being considerable of a politician as well as a farmer, was attending a political convention; for he was well known in those days as an old line Whig. He had been a member of the Iowa legislature, was a justice of the peace, and had held other offices. He was an excellent stump speaker and was often called upon to canvass the country round about for different candidates. The convention which he was attending at the time of the accident was being held at a crossroad tavern called "Sherman's" about a mile away.

Samuel and I had gone out together on horseback for the cows. He rode a vicious mare, which mother had told him time and again not to ride, as it had an ugly disposition. We were passing the schoolhouse just as the children were being dismissed, when Samuel undertook to give an exhibition of his horsemanship, he being a good rider for a boy. The mare, Besty, became unmanageable, reared and fell backward upon him, injuring him internally. He was picked up and carried amid great excitement to the house of a neighbor.

I at once set out with my horse at the top of his speed for my father, and informed him of Samuel's mishap. He took the horse and returned immediately. When I arrived at Mr. Burns' house, where my brother was, I found my father, mother, and sisters there, all weeping bitterly at Samuel's bedside. A physician, after examining him, pronounced his injuries to be of a fatal character. He died the next morning.

My brother was a great favorite with everybody, and his death cast a gloom upon the whole neighborhood. It was a great blow to all of the family, and especially to father, who seemed to be almost heartbroken over it.

Father had been greatly disappointed at the failure of his California expedition, and still desired to move to some new country. The death of Samuel no doubt increased this desire, and he determined to emigrate. Accordingly, early in the spring of 1852, he disposed of his farm, and late in March we took our departure for Kansas, which was then an unsettled territory. Our outfit consisted of one carriage, three wagons, and some fine-blooded horses. The carriage was occupied by my mother and sisters. Thus we left our Iowa home.

From A Boyhood Life in Iowa Forty Years Ago: As Found in the Memoirs of Rufus Rittenhouse (1880)

Rufus Rittenhouse

A much neglected figure in Iowa history, Dubuque's Rufus Rittenhouse penned one of the first and most valuable memoirs of northeastern Iowa, a small but fascinating volume printed by Charles B. Door in Dubuque and sold for fifteen cents. In the passage following, Rittenhouse recalls the religious fervor of the Mississippi Valley during settlement days, at which time Dubuque was little more than a scattering of houses up to 6th Street. In his Recollections of People and Events of Dubuque Iowa, 1846-1890, *John Conzett recalls the "castle-like" dwelling Rufus Rittenhouse, a bricklayer and contractor, eventually built himself on the bluff facing 14th Street—a home perhaps patterned after Father Simeon Clark's impressive homestead as described herein.*

In the summer of 1838 or 1839, we had a camp-meeting in a grove near Peter L. Sharp's place; it was largely attended, many coming from Dubuque and the adjacent settlements; the rain came down in torrents but notwithstanding a great outpouring of the spirit was manifest. I was soon converted; though I was young I knew I was a sinner; the power of the Lord was so greatly kindled for miles around, that a Dutchman and an Irishman were converted—Peter Bony and Felix O'Flaherty. Peter has remained among the faithful, but alas poor Felix soon sank below his first estate, and is not. All in the neighborhood were converted except two or three families which were looked upon as bad by the neighbors.

It was our custom in those days to watch the old year out and the new one in, and while we were fully determined to do better the coming year I am fearful that we did worse. I watched one year out at Brother John Paul's and the next at Father Simeon Clark's; I do not know which year I did the best, but I did nothing very bad.

Father Simeon Clark in those days never wore anything but a red handkerchief on his head—I never saw him with anything else and believe no one ever did. He was an excellent rifle-shot and a good bee-hunter. His residence some ten miles west of Dubuque was built near the head of a deep vale, in a sort of horseshoe; good springs on either side of the house went trickling down the valley some three-fourths of a mile to the south fork of the Little Maquoketa, whose general course was northeast, a stream so crooked that were you to follow its windings five miles you would have traveled twenty-five. The hills on either side were so high that no ordinary gun would reach to the top—if there was one it was one that afterwards came into my hands, of which I shall speak hereafter, but I never tried it at that range. The house was situated at an altitude of some six hundred feet above the level of the great Mississippi Valley. It was a heavy woodland section of country for miles; a small strip of table-land had been cleared a hundred feet or more above the house, and some two or three yards south near the dividing ridge. Deer were plenty, and black wolves were seen now and then; other species of game were very numerous, especially the catamount, and now and then the distant cry of the panther could be heard; occasionally a bald eagle could be seen flying over or perched on some high tree in search of prey, and the dismal hoots of the owl could be heard in the twilight.

Father Clark's house may have been fifteen feet by twenty-five, one end nearly all chimney, at the opposite end stood two beds, puncheon floors, doors the same, roof covered with clapboards and ridge poles, small cock-loft overhead. It was in the spring of 1840, I was at the house to hear him preach; puncheon benches had been brought in as was the custom, to seat all who might come; there may have been twenty persons present—four or five men, some long gaunt women, and the balance principally children; around the fireplace hung a dozen or more great venison hams swinging to and fro, drying for a time of need. Here Father Clark delivered his discourse, a masterly one. I have many times since listened to more eloquent discourses but never to any so impressive. The reader will pause for a moment and turn to the twelfth chapter and twenty-fifth verse, where he will find in Paul's advice to the Hebrews, "See that ye refuse not him that speaketh." Father Clark dwelt on depravity of mankind, that all men were sinners and finally wound up by saying that perhaps not more than two or three in that little assembly would be saved; 'twas a solemn time; Father Clark and Brother John Paul made two that I was sure would be saved, but as he said two or three might be saved, I thought Brother Morrison might make up the three; I looked upon the balance as lost; as for myself I had done nothing to merit salvation; true I had given the Spanish quarter that I had had in the root house, which my grandfather had given me, for the conversion of the heathen, and though I had taken the preacher for my mother to cook dinner for, I gave myself up for lost. I went away firmly resolved to tell no more lies about my grandfather in New Jersey, to whose princely fortune I would soon be sole heir.

Sometime after this I again attended service at Father Clark's; he was not the preacher at this time, but during class he told the brethren that he had a remarkable vision that he would die somewhere about the 14th of August that year; as the time was set so exact, we all watched, and though he was like good old

Simeon, ready and willing to die, for his eyes had seen the salvation of the Lord, yet his time had not come and though he had vision of his death thirty-nine years ago, I found him last summer, hale and hearty, minus the handkerchief, the postmaster of the enterprising village of Farley, twenty miles west of Dubuque.

Many of those good men of that day have since passed away, while but few remain whose lives and example would be well worthy of our imitation, particularly Father Simeon Clark.

From "Far from the Madding Crowd" (1882)

Emerson Hough

A Jasper County boy from Newton, Iowa, and a graduate of the State University of Iowa, now the University of Iowa, where he played on the football team and edited the newspaper, Emerson Hough worked for a short time after graduation as a surveyor in central Iowa, the setting for the outdoor scene that follows. After being admitted to the bar at Newton, and after a brief tenure at the Des Moines Times in 1884 as a business manager, Hough moved to Chicago to edit the "Chicago and the West" column for Field and Stream. The column gave him the perfect excuse to indulge his native interest in the Great Plains and the West, a fascination he mined in penning the dozens of popular novels set west of the Mississippi that would make him, according to Wallace Stegner, "the earliest writer of any prominence who can be legitimately considered Iowan." "Far from the Madding Crowd," Hough's first published magazine piece, demonstrates the wit and perceptiveness that would attract the attention of the editors at Forest and Stream, where this article appeared in the August 17, 1882 issue. The narrative, written less than forty years after Iowa entered the union, shows how quickly the state passed from pioneer territory to a thoroughly cultivated, thoroughly conquered land; after all, Hough's audience here is not the Iowan of pioneer stock, but the man with the desk job already longing for a return to a more primitive state, à la back-to-the-lander and future Emerson Hough friend and fan, Teddy Roosevelt. In singing the praises of Iowa's unheralded "wall" lakes—glacial lakes with rock-walled beaches—Hough takes up the mantle of countless Iowans since: namely, to convince tourists, as Meredith Willson put it in his famous lyrics to The Music Man, to "give Iowa a try."

There come days in the life of any businessman when the worries and perplexities of daily work seem almost unbearable. When he is sick of the treadmill walk, when he longs to throw from him the interests of his patrons, customers, and clients and live for a few blissful moments for himself alone. Take from him the possibility of doing this and you shorten his life and depreciate his usefulness. Any machine is better for rest. A razor cuts better from rest.

The desire for rest is gratified in various ways; but there is no more natural or effective way, even for the non-sporting man, than to merge for a time the artificial man into the natural; to sink civilized training in the instincts given us by our fathers, the savages, and rest for a little while near to nature's heart.

Now there are many men who long with a great longing for a few days' outing in the woods or on the streams, who suddenly become possessed to renew some of the innocent pleasures of their youth, but who are deterred by motives of economy, or by a lack of the experience which would make then "handy" in going at it. To these, for whom we have sympathy, we beg leave to speak a few words. The trouble is, we are too ambitious. We want to go to the Adirondacks, or the [Great] Lakes, or the Rockies, and the Yellowstone Country. Now, this is fine, but not needful. Rest and enjoyment can be found closer to home.*

Now suppose you live in the middle of the prairie state of Iowa, for instance, where the midsummer sun blazes hot and fierce, and the long, dry reaches of unprotected ground would seem to offer the least possible attractions to pleasure seekers. Even here you can have a pleasant trip. If you don't believe it, we will tell you of one of several we have made ourselves, being no better equipped than as we have described.

The [prairie] "chicken" season of [18]81 opened hot and dry; and as we started out for a trip to one of the so-called wall lakes of central Iowa, our friends assured us we should roast. But out on the road of the August breeze seemed all at once refreshing. The breath we breathed was all our own, the time we spent we did not count by the hour, and life again seemed worth the living.

The first night out it rained. The rain was wet. Our trusty old tent sprung a leak; water stood in pools upon the blankets, and trickled in streams through our beds of straw. In the morning, the Professor wanted to go home. He said he was going to die, and wanted to perish in the bosom of his family. We built a fire, hung him over a rail, and dried him out. A little later I saw him with an expression of wonder on his face, carefully feeling himself all over. Said he: "Heretofore no one could have persuaded me that so much moisture could be absorbed by the human tissues without producing serious complications. Yet I experience no ill effects. Hurrah! I'm prouder of myself than I was when I took the valedictory!" And he jumped up and began to harness a mule. He was a cured man.

We passed on our way under the overhanging willow hedges of Storey [Story] County. At noon we would halt and unsling the "grub-box," and the Judge would make the coffee. No matter how hot the weather, we had coffee three times a day.

The Judge was famous for his coffee. He would build the tiniest, hottest fire, and in less than no time have the water boiling; then he put in a double handful of coffee, set it back, and forthwith there arose a delicious fragrance, and with a musical gurgle the little black sheet-iron coffee pot announced itself "All ready!" God bless thee, little coffee pot! Foul fall the hand would mar the symmetry! Across the plains in [18]61, through the Gunnison country in [18]80, along many a wooded stream, by many a reedy lake in Iowa has they voice murmured sympathy.

A woman would despise thee; a hired girl would crush thee; but we tired men adore thee, and again exclaim, "All hail!"

We usually traveled about thirty miles a day, though on the level prairies we could have made fifty. We were in no hurry, and found as much pleasure in gypsying along the roadside as in the more exciting sport of hunting and fishing. The gentle Iowa scenery was soothing and restful.

At night we would select some high and breezy point for our camp, being too wise to camp near the streams, where mosquitoes, malaria, and much oppressiveness do abound. While one tended to the team, another brought wood and water and helped with the tent and bedding, while two were detailed to "get something for supper." Old Rex, noblest of a noble strain of settlers, could right easily in that country find a covey of "chickens," and enough were soon secured for our needs. We never killed a bird we did not eat and allowed just one bird per meal to each man. That made fifteen a day; we could easily have killed a hundred. I have often left a covey in the grass after bagging what I wanted.

Then at night about the campfire the Judge would tell us of the Sioux Massacre at Spirit Lake in [18]57, or of deer hunting in New York, or of fishing in the South, or would nudge Ned and ask him if he remembered his first night out on the skunk bottoms, when he thought the big owl was a wolf. I remember that night myself. We did not foresee in the blue-eyed six-year-old who "wanted to go home," the self-reliant youth who, before he was twenty, would foot it across the range from Leadville, shoot deer in the Rockies, and in his lonely camp never be frightened by the panther's scream. Steady as a veteran, modest as a girl, deadshot, expert fisherman, perfect horseman, with a heart as big as all outdoors and a politeness that is not of the house. Tell me it is wasting time to camp out!

Can I ever forget those days? Can I ever forget the evening when the Judge and I threw down our game bags (Tell it not in Gath! His was full of half-grown teal), and went down to the lakeshore to watch the "old gentleman" play the big pike which rose to the spoon from the lily pads. Do we not often catch that pike again? And will we not have some time to catch his mate? Aye, that we will, God willing. And you, men of toils and weariness, will you not come with us, and be strengthened so that you will go back to work rejoicing as a strong man to a run a race?

The old heathen god could not be killed while his feet were on the ground, which means that Mother Nature is kind to those who bring their troubles to her—which means that it will pay you to go.

And lest we be accused of digression from our original topic, let us add that for the eight days out on this trip, our expenses, above those to which we have alluded as preliminary, amounted for each man to just 55 cents. And this is true.

From **Iowa in War Times (1888)**

S. H. M. Byers

Samuel Hawkins Marsh Byers, whose family hailed from Mahaska County, was called the "Poet Laureate of Iowa" long before that office had officially been created. Byers, now mostly forgotten, was a true renaissance man, serving honorably as an adjutant in the Fifth Iowa Infantry during the Civil War and, later, as the Consul General to Rome, of all faraway places. But Byers was better known for his pen, from which flowed the famous poem "Sherman's March to the Sea" as well as "The Song of Iowa," which the state legislature adopted in 1911. The first verse of that classic anthem reads, "You asked what land I love the best, Iowa, 'tis Iowa, / The fairest State of all the west, Iowa, O! Iowa, / From yonder Mississippi's stream / To where Missouri's waters gleam / O! fair it is as poet's dream, Iowa, in Iowa."

To the Reader

Every state has its heroic age. Iowa, young as she is, has possibly passed the high-tide period of her existence. Scarcely once in a thousand years do states or nations fight for a principle really vital to the human race. All states worth preserving have wars. Fate stands at the side of the bravest, and in these times, as in all times, nations exist by the edge of their sabers and the caliber of their cannon. Yea, so long as men are human, wars will rage in the world somewhere. But war for the upholding of *Freedom*, for the unchaining of millions of human beings, such wars, are the epochs of the ages.

It is a happy people to whom fate gives the chance to strike a blow for human rights. That people's history is made. Had the Greeks no tale but Marathon, their fame would be complete; the Swiss no names but Morgarten, Winkelried and Sempach, their history would be perpetual. The traditions of heroic deeds outlive all the books of the world, and the sacrifice of life on the altar of liberty is a deed approved by angels. Liberty never saw a war waged in her name on so grand a scale as on the American continent. The battles of the Greeks, the Swiss, the early English and the Holland struggle, were petty encounters when compared with the mighty conflicts of the War of the Rebellion. Many northern states won imperishable renown in the struggle, but the state of Iowa, by common consent, stood first and foremost among them all. Of a population of less than seven hundred thousand, nearly eighty thousand were in the field. Of her arms-bearing men, every other one stood in the ranks of the union army. Two thousand one hundred and fifty-two of them were killed outright in battle; ten thousand two hundred and sixteen died in hospitals and from wounds and sickness; more than ten thousand were discharged for disability and bodies ruined by the service. It was an awful price for young Iowa to pay, in her valor and faith, but it brought her a renown as lasting as history. The soldiers of Iowa marched in columns from the Des Moines River to the Atlantic Ocean, and from the Gulf to the interior of every rebel state. Her flags floated at the front in every battle, and points of most awful danger in every conflict in the South were given to Iowa men. From chasing the murderous guerrillas of Missouri, to battling with the trained hosts in the Shenandoah Valley, from Donelson to Shiloh, from Atlanta to Mobile, from Cairo, in Illinois, to the heart of South Carolina, from the beginning of the bloody war until its very end, the history of the soldiers of Iowa has been the story of brave men. Ten thousand miles of marching, a hundred battlefields, and almost never a defeat. Men who had never seen a fort, went and took a dozen straight by storm. More prisoners were taken than the number of the captors; more cannon charged and captured than would man a dozen Sevastopols; more flags than the North had states. They marched to South Carolina, captured its treasonable capital, tore down its rebel banner, brought it home as a trophy, and hoisted the loyal flag of Iowa in its stead. Their cavalry rode to every town in rebeldom—and on horse or foot, helped to accomplish more harm to a foeman than had ever been done in the history of cavalry before. From the beginning until the end, the story of Iowa valor was the same as that of tried comrades from other states—not greater, for all were brave, but these conspicuously so. Their fortune kept them at the front; they were the first everywhere; at Wilson's Creek, Iuka, Donelson, Shiloh; at Vicksburg, Atlanta, Allatoona, Chattanooga and Mobile. Wherever Grant and Sherman led, they followed, and to victory. They were the heroes—the history-makers of the state. Their deeds will live. It is an impressive thought to realize that a thousand years from now schoolboys will be taught the story of these men. We owe the future something, we owe it to these men, that, as far as in us lies, the truth as to the heroism of these Iowa patriots, and the sacrifices of Iowa at home, shall be preserved.*

The War Governor

"Ten days ago there were two parties in Iowa," wrote Gov. Kirkwood to the President. "Now, there is only one, and that one for the Constitution and the Union unconditionally." What patriotic days those were in loyal Iowa—those Sumter days! For a while it seemed as if all party rancor had died out, with but one single sentiment animating every breast alike—the one resolve to avenge the insult at Sumter, and to save the union.

In the state's financial extremities, Gov. Kirkwood had secured the money for sending the first regiment to rendezvous by his own exertions, and the exertion of two or three personal friends. Money had to be had, and the governor gave his own personal bonds, pledging all his own property and earnings, many times over, that the first soldiers of the state might have shoes to wear, blankets to sleep on, and bread to eat.

Then came the patriotism of the banks of Iowa. Many of them offered the aid the state needed in its distress, without pledge and without bond. Men like Senator J. K. Graves, of Dubuque, offered loans to the state of many thousands of dollars without a thought as to when, if ever, the money might be returned. That meant patriotism, and Senator Graves was the first to risk his property that Iowa honor might be maintained. [The very morning after Sumter was fired on, J. K. Graves and R. E. Graves, his brother, telegraphed the governor, saying they would claim it an honor and privilege to honor his drafts to the extent of thirty thousand dollars; leaving repayment to the pleasure of the state, if it could help equip and send the boys to the front. It was the same spirit that later led these same men to hurry a carload of stores to the suffering of Chicago before the houses of the doomed city were done burning down. It was the prompt and splendid example of these men that soon led thousands of others to open their purses for the help of the state and its soldiers. They proved the maxim, too, that "he gives twice who gives promptly."] "You are authorized to draw on us for any sum you may need," was a common message telegraphed to the governor from the branch banks in different parts of the state. W. T. Smith, of Oskaloosa, and other strong war democrats, also came forward and promptly tendered money to the state. The railroads offered to carry the soldiers free, and private citizens in every town vied with one another in personal sacrifice to aid in the good cause.

Patriotism burned at its very height. The governor had called for but one regiment; that was on April 17th. Within a week, twenty-one companies were offered, and in a short time every organized militia company in the state, with one single exception, was tendered to defend the flag. Then commenced, too, the organizing of volunteer companies for the war. There was but one sentiment— "the Union." For a while party distinctions disappeared entirely. Even the old sympathizers with slavery were silent, and the mossback demagogues who had no patriotism in their thin-blooded veins shouted for the preservation of the union. Those who were not loyal kept it secret, and publicly cheered for the flag. The newspapers talked of nothing but the war, and many kept flags and patriotic songs permanently at the head of their columns. Their editorials were of loyalty to the country, and the very advertisements teemed with hints to stir the patriotism of the people. Republicans and Democrats met in the same rooms, forgetting their animosities, and talked only of Sumter and the South. In Martinsburg, Republicans and Democrats held a war meeting together and tore their partisan flags in pieces, to splice them in one common banner. At Aledo, the Democrats and Republicans took their party pole, cut them in two, spliced half of each together, and put the union flag on top.

At little Brighton, $1,250, cash, was raised in a few minutes from Republicans and Democrats alike, and as much more promised, to help feed and clothe the boys who volunteered. Jesse Bowen presented the state with a brass eight-pounder cannon, and eighty rifles. That was the kind of a present Iowa needed then, as much as money. The governor thanked Bowen for his patriotic gift, in the name of all Iowa. Those who could not fight gave of their substance. The little community of Amana, in Iowa County, sent the governor a present of a thousand dollars, to help clothe the Iowa soldiers. Later, the same society gave from its scanty means five hundred dollars more. Doctors offered their services to the enlisting soldiers, gratis. The women of the state did even more than the men. No sacrifice of means, of time, of labor of deft hands—no struggle of breaking heart, was too much for those, who, with their blessings and their prayers, were sending fathers, husbands, sons, brothers and lovers to battle to save the country. Wives of senators, representatives, and men in high place—women of position, of comfort, left their ease to sew and labor for the enlisting soldiers. In six days, the women of Burlington, with Mrs. Senator Grimes at their head, made three hundred soldiers' coats and haversacks. It was the same in every town and village and hamlet in the state—the "Woman's Relief Corps" being always the first and noblest organization of the place.

The church, with the press, took up the patriotic song all over the state. Ringing sermons of patriotism were preached from every pulpit. Every prayer ended with a benediction on the soldiers going to the front. To serve the state, at that hour, was to serve the Lord. The patriotism of the land was the religion of the land. Sermons were preached by men like William Salter of Burlington, Thomas Merrill of Newton, Asa Turner of Denmark, and scores of others, that made men shoulder their muskets to fight as they had prayed. The anti-slavery clergy saw in the action of the Rebels, the doom of slavery, and thanked the Lord. The Wyoming Conference resolved: "Whereas, Divine Providence has taken the work of emancipation into His own hands—therefore resolved, that we stand still and see the salvation of God."

There seemed but one sentiment abroad. "How many of the people of your town are in sympathy with this northern crusade on the South?" wrote a planter to a northern wholesale merchant; "we purchasers of your dry goods are interested in knowing." The merchant replied by expressing to the planter a copy or the *town directory.* The merchant's answer would have been a true index just then to the loyalty of every town in Iowa.

The first regiment was formed and ready for the march two weeks before the time designated by the government, and many companies all over the state waited anxiously for their opportunity. So far, only the one regiment had been demanded, but Gov. Kirkwood sent Senator Grimes to Washington to urge on the President the acceptance of more Iowa troops. In the meantime, he urged the people at home to keep up their military organizations, and to form from farm and village, bodies of "minute men," as did our fathers in the Revolution—neglecting neither plow nor anvil, yet prepared to march on an hour's notice. Uniforms and even arms were impossible to obtain; nor was there even legal authority for their purchase, were they obtainable by borrowed money. At his own risk, the governor sent the Hon. Ezekiel Clark, himself a most devoted patriot, to Chicago, to buy cloth for fifteen hundred uniforms. He reckoned on the deft hands of Iowa's loyal women for their making up for nothing. He did not reckon in vain. "Let the material be strong and durable," he added in his official note to Clark. There was to be no shoddy in the coats of Iowa soldiers, if bought by her loyal governor, and made by her loyal women.

The first regiment was ordered by the War Department to rendezvous at Keokuk. The governor urged Davenport as the better point, as Keokuk had no direct railroad east in those days, and not even a line of telegraph. The change to Davenport was not made, however. Keokuk's proximity to the distracted, half-rebel state of Missouri, made that city a near point to start from southward. It required a letter from three to five days to reach Des Moines, or the center of the state, and its lines of communication were poor in all directions. To reach the interior of the state quickly, the Burlington *Hawkeye* Company advertised for a "pony express" to carry its papers from Eddyville to Des Moines, a distance of seventy-five miles—time to be eight hours.

Never in the history of the state did a governor have such a burden, such a variety and such a vexation of duties. All fell upon his own personal shoulders. He had no aides, no staff—not even a private secretary, at first—and yet the pressing business, the overwhelming correspondence, permitted of no delay. Stenographers and typewriters were unknown at executive headquarters. Only an exceptionally strong body, and the kindness of a few friends who volunteered to help in the correspondence, made it possible for the accumulating business to be pushed along. A quiet, simple peace establishment had suddenly thrust upon it the burdens of a war footing. The cry for "muskets, more muskets," came up from every quarter of the state, and there were no muskets to send. "For God's sake send us arms," wrote the governor to Simon Cameron on the 29th of April, 1861. "I ask for nothing but *arms* and *ammunition*—we have the men to use them. Three regiments are waiting, and five thousand guns are required at once."

The Adjutant General's office was as much overrun with the new business as was the office of the chief executive; but fortunately it, too, was filled by a zealous patriot and a competent man. No labor was too great, no sacrifice too much, for the patriotism of Jesse Bowen, Iowa's Adjutant General at the breaking out of the battle storm.

On the 6th of May, the First regiment of Iowa infantry volunteers was ordered into rendezvous at Keokuk, by the governor. The Captains of the ten companies were, Matthies, Mahanna, Mason, Cummins, Streaper, Cook, Gottschalk, Wise, Wentz and Herron. Some of these names became famous as the war went on, and scores of the private soldiers comprising the regiment earned honorable commissions at the mouths of rebel cannon. Mr. I. K. Fuller went with the regiment as Chaplain, and Mrs. Fuller was the first regimental nurse to volunteer in the state.

Tenders of volunteer companies reached the governor daily, and the urgings for their acceptance for the country's defense were little short of angry declarations, so eager were all for the fray. The War Department thought it had no need for more than a thousand men from Iowa, and the governor was greatly embarrassed as to what to do with so many companies pressing for acceptance. He had not yet secured proper arms, spite of efforts made in every direction to buy in the market, or even to borrow of Illinois. The money he was borrowing of the state banks, to meet urgent expenses, was without sanction of law, leaving him personally liable for it all. All over the state, companies were kept together drilling, their subsistence furnished by boards of supervisors or by patriotic citizens, some of whom not only helped subsist the would-be soldiers, but furnished them uniforms at their own expense. Men who could not conveniently abandon business to volunteer, feared no sacrifice of labor and money that could add to the comforts of those who could volunteer. The extent of the patriotism, the sacrifices, the courage, the great loyal-heartedness of the men at home in Iowa, who stood like a bulwark behind the soldiers, cheering and supporting them and maintaining their families, is simply beyond reckoning. Without this phenomenal support, without this loyal holding up of the arms of the soldiers, success in the war would have been impossible. There were as great patriots, as sacrificing men and women, holding the plow and threading the needle at home in Iowa, as there were facing the cannon in the South. Their names should be written in letters of gold. They bore the sacrifice and the heartbreaks of war without the excitement and the glory of the contest as reward. Many of them impoverished themselves that our soldiers might have aid—quiet, duty-doing patriots and heroes, whose names never flamed in the bulletins, who did duty because it was duty. Their names in

Iowa are legion, and a grateful state will think of them, as it thinks of the sons, husbands and brothers whom it sent to the field.

From **Iowa Cranks: Or, The Beauties of Prohibition; A Political Novel (1890)**

E. N. Chapin

An exceedingly rare find is this satiric novel, held by less than a half dozen libraries in the world. A newspaperman by trade, E.N. Chapin moved Marshall County's first newspaper, the Iowa Central Journal from Albion to the county set of Marshalltown in 1857. Chapin, a Democrat, positively hated Iowa's Republican-passed 1886 prohibition law, the Clark Law, arguing that it was "passed through the blindest fanaticism since the time when Salem witches were hung in New England." In the foreword to Iowa Cranks, Chapin blasts the prohibitionists, declaring "No Russian Czar, or Nero himself, had such despotic power as the constables of Iowa. It was a diabolical outrage upon the rights of the private citizens." Chapin fingers Des Moines as the most puritanical city in the state in its enforcement of the Clark Law, and, therefore, sets his political parable in the mythical Iowa town of Sebastapol, "a little suburb of the Capitol near the Coon River bridge." The name conjures the Ukrainian port city of Sebastapol, which endured an eleven-month siege during the Crimean War; clearly Chapin felt the small cities of Polk County under similar siege by the prohibitionists. The author closes his preface with this note to his readers, "In the following story, while names have been suppressed, the facts are true, and can be proven in every line." The vignette to follow opens with the story of John Penny, an "English agriculturalist" in "P-K City" in Iowa who has twenty acres of apples and, given the political climate, can't sell them to make alcoholic cider.

"Hello! Penny, you look grumpy. What is the matter with you?" cried a cheery voice, and Farmer Wilkinson came along to the orchard fence, driving a good team.

"I am sick of fool Iowa," said Penny, "and as soon as I can sell I'll go to Missouri, or somewhere else."

"You cannot sell, John Penny, very well, for I've tried it for two years. There is no immigration, and all foreigners go round us, as if we had leprosy," remarked Wilkinson.

"Yes," and Penny looked half sorrowful, "my father and brothers in old England would not come here under this prohibitory law, I've told our folks just how it works. If prohibition prohibited, I wouldn't care much, but we all know that when a man wants a glass of liquor he can get it without any trouble."

Wilkinson nodded his head and slowly said, "This is a national campaign, and I don't want to give my vote or influence to the democrats, but next year I'll either stay at home or vote the democratic ticket. It is the only way to get rid of this confounded law." Penny thought a minute and replied slowly, "I hate to do such a thing, but if I don't sell and get out of the state, I shall vote the democratic ticket too."

The next spring in April days of 1889, Penny sowed a ten-acre lot with barley, for he found no customer for his farm, as word had gone out to Castle Garden—east, west, north, and south, that Iowa had raised bigger cranks than she did corn. The barley looked promising, and Penny hoped he could pay his debts in town. "I think it will pay better than corn anyway," he said.

One day, the Rev. Mr. Mossman, a sort of itinerant preacher, came along, and as Penny was fixing up his fence around the barley, the following conversation took place:

"I see you have a large field of barley out there, Mr. Penny. Do you expect to barley cakes next winter?"

"Oh no," said the farmer, as he wiped his forehead with a cheap cotton handkerchief, "I am raising barley to sell, not to eat it up in cakes."

"Don't they make good Milwaukee beer and ale out of it?" queried the preacher with a knowing look.

"Yes, I reckon they will, but I don't *know* it," said Penny.

"You ought to *know* it. Any man who will raise rye and barley to make whisky and beer is not the man for our neighborhood, or church; we live in a temperance community, and we expect every man to come up to our standard of right. Turn in your cattle and let them eat up the barley, or the curse of Almighty God may rest heavily on you and yours." With this warning, the pious itinerant drove to his home in the village.

Well! I'll be gumswizzled! What is a fellow to do? Asked Penny of himself. These cranks won't allow the corn and barley made up into alcohol here, and they would prevent its manufacture elsewhere. As it is, the railroads are paid to transport the corn to be manufactured into liquor at Peoria, or Milwaukee, and then paid to bring it back again for use in Iowa. We encourage manufactures for everything else but alcohol, yet we *must* at times have liquor.

If our whisky and alcohol could be made at home, made from our own corn, all we actually use in the arts and medicines—all made of Iowa corn, it would be worth something to the farmers. But my Farmers' Alliance never talks about anything but the monopoly of the railroads, trusts, etc. and it is of no use for me to say anything. I am simply disgusted with the situation."

Sunday, the Penny children went to the little Sabbath School in the village, and they heard a long lecture by the superintendent on the sin of intemperance, and the raising of barley for the Milwaukee brewers. "It ought not to be tolerated," said an old white-haired man from a corner of the room, and "I would be a party or empty the barley from the freight cars to the ground."

"Don't get excited," remarked Farmer Wilkinson, who was present. "This is not the place to berate our neighbors. We must talk and reason with them, before we take extreme measures."

The old man was about to speak again, when a young lady arose, and lifting up her voice, rang out these words: "The curse of God will rest on such sinners. A man who would raise barley and rye to make up into Milwaukee beer, or ale, would cut his neighbor's throat."

"Tut, tut," said Farmer Wilkinson, in the best of humor, "let us adjourn the Sabbath school, and try a temperance day some other time."

"The school stands adjourned, and four weeks from today we shall have Mr. D. M. Fox of Des Moines, to talk temperance to us." And the superintendent picked up his hat. There was some desultory talk among teachers and scholars, but as there was to be a program made out for "the temperance day" in the Sunday school, the barley question went out of sight.

John Penny, Jr. went home and reported the criticisms on his father's barley. "Yes, these temperance cranks drove off George Bartlett and all his married children, because he made cider to sell in Des Moines. And he was a good Christian man," said Mrs. Penny, a sweet, motherly person. "And now they want to get rid of me, because I raise barley. I'll sell, if possible, even at a sacrifice," emphatically remarked Penny.

"Mother, is there anything about prohibition in the Bible?" asked Mary, the oldest daughter.

"No, indeed?" Prohibition was never heard of until within a few years," answered the mother.

"I wonder if these cranks think that perdition is the portion of everybody who believes not in prohibition?" inquired John of his father.

"Yes, the most of them do, and for my part I long to get away from such folks. My father and grandfather were Baptists in the Old Country, and they drank ale, or beer, when at work. They were Christian men, and I do not believe they are lost, because they were not teetotalers. Christ says of the wine: "Drink ye all of it." This command is for sacramental purposes, and if there had been anything deleterious in the fluid, he would not have given the rule to his disciples. St. Paul says: "Take a little wine for the stomach's sake," but now this is scouted, as rumsellers' talk." And Mr. Penny took up his Bible, as if he had an unanswerable argument for someone to look after.

From "Student Life at Ames" (1894)

Tom Burke

Tom Burke's timeless memoir of student life at Iowa State University in Ames begins a stretch of a handful of readings dated 1894 to 1898 [Burke, Garland, Miller, Byers, Cole, Sharp, Smith, Horak, Colson, Ebersole] drawn from the pages of Des Moines's nationally known magazine, the Midland Monthly, *a journal edited in Iowa by Joseph Brigham, author and librarian and one-time part-owner of the Cedar Rapids* Republican, *for a few short, glorious years at the turn of the century before it was sold and reestablished in St. Louis. After the sale, Brigham eventually turned his sights back toward librarianship, as Iowa's Governor Shaw bestowed upon him the title of State Librarian in 1898. In this passage, Burke recalls the mainstays of campus life at Iowa Agricultural College. Though men still far outnumber women at Iowa State University, Burke's argument that women add refinement and balance to campus still compels, though his descriptions of the fairer sex are, by now, comically, even salaciously, outdated, as the last paragraph in this excerpt attests!*

My college days have drifted so far away among the spent years that it's difficult, at this distance, to drag them up through the memory rubbish that has since piled in over them.*

I will impose one other condition also. The students at Ames, while not wanting in urban manners, have a rural complexion that is quite marked; and, as I entered the institution fresh from the country, the personal character of this sketch must be taken as the reflection of a type, and not charged to lack of modesty.

The college of which I write is in Story County; but it's not located, as might be supposed, in the town which it made famous. It's in a healthy, picturesque region, about a mile west of Ames, and surrounded by a beautiful experimental farm of several hundred acres.

On entering at Ames, the first impressions that are made on a boy are apt to be lasting. Expansive grounds, beautiful in undulating surface, even before winter has relaxed from them his icy fingers; stately buildings scattered through the broad acreage of the campus and rising majestically among leafless branches of deciduous trees, or half obscured by clumps of evergreen; the winding gravel drive exposing at every turn new surprises in forestry or architecture; in short, the landscape, with its wealth of variety, is photographed indelibly on his youthful mind. And, as his fancy becomes stimulated, it leaps even beyond the surroundings and anticipates the scene when approaching spring shall have added the charms of flowers and foliage.

Suddenly Maxwell's bus stops at the front entrance to the main college building. I wonder if the old bus still runs. The new motor line I fear has retired it from service, with its bands of chattering passengers. But no doubt in going from town to college the students chatter just the same, whether in bus or car, and rapid transit for a nickel will be regarded by some as better than slow jolting for a dime.

As the occupants tumble out, they are met by a number of classmates already arrived. The greeting is tumultuous. Girls fall into each other's embrace, and boys tug away in couples, as if each were trying to jerk an arm off the other. It's the glad confusion of laughter and other expressions of joy in the meeting after vacation of college chums. There are no other sights nor sounds like it. None so full of unrestrained happiness. Our freshman, mute, with his mouth ajar, stands apart, smiling a plain country smile. How much at home in this vast place these young men and women see! They must be fine scholars, surely! It is another of his first impressions; and, like the landscape, it sinks into his memory.

Fares, please! The driver yells it this time. For a moment the tumult is turned, with slight interruption, into a hasty search for handbags and pocketbooks. The boys' wallets are the most accessible. One has been too quick for the others; the bill is settled; a clamorous protest from his fellows; reproving eyes from the girls; pardonable blushes. He must be a millionaire's son! They ascend the stone steps; the girls with arms entwined; boys bubbling over with delight; into the grand old building. At the crossing of the halls they separate—girls toward the south wing, chattering like magpies, laughing like chimes; boys up the spiral stairs, four steps at a jump. The freshman hesitates a moment at the entrance. He hears the echoes die away through the long aisles and among the upper stories. Only one thing is certain: he loves the whole crowd—boys and all! It's the opening day of the term. Recitations haven't as yet begun, and privileges are therefore taken by the older students, which admit of such freedom of the front steps.

Meantime, the organization is going in different offices. The freshman enrolls his name on the books of the college and, as I remember it, the name, residence, occupation, and nationality of his father also. He finds the custodian's apartment, deposits twenty dollars, and is assigned to a room in one of the dormitories. Happily, there's one left in the main building. When he goes to see the president, apprehension sets in a little stronger and he feels the sensation of having too many hands and feet. But he requires information in regard to the entrance examinations and, see the president, he must. A dozen other boys are seated in the office when he enters. They are freshmen also, beyond question.

This is reassuring. And yet, when he is asked his name by an old white-haired gentleman, he gives it with hesitation, intermixed with doubt. The president smiles a kindly smile, and shakes hands with him, and talks pleasantly, and gives him a list of printed instructions specifying the time and place for examination in the different branches, and hopes, in the gentlest voice possible, that he will pass without difficulty.

It is well the instructions were printed, for when he retires from the room there is left in his mind only a confused vision of the kindly face, and thin trembling hand, and those blue sympathetic eyes with a suggestion in them of humor, and, in the background, a row of raw freshmen like himself sitting expectant with their eyes and mouths open.

The examination covers, or used to cover, the common school branches and algebra to equations of the second degree. If he passes, he is admitted to the freshman class full-fledged. This gives him his first inkling of self-confidence. He feels identified with the institution. The gaslight that illuminates the great dining hall in the evening seems to have taken on an intenser radiance. His spirit it is that has lent the added luster. He begins soon to find his voiced in the mingled din of dishes and laughter that ascends from the surrounding tables. Acquaintance ripes rapidly with those who sit with him around the festive board, for they, too, are freshmen, and a common sympathy strengthens the courage and lifts the spirits of them all. Happy boy, if he secures a table where there are girls! It saves him from becoming a barbarian in manners. There's nothing so well calculated to restrain the voracity of a lot of hungry boys as the mild, reproving presence of girls. It gives a charm also to the dinner hour that nothing else can supply. Mealtime at Ames is a picnic! The sound of the gong strikes the ears of freshman like dulcet notes, and the thundering descent of freshmen, generally, down the winding stairway, is music to which he contributes the clatter of his boots. There never comes a time when the sound of that discordant old gong is unpleasant, but the response to it becomes more and more dignified as the years of the college course roll by.

The presence, in an agricultural college, of refined girls, with soft white hands, must not be regarded with surprise. The girls are simply there. Like the boys, they come largely from the smaller towns and country villages, and some direct from the farm. The city, however, is not entirely wanting in its contributions. There seems to be an affinity between the theory of this school and common sense everywhere, judging from the absence of fuss and feathers and affectation in the boys and girls attracted to it, both from city and county. It is, perhaps, needless to say that the girls are not required to pursue any study relating directly to agriculture. Nevertheless they have a special department of their own where, for an hour or two each week, they combine with the novel and interesting study of gastronomy. Most of the Ames girls regard the art of cooking as an accomplishment, and I suppose their idea is to preserve the art in those sections of the country which servant girls refuse to inhabit. Whatever there is in the science of domestic economy they learn practically and employ it in a manner most artistic. How refreshing it used to be, both to body and soul, when the girls of our table had samples of their cooking delivered at dinner, and they came in to grace the occasion, with white caps and aprons and rosy cheeks, late from the range! It was a question which to eat—the pies and things, or the girls.

"Boy Life in the Winter West" (1894)

Hamlin Garland

Many midwestern states, including Wisconsin, Missouri, Illinois, and South Dakota, can lay partial claim to the restless Hamlin Garland, but he spent his formative years—the very same that he would return to in later nonfiction—in Mitchell County and in Osage, in particular, where his peripatetic father finally homesteaded. There Garland helped his father farm while studying at the Cedar Valley Seminary, from which he graduated in 1881 just in time to see his father moved to the Dakota territory. But Garland stayed behind in the Hawkeye State, trying unsuccessfully to find a teaching position. After moving to Boston, where his writings turned, ironically, back to his early life on the Iowa prairie, he was convinced by William Dean Howells to return to Iowa to gather material. His fieldwork on Iowa soil would inform many of his future works, especially including the prose works Main-Traveled Roads *(1891), A Spoil of Office (1892), Boy Life on the Prairie, (1899) A Son of the Middle Border (1917), his Pulitzer Prize-winning, A Daughter of the Middle Border (1921) and Iowa, O Iowa (1935). Known for sounding some of midwestern realism's darkest notes, Garland instead crafts a warmly nostalgic piece below, a piece more closely resembling the author's exuberant, appreciative early poetry. The seemingly silly games boys once played in the Midwest (then called simply "The West") now make rich fodder for rural historians and sociologists.*

Boys are the great optimists. They can find comfort where a man would despair. They are great alchemists, indeed, extracting sunshine from cucumbers with ease. To prove this one has only to go back to the life of the boys on the prairies of Iowa in winter.

As I look out my window this morning, in Boston, it is snowing, and at once by some strange power I am caught up and whirled away from Boston. I travel back along one of the great trunk lines leading west from Chicago. All day through cold and snow. I get off at last at a little station four hundred miles west of Chicago.

A team, humped and shivering, stands waiting for me, and I leap into the seat beside the driver, who resembles a grizzly bear, so thick his buffalo coat. We set off at a tearing pace up the street lined with maples through whose branches the wind howls ferocious monody. The night is coming in the east.

But when we face the north we feel again the full powers of the weather. The sky is bright as burnished steel; the sun low down in the west is red and angry—partially veiled by the driving snow. The wind strikes the face like a lash, closing the nostrils and penetrating to the bone through every chink in one's clothing, as it drives upon us out of the frozen, level north.

I bow my head beneath the buffalo roe. I can see nothing, but I can hear the confused whirring, brushing sound of the driving, sliding snow—undertone to the clashing bells on the swift horses. I know every turn of the road. I know how every foot of it would look if I dared peer out. It is turnpike here, swept free of snow. There is no shelter, not even a fence, and the wind tears at us like a wolf. Now we go behind a cornfield and hedge and there is a moment's respite, and now again on the open road.

An hour of this riding and I look out to see the old schoolhouse standing just as it stood twenty odd years ago. Bare as a nose, not a bush, not a board to protect it from the pitiless winds. Not a vine to adorn it, not a line of beauty—a box, painted white, with six windows and two doors, set like a chicken-trap on the bare sod—and to crown all, the teacher, a stalwart young fellow, comes out as I used to do and leaps into the passing sleigh and instantly the twenty years between my Boston life of theaters, concerts, symphony orchestras, and that schoolhouse, are gone!

I am sitting at my "teacher's desk" hardly more than a boy myself, looking out into just such a wind, seeing the boys at play, unmindful of the cold. I hear their shouts, and see their eager eyes looking out of their mufflers. I hear their hoarse breathing as they re-enter at the sound of my bell!

The schoolhouse to these boys was the great meeting place for sports and entertainments of all sorts. Hardworking "hands" in summer, in the winter months these boys took a deeply pathetic delight in the hour or two which they could spend at "recess" at noon. I feel sure the readers of this page will be interested in knowing something of the games which they played (myself among them).

There is a great similarity in games for boys among the Teutonic races. Boisterous, full of action and hard knocks, they all have for unconscious aim the development of the lungs and muscles. But, other things being equal, these games are modified to suit the climate and the locality, as in our case.

Skating, so general an amusement in northern countries, was denied us in the midwinter for the reason that we had few ponds, and the few we had were buried deep under snow. Coasting was out of the question for we had no hills, (think of that, you eastern boys—no hills!) so the games were mainly those depending upon the fleetness of foot—"Draw gool," "Pom, pom, pullaway," "Dog and deer," "Fox and geese," and the like.

The last two games depended upon having new-fallen snow so that a track could be laid out—which was rather seldom—the snow was always in motion.

After a new fall of snow, when it lay out smooth and white on the sod, there always came a clamor at recess "Hurrah for dog and deer!"

Big Charley, the Swede, took the lead. (I can see him now, big, boisterous, tireless and jolly.) The leader runs out into the untracked field "scuffing" to plow a furrow in the snow, and the rest follow, the smallest boy bringing up the rear. The leader strikes out a series of loops encircled by the "home-stretch" leading back to "home."

The game was to set apart two fleet runners as dogs to chase the deer. The deer may leap across the necks of the loops in any direction and may rest at home, but the dogs are forced to run around the loops. "Home" is a safe place. The deer caught must become dogs.

Imagine the thermometer ten below zero, the wind blowing sharply, the pain dazzling in its whiteness and brightness—and these poorly clad boys alternately perspiring and shivering (the wonder is that any of them lived to tell of it), and yet enjoying it! Is this not sunshine from cucumbers? The girls, in the meantime stood about the stove, inside, melting snow in their dinner pails to satisfy the thirst caused by their breakfast of salted meat. The nearest well was a half-mile distant and snow-water was our daily drink.

When the weather was really bad, the boys played in the lee of the schoolhouse and a dilapidated little wooden shed. On sunny days—pleasant days—they played "gool," which was simply a game of "daring out," rushing, dodging and touching. The touching called the victim to the opposite goal. And the magic of the touch lay in his having left his goal last. This was a very exciting game indeed, and the displays of speed were really marvelous at times.

Wrestling was more often a sport entered into at night at lyceums, exhibitions and the like, or when two rival schools got together. Then came some great struggles. Each school had its champion and after various "Ring-rassels" and "Snap-the-whips," wherein all took part, the champions stripped their outer coats and stepped face to face. At such times excitement grew silent. All was good nature, but partisanship was astir.

Superb wrestlers some of those champions were, for they wrestled constantly. The best of all—after the "side holt" and "square-holt"—came the "no-holt" to end the contest. The champions, silent but breathing heavily, faced each other in this trial, with their hands deep in their trousers' pockets. With a peculiar, stealthy, menacing motion, they approached, each bending the right leg till their knees touched. Willowy, alert, and resolute. Now, one taps the icy ground with his foot, a challenge for the other to trip. He accepts, misses, recoils, saves himself, and amid cheers the two face each other again, rapid and graceful as fencers. When one falls, he falls heavily, as he has not the use of his hands.

Another game which I suppose is familiar to every country boy was "Pom, pom, pullaway."

> O, the phrase has magic in it,
> Sounding through the moonlit air,
> And in 'bout a half a minute
> I am part and parcel there.
> 'Cross the road I once more scurry,
> Through the thickest of the fray—
> Sleeve ripped off by Andy Murray—
> Let 'er rip—'Pom pullaway!'
> Mother'll mend it in the morning—
> (Dear old patient, smiling face!)
> One more darn my sleeve adorning
> (Whoop 'er up!') is no disgrace!
> "O, voices through the night air singing!
> O, thoughtless, happy, boisterous play!
> O, silver clouds the keen winds winging
> At the cry, 'Pom pullaway!'"
> I pause, and dream with strangest longing
> For that starlit, magic night,
> For my noisy playmates thronging,
> And the stars—moon's trailing light!

The game was played mainly when exhibitions or lyceums were being held at the schoolhouse—"The Grove Schoolhouse." And it was the roughest of all games. The games was very simple, consisting of the selection of two to "stand" in the middle of the road. After the cry, "Pom, pom, pullaway!" those standing strove to seize and thwack three times any of the runners who tried to cross the road. The runners so thwacked became in their turn aids to catch the rest. The result was a ferocious system of "tackling" quiet like the modern game of football. But with what zest we played it, and how many the coats torn from our backs!

If the schoolhouse was one center of boyish sports, the straw-stack was the other. The straw-pile! The western boy will begin to smile when the word meets his eyes, for around that word will spring up memories of booming, clattering, dusty threshing machine, and pictures of moonlit nights, and sunny slopes of yellow straw, wherein on winter noons the cattle fed. Nothing prosaic about an old-time western straw-pile to me. If I were a painter, like Enneking, I'd paint a couple of boys with their heads sticking out of a cozy cave, their faces round as the sun, and their gay "mufflers" flying loose. And every farmer boy of the great west would want to see that picture, and I'd not lack of buyers.

In those days of wheat-raising in northern Iowa, we had "worlds of straw." We burned it to get rid of it, and studied how to burn it with least injury to the coming crop. It was a nuisance. Each farmer, beside the great piles he burned in the field, had a great pile, or two or three of them, around his barn for use during the winter, especially reserving the oat straw because, being cut greener than the wheat, it retained more nutriment. In these huge piles of glistening yellow straw the boys plunged as soon as the dusty threshing machine was out of it, and while it lay light and easily penetrable their busy hands dug and pushed and burrowed into it, until in a few days it had devious tunnels leading to dim caves lighted by "wells and shoots" which ran obliquely from the top to the bottom of the stack, and runways leading from cave to cave. In short, it was honeycombed with round passages just big enough for a boy's body, crawling or sliding.

Passers-by were often astonished to see a boy standing on the top of such a strawrick suddenly dive with an exulting whoop into the straw, like a prairie dog into his den, to come into view a moment later at the foot of the pill, head foremost, with the rapidity of a shot through a tube, to finish his whooping as he shot out among the cattle lying in the sun below.

Writing of these runaways reminds me of another use each family of boys made of these secret chambers. On clear, moonlit nights, the neighboring boys used to assemble at some farm to play, much as in hill countries they meet to coast. Apples and popcorn were served by the hosts, and they then away with a whoop to the straw-pile and cattle-sheds for "Hi spy." There stood the straw-pile, roofed deep with snow, glittering in the moonlight and deeply hollowed in front, where the cattle have eaten caves, as the waves of Lake Superior eat into the rock. The boys roused up the cattle sleeping cozily in these sheds of their own making, and standing in a group began counting out with this weird verse chanted by a volunteer:

> Intry, mintry, cutry, corn,
> Apple-seed and apple-thorn;
> Wire, brier, limber lock,
> Three geese in a flock;
> One flew east, and one flew west,
> And one flew over the cuckoo's nest.

[This was] to be repeated till all were counted out save one, who was to be the "blind." I can hear the peculiar, chanting monotone as I write, as plainly as if I once more made up one of that little group of roughly clad urchins. I can hear the heavy sigh of the cattle, the stir of the horses in the barn, and see the vast, gleaming globe of burnished silver swing up from the level, snowy plain.

The "blinder" is counting in a loud voice, "one, two, three," standing with his head leaned into a stack. There is a scurry of feet, suppressed laughter, then silence again; and opening my eyes—not a boy to be seen! I am alone with the long piece of board which serves as "gool."

I look up and see etched against the dark-blue northern sky a black object like an eclipsed moon. "Hi spy, Rob Murray!" A derisive howl, and the head disappears. I prowl stealthily around the corner, tense and ready to hurry back. Too late! Like a shot the whooping Rob has whizzed down a hidden tunnel near which the board was cunningly placed, and he has reached goal before I could turn about.

And so the game goes on till nine, or mayhap [perhaps], ten o'clock; and then, tired and sleepy, we trudge along home again, the full moon riding high, our breath rising like smoke, our heavy boots, frozen stiff and hard as wood, slipping and sliding on the polished sled road. We reached our beds at last, hastily doff our outer garments (nightgowns were unknown with us), and creep into the icy bed, with chattering teeth and feet blue with cold—the room so cold our breath rises in a white cloud—so cold we could hear the snapping of rafters—so cold that the frost forms in the quilts drawn up around our faces.

I wonder if, far out in Iowa, the boys are still playing "Hi spy" around the straw-piles. I wonder if they still tunnel the straw-pile and dive into the bottom through the slippery "shoots." I suspect not. I suspect that barns have superseded the straw-piles in most cases; but that the modern western farmer boy plays "Hi spy" I cannot doubt, and that runic chant, with its endless repetitions, doubtless is heard on any moonlit night in far-off Iowa. I wish I might join once more in the game—with the privilege of going in, when my toes got chilled, to eat popcorn and apples with the girls. For alas! I've grown tender as I've grown older, and I could not play the whole evening through with the thermometer ten below zero, as we used to do then without overcoat, overshoes, or underclothing; and the boys would laugh as my cape-ulster and sealskin cap, and huge gloves and lambswool lined overshoes. I fear I could not enjoy "Hi spy" even were I invited to join. But I sigh with a curious longing for something that was mine in those days in the snowy Iowa plains. What was it? Was it the sparkle of winter stars? Was it stately march of moon? Was it the presence of dear friends? Yes; all of these, and more—it was *Youth*!

FROM "IOWA AT THE WORLD'S FAIR" (1894)

ORA E. MILLER

In her capacity as President of the State Board of Lady Manager's of the Iowa State Board of Commissioners, Cedar Rapids, Iowa's Ora E. Miller existed at the throbbing heart of the dramatic Chicago World's Fair of 1893, the exposition in which Frederick Jackson Turner famously declared the American frontier closed and Daniel Burnham and Charles Law Olmstead unveiled to the world the Exposition's white stucco, electrically lit, Neoclassically designed central campus—the "White City" at which Miller marvels in the passage to follow. Many, many Iowans traveled to Chicago for the unforgettable World Expo, taking justifiable pride in the home state's display, which included a building The Official Directory of the World's Columbian Exposition *describes as "undoubtedly one of the handsomest" of its peers; the walls of the Iowa showcase were decorated, not surprisingly, with cornstalks.*

It would be impossible to imagine a more delightful memory than that held by the millions who enjoyed the rare privilege of beholding the great White City. No pen has yet been able to fully describe the wonderful glories there presented, the great treasures of art and industry, resulting from the most brilliant genius and the broadest intelligence from every nook and corner of the civilized world. It was the universal verdict of visitors that the scene and the astonishing revealments were simply indescribable, and it is not too much to prophesy that none of the fifteen hundred million human beings of today will ever look upon its like again. The World's Fair was the climax of the grandeur of the centuries into which entered the knowledge, the pride, and the best efforts of the people of the whole world, and the memory of the scenes there presented will always be one of the rarest pleasures.

One day during the Exposition, a literary gentleman from an eastern state, after a round of sightseeing, wrote upon one of the state building registers the following, with his autograph, which as nearly expresses the feelings of those who beheld the glorious sight as words could possibly do: "This is not real; the midday sun may gleam / On many a column, and the night may set / On blazing dome and sparking minaret. / This is not real; it is a transient dream Foredoomed to perish / My own soul's regret / Is deeper than the raptures I had met; / For all must perish; it is but a dream."

The state of Iowa occupied no unimportant position in this, the grandest of all international events. No portion of the union, considering population and proximity, was as well represented. From the hour the gates were opened until they closed with the Exposition, there was no time when the Hawkeyes were not admirably represented in the numbers as well as in the evidences of their industry and progress. They were there not only to see, but to act. Present at the very birth of the movement in behalf of the Fair, they were always loyal, enthusiastic, and energetic in the prosecution of the wonderful work. Large rewards have already accrued to the commonwealth, not alone due to the knowledge gained by the people of the world concerning the grand position it occupies, and the inducements and opportunities it offers, but it has been benefited in a material and direct manner in various ways.

Two years ago the legislators of Iowa had before them for consideration the question of an appropriation to be used in the furtherance of the interests of the state at the International Exposition. Many may remember the heated discussion, and the persistency displayed by a few in opposition to providing the funds which the state commission had estimated would be required to place Iowa where she rightfully belonged during the Exposition. Indeed, the opposition was so strong that only about one-third of the amount asked was allowed. The final vote was very close and the appropriation of $125,000 came very nearly being reduced $25,000. It was not that the people of the state were unwilling to sustain their reputation for liberality, and strengthen their justifiable pride by giving to the commission sufficient financial support with which to properly represent the state, but it was due, I presume, to the fact that at that time the importance and vastness of the then approaching Exposition was not fully comprehended. It was doubtful if even the most ardent friends of the measure, to provide bountifully in behalf of the contemplated work, had any adequate conception of the real greatness of the approaching event which was to call the people of the world together.

The state commission was composed of men whose large experience and splendid abilities especially fitted them for the undertaking, and they proceeded energetically to meet the obligation which their state had imposed upon them. The hundreds of thousands who visited the White City from Iowa have seen, and consequently know from their own observation, how grandly and successfully the work of the commission was done, and how magnificently this commonwealth was there represented. The beautiful prairie state, richest in all the combinations of advantages that make it desirable for the home-seeker, occupied a correspondingly exalted position during the six months of international rivalry. Other hundreds of thousands, unable to attend, have read in detail the remarkable record won by the Hawkeyes. It would require volumes to fully and completely present a correct history of what was done, and more to portray the pleasures derived, and the benefits to accrue, from the part Iowa took at the Fair.

From "Resting at Okoboji" (1895)

S. H. M. Byers

Another rhapsodic prose selection from Iowa's unofficial, turn-of-the-century, poet laureate, "Resting at Okoboji" continues S. H. M. Byers's argument that Iowa's recreational resources could and did compete with the world's best natural wonders. On that score, he writes, "How few realize that within a hundred miles or so of Iowa's capital there is a lake as any lake in Italy!" Whether Byers's high praise for the Iowa "Great Lakes" was mere poetry, artful propaganda, or just a feeling-of-his-oats, it holds more than a kernel of truth—West Okoboji Lake is one of only a handful of "blue water" (water supplied by underground springs or some other source of fresh water) lakes in the world.

Somebody has written a magazine article telling people how to listen to Wagner's music. I am about to write an article, just a little one, to tell people how to enjoy Okoboji, that prettiest of all Iowa lakes. The Indians, our worthy predecessors in this lake region of the prairies, did not require someone to tell them that here was one of the loveliest spots in the world. The men who built castles and convents in former times all over Europe knew how to select the most telling scenery. Everybody who travels says that, and the Sioux Indians of the West evinced a taste as unerring when they placed their lodges near the beautiful waters of Minnesota, Okoboji, and Spirit Lake.

Nature rests the soul of man; tranquil waters, beautiful scenes inspire him.

We Americans work too hard, every mother's son of us, and here in the West the drive is even worse than in the East. Unfortunately we are noted for almost nothing except pork and politics—and work. It is dig, dig, dig, forever dig—and what comes of it all? Exactly nothing. Yes, something—exhausted nerves, irritable tempers, unhappiness, and at last—hopes crushed. Nature will not be hurried, the body breaks down, the intellect dwarfs. Look about and note the sudden wrecks, all over this country, of able men who drifted into the maelstrom of overwork. Every reader notes them among his own acquaintances. Every city is full of them. We have been a race of pioneers—everything was to be made and builded; in the making and the building we have done ourselves injury. Perhaps it could not be helped. But look at the pile of dead men's bones—lawyers, doctors, editors, statesmen, teachers, and men in commercial life, whose lives have gone out in early misery because of this everlasting rush.

But now we can stop. Our farms are improved; our towns and cities, churches, colleges, and railroads are built. If the building killed our fathers and crippled us, let us at least enjoy these things a little. Let us rest. The chase has done us no good. The rich man lost all in his last speculation. The overworked lawyer died before he got his fees, the statesman wrecked himself at the roadside before his fame was accomplished.

"But rest where? Resting costs money!" So it does. One need not go to Europe, nor to Saratoga, nor to the seaside. There are as delightful resting places right here in Iowa as there are in Europe or the East—if it is really rest and not excitement we are after. How few realize that within a hundred miles or so of Iowa's capital there is a lake as any lake in Italy! Only mountains and history are wanting to make Okoboji as enchanting as [Lake] Guarda or the Lake of Zurich. The very simplicity of Okoboji's surroundings, its unkempt woods, its magnificent prairie, the absence of everything artificial—all add to its charms. It is true Nature unspoiled by artifice. All the world is not looking on. When the sun rises, the air is as fresh, the scene as quiet, inspiring and beautiful as on that morning when the stars first sang together.

Minnetonka is beautiful; Okoboji is fairer still. I do not know of a more delightful, restful scene than that blue water with its fairy-like inlets winding back among shady headlands, its borders of young oak trees, its background of prairie.

I saw it first on a summer evening from the boat landing at Arnold's Park. Scores of lake dwellers had come to the Des Moines train to see the new arrivals. The ride from the capital had been long, dusty and hot. Ill-mannered people had littered the car with orange peels, refuse of lunch and tobacco juice. We were all glad when someone cried out, "Here we are!"

How delighted seemed the smiling faces out on the platform! Then the Manhattan Beach orchestra played—and the boat for Manhattan Beach steamed out into the blue lake. We all rushed up on the deck. It was evening; there had been a rainstorm, and the sun was setting in a midst of opalescent clouds. Every color seemed dazzling and illumining the wet western sky. On our right the banks were grassy green at Given's Point, and the white tents and beautiful cottages under the oak groves stretched off past Fort Dodge Point and into the distance. On the left loomed Pillsbury Promontory, abrupt and lonely.

Look at the sun!—look at the sky!—look at the green shore!—look at the white yachts!—such were the exclamations which came from eager lips, all about us.

We did look, and the band played, and the boat danced on the water, and the white sails skipped past us and around us. We were delighted. It was such a perfect summer evening! Such a delicious scene! We forgot the city with its racket of street cars and omnibuses, its weary lawyers and hurrying merchants. We were already resting! We did not think of the dirty streets, nor the loafers hanging over railings, nor the yelling newsboys, nor the mantle of coal dust and smoke—we were out of it all! Here all was clean, fresh, beautiful, and restful.

"It is like a scene on the Bosphorous," someone said, looking through his hands, having shaped them like a field glass. Only he saw no palaces out on the shore, no Turks in big trousers, no veiled women and no salaaming of grave seigniors. What he did see, however, was beautiful water, long; low banks fringed with oak trees and here and there a fir, pretty promontories, and inlets—and white sails. The bells of St. Sophia were not sounding in his ear, but in their stead the happy voices of men and women—made happy by this beautiful touch of nature's handiwork.

At different landing places the steamer touched, and other happy faces came on board. Dozens of fresh-looking pretty girls were in evening toilet, for it happened to be the very evening of the weekly ball at Manhattan Beach. The sun had set, the shadows gathered and the young girls in white dresses and satin slippers looked like real fairies coming of the green groves at Omaha Beach and clambering along the narrow gangway to the steamer. But young swains in black coats were not wanting there either. Where there is a woman there is a man. They were happy, and to all of them youth looked as if it might last forever.

One seldom sees a prettier sight than Manhattan on a "dance night,"—the white caps skipping along in the darkness over the lake, the water murmuring up over the sand close to the dancers—the happy people promenading along the great piazza of the brilliantly lighted pavilion to the sound of music.

Yet, within five minutes walk of all this is the rolling and boundless prairie, looking just as it looked a thousand years ago!

The very next day commenced our boating excursions, our fishing, our walks to the prairie. We went everywhere. I had never seen such fishing. Even ladies came in of morning with a string of fifty bass and perch and pickerel in their boat. Fish stories, "true ones," that I had never before heard, were told—marvelous, miraculous! Fish were caught just for the fun of the thing! There were too many to be eaten or sold. They just begged to be taken in out of the wet. Alas for me! No fish ever nibbled at my line! Fishing is not my forte. I was satisfied to see them on the table.

Little steamers ply daily between the hotel and the tent and cottage "settlements" on the lake, so there is much visiting of friends; much going to and fro, and no end of picnics and good times. There is a good society all about the lakes, too; and not much of the other kind.

Here at the lakes one meets in fact the best society from Des Moines, Omaha, St. Louis, Kansas City, Sioux City, and Dubuque, and an occasional southerner.

Many have delightful cottages of their own, expensive ones, too, fitted up with taste and elegance. Five-hundred-dollar cottages are not uncommon.

The beautiful villas at Badgerow's Bay at the upper end of Manhattan Beach would do credit to Newport. Badgerow's is one of the places to visit, for there in the grove one sees Indian graves and, near by, the trails of the buffalo. The views from the cottages are charming, and if one is really aiming, here are mineral waters for his infirmities, and for his stomach's sake. These waters, they say, contain large quantities of bicarbonates of lime and magnesia. They are said to have a favorable effect on diseased kidneys and stomach. The wonder is that enterprise has not conducted these mineral waters from Badgerow's down to Manhattan Beach pavilion where the public could really use them. Perhaps this is one of the advantages to be had in the future, for I am informed that Manhattan is itself shortly to undergo certain improvements of importance. As a bathing beach, nothing that money can do could improve Manhattan. The Manhattan company owns a stretch of lake shore here, a mile and a half long, and are selling it off in lots for cottages. It is not only the best of the numerous beaches on the lakes, it is one of the very best bathing beaches in the United States. The slope is long and gradual, and the sandy bottom perfect. Almost everybody who goes to Manhattan bathes in the lake, and the scene in front of the pavilion at bathing hours is full merriment. Boating and toboggan sliding are as common as swimming, rowing and fishing, and the season sees many expert oarsmen congregated there.

Beautiful Spirit Lake is only a few miles away and the streamers make frequent excursions there from Okoboji. It has its devotees and its Arnold's Park offers one of the most delightful views of Lake Okoboji. It is only a pity that so many careless tenters are allowed to litter the whole park till it looks like an abandoned camp. The more the pity that for here is where strangers get their first view of Okoboji.

The Okoboji Lake region has figured prominently in the early history of Iowa. In the pretty woods back of Pillsbury Point is the principle site of the fierce Indian massacre of 1857. The log house where the murdered Gardner family lived still stands there in perfect preservation. The only survivor of the horrible tragedy, a daughter of the Gardners, Abigail Gardner Sharp, lives in the cabin and relates incidents of the spectacle witnessed by her own eyes. Visitors to the cabin shudder at the narrative, and for a moment realize the dangers encountered by first settlers. A monument in memory of the massacred settlers is now being erected over their graves.

The sites of other Indian atrocities in the neighborhood of East Okoboji and Spirit Lake are also pointed out. They were a part of the same barbarous massacre.

One of the interesting features of Lake Okoboji is the long lake wall from Fort Dodge Point toward Dickson's Beach. It has the regularity of artificial masonry, but the real builders were the floods and the ice and the storm.

As a resort for rest, health, and pleasure, this chain of lakes cannot be excelled. Nothing can be more delightful in the hot season than tenting on their shores or living a life of ease in one of the handsome cottages so common there. The air is pure, the water clear, deep, and beautiful. West Okoboji Lake has a depth of from fifty to two hundred feet. Near Manhattan Beach is the highest point of land in Iowa. It is one thousand feet above Des Moines.

If somebody invites you to come to Lake Okoboji, or if you can see your way to invite yourself to go, don't wait—thank the gods, pack your trunk, stand not upon the order of your going, but go!

From "A Bit of Holland in America" (1895)

Cyrenus Cole

By the late 1800s, the cultural distinctiveness of Iowa's most conspicuous immigrant communities—the Dutch in Pella and the Germans in the Amanas—seemed threatened already by modern culture. In the overview that follows, Cyrenus Cole, himself a Pella native, graduate of Central University (now Central College), and U.S. Representative from Iowa, sets out to document the folkways of the "Hollanders" before their inevitable cultural twilight. Interestingly, Cole here invokes the founding Pilgrims as an analogy for Iowa's Dutch immigrants, a comparison by which Iowa itself becomes a promised land. Pella, home to the Tulip Festival and to Central College, remains one of Iowa's most culturally vibrant communities.

In the summer of 1847 a company of immigrants from Holland settled in Marion County, Iowa, on the divide between the Des Moines and Skunk Rivers. In their own country they had been persecuted on account of religion, being dissenters from the state Reformed Church, and so they called their new home Pella, the name meaning a place of refuge. Upon the seal of the new town they inscribed the words: *In Deo Spes Nostra et Refugium*, or, "In God Our Hope and Refuge."*

The Pella pilgrims in Holland believed in the complete separation of church and state. They were opposed to the established church because, in their opinion, it had become an institution of form, instead of being an expression of faith. They were separatists as the English pilgrims had been under Robinson and Brewster. The difference is mainly that between the seventeenth and nineteenth centuries. In creed they were adherents of the doctrine of which John Calvin was a later expounder. In faith and in history the Protestants of Holland, which term includes practically all Hollanders, are associated with the Waldenses of Switzerland, the Huguenots of France, the Puritans of England and the Convenanters of Scotland.*

It was a curious procession that made its way up the Des Moines River Valley. Quite a spectacle it must have been for the natives. There were more than seven hundred colonists in strange garb and speaking in a strange language. Some rode in wagons drawn by horses and some in carts drawn by horses and some in carts drawn by oxen, and some walked, no doubt, in wooden shoes. The men were broad shouldered and the women were rosy cheeked. The men were in velvet jackets and the women in outlandish caps and bonnets.

After a journey of several days, during which the houses became farther and farther apart and finally almost disappeared, for between Oskaloosa and Des Moines were only a few scattered settlers, they came, on August 26th, to a place where stood a hickory pole with a shingle nailed to the top, and on the shingle the word: *Pella*.

"But, Dominie, where is Pella?" asked Mrs. Scholte before alighting. "We are in the center of it, my dear," was the reply. But like the little girl in the fairy tale of Hans Christian Andersen, the dominie's four-year-old daughter, Johanna, now Mrs. John Nollen of Pella, could not see anything at all, and came to the conclusion that Pella was all make believe.

Iowa, as they saw it in 1847—no pen can describe it! It was billowy like the sea which they had crossed. There was wave after wave of grass, everywhere breaking into spray of wildflowers—wind-flowers and violets in spring; lilies and roses in summer; golden rod and asters in autumn, and great white stretches of snow in the winter. Far away were the forests along the rivers, green as emerald when they first saw them in August, and crimson and gold in October. And the sun and the stars in a beautiful Italian blue sky over them always—an infinite blue sky over an infinite green prairie, the sky studded with stars like flowers and the prairie with flowers like stars. So beautiful was their new home that they soon forgot the cultivated fields by the dikes and ditches over the sea and the windmills that stood over them; and now, after forty-seven years, the remembrance of it in the hearts of those who have survived is vivid enough and sweet enough to comfort them in old age.

But in 1847 Pella was beautiful simply as a country. As president of the colony, Mr. Scholte occupied a log cabin which stood on the center of what is now a beautiful park. This cabin was built as a claim pen, in 1843, by Thomas Tuttle and his wife. Farther north was another cabin which this pioneer couple used as a residence. The blood of heroes flowed in the veins of this man and woman. It is related that when Mr. Tuttle found it necessary to go east after supplies, his wife kept guard in the cabin for nine days and night, her only companion being a cat. Wolves that howled at night along Thunder Creek and Indians who passed stealthily, distance and loneliness—none of these daunted the courage of this brave woman.

This history would be incomplete without a mention of a band of pioneers who stood upon the site of Pella even before the Tuttles built their cabin there. They reached Pella on the 26th of April, 1843, five days before the New Purchase was thrown open for settlers, having made their way though the government lines. Of this band only three are now living, Robert Hamilton and Green T. Clark of Pella, and Robert B. Warren of Des Moines. Mrs. Sarah Nossaman, who came only a few weeks later, is also still living at Pella, and Mrs. Mary Butts and Mrs. Mary Todd who were there children. They were religious men and women and organized a Methodist church and afterwards, under Mr. Post, a Baptist church. Mr. Hamilton, writing of the Hollanders, says: "After living among them forty-seven years I can say I never knew a people more religious, church-going, and Sabbath-observing."

The commissioners from St. Louis had purchased most of these claims. The new settlers at once put the plow to the prairies and the axe to the forests. I will let Professor Newhall, a traveling writer of that time, tell of the magic transformation which they wrought here. "Methinks I hear you exclaim," he wrote in a letter to the Burlington *Hawkeye*, "'where is Pella?' Not the ancient city of Macedonia, but a foreshadowing of the famous Holland settlement which has recently been located upon our beautiful prairie of the New Purchase. To tell you this would be like telling you fiction.... Just about two months ago I halted about sunset at a lone cabin on the ridge midway between Oskaloosa and the Raccoon Forks.... Again today, (the 17th of September) about noon, I find myself dashing along this beautiful road. I did not dream, neither was I in a trance, for my eyes beheld the same beautiful earth clothed in its rich garniture of green—yet I discovered a new race of beings. The men in blanket coats and jeans were gone. And a broad-shouldered race in velvet jackets and wooden shoes were there.... Most of the inhabitants live in camps, the tops covered with tent cloth, some with grass and bushes. The sides, barricaded with countless numbers of trunks, boxes and chests of the oddest and most grotesque description.... They are all Protestants who have left their native land (much like the Puritans of old) on account of political and religious intolerance and persecution.... They appear to be intelligent and respectable, quite above class of European immigrants that have ever landed upon our shores." Professor Newhall speaks of his good fortune in arriving in time to see the male adults going through the ceremony of declaring their intention to become citizens of the United States, which was one of the first duties they performed after reaching Pella. He says:

"It was an altogether impressive scene, to behold some two hundred men with brawny arms upraised to heaven eschewing all allegiance of foreign powers, potentates, etc. And as they all responded in their native tongue to the last word of the oath, 'so help me God,' no one could resist the heartfelt response.... All appeared to feel the weight of the responsibility they were about to assume.... A fact worth recording during the ceremony before the clerk of the court was that of the whole number who took the intended oath of citizenship but two made their marks."

The first house built in Pella by the Hollanders was a long wooden structure of boards upright. So little were they acquainted with the nature of their new county that they built this in a low place, and the late autumn rains flooded it, setting all the beds in all the "sections" afloat. The first winter was by most of the people spent in dugouts with roofs of straw. This was called *Strooijstadt* or "Strawtown." But in these sheds, in which their descendants would hardly stable their cattle, these determined men and women were not unhappy. "Many times," writes one—H. de Booy—"I have looked back to that winter as one of the happiest of my life. There was love, unity, and helpfulness. The evenings were spent in psalm-singing and in edifying conversation." Pathetic it all was, but there were also amusing phases. For instance, a cow, finding better grazing on all the straw-covered roof of one of the dugouts than on the prairie, gradually climbed upon the roof, and finally fell through it on the floor of the cabin beside the bed on which a startled man and his wife were sleeping.

On the first Monday in April, 1848, the first election was held, Lake Prairie Township, comprising two geographical townships, having been organized under a special act of the legislature of 1848. Green T. Clark and Mr. Scholte were elected justice of the peace, Isaac Overkamp, clerk, and A. J. Betten, G. Awtrig and P. Welle, commissioners. A post office was opened, with the luxury of mails three times a week. Mr. Scholte was postmaster. Mrs. Post opened a hostelry and Wouters and Smink the first "store." The first child born in the settlement was named Bart Synhorst, and Lena Blanke was the first infant baptized in the church. Pella was platted in this same year by Standford Douds. The nomenclature of the streets, running east and west, and of the avenues, running north and south, was unique, a combination of religion and patriotism. Beginning on the north the streets were named in succession: Columbus, Washington, Franklin, Liberty, Union, Independence and Peace. Beginning on the east of the avenues were named: Entrance, Inquiry, Perseverance, Reformation, Gratitude, Experience, Patience, Confidence, Expectation, and Fulfilling.

While the mechanics were building houses, the farmers tilled the virgin soil with a willingness that has never been excelled, even in America. Everything was new to them—the oxen and the plows, the soil and the crops, the times of sunshine and of rain, but they were apt pupils in nature's great schoolroom. And, by the hand of God, as they believed, they had come to a place where, as Douglas Jerrold says, they had but to tickle the earth with a hoe to make it smile with a harvest.

But, to their honor be it said, no material considerations were allowed to take precedence of religion and education. At first they worshipped in "God's first temples," and then in G. H. Overkamp's log house, until a church was built. The first schoolmasters were Isaac Overkamp and James Muntingh, both of whom are still living. The first teacher in the English language was Benjamin Sturman. Education was at first under the control of the church and in the Holland language, but both features were soon abandoned. Since those first attempts, although nearly a score school districts have been under their control, all education has been in the language of their adopted country. Not a dollar of public monies has since been expanded for either sectarian or foreign education.

The religious and education liberality of these people was shown in the inducements they held out to the Baptists of the state, when early in the fifties this denomination was seeking a site for a college. As a result Central University came as a godsend to them.*

But if their hopes on the Des Moines and Skunk River came to naught, these people founded at least one other city which has become an honor to them and to the state. This is Orange City, in Sioux County, established under the leadership of Henry Hospers, in 1870. Motley says that the history of the people of Holland is "marked by one prevailing characteristic, one master passion—the love of liberty, the instinct of self-government." He might have added also the instinct of colonization, in which respect Holland as been second only to England, and today, after so much of her glory has departed, her colonial possession are those of a first-class European power, excelled in wealth only by those of England. This national instinct has regularly manifested itself among the settlers of Pella. In 1878 a Kansas colony was projected with H. de Booy as president and N. J. Geshman, secretary, but the droughts in that state cut the project short. Finding no satisfactory outlet farther west, the descendants have spread out on every side of Pella until now they are scattered over an area forty miles east and west and fifteen miles north and south, and the value of their farm lands has been steadily rising. They have written "yes," after the laconic question, "Does farming pay?"

I can speak briefly of their manners and customs. At first they were those of Holland. Many of these customs still survive among them, and some are too good to be allowed ever to perish. Family life among them is pure and noble. Its basis is the Christian religion, and its aim Christian character. Every home is a church and a school, each in miniature. The old-time family board was an elaborate event, not because of the things to eat, but because of the things that were said. A prayer preceded every meal and a Bible reading a longer prayer followed—three times a day, in winter or in harvest time. And it was all sincere.

There is no make-believe in anything that belongs to these people. And if they were strict in religion, they were equally strict in morals. Honest with themselves, they are also honest with other men. Debts among them are sacred, and the public conscience is as active as the private conscience. Municipal and other public affairs are as carefully administered as is private business. As to strong drink, they are temperate, many families to the verge of prohibition. Excessive drinking is among them almost wholly unknown and neither are they steady drinkers. Their social beverage is wine—not beer—and wine is generally homemade. While in Albany, Mr. Scholte recorded the fact that he was lodged in a hostelry where liquors were not served, and in the same pamphlet he records that among the sorrows that befell the colonists while at Keokuk were a death and a burial—and a case of drunkenness, which caused so much shame and humiliation to all "that the Christian organization no more recognizes him as a member of it." In their social life they are hospitable, and from nine to ten in the morning is coffee-time and from four to give in the afternoon teatime, and to these pleasant hours of social leisure friends are always welcome and strangers within their gates always invited.*

Here the curtain must be dropped on what Marshall Talbott, that strange genius who gave to Iowa art at least a local habitation and a name, called the most picturesque settlement in Iowa or in the West. Times and conditions have been changing. Much of the original coloring has been effaced. This bit of Holland I have tried to describe has been merging into America. But Rembrandt come to earth again might still repaint some of his great faces in Pella.

From "The Sole Survivor's Story of the [Spirit Lake] Massacre" (1895)

Abigail Gardner Sharp

The secondhand, textbook version of the Spirit Lake Massacre, so well known by so many students of Iowa history, pales by comparison with the eyewitness of Abigail Gardner Sharp, "sole survivor." Barely thirteen years old, Gardner watched as her entire family was slaughtered by renegade Sioux. Her firsthand account, written nearly forty years after the traumatic events of 1855 but with a child's eyes, pinpoints the horrendous winter weather of 1856–1857 as a possible factor in the Sioux's desperate incursions, though it neglects to mention one Henry Lott, a whisky dealer and horse thief whose murder of the Sioux Chief Sintomniduta in January of 1854 many believe provoked Inkpaduta's otherwise inexplicable attack on the settlers of Spirit Lake. In any case, Sharp's recounting shows how vulnerable pioneer children could be on the prairie, though it neglects to mention Inkapduta's atypicality—Iowa historian Joseph Frazier Wall has called the chief a "renegade among his own people." Sharp herself would go on to publish a book-length work on her capture, History of the Spirit Lake Massacre and Captivity of Mrs. Abbie Gardner *and to return to live in the old Gardner cabin not far from Okoboji.*

About the year of 1855 the wild and romantic region of Spirit and Okoboji Lakes began to be viewed as the "promised land" by the adventurous pioneer of that period. My father, Rowland Gardner, and his son-in-law, Harvey Luce, were the first white men to bring their families for settlement in this region. It was July, 1856, that heavy emigrant wagons drawn by ox-teams brought their passengers to the shores of the Okoboji Lakes. The family consisted of father, mother, two sisters and one brother. My brother was six years old, and I was thirteen. My eldest sister was the wife of Harvey Luce and was the mother of two small children.

A few families had settled that year—1856—on the headwaters of the Des Moines River in Minnesota, some eighteen miles north of Spirit Lake, where is now the town of Jackson. On the Little Sioux was also the settlement of Smithland in Woodbury County, Iowa. In Clay County, about forty miles south of the lakes, some six or eight families had located. These were the nearest neighbors to the settlers at the lakes when the Indian outbreak occurred of which I write. These settlements were all made on the extreme border and were absolutely unprotected.

The winter of 1856–57 was one never to be forgotten by the early settlers of Iowa and Minnesota. The bitter cold, deep snow, and violent storms that winter rendered communication between the scattered settlements almost impossible. Lakes and rivers were frozen to a great depth, and the ground was covered with four feet or more of snow on the level, and in the drifts the snow was fifteen to twenty feet deep. The settlers remained in their log cabins, not daring to attempt the dreadful elements, even for a short journey, unless necessity compelled them to do so.

The eighth of March, 1857, dawned bright and fair. The rising sun never shed brighter beams than on that ill-fated morning. Spring, that had already come in theory, now seemed near at hand, and the long winter of our discontent to have passed away.

As our family was about to sit down to breakfast, a solitary Indian entered the house wearing the guise of friendship. After the family had partaken of the frugal meal, and the visitor had warmed himself by the fire, my mother prepared a place for him and he ate his breakfast at our table. This Indian was followed by others, until Inkpaduta and his band of savages, squaws and papooses had all entered the house. They all wanted something to eat, and food was freely given to them.

They then asked for ammunition and numerous other things. While father was about giving to them a few gun caps, one of the band snatched the whole box from his hand. At the same time another one, as if by agreement, tried to seize a powder horn which hung against the wall. He was prevented, however, by Mr. Luce, who now suspected their intentions were so that we might not be able to protect ourselves. The Indian then drew his gun and would have shot my brother-in-law, had not the latter prevented him by promptly seizing the weapon pointed at his head.

The Indians prowled about the house and yard until noon, when they went off toward our neighbor's, Mr. Mattock's. They drove away our cattle as they went, and shot them down by the roadside.

After the Indians had gone, the matter was talked over by the family, as the situation was considered serious, and some measures should be taken for defense.

It was our desire to notify our neighbors of the danger; but if any should go it would weaken the force at home, and the Indians were liable to return at any time.

It was decided that Mr. Luce and Mr. Clark should go to warn the others of the impending danger, while father should remain at home to defend the family. They started out at about 2 P.M. An hour later we could hear reports of firearms in rapid succession from the house of our nearest neighbors, the Mattocks. We were then no longer in doubt of the awful conspiracy. Two long hours we passed in this fearful anxiety and suspense, waiting and watching, with conflicting hope and fear, for the safety of Mr. Luce and Mr. Clark as well as for our defenseless settlement.

As the sun was setting, father went out to reconnoiter. He hastily entered the house saying, "The Indians are coming and we are all doomed to die!"

His first thought was to barricade the door and return the fight with his two loaded guns. He said, "While they are killing all of us I will kill a few of them." But to this my mother, not having lost all faith in these savages, objected—she still had hope that they would spare our lives. "If we must die," said she, "let us go innocent of shedding blood."

Alas, for the faith placed in the stony-hearted savages! The Indians entered the house, and instantly shot my father through the heart. He fell dead. At the same time they seized my mother and my sister by the arms, beating them over the head with their guns and driving them out of doors; they there killed these defenseless women in the most shocking manner.

They next seized the children, tearing them from my arms one at a time. The little ones reached out their arms toward me, crying in terror for the protection that I was powerless to give them. Heedless of their piteous cries the savages dragged them out of doors and killed them with sticks of stove-wood.

During these awful scenes I was both speechless and tearless; but now, alone in the midst of the dying and the dead it seemed as though I could not wait for the missile of death to strike me, so I rushed forward to one of the band and begged him to "kill me quick!" He then roughly seized me by the arm with his brawny hand and said something which I could not understand, but well knew by his actions that I was to be taken captive.

Terrible as were the scenes through which I had just passed, others, if possible even more horrible, awaited me. A tramp of a mile through the snow brought me to their camp, near the house of our neighbors, the Mattocks. Here the sights and sounds that met my eye and ear were appalling. The forest was lighted by their campfires and the burning building; the air was rent with the hideous war-whoop of the savages, intermingled with the shrieks and groans of two helpless victims confined in the burning cabin. Scattered upon the ground were the dead bodies of thirteen persons—men, women and children.

Here, amid such scenes as these, in an Indian camp, I spent the first night of my captivity. No tongue or pen can portray the feelings and emotions I experienced during the long, sleepless night.

Early the next morning the warriors painted themselves black—which with the Sioux means war—and again sallied forth on the warpath.

Mr. Luce and Mr. Clark had the day before been overtaken and killed by the Indians a short distance from our home. The other settlers had consequently received no news of the outbreak while these terrible scenes were enacted in their very midst.

Throughout their whole course, the treacherous Indians got into the home of their victims through professions of friendship and the claims of hospitality, taking the men by surprise so that they could not defend themselves and their families.

Of the forty persons who were then residents of the lake region at the time of the massacre there was not one left to tell the tale! Everyone who was at home was killed except Mrs. Noble, Mrs. Thatcher, Mrs. Marble and myself, whom the Indians took with them as captives on their return to the North.

The massacre was first discovered by one Markham who, being absent from home, returned on the evening of the ninth of March. He found only the dead bodies of his friends and neighbors. He then proceeded to the settlement eighteen miles north of the lakes on the Des Moines River in Minnesota and carried the appalling news.

A rally was made and several families assembled at the house of Mr. Thomas for better protection. They also dispatched two men on snowshoes across the bleak country a distance of about two hundred and fifty miles to Fort Ridgeley to ask that troops be sent to their rescue.

Meanwhile Inkpaduta's band, with booty and captives, was moving in a northwesterly direction, camping at night in the groves along the streams and by small lakes, hunting for human game in the person of defenseless settler or unwary traveler.

On the twenty-sixth of March, we reached Heron Lake where the warriors left us with their squaws and papooses. Painting themselves again in the most warlike fashion, with rifle in hand and scalping-knife in their belts, they went forth the second time on the warpath.

I leave to ex-Governor Carpenter the description of the events which followed—the brave and successful defense of the twenty-one men, women, and children in the log house of Mr. Thomas.

The assault made by our captors on the Thomas house was vigorously kept up and as vigorously resisted until sunset, when the Indians became weary of firing at blank walls, and ignorant of the number of inmates, and not having the courage to charge the works, they returned to their camp bringing in the spoils. On their return they gave us captives to understanding that they had met with a repulse from the whites.

I also leave to ex-Governor Carpenter the account of the expedition formed in the settlements to the south of us for the threefold purpose of burying our dead, relieving the survivors if any should be found, and punishing the Indians if they could be overtaken, part of which expedition he himself was—and no unimportant part, either.

Scarcely twenty-four hours had elapsed since the attack on the house of Mr. Thomas when a company of United States soldiers arrived from Fort Ridgeley, under command of Captain Bee. Like the volunteers from Fort Dodge, they had endured almost unheard of hardships and surmounted all conceivable difficulties. They buried the dead found at Jackson, also Mr. Marble, who was killed at Spirit Lake, and came so near overtaking us captors and captives that they reached at 3 P.M. the camping-ground left by us in the morning. When their presence was discovered by our captors, the wildest excitement reigned among them. The squaws extinguished the fires by pouring on water that the smoke might not be seen, tore down the tents, and hastened from the camp down the creek, skulking like partridges among the willows and tall prairie grass.

We were encamped on a low piece of ground by the Little Sioux River. Between us and the soldiers was a high rolling prairie, so that the camp was not visible to the soldiers; but the Indians obtained a view from the higher ground, and could see all the movements of their pursuers. I observed one of the Indians creeping along the ground to the base of a tree, some rods from camp on higher ground. He then perched himself among its branches, where he could observe the movements of the troops.

One Indian was detailed to stand guard over us, and to kill us, they said, if there was an attack by the soldiers. The rest of the warriors prepared for battle. The company of United States troops above referred to had suffered much from exposure and fatigue in carrying out their orders to go to Spirit Lake and do what they could to suppress the Indians. When the lakes were reached, the Indians were gone. Their trail led to the west, and this pursuit was made by a portion of the command, some mounted on mules and some afoot. An examination was made of the deserted camp and fires by their half-breed guide, and the pursuit was then and there abandoned on the declaration of the guide that the enemy was by their signs several days in advance. The guides being half-breeds, their interests might have been more with the Indians than with the whites; but whether they were true or false, it was life to us captives. Had an attack been made it would have been certain death to us.

After six weeks of incessant marching over the trackless prairies and through what is now know as Lake Madison in South Dakota, we were visited by two strange Indians. They remained over night in Inkpaduta's camp, and were entertained by pantomimic representation of the massacre. The next morning they ventured to ask for one of the women. Mrs. Marble was the fortunate one. They paid for her all they had.

Just before starting on the unknown journey, Mrs. Marble came to my tent to bid me good-bye. She told me she believed her purchasers intended to take her to the whites. She said if they did she would do all in her power for the rescue of Mrs. Noble and myself.

Through thirty-nine eventful years have passed since that memorable day, the picture of her departure is still vivid in my memory. I can see her yet, as she marched away from the Indian camp, with her purchasers following in Indian file. The last account I had of her was some ten years since, when she was living in California, the wife of Mr. S. M. Sibaugh. She was taken by her purchasers to the agency, and delivered to Charles E. Flandreau, United States Indian agent for the Sioux, the Indians receiving five hundred dollars each.

Occasionally there would be a day so cold that even a Sioux would not travel. These days were even more dreaded by me than the wearisome marches.

Through the deep snow, across creeks, sloughs, rivers and lakes, we pushed on until we reached the Big Sioux River, on or about where is now the town of Flandreau, in South Dakota. There we found a bridge made in time of floods by the trees—tops, roots and all being borne downward by the current, forming a dam across the stream.

As Mrs. Thatcher and I were about to follow the Indians across one of these uncertain bridges where a misstep might plunge us into the deep, cold water, an Indian approached us and, taking the pack which Mrs. Thatcher was carrying, placed it on his own back and ordered us to go on.

This seeming kindness aroused our suspicions, as they had not offered us assistance under any circumstances whatever. It immediately occurred to Mrs. Thatcher, as well as to myself, that her time had come to die. She hastily bade me good-bye, and said, "If you are so fortunate as to ever escape, tell my husband and parents that I desire to live and escape for their sake."

Mrs. Thatcher was one of the four who were away from home at the time of the massacre.

When we reached the center of the river, as we anticipated, the Indian pushed Mrs. Thatcher from the bridge into the swollen stream. By what seemed supernatural strength she breasted the torrent and, making a desperate struggle for life, reached the shore and was clinging to the roots of a tree at the bank when she was met by members of the band, who were coming upon the scene. With long poles they shoved her back again into the angry stream. She was carried down by the strong current of the Big Sioux, while the Indians on either side of the river were running along the banks, whooping and yelling and throwing sticks and stones at her until she was carried beyond my sight. She was finally shot by one of the Indians in another division of the band, who was crossing on another bridge some distance below. Thus ended the sufferings, tortures, and agonies of poor Mrs. Thatcher.

While making this journey through the unbroken wilderness of the Northwest, we frequently met parties from the various bands of the Sioux Indians. On or about the first May we encamped near Big Skunk Lake. We were crowded in the tepee among the young Indians with their dirty faces, who now had good opportunity to show us their nature. They would fight, pull hair, scratch and bite until their faces were smeared with blood, the squaws not making any attempt to restrain them.

Some four weeks after the departure of Mrs. Marble, we fell in with a party of Yankton Sioux. One of them, named Wanduskaihauke, or End-of-the-Snake, purchased Mrs. Noble and myself from the mercenary Inkpaduta.

One evening, a short time after we were sold, just as we supposed we were settled for the night after a weary march, Mrs. Noble and I were about to lie down to rest when a son of Inkpaduta came into the tent of the Yankton and ordered Mrs. Noble to go out. She shook her head as a signal that she would not go. No sooner did she refuse to obey than the Indian seized her by the arm with one hand, and, with a big war-club in the other, he dragged her just outside the tent door and there struck her three blows such as only an Indian can deal. The piteous groans of his victim came through the tent and pierced my ears—deep, sorrowful and awful to hear. I did not dare venture out to go to her side, I was so terror-stricken.

Now I was left alone with them—no one to talk to, no one to share with me this bitter cup. Gladly would I have given up my claim on this life; but, for some reason, I was spared.

It was a beautiful spring, indeed, and nature was array in her fairest and freshest robes. As we journeyed across the vast prairies of Dakota, from the elevated points the scenes were really wonderful. Look in any direction, the grassy prairie was only bounded by the horizon. We traveled for weeks without seeing timber. The only things visible were antelope and buffalo and flocks of birds. We were moving farther and farther from civilization, and deeper into the heart of the unbroken wilderness.

A few days after the death of Mrs. Noble, we reached the Jim River, in the northern part of South Dakota. Here was an encampment of two hundred lodges of the Yankton Sioux, a powerful branch of the Sioux nation.

I was probably the first white person these Indians had ever seen, and was, to them, a great curiosity. They gathered around my tepee door to look me over, wondering and commenting on my flaxen hair, blue eyes, and fair, though tanned, complexion.

We had been in this camp a few days only when, to me, a most interesting event occurred. By this time nearly all hope had departed, and I was completely overcome by the thought that there was no way of escaping this servitude.

On the thirtieth day of May there appeared in the camp of the Yanktons three Indians wearing coats and white shirts with starched bosoms. I was certain they were from the white settlements as well I knew no Indian women were skilled in the art of laundering white shirts. I soon discovered that I was the object of their conversation. Councils were held after the Indian custom. They sat on the ground, in a circle, and talked and smoked, passing the peace pipe around. Each Indian took a whiff, then handed it to the next one who sat near him in the circle.

At the end of three days, I was delivered over to the "Indians with coats," and the journey toward civilization began. I was ignorant, however, of their good intentions. The price paid for my ransom was two horses, twelve blankets, two kegs of powder, twenty pounds of tobacco, thirty two yards of blue squaw-cloth, thirty-seven and a half yards of calico, and a quantity of ribbon, with which these Indians had been provided by United States Agent Flandraeu. The names of the rescuing party were: Mazaintemani, Ho-ton ho-washta, and Che-tan-maga. The last-named still survives, and had expressed his intention of being at Okoboji during the summer of 1895.

FROM "REMINISCENCES OF JOHN BROWN" (1895)

NARCISSA MACY SMITH

Often overlooked in Iowa schoolbooks is martyr/traitor John Brown's lengthy stay in the Quaker enclave of Springdale, just east of Herbert Hoover's West Branch. Herein, Narcissa Macy Smith recounts the tale of a messianic figure oddly polite and principled to a fault. Most impressive about Smith's little-known and little-cited account is its quotation of the mock legislature John Brown and his men held in December of 1857, in which they posited an independent, presumable secessionist State of Springlade [Iowa], the repeal of the Dred Scott decision and the Fugitive Slave Law, and, as a measure of their zealotry, a resolution that "John Brown is more justly entitled to the sympathy and honor of this nation than George Washington." Brown's indignation and maniacal imagination would soon prove his undoing. After leading a failed raid on the federal arsenal at Harper's Ferry in Virginia with the intention of inciting a slave rebellion, he was captured and hung for treason on December 2, 1859. While Brown is here portrayed as a pacifist, it should be noted that in Bloody Kansas, he and his antislavery guerillas gladly killed for their cause.

The deeds that men and women do, the principles for which they stand, the truths they utter, and the songs they sing, make for them a place in the hearts of the people.

When John Brown and his followers entered the quiet little village of Springdale [Iowa], in the fall of 1857, for a season of waiting, it was the voice of sympathy welling up from the hearts of her people, in the great cause of human liberty which bade them welcome. There never was a prophet or a leader who believed himself divinely called but had his garden into which he went for a deeper baptism of power and broader conception of the work before him. John Brown's Gethsemane was Springdale, and as he walked calmly in and out among her people, his great sympathetic heart was bearing the burden of the shackles of four million of slaves, as though bound with them, and whoever may have questioned his judgment, or the wisdom of his methods, none doubted but that he believed he was raised up by God to strike the death blow to human slavery.

That John Brown felt at home on reaching Springdale is evidenced by the immediate preparation he made for the restful sojourn. Even the gentle admonition of the plain, quiet, Quaker folk, "Thou art welcome to tarry among us, but we have no use for thy guns," did not in the least disturb him, for with their words of loyal testimony came the sweet smile of benediction; and although they would beat his swords into plowshares and his spears into pruning hooks, he well knew they would take every peaceable precaution that nothing should molest him.

John Brown's character was irreproachable. Many living witnesses testify to the fact that he was a total abstainer from all intoxicating liquors. He did not use tobacco in any form, and his language on all occasions was pure and chaste, making his life a beautiful exemplification of the Scripture text, "As a man thinketh so is he." Henry D. Thoreau, an intimate friend of John Brown, in one of his published books says: "I have heard John Brown say that at his camp he permitted no profanity. No man of loose morals was suffered to remain there, unless, indeed, as a prisoner of war. I would rather have smallpox, yellow fever and cholera, all together, in my camp, than a man without principle." Thoreau further says, "John Brown went to the great university of the West, where he pursued the study of Liberty; and after taking too many degrees, he finally began the public practice of Humanity in Kansas. Such were the humanities, and not any study of grammar; for he would have left a Greek accent slanting the wrong way, and righted up a falling man."

Springdale at that time represented Old and New England, Canada, New York, Ohio, Indiana, and other states, sections, and countries; and the harmonious blending of character, through years of pioneer life, had brought forth a citizenship which, for intelligence and high moral standing, was far in advance of the ordinary prairie village. With the mental activity and literary attainments of Brown's men, Realf, Kagi, Cook and Coppock [or "Coppoc"] added to the large array of home talent, both men and women, it is no wonder that in the forum of debate that winter passed into local history as a memorable period.

The writer has in her possession the secretary's book of the Mock Legislature held during that sojourn [in Springdale], and it reads like a veritable congressional or legislative record. That the public may see the range of thought and the varied questions which occupied their attention, I have taken the following from the minutes:

December 1, 1857

The Governor—Emmor Rood—was informed that the House was ready to receive his message. Among his recommendations was one to build a turnpike from Iowa City to Davenport through the capital of the State of Springdale.

Bill No. 1: To render operative the inalienable right of women to elective franchise.

Realf gave notice of a bill to render null and void the Dred Scott decision in all the courts and jurisdiction of the State of Springdale.

Cook introduced a bill to make null and void the Fugitive Slave law of this State.

Resolved, That the repeal of the Missouri Compromise was in accordance with the true principles of our national government.

Bill No. 13: Relating to the banking system of the United States.

Winn gave notice of his intention of offering a bill relative to the conduct of Commodore Paulding in the arrest of Walker.

The question of prohibition was discussed and it was decided that a prohibitory liquor law was both wise and practical.

A bill [introduced] for the establishment of a manual labor school.

Realf gave notice of is intention of speaking on the constitutionality of the Fugitive Slave law at the next meeting.

Kagi gave notice of a bill to establish a militia and harmonial college in the State of Springdale.

Resolved, That we look with regret upon the position which the *New York Tribune* has taken in regard to the reelection of Stephen A. Douglas to the United States Senate.

A bill to appropriate 50,000 acres of land, to be divided into small farms for the benefit of fugitives from slavery.

A bill for the establishment of a college for classical, physiological, and political education of women.

Resolved, That the law for the organization of the grand jury be and hereby is repealed.

Resolved, That John Brown is more justly entitled to the sympathy and honor of this nation than George Washington.

The political atmosphere at that time was not all serenity, in proof of which we give the following bit of unpublished history from the pen of Hon. William P. Wolf:

Tipton, Iowa, April 10, 1895

Respected Friend—In answer to your request, I gladly add to your reminiscences an incident which came under my personal notice. It is the account of the effort at Iowa City to raise a force to go out to Springdale and capture John Brown, Kagi, Stephens, and Coppock, together with about twelve or thirteen negroes, whom they were conveying to Canada and all of whom were stopping with the people at Springdale. In the spring of 1859 I had been getting law books to read from a certain firm in Iowa City, whose junior member was quite a rising young lawyer and Republican politician, and who was extremely solicitous lest the sentiments and doing of John Brown should be charged up to the Republican party, thereby convicting it of being composed of abolitionists; so that when I arrived at his office that morning, he seemed very much excited, and said he thought it the duty of the Republican party to have Brown and his men arrested and punished, and the negroes sent back to their masters. He went out of the office with the apparent determination to see that this was done, and in the afternoon I learned that a squad was gathering at a saloon on the east side of the street, near the corner of University Square. I also learned from Craft Coast that Jerome and Duncan, editors of the Iowa City *Republican*, might want to see me, as I lived three miles northwest of Springdale and could carry a message for them. I went to their office and they stated that they were in communication with the officials of the C. R. I. & P. R'y [Chicago, Rock Island, and Pacific Railway] at Davenport, in regard to getting a car for the purpose of transporting Brown's people to Chicago, and that they were awaiting an answer and desired me to wait till they received it, and carry it to Brown at Springdale. I waited until late in the afternoon, when they received an answer granting a certain boxcar at West Liberty, which was to be loaded at night, without being billed, and pulled out under the direction of the officers at headquarters, as the agent at West Liberty was an intense pro-slavery man. Jerome and Duncan's office was in a building near the southeast corner of University Square, and they told me to inform John Brown that they would provide him with a room in the same building, where he could spend the night. I learned from Craft Coast that by telling the saloon crowd bloodcurdling stories of how they would be waylaid in the woods on their way to Springdale, he had so worked upon their fears that the uncertain courage they had imbibed soon slipped away, and they at the same time slipped out the back door, some saying they would return after attending to certain domestic labors. It is unnecessary to state that they did not return. I then took the permit of the Rock Island officials and started for Springdale. It was stated in the city that the opposition had sent a scout out on horseback to Springdale in the morning. When about two miles out, in the timber, I saw a horseman approaching at the other end of a patch of brush that divided the wagon track, and who seemed desirous not to meet on the same track. When opposite, I crossed to his side, and in answer to my questions, he made evasive statements, the import of which I understood, and I said to him that I had an important communication that I must deliver that night, and that if he was friend of John Brown's, he would not deceive me. He asked if I had a letter. I replied that I had, and also something more important. He then said, "I guess you are all right. I am a friend of John Brown's. My name is Kagi, and John Brown has just passed among us." I then turned back with him and overtook Brown riding with a rag peddler in his wagon. He had a blanket over his head and shoulders, concealing his face, the rain then falling being a sufficient excuse therefore. I delivered the permit to him and told him of the efforts made in Iowa City to accomplish his arrest. He simply smiled and said, "Ah!" I told him of the room prepared for him where he could overlook the saloon rendezvous. He replied that he and Kagi would occupy it and observe any further proceedings. My brother has a little book by Richmond in which it was stated Realf and Kagi walked to Iowa City to get the permit, so you will see that the mistake is herein corrected.

Yours truly,

Wm. P. Wolf [District Judge, Eighteenth District of Iowa]

John Brown's kindliness of heart and strict integrity where shown in all the incidents of his daily life.

When he first arrived in Springdale, a gentleman seeing that his shoes were badly worn, purchased a new pair and gave them to him. He thanked the gentleman and said, "My shoes are all right and if you are willing I will be glad to give them to one of my negroes who has none at all."

One day John Painter, an old resident and successful farmer, met John Brown and said to him, "I understand you wish to sell your mules, and I want to purchase one of them." Brown replied, "Yes, they are for sale, and I want to ask you how much you think they are worth." Painter said, "I think they ought to bring one hundred and twenty-five dollars apiece." Brown replied, "The mules are all right only for one thing, and that is they have the habit of occasionally kicking, and I don't think they are worth but one hundred dollars each." "Very well," said John Painter, "I will give you one hundred dollars for the one I want, and donate twenty-five dollars to the cause in which you are engaged."

It is refreshing after the lapse of years to give to the public this golden rule method of settlement of a business transaction between two honest men.

Although Springdale, strictly speaking, is a prairie village, hard by is the beautiful Cedar River with its crystal clear water, pebbly bottom and rocky banks lined on either side with a heavy growth of trees of great variety, with here and there a little stretch of scenery such as an artist would be glad to gaze upon and transfer to the canvas. Nestled among the trees close to the byroad, leading to the timber, in a quiet sequestered spot, stood the home of William Maxson, where

John Brown and his men were welcome guests during their stay at Springdale. In this peaceful abode, the voices of friends, the birds in the trees, and the very air he breathed, betokened rest for the weary body, while his active, fertile brain was busy perfecting plans for the great deliverance.

In the spring of 1859, when the time of departure came, having no further use for his mules and wagons, they were purchased by the residents of Springdale. The wagon was the one made especially for his use by the Massachusetts Aid Society and sent to him at Iowa City in care of Doctor Bowen, the bill of lading for which is now in the Historical Society at that place. Moses Butler bought it of John Brown and soon after sold it to Gilbert P. Smith for seventy-five dollars in gold. It remained in use on the Smith farm for twenty years and was known as the John Brown wagon. At a general sale, in 1882, H. S. Fairall, of the Iowa City *Republican*, bought the wagon. He still retains it in his possession, though overtures from Massachusetts and Kansas have been made for its purchase.

When the day came for John Brown to take his final leave of Springdale, he rode on horseback from house to house—the deep mud making it impassable for a vehicle. He bade a tender farewell to friends whose kindness, sympathy, and love had given him courage and strength, and, when in tenderness of spirit, grave fears were expressed for his future personal safety, he replied, "God will take care of me, and of the cause for which I am ready to die."

Methinks the heart of our immortal Lincoln beat with stronger pulsations, and his hand held with firmer grasp and guided with surer stroke the pen which traced the words of the Proclamation of Emancipation, because of the human sacrifice on Freedom's holy alter at Harper's Ferry!

Iowa guarded well the lives of John Brown and his followers while their feet trod her soil, and she has sought on all possible occasions to do honor to the sons for their own sake, and as a tribute to the memory of their father.

From "Amana Colonies: A Glimpse of the Community of True Inspiration" (1896)

Bertha M. Horack [Bertha M. H. Shambaugh]

> "Behold how good and how pleasant it is for brethren to dwell together in unity." —*Psalm cxxxiii.*

A native of Cedar Rapids, Bertha Maude Horack graduated from Iowa City High in 1889. After attending the State University of Iowa from 1889–1895, she returned to her high school alma mater to teach natural science from 1893 to 1897, at which point she married Benjamin Shambaugh, a native of Elvira, Iowa, and who was then a professor at the University of Iowa and would later become the superintendent and editor of the State Historical Society. The article that follows, "Amana Colony," won the Midland Monthly *prize for best Original Descriptive Paper in 1895, laying the groundwork for Shambaugh's popular monograph* Amana: The Colony of True Inspiration *(1908) and an updated version,* Amana That Was and Amana That Is *(1933), both published by the State Historical Society of Iowa. Apropos to Shambaugh's final question in the essay below—whether the purity and simplicity of the Amana Colonies would be preserved, her 1933 book presents a community already somewhat compromised by its own novelty and subsequent popularity among tourists.*

Southeast of the center of Iowa stands a group of little villages, so unlike the neighboring towns in their arrangement, with people so different in customs and in dress from the people one is accustomed to see, that the visitor finds it difficult to realize he is only a few miles from Iowa's capital and not in a foreign country. Eight villages compose this picturesque little group, the home of the Amana Society or Community of True Inspiration.

The "Colonies" are in the northeastern part of Iowa County. They are situated on both sides of the Iowa River, the usefulness of which stream has been increased greatly by the construction of a millrace—a canal seven miles long which furnishes the waterpower for the several factories and mills scattered throughout the settlement. The millrace, with its fringe of grapevines and pickerel weed and the quaint little bridges that span it here and there, is as pretty as it is useful, and furnishes a never-ending source of enjoyment for Amana summer visitors.

Halfway between Amana and High Amana, with the millrace running through it, is a beautiful little lake, which is bordered sometimes to the width of sixty feet with the American Lotus or Yellow Nelumbo (*Nelumbium lutium*). It is worth a journey of many miles to see this little sheet of water in the month of July, when the lotus lifts hundreds of great buff blossoms above the water. The seed of the lotus, when ripe, is about the size of a small hazel nut, perfectly round, and hard enough to admit of a high polish. Every fall a priest from one of the neighboring towns collects these seeds in great quantities to be used in making rosaries.

Each Colony is a cluster of from fifty to one hundred houses, arranged for the most part along the main street or road. And how unlike the main street of the common country town! Instead of a ragged row of business buildings where neighboring farmers collect to discuss politics and the corn crop, we find on either side of the street a neat row of vine-covered houses—the only places of business being the store at one end of the street and the hotel near the other. Here the usual noise and bustle of the country store is wanting, and even the hotel has about it a quiet, soothing atmosphere.

Every now and then an oxcart comes meandering down the pretty little street. These great, patient, slow-moving animals would be strangely out of place in our own hurrying streets, but are in perfect keeping with the easy, steady, systematic movement of the Colony. The use of these animals is a matter of economy with the Colonists, as the ox, when speed is not required, can be used longer and worked harder than a horse, and, when no longer profitable for hauling, can be fattened and used as beef.

One never sees the Colonists collecting in any considerable number on the street. When they meet they usually greet each other with a shake of the hand and pass on—leaving the silver [currency] question, the latest candidate for the presidency, and other questions of the day untouched, or reserving them for some more appropriate place for discussion.

The houses are two-, sometimes three-storied structures of frame, brick, or a peculiar brown sandstone that is found in the vicinity; and some, as if to add still greater variety to scenes, are built of all these materials. The frame houses are all unpainted—the Colonists believing it to be more economical to rebuild when occasion requires than to preserve the buildings a little longer with paint. In summer the severe aspect of the houses is softened by the vines which partly cover dwelling house, school, church, and hotel alike. These vines are trained over a framework a few inches from the building itself, so as to prevent any injury to the wall, and afford a better support for the vines. For these vines are not simply the ornamental vines, but grapevines, which serve the purpose of shade and protection in the summertime and yield an abundant harvest in the fall. Here and there the trumpet vine with brilliant flowers will be seen climbing a trellis in company with the grape, it having won its way into the hearts of the people by its attractive blossom. But the woodbine, which has neither blossom nor fruit to recommend it, is not to be found, except where it creeps in unnoticed in some uncared for spot.

These houses are occupied by one, two or three families, depending upon the size of the house and the size of the family. There is no crowding, however; the same spirit that led these people to believe that the purity of the Society could better be maintained with more villages and fewer in a village has led them to provide plenty of room for other people. In spite of the fact that everything within these several Colonies is held in common, each man's home is his castle. Here he is at liberty to indulge his own taste in decoration—provided he does not go beyond his allowance. Here each child has a room to himself, where he may indulge his own hobbies and store his own keepsakes without being disturbed.

Two underlying principles govern the entire community—economy and utility; yet in one thing these seemingly ever-present motives are set aside, and that is in the matter of flowers. Around every house, even in the hotel and schoolyards, there are carefully kept flower gardens. Such masses of bloom! Such a display of color! Such a collection of quaint, old-fashioned flowers—petunias, marigolds, chrysanthemums, "pretty faces," bachelor's buttons, six-week's stock—with here and there a bed of geraniums, a rosebush, or a flowering shrub.

There are several "kitchens" in each Colony, by which is meant the houses at which the people take their meals. Long before the idea of cooperative housekeeping had dawned upon the minds of ardent reformers as a solution of the domestic problem, the Colonist had decided that this was the most economical mode of living. From sixteen to forty eat at one kitchen, the number depending largely upon the location. The places are assigned by the trustees.

The kitchen proper is usually a small room furnished with a long, low brick stove with an iron plate top. Back of this is a sheet of tin several feet high, which shines like a mirror; from its upper edge hang a great variety of strainers, spoons, dippers, and ladles. Everything from the floor to ceiling is kept scrupulously clean. During my visit at the Colony last summer I took a picture of the hotel kitchen. When I returned this year the housekeeper confided to me her chagrin on finding that the towel in the kitchen was not clean at the time the picture was taken, explaining just how it happened that it wasn't changed at the proper time. I had not noticed the presence of the towel at all, but to her it was the most conspicuous object in the picture. I tried to convince her the spots she saw were only shadows, but I am afraid I did not succeed.

It is one of the religious principles of this quiet, gentle people to care for those in sickness or in want, a fact the tramp element has not been slow to learn and take advantage of. At a certain season of the year the community is overrun with tramps—all posing as victims of misfortune.*

Throughout the entire settlement the same spirit is shown. "Malice toward none and charity for all," can be read upon every face that passes by. Generations of right-thinking and right-living can be seen on the faces of the Colonists. They need no garments of white, as *Die Weisen* [magi; wise elders] of old, for their faces are a better index of the pure, the noble, the spiritual lives that they lead than any spotless robe.

There is an indescribably restful atmosphere about the Colonies. Nowhere is work done more thoroughly than here; but, where each member of the community young and old does his honest share, the individual burden is not heavy. There are no drones in this hive. Everyone does his work conscientiously, but seems singularly free from worry.

The fact that very few children are seen by the average visitor has led many to believe and some to make the statement that there are not many here. This is a mistake. There are just as many little people to be found here as in any community of the same size. Long before the ordinary pleasure-seeker starts on his exploring tour, the boys and girls between the ages of five and fourteen are hard at work at school. Here they may be found six days in the week, all the year round. The sessions open early and close late—with the exception of Saturday—and there are no vacations. To those of us who are accustomed to the short sessions and long vacations of the modern public school this at first thought seems almost cruelty to the children, but a visit to *die Schule* very soon convinces one that these children fare quite as well as our own little people.

As each member of the Colony has his or her own appointed work to do—work which frequently keeps the parents away from home all day—the children must be taken care of, and the school largely supplants the home training of our children. That it is in every sense adequate, everyone who has visited the school must acknowledge. Never have I seen a group of children so uniformly well-mannered, pleasant spoken, courteous, and thoughtful as in the Colony school.

What would seem like an otherwise long, tiresome session is broken up into three parts—*die Lehr-schule*, where all the common branches are taught, *die Spiel stunde*, or hour of play, and *die Arbeits-schule*, where the girls and boys alike are taught to knit and sew, to care for the flowers and gardens, and in other ways to become useful members of the community.

During our last visit in Amana, we gave the knitting teacher candy to be distributed during recess, at which time luncheon is served to the children in the two vine-covered arbors, one for boys and one for girls—for here as everywhere throughout the Colony they are separated. Before the candy was distributed, the children named over one by one the schoolmates who were absent, and their share was put away first, then the remainder was divided among those present. After the candy had disappeared, every boy and girl, without a single expectation, came to us, offered a hand, thanked us in the most unaffected manner, and invited us to come again. As we sat in the arbor, one unfortunate little girl, whose mind was evidently blank, came bouncing in. Two of the older girls quietly arose, removed her sunbonnet, smoothed her hair, adjusted her little black cap, and led her gently to a bench nearby—an act so spontaneous, so considerate, that it was an effort for those of us who saw it to keep the tears back. We no longer wondered at the universal nobility of character, kindliness of manner, and genuine thoughtfulness of the men and women of Amana Colony.

While from the outside the vine-covered schoolhouse with its white-curtained windows and its neat flowerbeds is likely to be mistaken for a dwelling, the interior with its blackboards, charts, and globes is not unlike our own schoolrooms, with the exception of the unpainted woodwork and the sanded floors. The teachers in the school proper are all men, but there are women among the "working teachers."

Much of the reciting is done in concert, and, in the primary department where the little ones learn to spell syllables together and pronounce the word, the result is a sort of chant, the rhythm of which is fascinating. This same chant may be heard, during the long recess, when the children play their quaint little games—quaint to us because of their setting but in reality only equivalents of the "London Bridge," "King William," and "Drop the Handkerchief," of our own school days.

The children under five, whose parents are obliged to be away from home during the day, are kept in a nursery well-supplied with toys and sandpiles.

The dress of both men and women is plain in the extreme; utility and not adornment is the chief regard. There is nothing characteristic in the dress of the men aside from its severity. An Inspirationist is readily recognized anywhere by the short, round beard under the smooth-shaven chin. The dress of the women can never be mistaken for anything but the Amana dress. Fashions never trouble them. The dress of today is the same as it was at the founding of the Colony. Mothers and daughters, grandmothers and granddaughters, dress alike—not in the sober grays of the Quakers, nor in the more brilliant purples of the Amish, but in plain calicoes of gray or blue or brown. The waist is short and very plain, the skirt long and full. An apron of moderate length, a "shoulder shawl" of calico, and a small black cap completes the summer costume. The only headgear is a sunbonnet with a large cape. The winter dress differs from this only in being made in flannel; a hood takes the place of the sunbonnet. Thirty-five dollars for clothing is allowed each member of the Colony annually. A seemingly small sum, but sufficient when we remember that the clothing is all of the simplest and that this year's dress will answer for next year and for the year after—in fact, as long as it will last.

The secret of the prosperity of this communistic body is said to be the religion which binds its members together. The truth of this even the casual observer must recognize. Their religion is not a thing to be put aside Monday morning with the "best clothes" and donned on the following Sunday, but a thing ever-present with them—a part of their everyday life.*

The perfect equality maintained by the Colonists is shown even in death. In the cemetery there are no family lots, no monuments. The departed members are placed side by side in perfect rows, regardless of family ties. The graves are all marked by a low, white-painted board slab with the simplest kind of inscription on the side facing the grave. The grass in the cemetery is carefully trimmed, but there are no flowers there.

While the Colonists have to a certain degree tried to keep aloof from "the world," the latter, like Mahomet, has gone to the mountain, and has left its footprints in the form of modifications of the former austerity of the Community. Rag carpets have taken the place of sanded floors in many sitting rooms, ornamental trinkets are hung upon the wall, and here and there a piece of upholstered furniture is to be found. A few years ago instrumental music was strictly forbidden; now one occasionally hears the distant notes of the violin or the deeper tones of an accordion.

"What will the next half century do for the Colonists?" the visitor asks; and he is likely to follow up his question with expression of the hope that the Amana Society may prosper as it has prospered in the past, and that its purity and simplicity may be preserved.

From "Four Famous Iowa Girls in Chicago" (1897)

Ethel Maude Colson

Ethel Maude Colson, later to become Ethel M. Colson Brazelton, made it big in the Windy City as an instructor of women writers at Northwestern University's prestigious Medill School for Journalism. Author of the popular Writing and Editing for Women *(1927) and* How to Write Poetry *(1919), Colson preached empathy as a female writer's special province—a trait on display here as she translates the special achievements of Iowa girls in Chi-town for the mostly Iowa readers of the* Midland Monthly. *Contemporary readers will note that even Colson, a strong feminist in her day, finds it necessary to emphasize the femininity of these four successful businesswomen and artists.*

The colloquial title "an Iowa girl" has grown to mean much to the thoughtful resident of Chicago; it has become identified of late with no small amount of good and noteworthy work. During the past few years, the state of Iowa has contributed a large number of brilliant young women to the artistic circles of Chicago. Especially is this true in the line of musical work. A survey of the women musicians of Chicago brings to light the fact that over a third of those who have made enviable names for themselves, originally hailed from Iowa. Sara Herschell Eddy, the noted vocalist and teacher, wife of Clarence Eddy, the famous organist, was born and educated in Iowa; and so was Rose Ettinger, the popular singer, now in Paris; also Kate Funk, who, before her marriage with Jacobson, the well-known violinist, earned wide distinction by her own clever handling of the bow and strings. Many other distinguished names might be quoted in this connection. Of the four bright Iowa girls who are at present winning fame in Chicago two are musicians by profession and affinity, the third is manager of the Chicago orchestra, and the fourth, a journalist, possesses a strong interest in all things pertaining to or suggestive of harmony.

The last named is the latest acquisition to the "Iowa Colony," which is fast winning respectful recognition as a factor in the intellectual life and growth of Chicago. But little more than a year ago Miss Eleanor—or, to use the child-name by which she attracted public attention in her native state, "Nell"—Gilliland, came to Chicago in search of the larger newspaper work for which she had always longed. Within ten days she was hard at work on the *Chicago Tribune*, and in the short period of time since her introduction to the staff of a metropolitan newspaper, not only has she been remarkably successful, but she has also attained wide popularity and more than local fame. Prior to her advent in Chicago, Miss Gilliland had done some notable service on the daily paper of her birthplace, the Jefferson [Iowa] *Bee*, and had also contributed to the larger journals of her State. she was also, for a time, in charge of the Eldora [Iowa] *Herald*, leaving that position to come to Chicago. So great is the versatility of this clever girl that while still attending high school—from which institution she was graduated before her fifteenth birthday—she at one time composed fourteen of the required essays of her class, treating in a single subject in as many different ways, and so skillfully as to escape detection.*

Another Iowa girl whose success in Chicago has been as rapid as remarkable is Lucille Stevenson, the soprano singer. Three years ago this charming girl, only twenty-three at the present time, left her home in Des Moines to study vocal music in Chicago. She reached the city in April, and in the following October she was appointed to the position of soprano soloist in the New England Congregational Church. Another year saw her installed at the choir-desk of the Memorial Baptist Church. Twelve months later she began to sing in the Presbyterian Church at Hyde Park, and has recently been engaged by the Plymouth Congregational Church, thus holding, in unbroken succession, four of the best and most coveted positions in the music life of Chicago.*

Miss Anna Miller, the third member of this Iowa quartet, was born in Muscatine. She left that city seven years ago, to attend the University at Evanston. After spending several years in general work at that institution, she took up the study of music in Chicago, and labored hard with three instruments, the organ, the piano, and the violin. She also interested herself in voice culture. Becoming acquainted with Miss Electra Gifford, the singer, while planning a debut concert for that lady, she attracted the attention of the trustees of the Chicago Orchestral Association, and was requested to take charge of the season tickets for a time.*

While carrying on this work with the firm grasp and clear business comprehension of a trained businessman, and delighting in nothing so much as in study and severe intellectual labor, Miss Miller is as far removed from the so-called "strong-minded" woman as it is possible for a girl to be, and especially dislikes anything which suggests mannish women. Horses and dogs she loves devotedly, herself owning a pair of fine trotters and a beautiful saddle horse. These and her bicycle all come in for a large share of her affections. She is devoted to children and is ardently fond of flowers. She is an enthusiastic traveler, and will this year visit Europe to personally secure several continental soloists for the next orchestra season. She still calls the Muscatine farm her home, and pays her father and sisters frequent, though flying, visits. In person, this brilliant Iowa girl, who combines with unusual abilities the graceful tact which has made success possible under the most trying exactions and manifold cares of her position, is strikingly handsome and yet her manners are simple, direct, and unassuming as those of a child. Her figure is tall, athletic, and finely molded. She has a peculiarly mobile face. Her mouth is singularly fine and expressive, and her eyes are large, clear and steady. Looking at Miss Miller one feels instinctively that she was born to direct and organize, and her quiet, but warm and decided, hand-clasp suggests the secret of her strong hold upon her many friends.

Miss Julia Officer, the well-known pianist, is another Iowa musician who has won a speedy and delightful success in Chicago. Besides working enthusiastically with her private pupils, she finds time for much praiseworthy concert and parlor work, and also manages the affairs of the North Side Musical Club of Chicago, of which organization she is both president and musical director. She is also a member of the Amateur Musical Club, and of the famous Apollo Club, both formed, to a great degree, of the representative musicians of Chicago. With all these varied evidences of her success, it is scarcely seven years since Miss Officer first visited the city of her adoption.*

Iowa people in Chicago are proud of the work and influence of this charming compatriot. Like the other brilliant women mentioned here, she has added glory to both her native state and her adopted city.

"The First Violin in Amana Colony: A Sketch" (1898)

Maude Vary Ebersole

Maude Vary Ebersole appears to have been an editor's clerk for the Iowa General Assembly circa the time this short story—or, more accurately, this morality tale—appeared in the pages of the Midland Monthly. *In reading "The First Violin," one cannot help but think of Iowan Meredith Willson's musical* The Music Man *(1957)—where, as in the short fiction that follows, music transforms a conservative Iowa community's most sacred and unexamined notions of itself.*

If the elders of Amana Colony had known that there was to be found within its borders such a thing as a violin, there would have been great commotion until the sinful thing had been removed. Had the hotelkeeper at Amana known that that violin was in his daughter's possession, he would have forthwith destroyed it. The underlying principles of the Colonists' belief are economy and utility, and as the possession and use of musical instruments was believed by them to be in opposition to both these principles, musical instruments of all kinds were strictly forbidden.

No one but Frida Schwalm knew about the violin, and it was her only treasure. She kept it hidden in her own little room and only occasionally, when her father was resting of an evening on the vine-clad porch, would she dare steal away under the cover of the friendly darkness and, slipping noiselessly among the thick clumps of trees that skirted the riverbank, draw the bow across the strings.

The violin had once belonged to a wandering musician who, reduced to poverty and suffering from exposure and hunger, had sought aid from the charitable Colonists. While there, disease and death had overtaken him and he had confided his only property, the precious violin, to Frida's keeping. At first her conscience troubled her for having this secret from her father, and more than once she had determined to tell him. But every time she touched the strings they spoke to her in such sweet strains that she could not let it go. As time went on, the stolen moments by the riverside grew more and more precious, until the anticipation of them was her inspiration in her daily tasks.

I said no one knew the violin but Frida. One other shared her secret, and that was Ludwig. Poor Ludwig might be implicitly trusted to keep the secret, for he had been speechless all his life. Many an evening the old trees had stretched their protecting branches over these two and that violin, and listened as the faint, subdued strains of the stolen music floated up to them. Heaven must have hushed the sound ere it wandered out to bring trouble to the musician.

"Ludwig," said Frida one evening. "I am going away." Could she have seen the pained, surprised look in the speaking eyes she would have felt her resolution shaken; but the darkness hid it, and she only felt the pressure of his hand and guessed what he would say.

"Yes, Ludwig, I am going to run away. I cannot live here any longer, for I want to learn to play. I am going tonight, and shall take the violin with me. No, Ludwig, you could not go. You must stay here and wait for me. I will come back when I have conquered it, and I shall play it, oh, so beautifully."

The next morning consternation stalked through the village street. Frida Schwalm was gone! For many an evening the little groups that gathered in the chapels for prayers talked of her disappearance, and at the kitchens, when they all gathered for daily meals, Frida's name was in every mouth until there was nothing left to say.

The little hotelkeeper loved his daughter with the love that is born of loneliness and expended on the only companion of the last years of a troubled life. In the little cemetery there were five rude wooden crosses that marked the resting places of Frida's mother, brother, and sisters. Frida alone had been spared to cheer his home, and now she had deserted him—left him without a word or sign of her going!

Ludwig's heart ached for Frida and the violin. No one pitied him, as they pitied her father, for no one knew of his live. But he had what Johan Schwalm only dreamed of and tried to imagine, and that was hope. Had not Frida said she would return? Had she not asked him to wait and watch for her? And day by day the hotelkeeper, while he performed his tasks with a calmness that deluded the Colonists into the belief that he had ceased to grieve for his lost Frida, watched for her with the persistent habit of despair. Day by day Ludwig waited for her with the feverishness of hope long deferred. Five long years they watched and waited and prayed for her return.

At last she came, just as she said she would come. She came down the stairs from her little room one morning, as if those years had been but a night, and she was taking up her tasks where she had laid then down the evening before. Her face was older and changed, bearing traces of her experience out in the world. Instead of the severe Colony blue calico, the folded handkerchief about the neck, and the black cap on the head, she wore a simple white dress and upon her head only the glorious crown of sunny hair nature had given her.

Who could tell of the joy that came back to the father's heart that day? There was not a word of chiding, not a question asked; only a kindly, almost passionate greeting, his soul speaking its happiness through the stern old face that glowed with the love of his great, kind heart. He knew that his Frida would tell him all that had happened; and why and where she had gone, and he left it for her to choose the time and manner of telling him. And she did tell him—of the struggles she had had; how she had to toil and save to earn her way, and how at last her talent had been discovered, and she had been befriended by one who had taught her just for the joy of developing the gift of music God had given her.

"Father," she said, "I went to master it; I have just begun to see what I may do, but I wanted you to know now, and I want you to let me play for you."

The news that Frida had come spread through the village, and some neighbors came to the hotel that first evening to learn if it were true.

When they had all entered the room, Frida came forward, carrying her violin, and said: "My friends, I want to tell you a story—the story of the years that I have been away from you."

She stood before the open window, her white-clad figure clearly outlined against the red glow of the setting sun. First she drew from the violin a few quiet, gentle strains, setting forth the uneventful, monotonous life in the Colonies. She glanced at the faces before her, and in each one she saw pictured the prejudice of generations. She must dispel it; she must conquer their hearts by her playing. The music then burst into a wild, passionate longing, expressive of the soul hunger that led her away from home. Then followed the story of the years of patient, hard toil, and Frida was lost to her surroundings. She was a part of the music. The violin talked to them; it seemed to tremble with life; it had soul, for Frida had lent it hers. When her story was finished in a glad, exultant chord of triumph, it did away with the voice of pleading—that thought which has inspired the most beautiful and touching stains that mortal ears have ever heard—and the hand which held the bow dropped at her side: the violin was lowered. She saw tears in their eyes, and glistening down their cheeks, and she knew that she had conquered their hearts.

There was a light movement outside the window, and a hand touched hers. Turning, she saw the radiant face of Ludwig, his eyes fairly speaking the thoughts of his great, earnest soul, and her happiness was complete. *He* had heard her play, too. She could see it in his eyes.

The world outside the boasts of its superior civilization; its cultured social life; but there, in that room in the unpainted, homely hotel in the Colony of the True Inspirationists, a musician was receiving a higher compliment than ever courtier paid his queen.

The visitor who passes through the village now hears the occasional strains of a violin or an accordion; and it is because one girl, obeying the voice from within her, dared to brave the unknown world beyond her quiet home, and, flooding the very hearts of the Colonists with its music, swept out prejudice with the song of the first violin.

From **Uncle Henry's Letters to the Farm Boy (1897)**

"Uncle Henry" Wallace

The eldest Henry Wallace, the scion of the legendary Des Moines-based family that included son and U.S. secretary of agriculture Henry C. Wallace, and grandson, future vice president and candidate for president Henry A. Wallace, knew a thing or two about hard times. Nearly bankrupt and mired in a prolonged legal battle with his former employer, the Iowa Homestead *newspaper, the one-time theologian Wallace was once described by one of the leading journalists of his day, Ray Stannard Baker, as a "broken-down preacher of the United States Presbyterian Church" and, by his friends, as a "lion in torment." But out of troubled times arose Uncle Henry, the wise, generous, ever-forgiving yet tough-minded ethos Wallace conjured in his beloved Sabbath School Lessons in the magazine that bore his name,* Wallaces' Farmer, *and in a series of popular books, the first of which,* Uncle Henry's Letters to the Farm Boy *went through a remarkable five editions. Called by Baker "a sort of oracle for advice on everything from the best ways of feeding calves to brining up boys," Wallace here confronts, head on, a subject with which many Iowa farm families are intimately acquainted—the butting of heads between father and son.*

My Dear Boy:

It has occurred to me that matters might not be going just exactly right between you and your father, and that a word from one who has been both farm boy and father might do good to both of you. I do not think for a moment that there is anything seriously wrong, only that neither of you are as happy in your relations with each other as you ought to be and can be. I take it for granted that you love and respect your father—not quite in the same way that you love your mother, because the affection that you bear to the one is distinctly different from that which you bear to the other, and must be in the very nature of things. I take it that you have a good father who loves you dearly and who above all things else desires that you be a strong, true, brave, noble man, who will bear his name with honor when he is lying in the grave. I know he thinks more of you than he does of the farm and all that is on it, saving always your mother and your brothers and sisters. I take it that you are a good young man, and there is no reason why you and your father should not be as happy together as people can be in this world. If you are not, it is likely that both of you are somewhat to blame, and I will venture a guess as to why you are not as happy as I would like to see you.

You, perhaps, think your father is needlessly exacting in some things. He wants that stable cleaned out promptly and thoroughly, and wants the pigs fed just so every time, whether it is wet or dry, or a good day to go fishing or a bad one. He wants the cows milked clean, does not want any loud talking while milking, and he wants the milk cared for just so, and if you fail in any of those things he does not like it, and you do not see why he should be so particular. Now, I will tell you why. Your father was probably a little bit careless himself when a boy; he sees the mistake; he knows how difficult it was for him to get over this habit, and he does not want you to have the same kind of trouble.

You do not see why he disapproves of your going out with a lot of other boys whom you regard as good fellows, but who have some bad habits, such, for example, as using profane language or indulging in obscene talk. Now, I will tell you why he does not want you to go with those boys. He possibly went more or less with that class of boys himself and knows from experience that they are not the kind of boys with whom you ought to associate.

He objects to your going out at night unless it be to some literary event, or to make a social visit to your neighbor. Now, he is perfectly right about this because he has had experience and you have not. You do not see why he insists on your going to church every Sabbath and to Sabbath school, even if you are tired and sleepy and would like a good, long day's rest. Again I tell you why. He felt when he was a boy just as you do, but years have taught him the necessity of acquiring steady and regular habits of industry, morality, and religion. Your father has lived a long time, has had lots of experience, and knows a great deal that books can not teach, and he would like above all things else to be able to impart that experience to you, which he knows that he can not impart except by insisting on your acquiring it by the doing of it. That is the only way that anything worth learning can be learned. In all these things your father is exactly right.

You perhaps feel that he ought to give you a chance to earn something for yourself—that there ought to be something on the farm which is your very own, or, as your sister might say, your "ownest own." Well, I think so, too. I think you are entirely right in this, and if I were in your place I would, some day after supper when he was not troubled in any way, talk the matter over with him in a manly, open way. Nothing pleases a father so much as to see his boy develop manliness. I would talk to him about this, but I would make a square bargain that if you are to have a pig, or a calf, or a colt on the terms agreed on, it is to be your hog, or your steer, or your horse when it is disposed of, and you are to be the sole judge, after asking his advice, as to how you are to use that money.

You think your father should not bind you down so closely as to the plan you are to take in doing certain things about the farm. You want to exercise your own judgment, and have, so to speak, a little leeway. You are willing to do the things he wants you to do, but you would like to do a little planning and thinking for yourself as to the way of doing them. Here you may be right and again you may be wrong, but I think he had better say to you, "My son, there are certain results that I want accomplished: I think you had better do this way, but if you see a better way, try your hand." You will probably find that his way is the right way after all, but it will do no harm to find that out by experience.

You may think that your father is a little of an old fogy in some matters connected with farming. There is a possibility that his long years of experience enable him to see through the fallacy of theories that you may not be able to do as yet. Therefore, I would advise before condemning his ideas to study them quite thoroughly and weigh carefully what you may see on the other side. He may not be able to give you as good reasons as you may see on the other side on paper, but I suspect that he has the common sense of it pretty firmly fixed under his gray hairs, and may not have the patience to sit down and argue the thing out with you.

I would like for you to have profound respect for your father's views on all questions. They may be wrong—no doubt many of them are—but you should remember that "knowledge comes but wisdom lingers." It may be that you know a good deal more than your father. If so, it is because you take after your mother, but whether you really know it must be clearly established by actual results, and not assumed.

In order to have a proper respect for your father, you must not call him "dad," or "pap," or "pa," or "the old [man]," or "the governor," as I have heard a good many English boys call their fathers. There is but one name that he is entitled to, and he is entitled to that every time; and that name is "father," never "the old [man]." The very act of calling him father will make you respect him and respect yourself, and smooth out any little trouble that there may be between you. It is essential to your growth and future happiness that you and your father have the most perfect understanding with each other. By and by he will come to trust you implicitly. First, he will be to you a sort of older brother, and as the years go on he will learn to depend on you, to lean on you, so to speak, and by and by will be disposed, when he begins to lean heavily on his staff, to pay as much deference to your opinion as you did to his when you were a little boy. You thought then that father knew it all. He will think after a while that you know it all, and that whatever you do is about right because you do it.

I write this to you because I have known boys who took a different course from that which I advise you to take, and who have blighted their own lives and their fathers' lives, and broken their mothers' hearts, and I do not want you do to either.

Affectionately,

Uncle Henry

From **The Oldebolt, Iowa Chronicle** and the Iowa Supreme Court (1898-1901): Three Selections from the Cherry Sisters Controversy

An especially novel chapter from Iowa history—and a personal favorite—is the story of the famous, or rather infamous, Cherry Sisters of Marion, Iowa, whose wonderfully terrible, financially successful vaudeville act was promoted by Oscar Hammerstein I and described by the November 17, 1896 New York Times as the work of "four freaks form Iowa." When the rich and famous Cherries returned to tour their home state in 1898, Billy Hamilton, the editor of the Oldebolt Chronicle *in Sac County made ready his poison pen. His scathing "review" of the Cherries' show* Something Good, Something Bad *was reprinted by dozens of newspapers, including the Des Moines* Leader, *which the Cherries promptly sued for libel. The embattled sisters lost their case twice, the first in the Polk County Court, and the second, on appeal to the Iowa Supreme Court, whose opinion is excerpted as the third and final selection in the remarkable story that follows.*

"The Cherries Were Here" (February 17, 1898)
By Billy Hamilton, Editor, The Odebolt Chronicle

When the curtain went up on Wednesday evening of last week, the Cherries saw a good-natured audience, large enough to fatten their exchequer to the extent of $35, net.

The audience saw three creatures surpassing the witches in Macbeth in general hideousness.

Effie is an old jade of 50 summers, Jessie a frisky filly of 40, and Addie, the flower of the family, a capering monstrosity of 35. Their long, skinny arms, equipped with talons at the extremities, swung mechanically, and soon were waved frantically at the suffering spectators. The mouths of their rancid features opened like caverns, and sounds like the wailings of damned souls issued therefrom. They pranced around the stage with a motion that suggested a cross between the *danse du ventre* and a foxtrot, strange creatures with painted faces and hideous mien. Effie is spavined, Addie is knock-kneed and stringhalt, and Jessie, the only one who showed her stockings, has legs without calves, as classic in their outlines as the curves of a broom handle. The misguided fellows who came to see a leg show got their money's worth, for they never saw such limbs before and never will again—outside of a boneyard.

The first glimpse of the Cherries was worth the price of admission. One shriek of laughter swept over the house. Not even in the woods around Sac City, nor in the wilds of Monona County, could three such raw and rank specimens of womanhood be found. The men howled and the women shook with merriment. There were no vegetables thrown, but there was lots of talk. It would take the sisters six weeks to answer the questions that were fired at them. At intervals Effie and Addie would jaw back and threaten to stop the show, but the boys never let up. When Jessie came out in her bare feet, many solicitous inquiries were made about the condition of her corns, and she was freely advised to trim her toenails. And such feet! No instep, flat…and "Z" wide. Jessie, however, is not sensitive. She calmly went on with her part, evidently considering her feet her "strong" suit.

Finally the program came to an end and the audience left, well-satisfied, as a rule, although some who had never heard of the Cherries before were angry because the noise prevented them from hearing the girls.

The Cherries honestly believe that they are giving an entertainment surpassing anything on the stage, and that their audiences hoot them because they can't appreciate true merit. They have been systematically stuffed by every manager who has engaged them with the notion that they are away up. If they were not stuck on themselves, no money could induce them to stand the jeering they get. But having salted down $60,000 in the bank and purchased several large farms with the proceeds of their foolishness, they are willing to keep it up as long as they can make it pay. Their personal characters are above reproach; they are virtuous both from necessity and choice, as anyone will conclude at sight of them. The most skillful impersonator would find it impossible to burlesque the Cherry girls. They are nature's own raw material, unique and inimitable.

"Sued by the Cherries"

By Billy Hamilton (April 28, 1898)

The Cherry sisters evidently do not appreciate refined dramatic criticism. In February last the Des Moines *Leader* clipped from *The Chronicle* and published a paragraph of personal description of the Cherries as they appeared in Odebolt. The other day the proprietors of the *Leader* were notified that the three charmers had brought suit against them for libel, claiming $15,000 damages by reason of the publication of said "false and malicious" paragraph.

The attorney for the Cherries is one W. B. Crosby, of Des Moines. He announces that action will be begun against every newspaper which published *The Chronicle*'s comments; and as several hundred papers in Iowa and the Chicago dailies were guilty of the unpardonable sin, Crosby will have a job that will last him a lifetime.

Thus far no legal notice has been served on *The Chronicle*; but as it was the fountainhead of the alleged libel, it can hardly hope to escape. Should we have to defend an action, we shall set up a plea of justification, demand the appearance of the Cherries in court in full stage costume, the exhibition of certain physical peculiarities to the jury and the rendition of the vocal selection entitled "Cherries Ripe and Cherries Red." We shall also summon as witnesses the people who attended the Cherry performance in Odebolt. It will be a hard-hearted jury, indeed, that will give the sisters a verdict after hearing our defense.

To be on the safe side, we think of giving a bill of sale to the first man we can find who is foolish enough to want a newspaper.

"Cherry v. Des Moines *Leader* et al." (May 28, 1901)
By the Supreme Court of Iowa, Justice Horace
Deemer writing for the majority

The action is predicated on the publication of the following article: "Billy Hamilton, of the Odebolt *Chronicle*, gives the Cherry Sisters the following graphic write-up on their late appearance in his town: "Effie is an old jade of 50 summers, Jessie a frisky filly of 40, and Addie, the flower of the family, a capering monstrosity of 35. Their long, skinny arms, equipped with talons at the extremities, swung mechanically, and soon were waved frantically at the suffering audience. The mouths of their rancid features opened like caverns and sounds like the wailings of damned souls issued therefrom. They pranced around the stage with a motion that suggested a cross between the *danse du ventre* and a foxtrot, strange creatures with painted faces and hideous mien. Effie is spavined, Addie is stringhalt, and Jessie, the only one who showed her stockings, has legs without calves, as classic in their outlines as the curves of a broom handle." The defendants pleaded that plaintiff, with her sisters, were engaged in giving public performances, holding themselves out to the public as singers, dancers, reciters, and comedians; that their performances were coarse and farcical, wholly without merit, and ridiculous; that the Des Moines *Leader* is a newspaper published in the city of Des Moines, which the other defendants were conducting, and that the article appeared as a criticism of the performance given by plaintiff, and to expose the character of the entertainment; that it was written in a facetious and satirical style, and without malice or ill will towards plaintiff or her sisters. This is clearly a plea of privilege, and the direction to the jury to return a verdict for defendants was, no doubt, on the theory that the plea of privilege was established. That it was published of and concerning plaintiff in her role as a public performer scarcely admits of a doubt, and it is well settled that the editor of a newspaper has the right to freely criticize any and every kind of public performance, provided that in so doing he is not actuated by malice. In other words, the article was qualifiedly privileged…. The occasion was such that the presumption of malice arising from the publication is rebutted, and plaintiff, in order to recover, must prove actual malice…. By the term "actual malice" is meant personal spite or ill will, or culpable recklessness or negligence. Such malice may be shown by extrinsic evidence, or it may be gathered from the publication itself. There is absolutely no evidence, outside the publication itself, tending in any manner to show malice; hence, if malice be found, it must be from the article published. Ordinarily publication of such an article as the one in question would of itself be an indicium of malice, but, as applied to the facts of the case, we do not think it should be so held. Plaintiff described the entertainment she and her sisters gave, in part, as follows: "These entertainments are concerts—literary entertainments. I don't sing much. The others do. I have recitations and readings; recite and read in costume. In feminine costumes. Dresses as long as I have on, or shorter. I don't wear short dresses. Sometimes I have worn men's clothes. I never dance. I recite essays and events that have happened, I have written up of my own. I have none of them with me. One is, 'The Modern Young Man;' the other, 'An Event that Happened in the City of Chicago.' I sing an Irish song—an Irish ballad; also a eulogy on ourselves. It is a kind of a ballad composed by ourselves. I help the others sing it. I have forgotten it. It is about an editor. In the chorus I walked a little around the stage—kind of a fast walk. A *cavalier* is a Spaniard, I believe. I represent a Spaniard. That is given in the act that we call 'The Gipsy's [Gypsy's] Warning.' I wear my bicycle bloomer rig. They reach to my knees, and are divided like leggings—black leggings with buttons on them. I wear a blue blouse—a blue velvet blouse. Sometimes red and sometimes green. I have many suits; wear them in turn. The leggings are always black. In the chorus I walked a little around the stage—kind of fast walk or a little run. Had on different kind of clothes—mostly silk. We had a reproduction of the performance called 'Trilby.' The singing of Ben Bolt by my little sister. I would come in and hypnotize her in a farce way. I would tell the audience that I would hypnotize her while she would sing. I didn't appear at any show without stockings. My little sister was barefooted in one act—in very long dresses to her ankles. She also appears in a long robe in a tableau clinging to the cross. 'Cherries Ripe and Cherries Red' is a eulogy song. I was not asked to repeat only one verse. Q: What is the verse? A: "'Cherries red and cherries ripe, the cherries they are out of sight, cherries ripe and cherries red, Cherry Sisters still ahead.'" The defendant's evidence regarding the character of the performance is in part as follows: "It was the most ridiculous performance I ever saw. There was no orchestra there. The pianist left after the thing was half over. She could not stand the racket and left. There was no other music, except vocal music from the Cherrys. They had a drum, and I think they had cymbals. As near as I can recollect, the curtain raised at the beginning, and the Cherrys appeared and gave a walk around and a song. I think it was 'Ta, ra, ra, Boom de ay.' They read essays and sung choruses and gave recitations, interspersed with the remarks that, if the boys didn't stop, the curtain would go down. One young man brought a pair of beer bottles which he used as a pair of glasses. They threatened to stop the performance unless he was put out, but he was not put out, and they didn't stop. When the curtain went up the audience shrieked and indulged in catcalls, and from that time one could hardly hear very much, to know what was going on, to give a recital of it. There was no bad language used, however. When Jessie was on the stage she appeared in the Trilby act in bare feet and short dresses. She was asked to trim her toenails, and such irreverent remarks as that. She appeared more pleased than anything else. They had a washtub scene. I think Effie and Addie appeared with bare arms showing to the elbow, which was quite prominent. They went through the motions of washing, singing at the time. There was another piece called 'The Gipsy's [Gypsy's] Warning.' One of the sisters appeared in a male costume. Then there was a song, 'I want to be an editor,' and an explanation, accompanying the song, that an editor down at Cedar Rapids insulted them, and they made him pay dearly for it. The song was so jumbled up one could hardly make anything out of it, except, 'I want to be an editor, I want to be an editor,' whereupon the audience rose as one man and called on me to stand up. I did not stand up. My wife was there. While Jessie sang this she was rolling her eyes and swaying her body. I am not qualified to pass an opinion upon the merits of the singing. The discord was something that grated on one's nerves. There was short stepping around and swaying of the body. They went around the stage in one of their pieces—I cannot say which—sort of a mincing gait, shaking their bodies, and making little steps. That is what made me describe it as a cross between the *danse du ventre* and a foxtrot. They had their hands in front of them and at their sides. There was a tableau at the close, as I recollect. Jessie was the central figure in that piece, with her eyes uplifted, red lights, and so on. There was a 'Rock of Ages.' The audience was talking to the women, and they (the Cherry Sisters) would talk back. They would say: 'You don't know anything. You have not been raised well, or you would not interrupt a nice respectable show.' Nobody left during the performance except the pianist."

From "The Social Life of a Girl in Iowa College" (1898)

Helen B. Morris and Emeline B. Bartlett

Iowa College, now Grinnell, enters the act in the following article, penned by Helen B. Morris and Emeline B. Bartlett. Though the college, as the authors readily admit, was coeducational at the time, they describe, in an almost anthropological manner, the conspicuous behaviors and customs of the women of Iowa College as compared to those at women's colleges in the East. Notable in this reading is Iowa College's early support of women's athletics in general, and basketball in particular, and subsequent moves to codify physical education in the curriculum for women. And of course the sneaking of dormitory breakfast food to an overslept friend emerges as an especially long-lived Iowa collegiate tradition!

One feels as if he were in danger of falling upon Scylla or Charybdis in trying to tell of student life; for if much attention be paid to the scholastic, the real side of college training, if one only mentions the hours day after day spent in writing themes or working on abstruse problems, a reader might say, "All work and no play makes Jack a dull boy."*

As in every place the social life depends largely upon the influence of the women of the community, Iowa College is no exception to that rule. Although the men outnumber the women, it is the later who take the lead in social matters. This is seen, for instance, in the working of committees for class parties, where the girls do the greater part of the planning, leaving the boys to carry out their arrangements. Right here is to be noted one of the main differences between a girl's life in a western coeducational college and that in an institution in the East like Smith or Vassar.

There, where men are a rarity, a scarcity, and at a premium, if a girls wants a tack driven she learn to do it herself. If there is to be a party, she must give the invitation, send the flowers, and call for her "lady" in chivalrous a manner as her brother. If a play is to be given she is obliged to represent either hero or heroine, villain or lover, with equal versatility, till at last, upon receiving her degree, and coming out into the world, she is apt to discover that, owing to the long period, she has been almost ignorant of their existence; her needs for men are very few.

What wonder that the percentage of marriages among the graduates of women's colleges is small! There, although a girl may have gained the knowledge and ability to do anything and everything with a hairpin, and a certain independence and self-reliance, she is liable to have lost her contact with the world and the surroundings in which she must spend the rest of her life, while in a coeducational institution she is not shut off like a novice in a nunnery. Here she keeps in touch with her fellows, thus obtaining a knowledge of men as well as women, which is a valuable part of her college education. Not only is this done by the daily association in the classroom work, by the Friday evening calls, the class parties, the lectures and concerts, and the various forms of exercise to be participated in by two, where invariably the rule is followed, "the longest way round is the shortest way home."

But coeducation is not the only side to a girl's life in Grinnell. Living in little groups of six or seven around the town, there is opportunity for many a spread, or a fudge party, for which no chaperone, or permission of the faculty is necessary. From these houses the girls assemble for their meals in clubs of twenty or thirty which serve as a bureau of exchange for bits of news, where each one finds out "who is going with which," to the next party or lecture, who has been the recipient of the last box of flowers, etc. But this way of living in one place and boarding in another has its disadvantages. Even a tempting supper loses its attraction when the price to be paid for it is a walk of three or four blocks in a blinding storm, and, going to eight o'clock recitations, one frequently meets a pitcher and a mysterious bundle being carried to some roommate who prefers an extra half hour sleep to exercise at that early hour.*

When one thinks of the advantages connected with such a dormitory as this, it is easy to see that one of the greatest needs of Iowa College is to have enough such houses for all the girls, places where they would be constantly in the home atmosphere, and where the benefits coming from close mutual intercourse might be more easily reaped.

These later results are not the only ones which would be obtained, as, for instance, healthy rivalry might be shown in seeing which house could give the best play, and which the most original party or entertainment. In this way the latent possibilities in each girl's character for adding to the general fund of mutual enjoyment would be developed and brought out. An instance of what this rivalry may do was seen last year when basketball was first introduced to the College. Courts were laid out in the field adjoining the Cottage, and every afternoon one might see a busy bevy of girls tossing a ball about and making frantic efforts to land it in the basket. The Cottage girls, with characteristic enterprise, organized a team and challenged the rest of the College. For days before the match the coming contest was the one theme talked of, and the excitement arose to almost as high a pitch as before an all-important football game. Colors were chosen, the Cottage taking yellow and the College team wearing their rightful emblems, scarlet and black; yells were invented and nearly every member of the whole student body came out boldly as adherent to either the one team or the other. When finally the game was played, it was a close one, showing admirable practice and skill on both sides, and the enthusiastic support the players received from the spectators made the contest a most interesting one. It was only after forty minutes of hard-fought battle that the victory was carried off by the Cottage team and the supporters of the yellow and the jubilant. Then came a return match, the result of which made the sides equal, and after that it was decided to end all rivalry by celebrating peace with a sleigh-ride and oyster supper.

This year the new gymnasium has turned the interest rather away from basketball and tennis to regular gymnasium work. The constant moan used to be, "O, dear, must I go to the gym today," the speaker not having energy enough to put the final syllables on the word *gymnasium*. This year, the opposite complaint is heard because that form of exercise cannot be taken every day. A visitor sitting in the gymnasium gallery, watching the spirited movements and eager faces, would never think of asking if the work was compulsory, and might be sure that students take no "cuts" in those classes. Any girl who cares at all for her physical welfare must feel that such a gymnasium adds a new inducement to go to Iowa College. If the interest in this work continues as at present, we may have soon have a girl's field day that will rival Smith or Vassar, and surely none of the colleges in this state could compete with any hope of success, for even without this building, with its perfect equipment for physical development, our girls were able to win the prize in doubles and singles at the tennis tournament last year. Though the work in the gymnasium is done is done in the classes and strict discipline is maintained, still the minutes before it commences, and during the rests, offer opportunities for sociability and relaxation that add largely to the good results of the exercise. This is the common meeting ground for all girls. Bound together here by the mutual interest in the same work, deeper knowledge of one another is gained than would be in any other way.

Here it is one notes particularly the absence of an objectionable feature so often found in colleges, and so conspicuously absent in Grinnell—separate cliques are here almost unknown. In watching a class in the gymnasium, it is easy to see that here, as well as in every phase of the student intercourse, they are accustomed to work together for the accomplishment of whatever end they have in view. To a great extent the success of every Iowa College organization is due to this spirit of union, this common striving together for the good of all.

FROM **SOME AUTUMN DAYS**
IN IOWA (1906)

FREDERICK JOHN LAZELL

A professor of journalism at the University of Iowa and a faculty advisor to numerous student publications, Frederick John (F. J.) Lazell here engages in what might be called participatory nature writing in the tradition of Henry David Thoreau and John Burroughs. The foreword to the book, penned in Cedar Rapids, casts its aim as prophecy, as the author predicts, "By and by some writer with the learning of a naturalist and the soul of a poet shall tell of the beauties in this great of Eden which is embraced by two mighty rivers"—Iowa. The selection below comes from the chapter entitled "Some November Days in Iowa."

Poor Thomas Hood! He lived in England. For him the yellow fog, the gray skies, the bleak winds, the cheerless rains. If he could have spent one November in Iowa he would never have pictured Autumn sitting melancholy and tearful, alone upon a messy stone, reckoning up the dead and gone:

> This year's in the wane
> There is nothing adorning,
> The night hath no eve,
> And the day has no morning,
> Cold Winter gives warning."

Most of the British poets sang in a similar strain. Shelly writes a dirge for the "dead cold year," and asks the months

> From November to May
> Is your saddest array
> To follow the bier
> Of the dead cold year
> And like the dim shadows watch by her sepulcher.

The New England poets have been wont to follow these conceptions of the later autumn. Whittier sees all things around him stark and dumb, praying for the snows to come. Bryant mourns because "The south wind searches for the flowers, whose fragrance late he bore, and sighs to find them in the wood and by the stream no more." But the Iowa poet ought to sing in a happier strain. October in Iowa runs well into the month of November: for the first half of the month there is little difference. The many warm, sweet sunny days take all of the sadness out of the dying year. The sun smiles gently and benignly through the smoky air and gives a halo of amber and purple to the soft sepias and gleaming grays of the woodlands which a month ago were brilliant with crimson and gold.

"No flowers, no leaves, no birds," forsooth! If only Hood could have taken a walk through an Iowa wood, some bright sunny morning in early November. The willows stand guard at the very entrance to the wood. All through October when the wondrous coloration of the oaks and maples, alders and aspens, was running up and down the gamut of brilliancy, the willows retained their soft and restful green. Now the green is slowly searing to brown and the leaves are fluttering down in the sunshine while a flock of snowbirds (Juncos) with their bright yellow bills and their slate grey head and throats make merry among them. Down the trunk of the tree runs the white-breasted nuthatch and his incessant tap-tap-tap gives emphasis to the stillness of the mild November morning.

The savants say that there is no state in all the world more favored with bird life than Iowa. The state lies in the embrace of two mighty rivers with many fine long tributaries along and between these rivers the great flood of bird life goes northward in springtime and southward in the fall, filling the air with the matchless music and charming the eye with incomparable color. In his "Kim" [Rudyard] Kipling speaks of the Great Trunk Road as the highway for all sorts and conditions of Hindu life; so Iowa is a highway for the vernal and the autumnal flood of bird life. The robin and the hepatica, the bluebird and the spring beauty, follow the springtime up the valleys; the hepatica and the spring beauty show their beauty no more until the next spring; but the robin and the bluebird pass through again late in the fall.

A few robins are usually seen as late as the first week in November. Then there are some hardy little creatures which stay with us all winter through one must go to the woods to see them. Among them are the chickadee, the nuthatch, the waxwing, the American goldfinch, the blue jay, the crow, the snowbird, and some of the sparrows and woodpeckers; the Iowa woods and fields are never wholly deserted. The scream of the blue jay, the caw of the crow and the chick-a-dee-dee-dee of the little black-capped bird which bears the name are all familiar sounds in November.

No flowers, no leaves, said Hood. Once again, poor Hood! In this walk through the Iowa woodlands in early November, there are several varieties of late asters, some straggling blossom in the sheltered places, of the Indian tobacco (*Lobelia inflata*), pepper grass (*Lepidium Virginicum*) and sneezeweed (*Helenium autumnale*). If one should set out to swell the list and should call a few fading petals a blossom, he might doubtless swell the list to five times this number. The dandelion (*Taraxacum officinale*) may often be found in November, the yellow blossom forming the golden period at the end of the flowering season.

How many have seen a dandelion? Everyone, of course. Yes, but how many have really seen one? When is its stalk the longer? When is it drooping, and when does it stand erect? It was Darwin who first noticed that the stalk is short and drooping, while the flower is full of yellow gold, but long and erect when the flowers have developed into the white and fluffy seeds. Of course, everyone knew it after Darwin had recorded his observations. But no one had really seen it before.

As to the leaves—well, the common bramble shows the bronze green of its leaves to better advantage now than at any time during the summer. The same is true of the cat-brier or carrion flower (*Smilax herbacea*), the plant which has so offensive an odor in the flowering season, but makes up for it by its graceful season until well along into November. The oaks have shed many of their leaves by the end of the first week in November, though some linger much longer. The white willow falls about the same time.

Through the woodlands which slope gently upward toward the crest of the ridge, there is a thick carpet of the fallen leaves and among these another nature lover, which an eye for his table, is poking with a stick. He has been out for an hour and he carries a peach basket which he has almost filled with mushrooms (*Armaillaria mellea*). "You can hardly make a mistake at this time of the year," he says as he goes down on one knee and cuts off a fine bunch with the table knife which he carries. "See this growth like a cobweb from the stem to the gills?" When you see that you may put the mushroom in your basket and take it home for your dinner. Be sure to gather those that are fresh and firm. Those that have grown old and flabby are not good."

Over the crest of the ridge and down the slope to the river the grays and the sepias are brightened by the high notes of the late orange-colored pods and the scarlet seeds of the waxwork or bittersweet (*Celastrus scandens*), also, here and there, the burning bush, or wahoo (*Euonymus atropurpureus*) with its numerous and beautiful long drooping peduncles and deeply four-lobed crimson pods through which the scarlet seeds are bursting. This is one of the most ornamental of the native shrubs. The wonder is that more of them are not seen in gardens. And by the way, many of the wild shrubs, to say nothing of the wild herbs, might well find a place around the dwelling of the nature lover. They are far more beautiful and appropriate than some of the artificial ornamental oddities. The hard clematis, the common virgin's bower (*Clematis Virginiana*), the Virginia creeper (*Ampelopsis quinquefolia*), the steeple bush (*Spireae tomentosa*), the common meadowsweet (*Spirea salitcifolia*), the goatsbeard (*Spireae aruncus*), the black haw (*Viburnum prunifolium*), the honeysuckle (*Lonicera grata*), the catbrier (*Smilas herbacca*)—at least one town lot has many of these and many have wondered from what faraway state these beautiful shrubs were imported.

From **The Clara Hinton Diary (1907)**

Clara Hinton

Born in 1894, Clara Hinton survived a challenging childhood in Hedrick, Iowa, in Keokuk County, including the death of her mother and the caretaking of her father, her two brothers, and a sister who died shortly after their mother. Hinton went on to attended Central College in Pella, and, from there, chose the University of Wisconsin for a graduate degree in library science. A long-time librarian for the University of Iowa, Hinton donated her papers to the Iowa State Historical Society before her death in 1987. In the journal entries below, a teenage Clara Hinton makes history simply by reflecting on the everyday events of her southern Iowa childhood, including the first entry—May Day. For the sake of readability, Clara's adolescent spelling errors have been corrected in the entries that follow.

May 1, 1907

I am a good deal better today. Forrest stayed home from school too today. He is getting the pocks. So we are all at home today but Ruth. She complains because she has so much dishes etc. to do. This is Genie's worst day with the chickenpox. Forrest isn't very bad yet though. In the afternoon Papa went to the cow pasture, and there to Grandpa Hinton's, and then came home and telephoned to Bro. Campbell. Paul and Mrs. Campbell are sick. This evening one of the Bowlin boys brought a bouquet of "little boys breeches" and laid them on the porch and knocked and ran away. On them it said, "For Eugene and Clara. I hope you'll soon be well." I expect Annie Bowlin sent it. After that Papa and Ruth went to Prayer Meeting. Margeret and Marie Sheets were here this evening.

May 2, 1907

I feel almost well today except I look nearly as bad as ever because I ain't pealed off yet. It is a very nice warm day and the bees are humming and the birds are singing. I have been looking around hunting flowers. Papa is sawing wood. It is so nice outdoors. I can't hardly stay in the house. We had dinner. I dried the dishes. Papa went to town about 2 o'clock. At 2:30 it was 65 degrees above zero. Emily Bowlin brought my deportment card home and I got an F in Arithmetic—the first F I've got this term.

May 3, 1907

This is Friday. Us three are at home again today. Our church is now holding a B.Y.P.U. midyear meeting. M. C. Alexander at the Competine Church preached last night. Ruth and Papa went. This morning Papa went again. Gene is reading "Ruth Webster's Quest," but I doubt if he finishes it. It is cloudy and chilly today. It snowed about 2 inches deep. In the night it froze, and Papa thinks it killed all of the fruit. Eliza was here after 1 pint of milk. Tom Darner is in Ottumwa jail.

May 4, 1907

Ruth and papa went to church at 9 o'clock A.M. Gene and Forrest and I stayed at home. I made a cake and gem cakes for dinner. I went to Grandpa's in the A.M. a little bit.

From **The Chasm (1911)**

George Cram Cook

Seldom studied, George Cram Cook is not only one of Iowa's most important writers, but one of its most dynamic. Born in Davenport to a well-to-do, well-established family, his life took a sudden turn when his mother moved her family back to her childhood cabin in Buffalo, Iowa, south of the Quad Cities, introducing her family to a truly rural life. Precocious thanks to his mother's refinement and books, Cook enrolled at the University of Iowa at the tender age of sixteen, where he played on the baseball team in addition to studying literature and the classics. From Iowa, he went on to Harvard and, degree in hand, returned to teach at Iowa, and, later, at Stanford. In 1907, after meeting and falling under the influence of fellow Iowa writer and intellectual Floyd Dell, Cook joined the Socialist Party, earning his party's nomination for Congress from Iowa's second Congressional district. After two unsuccessful marriages and many travels, the romantic Cook ran away with a new flame, Davenport's up-and-coming writer Susan Glaspell, with whom he remained until his untimely death in 1924. The principal characters in the passage below, Minne Moulton (daughter of a wealthy Moline plow manufacturer) and Walt Bradfield (a Socialist gardener), evidence the ideological and class currents moving in Iowa at the time. Cook's political influences aside, the excerpt below offers a perfect recipe for an Iowa classic—a nervous mother, a dutiful father, a high-spirited daughter, a philosophical gardener, a storm on the Mississippi, and a forbidden love…what could be better?

Mrs. Moulton was alarmed about Marion when the storm first broke over Moline, but hoped the launch party would by that time be safe in the Camanche clubhouse. Since thinking evil things brings evil, it was her duty to believe them safe. Since nothing is but thinking makes it so, thinking of the party as not being at Camanche would very likely cause them not to be there. Her visualization of them there in the grillroom became so distinct that she could feel her astral self at Camanche seeing eight people, among them Marion, sitting at a certain table. Had anyone suggested to her that this vision might possibly be the optical memory of a party she had there chaperoned two years before, her will to believe the alluringly mysterious astral doctrine would have scorned the suggestion as emanating from the critical, that is from the Mephistophelian, spirit—"the spirit that ever denies." Yielding to this spirit would be evil because it would project from her mind a powerfully injurious thought-force.

When Mrs. Farnsworth, Mr. Moulton's sister, their guest at dinner, inquired for Marion, Mrs. Moulton replied that she had gone with a launch party to Camanche.

Mr. Farnsworth conjectured that the storm would compel them to leave their launch up there and return by train.

"I hope they got there before the storm struck," said Mr. Moulton.

A certain mysterious intonation in his wife's assurance that they had reached Camanche led him to suspect astral information. As soon as dinner was over he succeeded, in spite of the storm, in getting the steward at Camanche by telephone. Then he called Mrs. Moulton from her guests. "No launch party has reached Camanche today," said he abruptly.

Her real alarm made him relent.

"And none was expected there," he added. Now, Anne, don't get rattled, but tell me what you do really know about this launch party. Whose party was it?"

She had to explain that Marion, due at the river at ten-thirty, and not leaving the house till quarter to eleven, had departed hurriedly without giving her any details.

"How did she go?"

"On foot."

"Why didn't she take her electric?"

"I cannot say." She knew David imagined he had shattered one of her intuitions against a stone wall of fact, and resented the air of arrogant, incisive efficiency he always assumed on such occasions. If anything did happen to Marion it would be his fault for creating all this malicious thought-magnetism.

Mr. Moulton sent for one of the drivers and directed him to take Miss Moulton's electric down to the boat landing. She might be there with no way to get home through the rain. If she was not there, the driver was to find out and report at once what party she went with and which way they had gone.

Twenty minutes later, Mr. Moulton was informed by the driver, Eldridge, that it must have been Miss Moulton who had gone out alone with Walt Bradfield. About eleven o'clock they had gone through the lock, and so down the river, in Lew Anderson's launch *Nancy*.

"Bradfield?" repeated Mr. Moulton, trying to place the gentleman.

"He works here, sir," said the chauffeur, expecting to produce a sensation. "Sits beside me in the servants' dining room. He's one of the gardeners."

"Oh, yes," said Mr. Moulton, "—that plan of my daughter's. I didn't know she was doing that today. That's all, Eldridge."

Eldridge turned to go, but hesitated an instant at the door with the idea that he was to be told to keep this matter quiet.

"Was there something else?" inquired Mr. Moulton.

"No, sir," replied Eldridge, getting out. "I wonder if that old fox did know about that Bradfield deal?" he speculated.

Mr. Moulton sank back in his chair, irritation and perplexity in his soul. "What is that girl up to?" thought he. He looked out at the still-driving rain and swaying treetops. He was divided between concern for Marion's safety in the storm, and his effort to understand her motive in making a companion of a servant. Stories of refined women infatuated with strapping grooms and coachmen rose repulsively in his mind. He did not accept that explanation; but it remained in the background of his thoughts ready to reassert itself.

The affair looked worse to him when he found the girl had never mentioned Bradfield to her mother. Mrs. Moulton's amazement when she heard Marion had gone in a launch with the gardener made it impossible for her to bring the kindly side of her philosophy to bear. "Earth-forces" was her formulation of the same suspicion that had arisen in her husband. For her, once started along that path of thought, the very occupation of the man was symbolic. Was he not a digger in the earth? And Marion had gone with him upon the water. The affair was of earth and water, unsanctified of fire and air.

Mr. Moulton was tormented with the impulse to do something. Either the launch had swamped, or it had not. If it had, he wanted to know it. If it had not, Marion and her companion must now be someplace under shelter waiting for the storm to stop. He did not care to have them wait. He finally sent down the river a big launch with a closed cabin and a searchlight to find the *Nancy* and bring Marion home.

This launch left Moline about four o'clock manned by two old river men in charge of McChesney, a confidential agent in the detective service of the Plow Company. The rain stopped while they were searching. Near dark they located the stove-in Nancy on the shore of Round Island; but they found the log cabin there empty. The old fisherman in the houseboat on the Iowa shore told McChesney that when he came out after the storm to look at his nets, he had seen a couple on the island waving a shirt on an oar. He had taken them off, and they had started to walk to town.

The fisherman had told them they might make it by dark: but they had to pick their way along the edges of muddy roads, finally took to the gravel and ties of the railroad track; and as night fell, the electric lights of Davenport sprang up white out of the blackness of the eastern horizon. They came to a railroad bridge beneath which in the gloom a rain-swollen torrent ominously thundered. They stopped a moment, standing close together. The cold wind and the tumult of that unfriendly elemental force made the warmth and nearness of each other more precious.

"You don't suppose the bridge is out, do you?" said Marion, peering ahead. "No, I can see the shine on the rails." She clasped Walt's hand, and welcomed the support of his arm around her as they crossed, stepping from tie to tie.

He was seized with a wild happiness, a piercing realization of the present moment, an intense feeling of his identity and hers. The two of them crossing that bridge in the black night were to him the only man and woman in the world. When they felt the gravel once more underfoot she would have drawn away.

"A man, a woman, and Nature which made us!" he exclaimed. "There are no classes. There is no town. There is nothing but you and me and the night."

His feeling swept her like a poem creating a new mood. The thunder of waters behind them seemed no more a hostile voice, but the voice of great harmonious forces at work through eons and eons creating and maintaining man. She leaned and pressed her cheek against his shoulder; then, sighing, withdrew her hand and walked alone. "For me," she said, "there is town. There is Hillcrest, and in it another man and woman. They are worrying about me. They love me—in a way—not wisely, not trustfully, not realizing I must find or make my own path through life. They do not understand me: they have no sympathy for the things that I, being I, must seek and find. They will attack me tonight. I will have to defend myself. If he had his way, my father would reduce the real me to pulp."

The great tenderness then filling Walt turned into the channel of regret that she too should be subject to all the influences that shape our modern world and shape it wrong. "Shall I go in and help you defend yourself?" he asked.

"No. The best you could hope would be to defend yourself. After you left I should have my own fight just the same—or worse."

They caught the suburban car where it crossed the railroad at the lower end of Davenport. Three quarters of an hour later, they got off in Moline at an electric-lighted corner where the streets were thickly lined with workingmen's small frame houses, their paint grimed with soot from the factories. Back on the bluff towered Hillcrest, its four stories marked by half a dozen brilliant windows. Well to the right and left of it stood other great houses, each aloof on its own spacious eminence—as the castles of robber barons stood on the hills of Rhineland.

Walt and Marion ascended the hill, walking alongside a heavy terra-cotta retaining wall, from the top of which leafless, brittle-looking vines trailed downward. Between the base of the wall and the concrete sidewalk stood a row of low shrubs which Walt himself had planted. The return to use-and-wont, to Hillcrest, the end of his day with her, affected him gloomily. "I have a wretched premonition I am not going to see you very much any more," he said.

She had the same unpleasant feeling, but would not admit it. "I should think a monist like you would regard premonitions as superstitious."

"I did yesterday. Imagination was reason-guided—a light I turned at will upon the world. Therein lay my power. Today that monism of mine is split by war of reason and desire—and reason has the worst of it."

"Is that a reproach of me?"

"An analysis of me. I can no longer distinguish between the thing I desire and the thing that is true. I am no better than a bourgeois."

"That is humility!" she laughed. "But really, Walt, a little humility won't hurt you a bit."

He stopped abruptly. Once more, as on the dark bridge in the thunder of waters, there were no classes. She was woman to him, and he was man. An overpowering feeling of worship swept through him. "I could kneel here at your feet for that!" he breathed. "In fact—I must!"

"Oh, no!" she exclaimed. "No!" She caught hold of his arms to keep him from doing it. "It will make me cry if you do that!"

"No! Don't take it that way. I will be nice and quiet about it. It's a thing I have to do." He made her feel it as impulse and compulsion of the depths of life in him, and then he knelt as though it were an act of mere deliberate resolve. She found a beauty and richness in that union, in one act, of simple conscious will and some uncomprehended depth of feeling. The depth, and nothing of quietness, was in his voice when he stretched out his arms to her with the cry, "I worship you!"

She swayed back breathless, leaning against the wall, knowing clearly that this was something more than merely physical allurement. His cry—which she thought no woman in the world could have heard unmoved—and its echo in her were of the spirit, or more truly, of the whole and single being which man is. It felt like a great love. The great desire of all that day, thwarted but stronger inwardly for every thwarting, retreating only to advance through some new path of feeling, seized and subdued her. Not indirectly nor as an accident, not with manner unpurposive, she bent and kissed him—in the mood of answered prayer.

He rose. A beam from an arc lamp through the young buds showed her his face. In his arms she whispered: "I shouldn't have done it. I don't know why I did. I seemed to have to. It was too big for me, Walt."

"It was star-high above my hope!" he said.

"It's a pity to say it, but you mustn't, mustn't make too much of it. I must go in. I need to be alone and think." She saw a question forming in his eyes and did not dare listen. "Come!" she said, and using all her willpower moved on up the hill. She looked down and up the walk. Fortunately—no one! They turned in through the gate of Hillcrest and neared the door.

"Don't let this be the end of things between us!" he pleaded. "It has grown too strong to break."

"I'm utterly at sea," said Marion.

FROM **THE IOWA**

WILLIAM HARVEY MINER (1911)

William Harvey Miner, though credited as the author of this book by Cedar Rapids's Torch Press, actually provides little more than an assist here, as Miner reprints Thomas Foster's Indian Record and Historical Data *from 1876 while adding a few explanatory footnotes (here deleted). Dr. Foster, an earlier Indian historiographer, hoped to publish a weekly pamphlet, and, eventually, a scholarly monograph, on each of the country's Native American peoples; he began with the Iowa and the Winnebago, though finished neither book. The passage below describes the fascinating games and ritual dances of the Iowa, the people who gave our state its name. The importance of the Ioway, well understood by both Foster and Miner, returned to the state's consciousness in the form of the 2008 documentary* Lost Nation: The Ioway. *Miner and Foster likewise detail the separation and scattering of the Ioway people. In 1836, they write, the Iowa were assigned a reservation in northeastern Kansas, after having ceded all their Missouri lands. A part of the tribe later moved to another tract in Oklahoma allotted them in 1890.*

Like many other Mississippi Valley tribes the Iowa are not to any great extent associated with the tumuli of America. With the exception of some few mounds in Wapello County, Iowa, at a point near Iowaville, the site of an early trading post, there is little evidence that the Iowa were in any way connected with the mounds in that state. Along the valley located in this section, were many spots frequented by both the Sauk and Fox as well as Iowa and here also were situated the famous racetracks of nearly a mile in length, belonging to the latter tribe. The various games indulged in by the Iowa differed but slightly from those in vogue among kindred or allied tribes. As is almost universal, dice games, or games of chance, are more generally to be desired, while games of dexterity take second place. Catlin describes under the former class, once called Kon-tho-gra, or the game of platter which is played almost exclusively by women. It is said to have been exceedingly fascinating and consists of little blocks of wood marked with certain points for counting, to be decided by throw, the lot being shaken in a bowl and thrown out on a sort of a pillow. Bets were made after the bowl was turned and decided by the number of points and colors. Another game described by Catlin is called Ing-Kee-Ko-Kee, or, The Game of the Moccasin. It was played to a song accompaniment among the Iowa by two, four, or six people seated on the ground in a circle. In the center are three or four moccasins, under one of which the players in turn try to conceal some small article, as a stone or a nut. The opponents choose what appears to be the lucky covering and, if successful, win the stakes. The game, according to this writer, appeared simple and almost foolish, yet he professes to have seen it played for hours without intermission in perfect musical rhythm, and states that it "forms one of the principle gambling games of these gambling people." Among the Omaha, Ponca, Oto, and Iowa the game of Arrow, (Manmuqpe), was most common. This however was more of a religious game and now practically obsolete since the introduction of firearms. Arrows were shot up into trees until they lodged in the branches. The players then tried to dislodge them and whoever brought down the first, won. There were no sides or opposing parties. Probably the most exciting and to many the most important game among many of the tribes, aside from those of the mountain Indians, is that of Ball-playing or Racket. This is distinctly a man's game as opposed to double-ball and some other forms commonly played by women. There are instances however of by this having been played by women, and among the Santee Sioux it is at times played by both sexes together. This game has been divided into two principal classes, those of the single and those of the double racket or bat; the latter is more especially peculiar to the southern tribes. The racket may be likewise termed a throwing stick as it is used to pick up and throw the ball rather than for the purpose of hitting. The ball is either of wood or buckskin stuffed with hair, and the usual size is about two and one-half inches in diameter. Various kinds of rackets are used by the players, some preferring long and some short handles. Among the Oto of Oklahoma, one measured was forty inches in length. Catlin gives an excellent description of this game among the Iowa Indians. His details concerning the goals and byes and various points connected with the different features, make this sketch one of the most complete we have.

As among all tribes east and west, north and south, the Iowa were given to their numerous dances, many of which were of the highest importance. Mention is made here only of several of the more common or necessary dances, inasmuch as the subject is one if it were treated fully would occupy a volume in itself.

The Welcome Dance: This is a peculiar dance given in honor of one or more strangers whom the tribe may decide to welcome to their village. The musicians as well as spectators, out of respect, all rise to their feet while it is being performed. The song which accompanies it is at first one of lament, but ends in a gay and lively manner.

The War Dance: The most exciting as well as the longest and most tiresome of all dances. It is usually divided into three parts, i.e. Eh-Ros-Ka—the Warriors Dance—usually given after a party had returned from war as a boast and was oftentimes given as an amusement. The song used at this time entitled Wa-Sissica—the War Song—appeared to be addressed to the body of an enemy, from the name Eh-Ros-Ka, meaning tribe, war party or body.

Approaching Dance: The most spirited part of this greatest of all dances was called the Approaching Dance in which the dancers by their gestures exhibited the methods of advancing on an enemy. The song in this portion is also similar to that above mentioned.

The Eagle Dance: Ha Kon-E-Crase, or as more familiarly known "the soaring eagle," forms the third and most pleasing part or the War Dance and is in every respect a most interesting spectacle. Each dancer imagined himself a bird on the wing, and as they dance forward from behind the musicians, they take the position of an eagle headed against the wind and about to swoop down upon some unsuspecting prey. They have a peculiar method of singing and whistling at the same time.

The Calument Dance, the Ball-Play Dance, the Scalp Dance, the Buffalo Dance, and the Bear Dance, are all important but vary very slightly from those of similar import among other tribes of the same family. What we have said about the dances applies with equal force to the songs and music. The War Song, Death Song, Wolf Song, Medicine Song, Bread Song, and Farewell Song are all of much significance, indeed so much so that a large amount of space could well be devoted to this subject as well as to the dances.

From "Eight People Murdered in Their Beds in Villisca!" (1912)

The Villisca Review

The front-page article that follows tells the story of one of the twentieth century's most gruesome ax slayings—the Villisca, Iowa murders of 1912, in which the six-member Moore family, and two young neighbor girls on an overnight, Ina and Lena Stillinger, were killed in cold blood sometime before midnight on June 9, 1912. The next day the shock waves reverberated across the country; a lengthy article bearing the headline "Eight Slain In Home While They Slept" ran June 11 as a special to the New York Times. Omitted from the excerpted Villisca Review article below is, among others, the section "features of the tragedy," which explains how the Stillinger girls had planned to go to their grandmother's after church on that fateful Sunday evening, but instead decided, tragically as it turned out, to overnight with the Moores. The infamous crime remains to this day unsolved, and proved so vexing to Montgomery County law enforcement agents in 1912 that they enlisted the help of a Red Oak, Iowa "soothsayer," or psychic, by the name of "Aunty" Hamilton. Considered one of the most mismanaged investigations of the century, estimates suggest upwards of one hundred people were allowed to walk through the crime scene before it was secured by the National Guard. In 1994, Darwin and Martha Linn of Corning, Iowa, purchased the Moore home and arranged for its successful listing on the National Registry of Historic Places, and opened the home for tours. Several feature films and television shows have explored—and dramatized to the point of exaggeration—the homicides, including "ABC's Scariest Places on Earth." Historically, the Villisca crime, then thought to be a serial murder, is important for its foreshadowing of the increasingly brutal, senseless, multi-victim crimes of decades to follow.

On Sunday night or early on the morning of Monday, June 10, 1912, Villisca was the site of one of the most vicious crimes in all the history of the world. While the city lay sleeping, following a peaceful Sabbath, some fiend incarnate entered the home of Mr. and Mrs. J. B. More on East Third street, and, wielding an ax, murdered eight people while they slept in their beds. The dead are: Josiah B. more, age 43; Mrs. Moore, age 39; Herman Moore, age 11; Katherine Moore, age 10; Boyd Moore, age 7; Paul Moore, age 5; Lena Stillinger, age 12; Ina Stillinger, age 8.

The first six named constitute the entire family of J. B. Moore, one of Villisca's most prominent businessmen and the head of the J. B. Moore Implement company of this city. The two girls last named are daughters of Mr. and Mrs. J. T. Stillinger, living southeast of Villisca. Mr. Stillinger is a prominent and well-to-do farmer.

Mrs. Stillinger, who is in delicate health, is prostrated over the tragedy and there has been much anxiety shown over her condition. At one time her death was reported. Mr. and Mrs. C. C. Moore, parents of the dead man, are an aged couple, the former nearly eighty years of age, and by many it is thought that the burden to them is greater than they can bear. Mr. Moore is practically an invalid, and unable to leave his home. Parents of Mrs. Moore are Mr. and Mrs. John, Montgomery, of north of town, and to them, too, comes a measure of grief of a kind that but few have ever endured.

NO CLUE TO THE MURDERER

The discovery of the crime threw the city into the wildest state of excitement, and hundreds hurried to the scene of the tragedy. Few there were who were permitted to enter the house of carnage, and few, indeed, were there who cared to. The sight was one to make the stoutest hearts quail. Downstairs , in a bed of the northwest room, lay the bodies of the two Stillinger girls, their heads chopped open with an ax, and their blood and brains presenting a spectacle so repulsive that it was almost beyond comprehension that six more victims, murdered in identically the same fashion, lay in the two bedrooms upstairs. In the north upstairs bedroom were the bodies of Mr. and Mrs. Moore, who were on their backs, apparently as they were when asleep, and in the south room, in three beds were the four children, Herman Katherine, Boyd, and Paul. There were no signs of struggle on the part of any of the victims, except perhaps in the case of one of the girls downstairs, on whose arm a slight cut appeared. The bodies were not mutilated below the heads, and their faces had been covered up after the crime, either with part of the bedding or some discarded wearing apparel. So carefully was the deed accomplished that nowhere does there appear the slightest clue by which the murderer may be run to cover. The house does not present a deranged condition; there are no telltale blood stains leading to the door; there are no fingerprints discernible on the woodwork or the doorknobs. Every door and window was locked except the two windows in the room occupied by the Stillinger girls downstairs, and the evidences there showed that they had not been used either in entering or leaving the house. A cobweb and a dead fly on the windowsill in one, and a sewing machine laden with stockings and other clothing standing in front of the other, together with the undisturbed flowerpots outside, are ample proof of this. Although the front door to the dining room was locked there was no key to it, and the only solution of the problem of exit lies in the theory that the murderer escaped through the front door, locking it after him and taking the key with him. Before going, either before or after committing the fiendish deed, he had taken the precaution to pull down all the window curtains and to darken the doors, using an old black apron in one case and a black skirt in the other. In such condition was the house found at about half past eight o'clock Monday morning by Ross R. Moore and Mrs. Mary E. Peckham, who were first to enter and to look upon the terrible scene, so far as the downstairs portion of the house contributed to it.*

SIMILAR TO KANSAS CRIME

A theory carrying considerable weight is that the crime was committed by the same man who murdered Rolland Hudson and wife, Anna, at Paola, Kansas, on the night of Wednesday, June 5, four days previous to the Villisca murders, the circumstances being almost identically similar. At Paola, as at Villisca, a lamp, without a globe, was found sitting on the floor. At Paola, a pickax is thought to have been the instrument of death. There, as at Villisca, the motive was not robbery, for the murdered woman's diamond rings were unmolested on her fingers; and the murderer covered his retreat so carefully that not a vestige of a clue was found. The man and wife were murdered as they lay sleeping and showed no signs of a struggle. W. J. Hobin, a newspaperman representing the *Kansas City Post*, who was assigned to cover the Paola tragedy, came directly from that city to Villisca, and he told *The Review* that to all appearances the crime at Villisca was done by the same man as that at Paola, and, upon receiving a special permit to enter the Moore home here, found the missing globe from the lamp which sat on the floor in the downstairs bedroom. Fingerprints on the globe will be used as a means of identification, as will those on the ax found leaning against the wall close to the lamp. Mr. Hobin thinks the murderer at Villisca was secreted in the closet downstairs, and in support of his belief points out that a roll of cotton in a box there has been mashed down, as though sat upon, and a faint, but nonetheless evident, heel print impression invisible in the dust on the floor. A similar crime, in which six persons lost their lives, is reported to have occurred at Colorado Springs on the night of September 17 last, and on October 1, William E. Dawson, his wife and daughter were slain with an ax in their home at Monmouth, Illinois. An electric flashlight, with the words, "Colorado Springs, Sept. 4," was found near the Dawson home several days after the murder. Sheriff W. T. Fitzpatrick arrived from Monmouth yesterday morning, and in an interview with *The Review* man stated the methods employed here and at Monmouth were exactly the same, the windows and doors being darkened in both cases, and no robbery committed.

Mr. and Mrs. William Showman and their children were found murdered in their cottage at Ellworth, Kansas, October 15th last, and the arrest of Mrs. Showman's brother-in-law followed. The Colorado Springs, Monmouth, and

Villisca murders occurred on Sunday night, which gives some cause for thinking it may be the work of a religious maniac.

FOUR ARRESTS MADE

So thorough was the work of the Villisca murderer, and so completely has the earth swallowed him up, that the authorities now are at a loss to know which way to turn. Before the arrival of the sheriff and the coroner, no one seemed in authority, and much valuable time was lost in getting after the murderer. Mayor F. L. Ingman was in the country and did not return until about noon. Word was telegraphed to Beatrice, Nebraska, for bloodhounds, and Elmer Noffsinger, owner of the famous kennels at that place, arrived with two dogs on No. 12 Monday night. Posses were formed and spread out through the country, and one man, a tramp, realizing the danger that threatened, gave himself up to the police for protection. A previous suspect had been placed in the city bastille until such time as his innocence could be proven. Tuesday morning words came from New Market that two men there, of a rather bad countenance, one slightly taller than the other, had been seen, and that they boarded a fast moving freight out of town towards Clarinda. The authorities at Clarinda were notified but the men were not apprehended. Four negroes, said to have slept down by the hand car house in the Burlington yards at Villisca for three or four nights, disappeared on the night of the murder, and no trace has been found of them. Two men were taken into custody Tuesday night, but were latter released after identity was established.

WORK OF DOGS

Promptly upon the arrival of the dogs from Beatrice, Nebraska, Monday night they were taken to the Moore home, allowed to scent the ax handle, and started upon the trail of the murderer. The dogs seemed eager to go, and appeared to have a good scent although it was a matter of some eighteen or twenty hours since the trail was made. They left by the front door of the house, went off the east end of the porch, and up Sixth avenue north to Second Street where they turned west going clear to First Avenue in the opposite end of town. There they turned south and continued straight to John Green's farm, crossing the Green farm to the Mrs. E. A. Neillsson farm bringing up at the West Nodaway River, where they seemed to lose the scent. Taken to the other side of the river they were unable to pick it up again, and at last were brought back to town. The next morning they were taken out to the river again, but were unable to make progress, a slight rain having dampened the scent. They were brought back to the house and given a fresh start, and again made for the river. Once they seemed to have found the trail west of the river, but it availed nothing, and after a half dozen unsuccessful attempts the chase by bloodhounds was abandoned. The dogs had followed an apparently easy scent almost to the forks of the West and Middle Nodaway but could go no farther. Near the point where the trail seemed to enter the river, a couple of dirty handkerchiefs were found, but they bore no bloodstains, and apparently one of them had been used as a target for rifle shooting. Many persons followed the dogs, in autos, on horseback or on foot, in the hope that they might get upon some kind of a clue, but they might better have saved their energies. At times the dogs crosses soft tracks of ground where no tracks were visible; at other times footprints were plainly discernible, and measurements were taken. Villisca people are divided as to the merits of bloodhounds in cases presenting no better foundation for success than did this one. One of the dogs, the small black one, was used in running down Hez Rasco, the Maryville, Missouri, murderer. They are said to have been very successful on a number of occasions. They were taken out of Villisca on No. 9 Tuesday evening.

TOWN IS THRONGED WITH PEOPLE

Nothing that has happened since Mr. Thiele murdered his wife in Villisca twelve years ago has served to attract the attention and to hold the morbidly curious crowd as has this unparalleled crime. It is estimated that fully five thousand people gathered on the streets of the city Monday, hundreds coming from out of town, yet in all this crowd there was not the least sign of disorder or boisterous action. Everywhere pervaded a sense of oppression. The awfulness of the affair carried its lesson to the ear of every citizen, and each stood in respectful silence as the events of the day progressed. Groups formed and theories were discussed. Business was abandoned. Towards evening detectives and newspapermen from the cities began pouring into the town, and details of the awful tragedy were hurled to the world. Posses were formed every hour of the day; armed men scoured the country for many miles all day Monday and most of Tuesday.

FROM **AUTOBIOGRAPHY OF BILLY SUNDAY (1915)**

BILLY SUNDAY

Billy Sunday may well be the most fascinating Iowan of the twentieth century, though his name has been largely forgotten in his home state. Sunday tells his own story of an Iowa childhood in the passage below in the only Sunday autobiography scholars regard as both authentic and accurate. After being fostered by Colonel John Scott, a former Iowa lieutenant governor, Sunday moved to Marshalltown as a teen, where his skill on the baseball diamond attracted the notice of Marshalltown favorite son and future Hall of Famer Adrian "Cap" Anson. Sunday, a popular, speedy outfielder, went on to play professional for several teams, including the Chicago White Stockings, but a chance meeting on the streets of Chicago with gospel-singing preachers converted him to evangelical Christianity, and he abandoned a lucrative career in baseball for the pulpit. Drawing on his popularity as a ballplayer, Sunday was a charismatic sermonizer known to slide across the stage as if sliding into home plate. By some estimates, Sunday preached to as many as one hundred million people face to face, supporting claims that he was the most influential evangelist in early twentieth century America. Sunday's preaching began in Garner, Iowa, and, early on, sometimes included baseball games between local businesses—games in which Sunday wore his old pro uniform and played on both sides. A friend to Iowa's Herbert Hoover and likewise a supporter of prohibition, Billy Sunday and his wife Nell grew wealthy from his sermons, though their popularity was supplanted by radio and motion pictures after World War I.

HARDSHIPS OF PIONEER LIFE

I never saw my father. He walked from Ames, Iowa, to Des Moines, thirty miles, to enlist in the Civil War, and was assigned to Company E, Twenty-third Iowa Infantry, in August, 1862. I was born on my grandfather's farm one mile south of Ames, Story County, Iowa, the nineteenth of the following November.

My father was born near Chambersburg, Pennsylvania, and was of Pennsylvania Dutch parentage. He was a contractor and brick mason by trade, and built one of the first brick buildings ever erected in Cedar Rapids, Iowa.

He sleeps in an unknown grave beneath the eternal flowers and the perpetual sunshine of the southland, waiting for the trumpet of Gabriel to sound the reveille on the resurrection morning. Then, for the first time, I shall look into the face of him whose name I bear, and whose blood courses through my veins.

No more the bugle calls the weary one;

Rest, noble spirit, in your grave unknown.
I shall see him and know him among the brave and true
When a robe of white is given for his faded coat of blue.

His regiment forded a river which was partly frozen. He and scores of other soldiers caught severe colds that caused complications from which he and many others died. They were buried at Camp Patterson, Missouri, but all trace of the graves has been blotted out.

The old log cabin

Father wrote to mother from the front lines and said, "When the baby is born, if it is a boy, name him William Ashley." So my name is William Ashley Sunday. I was born in a log cabin and lived there for years until my grandfather built a sawmill, run by water power, cut lumber from black walnut logs, and built a frame house which stands today on the old farm near Ames.

The city of Ames and the county of Story were named after the families of Ames and Story, who lived in Boston and were among the capitalists who helped build the Chicago & Northwestern Railway, whose main line from Chicago to Omaha runs through Ames.

My grandfather was one of the men who helped locate the Iowa Agricultural College at Ames, now named Iowa State College. He had no money to give with which to start the college, and so he gave part of his land as his donation. He and two other men, pioneers of Story County, Dan McCarthy, and L. Q. Hoggett, aided in staking out the ground and locating the first building of what has become one of the greatest schools of its class in the United States.

He and General Grant were second cousins. Both were born in Ohio. After General Grant became President, he wrote a letter inviting granddad to visit him in Washington, but it was a long, tiresome journey in those days, and expensive, too, and money was as scarce as mosquitoes in January.

Granddad wore a coonskin cap, rawhide boots, blue jeans, and said "done hit" instead of "did it," "come" instead of "came," and "seen" instead of "saw." He drank coffee out of his saucer and ate peas with his knife. He had no "soup-and-fish" suit to wear, so he did not go.

During the first three years of my life I was sickly and could scarcely walk. Mother used to carry me on a pillow which she made for that purpose. There were no resident physicians in those pioneer days, and itinerant doctors would drive up to our cabin and ask, "Anybody sick here?"

One day Doctor Avery, a Frenchman, called at our cabin and mother told him, "I have a little boy three years old who has been sick ever since he was born."

The old doctor said, "Let me see him." He gave me the once-over, while I yelled and screamed like a Comanche Indian. Then he said to mother, "I can cure that boy."

She asked him how much he would charge, and he replied, "Oh, if you will feed me and my old mare, that will pay the bill."

Mother said, "All right; but you will have to sleep up in the garret. We have no stairs and you'll have to climb the ladder."

THE COUNTRY DOCTOR

He replied, "That suits me." He then went into the woods and picked leaves from various shrubs, including mulberry leaves and elderberries, dug up roots, and from them made a syrup and gave it to me. In a short time I was going like the wind and have been hitting on all eight ever since. From that day to this, elderberries and mulberries have been my favorite wild fruit, and I like sassafras tea.

My mother was born in Syracuse, Kosciusko County, Indiana. Her maiden name was Mary Jane Cory. She was the oldest of a family of eight children and she outlived them all. Her parents moved to Story County, Iowa, in 1848. They were three months making the journey. There were no bridges and they would often camp for a week waiting for the water in the rivers and creeks to fall so they could ford the stream. They lived on deer, wild turkey, ducks, geese, bear, and fish. Their home was the covered wagon, their cookstove the campfire. Today a fast airplane could make the trip in two hours.

Grandfather was the second man to take up government land in Story County. Mother helped clear the land, grub stumps, drop corn, plant potatoes, milk the cows, yoke the oxen, harness horses, plow the fields, chop wood, hive the bees, cook—say, I believe she could beat the world making biscuits, buckwheat cakes, flour gravy, and cooking raw-fried potatoes.

As civilization developed, the churches and schools came, Mother's two younger sisters were well-educated and taught school. The education which is rewarded by diplomas and scholarship was not Mother's, although in native shrewdness, born of contact with nature, she was miles ahead of her sisters.

MY GRANDFATHER

Mother married again some years after my father died. I didn't like the man whom she married, and I went to live with my grandparents. We all lived on the same farm. Then my stepfather died, and mother came to live with grandfather.

My grandfather was the most versatile man I have ever known. There was seemingly nothing that he could not make. He made wagons, the wheels and all parts of them. He could build houses and lay stone walls. He made a turning lathe and made bedposts, spindles for banisters, made bureaus, water wheels, and many other things.

He had a blacksmith shop and made horseshoes and wedges with which to split wood. He could dress a millstone on which to grind corn and wheat. Before he built the mill for sawing lumber and grinding grain, he and the neighbors had to drive to Burlington, two hundred miles away, to mill. He made all the ax handles sold by the hardware stores in Ames.

He made a loom upon which grandmother spun yarn and made cloth, from which she made dresses and cloth for suits. My clothes were made from homespun until I was sent to the orphans' home. While the clothes were ill-fitting affairs, they were warm. You couldn't tell from looking at my pants whether I was going or coming.

In those days, when people were sick, they used to bleed them by lancing a vein in the left arm, because it was near the heart and would bleed more profusely. Grandfather had a spring lance and had nerves of steel, and he was always sent for to perform the operation.

He gave a plot of ground, beautifully located on the bank of the river, and covered with oak and elm trees, for a cemetery. Hundreds are buried there, but the graves are grown over with trees and they could not be located by any research. The old family burying ground is there, and ten of the family sleep beneath the trees. I have cared for the graves for more than thirty years.

I remember one night a fellow named Sam Brandon, who lived in Ames, came bursting into our home, knocking the latch off the door as he came. He was pale and trembling, and screamed, "There's a ghost down at the graveyard. I saw it trying to jump out of a grave."

Grandpa got a lantern and we all went down there. We kids went with fear and trembling and clung close to Grandpa. We found a grave that had been dug for a funeral the next day, and one of our sheep had fallen in the grave and was trying to jump out. He would get far enough above the top so you could see his head and shoulders, and then he would fall back in. The supposed ghost proved to be a sheep, which we rescued.

When we were fighting for the Eighteenth Amendment, some scoundrels went to the farm; which was then owned by Captain Greeley, of Ames, and asked if my relatives were buried there. They were informed that they were.

Those black-hearted degenerates, so vile that the devil would duck up an alley to avoid meeting them, went to the graves, tore down the fence I had built, tipped over the gravestones, threw brush on the graves, and took photographs and had them published in whisky-sympathizing papers. Under the photograph was the caption, "This is the way Billy Sunday takes care of the graves of his relatives." I wish I had been there! Some of them would have gone away in the Red Cross wagon.

He was a great provider. The cellar was always filled with apples, potatoes, barrels of sauerkraut, salt pork, corned beef, and molasses made from sugar cane. The cabbage and parsnips and turnips we buried out of doors and dug up as needed. The garret was filled with rings of dried pumpkin, dried apples—peeled and quartered and strung on a string—dried sage, peppermint, catnip, red peppers, dried beef, and a supply of candles, for we used candles until kerosene lamps came into use.

Our house was the stopping place for visiting strangers. Everybody was welcome.

Newspapers were scarce, although the country editor, with his Washington hand press and grip filled with type, was only a step behind the pioneer. The newspaper was our bible.

I used to help milk ten cows night and morning. We had one old cow, a Hereford, that could open the gate with her head, and when we tied the gate with a rope, she would untie the knot with her horns and lead the whole herd into the cornfield. I can hear the call to round up the night raiders, "Oh, boys, get up! The cows are in the corn." My, how I did hate that white-faced cow, and how happy I was when the butchers got her!

I kept up my station in the harvest field with men when only eleven years old. That was before the days of the McCormick self-binder, when the grain was cut with a foot-dropping reaper; and we bound the bundle with a band we made from the grain. I can make that band today as quick as you can bat your eye.

Most every farmer planted a patch of sugar cane from which to make sorghum molasses. Grandpa made a cane mill. He cut down sycamore trees from which he made the rollers. There were three rollers. The master roller was twice as long as the others and had a long, curved sweep to which we hitched a horse that went round and round to grind the cane we fed into the mill. We were the only ones that had a cane mill, so all the farmers would bring their cane to us.

We had to keep the juice from each farmer's cane separate, and boil it separate until it became molasses. We would do the work gallon for gallon, giving them one and keeping one. Or, if they wanted to pay for it, we charged twenty-five cents per gallon. Often we would have to work until midnight, for we could not leave the sap once we put it in the vat to boil. We had to skim off certain residue that the boiling would bring to the surface.

THE WHIPPOORWILL

When my Aunt Elizabeth—we called her Libby—lay sick, one day she aroused herself from a comatose state and said, "Oh, I have looked into heaven and I saw mother."

That evening at dusk, a whippoorwill flew down in the yard. It was the first and last one I have ever seen. It was in the early spring and the door was open.

The bird fluttered into the house and perched upon the head of her bed and sang "Whip-poor-will, whip-poor-will, whip-poor-will," and out through the door it flew, and off into the darkening woods. From the depths of the gloom we heard his "whip-poor-will, whip-poor-will, whip-poor-will," and everybody trembled with dread and said, "That is a sure sign of death."

The bird sang "whip-poor-will" three times while sitting on the headboard of the bed and three times from the depths of the forest. "Libby will die in three days," they said; and sure enough, on the third day after the visit of the bird, and at the same hour, she died.

I am not superstitious. I do not believe it is bad luck to walk under a ladder, or to see a black cat run across the road, or to drown a cat, sleep in a room with number "13" on the door, to begin a journey on Friday, or to spill salt. I do not carry a rabbit's foot; but that incident carved a deep groove in my memory that "will be lifted, nevermore."

When my grandmother died, they would not tell me for two days. I sensed that something was wrong and asked, "Where is grandma?" They replied, "She is home." I said, "I'm going to see her." They said, "Willie, she wouldn't know you, and you wouldn't know her." I answered, "I would, too, know her."

I would leave her coffin only when forced to do so. The second day after the funeral my mother missed me. They called and searched everywhere; finally my dog picked up the scent and they followed my tracks through the snow to the graveyard, and there they found me lying across her grave, weeping and chilled through with the cold November winds. For weeks they feared that I would not live, but God spared my life and has led me where I am today.

The battle grew hard. The wolf of poverty howled and scratched at the cabin door. Mother decided to send Ed and myself to the Soldiers' Orphans' Home at Glenwood, Iowa. There were three such homes located in the state—Glenwood, Cedar Falls, and Davenport. One of the saddest memories of my life is the recollection of the grief I felt when leaving the old farm to go to Ames to take the train for the trip to Glenwood. I had never been farther away from home than Nevada, the county seat, eight miles east.

When we climbed into the wagon to go to town I called out, "Goodbye trees, goodbye spring." I put my arms around my dog named Watch and kissed him.

The train left about one o'clock in the morning. We went to the little hotel near the depot to wait. That hotel was left standing for forty years.

The proprietor awakened us about twelve-thirty, saying, "The train is coming." I looked into mother's face. Her eyes were red and her cheeks wet from weeping, her hair disheveled. While Ed and I slept she had prayed and wept. We went to the depot, and as the train pulled in she drew us to her heart, sobbing as if her heart would break.

The conductor called, "All aboard!" and the train pulled out. We raised the window. With my arms outstretched toward mother I cried, "I don't want to go to the Orphans' Home. Take me back to the farm with you." And today something tugs at my heartstrings, saying:

> I want to go back to the orchard,
> The orchard that used to be mine;
> Where the apples are redd'ning
> And filling the air with their wine.
>
> I want to wake up in the morning
> To the chirp of the birds in the eaves;
> I want the west wind through the cornfields
> To rustle the leaves.
>
> I want to run on through the pasture,
> And let down the dusty old bars;
> I want to find you there still waiting,
> Your eyes blazing like the twin stars.
>
> Oh nights! you are weary and dreary;
> And days! there's something you lack,
> To the old farm in the valley—
> I want to go back.

Shall I ever forget the home of my childhood? Yes; when the flowers forget the sun that kissed and warmed them. Yes; when the mountain peaks are incinerated into ashes. Yes; when love dies out in the human heart. Yes; when the desert sands grow cold.

A MOTHER'S LOVE

The last sound I heard that memorable night was mother's voice crying "Goodbye, boys," on the midnight air.

A mother's love is unselfish, and it has no limits this side of heaven. A mother's arms and a mother's heart are a safe anchorage for any boy. I do not believe there are devils enough to pull a boy or a girl out of the arms of a Christian mother.

It was my pleasure and privilege to provide a home for my mother during the last thirty years of her life. She died at our home at Winona Lake, Indiana, on Mrs. Sunday's birthday, June 25, 1918. I went to call her for breakfast that beautiful Sabbath morning and found that she had slipped away to heaven without bidding us goodbye.

We buried mother in the family lot on the old farm, by the side of her father and mother.

The Sunlit Hills

One of the brightest pictures that hang on memory's wall is the recollection of the days I spent when a boy on the farm. I went back years ago for a visit. I shut my eyes and visions of the past opened before me. I listened for the sound of voices forever still, and longed for the touch of hands turned to dust.

The man became a child again. The long, weary years of struggle and heartache became as though they had never been. Once more, with my gun on my shoulder and my dog at my heels, I roamed the woods, walked down the old familiar paths, sat on the old familiar stumps and logs. The squirrel chattered defiantly from the limb of an oak tree.

I threw myself into an interrogation point, and when the gun cracked the squirrel fell at my feet. I grabbed him by the tail and dashed home and threw him at mother's feet and received compliments for my skill as a marksman. Once more I listened to the "tinkling bells that lulled the distant fold."

I saw the cows wind slowly o'er the lea. I saw the crows winging their weary flight to the darkening woods. I heard the whippoorwill sing his lonesome song way over in Sleepy Hollow.

I saw the shades of night creep on. I heard mother call, "Oh, boys, come in to supper." Once more I ate my frugal meal of mush and milk. Once more I knelt and lisped the prayer millions have prayed:

> Now I lay me down to sleep—
> I pray Thee, Lord, my soul to keep;
> If I should die before I wake,
> I pray Thee, Lord, my soul to take—
> And this I ask for Jesus' sake. Amen.

Boyhood days

We reached Council Bluffs the next morning, tired, sleepy, cold, hungry, and homesick. We wandered down the streets and saw a sign, "Hotel." We went to the backdoor and asked for something to eat. The lady asked, "What are your names and where are you from? Where are you going? Did you run away from home?" She surely put us on the grill.

We replied, "Our names are Ed and Willie Sunday, and we're from Ames, and are going to the Soldiers' Orphans' Home at Glenwood. We didn't run away either. Here is our letter to the superintendent, Mr. Stephens."

She put her arms around us and said: "My husband was a soldier—he never came back. I never turned anyone away hungry, and I wouldn't turn you orphan boys away. Come in, Eddie and Willie."

We ate our breakfast. She did not put just so much on our plates, but put us about six inches from the table and let us eat until we touched. Oh, those buckwheat cakes and sausage, with sage ground in them! We sat in front of the fireplace and soon fell asleep. About noon she awakened us and asked: "Boys, do you want some dinner?"

We replied, "Uh huh."

After dinner we strolled over to the Burlington Railroad yards and saw a freight train being made up. We climbed into the caboose. When the train pulled out, the conductor came in and said: "Tickets!"

We said, "We ain't got no tickets."

He asked, "Where is your money?"

We replied, "We ain't got no money, Mr. Conductor."

He said, "I will have to put you off down at Pacific Junction."

Kindness for the friendless

We began to cry. "Where are you boys going?" he asked.

We said, "To the Soldiers' Orphans' Home at Glenwood. Our pa is dead." Then we handed him our letter of introduction from our guardian, Honorable Joe Fitzpatrick, state senator, of Nevada, Iowa.

He read it, and I saw the tears in his eyes as he handed back the letter, saying, "Sit still, boys; it won't cost you a cent to ride in my train."

We remained at the home until the legislature of Iowa discontinued that home and the one at Cedar Falls, and combined all three in one big institution at Davenport. Mr. S. W. Pierce, superintendent of the home at Davenport, came to escort all the children whose parents wanted them transferred.

Those who wished their children to return home were given that privilege. Most of them went to Davenport. None of the children ever liked the new home so well as they did the old home at Glenwood. There we had the freedom of the fields and the woods that surrounded the home. The institution was ideal in its location. The land was of rolling hills and dales and dense forests of stately trees. Nuts of all kinds grew in abundance. Every Saturday we could go hunting squirrels and rabbits, play ball, and run foot races. My granddad could outrun any young man in the county where he lived. I guess I inherited his speed, for I could do the same. I could outrun any boy in the Glenwood Home.

There were two boys older than I at Davenport, Frank Styles and Perry Howard, and it was nip and tuck between us three. Whoever got the start would win. That shows how closely we were matched for speed.

We had two dandy dogs that could tree squirrels and chase rabbits. They were pets with every child. When we left the home for Davenport, we wanted to take the dogs with us, but the "powers that were" ruled against us and sentenced them to be shot. When we saw the man going into the woods with the dogs, we began to hurl our protest and plead for the dogs. When we heard the reports of the gun that told us our dogs were dead, we all cried. We hunted and found them and dug one grave and put the dogs to rest side by side, covered them with leaves and grass, and filled the grave. We never liked the man who shot them and would never speak to him unless occasion required us to do so.

To reach Davenport from Glenwood, you take the Burlington to Council Bluffs, then the Rock Island to Davenport. En route to Davenport you pass through Des Moines, the capital of the state of Iowa. It is only thirty miles distant from the old farm at Ames. My brother, Ed, and I had it all planned out. I was to jump off the train when it stopped. Ed was lame and could not run fast. I could run all day and never tire. I knew every curve in the road, and figured I would be home before morning.

Ed confided to a chum and the "rat" squealed to Superintendent Pierce. As the train neared Des Moines, he came and sat on the arm of the seat so that I couldn't make my getaway. I was heartsick and boiling mad at that kid, and the first chance I had I cleaned up on him.

PUNISHMENT FOR RUNAWAYS

If ever the state of Iowa had two public servants absolutely fitted for the responsible position of caring for its orphans, they were Mr. and Mrs. S. W. Pierce, superintendent and assistant superintendent of the Soldiers' Orphans' Home at Davenport, Iowa. They were as opposite in their temperaments and methods of dealing with the boys as winter is from summer. Mr. Pierce was stern and a stickler for rules and discipline. He used the rawhide on tough, unruly fellows.

Every spring, as sure as the grass turned green and the flowers bloomed and the birds returned, some of the boys would be seized with the wanderlust fever, and would set the stage for a getaway. Over the fence they would go like sheep, but he would follow them to the farthest confines of the state and bring them back. If a boy reached home, he would bring him back, and if his folks wanted him home they would be required to place a formal request for his release according to the law.

He would bring the runaways back, and in front of the administration building was an oval park with a cinder driveway about an eighth of a mile around it. He would put the captured boys there and they would have to walk around and around that part for one week, starting every morning at eight o'clock, walk until noon, eat dinner, start at one, march until supper, and then come back for one hour after supper. Their feet would get so sore and their muscles so tired that they would almost fall over. No boy was allowed to speak to them until their term of "hitting the cinders" was finished.

Mrs. Pierce would talk to the boys, take them on her lap, and tell them how sad their mothers would be if they knew it. She would pray with them, and no one ever came from an interview with Mrs. Pierce dry-eyed. Any boy would rather have Mr. Pierce whip him than have Mrs. Pierce talk to him. Both are in heaven, but their memory blossoms sweet in the dust.

BLACKLISTED AT MEALTIME

At Glenwood, if you missed one meal without permission, you were compelled to miss the next meal as punishment. Believe me, the boys were usually there with the feedbag on.

The superintendent would tell the children what was going to be served— you as hungry as a wolf, and knowing you could only stand and watch the others. It was agonizing. He would read the names of those who were blacklisted for that meal, and they must stand during the meal.

Some kids would say, "Bill, do you want a drumstick?" Often they would pity you and take a long chance and sneak out a chicken leg; but if they were caught they had the same sentence passed on them! That method of dealing with us had more effect than a wagonload of switches.

At both homes religion had an important place in our training. All our teachers and officers were Christians. I never knew a boy from either home to be an infidel or a criminal. Of those of whom I have kept track, some became lawyers, merchants, farmers, railroad men, educators. I was the only one who ever became a big league baseball player.

We had prayers in each home once a day. On Sunday evenings, before we went to bed, each boy was required to recite a verse of Scripture. If he did not know a verse, he was given five demerit marks. Thirty demerit marks in a month would change your grade. You got three demerits if your face was not clean, three if your hair was not combed. Those who were detailed to make the beds received eight demerits if they failed to make them according to standard rules.

I was never in the bad grade, but I was often near the dead line. I had two strikes on me many times. As I look back, I wonder how I got by. I once got into a fight with the bully of a rival cottage, which would have put me "on the spot." But the gang stood by me, and we convinced the cottage manager that the other fellow started the scrap and I finished it, and so I escaped.

There were five grades, one, two, three, four, and five. Grades one and two were good. Grades three, four, and five were bad. Every boy and girl on entering the home was assigned to Grade two, so it was up to you to advance or retrograde.

Those in grades three, four, and five were never allowed outside of the grounds. Those in good grades were allowed to go to Davenport on Saturdays and also to the city churches on Sundays.

All the merchants knew by our uniforms who we were, and they would give us apples, candy, popcorn, and ice cream. That was an incentive to go straight. Only a certain number could go each week. Had the whole gang gone, we would have taken the merchants "to the cleaners." We would line up in front of Superintendent Pierce and ask, "Can we go to town?"

"What grade are you in, boys?" he would ask. He always trusted us. I never knew a boy to lie about his grade. Then he would say, "Take off your hat," and if our hair was not combed, "Step out of the line," would be the command. That meant we got the hook.

One more question, "Are your shoes shined? Turn and let me see the heels," and if they were not shined, you couldn't go. I never knew of a boy trained in that home that ever failed to shine the heels of his shoes.

We all dressed alike. Our winter suits were given us about October first. They were made of wool—a mixture of gray and brown, with four buttons straight down the front. The clothes for all the children were made by the older girls who were detailed to the sewing room. Our summer suits were made of denim, and the girls wore calico. On Sundays we all wore white collars with a little tie. Our shoes were square-toed, straight on both sides, so it made no difference which foot you put them on.

At Davenport they used the cottage system, with about twenty-five children in each cottage and a woman manager for each cottage. There were about thirty cottages. The superintendent and assistants and cottage managers and teachers, cooks and watchmen, in all made a faculty of 150 besides 600 or 700 children. The dining room was about half a mile from the cottages. The children marched in especially assigned divisions to their meals. No haphazard mob rush. There was a covered walk to protect us from the cold and storms.

At the home we never went to the dining room for Sunday evening supper. Attendants always brought our supper to our cottages. The supper for each child always consisted of a big piece of gingerbread, a piece of apple, peach, pumpkin, or mince pie—in season—and an apple. The boys used to trade their pie or gingerbread or apple for some trinket, and some shrewd traders would have three or four pieces of pie or gingerbread coming to them each week. Any kid who didn't pay his debt would be beaten up.

A YARN BALL

I have known boys to have their Sunday evening lunch traded for one month ahead. I would have been "sunk" many a time had it not been for my brother, Ed. He was detailed as assistant to the chef, and carried the keys to the pantry and would sneak me in and lock the door; and, oh, boy, I would make a hole in Uncle Sam's commissary department! In about fifteen minutes he would unlock the door and I'd beat it.

The age limit that boys could remain at the home was sixteen, girls eighteen. My brother had to leave because of that limit, and I would not stay. We both left and went back to the only home we knew, grandfather's, on the farm. Shortly after our return, Ed went to live with a neighbor who had no boys, a noble Christian man named Cyrus Simmons. After staying there for years, he returned to the home as one of the carpenters and watchmen. He married one of the girls, and they moved to North Dakota, where he entered land from the government and worked for the Northern Pacific Railroad Company.

Every child had some special work to do. I was assigned to the laundry. I became so expert that the lady manager had my length of time extended. We were detailed to one job for a short period, and then changed to another job. What I learned there opened the door in after years that had brought me where I am—I was taught to do my best. Do your best, that's all an angel can do. No one does his or her duty unless he does his best. More people fail from lack of purpose than from lack of opportunity. Their sparker and gas don't work together.

Little did I dream when I made me a yarn ball, and threw it in the air to see how far I could run and catch it, that I was training myself to become a member of the famous Chicago Cubs, and the Pittsburgh and Philadelphia baseball clubs of the National League.

One day on the farm, grandfather was in a hurry to go to town. We were helping him hitch up the horses. My half-brother, Roy, and I got hold of the neck yoke and were trying to pull it away from each other, and we pulled the rings out of the end. Grandfather was furious at our foolishness, as it delayed him. He swore at us and it cut me to the heart. I'm of a sensitive nature, and am still sensitive. I went to a neighbor's, Parley Sheldon, who for fifty years was a delegate to democratic national conventions.

After we husked the corn on our grandfather's farm, my brother Ed and I used to husk corn for Parley Sheldon. We could husk and crib one hundred bushels a day. We received three cents a bushel—Ed took two dollars and I one dollar.

I borrowed a horse from Parley and rode to Nevada, the county seat, eight miles away, to look for a job. I found a position working in a hotel.

I swept out the office and on Saturdays mopped out the office and dining room, chopped the wood, milked two cows, cared for the stable and went to the trains. I was the "barker" for the "beanery." I would call out, "Welton House, fine eats, clean beds only two blocks away, and a dollar a day." I would carry the traveling men's grips to the hotel, and if they had sample trunks, I would hitch up the team and drive to the depot and bring the trunks to the sample room. I used to sleep in the office behind the counter, and if anyone came in the night I would let him in and show him to his room. I was bellhop, too.

The proprietor of this little hotel in Nevada had a trotting horse of which he was very proud. She was a beautiful animal, sorrel, with white face and four white feet, and her tail dragged on the ground. They used to take great pride in showing her off to visitors. I would put the halter on her and trot her down the road a hundred yards or so, putting one hand on her shoulder and taking hold of the halter with the other.

I became so proficient in speed for that distance that I could "run her off her feet"—that is, she would stop trotting and go into a run. That training gave me my speed and breath for one hundred yards. I could go that distance and never breathe. I was not what you call a long-distance runner, like Nurmi, the great Finn, although I could run three hundred yards *in thirty-four seconds*!

FINDING A HOME

I worked there several months and became homesick for the old farm and a sight of familiar scenes and faces. I was given permission to go home and stay one day. I stayed two days, and when I returned I was fired—given the gate.

The next day I learned that Col. John Scott, then lieutenant governor of Iowa, wanted a boy. I got my hair cut, shined my shoes as I had learned at the orphans' home, and went to see Colonel Scott. He was a dignified Scotchman. I told him who I was and that my father was a soldier, and I had been to the orphans' home. That got under his vest, and he said: "Well, Willie, you're a nice-appearing boy; but, Sophy"—Mrs. Scott's given name was Sophia; he called her Sophy—"hires all the help, and you come back tomorrow and see her."

You bet I was back the next day as fast as I could go—Johnnie on the spot. She asked me, "What can you do, Willie?"

I replied, "Anything, and if I don't know how, I can learn."

She smiled at that answer and asked, "Can you milk cows and chop wood?"

I replied, "Yes, ma'am, I can."

"Can you scrub the floor?"

"Yes, I can."

"I need a boy who can scrub floors and steps. It's so hard for me to get down on my knees." She was a fleshy woman. "Well, I'll try you out and see what kind of a job of scrubbing you can do."

I was foxy. I didn't tell her scrubbing was my long suit, for I had been taught that at the Soldiers' Orphans' Home, and had she asked me to pick out the job for a tryout, I would have chosen to "scrub the floor." There was fourteen steps leading into the cellar. She said, "I'll scrub the first step and show you how. You scrub the others, and then I'll decide." Little did she dream that I could scrub rings around her.

I was soon through with the steps and she was amazed that I did it so quickly. So she said, "Oh, you are like all boys, a lick and a promise. I'll wait until they dry." When she put her critical eye on them, she patted me on the shoulder and said, "You'll do. You are hired. Here is your room. Go get your clothes."

I said, "I got 'em all on." They became godfather and mother to me; they were educated and refined.

From **Dominie Dean (1917)**

Ellis Parker Butler

A son of Muscatine, Iowa, humorist and novelist Ellis Parker Butler hit it big with his short story "Pigs is Pigs"—an expression that worked its way into the national vernacular thanks to the popularity of the short story by the same name. While a prolific writer of thirty two-books, Butler maintained a "day job" as the president of the Flushing Federated Savings and Loan after moving with his wife to Flushing, New York. Though Butler left Iowa for greener pastures, the fictional town of Riverbank, based on Muscatine, serves as the setting for his most beloved books, including Swatty (1920), Jibby Jones, (1923), Jibby Jones and the Alligator (1924), *and Butler's novel* Dominie Dean, *a work Marica Noe describes in the* Dictionary of Midwestern Literature *as "a social history of mid-nineteenth century life in a Mississippi River town." The passage that follows, from the aforementioned* Dominie Dean, *accurately portrays tensions along the Iowa side of the Mississippi during the Civil War, especially in Davenport and Muscatine, where a sizeable portion of Southern sympathizers—"Copperheads"—lived. The chapter, too, offers a timeless parable, as the young minister exemplifies mercy and tolerance for all, regardless of political views, while eschewing convenient scapegoats.*

When [Fort] Sumter was fired upon David Dean had been in Riverbank not quite a year, but he had passed through the first difficult test of the young minister, and Mary Wiggett's smile seemed to have driven from the minds of his people the opposition they had felt when it seemed he was, or might become, too fond of 'Thusia Fragg. Poor little 'Thusia! The bright, flirting, reckless butterfly of a girl, captured soul, mind and body by her first glimpse of David's cool gray eyes, knew—as soon as Mary Wiggett announced that David had proposed and had been accepted—that David was not for her. Mary Wiggett, inheriting much of hardheaded old Samuel Wiggett's common sense, was not apt to let David escape, and David had no desire to escape from the quite satisfactory position of future husband of Mary Wiggett. As the months of the engagement lengthened, he liked Mary more and more.

The announcement of the dominie's engagement settled many things. It settled the uneasiness that is bound to exist while a young, unmarried minister is still free to make a choice, and it settled the fear that David might make a fool of himself over 'Thusia Fragg. While his congregation did not realize what an attraction 'Thusia had had for David, they had feared her general effect on him. With David engaged to the leading elder's daughter, and that daughter such a fine, efficient blond young woman as Mary was, there was peace and David was happy. He had no trouble in stifling the feeling for 'Thusia that he felt had come dangerously near being love.

Until Riverbank was thrown into a rage by the news from Fort Sumter, David, with due regard for his motto, "Keep an even mind under all circumstances," had prepared to settle down into a state of gentle usefulness and to become the affectionate husband of the town's richest man's daughter. The wedding was to be when Mary decided she was quite ready. She was in no great haste, and in the flame of patriotism that swept all Iowa with the first call for troops and the subsequent excitement as the town and county responded and the streets were filled with volunteers, Mary postponed setting a day. David and Mary were both busy during those early war days. Almost too soon for belief, lists of dead and wounded came back to Riverbank, followed by the pale cripples and convalescents. Loyal entertainments and "sanitary fairs" kept every young woman busy, and there is no doubt that David did more to aid the cause by staying at home than by going to the front. He was willing enough to go, but all Iowa was afire and there were more volunteers than could be accepted. None expected the war to last over ninety days. More said sixty days.

Little 'Thusia Fragg, forgiven by Mary and become her protégé, was taken into the councils of the women of David's church in all the loyal charitable efforts. She was still the butterfly 'Thusia; she still danced and appeared in gay raiment and giggled and chattered; but she was a forgiven 'Thusia and did her best to be "good." Like all the young women of the town she was intensely loyal to the North, but her loyalty was more like the fiery spirit of the Southern women than the calmer Northern loyalty of her friends.

As the lists of dead grew and the war, at the end of ninety days, seemed hardly begun, loyalty and hatred and bitterness became almost synonymous. Riverbank, on the Mississippi, held not a few families of Southern sympathizers, and the position of any who ventured to doubt the right of the North to coerce the South became most unpleasant. Wise "Copperheads" kept low and said nothing, but they were generally known from their antebellum utterances, and they were looked upon with distrust and hatred. The title "Copperhead" was the worst one man could give another in those days. As the war lengthened, one or two hot outspoken democrats were ridden out of the town on rails and the rest, for the most part, found their sympathies change naturally into tacit agreement with those of their neighbors. It was early in the second year of the war that old Merlin Hinch came to Riverbank County. It was a time when public feeling against Copperheads was reaching the point of exasperation.

Merlin Hinch, with his few earthly goods and his wife and daughter, crossed the Mississippi on the ferry in a weather-beaten prairie schooner a few weeks before plowing time. He came from the East but he volunteered nothing about his past. He was a misshapen, pain-racked man, hard-handed and close-mouthed. He rested one day in Riverbank, got from some real estate man information about the farms in the back townships of the county, and drove on. There were plenty of farms to be had—rented on shares or bought with a mortgage—and he passed on his way, a silent, forbidding old man.

In the days that followed he sometimes drove into town to make such purchases as necessity required. Sometimes his wife—a faded, work-worn woman—came with him, and sometimes his daughter, but more often he came alone.

Old Hinch—"Copperhead Hinch" he came to be called—was not beautiful. He seldom wore a hat, coming to town with his iron-gray hair matted on his head and his iron-gray beard tangled and tobacco-stained. Some long-past accident had left him with a scar above the left eyebrow, lowering it, and his eyebrows were like long, down-curving gray bristles, so that his left eye looked out through a bristly covert, giving him a leering scowl. The same accident had wrenched his left shoulder so that his left arm seemed to drag behind him and he walked bent forward with an ugly sidewise gait. At times he rested his left hand on his hip. He looked like a hard character, but, as David came to know, he was neither hard nor soft but a man like other men. Sun and rain and hard weather seemed to have turned his flesh to leather.

In those days the post office was in the Wiggett Building, some sixty feet off the main street, and it was there those who liked to talk of the war met, for on a bulletin board just outside the door the lists of dead and wounded were posted as they arrived, and there headlined pages of the newspapers were pasted. To the post office old Hinch came on each trip to town, stopping there last before driving back to Griggs Township. Old Hinch issued from the post office one afternoon just as the postmaster was pasting the news of a Union victory on the board, and some jubilant reader, dancing and waving his cap, grasped old Hinch and shouted the news in his ear. The old man uttered an oath and with his elbow knocked his tormentor aside. He shouldered his way roughly through the crowd and clambered into his wagon.

"Yeh! You Copperhead!" the old man's tormentor shouted after him.

The crowd turned and saw the old man and jeered at him. Hinch muttered and mumbled as he arranged the scrap of old blanket on his wagon seat. He gathered up his reins and, without looking back, drove down the street, around the corner into the main street and out of the town. After that old Hinch was "that Copperhead from Griggs Township." Silent and surly always, he was left more completely alone than ever. When he came to town the storekeepers paid him scant courtesy; the manner in which they received him indicated that they did not want his trade, and would be better satisfied if he stayed away. The children on the street sometimes shouted at him.

Old Sam Wiggett, Mary's father, was by that time known as the most bitter hater of the South in Riverbank. Later there were some who said he assumed the greater part of his virulent fanaticism to cover his speculations in the Union paper currency and his tax sale purchases of the property of dead or impoverished Union soldiers, but this was not so. Heavy-bodied and heavy-jowled, he was also heavy-minded. That which he was against he hated with all the bitterness his soul could command, and he was sincere in his desire that every captured Confederate be hanged. He considered Lincoln a soft-hearted namby-pamby and would have had every Confederate home burned to the ground and the women and children driven into Mexico. In business he had the same harsh but honest single-mindedness. Money was something to get and any honest way of getting it was right. There were but two or three men in Riverbank County who would bid in the property of the unfortunate soldiers at tax sale, but Sam Wiggett had no scruples. The South, and not he, killed and ruined the soldiers, and the county, not he, forced the property to tax sale. He bought with depreciated currency that he had bought at a discount. That was business.

It was not unnatural that Mary Wiggett should have absorbed some share of his ultra loyalism from her father. The women of Riverbank were not, as a rule, bitterly angry. They were staunch and true to their cause; they worked eagerly with their hands, scraping lint, making "housewives" and doing what they could for their soldiers; they were cheered by victories and depressed by defeats, and they wept over their slain and wounded, but their attitude was one of pity and love for their own rather than of hard hatred against the South. With Mary Wiggett, patriotism was more militant. Could she have arranged it, the lint she scraped would never have been used to dress the wounds of a captured Confederate soldier boy. 'Thusia, even more intense, hated the South as a personal enemy.

David felt this without, at first, taking much notice of it. He was happy in his engagement and he liked Mary better each day. There was a wholesome, full-blooded womanliness in all she did and a frankness in her affection that satisfied him. The first shock to his evenly balanced mind came one day when he was walking through the main street with her.

The young dominie was swinging down the street at her side, his head high and his clear gray eyes looking straight ahead, when something whizzed past his face. They were near the corner of a street. Along the edge of the walk a half dozen farm wagons stood and in the nearest sat Mrs. Hinch, her sunbonnet thrown back and her paisley shawl—her finest possession—over her shoulders.

Old Hinch was clambering into the wagon and had his best foot on the hub of a wheel. The missile that whizzed past David's face was an egg. It struck old Hinch on the temple and broke, scattering the yolk upon the waist of Mrs. Hinch's calico dress and upon her shawl and her face. Some boy had grasped an egg from a box before a grocer's window and had thrown it. The lad darted around the corner, and old Hinch turned, grasping his whip and scowling through his bristly eyebrows. The corner loafers laughed.

What David did was not much. He drew his handkerchief from his pocket and gave it to the faded woman in the wagon, that she might remove the stain of egg. She wiped her face and began removing the egg from her garments, and David, and Mary moved on.

"Why did you do that?" Mary asked. "Don't you know them? They're Copperheads."

"She was badly spattered. She seemed at a loss what to do."

"Didn't you *know* they were Copperheads?"

"I did not know. That would have made no difference. She was distressed."

"Well, please, David, do not help any more distressed Copperheads when I am with you," Mary said. "Everyone in front of the store saw you. Oh! I wouldn't raise my little finger to help a Copperhead if she was dying! I hate them! They ought to be egged out of town, all of them."

Some weeks later old Hinch drove up to the little manse and knocked on David's door. He had the handkerchief, washed, ironed and folded in a bit of white paper, and a dozen fresh-laid eggs in a small basket.

"Ma sent me 'round with these," old Hinch said. "Sort of a thank you. She 'minded me particular not to throw the eggs at you."

There was almost a twinkle in his eyes as he repeated his wife's little joke. He would not enter the manse but sidled himself back to his wagon and drove away.

It was from 'Thusia Fragg that David had the next word of old Hinch. Even in those days David had acquired a great taste for a certain sugared bun made by Keller, the baker. Long years after the buns were still made by Riverbank bakers and known as "Keller buns" and the last sight many had of David was as an old man with a paper bag in his hand, trudging up the hill to his home for a little feast on "Keller buns." He used to stop and offer his favorite pastry to little children. Sometimes the paper bag was quite empty by the time he reached home.

It was no great disgrace, in those days, to carry parcels, for many of the Riverbankers had come from St. Louis or Cincinnati, where the best housewives went to market with basket on arm, but David would have thought nothing of his paper parcel of buns in any event. The buns were at the baker's and he liked them and wanted some at home, so he went to the baker's and bought them and carried them home. He was coming out of Keller's doorway when 'Thusia, as gayly dressed as ever, hurrying by, saw him and stopped. She was frightened and agitated and she grasped David's arm.

"Oh, Mr. Dean!" she cried. "Can't you do something? They're beating an old man! There!" she almost wept, pointing down the street toward the post office. David stood a moment, tense and breathing deeply.

"Who is it?" he asked.

"That Copperhead farmer," said 'Thusia. David forgot the motto over his desk in his study. He saw the small mob massed in front of the post office and men running toward it from across the street, and he too ran. He saw the crowd sway back and forth and a fist raised in the air, and then he was on the edge of the group, pushing his way into it.

"Stop this! Stop this!" he cried.

His voice had the ring of authority and those who turned knew him to be the dominie. They had done old Hinch no great harm; A few blows had been struck, but the old man had received them with his arm thrown over his head. He was tough and a few blows could not harm him: He carried a stout hickory club, and as the crowd hesitated, old Hinch sidled his way to the edge of the walk and scrambled into his wagon. Someone laughed. Old Hinch did not drive away.

"My letter," he growled, and David stooped and picked up the letter that lay on the walk and handed it to him. Then Hinch struck his horses a blow with the club and the wagon bumped over the loose stones and away. The letter had been trampled upon by dusty feet, and David's coat had received a smear of dust from the wagon wheel. He brushed his hands together, and someone began knocking the dust from the skirt of his coat. It eased the tension. Someone explained.

"We told the Copperhead to take off his hat to the flag," they told David, "and he damned the war. Somebody hit him."

"He is an old man," said David. "You can show your patriotism better than by striking an old man."

It was not a diplomatic thing to say, and it was still less diplomatic for David to preach, the next Sunday, on the prodigal son. Many shook their heads over the sermon, saying David went too far in asking them to prepare their hearts for the day when the war would be ended and it would be necessary to take the South back into the brotherhood of states, and to look upon the Confederates as returning prodigals. Old Wiggett was furiously angry. Forty years were to elapse before some of David's hearers were ready to forgive the South, and many went to their graves unforgiving. The feeling after the sermon was that David sympathized entirely too strongly with the South. Those who heard his following sermons knew David was still staunchly loyal, but through the byways of the town the word passed that Dominie Dean was "about as bad as any Copperhead in the county."

From In a Little Town (1917)

Rupert Hughes

One of America's most prolific authors, novelist-historian-screenwriter-director-poet Rupert Hughes was also one of the most jet setting. The uncle of the multi-millionaire-aviator-director-producer Howard Hughes, Rupert Hughes grew up in Keokuk just a few blocks from the Mississippi River. Of his more than sixty titles, Hughes achieved, arguably, his greatest success with his collections of short stories, including In a Little Town, *excerpted here and featuring stories about people in imaginary towns near Keokuk. In the March 18, 1917* New York Times, *a reviewer trumpeted, "[Hughes] finds vices as well as virtues among the people of these village streets.... But Mr. Hughes writes about them all with that tenderness of touch that comes of full comprehension." Nicknamed "History" for his scholarly looks, Hughes wrote a definitive, three-volume biography of George Washington, and, as a patriot, earned the rank of Captain in the U.S. Army infantry, serving as an intelligence officer in World War I. A favorite writer of Hollywood giants Samuel Goldwyn and Douglas Fairbanks, Hughes was destined to go to Hollywood. As early as 1912, he sold two short stories to none other than Thomas Edison, who planned to use one of them for the first "talkie" according to Hughes's own April 1935 memoir in the* Saturday Evening Post. *The selection below, reminiscent of the work of contemporary midwestern yarn spinner Garrison Keillor, consists of the foreword to* In a Little Town *and the short story "Daughters of Shiloh." "Daughters" shows what happens when the tango, a dance craze that hit New York just a few years before the publication of* In a Little Town *in 1917, reaches provincial Carthage. Carthage is, according to the author, a representation of Keokuk, though it should be noted that the real-life city of Carthage, Illinois, is located just across the Mississippi River.*

Foreword

There are two immortal imbecilities that I have no patience for.

The other one is the treatment of little towns as if they were essentially different from big towns. Cities are not "Ninevehs" and "Babylons" any more than little towns are Arcadias or Utopias. In fact we are now unearthing plentiful evidence of what might have been safely assumed, that Babylon never was a "Babylon" nor Nineveh a "Nineveh" in the sense employed by poets and praters without number. Those old cities were made up of assorted souls as good and as bad and as mixed as now.

They do small towns a grievous injustice who deny them restlessness, vice, ostentation, cruelty; as they do cities a grievous injustice who deny them simplicity, homeliness, friendship, and contentment. It is one of those undeniable facts (which everybody denies) that a city is only a lot of small towns put together. Its population is largely made up of people who came from small towns and of people who go back to small towns every evening.

A village is simply a quiet street in the big city of the world. Quaint, sweet happenings take place in the avenues most thronged, and desperate events come about in sleepy lanes. People are people, chance is chance.

My novels have mainly concerned themselves with New York, and I have tried therein to publish bits of its life as they appear to such eyes and such mind as I have. Though several of my short stories have been published in single volumes, this is the first group to be issued. They are all devoted to small-town people. In them I have sought the same end as in the city novels: to be true to truth, to observe with sympathy and explain with fidelity, to find the epic of a stranger's existence and shape it for the eyes of strangers—to pass the throb of another heart through my heart to your heart.

The scene of these stories lies pretty close to the core of these United States, in the Middle West, in the valley of the Mississippi River. I was born near that river and spent a good deal of my boyhood in it.

Though it would be unfair, false, and unkind to fasten these stories on any definite originals, they are centered in the region about the small city of Keokuk, Iowa, from which one can also see into Illinois, and into Missouri, where I was born. Comic poets have found something comic in the name of Keokuk, as in other town names in which the letter "K" is prominent. Why "K" should be so humorous, I can't imagine. The name of Keokuk, however, belonged to a splendid Indian chief who was friendly to the early settlers and saved them from massacre. The monument over his bones in the park, on the high bluff there, now commands one of the noblest views in the world, a great lake formed in the Mississippi River by a dam which is as beautiful as if the Greeks had built it. It was, in fact, built by a thousand Greeks who camped there for years. As an engineering achievement, it rivals the Assouan [Aswan] Dam and as a manufacturer of electricity it is a second to Niagara Falls. But it has not yet materially disturbed the rural quality of the country.

The scenery thereabout is very beautiful, but I guarantee you against landscape in these stories. I cannot, however, guarantee that the stories are even based on fact. Yet I hope that they are truth.

The characters are limited to a small neighborhood, but if they are not also faithful to humanity in general, then, as we would say out there, "I miss my guess."*

The news that Carthage had a tango teacher created a sensation rivaling the advent of its first streetcar. It gave the place a metropolitan flavor. If it only had a slums district, now, it would be a great and gloriously wicked city.

Prue was fairly besieged with applicants for lessons. Those who could dance a few steps wanted the new steps. Those who could not dance at all wanted to climb aboard the ark.

Mrs. Hippisley's drawing room did not long serve its purpose. On the third day the judge stalked in. He came home with a chill. At the sight of his wife with one knee up, trying to paw like a horse, his chill changed to fever. His roar was heard in the kitchen. He was so used to domineering that he was even afraid of his wife when he was in the first flush of rage.

Prue and Idalene and Bertha he would have sentenced to deportation if he had had the jurisdiction. He could at least send them home. He threatened his wife with dire punishments if she ever took another step of the abominable dance.

Prue was afraid of the judge, but she was not afraid of her own father. She told him that she was going to use the parlor, and he told her that she wasn't. The next day he came home to find the class installed.

He peeked into the parlor and saw Bertha Appleby dancing with Idalene Brearley. Prue was in the arms of old "Tawm" Kinch, the town scoundrel, a bald and wealthy old bachelor who had lingered uncaught like a wise old trout in a pool, though generations of girls had tried every device, from whipping the stream to tickling his sides. He had refused every bait and lived more or less alone in the big old mansion he had inherited from his skinflint mother.

At the sight of Tawm Kinch in his parlor embracing his daughter and bungling an odious dance with her, William Pepperall saw red. He would throw the old brute out of his house. As he made his temper ready, Mrs. Judge Hippisley hurried up the hall. She had walked round the block, crossed two backyards and climbed the kitchen steps to throw the judge off the scent. William could hardly make a scene before these women. He could only protest by leaving the house.

He found that, having let the outrage go unpunished, once, it was hard to work up steam to drive it out the second day. Also he remembered that he had asked Tawm Kinch for a position in his sash-and-blind factory, and Tawm had said he would see about it. Attacking Tawm Kinch would be like assaulting his future bread and butter. He kept away from the house as much as he could, sulking like a punished boy. One evening as he went home to supper, purposely delaying as long as possible, he saw Tawm Kinch coming from the house. He ran down the steps like an urchin and seized William's hand as if he had not seen him for a long time.

"Take a walk with me, Bill," he said, and led William along an unfrequented side street. After much hemming and hawing he began: "Bill, I got a proposition to make you. I find there's a possibility of a p'sition openin' up in the works and maybe I could fit you into it if you'd do something for me."

William tried not to betray his overweening joy. "I'd always do anything for you, Tawm," he said.

"I always liked you, always spoke well of you, which is more 'n I can say of some of the other folks round here."

Tawm was flying too high to note the raw tactlessness of this; he went right on: "Bill—or Mr. Pepperall, I'd better say—I'm simply dead gone on that girl of yours. She's the sweetest, smartest, gracefulest thing that ever struck this town, and when I—Well, I'm afraid to ask her m'self, but I was thinkin' if you could arrange it."

"Arrange what?"

"I want to marry her. I know I'm no kid, but she could have the big house, and I can be as foolish as anybody about spending money when I've a mind to. Prue could have 'most anything she wanted and I could give you a good job. And then ever'body would be happy."

Papa did his best to be dignified and not turn a handspring or shout for joy. He was like a boy trying to look sad when he learns that the schoolteacher is ill. He managed to hold back and tell Tawm Kinch that this was kind of sudden like and he'd have to talk to the wife about it, and o' course the girl would have to be considered.

He was good salesman enough not to leap at the first offer, and he left Tawm Kinch guessing at the gate of the big house. To Tawm it looked as lonely and forlorn as it looked majestic and desirable to Papa Pepper all, glancing back over his shoulder as he sauntered home with difficult deliberation. His heart was singing, "What a place to eat Sunday dinners at!"

Once out of Tawm Kinch's range, he broke into a walk that was almost a lope, and he rounded a corner into the portico that Judge Hippisley carried ahead of him. When the judge had regained his breath, he seized papa by both lapels and growled, "Look here, Pepperall, I told you to keep your daughter away from my boy, and you didn't; and now Ort has lost his job. Beadle fired him today. And jobs ain't easy to get in this town, as you know. And now what's going to happen?"

William Pepperall was so exultant that he tried to say two things at the same time; that Orton's job or loss of it was entirely immaterial and a matter of perfect indifference. What he said was, "It's material of perfect immaterence to me."

He spurned to correct himself and stalked on, leaving the judge gaping. A few paces off William's knees weakened at the thought of how he had jeopardized Ollie's position; but he tossed that aside with equal "immaterence," for when Prue became Mrs. Kinch she could take Ollie to live with her, or send her to school, or something.

When he reached home, he drew his wife into the parlor to break the glorious news to her. She was more hilarious than he had been. All their financial problems were solved and their social position enhanced, as if the family had suddenly been elevated to the peerage.

She was on pins and needles of impatience because Prue was late for supper. She came down at last when the others had heard all about it and nearly finished their food. She had her hat on, and she was in such a hurry that she paid no attention to the fluttering of the covey, or the prolonged throat-clearing of her father, who had difficulty in keeping Serina from blurting out the end of the story first. At length he said, "Well, Prue, I guess the tango ain't as bad as I made out."

"You going to join the class, poppa?" said Prue, 'round the spoonful of preserved pears she checked before her mouth.

Her father went on: "I guess you're one of those daughters of Shiloh like you said you was. And the son of Benjamin has come right out after you. And he's the biggest son of a gun in the whole tribe."

Prue put down the following spoonful and turned to her mother: "What ails Poppa, Momma? He talks feverish."

Serina fairly gurgled: "Prepare yourself for the grandest surprise. You'd never guess."

And William had to jump to beat her to the news. "Tawm Kinch wants to marry you."

"What?"

"Yep."

"What makes you think so?"

"He asked me."

"Asked you!"

Serina clasped her hands and her eyes filled with tears of the rescued. "Oh, Prue, ain't it wonderful? Ain't the Lord good to us?"

Prue did not catch fire from the blaze. She sniffed, "He wasn't very good to Tawm Kinch."

William, bitter with disappointment, snapped, "What do you mean? He's the richest man in town. Some folks say he's as good as worth a hundred thousand dollars."

"Well, what of it? He'll never learn to dance. His feet interfere."

"What's dancing got to do with it? You'll stop all that foolishness after you've married Tawm."

"Oh, will I? Ort Hippisley can dance better with one foot than Tawm Kinch could dance if he was a centipede."

"Ort Hippisley! Humph! He's lost his job and he'll never get another. You couldn't marry him."

"I'm not in any hurry to marry anybody."

The reaction from hope to confusion, the rejection of the glittering gift he proffered, infuriated the henpecked, chickpecked father. He shrieked:

"Well, you're going to marry Tawm Kinch or you're going to get out of my house!"

"Papa!" gasped Ollie.

"Here, Dad!" growled Horace.

"William!" cried Serina.

William thumped the table and rose to his full height. He had not often risen to it. And his voice had an unsuspected timbre:

"I mean it. I've been a worm in this house long enough. Here's where I turn. This girl has made me a laughingstock and a despisingstock long enough. She can take this grand opportunity I got for her or she can pack up her duds and clear out—for good!"

He thumped the table again and sat down trembling with spent rage. Serina was so crushed under the crumbled wall of her air-castles that she could not protest. Olive and Horace felt that since Prue was so indifferent to their happiness they need not consider hers. There was a long, long silence.

The sound of a low whistle outside stole into the silence. Prue rose and said, quietly:

"Ollie, would you mind packing my things for me? I'll send over for them when I know where I'll be."

Ollie tried to answer, but her lips made no sound. Prue kissed each of the solemn faces round the table, including her father's. They might have been dead in their chairs for all their response. She paused with prophetic loneliness. That low whistle shrilled again.

She murmured a somber, "Goodbye, everybody," and went out.

The door closed like a dull "Goodbye." They heard her swift feet slowly crossing the porch and descending the steps. They imagined them upon the walk. They heard the old gate squeal a rusty, *Good-by-e—Prue-ue!*

It was Ort Hippisley, of course, that waited for Prue outside the gate. They swapped bad news. She had heard that he had lost his job, but not that his father had forbidden him to speak to Prue.

Her evil tidings that she had been compelled to choose between marrying Tawm Kinch and banishment from home threw Ort into a panic of dismay. He was a natural-born dancer, but not a predestined hero. He had no inspirations for crises like these. He was as graceful as a manly man could be, but he was not at his best when the hour was darkest. He was at his best when the band was playing.

In him Prue found somebody to support, not to lean on. But his distress at her distress was so complete that it endeared him to her warlike soul more than a braver quality might have done. They stood awhile thus in each other's arms like a Pierrot and his Columbine with winter coming on. Finally Orton sighed:

"What in Heaven's name is goin' to become of us? What you goin' to do, Prue? Where can you go?"

Prue's resolution asserted itself. "The first place to go is Mrs. Prosser's boardin'-house and get me a room. Then we can go on to the dance and maybe that'll give us an idea."

"But maybe Mrs. Prosser won't want you since your father's turned you out."

"In the first place it was me that turned me out. In the second place Mrs. Prosser wants 'most anybody that's got six dollars a week comin' in. And I've got that, provided I can find a room to teach in."

Mrs. Prosser welcomed Prue, not without question, not without every question she could get answered, but she made no great bones of the family war. "The best o' families quar'ls," she said. "And half the time they take their meals with me till they quiet down. I'll be losin' you soon."

Prue broached the question of a room to teach in. To Mrs. Prosser, renting a room had always the joy of renting a room. She said that her "poller" was not used much and she'd be right glad to get something for it. She would throw in the use of the "pianna." Prue touched the keys. It was an old boarding house piano and sounded like a wire fence plucked; but almost anything would serve.

So Prue and Orton hastened away to the party, and danced with the final rapture of doing the forbidden thing under an overhanging cloud of menace. Several more pupils enlisted themselves in Prue's classes. Another problem was solved and a new danger commenced by Mr. Norman Maugans.

The question of music had become serious. It was hard to make progress when the dancers had to hum their own tunes. Prue could not buy a phonograph, and the Prosser piano dated from a time when pianos did not play themselves. Prue could "tear off a few rags," as she put it, but she could not dance and teach and play her own music all at once. Mrs. Hippisley was afraid to lend her phonograph lest the judge should notice its absence.

And now like a sent angel came Mr. Norman Maugans, who played the pipe organ at the church, and offered to exchange his services as musician for occasional lessons and the privilege of watching Prue dance, for which privilege, he said, "folks in New York would pay a hundred dollars a night if they knew what they was missin.'"

Prue grabbed the bargain, and the next morning began to teach him to play such things as "Some Smoke" and "Leg of Mutton."

At first he played "Girls, Run Along" so that it could hardly be told from "Where Is My Wandering Boy Tonight?" and his waltzes were mostly hesitation; but by and by he got so that he fairly tangoed on the pedals, and he was so funny bouncing about on the piano stool to "Something Seems Tingle-ingleingle-ingling So Queer" that the pupils stopped dancing to watch him.

The tango was upon the world like a Mississippi at flood time. The levees were going over one by one; or if they stood fast they stood alone, for the water crept round from above and backed up from below.

In Carthage, as in both Portlands, Maine and Oregon, and the two Cairos, Illinois and Egypt, the Parises of Kentucky and France, the Yorks and Londons, old and new; in Germany, Italy, and Japan, fathers, monarchs, mayors, editors stormed against the new dance; societies passed resolutions; police interfered; ballet girls declared the dances immoral and ungraceful. The army of the dance went right on growing.

Doctor Brearley called a meeting of the chief men of his congregation to talk things over and discipline, if not expel, all guilty members. Deacon Luxton was in a state of mind. He dared not vote in favor of the dance and he dared not vote against it. He and his wife were taking lessons from Prue surreptitiously at their own home. Judge Hippisley's voice would have been louder for war if he had not discovered that his wife was secretly addicted to the one-step. Old Doctor Brearly was walking about rehearsing a sermon against it when he happened to enter a room where Idalene was practicing. He wrung from her a confession of the depth of her iniquity. This knowledge paralyzed his enthusiasm.

Sour old Deacon Flugal was loudly in favor of making an example of Prue. His wife was even more violent. She happened to mention her disgust to Mrs. Deacon Luxton.

"I guess this'll put an end to the tango in Carthage!"

"Oh, I hope not!" Mrs. Luxton cried.

"You hope not!"

"Yes, I do. It has done my husband no end of good. It's taken pounds and pounds of fat off him. It brings out the perspiration on him something wonderful. And it's taken years off his age. He's that spry and full of jokes and he's gettin' right spoony. He used to be a terrible cutup, and then he settled down so there was no livin' with him. But now he keeps at me to buy some new clothes and he's thinkin' of gettin' a tuxeda. His old disp'sition seems to have come back and he's as cheerful and, oh, so affectionate! It's like a second honeymoon."

Mrs. Luxton gazed off into space with rapture. Mrs. Flugal was so silent that Mrs. Luxton turned to see if she had walked away in disgust. But there was in her eyes that light that lies in woman's eyes, and she turned a delicious tomato-red as she murmured, "How much, do you s'pose, would a term of lessons cost for my husband?"

"The Creed of Iowa" (1917)

J. Edward Kirbye

The first of a half dozen selections from the Iowa Press and Authors' Club 1917 anthology Prairie Gold *(presented here in their original order—Kirbye, Weitz, Sweet, French, Griffith, Patchin), J. Edward Kirbye's "Creed of Iowa" reads as a Hawkeye State affirmation or pledge of allegiance. Kirbye's quasi-religious zeal for Iowa came naturally; a theologian and one-time president of Drury University in Springfield, Missouri, Kirbye authored a well-known book,* Puritanism in the South *(1908), prior to accepting a post as vice-president of the Iowa Press and Authors' Club under honorary president Hamlin Garland.*

I believe in Iowa, land of limitless prairies, with rolling hills and fertile valleys, with winding and widening streams, with bounteous crops and fruit-laden trees, yielding to man their wealth and health.

I believe in Iowa, land of golden grains, whose harvests fill the granaries of the nation, making it opulent with the power of earth's fruitfulness.

I believe in Iowa, rich in her men and women of power and might. I believe in her authors and educators, her statesmen and ministers, whose intellectual and moral contribution is one of the mainstays of the republic—true in the hour of danger and steadfast in the hour of triumph.

I believe in Iowa, magnet and meeting place of all nations, fused into a noble unity, Americans all, blended into a free people. I believe in her stalwart sons, her winsome women, in her colleges and churches, in her institutions of philanthropy and mercy, in her press, the voice and instructor of her common mind and will, in her leadership and destiny, in the magnificence of her opportunity and in the fine responsiveness of her citizens to the call of every higher obligation.

I believe in our commonwealth, yet young, and in the process of making, palpitant with energy and faring forth with high hope and swift step; and I convenant with the God of my fathers to give myself in service, mind and money, hand and heart, to explore and develop her physical, intellectual, and moral resources, to sing her praises truthfully, to keep her politics pure, her ideals high, and to make better and better her schools and churches, her lands and homes, and to make her in fact what she is by divine right, the queen of all commonwealths.

"The Wind in the Corn" (1917)

Alice C. Weitz

President of the Iowa Press and Authors' Club, Polk County's Alice Carey Weitz's success in Iowa letters went well beyond publication of the club's anthology, Prairie Gold. *Weitz, a member of the General Federation of Women's Clubs, later published a successful book on the subject of young people and juvenile delinquency,* Youth and Your Community *(1945) and coedited the influential anthology* Women's Poetry To-day *(1929). In the mystical invocation of Iowa that follows, Weitz tunes in Iowa's siren song.*

There stands recorded in the Book of Time, a fascinating legend of the Sun, whose golden throne allured but for the day; and when the day was ended in great glee he hurried forth beyond the broad horizon toward a secret trysting place. All of his impassioned love, it is said, he poured upon the idol of his heart the boundless plains. Long years were they alone, the Rolling Prairie and the Golden Sun, until at last they found themselves spied upon by curious Man, who, captivated by the beauty of the two, remained and blessed the tryst thereby.

Here Sun and Soil and Man wrought out a work of art; and here Dame Nature smiled as was her wont, and brought rich gifts and blessings manifold. In sweet content Man's children toiled and wrought until upon the bosom of the sunlit plains there nestled close great fields and prosperous abodes.

And since that time a ceaseless music steals throughout the land in wooing cadences, now crying out in weird and wandering tones, now softly soothing in sweet, rhythmic chant.

'Tis the music of the wind within the corn—Iowa's Prairie Gold.

It sang itself into the lonely heart of the pioneer with its promise of golden harvest; it became the cradle song of restless souls that even in their youth longed but to free themselves in verse and song; and down through all the prosperous years, it steals like a sweet sustaining accompaniment to the countless activities which have builded a great commonwealth.

He who stood upon the hilltops in his youthful days and listened to the soft, alluring rustle of the wind-swayed leaves retains the music ever in his soul. It draws upon the heartstrings of the absent one, and like the constant singing of the sea insistent calls upon him to return.

Today in spirit come we all to Time's sweet trysting place with story song and jest, to add sweet comfort to the braver ones whose paths lie wide before them, and whose return lies not within our willing. God grant that even in their pains their troubled souls may yet to music be attuned, may know again the solace of that sweetly floating song, the rustle of the wind within the corn.

"That Iowa Town" (1917)

Oney Fred Sweet

A product of Hampton in Franklin County, Oney Fred Sweet was a feature- and short story writer for the Chicago Sunday-Tribune *and a popular lecturer on the famed Redpath Chautauqua circuit before settling back down in Hampton with his wife. Sweet's most popular lecture, "In the Other Fellow's Shoes" proved an apt title; he had, according to adverts from the time, worked as a beggar, a steeple jack, a Pullman porter, a railroad fireman, a trapeze performer, a gypsy, a marriage license clerk, a dogcatcher, a cemetery night watchman, a cowboy, a lumberjack, a jockey, a farmhand, and a film actor. He may not have achieved the dream of being a bestselling writer, but, for its sweet and spot-on nostalgia, as well as its historically-important documentation of the Fourth of July and Decoration Day at close of the nineteenth century, no can compare with Oney Fred Sweet.*

According to the popular songs, we are apt to get the impression that the only section of the country where there is moonlight and a waiting sweetheart and a home worth longing for is down in Dixie. Judging from the movies, a plot to appeal must have a mountain or a desert setting of the West. Fictionists, so many of them, seem to think they must locate their heroines on Fifth Avenue and their heroes at sea. But could I write songs or direct cinema dramas or pen novels, I'd get my inspiration from that Iowa town.

Did you ever drive in from an Iowa farm to a Fourth of July celebration? A few years back the land wasn't worth quite so much an acre; the sloughs hadn't been tiled yet, and the country hadn't discovered what a limited section of real good corn land there was after all. But she was Iowa then! Remember how the hot sun dawned early to shimmer across the knee-high fields and blaze against the side of the big red barn, how the shadows of the willow windbreak shortened and the fan on top of the tall windmill faintly creaked? The hired man had decorated his buggy-whip with a tiny ribbon of red, white and blue. Buggy-whip—sound queer now? Well, there were only three automobiles in the county then and they were the feature of the morning parade. Remember how the two blocks of Main Street were draped with bunting and flags, and the courthouse lawn was dotted with white dresses? Well, anyhow you remember the girls with parasols who represented the states, and the float bearing the Goddess of Liberty. And then the storm came in the middle of the afternoon. The lightning and the thunder, and the bunting with the red, white, and blue somewhat streaked together but still fluttering. And just before sunset, you remember, it brightened up again, and out past the low-roofed depot and the tall grain elevator you could see the streak of blue and the play of the departing sun against the spent clouds. Nowhere else; above no other town, could clouds pile just like that.

You remember that morning, once a year, when the lilacs had just turned purple out by the front gate, and the dew was still wet on the green grass, the faint strains of band music drifting out above the maples of the town, and flags hanging out on the porches—Decoration Day! How we used to hunt through the freshly awakened woods north of town for the rarest wildflowers! Tender petaled bloodroots there were in plenty, and cowslips down by the spring, and honeysuckles on the creek bank those late May days, but the lady's slippers and the jack-in-the-pulpits—one had to know the hidden recesses where they grew. Withered they became before the hot sun sank, sending rays from the west that made the tombstones gleam like gold. Somehow, on those days, the sky seemed a bluer blue when the words of the speaker at the "Monument of the Unknown Dead" were carried off by the faint breeze that muffled, too, the song of the quartet and the music of the band. But close in your ears were the chirps of the insects in the bluegrass and the robins that hopped about in the branches of the evergreens.

We had our quota of Civil War veterans in that Iowa town. We had our company that went down to Chickamauga in [18]98. And now—well, you know what to expect from the youth of that sort of a community. Prosperity can't rob a place like that of its pioneer virtues. That Iowa town is an American town and it simply wouldn't fit into the German system at all. There's nothing old world about it. The present generation may have it easier than their fathers did; they may ride in automobiles instead of lumber wagons; they may wear pinch back coats and long beak caps instead of overalls and straw hats, but they've inherited something beside material wealth. We who owned none of its surrounding acres when they were cheap and find them now so out of reach, are yet rich, fabulously rich, in inheritance. The last I heard from that Iowa town its youth was donning khaki for the purpose of helping to keep the Kaiser on the other side of the sea.

But it was of the town we used to know that I was speaking. Changed? We must realize that. It was the sort that improves rather than grows. But we remember the place as it was before the blacksmith shop was turned into a garage and before the harness shop was given an electric lighted front and transformed into a movie. I guess the new generation has long since passed up the old opera house above the drugstore for the rejuvenated harness shop and the actors that come by express in canned celluloid. But at county fair time, you remember, the Cora Warner Comedy Company used to come for a week's engagement, Cora Warner, noticeably wrinkled as she walked through the park from the hotel, donning a blonde wig that enabled her to play soubrette parts of the old school. And then there were the Beach and Bowers minstrels with their band that swung breezily up Main Street to form a circle on the bank corner and lift the whole center of the town out of the commonplace by the blare of trombones and the tenderness of clarinets. You remember how we Boy Scouts, who didn't know we were Boy Scouts, used to clamor for the front row of kitchen chairs after peddling bills for "The Octoroon" or "Nevada, and the Lost Mine"?

Oh, well, we're uninteresting old-timers now. And it used to be that I knew everyone in town—even the transient baker whose family had no garden and chickens but lived up over the furniture store, and the temporary telephone man who sat out in front of the hotel evenings with the pale-faced traveling man. That hotel—haunted with an atmosphere that was brought in from the outside world! Remember how you used to walk past it with awe, the hot sun on the plank sidewalk burning your bare feet, and your eyes wistful as you heard the bus man on the steps call a train? And the time came when we took the train ourselves. And when we came back—

When we came back, the town was still there, but the wondrous age when all life is roseate belonged to us no longer.

And yet that town, to me, will always be as it was in those days when the world was giving me its first pink-tinted impressions. And when my tussle with the world as it really is comes to a close, I want to go back there and take my last long sleep beneath one of those evergreens on the hillside where I know the robins hop along the branches. I know how each season's change comes there—the white drifts, the dew on the bluegrass, the rustling of crimsoned leaves. I'll know that off on the prairies beyond, the cornfields will still wave green in summer, and that from back across the creek, over in the schoolyard, there will float the old hushed echo of youth at play.

"The Captured Dream" (1917)

Alice French [Octave Thanet]

Raised in that hotbed of early Iowa writing, Davenport, Alice French (she used the gender-ambiguous Octave Thanet as an early pseudo to disarm biased male editors) would eventually come, as so many Iowa writers, to divide her time between the home state, and another—in French's case, Arkansas. A recipient of an honorary degree from the University of Iowa, French's work was perhaps better appreciated in her lifetime than today, as literary critics have, in hindsight, condemned some of the work for its traditional Iowa conservatism. Still, Iowa literary scholar Clarence Andrews anoints French as Iowa's first major literary figure, as, at the peak of her career, editors up and down the East Coast clamored for her short stories, which fetched more than five times the amount brought by Iowa legend Hamlin Garland. French also had many prominent admirers—Teddy Roosevelt and Andrew Carnegie among them—as well as influence over up-and-coming literary apprentices, most prominent among them Davenport's Susan Glaspell. Regardless of her reputation among critics, the story French tells below, of a starving Chicago artist called out on commission to do a portrait in Iowa, evidences what is often considered a fundamental of good fiction—the protagonist's transformation. Moreover, French flaunts literary convention in telling a story of true, rather than merely erotic, love as experienced on an otherwise nondescript Iowa farm.

Somers rode slowly over the low Iowa hills, fitting an air in his mind to Andrew Lang's dainty verses. Presently, being quite alone on the country road, he began to sing:

> In dreams doth he behold her
> Still fair and kind and young.

The gentle strain of melancholy and baffled desire faded into silence, but the young man's thoughts pursued it. A memory of his own that sometimes stung him, sometimes plaintively caressed him, stirred in his heart. "I am afraid you hit it, Andy," he muttered, "and I should have found it only a dream had I won."

At thirty, Somers imagined himself mighty cynical. He consorted with daring critics, and believed the worst both of art and letters. He was making campaign cartoons for a daily journal instead of painting the picture of the future; the panic of [18]93 had stripped him of his little fortune, and his sweetheart had refused to marry him. Therefore he said incessantly in the language of Job, "I do well to be angry."

The rubber tires revolved more slowly as his eyes turned from the wayside to the smiling hills. The corn ears were sheathed in silvery yellow, but the afternoon sun jeweled the green pastures, fresh as in May, for rain had fallen in the morning, and maples, oaks, and elms blended exquisite gradations of color and shade here and there among the open fields. Long rows of poplars recalled France to Somers, and he sighed. "These houses are all comfortable and all ugly," thought the artist. "I never saw anything less picturesque. The life hasn't even the dismal interest of poverty and revolt, for they are all beastly prosperous; and one of the farmers has offered me a hundred dollars and my expenses to come here and make a pastel of his wife. And I have taken the offer because I want to pay my board bill and buy a secondhand bicycle. The chances are he is after something like a colored photograph, something slick and smooth, and every hair painted—Oh, Lord! But I have to have the money; and I won't sign the cursed thing. What does he want it for though? I wonder, did he ever know love's dream? Dream? It's all a dream—a mirage of the senses or the fancy. Confound it, why need I be harking back to it? I must be near his house. House near the corner, they said, where the roads cross. Ugh! How it jumps at the eyes."

The house before him was yellow with pea-green blinds; the great barns were Indian red; the yard a riot of color from blooming flowers.

Somers wheeled up to the gate and asked of the old man who was leaning upon the fence where Mr. Gates lived.

"Here," said the old man, not removing his elbows from the fence bar.

"And, may I ask, are you Mr. Gates?" said Somers.

"Yes, sir. But if you're the young man was 'round selling *Mother, Home and Heaven*, and going to call again to see if we liked it, we don't want it. My wife can't read and we're taking a Chicago paper now, and ain't got any time."

Somers smiled. "I'm not selling anything but pictures," said he, "and I believe you want me to make one for you."

"Are you Mr. Somers, F. J. S.?" cried the farmer, his face lighting in a surprising manner. "Well, I'm glad to see you, sir. My wife said you'd come this afternoon, and I wouldn't believe her. I'm always caught when I don't believe my wife. Come right in. Oh, did you bring your tools with you?"

He guided Somers into the house and into a room so dark that he stumbled.

"There's the sofy; set down," said Gates, who seemed full of hospitable cheer. "I'll get a blind open. Girl's gone to the fair and Mother's setting out on the back piazza, listening to the noises on the road. She's all ready. Make yourself to home. Pastel like them pictures on the wall's what I want. My daughter done them." His tone changed on the last sentence, but Somers did not notice it; he was drinking in the details of the room to describe them afterwards to his sympathizing friends in Chicago.

"What a chamber of horrors," he thought, "and one can see he is proud of it." The carpet was soft to the foot, covered with a jungle of flowers and green leaves— the pattern of carpet which fashion leaves behind for disappointed salesmen to mark lower and lower until it shall be pushed into the ranks of shopworn bargains. The cheap paper on the wall was delicately tinted, but this boon came plainly from the designers, and not the taste of the buyer, since there was a simply terrible chair that swung by machinery, and had four brilliant hues of plush to vex the eye, besides a paroxysm of embroidery and lace to which was still attached the red ticket of the county fair. More embroidery figured on the cabinet organ and two tables, and another red ticket peeped coyly from under the ornate frame of a pastel landscape displaying every natural beauty—forest, mountain, sunlit lake, and meadow—at their bluest and greenest. There were three other pictures in the room, two very large colored photographs of a lad of twelve and of a pretty girl who might be sixteen, in a white gown with a roll of parchment in her hand tied with a blue ribbon; and the photograph of a cross of flowers.

The girl's dark, wistful, timid eyes seemed to follow the young artist as he walked about the room. They appealed to him. "Poor little girl" he thought, "to have to live here." Then he heard a dragging footfall, and there entered the mistress of the house. She was a tall woman who stooped. Her hair was gray and scanty, and so ill-arranged on the top of her head that the mournful tonsure of age showed under the false gray braid. She was thin with the gaunt thinness of years and toil, not the poetic, appealing slenderness of youth. She had attired herself for the picture in a black silken gown, sparkling with jet that tinkled as she moved; the harsh, black, bristling line at the neck defined her withered throat brutally. Yet Somer's sneer was transient. He was struck by two things—the woman was blind, and she had once worn a face like that of the pretty girl. With a sensation of pity he recalled Andrew Lang's verses; inaudibly, while she greeted him he was repeating:

> Who watches day by day
> The dust of time that stains her
> The griefs that leave her gray,
> The flesh that still enchains her,
> Whose grace has passed away.

Her eyes were closed but she came straight toward him, holding out her hand. It was her left hand that was extended; her right closed over the top of a cane, and this added to the impression of decrepitude conveyed by her whole presence. She spoke in a gentle, monotonous, pleasant voice. "I guess this is Mr. Somers, the artist. I feel—we feel very glad to have the honor of meeting you, sir."

No one had ever felt honored to meet Somers before. He thought how much refinement and sadness were in a blind woman's face. In his most deferential manner he proffered her a chair. "I presume I am to paint you, madam?" he said.

She blushed faintly. "Ain't it rediculous?" she apologized. "But Mr. Gates will have it. He has been at me to have somebody paint a picture of me ever since I had my photograph taken. It was a big picture and most folks said it was real good, though not flattering; but he wouldn't hang it. He took it off and I don't know what he did do to it. 'I want a real artist to paint you, Mother,' he said. I guess if Kitty had lived she'd have suited him, though she was all for landscape; never did much figures. You noticed her work in this room, ain't you—on the table and chair and organ—art needlework? Kitty could do anything. She took six prizes at the county fair; two of 'em come in after she was in her last sickness. She was so pleased that she had the picture—that's the picture right above the sofy; it's a pastel and the tidy, I mean the art needlework—put on her bed, and she looked at them the longest while. Her paw would never let the tickets be took off." She reached forth her hand to the chair near her and felt the ticket, stroking it absently, her chin quivering a little, while her lips smiled. "Mr. Gates was thinking," she said, "that maybe you'd paint a head of me—pastel like that landscape—that's why he likes pastel so. And he was thinking if—if maybe—my eyes was jest like Kitty's when we were married—if you would put in eyes, he would be awful much obliged and be willing to pay extra if necessary. Would it be hard? "

Somers dissembled a great dismay. "Certainly not," said he, rather dryly; and he was ashamed of himself at the sensitive flutter in the old features.

"Of course I know," she said, in a different tone than she had used before, "I understand how comical it must seem to a young man to have to draw an old woman's picture; but it ain't comical to my husband. He wants it very much. He's the kindest man that ever lived, to me, caring for me all the time. He's got me that organ—me that can't play a note, and never could—just because I love to hear music, and sometimes if we have an instrument, the neighbors will come in, especially Hattie Knight, who used to know Kittie, and is a splendid performer; she comes and plays and sings. It is a comfort to me. And though I guess you young folks can't understand it, it will be a comfort to him to have a picture of me. I mistrusted you'd be thinking it comical, and I hurried to come in and speak to you, lest, not meaning anything, you might, just by chance, let fall something might hurt his feelings—like you thought it queer or some sech thing. And he thinks so much of you, and having you here, that I couldn't bear there'd be any mistake."

"Surely it is the most natural thing in the world that he should want a portrait of you," Somers hastily interrupted.

"Yes, it is," she answered in her mild, even tones, "but it mightn't seem so to young folks. Young folks think they know all there is about loving. And it is very sweet and nice to enjoy things together; and you don't hardly seem to be in the world at all when you're courting, your feet and your head and your heart feel so light. But they don't know what it is to need each other. It's when folks suffer together that they find out what loving is. I never knew what I felt towards my husband till I lost my first baby; and I'd wake up in the night and there'd he no cradle there—and he'd comfort me. Do you see that picture under the photograph of the cross?"

"He's a pretty boy," said Somers.

"Yes, sir. He was drowned in the river. A lot of boys in playing, and one got too far, and Eddy, he swum out to help him. And he clumb up on Eddy and the man on shore didn't get there in time. He was a real good boy and liked to play home with me 'most as well as with the boys. Father was proud as he could be of him, though he wouldn't let on. That cross was what his schoolmates sent; and teacher she cried when she told me how hard Eddy was trying to win the prize to please his pa. Father and I went through that together. And we had to change all the things we used to talk of together, because Eddy was always in them; and we had to try not to let each other see how our hearts were breaking, and not shadder Kitty's life by letting her see how we missed him. Only once father broke down; it was when he give Kitty Eddy's colt." She stopped, for she could not go on.

"Don't—don't distress yourself," Somers begged lamely. His cheeks were very hot.

"It don't distress me," she answered, "only for the minnit; I'm always thinking of Eddy and Kitty, too. Sometimes I think it was harder for father when his girl went than anything else. And then my blindness and my rheumatism come; and it seemed he was trying to make up to me for the daughter and the son I'd lost, and be all to once to me. He has been, too. And do you think that two old people that have grown old together, like us, and have been through losses like that—do you think they ain't drawed closer and kinder and tenderer to each other, like the Lord to his church? Why, I'm plain, and old and blind and crooked—but he don't know it. Now, do you understand?"

"Yes," said Somers, "I understand."

"And you'll please excuse me for speaking so free; it was only so my father's feelings shouldn't get hurt by noticing maybe a look like you wanted to laugh."

"God knows I don't want to laugh," Somers burst in. "But I'm glad you spoke. It—it will be a better picture. Now may I ask you something? I want you to let me dress you—I mean put something about your neck, soft and white; and then I want to make two sketches of you—one, as Mr. Gates wishes, the head alone; the other of you sitting in the rustic chair outside."

"But"—she looked troubled—"it will be so expensive; and I know it will be foolish. If you'd just the same—"

"But I shouldn't; I want to do it. And it will not cost you anything. A hundred dollars will repay me well enough. I wish—I truly wish I could afford to do it all for nothing."

She gasped. "A hundred dollars! Oh, it ain't right. That was why he wouldn't buy the new buggy. And jest for a picture of me." But suddenly she flushed like a girl and smiled.

At this instant the old man, immaculate in his heavy black suit and glossy white shirt, appeared in the doorway bearing a tray.

"Father," said the old wife, "do you mean to tell me you are going to pay a hundred dollars jest for a picture of me?"

"Well, Mother, you know there's no fool like an old fool," he replied, jocosely; but when the old wife turned her sightless face toward the old husband's voice and he looked at her, Somers bowed his head.

He spent the afternoon over his sketches. Riding away in the twilight, he knew he had done better work than he had ever done before in his life, slight as its form might be; nevertheless he was not thinking of himself at all. He was trying to shape his own vague perception that the show of dainty thinking and the pomp of refinement are in truth amiable and lovely things, yet are they no more than the husks of life; not only under them, but under ungracious and sordid conditions, may be the human semblance of that "beauty most ancient, beauty most new," that the old saint found too late. He felt the elusive presence of something in love higher than his youthful dream; stronger than passion, fairer than delight. To this commonplace man and woman had come the deepest gift of life.

"A dream?" he murmured. "Yes, perhaps he has captured it."

"Tinkling Cymbals" (1917)

Helen Sherman Griffith

A 1915 edition of the Annals of Iowa *proudly announced that Helen Sherman Griffith, among other headliners, would attend the Iowa Author's Homecoming in Des Moines, an event which organizer James. B. Weaver hoped would prove to other states that "Iowa ears" resonated to something more than the "sounds of the dinnerbell." The short story below gives away Griffith as a playwright, as, though somewhat overdramatized, the dialogue between Margaret Durant and her husband Paul might have been more effectively staged. "The Marseillese," which Margaret hums in the passage, is the French national anthem, and moreover, a song that has come to symbolize spirited resistance, mobilization, and the hopes and dreams of the common laborer. In donning his khakis—the uniform of the Red Cross—Paul Durant takes a step toward civic engagement of the kind that distinguished Iowa in wartime.*

It was in the spring of 1915 that Margaret Durant came back to her home in Greenfield, Iowa, from a visit to friends in the East, and brought with her a clear, shining flame of patriotism, with which she proceeded to fire the town. Margaret had always been a leader, the foremost in civic betterment, in government reform, and in activities of her church and woman's club. She was a born orator, and loved nothing better than haranguing—and swaying—a crowd.

A fund was started for the purchase of an ambulance, which, Margaret insisted, must be driven by a Greenfield man. And she expressed sorrow on every occasion—particularly in the hearing of the mothers of young men—that she had no sooner to offer. The Red Cross rooms became the center of Greenfield social activity, and the young people never dreamed of giving an entertainment for any purpose save to benefit the Red Cross, the British Relief, or the Lafayette Fund. This last became presently the object of Margaret's special activities, since her husband, Paul, some four generations previously, had come of French blood. "So that is almost like working for my own country," Margaret said proudly. And she glowed with gratification whenever the French were praised.

So complete and self-sacrificing was her enthusiasm that she announced, as the spring advanced, her intention of taking no summer vacation, but to dedicate the money thus saved to the Lafayette Fund, and to work for that organization during the entire summer.

Her friends were thrilled with admiration at Margaret's attitude, and some of them emulated her heroic example. To be sure, staying at home that summer was a popular form of self-denial, since a good many families, even in Greenfield, Iowa, were beginning to feel the pinch of war.

One summer afternoon, Margaret strolled home from an animated meeting of the Lafayette Fund, exalted and tingling with emotion. She had addressed the meeting, and her speech had been declared the epitome of all that was splendid and noble. She had moved even herself to tears by her appeal for patriotism. She entered the house, still mentally enshrouded by intoxicating murmurs of "Isn't she wonderful.... Doesn't she make you wish you were a man, to go yourself!" and so forth.

Softly humming "The Marseillaise," she mounted the steps to her own room, to remove her hat. She stopped short on the threshold with a sudden startled cry. Her husband was there, walking up and down the room, and also humming "The Marseillaise." It was half an hour before his usual homecoming time, but that was not why Margaret cried out.

Paul was dressed in khaki! He was walking up and down in front of the cheval glass, taking in the effect from different angles. He took around foolishly when he heard his wife.

"Just trying it on," he said lightly. "How do you like me?"

"But Paul—what—what does it mean?"

"Just what you have guessed. I've signed up. I'm to drive the Greenfield ambulance," he added with justifiable pride.

"Margaret stared, grasped, tottered. She would have fallen if she had not sat down suddenly. Paul stared, too, astonished.

"Why, old girl, I thought it was what you wanted! I—you said—"

"Paul, Paul! You! It can't be! Why—why, you are all I have!"

"That is one reason the more for my going—we have no son to send."

"But Paul—It—I—the war is so far away! It isn't as if—as if we were at war."

"Almost—'France is the land of my ancestors'—your very words, Margaret."

"I know, but—"

"'and the cause is so just.'"

"But, Paul, I did not mean—"

"Did not mean what!" Paul turned and faced her sternly. "Margaret, your eloquence has sent a good many young men to the front. I wonder—" He paused, and a new expression dawned in his eyes; an expression that Margaret could not bear: an accusation, a suspicion.

Margaret cowered in her chair and hid her face.

"Oh, Paul, not that, not that! Leave me a moment, please. I—I want time to—to grasp it."

When she was alone she sat upright and faced the look she had seen in Paul's eyes.

"I am a canting hypocrite. I see it now, plainly. I read it in Paul's eyes. But I will show him he's mistaken. God! Is hypocrisy always so cruelly punished? Merciful God, have pity upon me!"

Rising to her feet, Margaret staggered to the door and called. The enthusiasm, the exaltation, had faded from her face, leaving it pinched and gray. But in her eye a new expression had been born, which lent a soft radiance to her features, the light of complete self-denial. Paul entered, gave one look, then knelt at his wife's feet.

"Forgive me, my love, for misunderstanding you. The fault was mine. You've been afraid I would not make good, and were testing me. Ah, my love."

For one terrible moment Margaret hesitated. Then she whispered, "No, Paul, you were right at first; but love has conquered. Not *our* love, but a greater, nobler sentiment: love of Right and Justice. Do you remember the verse: 'Though I speak with the tongues of men and of angels, and have not love, I am become as sounding brass or tinkling cymbal.' I—I am *not* a tinkling cymbal, Paul. I—Oh, Paul, take me with you! I can be of some use over there. We will go together."

Paul Rose and embraced her.

"My precious one! How Greenfield will honor you!"

Margaret winced and hid her face in his breast.

"No, Paul, no, no. Don't let them know! Let us go away quietly, in the night. Please, please, Paul. I—I could not bear any other way!"

Durant kissed her and said no more. And if he understood, he never let her know that he did.

"The Professor" (1917)

Calista Halsey Patchin

Celebrated by Iowa scholar and editor Johnson Brigham as one of the "three pioneer novelists of Iowa" along with Alice Ilgenfritz Jones and Maud Meredith, Des Moines's Calista Halsey Patchin is now largely, and sadly, forgotten. The short story below, similar in subject matter and style to the great midwestern writer Sherwood Anderson's work in Winesburg, Ohio, *touches on two important Iowa motifs: the legacy of compassionate teachers and the bittersweet experience of the estate auction. Though Iowa is not named until the story's conclusion, the* North American Review, *the prestigious literary journal published in Cedar Falls, offers a telltale clue to its setting.*

The professor had been dead two months. He had left the world very quietly, at that precise hour of the early evening when he was accustomed to say that his "spirit friends" came to him. The hospital nurse had noticed that there was always a time at twilight when the patient had a good hour; when pain and restlessness seemed to be charmed away, and he did not mind being left alone, and did not care whether or not there was a light in the room. Then it was that those who had gone came back to him with quiet, friendly ways and loving touch. He said nothing of this to the nurse. It was an old friend who told me that this had been his belief and solace for years.

When the professor had first come to town he had spoken of the wife who would follow him shortly, from the East. He did not display her picture, he did not talk about her enough so that the town, though it made an honest effort, ever really visualized her. She would come—without a doubt she would come—but not just yet. It was only that the East still held her. Gradually, he spoke of her less and less often, with a dignified reserve that brooked no inquiry, and finally not at all.

The town forgot. It was only when his illness became so serious that all felt someone should be written to, that it was discovered there was no one. The professor, when he was appealed to, said so. Then also, the hospital nurse noticed that at the twilight hour, when he talked quietly to his unseen friends, there was always One who stayed longer than the rest.

But he had been dead two months now, and the undertaker was pressing his bill, and there were other expenses which had been cheerfully borne by friends at the time, and indeed if there had been no other reason, it remains that something must become of the personal possessions of a man who leaves neither will nor known heirs. So the professor's effects were appraised, and a brief local appeared in the daily paper until it had made a dent in the memory of the public, apprising them that his personal property would be offered at public auction at 2 P.M. of a Thursday, in his rooms on the third floor of the Eureka Block.

It was the merest thread of curiosity that drew me to this sale. I did not want to buy anything. It was a sort of posthumous curiosity, and it concerned itself solely with the individuality of the dead man.

Not having had the opportunity of knowing him well in life, and never having known until I read his obituary what I had missed, I took this last chance of trying to evolve the man from his belongings. All I did know was that he was a teacher of music of the past generation in a Western town which grew so fast that it made a man seem older than he was. More than this, he was a composer, a music master, who took crude young voices, shrill with the tension of the western winds and the electric air, and tamed and trained them till they fell in love with harmony. When he heard a voice, he knew it. One of his contraltos is singing now in grand opera across the sea. A tenor that he discovered has charmed the world with an "upper note."

All the same, the professor had grown old—a new generation had arisen which knew not Joseph; he failed to advertise, and every young girl who "gave lessons" crowded him closer to the wall. Now and then there would appear in the daily paper—not the next morning, but a few days after the presentation of some opera—a column of musical criticism, keen, delicate, reminiscent—fragrant with the rosemary that is for remembrance. When "Elijah" was given by home talent with soloists imported from Chicago, it was the professor who kindly wrote, beforehand this time, luminous articles full of sympathetic interpretation of the great masters. And at rare intervals there would appear a communication from him on the beauty of the woods and the fields, the suburbs of the town and the country, as though he were some simple prophet of nature who stood by the wayside. And this was no affectation. Long, solitary walks were his recreation.

It was a good deal of a rookery, up the flights of narrow, dirty stairs to the third floor of the Eureka Block. And here the professor had lived and taught. Two rooms were made from one by the sort of partition which does not reach to the ceiling—a ceiling which for some inexplicable reason was higher in some places than in others.

The voice of the auctioneer came down that winding way in professional cadences. There were in the room about as many people as might come to a funeral where only friends of the family are invited. It was very still. The auctioneer took an easy conversational tone. There was a silent, forlorn sort of dignity about the five pianos standing in a row that put professional banter and cheap little jokes out of the question. The pianos went without much trouble—a big one of the best make, an old-fashioned cottage piano, a piano with an iron frame. One of the appraisers, himself a musician, became an assistant auctioneer, and kindly played a little—judiciously very little—on each instrument in turn.

Then came the bric-a-brac of personal effects—all the flotsam and jetsam that had floated into these rooms for years. The walls were pockmarked with pictures, big and little. There was no attempt at high art; the professor had bought a picture as a child might buy one—because he thought it was pretty. It was a curious showing of how one artistic faculty may be dormant while another is cultivated to its highest point. But no matter how cheap the picture, it was always conscientiously framed. And this was a great help to the auctioneer. Indeed, it was difficult to see how he could have cried the pictures at all without the frames.

By this time the rooms were fuller of people. There were ladies who had come in quietly, just to get some little thing for a remembrance of their old friend and teacher. These mostly went directly over to the corner where the music lay and began looking for something of "his." If it were manuscript music, so much the better. But there was little of this. It appeared that with the professor, as with most of us, early and middle manhood had been his most productive time, and that was long enough ago for everything to have been duly published in sheet and book form—long enough, indeed, for the books themselves to have gone out of date.

There they were—long, green notebooks, bearing the familiar names of well known publishers, and with such a hydra head of title as "*The Celestina, or New Sacred Minstrel; a Repository of Music adapted to every variety of taste and grade of capacity, from the million to the amateur or professor.*"

There were four or five of these. There was sheet music by the pile. There was an opera, "*Joseph*," the production of which had been a musical event.

Presently the auctioneer came that way. He had just sold a large oleograph, framed, one of those gorgeous historical pictures which are an apotheosis of good clothes. He approached an engraving of an old-fashioned lady in voluminous muslin draperies, with her hair looped away from her face in a "Book of Beauty" style.

"*He* liked that," murmured a lady.

"What do I hear!" cries the auctioneer, softly. "Oh, such a little bid as that—I can't see it at all in this dark corner. Suppose we throw these peaches in—awfully pretty thing for dining room—and this flower piece—shall we group these three?—now, how much for all? Ah, there they go!"

"Here, ladies and gentlemen, is a gold-headed cane which was presented to the deceased by his admiring friends. It is pure gold—you *know* they would not give him anything else. How much for this? How much? No—his name is *not* engraved on it—so much the better—what do I hear?"

"Look at this telescope, gentlemen—a good one—you know the professor was quite an astronomer in his way—and this telescope is all right—sound and in good condition"—the auctioneer had officiated at a stock sale the day before. "You can look right into futurity through this tube. Five dollars' worth of futurity? Five—five and a half? Case and all complete."

There was a pocketful of odds and ends; gold pens, lead pencils, some odd pocket knives; these inconsiderable trifles brought more in proportion than articles of greater intrinsic value. Evidently this was an auction of memories, of emotion, of sentiment.

There was a bit of the beam of the barn that was burned down when the cow kicked over the historic lamp that inaugurated the Chicago fire—no less than three persons were ready to testify to their belief in the genuineness of the relic, had anyone been disposed to question it. But no one was. Nearly all the people in the room were the dead music teacher's personal friends; they had heard the story of all these things; they knew who had sent him the stuffed brown prairie chicken that perched like a raven above the door—the little old-fashioned decanter and wine glasses of gilded glass—the artificial begonias—that clever imitation that goes far toward making one forswear begonias forevermore. There were lamps of various shapes and sizes, there was a kit of burglarious looking tools for piano tuning, there was a little globe—"Who wants the earth?" said the auctioneer. "You all want it."

There was a metronome, which, set to go, began to count time in a metallic whisper for some invisible pupil. Over in the corner just beyond the music were the professor's books. Now we shall find him out, for what a man reads he is, or wishes to be. There was a good deal of spiritualistic literature of the better sort. There was a *History of Christianity and Paganism* by the Roman Emperor Julian, a copy of *She*, a long shelf full of *North American Reviews*, a dozen or so of almanacs, a copy of *Bluebeard*. There were none of the "popular" magazines, and if there had been newspapers—those vagrants of literature—they had gone their way. There was a manuscript play for parlor presentation, with each part written out in legible script, entitled, "The Winning Card."

All these and many more things which only the patient appraisers can fully know were sold or set aside as unsalable, until all was done. And then those who had known and loved him and those who had not known or cared for him came down the stairs together.

Fate stood on the landing. As always, Fate ran true to form. She was a woman; a little tired, as a woman might well be who had come a thousand miles; a little

215

out of breath from the two flights of stairs. Her old-fashioned draperies clung about her; her hair was looped away from her face in a "Book of Beauty" style. The man who stood aside to let her pass was talking. "Of course," he was saying, "he was a sidetracked man. But I believe he stands the biggest chance of being remembered of any man in Iowa."

Swift protest at his first words clouded her face; sheer gratitude for his last words illumined it. She bent forward a little and went on up the stairs alone.

She faltered in the doorway, her hand fumbling at her throat. One of the men who had been talking below hastened to her side.

"It's all over," he said, then added, at the dumb misery that grayed her face "—the auction."

I—I—didn't come for that," the apathy in her voice holding it steady. "I—I am his wife. His last letter—he sent for me." A sob broke her speech. "It came last week—two months too late."

FROM **IOWA AND THE WAR (1917)**

CYRIL B. UPHAM

Cyril B. Upham was selected to lead off issue number five of the State Historical Society pamphlet series "Iowa and War," edited by Benjamin F. Shambaugh. A graduate of the University of Iowa and a research assistant for the State Historical Society, Upham was an active member of the American Economic Association in the 1930s and 1940s and an authority on monetary policy, a resume which lead him to coedit the important monograph Closed and Distressed Banks; A Study in Public Administration *(1934) for the Brookings Institute in Washington D.C. in the midst of the Depression. Upham's 1918 University of Iowa dissertation, still held by some two dozen libraries, was titled* The Speaker of the House of Representatives in Iowa. *But the author's most passionate scholarly interest was war, and Iowa's role in it, a topic he explores in this 1917 article excerpt detailing Iowa's contribution to the Great War.*

Although Iowa has not been the scene of any great battle—like Waterloo, Gettysburg, or the Marne—the record of events connecting with the history of Iowa with war and military affairs is long and varied.

THE GREAT WAR

Finally, in the year 1917 the United States became a participant in the Great War. For many months the people of the Mississippi Valley had been accused of being indifferent to the struggle going on across the seas. But the declaration that war existed brought unmistakable proof of the support of the Middle West—the "land of the singing corn"—the granary and garden of the nation, which furnishes a large part of the food so necessary to win the war. And so in Iowa a great storehouse of supplies became available for the soldiers in the trenches.

But it is not only as a food producer that Iowa is lending support to the government. At the time of this nation's entry into the war, the thirty-seventh general assembly was in session. On April 6th, Senate Joint Resolution No. 12 was introduced, pledging all the resources of the state of Iowa to assist in carrying on the war. Even before war had been declared, a similar joint resolution had been approved pledging support to the President in his stand for the preservation of national rights and dignity. To back up these pledges, a series of military measures were enacted and a total of $1,440,000 was appropriated for military purposes.

The early response has been well sustained. Organizations of every character have mobilized to lend aid to the government. Food conservation, care of soldiers' dependents, "smokes for soldiers," cantonment libraries, Red Cross activities, and

Y.M.C.A. work in its different phases have all been emphasized. Iowa is one of the foremost states in the union in the number of chapters of Red Cross which have been organized. Soon after our entry into a war, a state defense council was created with branches in every county. Furthermore, financial support to the government for carrying on the war itself has not been lacking. Iowa people have helped to make the liberty loans successful.

But Iowa is something more than a fertile farm and treasury of gold. In this war, as in the War of the Rebellion [the Civil War], the men of Iowa are responding to the call to the colors. The first opportunity for enlistment came in April. A twenty day emergency naval recruiting period was instituted. It closed with this state just fifty-three short of its quota of four hundred. The period was extended to May 5th, but the goal was reached on April 24th. An Iowa man—F. F. Fletcher—holds the position of admiral in the United States Navy.

The Hawkeye State was near the top in the list of states in filling its quota of enlistments in the regular army. The entire National Guard of Iowa has been filled up to war strength and mobilized. What was formerly the Third Regiment of the Iowa National Guard is now the 168th Regiment of United States Infantry and is "somewhere" in France. The two other regiments, the cavalry, the engineers, and the artillery have all been called from the state and mustered into United States service. At present, a new National Guard regiment is being recruited.

Various other units have been organized. Since the war began Iowa has furnished an ammunition train, two engineering units, a signal corps, a substantial medial and dental reserve, a field hospital corps, two ambulance units—one from the State College at Ames [Iowa State University] and one from the State University [The University of Iowa]—and a goodly number of officers for the various training camps. Iowa was allowed to send eight hundred men to the first Reserve Officers Training Camp at Fort Snelling. There were two thousand applications from which to select these eight hundred men. In the second camp, Iowa's quota was three hundred and fifty-five men.

The policy of choosing an army by selective draft received little opposition in Iowa. The total registration in the state was over 200,000. Iowa's quota for the first draft of the National army was 12,749. These men together with those from Minnesota, North Dakota, and the western half of Illinois are being trained at Camp Dodge, Iowa, one of the national cantonment camps.

Iowa came to "attention" when the time came for the forces of the United States to "fall in." In unison with the rest of the states of the union, "on right into line" was executed. Men and materiel are being furnished to the fullest extent. Already some Iowa men have seen service on European battlefields, while the name of one Iowa man appeared on the first list of casualties. One Iowan of wide reputation (James Norman Hall) served in Kitchener's Mob—the First Hundred Thousand—and is at present engaged in "High Adventure" in the service of the Allies. His thrilling, picturesque descriptions of solider life have brought the war closer to millions of American readers. Herbert Hoover is another Iowan whose services are of first importance in the progress of the war. The heritage of loyalty and honor handed down by Iowa men and women of past days, will be well sustained by Iowans of the present day.

"A Jury of Her Peers" (1917)

Susan Glaspell

One of Iowa's famed Pulitzer Prize-winners, dramatist and short fictionist Susan Keating Glaspell wrote "A Jury of Her Peers" first as a well-received one-act (Trifles, 1916) for the Provincetown Players before reworking it one year later as a short. Glaspell grew up in Davenport, attended Drake University, worked as a political reporter in Des Moines, and returned to Davenport only to run away with then-married novelist George Cram Cook in an affair that scandalized her hometown and prompted her de facto exile from Iowa. Cook and Glaspell settled in the East, summering in Provincetown, where they formed the Provincetown Players, promoted the work of Eugene O'Neill, and where, by and by, Glaspell turned her substantial talents to playwriting, a move which paid the ultimate dividend: a Pulitzer Prize in 1936 for her play Alison's House. In the lengthy short story below, originally published in Every Week and selected for the Best Short Stories of 1917, Glaspell shows her intuitive understanding of Iowans and, especially, Iowa women. "A Jury of Her Peers" is based on Margaret Hossack's murder trial as Glaspell reported it for the Des Moines Daily News. Hossack was tried for killing her husband John, a respected farmer in Warren County, with an ax as he slept. She was convicted of first-degree murder, and transferred from her cell in Indianola to the state penitentiary in Anamosa. Two trials later, including one before the Supreme Court, the verdict was overturned and Hossack released. The story of the Hossak murder has been retold in Midnight Assassin: A Murder in America's Heartland (2007).

When Martha Hale opened the storm door and got a cut of the north wind, she ran back for her big woolen scarf. As she hurriedly wound that round her head her eye made a scandalized sweep of her kitchen. It was no ordinary thing that called her away—it was probably further from ordinary than anything that had ever happened in Dickson County. But what her eye took in was that her kitchen was in no shape for leaving: her bread all ready for mixing, half the flour sifted and half unsifted.

She hated to see things half done; but she had been at that when the team from town stopped to get Mr. Hale, and then the sheriff came running in to say his wife wished Mrs. Hale would come too—adding, with a grin, that he guessed she was getting scary and wanted another woman along. So she had dropped everything right where it was.

"Martha!" now came her husband's impatient voice. "Don't keep folks waiting out here in the cold."

She again opened the storm door, and this time joined the three men and the one woman waiting for her in the big two-seated buggy.

After she had the robes tucked around her she took another look at the woman who sat beside her on the back seat. She had met Mrs. Peters the year before at the county fair, and the thing she remembered about her was that she didn't seem like a sheriff's wife. She was small and thin and didn't have a strong voice. Mrs. Gorman, sheriff's wife before Gorman went out and Peters came in, had a voice that somehow seemed to be backing up the law with every word. But if Mrs. Peters didn't look like a sheriff's wife, Peters made it up in looking like a sheriff. He was to a dot the kind of man who could get himself elected sheriff—a heavy man with a big voice, who was particularly genial with the law-abiding, as if to make it plain that he knew the difference between criminals and non-criminals. And right there it came into Mrs. Hale's mind, with a stab, that this man who was so pleasant and lively with all of them was going to the Wrights' now as a sheriff.

"The country's not very pleasant this time of year," Mrs. Peters at last ventured, as if she felt they ought to be talking as well as the men.

Mrs. Hale scarcely finished her reply, for they had gone up a little hill and could see the Wright place now, and seeing it did not make her feel like talking. It looked very lonesome this cold March morning. It had always been a lonesome-looking place. It was down in a hollow, and the poplar trees around it were lonesome-looking trees. The men were looking at it and talking about what had happened. The county attorney was bending to one side of the buggy, and kept looking steadily at the place as they drew up to it.

"I'm glad you came with me," Mrs. Peters said nervously, as the two women were about to follow the men in through the kitchen door.

Even after she had her foot on the doorstep, her hand on the knob, Martha Hale had a moment of feeling she could not cross that threshold. And the reason it seemed she couldn't cross it now was simply because she hadn't crossed it before. Time and time again it had been in her mind, "I ought to go over and see Minnie Foster"—she still thought of her as Minnie Foster, though for twenty years she had been Mrs. Wright. And then there was always something to do and Minnie Foster would go from her mind. But now she could come.

The men went over to the stove. The women stood close together by the door. Young Henderson, the county attorney, turned around and said, "Come up to the fire, ladies."

Mrs. Peters took a step forward, then stopped. "I'm not—cold," she said.

And so the two women stood by the door, at first not even so much as looking around the kitchen.

The men talked for a minute about what a good thing it was the sheriff had sent his deputy out that morning to make a fire for them, and then Sheriff Peters stepped back from the stove, unbuttoned his outer coat, and leaned his hands on the kitchen table in a way that seemed to mark the beginning of official business. "Now, Mr. Hale," he said in a sort of semi-official voice, "before we move things about, you tell Mr. Henderson just what it was you saw when you came here yesterday morning."

The county attorney was looking around the kitchen.

"By the way," he said, "has anything been moved?" He turned to the sheriff. "Are things just as you left them yesterday?"

Peters looked from cupboard to sink; from that to a small worn rocker a little to one side of the kitchen table.

"It's just the same."

"Somebody should have been left here yesterday," said the county attorney.

"Oh—yesterday," returned the sheriff, with a little gesture as if yesterday having been more than he could bear to think of. "When I had to send Frank to Morris Center for that man who went crazy—let me tell you. I had my hands full yesterday. I knew you could get back from Omaha by today, George, and as long as I went over everything here myself—"

"Well, Mr. Hale," said the county attorney, in a way of letting what was past and gone go, "tell just what happened when you came here yesterday morning."

Mrs. Hale, still leaning against the door, had that sinking feeling of the mother whose child is about to speak a piece. Lewis often wandered along and got things mixed up in a story. She hoped he would tell this straight and plain, and not say unnecessary things that would just make things harder for Minnie Foster. He didn't begin at once, and she noticed that he looked queer—as if standing in that kitchen and having to tell what he had seen there yesterday morning made him almost sick.

"Yes, Mr. Hale?" the county attorney reminded.

"Harry and I had started to town with a load of potatoes," Mrs. Hale's husband began.

Harry was Mrs. Hale's oldest boy. He wasn't with them now, for the very good reason that those potatoes never got to town yesterday and he was taking them this morning, so he hadn't been home when the sheriff stopped to say he wanted Mr. Hale to come over to the Wright place and tell the county attorney his story there, where he could point it all out. With all Mrs. Hale's other emotions came the fear now that maybe Harry wasn't dressed warm enough—they hadn't any of them realized how that north wind did bite.

"We come along this road," Hale was going on, with a motion of his hand to the road over which they had just come, "and as we got in sight of the house I says to Harry, 'I'm goin' to see if I can't get John Wright to take a telephone.' You see," he explained to Henderson, "unless I can get somebody to go in with me they won't come out this branch road except for a price I can't pay. I'd spoke to Wright about it once before; but he put me off, saying folks talked too much anyway, and all he asked was peace and quiet—guess you know about how much he talked himself. But I thought maybe if I went to the house and talked about it before his wife, and said all the womenfolks liked the telephones, and that in this lonesome stretch of road it would be a good thing—well, I said to Harry that that was what I was going to say—though I said at the same time that I didn't know as what his wife wanted made much difference to John—"

Now there he was!—saying things he didn't need to say. Mrs. Hale tried to catch her husband's eye, but fortunately the county attorney interrupted with: "Let's talk about that a little later, Mr. Hale. I do want to talk about that, but I'm anxious now to get along to just what happened when you got here."

When he began this time, it was very deliberately and carefully. "I didn't see or hear anything. I knocked at the door. And still it was all quiet inside. I knew they must be up—it was past eight o'clock. So I knocked again, louder, and I thought I heard somebody say, 'Come in.' I wasn't sure—I'm not sure yet. But I opened the door—this door," jerking a hand toward the door by which the two women stood, "and there, in that rocker"—pointing to it—"sat Mrs. Wright."

Everyone in the kitchen looked at the rocker. It came into Mrs. Hale's mind that that rocker didn't look in the least like Minnie Foster—the Minnie Foster of twenty years before. It was a dingy red, with wooden rungs up the back, and the middle rung was gone, and the chair sagged to one side.

"How did she—look?" the county attorney was inquiring.

"Well," said Hale, "she looked—queer."

"How do you mean—queer?"

As he asked it he took out a notebook and pencil. Mrs. Hale did not like the sight of that pencil. She kept her eye fixed on her husband, as if to keep him from saying unnecessary things that would go into that notebook and make trouble.

Hale did speak guardedly, as if the pencil had affected him too.

"Well, as if she didn't know what she was going to do next. And kind of—done up."

"How did she seem to feel about your coming?"

"Why, I don't think she minded—one way or other. She didn't pay much attention. I said, 'Ho' do, Mrs. Wright? It's cold, ain't it?' And she said. 'Is it?'—and went on pleatin' at her apron.

"Well, I was surprised. She didn't ask me to come up to the stove, or to sit down, but just set there, not even lookin' at me. And so I said: 'I want to see John.'

"And then she—laughed. I guess you would call it a laugh."

"I thought of Harry and the team outside, so I said, a little sharp, 'Can I see John?' 'No,' says she—kind of dull like. 'Ain't he home?' says I. Then she looked at me. 'Yes,' says she, 'he's home.' 'Then why can't I see him?' I asked her, out of patience with her now. 'Cause he's dead' says she, just as quiet and dull—and fell to pleatin' her apron. 'Dead?' says, I, like you do when you can't take in what you've heard.

"She just nodded her head, not getting a bit excited, but rockin' back and forth."

"Why—where is he?' says I, not knowing what to say.

"She just pointed upstairs—like this"—pointing to the room above.

"I got up, with the idea of going up there myself. By this time I—didn't know what to do. I walked from there to here; then I says: 'Why, what did he die of?'

"He died of a rope around his neck,' says she; and just went on pleatin' at her apron.'"

Hale stopped speaking, and stood staring at the rocker, as if he were still seeing the woman who had sat there the morning before. Nobody spoke; it was as if everyone were seeing the woman who had sat there the morning before.

"And what did you do then?" the county attorney at last broke the silence.

"I went out and called Harry. I thought I might—need help. I got Harry in, and we went upstairs." His voice fell almost to a whisper. "There he was—lying over the—"

"I think I'd rather have you go into that upstairs," the county attorney interrupted, "where you can point it all out. Just go on now with the rest of the story."

"Well, my first thought was to get that rope off. It looked—"

He stopped, his face twitching.

"But Harry, he went up to him, and he said. 'No, he's dead all right, and we'd better not touch anything.' So we went downstairs."

"She was still sitting that same way. 'Has anybody been notified?' I asked. 'No,' says she, unconcerned."

"Who did this, Mrs. Wright?' said Harry. He said it businesslike, and she stopped pleatin' at her apron. 'I don't know,' she says. 'You don't know?' says Harry. 'Weren't you sleepin' in the bed with him?' 'Yes,' says she, 'but I was on the inside. 'Somebody slipped a rope round his neck and strangled him, and you didn't wake up?' says Harry. 'I didn't wake up,' she said after him."

"We may have looked as if we didn't see how that could be, for after a minute she said, 'I sleep sound.'"

"Harry was going to ask her more questions, but I said maybe that weren't our business; maybe we ought to let her tell her story first to the coroner or the sheriff. So Harry went fast as he could over to High Road—the Rivers' place, where there's a telephone."

"And what did she do when she knew you had gone for the coroner?" The attorney got his pencil in his hand all ready for writing.

"She moved from that chair to this one over here"—Hale pointed to a small chair in the corner—"and just sat there with her hands held together and looking down. I got a feeling that I ought to make some conversation, so I said I had come in to see if John wanted to put in a telephone; and at that she started to laugh, and then she stopped and looked at me—scared."

At the sound of a moving pencil the man who was telling the story looked up.

"I dunno—maybe it wasn't scared," he hastened: "I wouldn't like to say it was. Soon Harry got back, and then Dr. Lloyd came, and you, Mr. Peters, and so I guess that's all I know that you don't."

He said that last with relief, and moved a little, as if relaxing. Everyone moved a little. The county attorney walked toward the stair door.

"I guess we'll go upstairs first—then out to the barn and around there."

He paused and looked around the kitchen.

"You're convinced there was nothing important here?" he asked the sheriff. "Nothing that would—point to any motive?"

The sheriff too looked all around, as if to re-convince himself.

"Nothing here but kitchen things," he said, with a little laugh for the insignificance of kitchen things.

The county attorney was looking at the cupboard—a peculiar, ungainly structure, half closet and half cupboard, the upper part of it being built in the wall, and the lower part just the old-fashioned kitchen cupboard. As if its queerness attracted him, he got a chair and opened the upper part and looked in. After a moment he drew his hand away sticky.

"Here's a nice mess," he said resentfully.

The two women had drawn nearer, and now the sheriff's wife spoke.

"Oh—her fruit," she said, looking to Mrs. Hale for sympathetic understanding.

She turned back to the county attorney and explained: "She worried about that when it turned so cold last night. She said the fire would go out and her jars might burst."

Mrs. Peters's husband broke into a laugh.

"Well, can you beat the women! Held for murder, and worrying about her preserves!"

The young attorney set his lips.

"I guess before we're through with her she may have something more serious than preserves to worry about."

"Oh, well," said Mrs. Hale's husband, with good-natured superiority, "women are used to worrying over trifles."

The two women moved a little closer together. Neither of them spoke. The county attorney seemed suddenly to remember his manners—and think of his future.

"And yet," said he, with the gallantry of a young politician. "for all their worries, what would we do without the ladies?"

The women did not speak, did not unbend. He went to the sink and began washing his hands. He turned to wipe them on the roller towel—whirled it for a cleaner place.

"Dirty towels! Not much of a housekeeper, would you say, ladies?"

He kicked his foot against some dirty pans under the sink.

"There's a great deal of work to be done on a farm," said Mrs. Hale stiffly.

"To be sure. And yet"—with a little bow to her—"I know there are some Dickson County farmhouses that do not have such roller towels." He gave it a pull to expose its full length again.

"Those towels get dirty awful quick. Men's hands aren't always as clean as they might be."

"Ah, loyal to your sex, I see," he laughed. He stopped and gave her a keen look, "But you and Mrs. Wright were neighbors. I suppose you were friends, too."

Martha Hale shook her head.

"I've seen little enough of her of late years. I've not been in this house—it's more than a year."

"And why was that? You didn't like her?"

"I liked her well enough," she replied with spirit. "Farmers' wives have their hands full, Mr. Henderson. And then—" She looked around the kitchen.

"Yes?" he encouraged.

"It never seemed a very cheerful place," said she, more to herself than to him.

"No," he agreed; "I don't think anyone would call it cheerful. I shouldn't say she had the homemaking instinct."

"Well, I don't know as Wright had, either," she muttered.

"You mean they didn't get on very well?" he was quick to ask.

"No; I don't mean anything," she answered, with decision. As she turned a little away from him, she added: "But I don't think a place would be any the cheerfuller for John Wright's bein' in it."

"I'd like to talk to you about that a little later, Mrs. Hale," he said. "I'm anxious to get the lay of things upstairs now."

He moved toward the stair door, followed by the two men.

"I suppose anything Mrs. Peters does'll be all right?" the sheriff inquired. "She was to take in some clothes for her, you know—and a few little things. We left in such a hurry yesterday."

The county attorney looked at the two women they were leaving alone there among the kitchen things.

"Yes—Mrs. Peters," he said, his glance resting on the woman who was not Mrs. Peters, the big farmer woman who stood behind the sheriff's wife. "Of course Mrs. Peters is one of us," he said, in a manner of entrusting responsibility. "And keep your eye out, Mrs. Peters, for anything that might be of use. No telling; you women might come upon a clue to the motive—and that's the thing we need."

Mr. Hale rubbed his face after the fashion of a showman getting ready for a pleasantry.

"But would the women know a clue if they did come upon it?" he said; and, having delivered himself of this, he followed the others through the stair door.

The women stood motionless and silent, listening to the footsteps, first upon the stairs, then in the room above them.

Then, as if releasing herself from something strange. Mrs. Hale began to arrange the dirty pans under the sink, which the county attorney's disdainful push of the foot had deranged.

"I'd hate to have men comin' into my kitchen," she said testily—"snoopin' round and criticizin.'"

"Of course it's no more than their duty," said the sheriff's wife, in her manner of timid acquiescence.

"Duty's all right," replied Mrs. Hale bluffly; "but I guess that deputy sheriff that come out to make the fire might have got a little of this on." She gave the roller towel a pull. "Wish I'd thought of that sooner! Seems mean to talk about her for not having things slicked up, when she had to come away in such a hurry."

She looked around the kitchen. Certainly it was not "slicked up." Her eye was held by a bucket of sugar on a low shelf. The cover was off the wooden bucket, and beside it was a paper bag—half full.

Mrs. Hale moved toward it.

"She was putting this in there," she said to herself—slowly.

She thought of the flour in her kitchen at home—half sifted, half not sifted. She had been interrupted, and had left things half done. What had interrupted Minnie Foster? Why had that work been left half done? She made a move as if to finish it—unfinished things always bothered her—and then she glanced around and saw that Mrs. Peters was watching her—and she didn't want Mrs. Peters to get that feeling she had got of work begun and then—for some reason—not finished.

"It's a shame about her fruit," she said, and walked toward the cupboard that the county attorney had opened, and got on the chair, murmuring: "I wonder if it's all gone."

It was a sorry enough looking sight, but "Here's one that's all right," she said at last. She held it toward the light. "This is cherries, too." She looked again. "I declare I believe that's the only one."

With a sigh, she got down from the chair, went to the sink, and wiped off the bottle.

"She'll feel awful bad, after all her hard work in the hot weather. I remember the afternoon I put up my cherries last summer."

She set the bottle on the table, and, with another sigh, started to sit down in the rocker. But she did not sit down. Something kept her from sitting down in that chair. She straightened—stepped back, and, half turned away, stood looking at it, seeing the woman who had sat there "pleatin' at her apron."

The thin voice of the sheriff's wife broke in upon her: "I must be getting those things from the front-room closet." She opened the door into the other room, started in, stepped back. "You coming with me, Mrs. Hale?" she asked nervously. "You—you could help me get them."

They were soon back—the stark coldness of that shut-up room was not a thing to linger in.

"My!" said Mrs. Peters, dropping the things on the table and hurrying to the stove.

Mrs. Hale stood examining the clothes the woman who was being detained in town had said she wanted.

"Wright was close!" she exclaimed, holding up a shabby black skirt that bore the marks of much making over. "I think maybe that's why she kept so much to herself. I s'pose she felt she couldn't do her part; and then, you don't enjoy things when you feel shabby. She used to wear pretty clothes and be lively—when she was Minnie Foster, one of the town girls, singing in the choir. But that—oh, that was twenty years ago."

With a carefulness in which there was something tender, she folded the shabby clothes and piled them at one corner of the table. She looked up at Mrs. Peters, and there was something in the other woman's look that irritated her.

"She don't care," she said to herself. "Much difference it makes to her whether Minnie Foster had pretty clothes when she was a girl."

Then she looked again, and she wasn't so sure; in fact, she hadn't at any time been perfectly sure about Mrs. Peters. She had that shrinking manner, and yet her eyes looked as if they could see a long way into things.

"This all you was to take in?" asked Mrs. Hale.

"No," said the sheriff's wife; "she said she wanted an apron. Funny thing to want," she ventured in her nervous little way, "for there's not much to get you dirty in jail, goodness knows. But I suppose just to make her feel more natural. If you're used to wearing an apron—. She said they were in the bottom drawer of this cupboard. Yes—here they are. And then her little shawl that always hung on the stair door."

She took the small gray shawl from behind the door leading upstairs, and stood a minute looking at it.

Suddenly Mrs. Hale took a quick step toward the other woman, "Mrs. Peters!"

"Yes, Mrs. Hale?"

"Do you think she—did it?"

A frightened look blurred the other thing in Mrs. Peters's eyes.

"Oh, I don't know," she said, in a voice that seemed to shrink away from the subject.

"Well, I don't think she did," affirmed Mrs. Hale stoutly. "Asking for an apron, and her little shawl. Worryin' about her fruit."

"Mr. Peters says—." Footsteps were heard in the room above; she stopped, looked up, then went on in a lowered voice: "Mr. Peters says—it looks bad for her. Mr. Henderson is awful sarcastic in a speech, and he's going to make fun of her saying she didn't—wake up."

For a moment Mrs. Hale had no answer. Then, "Well, I guess John Wright didn't wake up—when they was slippin' that rope under his neck," she muttered.

"No, it's strange," breathed Mrs. Peters. "They think it was such a—funny way to kill a man."

She began to laugh; at sound of the laugh, abruptly stopped.

"That's just what Mr. Hale said," said Mrs. Hale, in a resolutely natural voice. "There was a gun in the house. He says that's what he can't understand."

"Mr. Henderson said, coming out, that what was needed for the case was a motive. Something to show anger—or sudden feeling."

"Well, I don't see any signs of anger around here," said Mrs. Hale, "I don't—" She stopped. It was as if her mind tripped on something. Her eye was caught by a dishtowel in the middle of the kitchen table. Slowly she moved toward the table. One half of it was wiped clean, the other half messy. Her eyes made a slow, almost unwilling turn to the bucket of sugar and the half empty bag beside it. Things begun—and not finished.

After a moment she stepped back, and said, in that manner of releasing herself: "Wonder how they're finding things upstairs? I hope she had it a little more red up there. You know,"—she paused, and feeling gathered—"it seems kind of *sneaking*: locking her up in town and coming out here to get her own house to turn against her!"

"But, Mrs. Hale," said the sheriff's wife, "the law is the law."

"I s'pose 'tis," answered Mrs. Hale shortly.

She turned to the stove, saying something about that fire not being much to brag of. She worked with it a minute, and when she straightened up she said aggressively, "The law is the law—and a bad stove is a bad stove. How'd you like to cook on this?"—pointing with the poker to the broken lining. She opened the oven door and started to express her opinion of the oven; but she was swept into her own thoughts, thinking of what it would mean, year after year, to have that stove to wrestle with. The thought of Minnie Foster trying to bake in that oven—and the thought of her never going over to see Minnie Foster—.

She was startled by hearing Mrs. Peters say, "A person gets discouraged—and loses heart."

The sheriff's wife had looked from the stove to the sink—to the pail of water which had been carried in from outside. The two women stood there silent, above them the footsteps of the men who were looking for evidence against the woman who had worked in that kitchen. That look of seeing into things, of seeing through a thing to something else, was in the eyes of the sheriff's wife now. When Mrs. Hale next spoke to her, it was gently. "Better loosen up your things, Mrs. Peters. We'll not feel them when we go out."

Mrs. Peters went to the back of the room to hang up the fur tippet she was wearing. A moment later she exclaimed, "Why, she was piecing a quilt," and held up a large sewing basket piled high with quilt pieces.

Mrs. Hale spread some of the blocks on the table.

"It's log-cabin pattern," she said, putting several of them together, "Pretty, isn't it?"

They were so engaged with the quilt that they did not hear the footsteps on the stairs. Just as the stair door opened Mrs. Hale was saying, "Do you suppose she was going to quilt it or just knot it?"

The sheriff threw up his hands.

"They wonder whether she was going to quilt it or just knot it!"

There was a laugh for the ways of women, a warming of hands over the stove, and then the county attorney said briskly:

"Well, let's go right out to the barn and get that cleared up."

"I don't see as there's anything so strange," Mrs. Hale said resentfully, after the outside door had closed on the three men—"our taking up our time with little things while we're waiting for them to get the evidence. I don't see as it's anything to laugh about."

"Of course they've got awful important things on their minds," said the sheriff's wife apologetically.

They returned to an inspection of the block for the quilt. Mrs. Hale was looking at the fine, even sewing, and preoccupied with thoughts of the woman who had done that sewing, when she heard the sheriff's wife say, in a queer tone, "Why, look at this one."

She turned to take the block held out to her.

"The sewing," said Mrs. Peters, in a troubled way, "All the rest of them have been so nice and even—but—this one. Why, it looks as if she didn't know what she was about!"

Their eyes met—something flashed to life, passed between them; then, as if with an effort, they seemed to pull away from each other. A moment Mrs. Hale sat there, her hands folded over that sewing which was so unlike all the rest of the sewing. Then she had pulled a knot and drawn the threads.

"Oh, what are you doing, Mrs. Hale?" asked the sheriff's wife, startled.

"Just pulling out a stitch or two that's not sewed very good," said Mrs. Hale mildly.

"I don't think we ought to touch things," Mrs. Peters said, a little helplessly.

"I'll just finish up this end," answered Mrs. Hale, still in that mild, matter-of-fact fashion.

She threaded a needle and started to replace bad sewing with good. For a little while she sewed in silence. Then, in that thin, timid voice, she heard "Mrs. Hale!"

"Yes, Mrs. Peters?"

"What do you suppose she was so—nervous about?"

"Oh, I don't know," said Mrs. Hale, as if dismissing a thing not important enough to spend much time on. "I don't know as she was—nervous. I sew awful queer sometimes when I'm just tired."

She cut a thread, and out of the corner of her eye looked up at Mrs. Peters. The small, lean face of the sheriff's wife seemed to have tightened up. Her eyes had that look of peering into something. But next moment she moved, and said in her thin, indecisive way, "Well, I must get those clothes wrapped. They may be through sooner than we think. I wonder where I could find a piece of paper—and string."

"In that cupboard, maybe," suggested to Mrs. Hale, after a glance around.

One piece of the crazy sewing remained unripped. Mrs. Peter's back turned, Martha Hale now scrutinized that piece, compared it with the dainty, accurate sewing of the other blocks. The difference was startling. Holding this block made her feel queer, as if the distracted thoughts of the woman who had perhaps turned to it to try and quiet herself were communicating themselves to her.

Mrs. Peters' voice roused her.

"Here's a birdcage," she said. "Did she have a bird, Mrs. Hale?"

"Why, I don't know whether she did or not." She turned to look at the cage Mrs. Peters was holding up. "I've not been here in so long." She sighed. "There was a man round last year selling canaries cheap—but I don't know as she took one. Maybe she did. She used to sing real pretty herself."

Mrs. Peters looked around the kitchen.

"Seems kind of funny to think of a bird here." She half laughed—an attempt to put up a barrier. "But she must have had one—or why would she have a cage? I wonder what happened to it."

"I suppose maybe the cat got it," suggested Mrs. Hale, resuming her sewing.

"No; she didn't have a cat. She's got that feeling some people have about cats—being afraid of them. When they brought her to our house yesterday, my cat got in the room, and she was real upset and asked me to take it out."

"My sister Bessie was like that," laughed Mrs. Hale.

The sheriff's wife did not reply. The silence made Mrs. Hale turn round. Mrs. Peters was examining the birdcage.

"Look at this door," she said slowly. "It's broke. One hinge has been pulled apart."

Mrs. Hale came nearer.

"Looks as if someone must have been—rough with it."

Again their eyes met—startled, questioning, apprehensive. For a moment neither spoke nor stirred. Then Mrs. Hale, turning away, said brusquely, "If they're going to find any evidence, I wish they'd be about it. I don't like this place."

"But I'm awful glad you came with me, Mrs. Hale." Mrs. Peters put the birdcage on the table and sat down. "It would be lonesome for me—sitting here alone."

"Yes, it would, wouldn't it?" agreed Mrs. Hale, a certain determined naturalness in her voice. She had picked up the sewing, but now it dropped in her lap, and she murmured in a different voice: "But I tell you what I do wish, Mrs. Peters. I wish I had come over sometimes when she was here. I wish—I had."

"But of course you were awful busy, Mrs. Hale. Your house—and your children."

"I could've come," retorted Mrs. Hale shortly. "I stayed away because it weren't cheerful—and that's why I ought to have come. I"—she looked around—"I've never liked this place. Maybe because it's down in a hollow and you don't see the road. I don't know what it is, but it's a lonesome place, and always was. I wish I had come over to see Minnie Foster sometimes. I can see now—" She did not put it into words.

"Well, you mustn't reproach yourself," counseled Mrs. Peters. "Somehow, we just don't see how it is with other folks till—something comes up."

"Not having children makes less work," mused Mrs. Hale, after a silence, "but it makes a quiet house—and Wright out to work all day—and no company when he did come in. Did you know John Wright, Mrs. Peters?"

"Not to know him. I've seen him in town. They say he was a good man."

"Yes—good," conceded John Wright's neighbor grimly. "He didn't drink, and kept his word as well as most, I guess, and paid his debts. But he was a hard man, Mrs. Peters. Just to pass the time of day with him—" She stopped, shivered a little. "Like a raw wind that gets to the bone." Her eye fell upon the cage on the table before her, and she added, almost bitterly: "I should think she would've wanted a bird!"

Suddenly she leaned forward, looking intently at the cage. "But what do you s'pose went wrong with it?"

"I don't know," returned Mrs. Peters; "unless it got sick and died."

But after she said it she reached over and swung the broken door. Both women watched it as if somehow held by it.

"You didn't know—her?" Mrs. Hale asked, a gentler note in her voice.

"Not till they brought her yesterday," said the sheriff's wife.

"She—come to think of it, she was kind of like a bird herself. Real sweet and pretty, but kind of timid and—fluttery. How—she—did—change."

That held her for a long time. Finally, as if struck with a happy thought and relieved to get back to everyday things, she exclaimed, "Tell you what, Mrs. Peters, why don't you take the quilt in with you? It might take up her mind."

"Why, I think that's a real nice idea, Mrs. Hale," agreed the sheriff's wife, as if she too were glad to come into the atmosphere of a simple kindness. "There couldn't possibly be any objection to that, could there? Now, just what will I take? I wonder if her patches are in here—and her things?"

They turned to the sewing basket.

"Here's some red," said Mrs. Hale, bringing out a roll of cloth. Underneath that was a box. "Here, maybe her scissors are in here—and her things." She held it up. "What a pretty box! I'll warrant that was something she had a long time ago—when she was a girl."

She held it in her hand a moment; then, with a little sigh, opened it.

Instantly her hand went to her nose.

"Why—!"

Mrs. Peters drew nearer—then turned away.

"There's something wrapped up in this piece of silk," faltered Mrs. Hale.

"This isn't her scissors," said Mrs. Peters, in a shrinking voice.

Her hand not steady, Mrs. Hale raised the piece of silk. "Oh, Mrs. Peters!" she cried. "It's—"

Mrs. Peters bent closer.

"It's the bird," she whispered.

"But, Mrs. Peters!" cried Mrs. Hale. "Look at it! Its neck—look at its neck! It's all—other side to."

She held the box away from her.

The sheriff's wife again bent closer.

"Somebody wrung its neck," said she, in a voice that was slow and deep.

And then again the eyes of the two women met—this time clung together in a look of dawning comprehension, of growing horror. Mrs. Peters looked from the dead bird to the broken door of the cage. Again their eyes met. And just then there was a sound at the outside door. Mrs. Hale slipped the box under the quilt pieces in the basket, and sank into the chair before it. Mrs. Peters stood holding to the table. The county attorney and the sheriff came in from outside.

"Well, ladies," said the county attorney, as one turning from serious things to little pleasantries, "have you decided whether she was going to quilt it or knot it?"

"We think," began the sheriff's wife in a flurried voice, "that she was going to—knot it."

He was too preoccupied to notice the change that came in her voice on that last.

"Well, that's very interesting, I'm sure," he said tolerantly. He caught sight of the birdcage.

"Has the bird flown?"

"We think the cat got it," said Mrs. Hale in a voice curiously even.

He was walking up and down, as if thinking something out.

"Is there a cat?" he asked absently.

Mrs. Hale shot a look up at the sheriff's wife.

"Well, not now," said Mrs. Peters. "They're superstitious, you know; they leave."

She sank into her chair.

The county attorney did not heed her. "No sign at all of anyone having come in from the outside," he said to Peters, in the manner of continuing an interrupted conversation. "Their own rope. Now let's go upstairs again and go over it, piece by piece. It would have to have been someone who knew just the—"

The stair door closed behind them and their voices were lost.

The two women sat motionless, not looking at each other, but as if peering into something and at the same time holding back. When they spoke now it was as if they were afraid of what they were saying, but as if they could not help saying it.

"She liked the bird," said Martha Hale, low and slowly. "She was going to bury it in that pretty box."

"When I was a girl," said Mrs. Peters, under her breath, "my kitten—there was a boy took a hatchet, and before my eyes—before I could get there—." She covered her face an instant. "If they hadn't held me back I would have"—she caught herself, looked upstairs where footsteps were heard, and finished weakly—"hurt him."

Then they sat without speaking or moving.

"I wonder how it would seem," Mrs. Hale at last began, as if feeling her way over strange ground—"never to have had any children around?" Her eyes made a slow sweep of the kitchen, as if seeing what that kitchen had meant through all the years "No, Wright wouldn't like the bird," she said after that—"a thing that sang. She used to sing. He killed that too." Her voice tightened.

Mrs. Peters moved uneasily.

"Of course we don't know who killed the bird."

"I knew John Wright," was Mrs. Hale's answer.

"It was an awful thing was done in this house that night, Mrs. Hale," said the sheriff's wife. "Killing a man while he slept—slipping a thing round his neck that choked the life out of him."

Mrs. Hale's hand went out to the birdcage.

"We don't know who killed him," whispered Mrs. Peters wildly. "We don't know."

Mrs. Hale had not moved. "If there had been years and years of—nothing, then a bird to sing to you, it would be awful—still—after the bird was still."

It was as if something within her not herself had spoken, and it found in Mrs. Peters something she did not know as herself.

"I know what stillness is," she said, in a queer, monotonous voice. "When we homesteaded in Dakota, and my first baby died—after he was two years old—and me with no other then—"

Mrs. Hale stirred.

"How soon do you suppose they'll be through looking for the evidence?"

"I know what stillness is," repeated Mrs. Peters, in just that same way. Then she too pulled back. "The law has got to punish crime, Mrs. Hale," she said in her tight little way.

"I wish you'd seen Minnie Foster," was the answer, "when she wore a white dress with blue ribbons, and stood up there in the choir and sang."

The picture of that girl, the fact that she had lived neighbor to that girl for twenty years, and had let her die for lack of life, was suddenly more than she could bear.

"Oh, I wish I'd come over here once in a while!" she cried. "That was a crime! Who's going to punish that?"

"We mustn't take on," said Mrs. Peters, with a frightened look toward the stairs.

"I might 'a' known she needed help! I tell you, it's queer, Mrs. Peters. We live close together, and we live far apart. We all go through the same things—it's all just a different kind of the same thing! If it weren't—why do you and I understand? Why do we know—what we know this minute?"

She dashed her hand across her eyes. Then, seeing the jar of fruit on the table she reached for it and choked out, "If I was you I wouldn't tell her her fruit was gone! Tell her it ain't. Tell her it's all right—all of it. Here—take this in to prove it to her! She—she may never know whether it was broke or not."

She turned away.

Mrs. Peters reached out for the bottle of fruit as if she were glad to take it—as if touching a familiar thing, having something to do, could keep her from something else. She got up, looked about for something to wrap the fruit in, took a petticoat from the pile of clothes she had brought from the front room, and nervously started winding that round the bottle.

"My!" she began, in a high, false voice, "it's a good thing the men couldn't hear us! Getting all stirred up over a little thing like a—dead canary." She hurried over that. "As if that could have anything to do with—with—My, wouldn't they laugh?"

Footsteps were heard on the stairs.

"Maybe they would," muttered Mrs. Hale—"maybe they wouldn't."

"No, Peters," said the county attorney incisively, "it's all perfectly clear, except the reason for doing it. But you know juries when it comes to women. If there was some definite thing—something to show. Something to make a story about. A thing that would connect up with this clumsy way of doing it."

In a covert way Mrs. Hale looked at Mrs. Peters. Mrs. Peters was looking at her. Quickly they looked away from each other. The outer door opened and Mr. Hale came in.

"I've got the team round now," he said. "Pretty cold out there."

"I'm going to stay here awhile by myself," the county attorney suddenly announced. "You can send Frank out for me, can't you?" he asked the sheriff. "I want to go over everything. I'm not satisfied we can't do better."

Again, for one brief moment, the two women's eyes found one another.

The sheriff came up to the table.

"Did you want to see what Mrs. Peters was going to take in?"

The county attorney picked up the apron. He laughed.

"Oh, I guess they're not very dangerous things the ladies have picked out."

Mrs. Hale's hand was on the sewing basket in which the box was concealed. She felt that she ought to take her hand off the basket. She did not seem able to. He picked up one of the quilt blocks which she had piled on to cover the box. Her eyes felt like fire. She had a feeling that if he took up the basket she would snatch it from him.

But he did not take it up. With another little laugh, he turned away, saying, "No; Mrs. Peters doesn't need supervising. For that matter, a sheriff's wife is married to the law. Ever think of it that way, Mrs. Peters?"

Mrs. Peters was standing beside the table. Mrs. Hale shot a look up at her; but she could not see her face. Mrs. Peters had turned away. When she spoke, her voice was muffled.

"Not—just that way," she said.

"Married to the law!" chuckled Mrs. Peters's husband. He moved toward the door into the front room, and said to the county attorney:

"I just want you to come in here a minute, George. We ought to take a look at these windows."

"Oh—windows," said the county attorney scoffingly.

"We'll be right out, Mr. Hale," said the sheriff to the farmer, who was still waiting by the door.

Hale went to look after the horses. The sheriff followed the county attorney into the other room. Again—for one final moment—the two women were alone in that kitchen.

Martha Hale sprang up, her hands tight together, looking at that other woman, with whom it rested. At first she could not see her eyes, for the sheriff's wife had not turned back since she turned away at that suggestion of being married to the law. But now Mrs. Hale made her turn back. Her eyes made her turn back. Slowly, unwillingly, Mrs. Peters turned her head until her eyes met the eyes of the other woman. There was a moment when they held each other in a steady, burning look in which there was no evasion or flinching. Then Martha Hale's eyes pointed the way to the basket in which was hidden the thing that would make certain the conviction of the other woman—that woman who was not there and yet who had been there with them all through that hour.

For a moment Mrs. Peters did not move. And then she did it. With a rush forward, she threw back the quilt pieces, got the box, tried to put it in her handbag. It was too big. Desperately she opened it, started to take the bird out. But there she broke—she could not touch the bird. She stood there helpless, foolish.

There was the sound of a knob turning in the inner door. Martha Hale snatched the box from the sheriff's wife, and got it in the pocket of her big coat just as the sheriff and the county attorney came back into the kitchen.

"Well, Henry," said the county attorney facetiously, "at least we found out that she was not going to quilt it. She was going to—what is it you call it, ladies?"

Mrs. Hale's hand was against the pocket of her coat.

"We call it—knot it, Mr. Henderson."

From **In the Garret (1920)**

Carl Van Vechten

Another Cedar Rapids boy, Carl Van Vechten learned his literary chops in the Cedar Rapids Public Library his mother helped secure funding for while simultaneously filling his musical ear with the theatricals and operas put on at Greene's Opera House. While Van Vechten left Iowa to attend the University of Chicago, and departed Chicago for New York, his Iowa roots continued to shape his early career. Hired by the New York Times as an assistant music critic, the paper enlisted him as its Paris correspondent from 1908 to 1910, during which time he befriended Gertrude Stein, whose work he would champion for the rest of his life. Van Vechten's time in Paris also no doubt influenced his first and only novel about Iowa, The Tattooed Countess (1924), which tells the story of a Parisian noblewoman who returns to her Iowa hometown. In the essay below, "The Folk Songs of Iowa," Van Vechten combines his two great loves—writing and music—and intermingles both with an unusually broad-minded race and ethnic consciousness. For a man who once gratefully played piano at the church services of his African American housekeeper in Chicago, setting off to discover the "folk songs" of his home state—the Iowa blues, if you will—seemed a natural endeavor. Not coincidentally, Van Vechten is credited with seeing into print in Vanity Fair poems by black poets Langston Hughes and Countee Cullen. Note that this excerpt of "The Folk Songs of Iowa" begins midway through the second paragraph, before which time Van Vechten holds forth on the subject of Southern folks songs and spirituals.

I was born in a town in Iowa where at least half the population is of Slavic origin and I was brought up on Bohemian lullabies. When our cook was in good humor, she sang lusty Czech airs, redolent of foaming amber Pilsner and stamping booted feet, waving ribboned skirts, embroidered jackets, and elaborately flowered headdresses. In a different mood, she hummed Indian and Bohemian folk songs in Iowa (and I am certain that there is an unlimited field for the collector in this direction) I leave to others; it occurred to me to gather in the folk songs of the Iowa farmer, the epic of the corn.

There are villages in New England; there are hamlets in England; in Iowa there are cities and towns. Elsewhere these cities would be called towns, and the towns villages or hamlets. . . . In one of the typical cities the wide streets are brick paved, canopied with sweeping elm branches which meet like Gothic ogives overhead; there are rows of old wooden houses and new brick or plaster dwellings, in pseudo-English or colonial style, or, best of all, stately authentic American 1870 mansions and these are surrounded by gardens in which roses, day lilies, gladioli, and bleeding hearts bloom. The walls of many houses are clothed in purple or white clematis, or wisteria, or more often woodbine or English ivy. Everywhere you will find an attempt at amateur landscape gardening what with here a syringa, there a flaming mountain ash, here a clump of lilac bushes, there a row of blue hydrangeas. All the vegetation is clean-cut, attended to, matter-of-fact, and the buildings themselves, whether residences or outhouses, give the same impression of prosperity. So do the city parks, that facing the railway station in particular, with the name of the town embroidered in coleus and cockscombs on a sloping bank of well-clipped grass, suggesting a giant's grave. Churches, schools, libraries, theaters, moving picture auditoriums, rise in magnificence on every side. There must be a school for every tenth baby, a church for every third. Unconsciously priapic spires affront the tender sky in every direction. . . . Nor are business blocks lacking, multifloored business blocks with elevators and, slightly removed from the main thoroughfares, factories flaunt their gaunt stacks, factories employing thousands of men. Automobiles, countless automobiles, Fords, Rolls-Royces, and Packards, line the streets along the curbs, buzz along the numbered streets and avenues. I verily believe there are more motorcars in this Iowa town than there are in Monte Carlo. The very atmosphere spells prosperity, a certain animal comfort, and unfortunately, also, a certain sense of smugness. This then is an Iowa city, not only unlike everything else in the world in its newly painted freshness, its air of up-to-dateness, the greenness of its foliage, and the striking self-satisfaction of its inhabitants, but also sedulously aping corners in Paris, houses in Oxford, walls in Beaune, gardens at Hampton Court, country clubs at Rye, churches at Siena, farmhouses at Ronda, and banking houses in Chicago. This could be no place for the study of the folk song. Here one could hear only the music of Irving Berlin or Richard Strauss, Louis A. Hirsch, or Puccini.

So one very hot Iowa day—and hot days in Iowa are hotter and brighter than one can meet elsewhere west of Verona or east of Arizona—I set forth from this pleasant city in one of the few buggies which remained of the civilization of the eighties or the nineties, a civilization completely brushed aside by the rude rush of modernity in such a community. There is indeed more of the Rome of the Empire in the Rome of today than there is of the Iowa town of 1870 in the Iowa city of today. A not too loquacious driver lounged on the ample front seat, and I sat in the back under the shelter of a black leather canopy. Beside me on the seat I had placed a pile of blank music paper, a tuning fork, and an instrument capable of making phonographic records.

Iowa towns have no suburbs. You pass quickly from the town itself into the farming country, for the towns are built compactly so as not to interfere with the growing of the corn which is the chief occupation of the state. Indeed, for a certain time in the summer, the one concern, the unfailing topic of conversation is the weather, not only in the country but also in the towns. Dry hot weather is essential for the complete growth of the corn and on the complete growth of the corn depends the economic stride of the state. Bank stocks, the price of dry goods and green groceries, rents and dressmakers' bills are all affected by a bad corn year.

The Iowa scene has been infrequently described in literature and no writer, I think, has as yet done justice to it. There is, indeed, a feeling that the Iowa scene is unworthy of description, as it is usually imagined as a fecund but unbeautiful country laid out in flat squares. The contrary is the case. This fair land is unusually personal in its appeal, and its beauty, which may not be appreciated by those who glance at it casually from the back of an observation car on the Overland Limited, is in the end very haunting. Indeed to me the Iowa scene has a kind of picturesqueness which I do not find elsewhere in the United States. Pennsylvania or Connecticut, for instance, too often remind me of England, but Iowa is essentially American. Far from being flat the ground is constantly rolling so that when, as often happens, the unhindered view exposes only fields of corn in every direction, the light, dry wind playing over the green and tasseled stalks in the hot, the very hot sunglare, the effect is produced of the undulation of the waves in a southern sea, and the magnificent monotony of the prospect accentuates the comparison. There is, indeed, to be found in the state of Iowa a kind of inspiration usually only associated with great rivers, high mountains, or that mighty monster ocean, "that liest curl'd like a green serpent round about the world."

But there are other pictures which interrupt the cornfields. Brooks abound, bubbling joyously over white-stoned, sandy beds, over which bend willow trees…and now and then a copse of woods, not a stately Michigan forest but a delightfully brushy congeries of trees and underbrush, an overgrown spinny in which lindens, elms, and the comfortable maple, which later will illumine the landscape with all the hues of a [Léon] Bakst canvas, rear their modest heights over the heads of hazel shrub and sumac which in turn shelter the milkweed and the prickly thistle. The shade is never intense, the copse is never cool; the warm rays of the sun penetrate the fragile covering of leaves as easily as they would the laced panels of a sunshade held by a languid English lady on a maidenhead lawn. Striped chipmunks hustle and bustle through the dead leaves that carpet the sandy soil. Field mice and toads are friendly enemies. There are a few squirrels. Deer, fox, and bears have long since disappeared from a region which offers so little security to the pursued. The settled hum of the cicada becomes a burden in the overheated air at times too terrible to be borne, and then again in the intensity of its rhythm it becomes possible to forget it and to listen to the lesser chirping of the cricket.

The road passes over a wooden bridge, roughly railed; the boards clatter under the untired wheels of the buggy. We lean out to one side and catch a glimmer of silver trout in the stream below, the quick flash of a mammoth dragonfly, *darning needle* is the local name, a darning needle instinct with gorgeous sheeny sapphire and emerald. Now we are out of the woods and passing through acres of corn land again.... There are no rough rail fences in Iowa, no stone fences....only barbed wire, extended tautly from post to post. On these shining wires, like so many brazen wire walkers in blue tights, strut the tiny, saucy bluebirds, or they sit in straight rows. Lacking fence wires they seek the telegraph wires. Bronze grackles, rose-breasted grossbeaks, scarlet tanagers, yellow warblers, and redwinged blackbirds make a vast Manila shawl on the blue ground of the sky. The meadowlark soars, a hawk swoops low, and a crow calls *Caw! Caw! Caw!* The silly mew of the catbird assails our ear from the neighboring bush, the woodpecker taps in the maple tree and the cuckoo's thieving note is sounded.

We pass a workman in the fields. Is this the Iowa peasant? He guides a horse with a harrow through the straight aisles that separate the rows of corn. But he does not sing. He is silent, although occasionally he calls out "Gee up!" to the beast ahead, but he does not interrupt the cheruping of the pretty yellow warblers, the constant burden of the cicadae, the buzz of the locusts, so like the sound of an automobile. The horse neighs. The intense heat, serving as conductor, accentuates this symphony of nature, brings out the different voices.

But now ahead, over the brow of the hill, I do hear singing. I urge my driver to make speed. He clucks to our horse and the buggy rolls rapidly on. We make the top of the hill and a few steps below its crest a schoolhouse is exposed to view. This is the source of the music. The schoolchildren are singing, *Good morning, merry sunshine* . . . and as we disappear in the distance we hear *My country, 'tis of thee.*

The farm in Iowa is not a careless congeries. The yard is not strewn with rusting machinery and rotting wheelbarrows. The farm in Iowa is in its own way as magnificent as the chateau in France. The house, it is true, is often insignificant, a simple white, clapboarded structure, with a few shade trees, but the outlying buildings sound the true imperial note. An artesian well or windmill, a tower of gleaming steel, imitates the Tour Eiffel; the ample silos are as imposing in their cylindrical whiteness as the turrets of a robber baron's castle on the Rhine; the barns, the stables, the hog pens, and the chicken yards are beyond all eastern dreams of country grandeur. Business is abroad. Efficiency is in the land. The

Iowa farmer accepts orders over his telephone and delivers them in his motor truck.

Passing such a farm we note several more men silently working in the fields. They greet us soberly. There is no gaiety in the heart of the Iowa farmer. No joy... no song! The farmer's wife, a plain slender woman in simple calico, is standing on the porch of her little white house, partially hidden among the evergreen trees. We wave to her, and she waves her hand in return, although obviously somewhat puzzled over our identity. Then I quickly call to my man to stop and leaping out of my shandrydan [vehicle] into the road I run lightly up the gravel path.

"We don't want to buy nothin'," are the lady's first words; "nothin' at all."

"I don't want to sell nothin', neither," I retort. "Does anyone here sing?"

"Be you a music teacher? Or a piano tuner? My darter sings sometimes."

"No, I'm not a teacher. . . . I like music." The farmer's wife begins to look queer. I see her eyes wander to the spot in the yard where Towser's kennel stands. Towser's head protrudes, a wicked bulldog head. Towser growls tentatively and waits for the signal. I prepare to die . . . but the woman decides to humor my strange request or perhaps she is lonesome.

"Aggie," she calls, "Aggie."

"What is it, ma?" a shrill voice demands from the lima bean patch.

"Come here a minute."

In due time Aggie comes forward, a fat, freckled girl with hair which would be called in a cat show "any other color." She is dressed in a blue skirt and a red flannel dressing sacque. She carries a pan of pods in one hand. With the other she fingers the tied ends of a sunbonnet.

"There's a music man here."

"I thought perhaps I could hear some singing. . . . Don't you ever sing among yourselves?"

Aggie giggles. Ma even allows her worried, wrinkled face to break into a slight smile. Towser stops growling.

"Just you sit on the piazza a minute," Aggie suggests. She passes the portal. Ma and I sit down on two uncomfortable wooden chairs. I have forgotten my music paper, my tuning fork, my phonographic apparatus, but it is too late. Aggie touches the keys of an invisible piano; my God, folk songs are not composed for the piano; has she perhaps misunderstood? Aggie is singing, loudly and unmistakably, Aggie is singing:

> Oh, ev'ry evening hear him sing, It's the cutest little
>   thing,
> Got the cutest little swing,
> Hitchy Koo, Hitchy Koo, Hitchy Koo

"Very pretty," I gasp. "Very pretty."

"Come on in the parlor," Ma says. We go into a low-ceilinged room, with framed pictures from the Sunday supplements of the Chicago newspapers. High in the wall in one corner is the tin stopper of the stovepipe hole. Stove and pipe have disappeared for the summer. The furniture is early Grand Rapids, a trifle worn; the carpet is red and green ingrain. The piano is black and upright. Aggie is fumbling in a music cabinet. Presently she goes back to the piano and begins again:

"From the land of the sky bloo waaa—tur..."

Aggie's third choice is even more inspired:

"Pale haaands that float beside the..."

So do I discover a bond between Iowa and Mayfair! Did Cecil Sharp learn more in his Appalachian travels? I doubt it. I thank Aggie, I thank Ma, I even speak to Towser as I pass the kennel and hurry on to the buggy. I wake up my Sancho Panza, snoozing on the front seat, and we once more are underway.

More cornfields, more copses, more birds and butterflies, more stern and sober workers, occasionally an automobile passes us, occasionally a wagon loaded with crates of vegetables or chickens. A new sight is a duck yard. Hundreds of white birds, huddled in pens with stretches of water like canals in Holland. In the next cornfield a quaint scarecrow, clothed in blue overalls and a long frock coat. On his head a sombrero tied with a gay red bandana.

An hour later we drive up to another farmhouse to give our Rozinante food and water. Our companion on the front seat drives the steed to the stables. I enter the farmhouse kitchen where the gaunt housewife prepares the midday meal, dinner, it is called in Iowa. She nods a curt good day and answers my request for dinner in the affirmative. I have become more circumspect. Tea stands on the stove stewing; tea is always stewed in Iowa; black and strong it stews in the kettle. Sometimes the kettle with its strong black residue stands for days unmolested at the back of the stove, save for the pouring out of cupfuls of the liquid and the replenishing of water and green tea leaves. Steaks cut as thin as sandwiches in Mayfair are frying. Grilling is an unknown art in these regions. Vegetables are boiling in pots of milk. Watch the patient housewife as she cuts the long and splendid asparagus stalks into minute bits which she tosses dexterously into the boiling kettle. A great green head of lettuce fresh from the garden is thrown into the wooden chopping bowl and soon reduced to atoms which are presently drowned in vinegar. But during all these operations and the preparing of griddle cakes, buckwheat griddle cakes, there is no singing, except that furnished by the teakettle, nor is there much conversation, although two women are assisting the housewife. The women bustle about but they do not talk. The farmhands come in and eat from the heavily laden unclothed table. Food is shoveled into the mouth without respite but still the tongues do not speak. Only occasionally someone asks a question, which is usually replied to monosyllabically. Dinner over, I tremblingly ask for a song.

"Song," says the farmer. "We haven't got no time for songs."

A maidservant titters. So does my Sancho.

"I guess the city feller's crazy," I hear a husky whisper from the corner.

The farmhands file out. I thank the housewife and attempt to pay the reckoning but she waves away the money.

"We don't take no boarders," she says, "but strangers is always welcome, leastwise if there ain't too many of us eatin'. We can't take 'em in at harvest time."

Sancho puts the steed back into the traces.

The buggy starts, leaps forward into the road and soon we have left the farmhouse far behind…. The sun is lowering, the shadows fall long. Sancho leans back confidentially.

"Say, feller," speaks our squire; "say, feller, if you want ter hear some singin' there's a farmer over here that's got a religion bug. Most every day after dinner somebody's singin' hymns for an hour. 'Onward', 'Christian Soldiers', 'At the Cross', and all those."

I smile feebly and shake my head. Why is it that Natalie Burlin, Loraine Wyman, Frances Densmore, and Cecil Sharp can go out in the morning and return at night with a bundle of songs in Mixolydian, Dorian, and Aeolian modes? Reluctantly, I give the signal to proceed back to the city. I remember that once in Shoreditch I had a similar experience. Seeking the cheapest of the music halls, I entered to find myself surrounded by cockneys so bebuttoned that they seemed to have ransacked all the button factories, the females so befeathered that all the bedraggled plumes in the world seemed to have been collected in that house. At last, I muttered to myself, I will hear a good racy Cockney comic song. The lights went low; a white screen replaced the drop curtain…. It was before the days of moving pictures; the evidence pointed to an illustrated song. A scrawny female in a dirty pink satin dress walked out. "Tike me 'ome to owld New 'Ampshire, mother dear," were her very words. The picture on the screen was Times Square by moonlight.

The tongues of the farmers had been still; even the farmers' wives had been comparatively silent. They had not worked in the cornfields to the accompaniment of some broad sweeping rhythm; I had not heard the suggestion of a pentatonic scale. . . . But as we drove back in silence through this splendid region it came to me that Iowa has her own folk songs. The melody of the yellow warbler, the soft low call of the brown thrasher, the entrancing aspirational cry of the meadowlark mounting to heaven, the whippoorwill shouting his own name, the caw of the crow, the *tap, tap, tap* of the redheaded woodpecker, the shrill raucous shout of the magisterial and quarrelsome blue jay, the heartbreaking dirge-like moan of the mourning dove, the memory of all these reminded me that Iowa has her folk songs, but the corn itself, the unserried ranks of green tassel-bearing stalks growing, almost visibly growing, in the hot cicada-burdened atmosphere, sings, it seems to me, the noblest song of all. The corn song, beginning, no doubt, if one could transcribe its runic accents into our rude Iowa English, "I am the corn!" a noble line, a magnificent refrain which is repeated as far as the eye and ear can reach.

I Am the Corn! is the folk song of Iowa and can it be said that any other state or nation has produced a better song?

From A History of the People of Iowa (1921)

Cyrenus Cole

Cole, introduced previously in this volume (see "A Bit of Holland in America"), penned his complete history of the home state in 1921. Exhaustive in his scholarship, Cole must have reached the last chapter, Chapter LXXXV, winded and research-weary, as he indulges here in memoir. The result is, "A Postscript, Personal"—the final, and most delightful chapter in an otherwise informative book. In it, Cole pays tribute to his mother, and by extension, to all the Iowa women upon whose sacrifices the state rose to prominence.

She [Cole's mother] came to Iowa in 1847, before the state was a year old, and while she herself was still a girl. Sitting by the side of her father on the front seat of a mover's wagon, she first saw the wonderland of the prairies in the waning summertime of that year. To her eyes, it was like the unfolding of a dream in some fairy land. Blashfield's picture in the statehouse at Des Moines, with the winged spirits hovering over the pioneer's wagon, might have been painted from her visionings. Her father, Mathias de Booy, grandson of Cyrenus de Booy, of ancient name, was a man already burdened with years, but he was permitted to live in the land of his adoption until he had increased the psalmist's limit by more than a score. I can just remember him—a man who had participated in the wars of Napoleon in Europe, and who might have witnessed the inauguration of Washington had he been an American citizen. It takes only three generations to encompass all of the marvelous history of America.

They journeyed from Keokuk up the valley of the Des Moines River, following, perhaps, in part the route of the Dragoons in 1835. There were scattered settlements, but the country generally was still an open prairie. It must have been a hard journey, but my mother always spoke of it as a beautiful one. In her old age she seemed to think of it as something she had dreamed when she was a girl. She was young and she was impressionable, and all the things of earth and sky were lovely in her sight. The skies were so vast and so blue, and the flowers were so many and so fair. Doubtless she added to them something of her own loveliness, and sweetened them in her remembrance. But I have tried to write of the prairies as she saw them then, and as she remembered them afterwards. Nor have I found her personal impressions of them at variance with the testimonies of any of the earlier writers, whether French or American. George Catlin, the artist, said over and over that he could find no words to describe the beauties of the prairies, and so did Albert Lea, the soldier and engineer.

I have written not only of the prairies, but I have written of savages who paddled canoes on unmapped rivers; of explorers and adventurers and missionaries; of men who felled the forests and subdued the land; of those who toiled and fought and died; of the sturdy and the strong; of the determined, and the valiant who helped to make this state; of the wise and the unwise who made and unmade her laws—but with all my writing I have felt that there was something omitted, something left out of the story. And that something is the part that women played in the making of Iowa.

History is largely made up of the visible deeds of men. It omits the invisible deeds of women. What wives and mothers suffered and endured and achieved in the seclusion of their homes did not always finds its way into their narratives. The pioneer women did as much as the pioneer men. They ventured as far and often as they hazarded more. By so much as their bodies were weaker and their souls more sensitive, by that much they suffered more. If the labors of men and of women differed in kind, yet were they equal. Men's labors were sometimes done, and but those of women were unceasing. Mothers were busied with their household cares while the men dozed before fires, or slept in their beds. And what the women contributed to the future was as much, or more. They were the conservators of the traditions of the human race, and the perpetuators of the things that are in all times holiest. If the men made the farms and built the cities, the women made the homes and re-created the race. And so I have thought, and I am still thinking, that anything that I may write about my own mother may stand as a tribute to all the pioneer women of Iowa.

In many books that I have been written about pioneer life in the middle west, it has been pictured as petty and monotonous, and as steeped in the melancholies of isolation and despair but while it often partook of such qualities, there was much more in it. Pioneer life had a sweetness and a nobility of its own. It was vast in visions for those who learned to love it, and who by that love were reconciled to its hard labors. But it was worse than misery for those who despised their surroundings and who quarreled with their fate. Its hardships were indeed many, and its discouragements were multitudinous. There were dismal days in summer and stormy ones in winter. Drizzling rains and driven snows found every leak in the roofs and every crevice in the walls of the cabins. In a few cramped rooms the women had to carry on the interminable work of living. Cooking and washing and sewing and sleeping all had to be done in a few rooms, and often in only one. Broods of children had to be cared for, and there must always be a welcome for even the stranger. But for the best of them and for the noblest, labor was love, and love was labor. In such surroundings and so hampered, even the golden threads of romance were woven into the textures of life, although the romances might be of their own thoughts and of the future. At least I like to think this was true of the mother of whom I am writing. Over her memories of the past in Iowa there always seemed to linger the scent of roses, of faded petals in a beautiful jar.

The mother of whom I am writing was not born, nor was she reared, in the west. The blood of the movers did not course in her veins. To her a home was not something on four wheels; it was a fixed place where year after year the same flowers bloomed like familiar faces returned, and where year after year the same birds came to nest and to sing. She belonged to one of the oldest and proudest civilizations of Europe. She came out of surrounding that were ages old, to live in those that were ages young. If the new things thrilled her, the memories of the old must sometimes have depressed her. She was often bewildered. She spoke of wandering out into the prairies like a child lost in a strange land. They seemed so wide and the sky stood so high over them. At night their stillness broken by the howlings of the wolves made her think of death. And when the winds moaned through the grasses by day, their billows reminded her of the seas she had crossed.

I never fully understood what she told me about such feelings and impressions until many years afterwards when for the first time I heard Dvorak's *New World Symphony*—as I listened to that beautiful music I recalled what she had told me, and the meaning of it was made plain to me. She had been homesick amid her new surroundings; she had longed for the old scenes. The composer of that music had lived on the same prairies and he had mingled their moanings with the same memories and longings of an alien soul. As she might have painted Blashfield's picture, so she might have composed Dvorak's music, if the gift and the genius of the painter and the musician had been hers.

But when she had children of her own, the past must have vanished from her mind, for children belong to the future. She was soon dreaming and planning for them in her new multitudinous land. She hoped for them better things than had befallen her—for that is the ever recurring hope of all mothers. When they began to build a college in the town near where she lived—a university they called it in those days—she dreamed and hoped all the more. The projectors of that college thought of it as a voice crying in the wilderness, but she thought of it as a doorway and a gate for her children, for the born and the unborn. In that doorway, they would stand on the threshold of other worlds, and by that gate they would enter the future which she craved for them. Glimpses of other worlds had come to her, and dreams of places whose walls were wider and whose roofs were higher than cabins on the prairies. She told me that as she watched the builders of that college she thought that every brick they laid in mortar was like a kind and comforting word spoken to her. And perhaps her happiest and proudest days were those when her children went to school in that college.

And they were beautiful days—they are still beautiful to me in memory. Bright mornings, noondays steeped in sunshine, and lingering twilights. Balsams and four-o'clocks blossomed in the gardens, verbenas and portulacas crawled out of their beds to burst into bloom, mignonette sweetened the air, and hollyhocks and sunflowers and trailing morning glories vied with each other. Creaking wagons passed slowly by and disappeared on dusty roads. No one was in a hurry, and, perhaps, no one was ever worried over many things.

How times and manners and customs have changed! How simple were human wants in those days, and how complex they are today! What was then a luxury is now hardly a subsistence. What was then a day's journey is now the flight of a moment. In those days they still scanned the almanacs, and every year they read the Bible through to their children from the dewy morning in the Garden of Eden to the effulgent splendors of New Jerusalem of which the seer dreamed in the sunset of his life on Patmos Island. Now in every home in Iowa they read what happened in the world yesterday. The rising sun brings the messages from the four corners of the world, and from the seven seas thereof. What was done in Africa or Asia last night is talked over at the dinner tables of the four corners of the state. Marvelous and miraculous! But if we think of things they dreamed not of, have we not forgotten others which they knew? Even in her day, George Eliot sighed because leisure was gone—"gone where the spinning wheels are gone, and the pack horses, and the slow wagons, and the peddlers who brought bargains to the door on sunny afternoons." Men, and women also, live faster now. They think they live. And yet do they take time to live?

But those days are gone. They will not return. Three hundred thousand automobiles have displaced the creaking wagons. Humanity is now on wheels. It is going up into the air. We call it progress and we boast of it and rejoice in it. But if we must think of those other days as slow and prosaic and uninteresting, still let us not forget that we are the beneficiaries of those who have lived so leisurely then, and who planned so much for the future. We are their debtors—let us pay our debts to them at least in the tokens of remembrance. And let us not despise their ways, lest those who come after us despise our ways.

"The Little Brown Church in the Vale" (1921)

Charlton G. Laird

In the article that follows, reprinted from the 1921 Palimpsest, *then University of Iowa undergraduate and future historical novelist Charlton G. Laird spins one of the strangest, and most inspiring embodiments of the now-classic Iowa mantra "If you build it, they will come," only in reverse. As Laird tells it, William Pitts, on his way to visit his fiancée in Fredericksburg, Iowa, back in 1857, spotted an empty, forested glade in Bradford, Iowa, that inspired a song. When Pitts returned home to Wisconsin after visiting his beloved, he put the sentiment he felt in that valley, "vale" for short, into words, calling it "The Church in the Wildwood" even though no chapel yet existed there. Five years later Pitts returned to teach music at the Bradford Academy and found the church he had imagined miraculously built, and painted brown. In 1865, cash-strapped, he sold the song to a Chicago music publisher for $25, using his profits to enroll in Rush Medical College. After graduation in 1868, Pitts returned to Fredericksburg where he practiced medicine until his retirement in 1906. By the late 1800s Bradford itself had largely been supplanted by Nashua and New Hampton, and the church closed in 1888. The song fell into obscurity until the church was reopened and the tune that inspired it became the signature song of the Depression-era musical group Weatherwax Quartet as they toured throughout North America. In the years since, the song, now known as "The Little Brown Church" has become a standard, and the church that inspired it a major tourist destination reported to be the site of nearly 70,000 weddings since 1918. The church still holds weekly services, gives tours and, of course, hosts weddings—hundreds of them each year. Incidentally, Laird's own story evidences a bit of the Little Brown Church magic. His grandfather had helped build the sanctuary, and this article, written as a term paper encouraged by his teacher Luella Wright, helped introduce him to the world of professional writing.*

At the edge of the now-deserted village of Bradford stands a little, weather-beaten old church, painted a quiet brown and half-hidden among the trees. The bit of forest that civilization has left clustering about the building half hides and half discloses it; the short square belfry is only partly screened by the boughs of several oaks and a towering pine. This is the church immortalized in Dr. William Pitts's lyric song, "The Little Brown Church in the Vale."

The church itself is very plain—plain in a simple, homely way that gives to it a rare charm and beauty. In the simplicity and dignity of the structure are reflected the New England ancestry and training of the architect, the Reverend J. K. Nutting. The main gabled building, low and rather broad, is fronted with a dignified little tower. Everything is neat and unadorned; even the old doors of the Gothic portal are without ornament.

Little and plain as the church is, it represented courageous undertaking on the part of the inhabitants of the village. It was built just after a panic and during a period of inflated war prices. Money was practically unknown; Mr. Nutting indicated this when he wrote that his cash salary for 1859—four dollars—had been brought into the community by an Easterner. In the year 1862 poverty because of war conditions compelled the parish to reduce the minister's salary from five hundred dollars to four hundred and fifty dollars, payable in goods. Wedding fees were in addition, but they might be paid in apples or vegetables. With his characteristic energy, the young pastor not only accepted the reduction, but increased his already heavy burdens by making his acceptance conditional upon the building of a church.

The young men were in the army; those who remained were practically penniless, but they enthusiastically undertook the task. One man donated the lots, a second gave logs, and a third sawed them into lumber. A "bee" quarried the stone, which Leander Smith fitted into a slanting wall. Since his knowledge of masonry came from experience with the fences of Massachusetts, it happens that the foundations of the church have the same inward pitch that he habitually used in New England. The Reverend Mr. Todd, a friend of Mr. Nutting's father, now came to the aid of the little church. A collection from his Sunday school at Pittsfield, Massachusetts, bought the finishing lumber, which was hauled eighty miles by wagon from McGregor . "And so," Mr. Nutting wrote, "we finished the building."

Meanwhile the words of the song "The Little Brown Church in the Vale" had already been written. They had been inspired by the beauty of the spot upon which the church stands, but the picture of the building itself was purely imaginative. Dr. William Pitts, while visiting Bradford in 1857, was impressed by the beauty of the valley that sheltered the little village. Leading from Bradford to Greenwood, a shaded nook on the Red Cedar River was an inviting path that became the haunt of the young physician-musician. Nearly every afternoon of his visit found him following the trail up through the grove of oaks and out across the plain to Greenwood. Just where the verdure of the forest merged into the blossoms of the prairie was a little glade that Dr. Pitts described as "an attractive and lovely spot." And this broadening of the wooded lane into the more open country held for him an enchantment that found expression in his favorite song. The place was also a favorite with the people of Bradford, and it was here, a few years later, that they built the Little Brown Church.

The song was written at Dr. Pitts's home in Wisconsin, but it was first publicly sung in the church which it eventually named. A passionate lover of beauty, the young doctor carried home with him a vivid picture of the little prairie valley, and embodied this vision in what the world knows as "The Little Brown Church in the Vale." Five years later, Dr. Pitts moved to Iowa and settled in the neighboring town of Fredericksburg, but twenty miles from the Little Brown Church, then in the process of construction. In taking charge of the musical organizations of southern Chickasaw County, he became the teacher of a little singing school at Bradford. In the spring of 1864, Mr. Nutting, who was a member of the doctor's class, led the party to the church which, although enclosed, was as yet unfinished; and here, to an audience seated upon improvised board benches, Dr. Pitts sang from his original manuscript the song. Thus the bare, unplastered walls that the lines immortalized were the first to echo their sweet melodies.

The song became immensely popular. It was sung throughout the country and before the royal courts of Europe. Bradford's little church, already closely connected with the song, soon became definitely identified with it. The building, dedicated on December 29, 1864, only a few months prior to the publication of the song in Chicago, had been appropriately painted brown. Whether this was due to the cheapness of brown paint or whether it is traceable to a desire to conform with the published poem will probably never be known.

The building that we know as the Little Brown Church expresses very well the sentiment of the lyric whose name it bears. It may be interesting to note just how the little church has fulfilled the statements and predictions of each stanza of the poem. Allowance must be made, however, for the fact that at the time of writing the nook selected by Dr. Pitts had never been popularly considered as the site for a place of worship, and that the church and graveyard of the song are the product of an idealistic imagination that felt no necessity for conformity with the real.

> There's a church in the valley by the wildwood,
> No lovelier spot in the dale.
> No spot is so dear to my childhood,
> As the little brown church in the vale.

The valley that shelters the church is charming in its simple beauty. The building stands at the edge of the break in the prairie. To the east, and yet really including the church within its borders, lies the vale, scatteringly wooded and appropriately set with the old-fashioned buildings. To the west stretches the blossoming prairie until it ends in the wooded skyline along the Red Cedar River. A few rods from the church a wooden bridge spans the grassy-banked creek that courses through the valley. It all reminds one very much of an etching of an

English landscape. Lofty oaks and stately pines still enshrine the little church, but the wildwood of the poems has gone with the life of the village that it surrounded. In the days when Dr. Pitts described the village as "a veritable beehive of industry," Bradford boasted of two saw mills, and these were so busy that the logs for the frame of the church had to wait several months before there was room for them in the millyard. The size of the forest monarchs that once surrounded the church is indicated by a black walnut timber, three feet square and forty feet long, which supported the top saw in one of these mills. A very pretty grove still clusters about the little building, and though it is but a suggestion of the former wealth of verdure, it forms a glade that at once secludes and dignifies the structure. This simple little church has sequestered itself among the protecting foliage, and there, enshrined in memories, it continues in its quite homely way.

> How Sweet on a bright Sabbath morning,
> To list to the clear ringing bell,
> Its tones so sweetly are calling,
> Oh come to the church in the dell.

The praise of the bell is upheld in the love that the community bore it. Bells play a prominent part in many of Dr. Pitts's songs, but no other ever held for him the charm of the one whose soft enticing tones he immortalized. "The Bells of Shannon" may be as grand as the poet has pictured them, but you will never convince an old Bradfordite that they can rival the dear sweet tones of the bell that calls for the Little Brown Church. "The bell," it was called throughout the countryside, for it was the only one in the country and was the pride of all Bradford. Cast in Meneeley's famous foundry at Troy, New York, it was personally selected by Mr. Nutting because of its clear, sweet tone. The bell was obtained through the benevolences of the young pastor's eastern friends; the inscription proclaimed it the gift of Mr. Thomas Cole and Catherine, his wife. Brought from Dubuque by wagon, the bell was rung almost the entire distance, and a considerable crowd gathered to view its entrance into the village, for the arrival of the "the bell" was an event in Bradford's history.

> There close by the church in the valley,
> lies one I loved so well.
> She sleeps, quietly sleeps 'neath the willow,
> Disturb not her rest in the vale.

A pretty myth to the effect that Mrs. Pitts was buried at the Little Brown Church has grown around the sentiment expressed in this stanza. To the rear of the church is a little swale that would have been beautiful as a graveyard. This is the mythical resting place of Mrs. Pitts, and here the willows still grow, just as the poet described them. But there are no signs that the spot was ever used as a burying ground. The writing of the lyric seven years before the dedication of the church accounts for the inconsistency in regard to the graveyard. At the time of writing, Dr. Pitts never suspected that a house of worship would later be built upon the very spot on which he erected his dream church. With his usual sense of aesthetic fitness, he not only created the church for which nature had supplied the setting, but he added the churchyard that completed the picture.

> There close by the side of the loved one
> 'Neath the tree where the wildflowers bloom,
> When the farewell hymn shall be changed,
> I shall rest by her side in the tomb.

The sentiment of this stanza was fulfilled in the case of Dr. Pitts, though the burial did not take place at the Little Brown Church. In his later life, the doctor moved to Clarion, Iowa, and then to Brooklyn, New York, where he died in 1918. The ceremony for him at Fredericksburg was fittingly simple; the singing of "The City Four Square" by his eight-year-old grandson was the only distinguishing feature. He was buried beside his wife in the local cemetery at Fredericksburg where at last he "rests by her side in the tomb."

The very simpleness of The Little Brown Church endears it to all who knew old Bradford. After all, it is only a little, very plain, storm-beaten church. But within it dwell the hope and love of God-fearing pioneers; around it cling the fondest memories that a scattered people cherish for their deserted village.

From **Vandemark's Folly (1922)**

Herbert Quick

A favorite by those who find Iowa Realists Hamlin Garland and Ruth Suckow too depressing, [John] Herbert Quick proved a late bloomer as an imaginative writer, publishing the first book in his so-called "Iowa Trilogy" (Vandemark's Folly in 1922; The Hawkeye in 1923; and The Invisible Woman in 1924) after the ripe old age of sixty. But Quick, born on a farm near the Grundy-Hardin County line not far from the town of Steamboat Rock, was plenty busy before that, working as a teacher, school principal, lawyer, and mayor of Sioux City from 1898 to 1900. That taste of government and its efficacy led Quick to an appointment by President Woodrow Wilson to the newly created Federal Farm Loan Bureau and to an editorship at the national ag journal Farm and Fireside. While the selection that follows, from Vandemark's Folly, is a fiction, as is its setting, Monterey County, it portrays faithfully the spirit of the journey many Yankee pioneers made from New York to Iowa in the days before the Civil War. A passionate devotee of Iowa, Quick often leaves the expression of his high regard to his somewhat autobiographical characters, such as Fremont McConkey, who in The Hawkeye says, "I know if the artist born in Iowa could only be allowed such a life of the soul as would impel him to respect his Iowa materials, and to ponder them long enough and deeply enough, every element of great art would be found here." Quick's sentiments, here given voice by McConkey, anticipate the Regionalist manifesto later articulated by Grant Wood. Above all, Quick was, as many an Iowan before him, a survivor, having beat polio as a child and survived a hemorrhaging ulcer while heading up the Red Cross Commission in Vladivostock. Quick's protagonist in Vandemark's Folly, J. T. Vandemark, is likewise possessed of sturdy body and sweeping vision, as the selections below (collaged from the chapters entitled "I Become Cow Vandemark," "Adventure on Ridge Road," "An Embarrassing Addition," and "Rowena's Way Out") make clear.

The work of writing the history of this township—I mean Vandemark Township, Monterey County, State of Iowa—has been turned over to me. I have been asked to do this I guess because I was the first settler in the township; it was named after me; I live on my own farm—the oldest farm operated by the original settler in this part of the country; I know the history of these thirty-six square miles of land and also of the wonderful swarming of peoples which made the prairies over; and the agent of the Excelsior County History Company of Chicago, having heard of me as an authority on local history, has asked me to write this part of their new History of Monterey County for which they are now canvassing for subscribers. I can never write this as it ought to be written, and for an old farmer with no learning to try to do it may seem impudent, but sometimes a great genius may come up who will put on paper the strange and splendid story of Iowa, of Monterey County, and of Vandemark Township; and when he does write this, the greatest history ever written, he may find such adventures as mine of some use to him. Those who lived this history are already few in number, are fast passing away and will soon be gone. I lived it, and so did my neighbors and old companions and friends. So here I begin*

After a few miles, we reached a point from which I could see the Iowa prairie sweeping away as far as the eye could see. I drew out by the roadside to look at it, as a man appraises one with whom he must live—as a friend or an enemy.

I shall never forget the sight. It was like a great green sea. The old growth had been burned the fall before, and the spring grass scarcely concealed the brown sod on the uplands; but all the swales were coated thick with an emerald growth full-bite high, and in the deeper, wetter hollows grew cowslips, already showing their glossy, golden flowers. The hillsides were thick with the woolly possblummies in their furry spring coats protecting them against the frost and chill, showing purple-violet on the outside of a cup filled with golden stamens, the first fruits of the prairie flowers; on the warmer southern slopes a few of the splendid birdsfoot violets of the prairie were showing the azure color which would soon make some of the hillsides as blue as the sky; and standing higher than the peering grass rose the rough-leafed stalks of green which would soon show us the yellow puccoons and sweet williams and scarlet lilies and shooting stars, and later the yellow rosin-weeds, Indian dye flower and goldenrod. The keen northwest wind swept before it a flock of white clouds; and under the clouds went their shadows, walking over the lovely hills like dark ships over an emerald sea.

The wildfowl were clamoring north for the summer's campaign of nesting. Everywhere the sky was harrowed by the wedged wild geese, their voices as sweet as organ tones; and ducks quacked, whistled and whirred overhead, a true rain of birds beating up against the wind. Over every slew, on all sides, thousands of ducks of many kinds, and several sorts of geese hovered, settled, or burst up in eruptions of birds, their back-feathers shining like bronze as they turned so as to reflect the sunlight to my eyes; while so far up that they looked like specks, away above the wind it seemed, so quietly did they circle and sail, floated huge flocks of cranes—the sandhill cranes in their slaty-gray, and the whooping cranes, white as snow with black heads and feet, each bird with a ten-foot spread of wing, piping their wild cries which fell down to me as if from another world.

It was sublime! Bird, flower, grass; cloud, wind, and the immense expanse of sunny prairie, swelling up into undulations like a woman's breast turgid with milk. I forgot myself and my position in the world, my loneliness, my strange passenger, the problems of my life; my heart swelled, and my throat filled. I sat looking at it, with the tears trickling from my eyes, the uplift of my soul more than I could bear. It was not the thought of my mother that brought the tears to my eyes, but my happiness in finding the newest, strangest, most delightful, sternest, most wonderful thing in the world—the Iowa prairie—that made me think of my mother. If I only could have found her alive! If I only could have had her with me!*

This last bit of it [the Old Ridge Road] ran across a school section that had been left in prairie sod till then. The past came rolling back upon me as I stopped my horses and looked at it, a wonderful road, that never was a highway in law, curving about the side of a knoll, the comb between the tracks carrying its plume of tall spear grass, its barbed shafts just ripe for boys to play Indian with, which bent over the two tracks, washed deep by the rains, and blown out by the winds; and where the trail had crossed a wet place, the grass and weeds still showed the effects of the plowing and puddling of the thousands of wheels and hoofs which had poached up the black soil into bubbly mud as the road spread out into a bulb of traffic where the pioneering drivers sought for tough sod which would bear up their wheels. A plow had already begun its work on this last piece of the Old Ridge Road, and as I stood there, the farmer who was breaking it up came by with his big plow and four horses, and stopped to talk with me.

"What made that old road?" I asked.

"Vell," said he, "dot's more as I know. Somebody, I dank."

And yet, the history of Vandemark Township was in that old road that he complained of because he couldn't do a good job of breaking across it—he was one of those German settlers, or the son of one, who invaded the state after the rest of us had opened it up.

The Old Ridge Road went through Dyersville, Manchester, Independence, Waterloo, and on to Fort Dodge—but beyond there both the road and—so far as I know —the country itself was a vague and undefined thing.

So also was the road itself beyond the Iowa River, and for that matter it got to be less and less a beaten track all the way as the wagons spread out fanwise to the various fords and ferries and as the movers stopped and settled like nesting cranes. Of course there was a fringe of well-established settlements a hundred miles or so beyond Fort Dodge, of people who, most of them, came up the Missouri River.

Our Iowa wilderness did not settle up in any uniform way, but was inundated as a field is overspread by a flood; only it was a flood which set upstream. First the Mississippi had its old town, away off south of Iowa, near its mouth; then the people worked up to the mouth of the Missouri and made another town; then the human flood crept up the Mississippi and the Missouri, and Iowa was reached; then the Iowa valleys were occupied by the river immigration, and the tide of settlement rose until it broke over the hills on such routes as the Old Ridge Road; by these cross-country streams here and there met other trickles of population which had come up the belts of forest on the streams. I was steering right into the wilderness; but there were far islands of occupation—the heft of the earliest settlements strongly Southern in character—on each of the Iowa streams which I was to cross, snuggled down in the wooded bottomlands on the Missouri, and even away beyond at Salt Lake, and farther off in Oregon and California where the folk freshet broke on the Pacific—a wave of humanity dashing against a reef of water.

Of course, I knew very little of these things as I sat there, ignorant as I was, looking out over the grassy sea, in my prairie schooner, my four cows panting from the climb, and with the yellow-haired young woman beside me, who had been wished on me by the black-bearded man on leaving the Illinois shore. Most of it I still had to spell out through age and experience, and some reading. I only knew that I had been told that the Ridge Road would take me to Monterey County, if the weather wasn't too wet, and I didn't get drowned in a freshet at a ferry or slowed down and permanently stuck fast somewhere with all my goods.

"Gee-up," I shouted to my cows, and cracked my blacksnake over their backs; and they strained slowly into the yoke. The wagon began chuck-chucking along into the unknown.*

I know communities in Iowa that went into evil ways, and were blighted through the poison distilled into their veins by a few of the earliest settlers; I know others that began with a few strong, honest, thinking, reading, praying families, and soon began sending out streams of good influence which had a strange power for better things; I knew other settlements in which there was a feud from the beginning between the bad and the good; and in some of them the blight of the bad finally overwhelmed the good, while in others the forces of righteousness at last grappled with the devil's gang, and, sometimes in violence, redeemed the neighborhood to a place in the light.*

[I] set out on my way over the Old Ridge Road for the West. The spring was by this time broadening into the loveliest of all times on the prairies (when the weather is fine), the days of the fun blowth of the upland birdsfoot violets. Some southern slopes were so blue with them that you could hardly tell the distant hill from the sky, except for the greening of the peeping grass. The possblummies were still blowing, but only the later ones. The others were aging into tassels of down.

The Canada geese, except for the nesters, had swept on in that marvelous, ranked army which ends the migration, spreading from the east to the west some warm morning when the wind is south, and extending from a hundred feet in the air to ten thousand, all moved by a common impulse like myself and my fellow migrants, pressing northward though, instead of westward, with the piping of a thousand organs, their wings whirring, their eyes glistening as if with some mysterious hope, their black-webbed feet folded and stretched out behind, their necks strained out eagerly to the north, and held a little high I thought as if to peer over the horizon to catch a glimpse of their promised land of blue lakes, tall reeds, and broad fields of water-celery and wild rice, with dry nests downy with the harvests of their gray breasts; and fluffy goslings swimming in orderly classes after their teachers. And up from the south following these old honkers came the snow geese, the Wilson geese, and all the other little geese (we ignorantly called all of them "brants"), with their wild flutings like the high notes of clarinets—and the ponds became speckled with teal and coot.

The prairie chickens now became the musicians of the morning and evening on the uplands, with their wild and intense and almost insane chorus, repeated over and over until it seemed as if the meaning of it must be forced upon every mind like a figure in music played with greatening power by a violinist so that the heart finally almost breaks with it—*Ka-a-a-a-a, ka, ka, ka, ka! Ka-a-a-aa-a-a, ka, ka, ka, ka, ka, ka, ka! KA-A-A-A-A-A-A, ka, ka, ka, ka, ka, ka, ka, ka!*—Oh, there is no way to tell it—and then the cock filled in the harmony with his lovely contribution: facing the courted hen, he swelled out the great orange globes at the sides of his head, fluffed out his feathers, strutted forward a few steps, and tolled his deep-toned bell, with all the skill of a ventriloquist, making it seem far away. When he was on a nearby knoll, like a velvet gong sounded with no stroke of the hammer, as if it spoke from some inward vibration set up by a mysterious current—a liquid *Do, re, me,* here full and distinct, there afar off, the whole air tremulous with it, the harmony to the ceaseless fugue in the soprano clef of the rest of the flock—nobody will ever hear it again! Nobody ever drew from it, and from the howling of the wolves, the honking of the geese, the calls of the ducks, the strange cries of the cranes as they soared with motionless wings high overhead, or rowed their way on with long slow strokes of their great wings, or danced their strange reels and cotillions in the twilight; and from the myriad voices of curlew, plover, gopher, bobolink, meadowlark, dick-cissel, killdeer and the rest—day-sounds and night-sounds, dawn-sounds and dusk-sounds—more inspiration than did the stolid Dutch boy plodding west across Iowa that spring of 1855, with his fortune in his teams of cows, in the covered wagon they drew, and the deed to his farm in a flat packet of treasures in a little ironbound trunk—among them a rain-stained letter and a worn-out woman's shoe.*

I let my horse walk. The fire was farther off, now; but the sky, now flecked with drifting clouds, was red with its light, and the sight was one which I shall never see again, which I suppose nobody will ever see again; for I do not believe there will ever be seen such an expanse of grass as that of Iowa at that time. I have seen prairie fires in Montana and Western Canada; but they do not compare to the prairie fires of old Iowa. None of these countries bears such a coating of grass as came up from the black soil of Iowa; for their climate is drier. I can see that sight as if it were before my eyes now. The roaring came no longer to my ears as I rode on through the night, except faintly when the breeze, which had died down, sprang up as the fire reached some swale covered with its ten-foot high sawgrass. Then, I could see from the top of some rising ground the flames leap up, reach over, catch in front of the line, kindle a new fire, and again be overleaped by a new tongue of fire, so that the whole line became a belt of flames, and appeared to be rolling along in a huge billow of fire, three or four rods across, and miles in length.

The advance was not in a straight line. In some places for one reason or another, the thickness or thinness of the grass, the slope of the land, or the varying strength of the wind, the fire gained or lost ground. In some places great patches of land were cut off as islands by the joining of advanced columns ahead of them, and lay burning in triangles and circles and hollow squares of fire, like bodies of soldiers falling behind and formed to defend themselves against pursuers. All this unevenness of line, with the varying surface of the lovely Iowa prairie, threw the fire into separate lines and columns and detachments more and more like burning armies as they receded from view.

Sometimes a whole mile or so of the line disappeared as the fire burned down into lower ground; and then with a swirl or flame and smoke, the smoke luminous in the glare, it moved magnificently up into sight, rolling like a breaker of fire bursting on a reef of land, buried the hillside in flame, and then whirled on over the top, its streamers flapping against the horizon, snapping off shreds of flame into the air, as triumphantly as a human army taking an enemy fort. Never again, never again! We went through some hardships, we suffered some ills to be pioneers in Iowa; but I would rather have my grandsons see what I saw and feel what I felt in the conquest of these prairies, than to get up by their radiators, step into their baths, whirl themselves away in their cars, and go to universities. I am glad I had my share in those old, sweet, grand, beautiful things—the things which never can be again.

An old man looks back on things passed through as sufferings, and feels a thrill when he identifies them as among the splendors of life. Can anything more clearly prove the vanity of human experiences? But look at the wonders which have come out of those days. My youth has already passed into a period as legendary as the days when King Alfred hid in the swamp and was reproved by the peasant's wife for burning the cakes. I have lived on my Iowa farm from times of bleak wastes, robber bands, and savage primitiveness, to this day, when my state is almost as completely developed as Holland. If I have a pride in it, if I look back to those days as worthy of record, remember that I have some excuse. There will be no other generation of human beings with a life so rich in change and growth. And there never was such a thing in all the history of the world before.

FROM **DRUIDA (1923)**

JOHN T. FREDERICK

John Towner Frederick embodies, in his literary work, a quintessential Iowa spirit—the dual spirit of husbandman and midwife. Though a writer of considerable talent and vision, the Corning, Iowa-born Frederick spent most of his energies championing the work of fellow Iowa scribes Paul Engle, Ruth Suckow, Paul Corey, Marquis Childs, MacKinlay Kantor, and Phil Stong, among many others, in the pages of the legendary journal he founded, the Midland. *But Frederick was no ivory tower intellectual, as he balanced various professorships (at the University of Iowa, at Northwestern University and Notre Dame) with literal field work with his father and two sons on the farm. As early as his first attempt at earning a degree from the University of Iowa, Frederick scrubbed floors and washed dishes at the YMCA to pay his way. He made it one year at the U of I, then dropped out to serve as principal and superintendent of a tiny school in Prescott, Iowa, where he coached football and earned a whopping $75 a month to add to the savings that would eventually allow him to re-enroll at Iowa. While he moved the* Midland *to Chicago in 1930, from where he served as a professor at Northwestern, directed that city's WPA Writers' Project, and hosted a weekly book review program,* Of Men and Books, *for CBS Radio, he eventually returned to teach at the University of Iowa, retiring in 1970. Forever caught between two worlds—as the title of the 2005 anthology of farmer-writers* Black Earth and Ivory Tower *captures it—Frederick consistently advocated for the visceral life of the farm, as in this passage from the pages of the May-June 1928 issue of the* Midland: *"Increasingly numerous and influential in American letters are those writers and critics who are urban to the core of their experience. The older American writer, like Americans of an earlier generation generally, was typically a man or woman familiar with farm and village life, acquainted with occupations and emotions intimately related to the earth. His study window opened on the fields. Sky, soil, and sun were real to him." In the passage below, from his first novel,* Druida, *the protagonist, Druida Horsfall finds herself at loose ends in a rural town, contemplating her future at a teacher's college. Fortunately, she finds a mentor in the doctor, whose platonic interests propel young Druida into a wider, more cosmopolitan world, a world which she ultimately abandons in favor of a life on the farm. Frederick's advice to Iowa young people is ably expressed in the words of the protagonist in Frederick's second and final novel,* Green Bush *(1925), in which Frank Thompson concludes, "It isn't what a man does that counts to him. It's what he thinks and feels that make his life."*

The afternoon visit to Bella was duly made, and her chatter over the hairdressing held Druida at the store until dark. "I must hurry," she told Bella, and wearing the newly fitted dress and leaving her hair in its heavy coils high on her head, she ran lightly down the street and up to the doctor's door. As she hung her coat and cap on a hook and turned toward the fire, she caught in the doctor's face a look which surprised her.

"You—" he hesitated, flushed—"is that the dress you told us about at noon, then? It most certainly is becoming." Her run in the cold air had colored Druida's cheeks brilliantly, and as she turned slowly at the doctor's request to show the effect of the dress from all angles, the black and purple made her truly what Bella had said—"a regular beauty."

"Supper's waiting," observed Emma from the kitchen door. Her mouth was grim. "I'll do the dishes myself," she stated firmly after the meal. "You don't want to splash up that fine dress."

Druida hesitated unhappily. "Just sit down then a while," said the doctor quietly. "I can talk to you while I smoke my cigar." In a few minutes he was talking of China. Druida did not notice when Emma went to bed, so absorbing was his broken narrative. In the evenings that followed, she learned to know Dr. Thompson as she had known no other person. Now consciously, with a pathetic outreaching for sympathy and understanding, now unconsciously as though thinking aloud, he revealed himself to her. She saw through his eyes the pageant of oriental life, with its opulent coloring heightened by the strangely contrasting bareness of Stablesburg. She perceived that the man's real life for twenty years had lain in that brilliant subjective world, made luminous and poignant for him by its final memories. "You may wonder why I don't show you coins or curios," he remarked one time. "When I came from Shanghai I brought with me nothing—nothing that I could carry in my hands."

"I have no longing to see the outside world," he told her at another time, his mild blue eyes assuming that piercing, abstracted look which she learned to associate with his gravest utterances. "My world is bigger than it seems."

She caught glimpses of his practice—the strange, the pathetic, the sordid. He confessed to her, with tears in his eyes, errors of which he had never spoken. She sensed the singleness of his devotion to his work, his generosity, his tolerance. Once he spoke of the time of her birth: the cold drive, Ma Beck. Then he fell silent, his eyes impenetrable; at this she wondered.

In her turn Druida confided to the doctor some of her enthusiasms, spoke haltingly of vague aspirations. "I want to do something with my life; I don't know what," she said.

"I suppose I ought to advise you," he spoke slowly. "But I cannot—I seldom offer advice except of a medical nature." He chuckled a little, then his eyes became serious. "Human lives touch each other so uncertainly. The bridges from one set of experiences to another are so unsteady and unsure. Here I have been telling you things I have never told before. Strangely, you have come nearer to me than has anyone—for twenty years. And yet I do not know what your life will be tomorrow—I do not know."

"I appreciate your confidence," she said softly.

"I do not feel worthy of it. It seems very wonderful to me."

"Say nothing of that," he answered. "You are giving me far more than I give you—just in response, understanding. I had not known how lonely I was for someone I could talk to." He smoked a while in silence, then spoke defensively, as to himself. "It is not your physical attractiveness that is responsible, though you have beauty—beauty of a purity and strength I have seen most rarely. It is because your mind is beautiful, too." His face clouded. He puffed vigorously. "Young Hiram Cassidy spoke to me about you today. He wanted me to persuade you to take a business course; said he would give you a place in the bank; offered to lend you money; I promised to tell you about it."

"I told him I am going to the Normal," said Druida positively.

The doctor did not reply at once. "Good looks will not be your undoing," he said finally. "But it may bring some annoyances."

Emma's hostility increased from day to day. "I can't keep up the pretence of working for my board," Druida told the doctor. "I must go somewhere else."

"No, no—do not mind Emma. She is a good housekeeper, but she is not a companion. I fear she is a little jealous, absurdly enough. But I am very sorry she makes things unpleasant."

"But I can't stay—just as a guest, Doctor. It isn't right to you."

"I am enjoying your presence more than that of any visitor I can think of. But if you are going to worry about it, you may pay board for the rest of the time. We'll tell Emma that, and you can settle with me when you go."

Bella's interest in Druida led her to suggest certain real bargains in various materials which the girl would need for aprons and lingerie, and Druida spent much of her time sewing in her room, or even at the store, where Bella proffered the use of "the machine," and helped her with the cutting and planning. "You'd make a dandy dressmaker," she told her pupil.

One day Druida ate little at noon, and when the doctor pressed her she admitted a slight headache.

"You were up too late last evening, I should certainly suppose," said Emma venomously. "You were still downstairs when I went to sleep. You must like the smell of cigars."

"Come with me for a drive this afternoon," the doctor told her. "It will be good for you—you're staying in too closely."

He had been taking his rickety Ford on recent drives, since the roads had partially dried. But this afternoon he ordered a team, and they jogged slowly over the level miles toward the northwest. Everywhere discs and seeders were traveling back and forth across the vividly black fields.

"I wish I were younger," the doctor told Druida wistfully. "I would go out and farm. If I didn't get out in the country on drives I don't know how I could stand it. The soil calls me. I was raised on a farm in Illinois: maybe I should have stayed there, as my father wished. But my father and mother are dead long since, the farm is sold—and I'm an old man, Druida. I did buy some land a few years back—a big tract of wild land—not paid for yet by a good way. Guess it will make me some money if I can hold it long enough. But that isn't what I wanted—I dreamed of farming it—but I'm too old."

Druida was silent.

The call was at a tiny farmhouse by a marshy lake. Druida watched the brown ducks dipping for food among the broken reeds, their tails up, their feet kicking to keep their heads submerged. The slow drive home was infinitely restful. The girl seemed to feel strength filling her from the fields ready for the seeding, the stainless sky, the gentle man who rode beside her.

As they neared the town the cloudless sunset behind it climbed swiftly to an orange blaze of consummate brilliance, against which the elevator and the stores and dwellings along the level streets were outlined in sharp black masses, weirdly portentous.

"Iowa" (1926)

Ruth Suckow

Another of Iowa's well-known authors now sadly slipped from national view, Ruth Suckow's life touched many Iowa communities—Hawarden, where she was born, Grinnell, where she attended college, and Earlville, where, post graduate school, she established an apiary. Her father, a traveling Congregational minister, also exposed her to other small Iowa communities, including LeMars, Algona, and Manchester. Suckow thrived with a little help from her friends—H. L. Mencken, who helped placed her work in Smart Set *and* American Mercury, *and John T. Frederick, who saw to it that her work appeared in the* Midland. *Having found an audience, Suckow the short story writer turned into Suckow the novelist, publishing a handful of respected novels, most concerning the struggles of Iowa farm families, and especially women, to find happiness and beauty amid restrictive cultures. Restless, Suckow and her husband lived, at various times, in New Mexico, Virginia, Arizona, and, of course, Iowa, which affected her more deeply than any other place, as her essay "Iowa," originally appearing in* American Mercury, *demonstrates. The tone is perhaps best described as "tough love," evident in the unapologetic utterance of Iowa truisms such as: "Many young people forced themselves away and doomed themselves to a kind of rootless exile simply to prove themselves socially or intellectually and artistically enterprising, and to escape the stigma attached to 'just settling down at home.'"*

Iowa is, in a way, the center of the big region called the Middle West. It combines the qualities of half a dozen states; and perhaps that is the reason why it so often seems, and more to its own people than to any others, the most undistinguished place in the world. Its northern corner borders on Minnesota, and is windy and sloughy, with numerous lakes and Scandinavian towns. The beautiful northeastern portion is like an extension of the woods and dells of Wisconsin. The southern part is tinged with the softness, laxness and provincialism of Missouri and Arkansas. Much of the west is flat, windy, harsh, like Kansas, Nebraska or the Dakotas. The central portion is the very heart of the prairie region—smooth, plain, simple, fresh, and prosperous. All these differing elements, however, are smoothed down with a touch of gentleness into that lovely, open pastoral quality which is peculiarly Iowan after all.

The culture of the state is composed of elements seemingly as various. The early influx from the South softened the intense fiber of its Puritan inheritance and gave it a certain easy-going quality. This Southern influence lingers now about the Mississippi and in out-of-the-way hill and timber regions where little settlements unbelievably primitive can still be found. The state is dotted all over with communities of Europeans: German, Dutch, Scandinavian, Welsh, Bohemian, Scotch, and Irish, and English of fairly recent immigration. But many of these have been so thoroughly assimilated into the life of the state as to be virtually indistinguishable from what we call the native stock. Even their churches are rapidly going under and the few old people who cling to their native languages are relegated to the evening services which no one else wants to attend.

These are all, however, underlying fertilizing elements. "Culture" as it has been known in Iowa—and it is a term of great repute—has been derived almost wholly from the Eastern States and particularly from New England. New Englanders brought culture to the new state as once they had brought their religion to the new continent. But with an important difference. It was not a primary but a side issue. These people did not come to Iowa to plant this sacred culture in the wilderness. They came to farm and to acquire land. The settlement of Iowa (in spite of all its band of home missionaries) was frankly material in its nature, as was that of the whole Middle West. Therefore, culture was cherished with devotion, perhaps, but not with confidence. In spite of the number of colleges early dedicated to it, Iowans never have, and do not to this day, quite believe in the possibility of its existence among them in any strong degree. When their forefathers went out to the raw country, it was with the belief that they were leaving culture behind. Thus Iowans have always felt themselves in the nature of intellectual poor relations to the Eastern states. And New Englanders, especially, have never got over a home missionary attitude toward them.

Thus has grown up a timid, fidgety, hesitant state of mind. Iowa has never had a rampant boosterism of Kansas and Minnesota, although Rotary and Kiwanis are now laboring hard. It has always been far too deprecatory and self-doubting for that. It has even railed at its generally healthy climate. Its "well-fixed" ancients have sought climate in the West, and its aspiring young intellectuals culture in the East. Iowans are great travelers. Their foreign colonies in California, Florida, Boston and New York are always among the largest. This comes chiefly from their humility. Some are dissatisfies and come back; but the most that is permitted them to say is: "Well, I guess old Iowa isn't such a bad place after all." Anything more would be a proof of ignorance.

Iowa is proud—fairly proud—of its material prosperity, its land and corn and hogs. But like an old farmer—or rather, like a timid farmer wife—it has taken it for granted that other things are really above it. It has copied its best houses from New England and California, disregarding climatic and topographical conditions in its faith that only something from somewhere else can really be artistic. Until the last very few years it has been accepted almost without question that its young intellectuals must go away preferably to New York, but at least away!—in order to find something "interesting" to write about. Interest in Iowa's own towns and plain people was a direct blow to "culture."

This thing called culture, in Iowa, has always been accepted as a distinctly feminine affair. The men went out here for business. They left all such things to the women. Puritan mothers brought along their cherished ideals of New England culture as they brought family heirlooms and slips for houseplants. Schoolteachers, especially in colleges, taught these ideals with the zeal of devotees. Twenty years ago, every Iowa schoolroom had a picture, enlarged, of its own poet on the wall; and the poets were, of course, Henry Wadsworth Longfellow, John Greenleaf, Whittier, James Russell Lowell, Oliver Wendell Holmes, and Cecilia Thaxter. Emerson was above our heads. Whitman, needless to say, was beyond the pale. Such a native genius as Thoreau was far too rugged for genuine culture esteem. Mark Twain was a rude Westerner. *Huckleberry Finn* and *Tom Sawyer* might be exciting, but they were bad, rough books, and the librarian really did not think they should be given to children. Thus were the best elements of our national culture preserved.

But always, in this noble striving to keep the lamp of culture burning, there was a sad and hopeless feeling that it must be against terrible odds. How could we—so young and crude and raw, so far from the center of refinement in Massachusetts—aspire to do more than keep the little light from flickering out, and perhaps kindle a tiny flame that would show the rich relations we were not wholly benighted? We had our colleges—dozens of them—with their traditions cherished all the more fervently because so new. And they did very well—if we did not have the money to go East to school.

There was good reason for this hopelessness. The whole Middle West was big, breezy, and plain. It was miscellaneous. The spare, narrow intensity of New England was out of place on the prairies. Even the type of face (as Sinclair Lewis noted in *Main Street*) changed from the thin and bleak to the round and pink. Prosperity came with the second, sometimes even with the first, generation. There was hard work and plain living; but why should there be spare living in the midst of acres and acres of great far cornfields growing out of the richest, most fertile soil on earth? Spare living and transcendental thinking did not go with the Iowa landscape, but with

> ...the stony fields where clear
> Through the thin trees the skies appear,
> In delicate spare soil and fen,
> And slender landscape and austere.

Really heroic efforts were made to preserve the old ideals. Little delicate children of New Englanders were carefully set apart, guarding in speech and action from the common herd, and destined for Wellesley. Every religious denomination set up two or three colleges. The Colonial Dames and the D. A. R. [Daughters of the American Revolution] held off the rabble. One family even papered the walls of a necessary building with quotations from Emerson for the spiritual edification of its children; devotion to the finer things can not be expected to go much farther than that. But it was like holding a little fort against the barbarians. And instead of being sent reinforcements from the central citadel, the poor meek outlanders were sneered upon and neglected.

It might have been a simpler problem had our earlier settlers actually been aborigines. But they were beings from nations that had already reached a degree of civilization. Distance could differentiate, but not completely separate them. Cultural activities had to be suspended for a time while the people made for themselves a secure shelter in this new wilderness. Raw nature was conquered almost within the space of generation. The material basis was quickly established and invigorated by change, the other activities should be quickly resumed.

This was where the difficulty came in. For the sheer distance had wrought a difference, just as the loyal torchbearers had feared. The elements of population were diverse. They could not fit into that New England mold of culture which was the only conceivable mold. It was as if a young sculptor had been given tools carefully preserved for him but designed for a material not his, and told at the same time that it would be a crime against art to devise others; or as if with unused clay all about him and tempting him to design, he had been warned that only that far away somewhere, the nature of which he did not understand, could ever be fit for design at all. There were books, and reading was not a lost art. But there seemed to be no bridging of the gulf between the experience of life and the experience of books. Culture, art, beauty, were fixed in certain places.

This faith was so drilled into the children in various and subtle ways that all our bright young people grew up with the most curious sense of exile. An instance may be taken from *Main Street*, for the thing was true of the whole Middle West. At first glance, it would seem incongruous that Carol Kennicott, born in Mankato, Sinclair Lewis carefully tells us, was not a prairie town but "green-and-white New England reborn." Had Carol been born in Gopher Prairie itself, of devout New England parents, she would have felt the same. And had she been born in Iowa, her faith would have been disputed by no one, not even by Doc Kennicott himself.

It was an axiom of youth that the hometown was "dead." All sorts of changes, from the facetious to the agonizing, were rung upon this theme—and with partial truth. Many young people forced themselves away and doomed themselves to a kind of rootless exile simply to prove themselves socially or intellectually and artistically enterprising, and to escape the stigma attached to "just settling down at home." To say of a bright young man when college was over, "Oh, he's gone back to Cornville and he's living there," was to prove him without ambition. The flocks of talented girls graduated every year from the colleges must go East if they were to live up to the flowery expectations held for them. Boys and girls no sooner got away to college, perhaps eighty miles from home, than they began to regard the hometown from standpoint of detached superiority, with a lightly humorous and patronizing touch. Some of this, of course, was assumed from youthful smartness, but the peculiar thing is that most of it was genuine. Those who went on, seeking something indefinable in far places, some stamp of mystic authority, repudiated the hometown with a feeling of bitter alienation.

This sense of exile has colored nearly all the expression of the Middle West, in whatever medium; and for years it kept timorous and reverent Iowa from any expression. It is the spirit of colonialism at its last gasp, and to some extent the counterpart of that pathetic lack of self-dependence and uncertain nostalgia for something fixed and certain of the semi-Europeanized American, which is reflected in so many of the novels of Henry James and Anne Douglas Sedgwick. It is the thing which differentiates the provincial of America from the provincial of Europe. The wandering children of our Middle Western small towns do not own that deep loyalty to the province and the village of their birth sung in old ballads (although they may have tremendous loyalty to European villages!) Instead, they labor for years to obliterate all traces of it. They delve into the remotest branches of their ancestry and announce themselves "from Virginia," of "from California" after their parents have spent a winter in Los Angeles, south or west of the Fiji Islands—but not the hometown. The most noticeable thing about this attitude is not so much its existence, however, as its intense self-consciousness.

The thing which gave this sense of exile its peculiarly American quality was the fact of distance without the more complete separation which a great body of water gives. The East was far away, but not too far to be reached. Therefore, the timid Middle Western states could never forget its existence. Its eye might be upon them, even if negligently.

Of all these meek states, Iowa, which is on the fence geographically, politically, religiously, and aesthetically, has been the meekest. A trifle more of even Babbitt bumptiousness would have helped it long ago. It was far too deeply imbued with a reverence for Puritan culture to attempt even a youthful swagger. It is, therefore, this very distance which has proved the one saving necessity, rescuing Iowa from the neither-this nor-thatness of such a state as Ohio.

For, placed inland, far from every coast, Iowa was hopelessly far from Europe. New England looked to England; Iowa looked to New England and the Eastern seaboard. New England took culture at secondhand; Iowa took it at "thirdhand." And while the whole Middle West had the East as a bugaboo, it did not have the hypothetical opinions of that "highly civilized European" which so long made the cultured Easterner shake in his shoes. Here, pure ignorance and pure humility saved Iowa. "He that is down need fear no fall," Bunyan sang. Almost the only claim of Iowa among these United States (aside from a little pride in the matter of corn and hogs) has been for the place of the lowest. But yielding itself thus, not only submissively but with ardor, to the charge of provincialism, it lost colonialism, by far the more insidious disease of the two.

There can be some pretension about a garment worn at secondhand. But that worn at thirdhand gets too threadbare. Yet there was pioneer blood in Iowa for all its meekness. It could not stay away forever because lack of the proper clothes. Its first literary efforts, largely poetical, had been naturally the dilution of a dilution. It was perhaps unforgivable impudence even to contemplate poetry in a country where the lanes were dirt roads, the rills "cricks," and the villages "burgs." These early poetizers used a manner that sat as stiffly upon their material as his Sunday suit upon a farmer. They called it "style." Little real roughnesses which kept creeping in were quickly put out of sight for fear of "the opinion the east would get of us." Our culture must always be dressed up in its thirdhand garments to meet the eye of the East. At last the garment went to pieces. The awkward, growing young creature could no longer attempt to hide his big hands and feet. The culture of Iowa either had to shut itself up or appear in homemade clothes.

It appeared, but still with the customary note of fear and apology. A gentleman pleaded in the now deceased *Grinnell Review* for an Iowa literature; but for one which would deal, not with the "uncouth characters" of Hamlin Garland, that gave such a bad impression to the East, but with our best people. Herbert Quick wrote his loveable records of pioneer life in *Vandemark's Folly* and *The Hawkeye*. But he was careful to link this life to the life of books. "I know this is a raw country," he said in effect. "These are only common folks. But remember that these young people of mine were lovers, and don't entirely despise them." This attitude was not so surprising when you consider that for years Mr. Quick had been wanting to write these stories and had been told by editors that "Iowa was not literary material." The point, however, is the customary docility and lack of conviction which led him to accept this dictum for so long, and not, like the old Scotchman, feel that he "must do it whatever."

But Mr. Quick kept faith with his material in the end and his achievement is to be respected. Long before, Hamlin Garland, with his "uncouth characters," had made the first vital attempt to deal with the raw material of art in a new country. He fell by wayside. After writing his saga of the Garlands and the McClintocks in *A Son of the Middle Border*, we find him in the succeeding volume thanking his readers with lowly amazement for their interest in such commonplace chronicles. *A Daughter of the Middle Border* is the sum total of this whole matter of the mental meekness and uncertainty of the Middle Western. It is an intellectual and spiritual tragedy with terribly comic elements. The attitude of Mr. Garland that is revealed with only too much transparency in this book has been the attitude of the Middle West, and of Iowa above all, for many years. Mr. Garland's people moved West and he had to go out into the fields. But he knew that farmer clothes were not the thing for a literary man. He ought to dress up in either a cowboy suit or a silk hat, or perhaps a velvet tam-o'-shanter. The sad thing is that his native gift was far superior to Mr. Quick's. It was courage rather than ability which failed him.

Later writers have been most uncomfortably aware of the home state and the hometown. They have tried to deal with each from a perch of humorous aloofness, attained after an absence of five or six years, introducing characters from the great world with all the fidgety awareness of a youth ashamed of his humble antecedents and trying to pass them off as funny. This cringing attitude is apparent in all the admitted culture of Iowa. It is extremely self-conscious, uncertain now of the old and still more uncertain of the new. The thin grasp of New England has gradually weakened. New York has to a great extent taken its place in the people's awe, but New York is full of Middle Westerners and therefore attainable. The raw vigor of other elements in the life of the state is working into its sacred culture as well. The fog of old timidities still hangs over its intellectual life like a damp cloud; but—tentatively, humbly, with sad disillusionment mingled with a faint hope—a native culture has begun to work its way out.

The foreign element is important here. The prairies more than cities, it may be, have been a melting pot, for on them the foreign element has been welded into the life of the place and something that goes far towards being genuine is resulting. Some of the old Germans and Dutch and Norwegians have clung tightly to their ancient customs, but the majority, when they came to this country, definitely left the Old World behind. They looked back with affection, very deep and real, to the "old country," but it was not the "mother country"; and there was an immense difference of viewpoint in this very difference of phrase. These people were coming on a desperate adventure. They had to strike their roots deeply and finally here. It is not the English of the second or third generation in Iowa who look back with awe to England. Strangely enough, it is those who have been longest established on this young continent and proudly call themselves its native stock, who are most worried and timid about the American attitude and unable to accept it naturally. The same thing is true, in its slightly differing way, of our oldest families in Iowa.

To be sure, there have been great culture lacks and disadvantages in this attitude of the foreign stock. Part of a very precious heritage has been lost. Crudeness has inevitably resulted. But crudeness is after all of less importance than the quality of the metal. And it has had its rough value, like the old method of plunging a boy straight into the water and making him sink or swim in the new element. It has added a certain tough hardiness to the pale remnant of transcendentalism.

The thin little stream of colonialism has almost dried up on the prairies. They are too big for it. Simple space defeats it. Besides, hundreds of ignorant young "foreigners" on the farms have never heard of it. They are so simple as to accept their own country as having its natural claims to a natural place in the world. One after another of the prairie states has begun to find this out, the least cultured first, until at last timid Iowa has dared to lift its eyes even in the presence of the East. Even those old and final strongholds, the colleges, are weakening. Professors, uncomfortably although disdainfully aware of iconoclastic young instructors, retreat farther as they hold their standards against the onslaught of the mob.

The effect of this general breakup of culture has been distinctly and amazingly noticeable during the last three or four years. A terrific rattle of typewriters has broken out. Newspapers are beginning to carry book columns of their own. People dare to send their own unsubstantiated opinions to the liberal and lively book page of the *Des Moines Register*. The group at the state university [The University of Iowa] has at last been accepted as culturally respectable in spite of its native origin. The barriers have come down, to the horror of the old guard, who can really recommend no American contemporaries except Mrs. Wharton. No longer is our literature in the hands of a caste. It is snatched at by everybody—farmer boys, dentists, telegraph editors in small towns, students, undertakers, insurance agents, and nobodies. All have a try at it. Every good-sized town has its band of ladies who meet and discuss the literary markets (wearing smocks in one instance as a bandage of aesthetic dignity), and who yearn to desert their husbands for a year at Columbia. A gathering of the literary clans is enough to bowl over the observer with the sight of its astounding and delicious diversity. All the elements, old and new, are jumbled up together until it seems impossible to guess what can be fished out of the muddle. But miscellaneous as the thing is, it is at least active, which under the old regime was the very last thing it dared to be.

And this very activity is a sign that a settling process is going on. The old self-deprecation is still on top. It persists among our best people and our expatriates. Just a layer below this is the mild idealism of the colleges, very milk-and-watery, into which the faith of the Pilgrims has developed under the impetus of material prosperity. It trusts that all things can be tested upon an ethical basis according to the moral value of their service to humanity, and is touchingly innocent of the cold rigor of aesthetics. Below this, and supporting it, is good prosperous Babbittry that judges life in terms of houses, automobiles, and radios, and lets its womenfolk go in for books and frills in the women's club. There is the main street element of small town hardness, dreariness, and tense material ambition. Still below this, solid and unyielding, is the retired farmer element in the towns: narrow, cautious, steady and thrifty, suspicious of "culture" but faithful to the churches, beginning to travel a little in big automobiles; of varying nationalities, but in the main Anglo-Saxon, Teutonic and Scandinavian; whose womenfolk still apologize if caught spending good time (which might be given to fancy work) over a book. And then there are the working farmers, the folk element and still the very soil and bedrock of our native culture. Raw, book-ignorant, travel-ignorant, stubborn, and hardheaded; but in their best aspect hardworking, serious-minded, strong and fresh. They give a saving rudeness, vigor, and individuality to the too mild brew which—now that pioneer days are over—would be the spirit of Iowa without them.

Whatever real intrinsic value the culture and art of Iowa can have is founded upon this bedrock. Other elements may influence and vary it, but this is at the bottom of them all. Our varying nationalities meet in its rich soil which has still some of the some of the old pioneer virtue of sturdy freshness—perhaps the only virtue, genuine and clearly distinguishable from all others, which the native culture of this young country has to offer. Certainly, without this underlying strong basis, and if it depended merely upon our best people, what we call culture in Iowa would still be as insipid as cambric tea.

Now that all these diversities have at last come together, they begin to suggest something distinctive. That something is at its worst, timid, deprecating, wishy-washy, colorless, and idealistic in a mild fruitless way. At its best, it is innocently ingenuous, fresh and sincere, unpretentious, and essentially ample, with a certain quality of pure loveliness—held together and strengthened by the simplicity and severity of its hardworking farmer people.

FROM LITTLE STORIES OF MASON CITY'S PAST (1928)

EDITH RULE

A graduate of the University of Iowa, Edith Rule writes here about her beloved home community, Mason City. The coauthor of True Tales of Iowa *(1932), Rule devoted much of her adult life to researching the state's varied history, as the passage that follows, Chapter XXVI, "The Coming of the Railroad," attests. Unusually contemporary and best described as creative nonfiction, Rule's style is invoked in her preface to* True Tales: *"Let us write the true tales of Iowaland as we write romance—with life, action, and color—that the history of our commonwealth may live."*

A small city sprang up on the north Iowa prairies, grew steadily, swiftly, with no more self-consciousness than a healthy young boy absorbed in his own play, unconcerned with questions of who he is, or why he is here. Its townspeople lived and died, names appeared and faded, life and the city were taken for granted. Until in June 1928, seventy-five years after the father of the city first looked out at the prairie lands flushed with autumn beauty, there came a break in historical lethargy. A four-day birthday celebration was held, and with it came awakening and the full measure of civic consciousness.

Eyes opened, the people of Mason City proudly saw themselves as an integral part of the history that had made and was making a city. Only four days were given to actual celebration, but the newfound pride in the town and all that had gone to build it was lasting.

In delving into Mason City and Cerro Gordo County history, both in books and in long talks with the city's old settlers and their descendants, the writer saw the romantic qualities that can be used to transform history into romance. These little stories, beginning with the earliest settlements in the country, were printed daily in the Mason City *Globe Gazette*. They carry the story up to the coming of the first railroad into the city. They do not seek to present a year by year history of Mason City but rather attempt to extract the full flavor of the past; to bring back the flesh and blood lives which have gone to make a city; to paint for those who are now enjoying the full fruits of early sacrifices the real dramas of pioneer days, exciting, tragic, absurd, heroic, as the case may be. The stories are based on authentic facts—the settings, actions, and speeches are productions of imagination, those pigments used to convert history's dull print into a colorful romance of the past.*

November 7, 1869, opened like any other day in an Iowa fall. The trees made black webs across a lowering sky—chill omen of snow was in the air and, in the early morning, warm beds and the drowsy languor of a last sleep should have held sway. However, all over the little village of Mason City there was energetic hopping out of bed, hurried dressing, and a feeling of anticipation, for today the Milwaukee railroad was to send the first train into Mason City.

For days they had looked forward to the 7th of November and that glorious hilarity would ride high was evident by the little piece in the *Press* of the night before. Mayor Stanbery had issued orders for an enormous celebration and if any man was found sober on the streets that day he was to be put in the calaboose.

On the way to school that morning young Ed Harding scuffed along kicking at the frozen earth, looked speculatively at the gray sky above him and longingly in the direction of the Milwaukee sheds where already a crowd of people were bustling about. Had it not been for rather peremptory orders from headquarters at home, Ed would have played hooky and been among those present when the iron horses came in. No wonder he scowled and kicked at the roadway.

A bell rang just as the boy entered the little building and the score or so of children were assembled. Then what heaven-blessed words was the teacher saying? "School will be out for today, children. You may all go down and see the train—the first train—come into Mason City." With a whoop they were out and down the road running pell-mell through the first flurry of early snowflakes. The boys tore ahead wild with joy. The girls forgot to be sedate little ladies and came flocking after, curls and hoops flying in the breeze.

They were everywhere in the crowd, in and out, very confident, very important, and gloriously happy. And then from far down the shining tracks there came a faint whistle. They waited, holding their breath; they were going to see their first train. Nearer, nearer it came until like an avalanche of noise it thundered down upon them, big and black, belching white smoke and taking their breath away with its size. Some of the children, terrified, fled to protective maternal skirts. Some were fascinated by the sight, and when the great beast gave a long drawn out howl as it came to a standstill in Mason City, the little boy who grumbled about having to go to school shrieked in terror and fled down the road toward home.

That night the joking edict of Mayor Stanbery was taken seriously by most of the town and all of the men who had come in on the first train. Glasses were filled and emptied and filled again. There were shouts and riotous singing on the street.

On the first floor of the hotel, most of the city's male population gathered to talk it over and to have "just one more." One jubilant individual did a buck and wing and another tried to be a whole Virginia reel in himself. It got so bad that the boys below, playing billiards, called up and told them to keep quiet, they were shaking the house.

The message had hardly more than gone up than there came a sudden ripping, tearing noise and floor and all gave way—the hilarious ones found themselves precipitated in a mass of flying boards down upon the billiard tables. For a stunned moment they examined themselves—took the roll call of bones, searched for blood and then pulled themselves out of the melee. They were all safely out when there came a call from one corner of the room and there was Del Thompson pinned between fallen floor and billiard table—unhurt but unable to move. Somewhat shaky with both laughter and shock, the men extricated him and the celebration came to an end.

With the coming of the railroad the last of the pioneer days came to a close. Mason City had gone through her infancy—had been carried gloriously, bravely, tragically, or absurdly through her early history. Now with the coming of the first train a brilliant future lay open before her.

From **Iowa Federation Home,** **Operated by Iowa Federation of** **Colored Women's Clubs (1929)**

The Iowa Federation Home

The pamphlet that follows was printed with pride, publicizing what it describes as the "the only home in America maintained by colored women at a state university, with the aid and assistance of popular subscription." The house, located at 942 Iowa Avenue in Iowa City, helped make African American women students at the University of Iowa feel truly at home. The cost for staying was $2.50 per week without meals, $6.00 with. The publication, excerpted here, offers still more evidence of Iowa's unusually open, even pioneering, racial attitudes, while also attesting to a too-belated recognition of minority rights; integration of the University of Iowa dormitories did not happen until 1946. Of course, the off-campus residents of the Federation Home were to be treated as other female boarders at the university, which meant they had to comply with the seemingly draconian "Iowa University Social Regulations" printed in the pamphlet as fair warning.

Since the fall of 1908, there has been an increasing number of negro young women enrolled at the State University [University of Iowa]

For several years, these young women, being few in number, easily found homes with the various faculty members, where they served as domestics, earning their board and room and sometimes a little spending change; but by the year 1915, the number had increased to about seven, some of whom could not find suitable homes in which to live, the negro population of Iowa City, being quite small, so a delegation of these young women visited the State Federation of Colored Women's Club, in session at Cedar Rapids, and pled with these women to give them some assistance in the procuring of a dormitory, where they might have comfortable quarters at a nominal price as well as more time for study and some social environment, similar to that in the regular university dormitories where on account of their race they felt that their presence would not be desired, and where few of them would be able to pay the scheduled fees.

Location
In May, 1917, Mrs. S. Joe Brown, retiring president of the Federation, appointed a committee to devise some means of assisting the negro young women at the university, and in August, 1919, this committee, headed by Mrs. Helena Downey,

selected the present building, a twelve room, modern, two-story residence, at 942 Iowa Ave., a wide boulevard which is exceedingly beautiful as well as famous in the history of Iowa City and the university. It is nine blocks east from the Old Capitol campus, and launched a statewide drive to procure $5,500 with which to purchase it; and in September 1919 the home was taken possession of and turned over to the young women, each of whom contributed what she could toward the furnishings and upkeep and lived together as a large family presided over by Mrs. Jas. L. Dameron, the matron selected by the trustees of the Federation.*

NEED FOR HOME

That this home has justified its existence and filled a long-felt need during the past ten years is demonstrated by the increase of from seven young women in our State University ten years ago, to twenty-five at the present time; but because of the congested condition only seventeen are housed in the home at this date (September, 1929) of whom seven are from Iowa, six from Missouri, and one each from Illinois, Alabama, Mississippi, and Oklahoma, which is evidence of the fact that the home is not only benefiting the young women of Iowa, but has during this period been an incentive for young women of our group from the various sections of the country, being the only home in America maintained by colored women at a state university, with the aid and assistance of popular subscription as is this one. It would appear, also, that the presence of this aggregation of young women at the Iowa University has had a tendency to increase the attendance of our young men; for, during this same period there has been an increase of from about ten to about one hundred negro young men, according to the record of Atty. S. Brown, who finished there about thirty years ago, when there were only two young men and no young women of our race enrolled and prior to which time no negro young woman had ever been enrolled. The record shows that at this time the university has a total enrollment of about nine thousand, of which about four thousand are young women; for the accommodation of which the state maintains only two dormitories, housing about three hundred eighty-four young women, leaving the vast majority to seek shelter elsewhere; and the colored women of the State Federation, taking cognizance of this situation and realizing the improbability of our girls being numbered among these less than four hundred housed in the regular state dormitories, felt that they could render no more commendable service than the establishment of his home.

Iowa University Social Regulations

University regulations are never suspended but are in operation throughout the entire year. The university expects all students to conduct themselves according to the usages of good society. Failure in this respect will be considered a violation of social regulations.

Young women may not room in houses which are not on the approved list except by special permission of the dean of women. Young men and women shall not lodge in the same house. Young women shall not entertain callers in their sleeping rooms, however furnished.

Houses shall be closed to callers at 10:30 o'clock each night except on Friday and Saturday when the hour shall be the same as that for returning from parties.

Dancing parties may be given and attended only on Friday and Saturday nights or the night preceding a holiday. All evening parties must conclude by 12 o'clock, including time for refreshment. It is a misdemeanor for young women to remain out after 12:30 o'clock following attendance at an approved dance or party. Chaperones are required to report such cases to the dean of women.

"Corn Husking" (1930)

Frank Patterson

Imagine Burlington high schooler Frank Patterson's delight in winning first place in the essay contest sponsored by the National Society for High School Journalists and having the essay that follows debut in the book Best Creative Work in American High Schools, *edited by H. A. Berns. Of course he had a little help from sympathetic readers; that year's judges included Iowan Frank Luther Mott, then editor of the* Midland, *and Jefferson, Iowa's, George Gallup, editor of the* Quill and Scroll, *and the man who would develop the world-famous Gallup Poll later in the 1930s. Patterson's woe-is-me tale, suffering though it does of "adjectivitis," must nevertheless have impressed the illustrious judges, proving the maxim "once an Iowa farm boy, always an Iowa farm boy."*

The large cookstove in the kitchen belched little puffs of smoke and kerosene fumes as the newly built fire struggled to warm the chilled room.

It was to be another dreary farm day for me—a day of chores, followed by corn husking, and then bed. Poets foolishly write of the joys of country living; poets who know nothing of its monotonous hardships. So my sympathies after seventeen years, my lifetime spent on a farm, are with realists like Hamlin Garland and Walter Muilenberg, who tell the truth about farm life, men who realize that with the amber and amethyst leaves of autumn, there come hours of cramped fingers, aching muscles, and feet heavy with mud-caked shoes.

Before I was ready to husk corn that morning there were the usual chores. I had first to break the thin scum of ice on the water pail and wash it in the stinging water. Then buttoning mackinaws about us, Father and I buckled on overshoes and with milk pails and lanterns stepped out into the blue-dark morning. Not a star shone through the shawl-like clouds. The light of the lanterns wove shadows of long spider-like legs on the snow. The darkness seemed mocking and empty. The occasional clanking of the milk pails and the steady *crunch, crunch* of our overshoes on the snow competed with the rasping screech of the barn door on its rollers as we shoved it partly open. Father placed his lantern on a nearby salt barrel. The horses nickered as he neared them with a measure of oats. Rusty, a big bay, lipped the oats. He was something of a favorite. But I was in no mood for touching his dusty hair. So I stumbled on to the warm straw pile north of the barn, where three milk cows lay. They stopped their chewing to snort suspiciously. Then with clicking hoofs they preceded me to the cow barn. The brutes lumbered through the doorway. With an air of dejection they took their places. I locked the three stanchions. Then hanging up on my lantern and taking a pail from a hook on the wall, I drew a milk stool to the flank of the nearest cow. Two streams of milk struck the bottom of the pail.

As the milk, white and cloying smelling, rose higher, the sound of the throbbing streams became a dull thud in the foam. At times steam rose from the milk so thickly as to hide the bucket. Then a poor aim of a stream of milk ended in a splattering spray upon my pants leg. Here it froze almost as soon as it touched. It was cold. At last, finishing the third cow, I raised the stanchions and opened the barn door. The cows gone, I shut it again.

"It's going to be clear and cold today. Good for husking," Father grunted.

"Yeah," I answered. I couldn't think of anything else to say. We never talked much—just did our work.

Father had finished harnessing the horses. With two buckets of milk we left the barn. We did not need the pale light of the lanterns, for in the sky the first gray streaks of dawn had come. Life was just awakening on our farm. An ambitious rooster crowed. From somewhere a sparrow chirruped a half dozen uninteresting notes.

Breakfast waited on the table in the warm kitchen. Mother was bending over the stove. She raised her flushed face to day, "Good morning. Hope you'll like the waffles." There was a place of crisp brown ones. And the fragrance of maple syrup struck my nostrils.

"Well, Frank," remarked Father, "Think you will finish the south forty today?"

"Hope so," I replied. "Another inch of snow and it will be too late to get the rest of the corn."

I finished the breakfast and prepared to leave for the field. Father would finish the chores before he left.

The bridle bits became coated with frost as I warmed them with my breath before placing them in the horses' mouths. I led my team to the watering tank. After breaking the thick ice, I took down the lines and snapped the checks while the horses drank. Then I fastened the bridle reins and drove to my wagon. Quickly snapping up the neck yoke, and hooking the tugs, I climbed over the high sideboards into the wagon. I flipped the lines, then bounced toward the cornfield.

After a time, I stopped husking to look at the sky. Feathery clouds lay waiting for the evening sun to slide behind the hills. A queer grayness filled the air—the sign of a coming storm. I spoke to the horses. Again I dragged tired legs from stalk to stalk in the endless cornfield, a field of endless rows of stalks, crooked, broken, twisted stalks that tripped me so that once or twice I fell on the hard snow.

Mechanically, I reached for the ears, ripped the husk with my husking peg, and with a twist of the ear, tore it from the stalk and banged it into the wagon. My fingers and arms no longer ached. They were numb with cold. The horses stooped at the fence. As I turned them back through the field, I counted the remaining rows. Eight were left. And the sun was out of sight. Stimulated by frosty evening air, I began, after a time, to husk faster. If I didn't finish the field that night it would be too late. Storm clouds were already piled in the sky.

At last I started on the thirty-fifth row. With only the gleam of snow for a light I reached for the ears when a stalk caught my foot. I fell. Silently cursing, I stumbled on. At times the wide flung ears missed the wagon. I had no time to pick them up.

Then the team stopped. When I had jerked the last ear from its stalk, I pulled myself into the heaped wagon that seemed to bulge with pale ears of husked corn. The team started homeward. The heavy wagon sang and squeaked alternately as the iron wheels scrapped through the crusted snow. Harness buckles rattled, creaked, snapped, as the horses strained forward. The sky was almost blank. A few stars still shone at its rim. The rest, perhaps, hid behind the warmth of drifting clouds.

Father, lantern in hand, came out of the house as I drove into the yard.

"You got through?" he asked as he started unhooking the horses.

"Yes, but that's about all." We always talked about getting through. Always the same words. Father always talked farm things.

"Better go into the house. I'll take care of the team tonight." His tones were kind.

"Thanks," was all I answered. I was glad to be free from chores. As I neared the house, I felt a soft, damp flake on my face. I looked up—it was snowing.

"Supper," Mother called. "Come, Frank, supper's waiting."

I was almost too tired to eat. I was hungry, though. The table was covered with hot, steamy things that all tasted the same.

"But farming is going to be better. The farmer's day is coming." Mother's voice sounded strangely far away. Too tired to argue, I nodded to her statements. Yes, the farmer's day was coming. But when?

"And besides, you are your own boss. You can do as you please on the farm." Thinking she had changed my gloomy point of view, Mother talked on. Father said nothing. He seldom spoke when he talked about my staying on the farm. Perhaps he remembered other days when he, too, had loathed the dreary routine of farm life.

I rose from the table. Taking a book from the bookcase, I pulled a squeaky rocking chair up to the bowlegged heating stove in the living room. There was no use trying to read. Masses of words with no meaning blurred the page. I was too tired to understand the words.

Grunting a good night to mother and father, I dragged up the steep stairway to my room. I undressed in cold darkness and pulled the covers up to my chin. Then I remembered mother's words. "But farm life is going to be better."

I tried to think of an answering argument. My senses, though, were dull, and I was sleepy.

Outside, the withered maple trees cracked and snapped as the wind caught their frozen boughs.

FROM **BLACK SOIL (1930)**

JOSEPHINE DONOVAN

Another surprise prizewinner, Granville, Iowa's, Josephine Donovan wrote her novel, Black Soil, *as a Master's thesis, but a two-thousand-dollar prize and the promise of publication lured her away from a graduate degree at the University of Iowa.* Black Soil *is set in O'Brien County in northwest Iowa, where the Irish Catholic Connor family (Tim, Nell, their children, and an orphan, Sheila) put down roots among the Dutch and Germans. While the novel deals with the cultural misunderstandings among rival ethnic groups, the passage below finds those factions brought together by true calamity—the great grasshopper plagues of the 1870s, which Donovan heard recounted by her father. The infestation proved almost biblical for many Iowa farm families, who took the swarm as an omen they should head back East.*

One June morning Johann, as usual, was hoeing in his patch of sod corn when the sun, baring the nightly mysteries of the sky and prairie, pushed up its face over the rim of the world. A quivering breeze stirred the phlox and made music in the coarse slough grass. The reach of the prairie was limitless. In its waving motion, its distant shanties and soddies bobbed like flotsam. Wee fluffs of cloud, enhancing the blueness of the sky, sailed by, became a mist, and melted away. And the sky remained as blue.

The morning slipped away. The sun was in the zenith; still Johann remained in his field. He saw Nell Connor hoeing potatoes nearby, working also without regard for time.

Suddenly a large, dark cloud appeared in the west.

Broadening out and roaring, it moved directly toward them. Terrified, Johann recalled confusedly strange phenomena. What was it? Anything might happen in a new country. The apparition as it settled lower became more and more terrifying. Its rumbling sound changed to a sonorous hum. The sun lost its light.

"Bad storm!" he shouted, as he ran toward Nell, who with uplifted face stood like a statue, staring into the sky.

The sky was filled with a storm of black flakes, the dark particles singling out and becoming more defined in shape as they descended. He heard a buzzing, saw shining wings, long bodies, legs.

"Grasshoppers!" Nell's agonized voice rang out. "Grasshoppers! May God preserve us—the scourge of the prairie is upon us."

He saw her sink to the ground and cover her face with her hands.

Johann shouted and brandished his hoe. The horde descended. He tried to defend his field...his corn was a mass of shining bodies sucking, sucking the tender juices. He worked feverishly, knocking off feeders only to give place to others. He himself was covered with grasshoppers. They crawled over his face, his eyes, and invaded his clothes. The limitless stretch of prairie was not vast enough to hold them all. He surrendered to them, and went toward Connors'. As he walked, his boots became slimy with crushed bodies.

The succulent prairie grass was converted into a moving mass as the hoppers piled up in their greed.

Nell joined him in the yard. "Thank God we're safe, anyhow," she said.

Tim, who was at the county seat with Weiss, could not return home before evening; but Sheila, who was herding, and Danny, who was taking his father's place plowing corn, soon came running in. "The horses are gone," Danny announced, crying with fear and excitement. "When it got so dark they acted so funny I unhitched their tugs and they ran away. I can't even see where they went."

"They'll come back. Don't bother about them. It's a miracle they didn't kill you." Nell's face was as white as chalk. Her blue eyes were dark. She was trying hard to regain her self-control.

"The cattle went wild, too," Sheila broke in, all out of breath. "They bellowed so and sniffed the ground like when they see blood. I put for home."

"Let 'em go. Don't go near 'em. They can go where they want now—there's nothing to save, I guess," Nell said with resignation.

Robert Emmet and Ellen, still terrified, clung to Nell. She held them closely, wishing to impart to them some of her trust, her thanks.... "The children might have been killed by those frightened animals."

Hysterical shrieks broke in on the temporary calm.

From across the field they saw Katto Schwartz approaching. Johann moved back toward the house as she faced him. Shaking her fist first in the direction of the sky and then at the pests at her feet, she went through her repertoire of imprecations. Stamping her calloused bare feet, she crushed the slimy horde with a vengeance. While the sun shone on her glazed calico dress and disclosed tawny strands in her disheveled hair, she ground her teeth and was shaken by a tremor which agitated her excess of flesh.

Mrs. Connor's attempt at calming her was of no avail. "Come," she said finally. "I'll make the coffee."

"All right," Katto acquiesced, her voice lowered considerably. "We'd better drink it once before something gets it from us. I said the devil would get the crop; but we got good measure—all hell is turned loose."

Johann declined to have coffee with the women. Bewildered, he moved toward his soddy [sod house] which he found veneered a shiny brown. He had never had a door, so the invaders had entered and taken possession of his house, even testing the edibility of his old red stove. He went to the field for his hoe, and began his futile struggle to dislodge them.

The Connor children watched for their father, while they worked in the garden helping Nell wrest what was possible from the plunderers.

Danny talked glibly. "Hey, you old pigs! Get off of those carrots." It was really a hand-to-hand struggle, for the invaders persisted in having their share, even while the vegetables were being pulled.

Margaret spied a dark speck in the east. Soon they recognized horses' bobbing heads, and like a flash they ran to meet Tim and Weiss.

There was an exchange of waving, then a series of: "Hello, Pop," and the children climbed into the wagon.

"Pop, we got the grasshoppers!"

"And they put out the sun…!"

"My, we were so scared!"

"They ate everything up, Pop. John thought it was a cyclone; but when Mom saw their wings and everything, she knew it was grasshoppers."

"—and she cried, too."

"We fighted with them in the garden. Our cave is full of stuff."

Peter Weiss stood silently in the wagon. The joints of his hands were knobbed as he held the reins tightly. An occasional tear trickled down his beard…. He could see his farm.

The children spied a wooden pail. "What's that?" they asked at once.

"I see that they didn't carry you or your curiosity away," Tim said lightly. "I brought you some jelly."

"Jelly? What's jelly?"

Tim drew out his knife, ripped up the lid of the pail, and gave each child a quivering, ruddy slice. "Here's a bit of a taste now and you can put some on bread when we get home."

"M-m-m, it's good," they commented in unison.

"And Pop," Margaret took up the recital of events again, "Katto got mad and sent her curses up to God. She won't go to Heaven, will she, Pop?"

"Even as you and I, childer. Katto's all right. There's no harm in Katto."

Tim could see the destruction in his own fields now. His usually erect figure slumped dejectedly and he swallowed hard. "Everything all gone, eh? Wheat patch, too?

"Yes," Danny answered. "They bent the stalks. See, Pop, the patch is all brown."

That evening they spoke little of grasshoppers, although the insects were omnipresent, clicking, jumping, and dashing their bodies against the house. Tim, as usual, related his experiences at the county seat and told the news picked up that day.

Nell, lulling Ellen on her knees, asked: "Did you get Weiss's trouble fixed up all right? Was it so serious as he imagined?"

"Well, serious enough," Tim answered with a reminiscent smile. "A St. Paul concern had a chattel mortgage on his two hogs and a spavined mule that he'd brought back from the Black Hills. Last winter his family ran short of food, so they ate the hogs; and to cap the climax the old mule died. So Weiss was in a terrible way; he was afraid it was to jail he'd have to go."

"Did you settle it for him?"

"I don't think they'll bother Weiss any more about it. Young Peck was there to represent the company—Peck's a fine, decent fellow. After he had made his plea, I stood up and told them that the family was forced to eat the hogs or starve, and that the old mule had withstood all other calamities in its cosmopolitan life, but the chattel mortgage had proved fatal. The court had a great laugh, and the case was dismissed."

"Childer, you should have seen the funny fellow they had there today," he went on. "His clothes were a mass of rags sewed and quilted together. They said he'd been around the country for some time and when people spoke to him he got down on hands and knees and crept into the cornfields. As he was scaring the people, the sheriff rounded him up and brought him in. And he discovered that in between the layers of his tatters was money, paper money, gone to chaff with dry rot. And he had gold on him, too. I saw him there. He wasn't old: he had a fine face and looked bright. I couldn't help but think he had good connections. He wouldn't give his name. He only said; 'Call me John Doe.' I believe they took him to Cherokee."

"What else did you see, Pop?"

"There was a hay twister for sale there. Twisted the hay up slick as a whistle. Bunch of us settlers looking at it in the morning thought we might buy one together in the fall; but after we saw that scourge of hoppers land, I guess we thought no more of hay twisters…. That white courthouse was painted brown in a few minutes."

The impending depression forced itself in. Tim got up and walked out of the house.

He went through the grove and stood on the edge of the cornfield. The moonlight, bright as day, revealed the luster of the shiny pests, and the snapping and crackling of corn was like the subdued noise of cattle feeding.

Tim thought of neighbors who shared his fate as he saw their groves—dark rectangles against the sky. By their height one could determine the length of time the owner had been in the country. Schwartz's grove completely hid his house. Van Den Hull had one peeping window in which a yellow light gleamed. Johann's shack remained a clod of black earth.

In the grove behind him and in the fields before him was the eerie rustling, a sucking away of the food of his family. Just when they had dared to hope and had been so bold as to involve themselves more deeply in debt—the well, Sheila's room, the harvester—had come this calamity. Surely they would not force him to take that harvester when there was no harvest. He would write and cancel the order.

The children's words returned to him…Mom had cried. "Poor girl! Poor childer! I picked the devil's own country for them. This prairie charmed me like a snake, to strike not only me but Nell and the young ones as well…Yes sir, the devil's own country! Still, can fortune always be so bad? It's a long lane that hasn't a turn!"

He walked back to the house. The light was turned low. The even breathing and sleepy mutterings of healthy children filled the house. Nell was kneeling by the open window of the bedroom, her dark hair hanging down her back, her face resting on the sill. She was praying, in an attitude of dejection. The hundreds of eyes watching her through the window completely shut off her vision of the stars.

"Nell," Tim spoke out. "Good luck will come to us yet, I'm a-thinking. The darkest hour is just before the dawn."

Johann could not accept this calamity so philosophically as did the Connors. He tried to seek out a reason, but there was no reason; there was no justification for such a phenomenon.

"It's God's will, John. Accept it as such and you can bear it better," Nell repeated. "Remember, God never closes one gap but He opens another. Keep your trust in God."

But Johann could not be convinced. Often he stood in the doorway where he had succeeded in scraping a pile of the pests, and allowed them to become scattered again as he leaned on the handle of his hoe asking: Why? Why? Why the incongruity in the scene before him? Sometimes he felt raised to the capability of real struggle when he contemplated the sky so blue, so guileless, the prairie—a strange place, holding the answers to his questions in its sinister silence. In his meditations he felt cut off from the world. All about him nothing was distant, yet all was distance.

From **Memories of Fourscore Years (1930)**

Charles August Ficke

Father of the well-known Iowa writer Arthur Davison Ficke, Charles August Ficke was born in Germany and came of age on the family farm in Long Grove, Iowa, just north of Davenport. A lawyer and a Democrat, Ficke moved his family to Davenport, where he served as Scott County attorney from 1886-1888 and mayor of Davenport from 1890 to 1891. According to Iowa literary scholar William H. Roba, C. A. Ficke was the richest man in eastern Iowa at the time, as well as leader of the immigrant German community. The excerpts following, drawn from chapters entitled "The Trying Early Years," "School Years at Long Grove," and "Leaving the Farm," make for a memoir that goes well beyond navel-gazing and hermetic family history to a historically valuable, wide-angle window on the times.

In the [eighteen] fifties, correspondence with persons in Germany was carried on under difficulties. It required from three to four months to get a reply to one's letter to that country. Besides the rate of postage was almost prohibitive. America had just begun using adhesive postage stamps. Germany was already using these, on local letters, but not on letters to America. It gave senders of letters the choice between paying sixty cents on such of minimum weight, in advance, or sending them "collect." Some of father's correspondents, assuming, perhaps, that he was rolling in wealth, had the bad habit of sending their letters "collect" although, in these, they were asking favors. Letters from Germany, of which several hundred are extant, sometimes were great curiosities. To keep them within the minimum weight, and yet allow them to be of great length, they were written on the thinnest of paper, in script so small, that often a magnifying glass had to be employed to decipher them. To minimize weight, envelopes were dispensed with. A blank space would be left on the last page, which after the letter was folded, the size of an envelope, and sealed with a wafer, would be used for the address.

Mother, on an average, wrote four letters a year to her mother and received an equal number in return. Father, on an average, wrote two letters to each of his two brothers a year. His brothers exchanged the letters received so that each of them heard from us at least every three months. To friends my parents would write perhaps only once a year. All the letters which my parents received from relatives and friends, until these one after another passed to the Great Beyond, they carefully preserved. These make most interesting reading. In all of them deepest interest is expressed in our welfare. Many of them request minutest details regarding our activities, mode of life, and measure of success.

One of father's brothers wrote: "I am delighted that [Wilhelm] Fischer is staying with you, and that your wife and daughters so bravely took hold of the housework. Write me more particulars about your farm. Do you plow with oxen or horses? What did you harvest? How much maize and how much wheat per acre? What crop changes are necessary or customary? How often must you plow and how deep? Do you use fertilizers? Have you a garden behind the house, and if so, how large is it? Is your house surrounded by trees? Where is the barn? Let Herman, the good draftsman, send me a sketch of your place. Is there any timber near you and how old is it? How was the crop this year, and how were the prices? What livestock have you? How much milk do you get, and what do you do with it? Do you raise potatoes, cabbage, and other vegetables? At what hour do you rise, when do you breakfast, and when do you retire? What kind of neighbors have you? Do they visit you, do they love music, and do they play whist in winter? You will perhaps laugh at my asking all these questions, but the great distance that lies between us, and my deep interest in your welfare, prompts me to ask them, and I hope you will answer them. Go fully into details. I measured up an area the size of your farm, and find it so large that it seems to me that it is impossible for you to farm so much land. It is possible that agriculture with you is more simplified than with us, and that you have better agricultural implements than we, otherwise this would be impossible."

Could a lawyer have asked more searching questions than did Uncle August in this letter? Father, of course, answered fully every question asked. The next letter from Uncle August overflowed with joy over the full report he had received and the rosy pictures father had drawn of conditions in Iowa. He stated that his wife, after reading father's letter, had expressed a wish to go to America and perhaps some day the three branches of the family could be united in that country.

Had father given a true picture of conditions in Iowa, and of his own troubles, his brother would not have expressed a wish to make his home in that state. It was one of father's and mother's failings, if it was a failing, that in letters to relatives in Germany, they minimized adversities and magnified blessings. Instances of good fortune were promptly reported while reverses were minimized or passed over in silence. Their pride would not permit them to let the home folks, who had opposed their going to America, know how narrow had been the margin between success and failure, and how often failure instead of success, had rewarded their best efforts.

Father's first eight years in America were not a financial success. Although he was one of those farmers, who in common parlance were called "Latin farmers," because they knew more about Latin and other languages or about business than about farming or hard work on the farm, his want of success was not due to any shortcomings on his part but to causes from which others, who had followed farming all their lives, suffered as severely as he: crop failures, low prices, scarcity of money, and hard times in general. The only dream of my parents which had become a reality was the one of establishing a home for their children in a country in which there were no class distinctions, where people were rated at their real worth, and in which supposedly they could become masters of their own fortunes.

The letters which my parents wrote to relatives in Germany and which brought joy to those who received them, touched me deeply, when I read the copies which had been retained, knowing, as I did, that they concealed the true conditions. Between the lines of mother's letters, in particular, I read how during the early years on the farm, homesickness was gnawing at her heart. "Nightly, when I lay my head on my pillow," she wrote to her mother, "my thoughts are with you, dearest mother, and I pray to God to reward you for all that you have done for me, as it is not in my power to do so."

In letters to friends, father would sometimes be more candid than in letters to relatives. In these he admitted that he had not found either the Utopia or the El Dorado which he had expected to find. In one of his letters he describes the difference between life in Germany and America. One had to give up such habits as smoking and indulging in an occasional glass of beer. This could not have been difficult for father, because I never knew him to smoke or to care for beer, which he claimed did not agree with him. He brought from Germany a long stemmed pipe, the bowl of which, six inches in length, bore the portrait of Louis Phillipe of France, but never smoked it.

In one letter father wrote that his wife and oldest daughters were suffering privations, because they lacked servants and because the large amount of housework they had to do, left them no time for recreation. He mentioned that the piano was proving a great blessing because it brought them visits from Scotch neighbors, to whom music was a gift of God. He added that the music must not be too frivolous because they were very pious. In another letter he wrote that visits from neighbors usually occurred about three in the afternoon, that there would be conversation until five which progressed smoothly because these neighbors were intelligent people. Then a repast would be served, and that as soon as the guest had finished his last morsel he would pick up his hat and say "goodbye" and the visit would be over. He stated that only the "real Yankees" acted thus, and that the manners of the Scotch neighbors were more refined, because they would remain a while after the repast.

That father was not the only new arrival who met with difficulties, appears from another letter. In that he relates the fate of some former officers of the Schleswig-Holstein army whom his correspondent evidently knew. Von Schuck and Von Schomansky, he stated, had worked for their board for a farmer who was single, Von Schuck acting as cook and chambermaid. Then they had been engaged in floating firewood down the Mississippi to Davenport. Now they were in Missouri in want. Another ex-officer, Von Schumann, had first worked a year for a farmer for his board, and was now a fireman, in a Davenport flour mill at twelve dollars a month. A fourth ex-officer, Baron Von Herzberg, had invested his means in a farm, which he neglected, and finally rented to another. He was now acting as a surveyor. A fifth, Von Gabien, had had no better luck on the farm. He was now a cigar maker. He mentioned two other ex-officers who were now running a threshing machine.

As has been stated, my memory is a blank regarding what happened during the first five years of my life. My earliest recollections are associated with a scene in which my mother is holding me on her knees, and on a slate is drawing a picture of a cat on geometrical lines, giving the creature a triangular head. Judging the picture by ultra-modernistic standards, it would perhaps have been called a great work of art. To me, in any event, it appeared to be a wonderful production. It filled me with admiration for mother's accomplishments as an artist, and so indelibly imprinted itself on my memory that I was able to reproduce it, for my children and grandchildren, innumerable times. The evenings in which mother would draw pictures for me, or hold me on her knees, telling me stories, while ceaselessly working her knitting, are among the most precious memories of my childhood.

I next recall with what profound apprehension I listened to the nocturnal concerts of the wolves, of which there were many in the hills, up the creek, which crossed our farm. Nightly these creatures assembled, in far too close proximity to our home, to serenade us, the nearest intruders of their preserves. In later years, I was told that I would turn pale with fear when nightly these concerts opened. It took me years to overcome this early implanted terror. Even when I was old enough to be sent out into what then, to me, was a limitless wilderness, to search for our cattle, I would look for them in the hill country only as a last resort.

Next I recall a visit from a man by the name of Meyer, who was called "Bartmeyer" because of his long beard, who lived at some distance but would frequently call on father, accompanied by his large dog, of which I was mortally afraid. One day when I saw him approaching, accompanied by his dog, I hid under the bed in my parents' bedroom, and there fell asleep. When I was missed every room in the house, every building on the farm, and every conceivable place where I might be hiding, except the one where I was asleep was searched for me in vain. There was great consternation. When, after having finished my nap, I emerged from my hiding place, I beheld a room full of weeping people. Quickly the scene resolved itself into one of joy. No favor that I had asked at that moment would have been denied me.

Judging from one of father's letters, the years which I do not recall must have been carefree ones for me. Father, when I was three, wrote that I was romping about the farm in sunshine and storm, knew the name of every animal on the place, the English name of every farm implement, was a smart little chap, and as his friend had predicted, would doubtless some day become president of all the agricultural societies of America.

At the age of six I accompanied my parents to Davenport for the first time. On this occasion I received my first lesson in perspective. When we reached the brow of the hill on Brady Street I saw at its bottom between Fifth and Front streets numberless moving objects, apparently not larger than ants. To my amazement I learned that these were human beings and horses and vehicles whom distance made seem so diminutive. When I learned that the silvery sheet, which I saw at the end of Brady Street, was the Mississippi, I became alarmed lest in descending the hill, the like of which I had never beheld, we should be unable to stop in time to prevent our plunging into the river.*

Three years after father arrived in Iowa he decided to build a gristmill. The west branch of the Walnut Creek, which crossed our farm, it was believed, would provide enough water to operate such a mill. He entered into a contract with a millwright, in which the latter agreed to install complete mill machinery within six weeks after the completion of the mill building. Father's discouraging experience at farming, presumably, induced him to go into so risky a venture. With money almost unobtainable, and rates of interest extortionate, this venture should have impressed him as being doubly hazardous.

When father announced his intention of building a mill, there was great rejoicing in the northern part of Scott County. In one of mother's letters to her mother she told how the settlers from near and far offered their services, gratis, in hauling the material, and that when there was not enough of this to go round those who were left out expressed deep disappointment. Willingness to cooperate with their neighbors was one of the great virtues of the early settlers.

When the mill and the dam, which impounded the water of the creek, had been completed and the "Elizabeth Mill," so named after my mother, was ready to start, there was even greater rejoicing. The settlers came to congratulate father upon his public spirit and the courage he had shown in building the mill. They brought grain, to be converted into flour, in such quantities that some of them had to wait months before they received their flour.

Prosperity seemed to be at father's door. Years of worry, however, lay ahead. No one had foreseen that in spring, when the snow suddenly melted on the hillsides, upstream, and in summer after heavy rains or cloudbursts, the quiet Walnut Creek would become a wild torrent and carry away the milldam. That calamity happened the very next spring. Months were required to rebuild it. This calamity repeated itself a number of times, as the years passed. Another unforeseen difficulty arose. The mill was built when the land upstream, which constituted the watershed, was still prairie. Prairie, after rains, readily allowed the water to find its way to the creek. Slowly but surely this prairie was converted into cultivated land and this retained the water. The supply required to run the mill began to dwindle and finally the mill had to be closed. The mill, however, was not closed until after a long, hopeless, and costly struggle with these unconquerable forces. At first, after the water had begun to dwindle, the mill ceased running two or three days a week. When finally the pond went all but dry, the long foreseen and inevitable end came. The mill was closed, the machinery sold, and the building removed to a site near our home. The agony was at last over. When the "Elizabeth Mill" shall have passed out of the memory of the oldest settler, people will wonder what prehistoric people were the builders of the earthworks, once the dam of our mill, which though slowly dwindling in height, will be visible during centuries to come.

The mill with its large waterwheel, and the millpond, richly stocked with fish for a while, had a great fascination for me. The mill, however, lost this fascination when it became my duty daily to turn the grindstone on which the picks, needed to re-cut the millstones, had to be sharpened. I never lost my interest in the millpond. I sat on its banks by the hour fishing but usually caught only sunfish, because the suckers, catfish, and pike, though plentiful, scorned my bait, which consisted of grasshoppers or angleworms.

After heavy rains, however, the fish which had despised my bait, got themselves into trouble, and many of them were caught. Following such rains the sluices of the dam had to be opened, to relieve the pressure on the latter. Following the closing of these, the water in the ditch below would be lowered so suddenly that the fish had not time to escape, and hundreds of them would sometimes be imprisoned in the larger or smaller depressions in the ditch. Armed with garden rakes, we would descend upon these prisoners. Sometimes we would fill washtubs with them. Then mother would call on the entire family to assist in cleaning the catch, and for weeks thereafter fish in aspic was our daily diet.

To the settlers for miles around, our pond was a great attraction. It afforded good bathing, and in spring and autumn, when migrating ducks and geese were its visitors, it attracted lovers of sport. From a blind on shore, they made war on these unsuspecting creatures. My brother Herman, from this point of vantage, one morning shot a beautiful swan. He greatly regretted his act when he discovered what a majestic bird he had slain.

Our pond, on several occasions, was used for baptismal purposes. Once this happened when the pond was still covered with ice. New converts ready to join the Long Grove church came accompanied by the entire congregation, to be baptized. A large hole was made in the ice near the shore, where the water was of the needed depth but not too deep. Into this descended the minister and the convert. The congregation sang while the act of baptism was being performed. As each convert emerged from the icy water with chattering teeth he was wrapped up in warm blankets and with the last convert baptized the interesting ceremony was over.

Our mill played its part in the Civil War drama. My father, like all the German pioneers of the fifties and sixties, was a staunch Republican, and a loyal supporter of the Union cause. He had become an American citizen as soon as the law permitted him to do so, and had voted for Lincoln. He and all the members of our family followed closely the events of the war. To the north of us, along the Wapsipinicon [River], lived a number of settlers who in common parlance were styled "Copperheads," and whose loyalty to the Union was questioned. During the war, the Union men of our locality organized a secret society in support of the Union cause. Father and my two brothers were among its most active members. Unbeknown to me this society held its secret meetings in father's mill. I did not even know that there was such a society. When I accidentally learned of its existence, and that it was holding its meetings in our mill, I was made to promise that I would disclose, to no one, what I had discovered lest the Copperheads on the Wapsi would learn for what purpose our mill was being used, and set it on fire.*

During my school year the Civil War was in its most critical period. From every front, at which our armies were fighting for the preservation of the Union, came calls for reinforcements. Wards and townships, desirous of filling their quotas of recruits, offered bounties to those who would enlist. The city papers were filled with advertisements of firms offering to furnish substitutes for men who had been drafted, and with advertisements of wards and townships, which were overbidding each other in the amount of bounty they offered recruits. Several Davenport wards, in their advertisements, first offered $150 bounty. Then they increased their offer to $200, with ten dollars to the party who brought a recruit. Le Claire Township finally outbid all seekers of recruits by offering $550 to recruits who would enlist for five years.

The country was filled with professional bounty hunters. These were called "Professional Bounty Jumpers." These persons would enlist, pocket the bounty, and desert before they could be sent to the front, in order to repeat their crookedness in another county or state under another name. At Camp McClellan there was a strongly guarded enclosure in which were the substitutes for drafted men and recruits who had enlisted for bounty. The drafts were held in Metropolitan Hall. The days on which these took place were days of gloom. Many of those who were of military age attended to learn their fate.

One evening I was present when General Joe Booker, called "Fighting Joe," was addressing an open-air meeting from the portico of the LeClaire hotel. While he was making his most eloquent appeal in support of the Union cause a well-known Front Street innkeeper, a Democrat of the class styled "Copperheads," stationed himself by his side and in a stentorian tone called for three cheers for Jefferson Davis. Imagine what would have happened to a sympathizer with Germany who, during the World War, at a patriotic meeting, had called for three cheers for Emperor William. In the case referred to, the general proceeded with his address and the incident was deemed closed after the unpatriotic citizen had been unceremoniously thrown into the street.

During the autumn of 1864 twenty thousand prisoners were confined in the Rebel prison on Rock Island. Shortly after the discovery of a plot to release the Rebel prisoners confined in Camp Douglas, near Chicago, Adjutant General Baker, late one evening, caused a general alarm to be sounded, and the Davenport militia companies to be ordered out, upon his being apprised by the Rock Island prison authorities that they had discovered a plot which had as its goal a break for liberty by the Rebel prisoners that night. No such break was made, but Davenport people obtained little sleep that night.

One evening, a little later, there was another alarm. A report had gained credence that the prisoners had broken out; that they had made a rush for the railroad bridge after killing their guards; that many of them had crossed to Davenport before the bridge tender had opened the draw; and after this had been done many prisoners had been pushed into the river by their comrades who did not know that the draw had been opened. There was again tremendous excitement. People ran hither and thither, wildly repeating the story they had heard. I myself repeated it to whomever I met. I expected every moment to encounter one of the escaped prisoners. It was again a false alarm. No prisoners had even attempted to escape.

In the presidential election of 1864 General McClellan was the democratic candidate against Lincoln. I had heard Copperheads so often denounced as enemies of the country that when I heard McClellan spoken of as a Copperhead, I could not understand how so dangerous a person could be trusted at the head of the Union army. When I heard Hiram Price, candidate for Congress, who I highly respected, in a joint debate with his Democrat opponent, George H. Parker, pronounce McClellan a Copperhead in unmeasured terms, I decided that he must really be a very dangerous man. I had not yet learned that political speeches should not be taken too seriously.

During the closing months of 1864 and the early months of 1865 stirring events followed each other in rapid succession. The battle of Winchester, which inspired the well-known poem "Sheridan's Ride," was fought and won. Sherman made his famous march from Atlanta to the sea. The Thirteenth Amendment abolishing slavery was adopted. Then Richmond fell.

When the news of Richmond's surrender reached Davenport, pandemonium broke loose. Church bells, school bells, and the fire bell were rung. Every steam whistle joined in a concert. As if by magic the streets became filled with a seething mass of humanity. Men, women, and children formed themselves into a procession and paraded through the streets singing patriotic songs. At the levee bonfires were lit and salutes were fired by a battery of guns. I witnessed an unfortunate premature discharge of one of the guns which came near costing two of the gunners their lives. Finally from the portico of the LeClaire Hotel prominent speakers addressed the multitude. Never in its history had Davenport witnessed so great an outpouring on short notice.

A few days later further good news arrived. General Lee had surrendered with his army. The rejoicings which followed the surrender of Richmond were repeated. Surely this was the end of the war. Again there was ringing of bells, blowing of whistles, singing and cheering and processions. This time, however, the rejoicings were spread over two days. The news of Lee's surrender had arrived on Sunday. That day there was a spontaneous celebration. Next day this was supplemented by a dignified celebration in front of the LeClaire Hotel at which speakers addressed the assembled thousands from the portico of that building.

Those who witnessed the pandemonium which reigned in the streets of Davenport, after the armistice which ended the World War had been signed, can understand why the celebrations which followed the fall of Richmond and the surrender of Lee remain as vivid in my memory as if they had occurred but yesterday, although sixty-five years have elapsed since. When Lincoln, a few days after Lee's surrender, issued a proclamation that recruiting and the draft were to cease, the country was tremendously relieved.

Hardly had the echoes of the demonstrations of joy, that had recently been staged throughout the North, died away when there came a bolt out of the blue sky. Five days after Lee's surrender the news that Abraham Lincoln, our beloved president, had been shot down in cold blood by an assassin, shook the North to its foundation. Crowds besieged the telegraph and newspaper offices. Was the South, through murder, aiming to gain what it had not been able to accomplish by war? Deep gloom settled over the city. People spoke to each other in a whisper. Flags were hung at half-mast. Public buildings and business houses were draped in mourning. A public meeting was called at Metropolitan Hall at which speakers gave utterance to the nation's sorrow.

A month later the North had once more cause to rejoice. Jefferson Davis had been captured. Now surely the war was over. The fathers, sons, and husbands, who had been absent so long, would now surely soon be home.

Then the troops began to return. Those from Iowa, which had been mustered into the service at Davenport, were returned to that city to be mustered out. They had seen hard service. New uniforms had not been furnished them any too often, those of some being ragged with long service. Men were glad to discard their uniforms and once more don civilian clothes. Upon receiving their pay, they hastened to supply themselves with these regardless of cost. The city then had more dealers in ready-made clothing than it has had at any one time since. The representatives of these dealers hovered about the camp in which were quartered the men waiting to be mustered out. They resembled vultures gathered around carrion. They sought out company officers to whom they offered inducements to march squads of their men to this or that dealer.

During the war my father had kept my uncle, August Ficke, informed in regard to its progress. My uncle, therefore, had a faith equal to that of my father in its successful outcome.

On April 12, 1862, Uncle August wrote to my father: "Your war with the Southern states creates profound excitement here. All the enemies of freedom here are rejoicing over your misfortune and are predicting the downfall of your republic. The officers are laughing about your soldiers, and I have many bitter word combats with them. My trump card is always my statement that seven hundred thousand volunteers have offered their services to fight for the Union and the Constitution. Then I ask them whether it would be possible to find that number of volunteers in Germany who would offer their services to fight for their rulers. Now that Europe is sending military experts to America to study her military methods, I take great pleasure in rubbing this into our headswelled militarists."

In 1864, when the prospects of saving the Union were at their worst and most fervent appeals were being made to its friends for financial assistance, my uncle gave still stronger proof of his confidence in the Union cause. He sent my father a very considerable sum for investment in United States bonds. The investment was instantly made. Uncle's remittance came in a draft payable in gold dollars. Gold dollars then brought approximately two dollars and fifty cents in paper. Uncle's bonds, therefore, cost him but about forty dollars per one hundred dollar bond. When, after the war, these bonds went not only to par with gold but to a premium, my uncle received the reward for his confidence in our Union which he so richly deserved.

"Puddles" (1930)

Jay G. Sigmund

Originally from Waubeek in northern Linn County, Jay G. Sigmund is arguably America's most forgotten Regionalist. An insurance executive by day in Cedar Rapids, Sigmund quietly built a reputation as one of the leading Iowa literary figures of his time, a reputation endorsed by the likes of Grant Wood, Carl Sandburg, and Sherwood Anderson. In his introduction to Sigmund's short story collection Wapsipinicon Tales *(1927),* Newberry Prize-winning author Charles Finger, effused, "Someday, when historians of the future cast about in newspapers and magazines for material to enable them to reconstruct ways of life in the Middle West, someone may exhume Sigmund's books and great will be the joy of the discoverer." Sigmund's heart belonged to the Wapsi River and its quirky, backwater villages, towns like the mythical Ontarns, which serves as the backdrop for his quintessentially Iowan, grass-is-greener story, "Puddles," from* The Ridge Road. *Gorge Rapids, the antithesis of Ontarns in this short fiction, represents Cedar Rapids and its ilk.*

Morning came to the little Wapsipinicon town of Ontarns in much the same way as age crept on its inhabitants—slowly, with a strange grayness, yet with a surefootedness that impressed one of a practical thoroughness.

Delbert Montcarn, the storekeeper, for all of the romantic sound of his name, was almost the same color as Ontarns. Clay Street and he matched their environment—even to the morning which was gray with river mists—as a grub fits into the protective color scheme of the old post which houses it in its center.

Delbert Montcarn could not remember that he had ever had a feeling of nostalgia before; in fact, there has never been reason for any periods of homesickness, for he had seldom, in the sixty-eight years of his uneventful life, been away from his natal town except on an occasional visit or a buying trip to Chicago. But today, suddenly and ruthlessly, there was to come to him the first radical change in his life. Today he was leaving Ontarns. The store had been sold, the new proprietor was already in town, and they were moving, he and Ma and Luella, to Gorge Rapids, the county seat and a city of sixty thousand people.

The door of the store opened and broke the reverie into which Delbert had allowed himself to drift, as he sat by the sheet-iron heater near the candy case of his general store.

His visitor greeted him with a grunted "Good morning." It was Horace Diltz, postmaster of Ontarns and likewise mayor. Horace and Delbert had pulled in double harness for the good of their native town for many years, and if the town bore scant evidence of their efforts to improve its streets, its buildings and its riverfront, it did not mean that these two somber men and their loyal coworkers had been lacking in enthusiasm.

Horace slumped into a burlap-covered chair opposite Delbert. His face, which was thin and expressionless, was covered with a week's growth of bristles, and except for brownish tobacco stains that reached out from the corners of his sagging mouth, there was little variation in the monotonous grayness of his whole person from the scanty mop of hair protruding from under his ancient felt hat to the frayed laces of his shoes.

"Is this the day you're goin'?" asked Horace. His voice was throaty and the question carried nothing to indicate that there was enough interest back of it to justify its asking.

"Yes," replied Delbert, turning the cigar stub which protruded from his mouth with a deft movement of the tongue, "this is the day. I'm just watchin' the store here for Meigs until he goes to breakfast. He's got possession now. The truck will be here in an hour from Gorge Rapids for our household goods, and Ma and I and Luella will drive in ahead of them and be there in the house to straighten things around. We're comin' back here tomorrow to clean up the house. Meigs is movin' in there, you know, and Ma says she don't want them to move into a dirty place."

"You'll be back here now and then, though?" queried Horace. There was almost a note of plaintiveness in his voice.

"Oh, it may be we'll get out once in a while, but I'm afraid not very often," Delbert answered with a readiness that covered up a strange note in his words. "You see, we'll be pretty busy for a spell. Luella will go right to work and she's goin' to board at home, so Ma will be kind of tied down. Then there'll be a lot for me to look after. I've got some business that I've been puttin' off in Gorge Rapids, and the place we've bought, while it's a good house and all that, needs some fixin' up. The back yard is all sodded, and I want to get that plowed and ready for a garden next spring. Ma wants a trellis put up beside the porch, and if I get time this fall, I want to paint the house. There'll be plenty to keep a fellow busy."

"You know, Delbert," Horace spoke in a low tone and leaned over in his chair toward his friend, "I can't help but think you're makin' a mistake in leavin' Ontarns."

"Why?" Delbert started as though some secret which he had hugged to himself had suddenly been discovered by another.

"Well," drawled Horace, "here you are somebody. This may be a little puddle, but in it you're quite a good-sized toad. Gorge Rapids is a good-size puddle. There a fellow can croak hard and not be heard much."

"Well, but Horace," answered Delbert in a tone that seemed anxious, "I've got something to think of besides myself. I've done good here, I know, and I'm kind of sorry to leave, but what good does it do to educate a girl and then keep her in a place like this? We've worked hard and saved and sent Luella through college and then sent her to business college. She wants to get into the business world, and so I got her this secretary's job in the wholesale house. Ma would never be satisfied to see her go to the city alone, and neither would I. I'll tell you, Horace, it's pretty dull in a place like this for young folks. I can't blame 'em for wantin' to get away. Of course you've managed to keep Alice with you. She took to teachin' and she was lucky and got the home school, but Luella wanted to get into business, and the store here didn't suit her. I don't see no other way out of it but to get her where she's got a chance, and, then, I'm gettin' on in years too. And besides, I've got enough to keep me without workin' anymore." This last remark was made in a tone of pride, well suppressed.

"Oh, I know," Horace answered hastily, "you're fixed so you can do it. It wasn't *that* I was thinkin' of. You've always done better than me. I couldn't go to Gorge Rapids and live if I wanted to. I ain't fixed well enough, but I was just thinkin' of all you meant to this community, and what you'd leave, and how you'd miss it, maybe. You've got a good business here. You've been a church leader. You've been mayor of the town. You've been president of the school board. You've been Republican delegate. You've been county supervisor, and I don't know what else. Everybody knows you for miles around. You stand ace-high with everyone. It takes years to build up a reputation like you've got, and when a man's your age he don't make acquaintances as fast as a younger man. That's what I was thinkin' of."

The two men remained silent for a few moments, but the swinging of the door interrupted their thoughts, and a girl of perhaps twenty years entered the store. She was dressed in a fashionable though rather shoddy frock, and her closely-cropped blond hair was waved in the latest mode. Laughter was in the blue eyes, and though her cheeks were over-rouged and her lips too scarlet for real freshness, there was a certain prettiness of feature that seemed strangely out of place against the somber background of the cluttered old store.

"Pa, why aren't you coming to breakfast?" said the girl in her high-pitched voice.

"I'm waitin' for Meigs to come back," answered her father in the tone men use when they are in the presence of domineering members of their household.

"Oh, hang Meigs," said the girl impatiently. Lock the dump up. I'd think you'd had enough of this. Do you know," this to Horace, "Pa has been mooning around like he was homesick. I almost believe he hates to leave this burg!"

"How about *you*, Luella?" asked Horace in his colorless tone.

"*Me?*" The girl broke into laughter. "Why I'm floating in air, I'm that tickled. Say, Mr. Diltz," said the girl in her nervous accents, "do you know the last week has seemed like an age to me. I simply can't stand it here any longer. I'm sick of the town, sick of the faces, sick of the very songs they sing in the church. The sight of that river on a morning like this makes me shudder. I guess I never was cut out to live in a small town. I told my girlfriend in Gorge Rapids a few days ago that it was funny how I never took to this place. It's mighty strange, my being born and raised here, too. But from the time I was old enough to realize anything, I've always wanted to get out of here and go to the city. Of course I stood it until now, but Pa is getting old and Ma ought to have a better house, and after I came home from Gorge Rapids, I just put my foot down and insisted that the folks had to get out of here. Lord, I'd die if I couldn't get away."

"Alice is quite contented here," said Horace feebly. It seemed he could offer no other defense to the girl's indictment of the town.

"Oh, I know," answered Luella. "Alice is very happy here, and I'm so glad, but," she patted her blond hair at the temples, "Alice is quite a different person. She and I are much different in temperament. Alice is quieter. She is satisfied with the commonplace. As for me, well," the girl broke into laughter again, "I guess there's a sort of romantic streak in me, though for the life of me I don't know where it could come from, but I love cities. I crave something exciting. I simply can't stand the humdrum existence of a place like this. I'm going into business, not because I'm so much in love with business, but because business means the city and the city means people—lots of people, and where there's people, things happen, and, when things happen, life has color—but," looking toward her father, "Pa and Ma find it hard to understand me. It's no wonder. I'm so different from them."

The two old men walked toward the door. The young woman followed them. At the door they met a man who, though he was well past middle age, looked young and his clothes were suggestive of the city. He paused to take the key to the door from Delbert Montcarn. Awkwardly Delbert introduced him to his daughter as Mr. Meigs, the new proprietor of the store.

Meigs acknowledged the introduction with an easy friendliness and took in Luella from head to foot with a swift glance of appraisal.

"Well, Miss Montcarn," he said laughingly, "here you go to Gorge Rapids while I come from Gorge Rapids to take your place in Ontarns. Your father tells me you do not regret leaving here."

"Quite the contrary," laughed Luella. "I'm glad to go, to fill up the place you leave in the great city."

"Well," answered Meigs, "Good luck! I'm glad, for my part, to get away from the city. I come from a long line of farmer folk, and as I grew older I felt an urge to get back to a place like this. I nearly went on a farm, but finally compromised on this store. I'm going to be satisfied here, I'm sure. I hope you will be, with your new life in the city."

The two old men walked on ahead. For a moment they were both silent. At last Horace Diltz spoke.

"There's something I can't understand. There's a man who's always lived in a big city comin' here to this small town, and here you're leavin' here and goin' to the city. I can't make it out. His folks, he says, was country folks. Now he feels like gettin' back to the country again. But your folks was here before you, Delbert, and here's your daughter wantin' to get out of here and get to a bigger place. It's more'n I can understand, unless it's some kind of a throwback. Somewhere there must of been some of your folks that was in big puddles."

The two men parted at Delbert Montcarn's gate.

"I'll be in to see you before I go," said Delbert as they parted.

Mrs. Montcarn met her husband and daughter at the door. Her ample form was clad in a gingham dress and a "dust-cap" was above her perspiring, round face. As they crossed the door sill, she sank into a rocker and addressed her husband:

"Pa, I wish you'd look over everything in the attic before we go. There's loads of trash up there in them old trunks your mother left, and I don't believe we want to take any of it with us. But you look it all over. The trunks ain't been touched since your mother died."

Slowly Delbert Montcarn climbed the stairs which led up to the dusty attic. It had been a number of years since he had visited the musty old room above the rooms where he had lived so many years. He was the youngest of five children and the only one of the family surviving. His mother had died under his roof at an advanced age, and her few poor effects, including two ancient battered trunks, had been stored at her son's house since her death.

Delbert had never really known his mother. She had seemed, outwardly, much like the other farmers' wives in the neighborhood, but her silence, which was broken only on rare occasions, covered well her real self, and the shy soul of her youngest son had never broken beyond the wall of it.

Delbert stood for a long time over one of the ancient trunks. At last he lifted the lid, showering dust on the pine floor as he did so.

The trunk was full of old dresses, old books, two or three family albums and some newspapers yellowed with age. Delbert rummaged among the musty things. One album was filled with tintypes of people dressed in garments long gone out of fashion, and the styles of beards and hairdress made even the somber storekeeper smile. As he turned the pages, he came upon a yellowed envelope.

The address was so faded as to be almost illegible, and even the postmark was blurred from age.

Delbert inserted a soiled forefinger into the envelope and drew out the letter. It was yellowed and faded too, but not so much but it could be easily made out. The writing was a woman's, and Delbert saw that it was a message written to his mother by his grandmother. The letter said:

> *Dear Daughter:*
>
> *I received your note, and I make haste to answer. Do not, I beg of you, do as you say you feel like doing. Your husband is a splendid man and though he is only a farmer, as your own father was, he is a man who is worthy of you, a man of principle, and thrifty. I know how you dislike the life of a farmer's wife, and how you long for the city, as I once did. But this, my daughter, you will get over, and in time you will learn to make the most of your lot, as I have done. Remember your child. Be silent and remember that as the wife of your husband, you are a person of some note among your neighbors. I find that discontent is in the hearts of many people. It is not alone the farm folk who feel it. How do you know that you would lose it in the city? To leave your husband will only bring unhappiness to him and disgrace to you.*
>
> *—Your Mother*

For a long time Delbert Montcarn sat and held the yellowed sheets in his hand. In his eyes was a look which comes to the eyes of one who only half understands a newfound truth, but who accepts and gropes no farther.

"Horace was right," he muttered. "It's a throwback. That's what makes 'em want to get into big puddles, and sometimes when they're there, makes 'em want to get out."

Up the stairway came Luella's high-pitched voice.

"Hurry up, Pa, the truck's here!"

FROM **THE GREEN TREE (1931)**

FRITIOF FRYXELL

A slight editorial exception is here made for Fritiof Fryxell, who grew up on the wrong side of the Mississippi to be considered a full-fledged Iowan, but who wrote exquisitely about Le Claire, Iowa and the Mississippi Valley from his home base in the Quad Cities. An Augustana College graduate, Fryxell served as the first chair of the geology department there. A frequent researcher at Grand Teton National Park in Wyoming, which he helped establish, somehow Fryxell managed to find equal natural beauty and history in the famous "Le Claire Elm" or "Green Tree" on the banks of the Mississippi River. This Iowa arboreal ode reminds of the best writing of Henry David Thoreau, John Burroughs, and John Muir, only set right here at home.

The noblest among the tree celebrities of the upper Mississippi Valley is the famous elm claimed by the old river town of Le Claire, Iowa. From considerations of size, beauty, and historic associations, this is s a tree of exceptional interest and personality. It was eminently fitting in 1912 it should be elected to a place in the "Hall of Fame for Trees" at Washington.

"The Le Claire Elm" is the name by which this tree has become known far and wide through the Mississippi Valley, but to the residents of the village and the surrounding countryside it is known as "The Green Tree." Back of this somewhat enigmatic name lies a fascinating story.

In the antebellum river days, the days immortalized by Mark Twain in *Life on the Mississippi*, the village of Le Claire was an important river port because of the strategic position which it occupied at the head of the Upper, or Rock Island, Rapids. Steamboats and rafts plying the upper Mississippi were compelled to stop here before starting across the rapids or after having passed them. Thus Le Claire became a great river town. "When the river business was at its high mark," says a historians of those early days, "Le Claire could boast without fear of contradiction of furnishing more pilots and engineers than any other town or city on the Mississippi."

A few rods upstream from the Le Claire landing place there stood by the water's edge a shapely elm whose branches overarched a large plot of sloping ground. This naturally became a rendezvous for river men from far and near who, often penniless, came to Le Claire looking for jobs as river hands, or to catch a ride up or down the river (in many cases it mattered little which). Under the grateful shade of the elm, they congregated, spread their blankets, and cooked their meals, often making this spot their home for weeks at a time. With characteristic Yankee humor they dubbed this inexpensive open-air lodging house "The Green Tree Hotel," and by this name it came to be known among the river men from St. Paul to New Orleans.

The scene has changed. Now the river is silent and deserted compared to what it was in those heydays of steamboat traffic. It has been so for soon half a century. The rough and picturesque river men no longer crowd the wharves or gather in the shade of the elm to cook, sleep, or swap river yarns and river gossip while waiting for their ships to come in. They are a vanished generation. But the grand old tree stills stands, grown patriarchal with the passing years, and its local name, The Green Tree, perpetuates the faded glory of the all but forgotten days of the '40s and '50s.

In the early days the Father of Waters lapped against the very foot of the Green Tree. The town youngsters—The Tom Sawyers and Huck Finns of this community—frequently met under the elm, played games, and doubtless concocted much mischief. Perched on the roots of the tree they could dangle their bare feet idly in the current and wriggle their toes in the sand.

One day in the summer of 1852 a new boy ventured into the circle, a stranger belonging to the family just moved down from a farm located a few miles back on the prairies and now living in the frame house "up the road a piece." Upon invitation the newcomer stripped and, leaving his clothes under The Green Tree, joined his future comrades in a swim.

A few minutes later, from the direction of the shore came derisive yells of "Chaw beef!" Breathes there a boy with a soul so dead that he doesn't instinctively feel the urge of battle at the call of "Chaw Beef?" Well—the newcomer did chaw beef, of course, but when the knots in his sleeves and shirt tails were all solved, he unhesitatingly set himself to the task in hand, and because he was tall, sturdy, and a born scrapper, he soundly thrashed the ringleader of his tormentors. So the stranger won for himself a place of honor in that pioneer community.

Today there stands a granite monument under The Green Tree dedicating the elm to the memory of the newcomer of that faraway day. It was erected by another of the youngsters then present, a little fellow who went by the nickname "The Runt" and how with the rest had lustily shouted "Chaw beef!" The inscription on the granite slab will tell the rest of the story—

Dedicated to
Col. Wm. F. Cody
"Buffalo Bill"

By his friend and boyhood playmate
Joe Barnes
Erected in 1924

Of the house near Le Claire in which William Cody was born, not a vestige remains today. It was located a couple of miles inland from the elm. It is to be hoped that at some not distant day a marker will be placed to indicate the spot where the house stood. The frame house "up the road a piece" in which Cody spent part of his boyhood days still stands and the new hard road passes in a few yards of its aged and rickety threshold. The country roundabout is rich in associations of the Cody family, but that is another story.*

And a picture of the Green Tree itself, placed in this attractive setting. It stands in the heart of the village about forty feet from the water's edge. The massive, well-turned bole, four feet in diameter, springs unbuttressed from the ground and rises with scarcely perceptible taper to a height of twenty feet, where it bursts into that magnificent crown which, once seen, is not to be forgotten.

Rarely, if ever, may one find a nobler example of intricate and majestic branching than that afforded by this lordly old elm. The huge lower limbs are thrust far out horizontally, and at their extremities almost sweep the ground. The others are tossed skyward, but because they are shorter, the crown of the tree is given an oval shape, being more than twice as broad as high. Though the total height of the tree is not much in excess of fifty feet, the crown canopies an area measuring over one hundred feet north and south and eighty feet east and west.

All of the limbs are grandly twisted and contorted, yet in their ensemble they give the crown a symmetry that is irreproachable. This marvelous symmetry and beauty of branching can best be appreciated if the tree be studied in late winter, when not a leaf remains to obscure the exquisite tracery, and every tortuous limb may be followed from its thick knotted base to its countless tips. To me The Green Tree has always seemed most appealing so, when displayed in the stark bareness of winter, but others prefer it in summer, when the foliage is so dense that the magnificent framework which supports it is quite lost to view.

The Green Tree is redeemed from the flaw of painful perfection in that it leans pronouncedly toward the river. Perhaps this inclination is lightward, perhaps it is the result of the settling of the riverbanks, long ago. Whatever the cause, it serves rather to heighten the individuality of the tree than to detract from it.

It has pleased me to fancy that when The Green Tree was yet but a slender sapling on the banks of the Mississippi, it was singled out to be henceforth the object of special dispensations, that some day it might be displayed as the very exemplification of tree nobility. Does it not seem so? How The Green Tree was rescued from the river and from the railroad has already been told, but that is not all the story:

The Green Tree has never been torn by lightning or rent by storm, and the "globe" character of its crown makes the splitting off of limbs extremely improbable in the future. Thus it is spared the greatest menace which ordinarily threatens the elm.

Its roots are sunk in beds perennially saturated from the river; hence The Green Tree has never experienced drought, and never will.

Nor has the tree been denied its full measure of the life-bestowing sunlight, for to the east, northeast, and southeast stretches only the broad expanse of the Mississippi.

The full, rounded contour of the crown of The Green Tree testifies that at least for many decades no crowding neighbors have contested its ground. Now the elm stands quite alone, and it is the more majestic and imposing for being so.

Through the campfires have doubtless often been kindled beneath The Green Tree since the early days when the Sacs and Foxes held this land against the claims of rival tribes, there is no evidence to indicate that any of them ever seriously marred its shapely trunk.

From these dispensations—and the list might be lengthened—is one not justified in concluding that here indeed is a veritable "Nature's darling"?

From **A Boyhood in Iowa (1931)**

Herbert Hoover

The bullet points of Herbert Hoover's remarkable life are well-known by Iowans everywhere—Hoover the Engineer, Hoover the Great Humanitarian, Hoover the Secretary of Commerce under Harding and Coolidge, Hoover the hard-pressed President during the Great Depression. But more than a few students of Iowa forget that Hoover actually spent only his first ten years in the Hawkeye State—the bulk in West Branch during which time both of his parents died, and a shorter stay in Kingsley, Iowa, prior to joining his uncle John in Oregon. Still, Hoover, the first president born west of the Mississippi, kindled a lasting warmth for Iowa as home. In the delightful reminiscence that follows, Hoover purposefully abandons an engineer's logic and recalls the boy-life that, as he put it, "reminds me that I have the brand of Iowa still upon me." Note that Hoover originally delivered this speech during his tenure as Secretary of Commerce, hence the opening reference.

As the head of the Department of Commerce, I am presumed to deal on all public occasions with heavy economic discussions, with terrific volleys of statistics, diatribes on national delinquencies, or sovereign remedies for national economic woes, or solemn assurances as to the progress of national welfare. I suppose I could talk about Iowa in this fashion. I could summon a battalion of experts from the Department and, having skimmed their intellects, I could churn out something in compliance with the Organic Act creating my job. But if I did, I should probably be accused of trampling on the feet of the Interstate Commerce Commission if I mention railways, of the Highway Bureau if I mention roads, of the Bureau of Education if I mention schools, or of the Treasury if I mention taxes, and above all upon the Department of Agriculture if I mention farms; and Iowa is mostly made of such economic compounds.

But I prefer to think of Iowa as I saw it through the eyes of a ten-year-old boy—and the eyes of all ten-year-old Iowa boys are or should be filled with the wonders of Iowa's streams and woods, of the mystery of growing crops. His days should be filled with adventure and great undertakings, with participation in good and comforting things. I was taken farther west from Iowa when I was ten, to Oregon and thence to that final haven of Iowans—California—where I have clung ever since. Someone may say that these recollections of Iowa are only the illusions of forty years after, but I know better—for I have been back and checked them up. I was told that when I went back everything would have shrunk up and become small and ordinary. For instance, there was Cook's Hill—that great long hill where, on winter nights, we slid down at terrific speeds, with our tummies tight to homemade sleds. I've seen it several times since; it's a good hill, and except for the older method of thawing out frozen toes with ice water, the operation needs no modern improvement. The swimming hole under the willows down by the railroad bridge is still operating efficiently, albeit modern mothers probably compel their youngsters to take a bath to get rid of clean and healthy mud when they come home. The hole still needs to be deepened, however. It is hard to keep from pounding the mud with your hands and feet when you shove off for the thirty feet of a cross-channel swim. And there were the woods down the Burlington track. The denudation of our forest hasn't reached them even yet, and I know there are rabbits still being trapped in cracker boxes held open by a figure four at the behest of small boys at this very time. I suspect, however, that the conservationists have invented some kind of a closed season before now. One of the bitterest days of my life was in connection with a rabbit. Rabbits fresh from a figure-four trap early on a cold morning are wiggly rabbits, and in the lore of boys of my time it is better to bring them home alive. My brother, being older, had surreptitiously behind the blacksmith shop read in the *Youth's Companion* [magazine] full directions for rendering live rabbits secure. I say "surreptitiously," for mine was a Quaker family unwilling in those days to have youth corrupted with stronger reading than the Bible, the encyclopedia or those great novels where the hero overcomes the demon rum. Soon after he had acquired this higher learning on rabbits, he proceeded to instruct me to stand still in the cold snow and to hold up the rabbit by its hind feet while with his not oversharp knife he proposed to puncture two holes between the sinews and back knee joints of the rabbit, through which holes he proposed to tie a string and thus arrive at complete security. Upon the introduction of the operation, the resistance of this rabbit was too much for me. I was not only blamed for its escape all the way home and for weeks afterwards, but continuously over the last forty years. I had thought sometimes that I would write the *Youth's Companion* and suggest they make sure that this method is altered. For I never see rabbit tracks across the snowy fields that I do not have a painful recollection of it all.

There were also at times pigeons in this great forest, and prairie chickens in the hedges. With the efficient instruction of a real live American Indian boy from a neighboring Indian school on the subject of bows and arrows, we sometimes by firing volleys in battalions were able to bring down a pigeon or a chicken. The Ritz Hotel has never yet provided game of such wondrous flavor as this bird plucked and half-cooked over the small boys' campfire. And in those days there were sun- and catfish to be had. Nor did we possess the modern equipment in artificial lures, tackle assembled from the steel of Damascus, the bamboos of Siam, tin of

Bangkok, the lacquer of China or silver of Colorado. We were still in that rude but highly social condition of using a willow pole with a butcher string line and hooks ten for a dime. Our compelling lure was a segment of an angleworm, and our incantation was to spit on the bait. We lived in the time when fish used to bite instead of strike, and we knew it bit when the cork bobbed. And moreover, we ate the fish.

And in the matter of eating, my recollections of Iowa food are of the most distinguished order. You may say that is the appetite of youth, but I have also checked this up. At later stages in my life I had opportunity to eat both of the presumably very best food in the world, as well of the very worst. When I ate the worst, my thoughts went back to Iowa, and when I ate of the best I was still sure that Aunt Millie was a better cook. Some thirty years after this time, in visiting Aunt Millie, I challenged that dear old lady, then far along in years, to cook another dinner of the kind she provided on Sabbath days when we were both youthful. She produced that dinner, and I am able to say now that if all the cooks of Iowa are up to Aunt Millie's standard, then the gourmets of the world should leave Paris for Iowa, at least for Cedar County.

I mentioned the Burlington track. It was a wonderful place: the track was ballasted with glacial gravels where, on industrious search, you discovered gems of agate and fossil coral which could with infinite backaches be polished on the grindstone. Their fine points came out wonderfully when wet, and you had to lick them with your tongue before each exhibit. I suppose that engineering has long since destroyed this inspiration to young geologists by using mass production crushed rock.

My earliest realization of the stir of national life was the torch parade in the Garfield campaign. On that occasion I was not only allowed out that night—but I saw the lamps being filled and lighted. There was no great need for urging voters in our village—there was a Democrat in the village. He occasionally fell to the influence of liquor, therefore in the esteem of our group, he represented all the forces of evil. At times he relapsed to goodness in the form of rations of a single gumdrop to the small boys who did errands at his store. He also bought the old iron from which the financial resources were provided for firecrackers on the Fourth of July. He was therefore tolerated and he served well and efficiently as a moral and political lesson. But Iowa through the eyes of a ten-year-old boy is not all adventure or high living. Iowa in those years, as in these years, was filled with days of school—and who does not remember with a glow that sweet-faced lady who with infinite patience and kindness drilled into us those foundations of all we know today? And they were days of chores and labor. I am no supporter of factory labor for children, but I have never joined with those who clamored against proper work of children on farms outside their school hours. And I speak from the common experience of most Iowa children of my day in planting corn, hoeing gardens, learning to milk, sawing wood, and the other proper and normal occupations for boys. We had no need of Montessori schools to teach us application. But of more purpose I can bespeak for the strong and healthy bodies which come from it all. Nor was Iowa of those days without its tragedies. Medical science of those times was powerless against the contagious diseases which swept the countryside. My own parents were among its victims.

There was an entirely different economic setting of farm life in Iowa in those days. I am not stating to you that I had at that time any pretense of economics or the farm problem. Upon the farm of the uncle with whom I lived we did know of the mortgage as some dreadful damper on youthful hopes of things that could not be bought. I do have a vivid recollection that the major purpose of a farm was to produce a living right on the spot for the family. I know by experience that a family then produced all of its own vegetables, carried its grain to the nearest mill for grinding on toll, cut and hauled its own fuel from the wonderful woods ten miles away, and incidentally gathered walnuts. The family wove its own carpets and some of its clothes, made its own soap, preserved its own meat and fruit and vegetables, got its sweetness from sorghum and honey. These families consumed perhaps eighty percent of the product of their land. Twenty percent of it was exchanged for the few outside essentials and to pay interest on the mortgage. When prices rose and fell on the Chicago market, they only affected twenty percent of the product of the farm. I know, and you know, that today as the result of the revolution brought about by machinery and improved methods of planting and breeding animals, and whatnot, eighty percent of the product of the farm must go to the market. When the price of these things wobbles in Chicago, it has four times the effect on that family on the farm that it did in those days. If prices are high—they mean comfort and automobiles; if prices are low—they mean increasing debt and privation. I am not recommending the good old days, for while the standards of living in food and clothing and shelter were high enough for anybody's health and comfort, there was but little left for the other purposes of living. That is probably one reason why the people of Iowa of that time put more of their time into religious devotion than most of them do now. It certainly did not require as much expenditure as their recreation does today. However, those of you who are acquainted with the Quaker faith, and who know the primitive furnishing of the Quaker meetinghouse of those days, the solemnity of the long hours of meeting awaiting the spirit to move someone, will know the intense restraint required in a ten-year-old boy not even to count his toes. All this may not have been recreation, but it was strong training in patience. And that reminds me that I have the brand of Iowa still upon me, for one of my earliest recollections of that great and glorious state was stepping barefooted on a red hot iron chip at my father's blacksmith shop, the scar of which I still carry.

But there are few scars that people carry from the state of Iowa. The good Lord originally made it the richest stretch of agricultural land that ever blessed any one sovereign government. It was populated by the more adventurous and the more courageous, who fought their way along the ever-extending frontier. They builded here in so short a period as seventy-five years a people who today enjoy the highest standard of living, the highest average intelligence, the highest average degree of education that has ever blessed a single commonwealth. There is no man or woman born of Iowa who is no proud of his native state.

From **Stories of Iowa for Boys and Girls (1931)**

Ruth A. Gallaher and Bruce E. Mahan

The best way to quickly apprehend the essence of any historical event is often to read a young adult treatment of the subject, a fact well understood by Ruth Gallaher and Bruce Mahan in Stories of Iowa for Boys and Girls. *Both came to the task well-qualified—Mahan as a lecturer in history at the University of Iowa; Gallaher as a library research associate of the State Historical Society—though they insisted on decidedly nonacademic "concrete incidents rather than lengthy and abstract narrative." In their introduction, Gallaher and Mahan write, "An attempt has been made to tell the story of Iowa as a colorful drama enacted upon the prairies and along the rivers of the Iowa country. The demand of boys and girls for life and action and movement in stories has been kept in mind." The result is this short, plainspoken chapter on how Iowa soldiers spent their first Christmas in France. Easily missed in this understated narrative is the symbolic importance of Merle Hay of Glidden, Iowa—arguably the first American killed in World War I and the namesake for Merle Hay Road and Merle Hay Mall in Des Moines.*

In the summer of 1914 a great war began in Europe. On one side were Austria, Germany, Bulgaria, and Turkey, countries in the central part of Europe. Against them were Russia, Serbia, France, Belgium, Great Britain, Italy, Romania, and Portugal.

As the war went on, Germany tried to destroy all the commerce of Great Britain, so the people could not get food. The German submarines—boats which can run under the surface of the water—were sent out to sink ships going to England. The United States told the Germans that they must not sink American ships; but sometimes they did, and a number of Americans were killed.

Finally President Woodrow Wilson asked Congress to declare that the United States was at war with Germany. This was done on the sixth of April, 1917. Of course there was great excitement everywhere. People knew that many young men would be sent across the Atlantic Ocean to help fight the German army.

Soon after the war with Germany began, the United States government decided to send a division of National Guard troops to Europe. This was called the Forty-second Division, but it soon came to be known as the Rainbow Division, because it contained regiments from many parts of the country.

At this time the three National Guard regiments of Iowa had just returned to their homes from the Mexican border, where they had been doing guard duty.

They had not been home long, however, before they received orders to assemble at Des Moines.

The Third Iowa Regiment had been chosen to represent the state in the Rainbow Division. As there were not enough men in this regiment, several hundred were taken from the First and Second Regiments to give the Third Iowa a war-strength of 3600 men. In August, 1917, the Third Iowa was made a part of the United States Army. It was then called the 168th United States Infantry.

The 168th Infantry joined the others which belonged to the Rainbow Division at Camp Mills in September. They did not stay there long. The Rainbow Division was one of the first sent to France. On December 9, 1917, the men of the 168th Infantry arrived at the port of Le Havre, France. The weather was cold and rainy. Three days later the Iowa boys were sent to a little French village called Rimaucourt. How strange everything seemed to the men from Iowa. They could not understand the people, for everyone in the village spoke French.

The soldiers had to live in barns and attics or anywhere they could find shelter from the cold. There were tiny stoves in some of the rooms, but there was not much wood, so the men were often cold. They even had to eat their meals outdoors. The French people, however, were kind to the soldiers who had come so far to help them, and the men were cheerful.

But Christmas was coming. The soldiers thought of their homes back in Iowa. They could not go back to see the Christmas trees or to get their presents. They were cold and sometimes hungry. What were they to do? They talked it over among themselves and decided that it would be great fun to have a Christmas tree for the little French children in the village.

You see the fathers of most of these children had been fighting since 1914. Many of them had been killed. Food was very high and they did not have any money to buy toys or candy. The Iowa soldiers planned to surprise these little French children. They invited them all to a celebration on Christmas Eve.

How the men worked! They asked the *curé*, or priest, in the village if they might have the program in the little stone church. They were afraid the German aviators might see the lights on the tree and drop bombs on them if they had it out-of-doors. The priest was very glad to let them use the church

Then they had to have a tree. They went to the lady who owned a beautiful home or chateau near Rimaucourt and asked if she would give them a tree from her park. She said they might have one.

Of course a Christmas tree must have lights. So the men of the Signal Corps, who take care of such things as lights, radios, and telegraph wires for the army, fixed the lights. They put colored bulbs all over the tree.

But a Christmas tree needs something besides lights. There should be presents. There were not many toys in Rimaucourt and not much candy. But Chaplain Winfred T. Robb, after much searching, found both toys and candy. There had to be a lot, too, for there were two hundred children in Rimaucourt and as many more were expected from nearby villages.

Christmas Eve came. More than four hundred French children crowded into the little church. There was the tall tree ablaze with lights. The band played. How excited the children were. They were almost afraid of the tall American soldiers who could not talk to them in French. But up in front were two Santa Clauses. The children were told to go up to them and get their presents. They were very polite and said *merci*, which was the French for "thank you."

The old priest repeated a prayer and tried to thank the American soldiers in English for being so kind to the French children. Then the band played the "Star Spangled Banner," and the children started for home, laughing and tooting their new horns. In, the streets the snow was falling softly.

The next day was Christmas. The soldiers were disappointed because the mail did not reach Rimaucourt. Most of all they wanted to hear how their people were back home in Iowa. It was clear and cold. One thing pleased them. There were turkeys for dinner, with English walnuts, apples, and figs, besides the things they usually had.

Perhaps you would like to know what happened to the men of the 168th Infantry after this Christmas celebration. For a while they were kept in training camps. Then in February, 1918, they were taken to the front and put in charge of some trenches. These trenches were deep ditches which helped protect the men from the German shells and bullets. Beyond them were others in which were German soldiers. Between the two lines were fences and networks of barbed wire so the men could not cross to capture the enemy trenches.

For months the men of the 168th Infantry fought the men of the German army. Many of the Iowa boys were killed. Many others were wounded and sick. Some of them were sent home. And then on the eleventh of November, 1918, which you know as Armistice Day, the day agreed upon with the Germans, the fighting stopped. After that the Iowa soldiers did not have to live in the muddy trenches or see their friends killed by the shells.

They hoped that they would be sent home to Iowa very soon, but the war was not yet over. The American army was sent into Germany. They were to stay there until the terms of peace could be decided. There was no fighting, but again the men of the 168th Infantry had to make long marches in the cold. Their shoes wore out, and the new supply did not reach them until they were nearly at the end of their march. The Iowa regiment, however, was soon settled for the winter in a number of German villages along the Rhine River. There they spent their second Christmas away from Iowa.

They stayed here until April, 1919. Then they were sent to Brest, France, where they boarded a great steamship, the *Leviathan*, which carried nearly 12,000 soldiers. Soon they were back in New York, and on May 14th, the 168th Infantry reached Des Moines. The day was clear and warm as the men in full equipment marched through the streets to the Capitol grounds.

The old Third Iowa had returned, but not all the men came back. More than half of the men who had left Des Moines in the spring of 1917 had been killed in battle, died of disease, or been so badly wounded that they were sent to the hospitals. Many things had happened to the regiment since the Christmas Eve at Rimaucourt in 1917.

The men in this regiment were not the only ones from Iowa in the World War. More than 113,000 Iowa men served in the United States Army, Navy, and Marine Corps. One of the first American soldiers killed in battle was Merle Hay of Glidden, Iowa. During the period of the war more than two thousand soldiers and sailors from Iowa were killed in battle or died from disease.

Near Des Moines the War Department established Camp Dodge, named for General Grenville M. Dodge. Here thousands of men from many states were trained for war service overseas. These soldiers lived in large unpainted frame buildings, called barracks. Not far away was Fort Des Moines, which had been established in 1901. This was first used for a training camp, but was soon used as an Army hospital.

FROM STATE FAIR (1932)

PHIL STONG

Phillip Duffield Stong easily qualifies as one of Iowa's most prolific, and most popular writers, and his novel State Fair, *from which the chapter below is drawn, stands as his most beloved. Born in Pittsburg, Iowa, just west of Keosauqua where the Des Moines River takes its conspicuous "Big Bend" on the way to the Mississippi, Stong attended Drake University and took graduate classes at Columbia University in New York for a year before returning to the Midwest to teach high school, and, ultimately, college courses at his alma mater. At Drake, Stong had an epiphany—if he kept on teaching, he'd be stuck as a professor forever. A newspaper job, however, like the one he was already working part-time at the* Des Moines Register, *would allow him to practice rather than preach. And so he did, eventually earning a coveted staff position at the* New York World. *Even journalism, though, paled by comparison with the thrills of imaginative writing, so when Stong published* State Fair *to rave reviews—and a selection by the Literary Guild—he quit his newspaper gig, too.* State Fair *became a cultural phenomenon; just a year after its publication the film version appeared staring Will Rogers as farmer and champion hog-showman Abel Frake. In 1945, the legendary Rodgers and Hammerstein made the story into an Oscar-winning musical. In fact,* State Fair *was just one, albeit a popular one, of Stong's forty books and merely a single installment in the larger narrative of the "Pittsville" series—named for the mythical Iowa town at the center of the episodic storylines. Forever on Stong's mind, Iowa was also the subject of what the author called his "biography" of the state,* Hawkeyes *(1940), as well as a historical novel about his pioneer Iowa family,* Bucksin Breeches *(1937). Here, then, is the climactic, hog-judging chapter, "Blue Boy," from* State Fair, *a book praised by Louis Kronenberger in the* New York Times Book Review *in May of 1932 as a "brilliant rendering of the state fair setting...not forgetting Blue Boy, one of the most famous animals in American literature." The last line in the reading references the provocative bet made by the hometown storekeeper that brought the Frakes—father Abel, mother Melissa, and children Margy and Wayne—to the fair to show Blue Boy in the first place.*

"Wake up," his father said. "Today's the day they pick out Blue Boy for the finest boar was ever raised. Everybody out!"

He heard his mother rise quickly in the next cubicle. Then he heard his sister cry, out of broken sleep, "No-no—oh, I'm still half-asleep!"

He made some definite swishes and thuds which would indicate that he was dressing in all haste. Then he lay down quietly and allowed his eyes to droop half-shut. His father's pallet was rumpled and mussed—today was the day they judged Blue Boy.

Had it been an accident that Emily had touched her fingers to her lips before she waved at him last night? If he had only had opera glasses! She had worn some kind of a shimmering white dress which made her look like a wheat stalk across the sun. But he could not see her face, half across the auditorium from him. She had lifted her arm, when she saw him, and when she waved she—or did she? Certainly she waved.

"Wayne! You're going to be late for breakfast!"

"All right, Mother."

The bathhouse was a hundred yards away. He jerked on the minimum essentials of clothing and rushed out of the tent at a sprint. He liked the showers. He wished that they had showers at home. Quickly he shaved, arranged his clothing, and walked back up the hill.

Miss Iowa was a silly-looking fool. Any girl who would go in for that sort of thing must be pretty dumb and pretty cheap. She'd been brought out and introduced like an unusual heifer, or a prize sow. Next week, Emily's father had announced, Miss Iowa was to compete for the title of Miss America in Atlantic City. Champion human sow of America! But she'd never get it—they raised them better for that purpose in California. Rot! It was filthy to think about.

He spat on the grass and strode in to the breakfast table. The whole family was waiting. His father, at the head of the table, was in the act of loading his plate with poached eggs and bacon, cut thick.

"Well, Wayne, you finally got up."

"I couldn't have been much behind Margy. I saw her coming back from the ladies' baths just as I came out of the bath door."

His father laughed, but with a high pitch in his laughter. "No harm done. Come on, gobble this up. Today's Blue Boy's big day."

"What time is the judging?"

The animals will be shown tonight. But they ought to put the ribbons on the crates around four o'clock. Those judges have sized the animals up pretty well, right now. Once I know Blue Boy's taken sweepstakes, I don't care whether they parade him in a Prince Albert or a pink kimono tonight. I don't care about watching his triumphal progress."

"Maybe we could all go down together—around three thirty," Mrs. Frake suggested.

"I'd have to be down earlier than that," said Abel, "but if all of you will wait around Blue Boy's crate for me when you come in, I'll find you and we'll look over the show."

"What do you children plan to do?"

Margy waited for her brother to speak. "I didn't plan anything till evening," Wayne said. "My friend in Des Moines got a pair of tickets for a show called *Blossom Time*. I thought I'd go with him."

"That won't be over till late," Mrs. Frake said, thoughtfully. "Were you going to come back out to the grounds tonight?"

"Oh, sure—anyway, I suppose I will. He didn't say anything—" Wayne paused, confused, and wondered why he had said that.

"Well," Mrs. Frake smiled kindly, "we won't wait up for you. If you come in late, try to come in quiet."

"What are you going to do, Margy?"

The girl answered indifferently. "I'll go down with you folks to see Blue Boy get his prize. If Wayne's going in to town, I guess I'll go and see the moving-picture show this evening, and maybe ride once on the rollercoaster afterwards—maybe twice."

"I'm glad you can amuse yourselves," said Mrs. Frake. "I've just been running around so that I'm all tired out. I'm going to bed early this evening and get a good long sleep. The heat, and the people and the excitement and winning the prizes and so on kind of wore me out. And I've got lots to do tomorrow. I met that Mrs. Whittaker from Sac County at the contest yesterday, and she and her husband are coming over to eat supper tomorrow evening. Then I've got to look up some folks I met last year on the steps of the Administration Building. I'd told them I'd find them there again this year, and I've been so busy I haven't been near the place."

Abel put his arms around her shoulders and laughed. "Mama, every year you plan to come to the Fair all year, and then when you get here, as soon as you get settled and get the sewing and the washing off your hands, you begin serving company meals to all the hungry people in the state of Iowa. Now I want you to quit it and make Margy and Wayne do all the work, and go out and see a State Fair once."

"Abel Frake, I've planned and managed every one of our Fair trips, and never once has anything gone wrong—except maybe a cup or two—and everyone has had a perfectly lovely time; me, most of all." She smiled good-naturedly. "If your hog was where my pickles are, you wouldn't be so bossy all of a sudden." It was a worn family joke that Abel and Melissa should accuse each other by innuendo of unsteadiness, irritability, and Napoleonic complexes.

"Where were you last night?" Wayne asked his sister, suddenly. "I heard you come in."

There was a crash of china and a silence. "Oh, my Lord," said Margy. "Do you have to shriek at a person, Wayne? Oh, I'm sorry—I didn't mean to be cross. It's so hot my fingers were wet."

"It isn't one of the set," said Mrs. Frake. "Now, Margy, you remember the argument we had about planning things? That might just as easy have been one of the set. Why wasn't it? Because, I said to myself, 'There's two things you've got to watch out for to save your china: company, because you don't know anything about them, and Margy.' Women know how to handle china and so they get careless. Men are awkward, so they're safe. That, Margy, is why I saw to it you weren't drinking out of the one from the set."

Margy giggled, and there was an almost hysterical note in her voice. "I'm sorry, Mother. I was thinking about something else."

"Say," said Abel, "I'm not going to be cheated out of my last word, and that was, that if my hog was where those three judges put your pickles, there'd be three of the awfulest bellyaches in this town today was ever seen or known of in the state of Iowa—but I wouldn't have any chance for a prize."

Wayne wandered down to the grounds after breakfast and roamed disconsolately from stand to stand. He tried his luck on a wheel of fortune and after spending forty cents found himself in possession of a kewpie doll. It was a rather silly kewpie doll, but it was not as silly as he was when he carried it. He tried lugging it nonchalantly by the legs but immediately discovered that despite its elaborate lace dress it wore no underwear. He right-ended it and wished to God that Emily were there.

The rollercoaster was rather good the first time, but very dull after that. By and by noon came, and after lunch he read a newspaper in front of the tent and waited for three o'clock. The three of them started for the Stock Pavilion a few minutes after that hour.

The Stock Pavilion consisted of a great central auditorium with six wings running out from it at equal intervals. The hogs had been housed in the Swine Building and horses had held the Stock Pavilion until this afternoon, but the development of two new strains in the state had given hogs a special importance on this year's programs, and for one day they were given the larger building.

Abel's family found him near Blue Boy's crate in warm but genial argument with the owner of an immense red beast.

"Smoked right, I admit," said Abel. "You take Virginia ham, that's famous, but it's made from measly razorbacks we wouldn't tolerate in this part of the country. If you want to spend more than a critter is worth curing him and dressing him up, you'll get a pretty good piece of meat, no matter what. You give a Hampshire shoat the same opportunities an ornery piece of Virginia razorback gets and you'd have manna—yes, sir, just manna. As for me, there's no ham I like so well as Pella ham."

"Smithfield—" said the owner of the red animal.

"When you buy a piece of Smithfield—which I never do," said Abel, "what are you buying? You're buying fifty cents' worth of curing and ten cents' worth of moral and physical ruin the way it's worked up by the scrawny hogs of Virginia. They don't raise any hogs in Virginia. A hog's got temperament. In Iowa, he's unhappy. Anywhere else he's miserable. Iowa'll always raise better hogs than any state in the Union. Hello, folks!"

Winning his argument by this simple device of recognizing his family, Abel smiled and shook hands with the owner of the red boar and moved up toward Blue Boy.

That animal was still standing looking as much like the Apollo Belvedere as his species would permit. What he lacked in contour he partially made up in intensity, in eagerness. Adaptable, intuitive, Esmeralda had long before decided that Nature was for the moment fundamentally and unfavorably disordered. She was not altogether certain whether Blue Boy was a hog or an illusion. She had lain down to sleep out the depression.

Blue Boy for four days had grown rapidly more conscious that he was a hog. Each morning he spent an observant ten minutes in touring his cage; then he took up his post with his snout against the wires, pointed at Esmeralda. The powerful hind hocks which would one day ornament a jar filled with white vinegar and bay leaf, touch the floor only with a foremost crescent. Blue Boy was great enough to assume this attitude; he was too great to change it.

"But, Dad," cried Margy, with excitement, "Blue Boy's already won! See, they've pinned a blue ribbon on his cage!"

"That's just the class award," Abel said with an indifference which was betrayed by the trembling of his voice. "Best Hampshire boar. They're looking 'em over now to find the most physically perfect boar—all classes, sweepstakes winner. Ought to come pretty soon now. They don't have near so many entries to judge."

"Where are the judges?"

"They're in the next wing. There's a pretty good animal—no, here they come."

The judges paused at a crate up the line. They discussed a black-and-white animal with considerable animation, taking plentiful notes. Then they bore down directly on Blue Boy. All three of the judges, department heads from Nebraska U. and the State College at Ames, smiled at Margy and Mrs. Frake.

"Don't worry, ladies," a goateed man who might have been an etcher, apologized to Mrs. Frake. "We won't keep you waiting much longer." Then they looked at Blue Boy from all angles, moving around and around the cage and checking up on each other's notes in low voices. Blue Boy was bored, disdainful, and annoyed. One of the judges reached into the pen and scratched the boar's back. Blue Boy voiced his resentment in no unmistakable, though rather indolent, terms.

"Poise," said the judge, and laughed.

Blue Boy looked at the judge closely and then shifted his glance significantly to the cage opposite. "Ahoonk," he suggested, with relative mildness. "Ahoonk!"

The judge scratched him again and his attitude became even more tense.

They checked once more on Blue Boy's printed record and then moved off to the crate of the red hog.

"Aren't they going to give it to him?" asked Margy, in a repressed tone, when the judges were quite out of earshot.

"Of course they're going to give it to him. But they have to look at all the rest—just as a matter of form." Abel was nervous. Blue Boy uttered an asthmatic wish for his mudhole and his mistresses.

Blue Boy allowed his heels to touch the pen floor. Slowly the approximate conviction to which Esmeralda had attained forty-eight hours before was forcing itself upon Blue Boy's masculine mind. He submerged the repressions of four days in the one philosophic consolation left to him. After all, it was quiet here for hours at a time, sometimes. Blue Boy considered sleep.

The judges passed on, comparing notes.

And they did look at all the rest. At four thirty o'clock, when the family was at a breaking tension and Abel had become almost ill-natured, the judges returned to Blue Boy's crate and chalked "1" in a large figure on the corner of the crate.

"Most remarkable boar I've seen in twelve years of judging and thirty-five years with hogs," said the Nebraska dean. The others congratulated Abel and added their assurances that Blue Boy was an unparalleled animal.

"Hardly ever you see an animal so well-developed that's got the spirit he has," said the Ames man. "I like to see a boar up on his toes, full of vitality."

Quite by accident, Esmeralda lifted the lid of one eye and looked at the judges. She could not smell her owner, so she gave one speculative glance at Blue Boy and went to sleep again. Blue Boy went back to the corner of his cage where the water gurgled, and lay down. The judges shook hands with Abel once more.

When they had gone, "Oh, my Lord," said Abel. "I own the finest hog that ever was, and the Storekeeper owes me five dollars."

From **True Tales of Iowa** (1932)

Edith Rule and William J. Petersen

Introduced earlier in this volume (see Little Stories of Mason City's Past), *the work of Edith Rule (and the State Historical Society's William J. Petersen) deserves second airing, this time from their uncanny 1932 text* True Tales of Iowa. *As always, Rule knew her readers, writing this of the dynamic history offered by her unorthodox text: "Historical characters have been made to live, move, and have their being, so that the study of the making of a great state will seem an absorbing story to enjoy, rather than a laborious lesson to be learned." Following, are reprinted two chapters, "The Honey War," and "Meat and Wool," covering two widely forgotten and little understood aspects of state history—the "war" with Missouri and Iowa's Underground Railroad.*

The Honey War

The people of Van Buren County in the territory of Iowa were in a rage. Some thief had cut down the bee trees in whose hollow trunks was sweet wild honey. The thief had been chased but he had escaped over the boundary line into his state of Missouri and got away. He probably would have said he had not crossed the boundary line for that boundary line was just what the trouble was all about.

For the beginning of the story it is necessary to go back to 1816 when the United States government sent J. C. Sullivan to survey the northern boundary of what was to be the state of Missouri. He had run a line east from a point one hundred miles due north of the junction of the Kansas and Missouri rivers to the Des Moines rapids of the Mississippi. But by 1837 a number of settlers had come into northern Missouri and southeastern Iowa, and Missouri began to cast an envious eye at the rich far lands and the bee trees just over the border.

Accordingly, the Missouri legislature sent J. C. Brown, in 1836, to re-determine the boundary according to the state constitution which said the northern boundary was a line west of the "Rapids of the river Des Moines." Mr. Brown proceeded up the Des Moines River in 1837, found a slight ripple in its surface near the present site of the town of Keosauqua, and surveyed his line due west from there.

The Missouri legislature in 1838 passed a law claiming the Brown line as the northern boundary of the state of Missouri. Thereby they cut off twenty-six hundred square miles of the territory of Iowa, by taking a strip nine miles wide at the Mississippi and thirteen miles wide at the Missouri end.

In the late summer of 1838, Martin Van Buren, the President of the United States, sent Albert M. Lea as a commissioner to decide the correct line. He returned with the report that the old Sullivan boundary was the correct one, but Missouri paid no attention to this.

Presently, the people of Van Buren County were visited by Missouri officers who came to collect taxes. These Iowans rushed to Robert Lucas, governor of the territory of Iowa, with their troubles. He answered by issuing a proclamation that Van Buren County was in Iowa territory and all officers should uphold its laws as it was federal land. The Missouri Governor, Lilburn W. Boggs, retorted with a proclamation denying they had any right. And in his second annual address to the Iowa territorial legislature, assembled at Burlington, he said that the discussion might finally "lead to the shedding of blood."

It seemed probable when some desperate character destroyed the precious bee trees in Iowa. The furious Iowans failed to capture the culprit, but when the sheriff of Clark County, Missouri, came again across the line to collect taxes, the sheriff of Van Buren County arrested him and took him to Burlington.

That was the signal for the action south of the disputed boundary. A special session of the Clark County court was held and the militia of several counties was called out. They came through the bitter cold of December 7, 1839, and encamped in Waterloo in Clark County, Missouri. They did not have blankets, tents, arms, or ammunition enough, but in spirit they were all ready for war.

Rumors reached Iowa that the Missourians were rising in arms, and Governor Lucas set his grim mouth tighter, and his deep eyes flashed as he, too, issued the order for Iowa militia commanders of the whole territory to lead forth their men.

At first there was little interest shown, but as the tale of the wrongs of Van Buren County and the destruction of the bee trees spread, companies began to crop up in Burlington, Bloomington, Davenport, and Dubuque, as the men volunteered. Old Zion Church in Burlington became the headquarters, and the wave of war washed even as far north as the Turkey River. There is a company enlisted but got lost before they reached the border.

From shop, fireside, and farm came the men. Their uniforms were what they wanted to wear, or what they happened to be wearing at the time. Their arms were anything from a hunting knife to a blunderbuss or musket that had seen service at the Revolutionary War. One man even brought a plowshare, slung over his shoulder by a chain. A company called "The Grays" of Burlington was commanded by James W. Grimes, destined to be an Iowa governor. One commander at Bloomington got behind his men, an Indian spear in his and, and told them to march on, and the first man to desert would get the spear in his back.

So the Iowa army, about twelve hundred strong, with a generous supply of commanders—four generals and one hundred and thirty-two lesser officers, assembled at Farmington.

Although Governor Lucas was heartily in favor of war, the Iowa legislative assembly was not, and sent a commission to Clark County to confer with the court there on December 12, 1839. The result was that both sides agreed to cease hostilities and leaves the decision of the boundary to the United States Supreme Court. Thereupon the Missouri troops were disbanded. They had been bloodthirsty and ready for a fight so they let their feelings out by dividing a haunch of venison in two pieces, one of which they called Governor Boggs, the other Governor Lucas. These they filled full of bullets and buried them with all military honors. Then they went home.

The Iowa army, however, had heard nothing of all this, and that was their surprise to march down upon the foe and find none there. It did not seem quite possible to have a war without any enemy so they sent a commission headed by Augustus Caesar Dodge, to ask what had become of the enemy. It returned with the news that the Missouri army had gone home and they might as well do the same, since the Honey War seemed to be all over. Joyfully, the troops started back, often meeting fresh volunteers on their way down, who turned about and proceeded home with them.

The Honey War was a joke and many there were who told it. A Missourian, John I. Campbell, chose to say his version in rhyme, to be sung to the tune of Yankee Doodle:

> Ye freemen of the happy land,
> Which flows with milk and honey,
> Arise! To arms! Your ponies mount!
> Regard not blood or money.
> Old Governor Lucas, tiger-like,
> Is prowling round your borders,
> But Governor Boggs is wide-awake—
> Just listen to his orders.

The Honey War caused plenty of merriment, but it did not settle the boundary question. For a long time Congress considered the knotty problem. Finally in 1849, three years after Iowa had been admitted as a state, the United States Supreme Court decided in favor of the original Sullivan boundary and sent men out to resurvey and remark the line.

"Meat and Wool"

A road stretched, narrow, dry, and rutty across central Iowa. Hemming it in closely on both sides were tall prairie grasses or fields of grain. Now and then these would be broken by tassels of tall corn, and here and there a zigzag rail fence marked off a grazing meadow. Off in the distance, an occasional farmhouse nestled in a grove, or a little settlement of many frame houses could be seen.

It was a breathless summer day. The air was still. Yet there was a wave in the sharp prairie grasses, a movement as if something were crouching, hiding. A number of black slaves, escaped from their master in Missouri, were traveling on the Undeground Railroad through Iowa to Canada and freedom.

The Underground Railroad was a ghost train, never seen nor heard. The men who ran it kept no papers or books. It was a secret route, known by word of mouth only, to fugitive slaves. It meant simply the way they were to take, and the houses of friendly white people, who would feed them, hide them, and aid them on their way to safety. The negroes traveled only at night. By day they hid, if possible, in a kindly farmer's house, barn, orchard, or haystack—if that were not possible then they took to the tall grass of the open fields.

In Iowa one of the principal routes of the Underground Railroad entered the state in the southwest corner near Tabor and ran through Lewis, Des Moines, Grinnell, Iowa City, West Liberty, Tipton, DeWitt, Low Moor and Clinton where it crossed the Mississippi River into Illinois. Denmark, a New England village in Iowa, and the Quaker settlements of Salem, Springdale, and West Branch, were other stations on this mysterious road. Indeed the quiet, gray-clad Quakers felt it a moral duty to help the negroes to escape, for, under God's law, all men were free and equal. They would not fight, or lie to the slavemasters, but they helped in every way they could.

On this particular day when dusk descended upon the prairies, shadowy forms rose out of hiding and sped to the home of Laurie Tatum, a Quaker farmer. That night he gave them food and hid them. The next day he concealed them in his wagon to take them to Mechanicsville, where other conductors would pass them along. On the way he had to cross the treacherous, shifting sands of the Cedar River at Gray's Ford. There the big wheels slid down, hub deep, and all the straining and pulling of the horses would not loosen them. Tatum was worried. He dare not get one of the negroes to help him, for not all the countryside was in favor of aiding fugitive slaves.

A house stood nearby and the Quaker, warning the negroes not to move, started off to get the farmer to help him. The man came, a stranger, and looked at the slowly sinking wagon.

"It's a pretty heavy load," he remarked. "Here, we better unload."

Tatum held out his hand. "No, no," he said, "I think we can get it out without that."

The stranger looked surprised, then staring keenly at the Quaker he asked, "What do you have on your wagon?"

Tatum looked the man straight in the eye. "Meat and wool," he said.

There was a moment's silence. The stranger looked at the covered load, lying very still. Then he shrugged his shoulders. "Well, I guess if we get a fence rail and pry up those hind wheels we can get her out." With no further questions they set about their work. A mighty wrench and the horses pulled the wagon out. Tatum, waving his hand and calling his thanks to the stranger, went on with his load of meat and wool. A collision on the Underground Railroad had narrowly been avoided.

It was not always negro men who traveled through Iowa on the mysterious road. Sometimes there were women with small children, sometimes whole families. One day two lone negro girls sought protection of a Quaker and his wife who kindly took them in. Suddenly, the master and a posse of men appeared at the door and demanded to be let in to search the house. The gentle Quaker for a moment forgot his teachings against anger or force and spreading his arms across the doorway, he flung back his head and looked the men in the eyes.

"Thee will not search my house. And if thee tries to force thy way in I'll defend my home."

Just then there was a gentle touch on his farm. His wife, demure in her gray dress and cap, stood beside him. "Let the men in," she said. "Thee knows that they will not find any slaves here."

The husband, too astonished to say another word, stepped aside and let the men pass. He knew the two negro girls were hidden in his house. He knew, too, the heavy fine the men could collect from him for harboring them, but he gave his wife her way.

The slavemaster and his men searched in every room but found no trace of the girls. With a word of apology, they left. Then the Quaker housewife went to one of the beds, and there under the feather mattress lay the two terrified negro maids.

"But thee said they would find no slaves in here," protested the husband.

"Nor did they," replied the little Quaker woman. "Thee knows there is no such thing as a slave in the eyes of God."

From **Why Wars Must Cease (1935)**

Carrie Chapman Catt

Though Carrie Clinton Lane was born in Wisconsin, she spent her childhood in Charles City, and graduated as the only woman in her class from Iowa Agricultural College (Iowa State University) in 1880, paying her way by washing dishes, working at the college library, and teaching. After college, she law clerked back home in Charles City before accepting an appointment at Mason City as one of the first female school superintendents in the nation. In 1885, Catt married Leo Chapman, editor and publisher of the Mason City Republican; one year later Chapman died of typhoid fever. Bowed but not broken, she joined, in 1897, the Iowa Woman Suffrage Association as a writer and lecturer and, from 1890 to 1892, as the state organizer for the association. In 1890, Carrie Chapman became Carrie Chapman Catt after marrying George Catt, likewise a graduate of what would come to be called Iowa State University. That same year, Catt joined the National American Woman Suffrage Association (NAWSA), succeeding Susan B. Anthony as that organization's president in 1900. Catt spent the next two decades working tirelessly to get women the vote, a momentous event which came to pass with the Nineteenth Amendment in August of 1920. Later in her life, Catt's belief in social justice led her to the peace movement, a subject she takes up in the chapter excerpt, originally entitled "Because If We Do Not Destroy War Now, War Will Destroy Us," that follows. Compiled by Catt on behalf of the National Committee on the Cause and Cure of War, the anthology Why Wars Must Cease includes Catt's essay alongside contributions from luminaries such as Eleanor Roosevelt and Jane Addams. The excerpt that follows, while not parochially or reductively Iowan, concerns Iowans directly, especially women, who Catt prophecies will lose their "noncombatant status." The great suffragist also predicts in these pages an apocalyptic scene eerily reminiscent of the 9-11 terrorist attack on the World Trade Center towers. It must be read to be believed.

> "If my soldiers would really think, not one would remain in the ranks." —Frederick the Great

The world is again talking of war. When it will begin and what nations will start it are predicted. It must be admitted that so long as every great power, including the United States, continually expands its preparation for war and does so to the point that suspicion of its motives is amply justified by all other nations, it follows that there is no guarantee that any peace agreement, such as the Covenant of the League of Nations, or the Paris Pact, will prevent another war. While nations spend approximately 85 cents out of every dollar of annual income upon preparedness for war, and take a spineless, hesitating, uncertain attitude toward preparation for peace, competition in armament will proceed, hindered only by empty war chests and scant credit.*

When and if a "Next War" comes, all authorities appear to agree that it will be more hideous than the last. They further agree that no weapon or equipment used in the last war will be abandoned in the next because it was too ruthless. On the contrary, every nation, if it can, will have improved each instrument of war by making it more powerfully destructive. More, if possible, it will invent and produce new weapons that will be more deadly than any yet used. The possible new weapons that may appear with the coming of the threatening "Next War" are the dread of all nations.

Efforts are certainly being made in some gun factories, and perhaps in all, to prevent the flash of explosion and to create more perfectly smokeless powder, because the flash may reveal the position of the firer of the gun to the enemy at night and the smoke may reveal it by day. Steadfast endeavor to produce a noiseless gun explosion is also a part of the hoped-for improvements before the next war. When a rifle can be fired without noise, smoke, or flash, it will be more deadly than those now in use, but it will also follow that every army must be equipped anew with rifles or ammunition, which will mean a fine profit to the munitions factories and a new burden to the taxpayers.

Already several nations have announced that they now have a gas more poisonous than any used in the last war. The United States of America told the world, in the closing months of the war, that it had discovered Lewisite, a gas more destructive than any yet used, but had refrained from producing it. Now, however, it has outdone itself by announcing two new poison gases, each more destructive than Lewisite.

All the chief powers have advertised the fact that they now have a larger "Big Bertha" than the Germans had. The United States describes its new gun, planned by its Army ordnance experts, as "the heaviest and most powerful gun of its type in the entire world." It has been officially stated in the press that it is capable of hurling an armor-piercing projectile of 1,560 pounds for a distance of twenty-three miles. Larger submarines, also, have been constructed, much improved in mysterious ways and made capable of projecting larger, heavier torpedoes than any used in the last war.

A brisk competitive race in the building of airplanes has been in progress. Many military authorities have declared that the next war will be fought in the skies. At the close of the Great War, no nation possessed airplanes in excess of one hundred. At the close of the year 1931, an official statement of the number and character of airplanes then possessed by each state was made by the League of Nations. At that date, France had 2,375, Great Britain 1,434, Italy 1,507, Japan 1,639, the United States 1,752, the total of these five nations being 8,707. Since that date, the race for quantity, size, and quality has continued, but nations refrain from frank confession as to their present air equipment. The correct number owned by each nation is also difficult to ascertain because airplanes have been accidentally destroyed, purposely abandoned for better designs, and many new types have been built without known value.

At a hearing of the President's Aviation Commission (October 19, 1934, Washington) a designer of airplanes announced that airplanes carrying two hundred pound bombs, one hundred to a plane; and seaplanes with a range of 4,600 miles, carrying fifty-six passengers and one hundred pounds of cargo, were well on their way to perfection. Imagine a fleet of airplanes hovering over New York, loaded with bombs, some filled with the new varieties of poison gas, incurable disease germs or explosives to set our skyscrapers on fire, while in defense the promised "death rays" are blinding or killing the pilots, thus leaving no control of the airplanes which, in nose dives, will speedily spill out the precious bombs, germs, poison, and fire setters over our greatest city! Once, it is claimed, God sent a flood and destroyed most of the human race because it had been such a failure. This picture of war in the skies, actually painted by those who believe the prediction well founded, calls loudly for another fresh start for the human race.

There probably has been more talk about the competition of naval building of a few Great Powers than any other phase of war preparation. The largest expense of preparedness for these nations is the construction of new warships and the maintenance of the navy.

It is clear that the number of men engaged in war has increased out of proportion to the increase in population, that weapons have grown more destructive and war has become more complicated. It now includes not only all the men of the world, but there is a threat to conscript all women in the chief nations when and if there is another war. Certainly, if one country conscripts women, other nations engaged in the same war will also do so, for that is the usual war policy. Apparently, the Powers That Be propose to add a competition in the use of women for war purposes to the competition in armament which, for many years, has lain at the foundation of preparedness for war. Women need expect no protection as non-combatants in another war. More, the new weapons of airplane bombs, poison gas, and disease germs, which may or may not be so deadly as some authorities think, will threaten the lives of women and children in every warring nation. Grown desperate enough, any country might logically agree with General Ludendorf and carry out his theory. He said "All the means to weaken an enemy nation become legitimate. By killing women and children, for example, one destroys future mothers and eventual defenders of the country."*

An army so gigantic, equipped with weapons more destructive than any previous army had had, left behind it an astounding number of dead. Field Marshall Sir William Robertson, chief of the British General Staff during the World War, is sponsor for the statement that the dead in the Great War numbered 10,873,000. General Tasker Howard Bliss gives the total death as 12,991,000. [Original footnote cited "What Really Happened at Paris," page 385]. The number of those killed in all war of the preceding one hundred and twenty years (1790-1913) has been estimated at 4,449,300. [Ibid, page 384].*

Lord Balfour said in this country in 1917, "Behind every man in the trench, there are ten persons making it possible for him to stay there, and at present seven of the ten persons are women." General Joffre said: "We have two armies, one in the trench, and one behind the trenches. The one in the rear is composed largely of women." So wrote General Tasker H. Bliss: "A nation in arms is a nation of combatants, men, women, and children—some drafted to the front, the labor of others commandeered and directed to maintain the former."

Women would now do well to transform their traditional habit of helpless surrender when war comes to one of righteous opposition to war itself while it merely threatens. War does not creep upon a nation as did smallpox before vaccination. It comes because the people of the nation have no freedom to express their opinion or because they are too ignorant to know the history of war or the facts that keep it going. I urge you, women, to know more, think more, do more, about this world's war system.

Men and women will do well to march together toward the abolition of war. It will require all the bravery, information, and understanding the people of this and other nations can muster to bring this mighty and terrible institution to its close. Let me repeat, the progress of the human race demands the speedy abolition of war.

From **Revolt Against the City**

Grant Wood (1935)

Like Herbert Hoover, the touchstones in Grant Wood's Iowa biography are well known—born in Anamosa, moved to Cedar Rapids, graduated from Washington High School, taught art in the Cedar Rapids community school district, painted American Gothic *to include a backdrop he recalled from Eldon, Iowa, founded the Stone City, Iowa, Art Colony during the Depression, and accepted a position at the University of Iowa's School of Art in the mid 1930s. Not as well understood is Grant Wood's literary acumen and advocacy; he befriended and championed, for example, fellow Cedar Rapids greats Paul Engle and Jay Sigmund, and set down in writing a kind of manifesto for the Regionalist movement his canvases defined. Published by Iowa City's Clio Press in 1935—run by Iowa writer Frank Luther Mott—Wood's little book* Revolt Against the City, *excerpted here, captures beautifully the spirit that made Iowa an unlikely, if not glorious, literary and artistic center throughout the late 1920s and early 1930s. In his editor's preface to* Revolt, *Mott writes, "It is fitting that he [Wood] should turn to the written word, in a brief respite from palette and brush, for his is a mind so active, so crackling with ideas, that it demands more than one medium of expression." This excerpt begins with page twenty-four of the original.*

When Christopher Morley was out in Iowa last fall, he remarked on its freedom, permitting expansion "with space and relaxing conditions for work." Future artists, he wisely observed, "are more likely to come from the remoter areas, farther from the claims and distractions of an accelerating civilization."

So many of the leaders in the arts were born in small towns and on farms that in the comments and conversation of many who have "gone East" there is today a noticeable homesickness for the scenes of their childhood. On a recent visit to New York, after seven continuous years in the Middle West, I found this attitude very striking. Seven years ago my friends had sincerely pitied me for what they called my "exile" in Iowa. They then had a vision of my going back to an uninteresting region where I could have no contact with culture and no association with kindred spirits. But now, upon my return to the East, I found these same friends eager for news and information about the rich funds of creative material which this region holds.

I found, moreover, a determination on the part of some of the Eastern artists to visit the Middle West for the purpose of obtaining such material. I feel that, in general, such a procedure would be as false as the old one of going to Europe for subject matter, or the later fashion of going to New England fishing villages or to Mexican cities or to the mountains of our Southwest for materials. I feel that whatever virtue this new movement has lies in the necessity the painter (and the writer, too) is under, to use material which is really a part of himself. However, many New York artists and writers are more familiar, through strong childhood impressions, with village and country life than with their adopted urban environment; and for them a back-to-the-village movement is entirely feasible and defensible. But a cult or a fad for midwestern materials is just what must be avoided. Regionalism has already suffered from a kind of cultism which is essentially false.

I think the alarming nature of the Depression and the general economic unrest have had much to do in producing this wistful nostalgia for the Midwest to which I have referred. This region has always stood as the great conservative section of the country. Now, during boom times conservatism is a thing to be ridiculed, but under unsettled conditions, it becomes a virtue. To the East, which is not in a position to produce its own food, the Middle West today looks a haven of security. This is, of course, the basis for the various projects for the return of urban populations to the land; but it is an economic condition not without implications for art. The talented youths who, in the expansive era of unlimited prosperity, were carried away on waves of enthusiasm for projects of various sorts, wanting nothing so much as to get away from the old things of home, now, when it all collapses, come back solidly to the good earth.

But for those of us who have never deserted our own regions for long find them not so much havens of refuge, as continuing friendly, homely environments.

As for my own region—the great farming section of the Middle West—I find it, quite contrary to the prevailing Eastern impression, not a drab country inhabited by peasants, but a various, rich land abounding in painting material. It does not, however, furnish scenes of the picture-postcard type that one too often finds in New Mexico or further West, and sometimes in New England. Its material seems to me to be more sincere and honest, and to gain in depth by having to be hunted for. It is the result of analysis, and therefore is less obscured by "picturesque" surface quality. I find myself becoming rather bored by quaintness. I lose patience with the thinness of things viewed from outside, or from a height. Of course, my feeling for the genuineness of this Iowa scene is doubtless rooted in the fact that I was born here and have lived here most of my life. I shall not quarrel with the painter from New Mexico, from further West, or from quaint New England, if he differs with me; for if he does so honestly, he doubtless has the same basic feeling for his material that I have for mine—he believes in its genuineness. After all, all I contend for is the sincere use of native material by the artist who has command of it.

Central and dominant in our midwestern scene is the farmer. The Depression, with its farm strikes and the heroic attempts of government to find solutions for agrarian difficulties, has emphasized for us all the fact that the farmer is basic in the economics of the country—and, further, that he is a human being. The farm strikes, strangely enough, caused little disturbance to the people of the Middle West who were not directly concerned in them; but they did cause both surprise and consternation in the East, far away as it is from the source of supplies. Indeed, the farm strikes did much to establish the midwestern farmer in the Eastern estimation as a man, functioning as an individual capable of thinking and feeling, and not an oaf.

Midwestern farmers are not of peasant stock. There is much variety in their ancestry, of course; but the Iowa farmer as I know him is fully as American as Boston, and has the great advantage of being farther away from European influence. He knows little of life in crowded cities, and would find such intimacies uncomfortable; it is with difficulty that he reconciles himself even to village life. He is on a little unit of his own, where he develops an extraordinary independence. The economics, geography, and psychology of his situation have always accented his comparative isolation. The farmer's reactions must be toward weather, tools, beasts, and plants to a far greater extent than those of city dwellers, and toward other human beings far less: this makes him not an egoist by any means, but (something quite different) a less socialized being than the average American. The term "rugged individualism" has been seized upon as a political catchword, but it suits the farmer's character very well.

Of course, the automobile and the radio have worked some change in the situation; but they have not altered the farmer's essential character in this generation, whatever they may do in the next. More important so far as change is concerned have been recent economic conditions, including the foreclosing of mortgages; and these factors, threatening the farmer's traditional position as a self-supporting individual, threatening even a reduction to a kind of American peasantry, brought on the violent uprisings of the farm strikes and other protests.

The farmer is not articulate. Self-expression through literature and art belong not to the set of relationships with which he is familiar (those with weather, tools, and growing things), but to more socialized systems. He is almost wholly preoccupied with his struggle against the elements, with the fundamental things of life, so that he has no time for Wertherism [self-indulgent melancholy and romance] or for the subtleties of interpretation. Moreover, the farmers that I know (chiefly of New England stock) seem to me to have something of that old Anglo-Saxon reserve which made our ancient forebears to look upon much talk about oneself as a childish weakness. Finally, ridicule by city folks with European ideas of the farmer as a peasant, or, as our American slang has it, a "hick," has caused a further withdrawal—a proud and disdainful answer to misunderstanding criticism.

But the very fact that the farmer is not himself vocal makes him the richest kind of material for the writer and the artist. He needs interpretation. Serious, sympathetic handling of farmer-material offers a great field for the careful worker. The life of the farmer, engaged in a constant conflict with natural forces, is essentially dramatic. The drought of last summer provided innumerable episodes of the most gripping human interest. The nomadic movements of cattlemen in Wisconsin, in South Dakota, and in other states, the great dust storms, the floods following drought, the milk strikes, the violent protests against foreclosures, the struggles against dry-year pests, the sacrifices forced upon once prosperous families—all these elements and many more are colorful, significant, and intensely dramatic.

It is a conflict quite as exciting as that of the fisherman with the sea. I have been interested to find in the little town of Waubeek, near my home, farmer-descendants of the folk of New England fishing villages. Waubeek has not changed or grown much since it was originally settled, because it was missed by the railroads and by the paved highways. The people of this community have kept as family heirlooms some of the old whaling harpoons, anchors, and so on which connect them with the struggle which their ancestors waged with the sea. But their own energies are transferred to another contest, and their crops come not out of the water but out of the land. I feel that the drama and color of the old fishing villages have become hackneyed and relatively unprofitable, while little has been done in painting at least, with the fine materials that are inherent in farming in the great region of the mid-American states.

My friend and fellow townsman Jay Sigmund devotes his leisure hours to the writing of verse celebrating the kind of human beings I have been discussing. He is as much at home in Waubeek—perhaps more so—as in the office of his insurance company. I wish to quote a poem of his in this place.

Visitor

I knew he held the tang of stack and mow—
One sensed that he was brother to the soil;
His palms were stained with signs of stable toil
And calloused by the handles of the plow.

Yet I felt bound to him by many ties:
I knew the countryside where he was born;
I'd seen its hillsides green with rows of corn,
And now I saw its meadows in his eyes.

For he had kept deep-rooted in the clay,
While I had chosen marketplace and street;
I knew the city's bricks would bruise his feet
And send him soon to go his plodding way.

But he had sought me out to grip my hand
And sit for one short hour by my chair.
Our talk was of the things that happen where
The souls of men have kinship with the land.

I asked him of the orchard and the grove,
About the bayou with its reedy shore,
About the grey one in the village store
Who used to doze beside a ruddy stove.

He told me how the creek had changed its bed,
And how his acres spread across the hill;
The hour wore on and he was talking still.
And I was hungry for the things he said.

Then I who long had pitied peasant folk
And broken faith with field and pasture ground
Felt dull and leaden-footed in my round,
And strangely like a cart-beast with a yoke!

There is, of course, no ownership in artistic subject matter except that which is
validated by the artist's own complete apprehension and understanding of the

341

materials. By virtue of such validation, however, the farm and village matter of a given region would seem peculiarly to belong to its own regional painters. This brings up the whole of the ancient moot question of regionalism in literature and in art.

Occasionally I have been accused of being a flag-waver for my own part of the country. I do believe in the Middle West in its people and in its art, and in the future of both—and this with no derogation to other sections. I believe in the Middle West in spite of abundant knowledge of its faults. Your true regionalist is not a mere eulogist; he may even be a severe critic. I believe in the regional movement in art and letters (comparatively new in the former though old enough in the latter); but I wish to place no narrow interpretation on such regionalism. There is, or at least there need be, no geography of the art mind or of artistic talent or appreciation. But painting and sculpture do not raise up a public as easily as literature, and not until the breakup caused by the Great Depression has there really been an opportunity to demonstrate the artistic potentialities of what some of our Eastern city friends call "the provinces."

Let me try to state the basic idea of the regional movement. Each section has a personality of its own, in physiography, industry, psychology. Thinking painters and writers who have passed their formative years in these regions will, by caretaking analysis, work out and interpret in their productions these varying personalities. When the different regions develop characteristics of their own, they will come into competition with each other; and out of this competition a rich American culture will grow.

FROM **THE COUNTESS FROM IOWA (1936)**

COUNTESS NOSTITZ [LILIE DE FERNANDEZ-AZABAL]

Utterly forgotten by most Hawkeyes, Countess Nostitz lived a storybook life of international intrigue, quite literally, as she was widely believed to be a spy during World War I. Born in Hamburg, Iowa, in the far southwestern corner of the state (Fremont County), Lilie Bouton was a natural thespian, making her way on stage in San Francisco and New York City, and from there, via a marriage to a German aristocrat, to Germany. Cinderella-like, she met Count Nostitz, a military attaché of the Russian Embassy, at a ball for princes, and divorced the Baron to marry the Count in 1907. A fervent anti-Bolshevik, Countess Nostitz eventually escaped Russia with her husband and returned to the States, telling that harrowing tale, and others, in her 1936 memoir, The Countess from Iowa, *the first chapter of which is here excerpted.*

Sunshine dappled the lush grass of the orchard with patches of jade among the cool emerald. From the fields lining the banks of the sluggishly-moving Nishnabotna River came the lowing of cattle, and the shouts of men at work, the harsh, guttural voices of the Germans who had founded the little town of Hamburg, Iowa, mingling with the soft, lazy drawl of the Southern settlers.

Familiar sounds to the three little girls who lay sprawled at the foot of a tree so heavily laden that its lower branches dipped almost to the ground, munching their stolen harvest of apples. Three sunbonnets tossed back from flushed faces hung suspended round three slender necks—a dainty pink percale, a blue covered with tiny frills, a plain checked gingham.

She of the pink percale sat up suddenly. Gray-blue eyes set in a lovely heart-shaped face crowned with dark curls—that was Della…

"When I'm grown up, I'm going to be very rich—and have horses and carriages—and jewels—and everything I want. What are you going to do, Ida?"

Gingham sunbonnet turned slowly. Her sweet, freckled face was serious, her strong little jaws crunched meditatively on her apple for a moment before she answered, "Me?—I'm going to serve my generation…"

"That's out of the Bible," said I, the owner of the blue-frilled bonnet, proud of my superior knowledge. "But Ida, how will you do it? Are you going to be a missionary or something?"

"No." She fidgeted, twisted her faded gingham dress between her childish fingers. "Somehow I'll find a way."

Della's soft voice cut in. "And you, Lilie?"

"I'm not sure yet. I only know I want to see everything I can, and learn a lot."

Della shrugged contemptuous shoulders.

"Is that all? You won't need to learn after you quit school."

"I don't think Lilie meant that sort of learning," said Ida in her weightiest manner. "I guess she meant something else...learning how to live."

Then, feeling that the conversation was getting rather deep, and spurred on by the distant approach of the German farmer whose orchard we had raided, we sprang to our feet and raced across the meadows.

The years went by and we set about realizing our several ambitions. Gingham bonnet served her generation. Known now as Ida B. Wise Smith, she is national president of the W.C.T.U. [Women's Christian Temperance Union]. How different a life from mine, passed in the last glitter and glory of a fading European aristocracy!

And Della of the brown curls? Long afterwards I came across a woman's photograph in one of the drawers of my husband's writing table in St. Petersburg. Something in the delicate oval of the face, the setting of the wistful eyes struck me as oddly familiar. I searched my memory.

"Why, it's Della, my school friend in Iowa," I exclaimed joyfully. "Where did you meet her?"

My husband snatched the photograph out of my hand. "How can such a woman possibly be a friend of yours?"

"I lost sight of her after my childhood," I said, aghast.

After persistent questioning, he told me where he had met her. It was during the Chicago Fair in 1893 when he and some of the richest young bloods of the Windy City set out to see nightlife. In a palatial "house," he met a very young girl whose charm, grace, and beauty struck him as being utterly at variance with her sordid surroundings, but beyond the fact that her name was Della, she told him nothing of herself. Before he left she gave him her photograph. He never saw her again.

Poor little Della, where did your quest for riches lead you?

And I? I have not yet achieved my ambition, for never while I live can I feel I know enough of this fascinating game called living. The years have sped by since those summer days in the orchard of my home and with them I have passed through storm and sunshine. A whole rosary of experience slips through my reflective mind. I have been fêted—the incense of adoration has been burned at my feet. I have known love as it is given to few women to know it—and I have known devouring jealousy. I have seen the splendors of the greatest courts in Europe before the curtain fell on an era that has passed forever. I have seen empires swept away. I have had a vast fortune lavished on me by the husband I loved, and lost it in the tragedy of a nation.

Yet I would not have it otherwise. I would not have lived in an epoch other than this, which will, I believe, be known to future generations as one of the greatest, the most eventful in the history of humanity.

And because I have been privileged to live through events that have made history I want to record them at firsthand knowledge, to write of them as I saw them.

My destiny has been cast in a wide setting. It has taken me to many places, shown me many sides of life. My rise to fame on the New York stage…the uncompromising, autocratic, Kaiser-ruled Germany of William II…the splendors of the Imperial Court of the last Czar of Russia…the hell of the Revolution…I have experienced them all.

And now let me tell of them as I sit here in my peaceful villa in Biarritz…roll back the curtain…

First a haze of childish memories. Sleepy little Hamburg in Iowa where I was born, the big straggling brick house nestling in its park of fine old maple trees. Rambles in the low-lying hills looking for hazelnuts in the glory of the golden russet fall; fishing with my brothers in the sluggish waters of the Nishnibotna; firelit evenings in the old playroom, telling stories to each other after a raid on the kitchen for cookies. Sundays with their interminable boredom of long family dinners enlivened by religious disputes of decidedly un-Christian vehemence between my four uncles—old clerics of different denominations.

Ours was a laughing, carefree household. My father who had built up a prosperous grain elevator business was a contented man, proud of his children and of his pretty wife. My mother, who came from an old Irish family and was a niece of the famous geologist John Tyndall, had a gay expectancy towards life that was infectious. She had the Irish richness of imagination, saw even the most humdrum circumstances "couleur de rose," and was always waiting for something wonderful to happen—as it invariably did—for she made it so out of the charm of her own vivid personality. To each of her children she gave the priceless heritage of joy in living.

When the illness of my little sister Mabel, whose lungs proved incapable of withstanding the long Iowan winters, uprooted us all from the peace and plenty of the Middle West and forced us to migrate to California in search of health for her, Mother took it characteristically. It was a hard blow to her and my father, for it meant the severing of old friendships—the renunciation of cherished ambitions, but she managed to turn it into a joyous adventure. She painted such a glowing picture of the future, filled our little minds so full of the fun we would have, that there was no room left for regrets at the parting from familiar surroundings.

From **Remembering Laughter (1937)**

Wallace Stegner

Identified more with the West than the Midwest, Pulitzer Prize-winning Wallace Stegner was born in Lake Mills in Winnebago County in north central Iowa. An environmentalist and conservationist par excellence, Stegner first learned a love for the land in the Hawkeye State, a subject he touches on in his first novel Remembering Laughter, *from which the excerpt below appears. In truth, the deep well of Iowa memories from which the author drew belonged as much to his wife as to Stegner. In her afterword to the Penguin reprint edition, Mary Stegner recalls how, in 1936, her husband saw an announcement for a Little, Brown, and Company prize for a "novellete" (novella) but didn't know what to write about. "I remembered a family account about my two gaunt aunts," Mary explains, "who lived with their son in western Iowa.... From that little seed* Remembering Laughter *grew." This passage demonstrates Stegner's intimate knowledge of the farm—its beauties, its tensions, and its grim realities and sublime comedies. Iowa farms have always been a refuge for family members and wayfaring strangers, as the Stuart Farm is for young Elspeth MacLeod. Here the arrival of a difference-making visitor to Iowa is greeted with characteristic excitement and trepidation.*

On the afternoon that Elspeth MacLeod was to arrive from Scotland, Alec Stuart and his wife were waiting in the town of Spring Mill a full hour before the train was due. Still pretty at twenty-nine, Margaret hung on her husband's arm and walked him up and down the platform, happy and excited and talking in quick bursts.

Alec, dressed in his best, looking the landowner he was, kept his arm stiff for his wife to hang on, stiffened it still more until the muscles were ridged and hard when she pinched it in anticipation.

They were a handsome couple, and he knew it, and he grinned down at Margaret in her tight-waisted, puff-shouldered, high-necked dress, tipped the absurd bonnet perched on her brown hair. She was tall, but not so tall as he, and she was slender, and the bloom still on her.

"You haven't been so excited since your wedding day," he said.

"I wish the train would hurry."

"Well, she'll never come the sooner for our walking ourselves to death, my lady. Let's sit down."

"I can't keep still," said Margaret.

"You walk, then. I'll sit down," said Alec good-humoredly.

He sank on a rough bench against the wall of the little station, and Margaret sat dutifully beside him. The town ended abruptly at the tracks, and before them across the few rods of cinders and the double bands of ribboned steel was open country sloping up the long roll of a hill, dark cultivated earth lined with spear-ranks of young corn, white gabled houses half-hidden by flourishing oaks and elms, tufted green woodlots tonguing down through swales, the angles of fences and rutted country roads cutting off black fields from intense green squares of meadow and pasture.

"Think she'll like it?" Alec asked.

"I hope so. I described it as well as I could, but maybe I didn't say enough about the winters, and the summer heat, and the flies, and the like."

"It's a good country enough," Alec said. "She'll like it."

Two men crossed over from the water tank, angling across the street toward the block of stores and shops concealed from Alec and Margaret by the station building. They waved at Alec, and he craned around the corner to watch them. They went in the swinging doors of the Corn Belt Saloon.

"Where'd they go?" asked Margaret sharply. "Into that tavern?"

"Na, na," Alec said vaguely. "They're just walking down the street."

Margaret took hold of her husband's arm again in an almost fierce gesture, as if to hold him beside her by force, but he made no move to rise. They sat for ten more minutes quietly absorbing the spring sun, waiting, Margaret's excitement cooled now by her distrust.

Finally Alec rose. "The horses'll need their flynets, I'm thinking,"

While she watched suspiciously, he strolled to the other end of the platform where the horses were tied, and threw over them bright yellow nets of string. Big and casual, he stood there a moment with his hands in his pockets, staring across the street, before he sauntered back to his wife.

"I see Henning Ahlquist across the street," he said, "You wait here a minute, I want to talk to him about working this summer."

"Alec!"

Alec's overacted look of surprise broke down before his wife's look. He tried to laugh away the guilty air that he felt he wore, but the laugh, too, died in an embarrassed cough.

"I *did* see Ahlquist," he said.

"Maybe you did. But if you go over there you know as well as I do that you'll come back drunk as a brewer, and Elspeth coming in a few minutes, 'Twouldn't be the welcome she'd like, Alec."

Alec eased himself back down on the bench and leaned his elbows on his knees.

"Ah, weel," he sighed comically. "I can see Ahlquist any time."

Half-humorously he studied his wife's face with its little frown and its lips pursed in almost petulant disapproval.

"Why do you drink, Alec?" Margaret's voice was plaintive, the echo of a thousand repetitions.

"Why don't I, you mean," Alec said lugubriously. "Ye'll make me a drunkard yet, just by keeping me from getting full once in a while."

Looking at each other, friendly again, reconciled, half-joking, they were both aware of the clash of their wills, neither willing to quarrel but with something between them that showed as a pained puzzlement in Margaret's face and an obscure stubborn tightening in Alec's. Alec's stubbornness, his wife thought, was like a rubber wall. It gave, but the more one pushed against it the harder it became. And Margaret's disgust with drink, Alec was thinking, was too extreme. A little nip with a friend was deadly sin. And so they sat with a nebulous cloud of mutual recrimination between them until the whistle of the train announced Elspeth's arrival.

The train slowed for the station, the engine passed them with a prolonged hiss of escaping steam, its iron underparts smoking and its high wheels dragging, slowing, the drivers moving jerkily like a runner's stiff elbows, and before the cars were completely stopped, the two waiting saw Elspeth ready at the door. Then she was down, running toward them across the plank platform into Margaret's arms for a long hug, and out to be whirled high and kissed roundly by big Alec, and back to Margaret's arms. There were exclamations and a few tears, and the smiles of the three were broad and delighted, and then, all a little breathless, they were walking over to the buggy with Elspeth rattling about her trip and the things she'd seen, and the miles and miles and days and nights on the train, and what a tremendous country they had here.

As Alec tossed her bags into the buggy and took her arm to help her into the high seat she stopped short.

"Ooooh! Your own carriage!"

Alec laughed. Then, solemnly, as he lifted her in, "I had to get something to haul away the bodies of Indians Margo and I killed prowling around the house."

Margaret answered Elspeth's startled look with a smile.

"He'll tell you more lies in a minute than you can soak up in a year. Never mind a word he says."

"But aren't there…Indians?"

"Not many now," Alec said. "Margo got fourteen with the shotgun off the back porch last year. They used to come around to steal feathers off the chickens for their hair, but Margo's discouraged 'em."

Through the six-mile drive back to the farm Alec was in a constant roar of laughter at Elspeth's questions. They passed several farms with new cylindrical silos, and after the third one Elspeth could no longer restrain her curiosity.

"What are the round things?"

"Wells," Alec said.

"Wells? So high?"

"Artesian wells," Alec said. "They have to be capped or they'll flood the country, and sometimes the water is so strong it lifts the cap way up in the air. Then people have to build up walls to support the cap for fear it'll get tipped a little and fall off the water on somebody. Sometimes they get up two or three hundred feet."

"I don't believe you," said Elspeth. Then to Margaret, "Is he lying again?"

"Alec," said his wife, "stop teasing the child."

"She's no child," said Alec, "She's twenty-two. She has a right to know about things."

And throughout the rest of the ride he devoted himself to telling her about things. He told her of the Mississippi Valley angleworms that were so long a hen worked a whole day to eat one. The hen, he said, would get hold of one end of the worm and start backing away, to pull it from its hole. If it was a really grown worm, that hen would back away from eight in the morning till three in the afternoon, with an hour's rest at noon. When the tail end finally came loose from the hole the worm, snapping together after its long stretch, would knock down trees for miles; and if it happened to slip around a house or a barn, would snap that off its foundations slick as a whistle. Then the hen, if she recovered from the elastic backlash, would start eating her way back toward home, arriving there generally after nine in the evening, dusty and footsore and completely spent, and so gorged with angleworm that she couldn't get in the door of the henhouse.

And he told her of the corn he had raised last year, with cobs as big as the trunk of an elm and kernels like penny buns. It took a four-horse team to haul one of those ears out of the field, and it was a half-day job for two men with a saw to cut down the stalk. And in the night, before it was ripe, the noise of its growing was like a tornado through a forest, snapping and popping and whining till you couldn't sleep.

And he told her about the winds of winter that piled snow thirty feet high over the roofs of houses, so that it took forty-eight hours for the smoke from the chimney to melt a hole through to the air, and when it finally got out it was too tired to rise but lay panting on top of the drifts and froze solid. He promised to show her a stick of it he had preserved in the icehouse.

And Margaret, watching him delightedly pour out a lavish stream of nonsense, watching her young sister with bright eyes and pert disbelieving merriment drink it all in, was contented to sit sedately beside them and let her own questions wait. There was much about Scotland, about their father's death, about friends and relatives, that she wanted to know; but meanwhile Alec was telling about the cannibal eels in the Coon River, which seeing their own tails following them, turned and snapped and ate themselves at a gulp in a swirling eddy of water.

They rolled along the country lane, past thickets of wild plum, across two muddy, jungly creeks where the hoofs of the horses and the iron wheels of the buggy beat hollow thunder from the plank bridges, over a low hill where workmen putting up a farmhouse waved at them, along a stretch of white dusty road to where the drive turned in between rows of thrifty young elms that Alec had planted six years ago. At the end of that elm-lined drive the two-story white house shone clean and spotless against a spruce windbreak with the barns looming red off to the right and the henhouse a long red bar across the lower lot.

"Here we are, Elspeth," Margaret said. "Here's your new home."

The buggy stopped on the hard-packed drive before a broad sweep of lawn shaded by two wide-crowned elms as graceful as giant ferns. A cement walk bordered with peonies led to the pillared porch, from either side of which flowers and shrubs spread to girdle the foundations of the house. Elspeth noticed that even the yard beyond the grass plot was clean and well-kept, that it was not, like the yards of most of the farms they had passed, cluttered with machinery and rubbish. The house, too, was bigger, the barns redder, the outbuildings more numerous and in better repair.

Margaret was watching her. "Like it?"

"It's big," Elspeth breathed, "and lovely, and grand. You didn't tell me. I expected a farm. This is a great estate."

They jumped down and followed the luggage-laden Alec into the house. A wide hall opened to the left into living and dining rooms, and on the right a closed door indicated either front bedroom or parlor. Back of the dining room was a huge kitchen where a red-faced Scandinavian woman turned to meet them with flour-coated hands outstretched.

"This is Elspeth, Minnie," Margaret said. The red-faced woman threw her arms about Elspeth and kissed her boisterously, leaving white tracks on the girl's back. Margaret brushed them off, frowning.

"You should be more careful, Minnie. You'll spoil Elspeth's dress."

"I'm sorry," the hired girl said, still grinning. "I've heard so much about you it was like seeing my own sister."

"It's all right," said Elspeth. "Show me your kitchen. It must be gay cooking in such a place."

"Ya," Minnie said. "Look."

For fifteen minutes she opened cupboards and cabinets, displayed flour and sugar bins, showed stove and oven and pantry, led them outside to the cemented dugout, damp and cool and smelling of smoked meat and storage. Behind the cave was a tiny smokehouse, and beyond that the dark windbreak of spruce and Lombardy poplar. As Elspeth looked, two squirrels chased each other across the back lawn and up the oak at the corner of the house, then out of the oak to the roof, where they sat ten feet apart and ratcheted at each other with flirting tails.

Inside again, Elspeth was shown the two downstairs bedrooms with their tall beds of carved and burled walnut. She examined with a seamstress's approving eye the bright quilt spreads and the dresser covers crocheted in matched patterns of twined ivy leaves.

Everything about the house delighted her except the parlor that opened off the main hall. There, after the light and the bowls of flowers and the comfortable furniture of the other rooms, she was vaguely depressed. The room looked so painfully clean, so formal and unlivable; the sea shells on the mantel looked so rigorously dusted, like a child with scrubbed ears; the walls were so shadowy in the gloom behind the drawn shades; the horsehair couch on which she sat gingerly was so uncompromisingly hard, that for a moment she felt almost like that child with the scrubbed ears, visiting at a strange house with people she did not know.

Margaret saw the look and apologized. "This is the company parlor, I have to keep it closed most of the time, and the shades down so the sun won't fade the carpet."

She walked over and raised the blinds halfway, so that through the window Elspeth could see two men working by the barn, and Alec driving the team down to be unhitched.

Then the older sister came back to sit beside Elspeth, and they talked with Elspeth's hands tight in Margaret's. But even while she was answering questions about how their father had died, and how she had had to live by teaching for almost a year, and saying, "Yes, yes, I'm not lonesome for home one bit," she was thinking: "She's a dear, she's my only sister and I love her dearly, but there *is* something about this room, something about the way Margaret's clothes look so unwrinkled and the way her hair looks as if it could never get out of place... There's something in this cold room that matches something in her—it's almost prim, but prim's hardly the word. Prim, starched, stiff, formal, dignified, haughty—none of those. But there's *something*, and it isn't the real Margaret at all, it's only laid on, as this grim parlor is laid on the rest of the house. The rest of the house is really Margaret; but she brings me in here with the sea shells and the drawn blinds and the chairs that dare you to sit down in them..."

Margaret's cool fingers tightened on hers, her voice was soft with maternal fondness.

"Do you think you can learn to like it here?"

"Learn to like it!" Elspeth jumped up as she heard Alec's step on the porch. "I love it already! Let's go up and see my room."

Margaret rose beside her. They were of even height, with the same rosy complexion, the same straight slim figure, the same brown slightly wavy hair, the same bright birdlike eyes. With their arms around each other they went out into the hall.

Pleased by Elspeth's insatiable curiosity, Alec and Margaret devoted much of the next week to showing her about the farm, through sheds and coops and barns, up into the hayloft, almost empty now and smelling faintly of mold and dust, the packed hay in the corners rustly with field mice. Pigeons roosted there, and Elspeth climbed the ladder Alec held so that she could examine a nest with its four spotted eggs.

From the window of the loft they looked out over the gently rolling land quilted with cornfield and pasture, where Alec's Jersey cattle were tawny quiet spots and a Poland China sow with her trailing brood rooted in distant miniature. Across the corner of Alec's land the sunken line of a creek was a belt of vivid jungle.

"And is all this yours?" Elspeth asked.

"That and more," Alec said. "I've four other farms, over beyond, that I lease." He waved vaguely eastward.

"The stream is yours too?"

"About a mile of it. We'll walk down if you like."

With Alec and Elspeth swinging ahead and Margaret trailing behind, composedly taking her time and stepping carefully over the rough ground, they went down through the gate of the vegetable garden and out across a field geometrically lined with hills of six-inch corn, through a barbed-wire fence which Alec held up for them, across a strip of unplowed land, and down into the shallow flood plain of the creek. On each side of the sluggish stream elms, oaks, cottonwoods, and birch pillared an interlaced roof of branches and leaves so thick that little sunlight pierced through it. Many of the trunks were almost strangled with creeper and wild grape. Cattle trails shouldered through thickets of willow and dogwood, and the black mud of the bank was pocked with deep tracks.

"Don't go near the bank," Alec said, "There's quicksand here that'd swallow a barn. A man fell in here three years ago and his relatives have been putting tombstone on top of tombstone ever since. There must be a hundred feet of granite on top of him by now."

Margaret, who had settled herself carefully on a fallen trunk, shook her head at him with a slight frown.

"Alec!"

But Alec blithely ignored the look. "Fact," he said to Elspeth. "You remember that spotted cow that fell in, Margo? I got a rope around her horns before she went down, and when we got her hauled out she was a perfect giraffe and permanently dry. The suction milked her completely out. Never gave a drop after that."

Elspeth's lips curved and her eyes twinkled at him. "Where is this beast now?"

"Oh, I sold her. A circus gave me two hundred dollars for her."

The girl's laugh pealed gaily among the gray trunks and startled a magpie across the stream into investigative flight. Still laughing, Elspeth watched the bird, turning toward the house to follow it, and saw a man approaching across the sunlit field.

"I wonder if that man's looking for us?" she said.

Alec stared a moment.

"It's Ahlquist."

They walked out to the edge of the timber to meet him.

Henning Ahlquist was blond, slow, powerful, dressed in overalls and blue shirt with the sleeves rolled up, showing huge corded forearms matted with golden hair and glistening in the sun as if oiled. He pulled off his cap with a clublike fist when he saw the women.

"Hello," he said. "I hear you need a hand."

"I do," said Alec. "I thought of you when they told me you'd sold out and sent your family back to Norway."

"Ya, I sold out," Ahlquist said. His voice had the plaintive, chanting singsong of the Nordlander. "I don't want to work long. Just while I get enough money to pay some debts and get back myself."

"Aye," Alec said. "As long as you want, Henning. There's an extra bed in with the Grimmitsch boys."

On the way back to the house Elspeth was silent, watching this huge slow Norwegian with the grave face and the melancholy eyes, wondering what would drive such a Viking away from a land of plenty back to some bleak, rocky coast, wondering whether or not he was typical, whether or not she too would want to go back.

"Why do you want to leave here, Mr. Ahlquist?"

The heavy head turned; blue eyes, grave and quiet, searched her face.

"I'm a sailor, miss, a fisherman. I don't like this country."

"Have you been here long?"

"Four years. Four years too long."

In the days to come Elspeth went out of her way to speak to Ahlquist, feeling the loneliness around him, pitying him when she saw him lean on a pitchfork and stare out across the growing corn to horizons shortened by the slow oceanic roll of the earth. He was like a great unhappy dog—slow, sad-eyed, indifferent to the people as to the country around him.

The Grimmitsch brothers—lank, grinning, tobacco-chewing farmhands— did not interest her; but this man eaten by homesickness fascinated her until at times she caught herself wanting to reach out and stroke his blond mane as she would have given an encouraging pat to a Saint Bernard.

Sometimes she would hear Ahlquist singing around the barn in a clear tenor that matched oddly with his ponderous size, singing strange Norwegian songs made stranger by the unfamiliar language. Catching him once, she made him spell out the words, and in her room at night she wrote down all she could remember of them, recalling in the quiet lamplight the melancholy nostalgia of the tune, and the tawny quiet Viking who sang the song to her completely without embarrassment, watching her with grave blue eyes—

> Millom bakkar og berg ut med havet
> Heve Normannen fenge sin heim,
> Der han sjølv heve tuftene grave
> Og sett sjølv sine hus uppaa deim.

Ahlquist wouldn't, or couldn't, tell her what the song meant. He only said: "It's just a Norsk song. Fishermen sing it a lot."

And in the dreamful reveries before sleeping Elspeth would imagine the little fishing boats sailing in late afternoon into the mouth of a rocky fjord, with fishermen singing across the black water, and women waiting on shore, and skiffs rocking gently against crude wharfs. At such times she could understand Ahlquist's loneliness; she would lie wide-eyed in the breathless summer night and think, "I'm the only one who does understand him, with his wife gone and his children."

Several times too she took apparently aimless walks that brought her up with Ahlquist where he worked in the field, and he would stop his team and sit quietly listening to her talk, wiping his hot face with a soiled bandanna, and after a few minutes he would cover his glistening hair again with the shapeless hat, shake out the lines, and say "I have to get back to work now, Miss MacLeod," and leave her standing in the rough, black field.

Then one day after she had been talking with the hired man while he sharpened a mower blade behind the barn, she came up to the house and met Margaret, who smiled at her reprovingly, maternally, softening the rebuke with smiling fondness but not completely covering the stiff puritan disapproval behind her words.

"I wouldn't be seen too much with Ahlquist, dear," she said. "He's only a hired man, remember, and you've a certain position to keep. People might talk."

"But he's nice," Elspeth said. "And he's lonesome. I think it cheers him up to have me talk to him."

"Yes," said Margaret, as if to a stubborn child; "but he's a married man, Elspeth, and his wife is away."

"Oh!" Elspeth said hotly. "I think that's…" She turned and went out in the back yard, where she threw herself on the bench against the windbreak, thinking furiously how innocent she was of Margaret's suspicions, how Margaret wronged a pleasant friendship with her stiff conventional avoidance of anything that would cause "talk," how she was just interested in Ahlquist because he was lonesome. One would think from the way Margaret took it that she was in love with him!

But in her heart she knew that Margaret didn't think that; she knew that this was only what she mentally called the "parlor" part of Margaret speaking. This was only the rural society woman, the style-setter of a county, the rather proud wife of a wealthy farmer who tightened herself up to what she thought her position and built her life on its conventions. In justice to her sister, Elspeth had to admit that the actual suspicion of anything wrong had never entered Margaret's head, and that Margaret had been merely looking out for her respectability. But even so, Elspeth from that time on saw less of Ahlquist.

To compensate for her thwarted interest in the Viking—an interest that still showed itself in greetings and an occasional conversation—Elspeth gave herself to learning about the farm with the abandon of a child. Everything interested her. She spent hours weeding and trimming and cutting flowers with Margaret in the beds that surrounded the house. She took over the daily chore of gathering eggs from the long chicken shed, and every morning the sight of her white dress brought the hens running and cackling to the wire for the wheat she scattered.

The hens amused her immensely. There was nothing, she told Margaret, quite so ridiculous. She could stand for hours watching the stiff, pecking walk of them, the excited scramble when one found a bug, the wandering, aimless search that led them jerkily around the pen.

The imperial strut of the roosters, too, amused her, and she delighted in taunting them aloud—berating them as stupid, conceited coxcombs, putting a hand through the screen to entice them near, and shooing them off with a flutter of her apron to see their suspicious high-toed strut change instantly to dismayed terror and disorderly retreat.

"Poof!" Elspeth would say. "Absurd beasts!" and walk on down to the barn to caress the silky muzzles of two young calves she had adopted, or to scratch between the horns of the placid mothers.

All the animals on the farm the girl liked except one ugly old brood sow which had littered after her arrival, and which two days later had turned savagely cannibalistic, eating all but two of her own young. Every time she passed the pen Elspeth shuddered at the hideous gray mud-covered brute with the meaty snout and the little bloodshot eyes and the scalloped sagging teats.

"Why don't you kill the beast?" she asked Alec, and when he explained that slaughtering wasn't done until fall, and that anyway the destruction of the litter had been his own fault because he hadn't watched her closely, Elspeth burst out angrily: "Your fault? Is it your fault if a mother eats her own children? I could kill that old cannibal myself!"

"Sows do it all the time if they're not watched," Alec said. "Boars too, only they don't very often get the chance."

"Then I don't have any use for pigs, and I won't eat their filthy meat again, ever!"

"You're tender because of the little ones," Margaret said. "You can't judge animals like humans, Elspeth."

"Why not? A mother's a mother. Even a silly hen takes care of her chicks. I hate that old sow."

Smiling broadly, Alec winked at Margaret, playfully tweaked the girl's ear.

"She's pretty when she's boilin', eh?"

"Oh, you!"

Elspeth flounced out. Watching her thoughtfully throughout the afternoon, Margaret saw her picking tender tufts of grass along the stable wall and poking the green handfuls into the nibbling lips of the two young calves.

A little later the girl was leaning with her fingers hooked into the screen surrounding the chicken pen. Inside the pen the aimless search for bugs and grain was broken suddenly by the amorous rush of a rooster. Hens scattered and flew. The selected victim ducked and scuttled, but at last submitted meekly to her lover, enduring him with a placidity that was almost insulting. Although the rooster pranced a little higher and more pompously for a few minutes, the hen apparently thought no more of it than she did of pecking up a worm.

Elspeth, fresh, high-colored, stood watching, and when it was over she hissed through the wire at the degraded hen.

"You're a disgrace to your sex, you vixen. You've laid too many eggs. Let that pompous dandy treat you so! S-s-s-s-s-s-s! And to the smug rooster: "S-s-s-s-s-s-s-s! You Mormon, you. You Brigham Young! And so proud of yoursel'! So *ver-ry* proud of yoursel'!"

She bent her arms into wings and strutted back and fourth outside the screen, mocking him, while the rooster inside watched suspiciously, stopping with one foot in the air, his combed head perking to see her better, ready to fly at the first flutter of her apron.

"Shoo!"

The apron billowed out, and the rooster took off in a stretch-necked run, wings spread, legs desperately pumping. At a safe distance he stopped, adjusted his wings, and resumed his dainty, slow, high-stepping walk, eyeing her suspiciously still.

And Margaret, who had watched the whole thing through the living room window, turned away with a thoughtful face, thinking of the girl's hatred of the cannibal sow, of her ecstatic devotion to the two awkward little calves, of her bright interest in Ahlquist's melancholy expatriation; thinking of the tense fixity of the girl's figure while she watched the rooster cover the hen.

Later, when Alec came up from the garden eating a raw carrot, she met him in the yard. Elspeth was walking slowly down the lane of elms leading to the state road, and the two stood looking after her for some time before Margaret spoke.

"I'm afraid she's lonesome, Alec."

"Na. She has a grand time. What would she be lonesome for?"

"People her own age—boys."

"Boys?"

The carrot stopped halfway to Alec's mouth as he turned on her in surprise.

"She's ripe to fall in love. I've noticed her with the calves, and the chickens."

"What've the calves and chickens got to do with it?"

"Oh, nothing. But I know. I'm going to give a party, Alec. Not just a dinner, but a party. Young people."

"Um" said Alec, munching on the carrot, his eyes on the white dress down the row of elms. "I wouldn't go too fast, Margo."

"You think I'm being a matchmaker?"

"Why, it sounds like that," Alec said. "She's met a few people. Give her time. She'll find someone."

Margaret's lips tightened with determination.

"I want to give the party anyway. May I?"

Alec hurled the stub of the carrot high and far into the chicken pen.

"Suit yourself," he said.

From **The WPA Guide to Iowa (1938)**

The Federal Writers' Project of the Works Progress Administration for the State of Iowa

Established under the auspices of the WPA [Works Project Administration], the Federal Writers' Project gave struggling writers across the country a chance to earn a buck by way of Franklin Roosevelt's New Deal. The deal in Iowa was this…for $73 a month Iowa writers, so long as they accepted a thirty-hour work week, would complete documentary writings with the goal, as native Iowan and national administrator of the WPA, Harry L. Hopkins, put it, of producing a "portrait of America—its history, folklore, scenery, cultural backgrounds, social and economic trends, and racial factors." Each state project, as it turns out, needed a sponsor, so Iowa director Raymond Kresensky, a Presbyterian minister from Algona, joined forces with Benjamin Shambaugh's Iowa State Historical Society, as directed by the Iowa legislature. Though initially wary about the quality and longevity of the writing, the State Historical Society beamed when, upon the publication of the WPA Guide, positive reviews started rolling in from on high. Ruth Suckow's review in the Des Moines Register *called the effort "splendid" while Phil Stong raved, "One of the most engaging collections of anecdotes and one of the best descriptions of an American people in an American place that I have ever seen—or you either." Iowa had done herself proud, as it had been fourth among the states to finish its guide; Iowa, too, could boast a larger audience, as Viking published the text under the title* Iowa: A Guide to the Hawkeye State. *The selection that follows consists of two separate chapters, "Iowans: The Social Pattern" and "Racial Elements and Folkways" and is presented as one continuous reading with subheadings drawn from the original chapter heads.*

Iowans: the social pattern

An Iowan is as likely to be found in any other of the forty-eight states as in his native one, if the term be taken simply to mean a person who was born in Iowa. By 1930, according to a survey made for the National Resources Board in 1935, more than one-third of all the children of Iowa were living elsewhere—1,084,000 persons. In that same year the state's population was 2,470,939. Between 1920 and 1930, nearly 160,000 emigrated from Iowa, and during the same period many thousands left their cornfields to find a richer living—or merely a living—in the larger industrial centers within the state.

The Iowan who remains at home has a choice of physical environments similar to those he would find beyond the state's boundaries. The beautiful lake region of northwest Iowa is not very different in natural setting or social customs from parts of Minnesota and Wisconsin; the western edge is like Nebraska; and the large towns, Sioux City and Council Bluffs, have characteristics that are definitely western; the southernmost tier of counties is indistinguishable from adjacent Missouri; and along the Mississippi the population looks to Chicago and the East. In Davenport, Dubuque, and the smaller river cities the economic, political, and artistic standards of eastern United States are quickly reflected.

But the real Iowa to the majority of Americans is the great central region, with Des Moines as its focal point; an expanse of fertile farmland, originally prairie, across which the state's own river flows. Here are the corn- and wheatfields, the characteristic white houses, big red barns and tall silos; and, at regular intervals, grain elevators and church spires dominating the little towns. It is from this area largely that the state's agricultural prestige is derived.

With a larger total acreage of grade-one agricultural land than any other state—possibly twenty-five percent of the country's total—Iowa is unquestionably rich. It has excellent educational institutions, kindly citizens, and considerable natural beauty. How then explain the phenomenal emigration of its people, especially of the young and middle-aged? That question the state itself is undertaking to answer.

Setting about making surveys and long-term plans is a tradition in Iowa, one of the earliest states to experiment with extension service from the colleges and the university to the farm. But there is evident now a new perspective and a new emphasis. In the past the test of any economic doctrine or political program was its possible effect upon agriculture. The Grange movement was a direct result of the people's insistence that the railroads should conform to agricultural needs—incredible as it may seem, there is no place in the state farther than twelve miles from a railroad. The innumerable small towns grew up in the center of farming populations, near a gristmill or a railroad station. The railroad often determined the town site on the prairie, loaded a tiny depot on a flat car and bought it to the spot. Next came the freight house for supplies and a stock pen for loading cattle; then a tiny grain elevator, a general store; a doctor, a lawyer, a newspaper—a new town in Iowa.

The long struggle against spending money for highway improvement was due largely to rural opposition, and was ended when the farmer saw its value in terms of the farm. The size of the larger cities, scattered fairly evenly throughout the state, may be traced directly to the number of grain processing, meatpacking, farm implement, and tractor manufacturing plants; and their prosperity depends largely on the prosperity of the farmer. With the coming of the nationwide depression in the 1930s, the Iowan was slow to realize that anything could affect for long the value of the farm or nullify the results of the farmer's labor, for generations, as unquestioned realities as the hot sun and the abundant corn.

But at length he realized that he was no longer independent as once he had been. On his neatly fenced farm of 80 to 200 acres, the Iowan was accustomed to being his own manager, a businessman as well as a tiller of the soil. In the World War period, he followed a national trend and speculated heavily in the land. Farms sold at high prices and mortgages were common, one farm frequently being mortgaged to purchase another. Beginning in 1929 many of these mortgages were foreclosed and much of the land turned over to banks and insurance companies. The farmer today faces the fact that tenancy is common in this great farming state, and that more than half of the farms are rented properties. Unrest and dissatisfaction brought the farmers to organize, to strike, to declare farm holidays—cooperating as in pioneer days to maintain the established pattern of their lives.

In addition to the strictly agricultural problems, the Iowan faces, with the rest of America, the increasing pressure of modern industrialism. From the time that the state reached its peak in farm production, about the beginning of the present century, industry began to develop on a large scale. The small town began to feel the competition of the big manufacturing center. Potential farmers and farmwives began to work in office, store, and factory. With the Depression, unemployment and social unrest became realities to a hitherto more or less self-confident people.

Owing to its fertile soil and the hardworking farmer and farmhand, per capita income in Iowa had been for many years greater than that in the country as a whole. But a gradual decline in farm income had reduced the state's per capita income until it is (1938) approximately equal to that of the nation. Industrial income, however, is growing proportionately larger and has shown greater stability, on the whole, than that of the United States.

With the development of industry and dissatisfaction with farm life began the unusual flow of rural people to urban centers within the state; and this movement from the farm to the manufacturing towns was—and continues to be—but a step in the exodus to the great industrial and commercial cites of the rest of the country. It is this problem that the contemporary Iowan is attempting to solve—how to make Iowa a place where Iowans may live securely and happily.

No longer is the value of a plan or a development tested only by its value to the farm. How, the Iowan asks, can this state give a full and satisfying life to its people? In a sense this is not a new perspective; it is more a picking up of an early tradition simply lost sight of for a while, neglected because of the needs of the farm, often indeed from strict necessity.

With the first settlers, education was a primary interest. In the early [18]40s, [18]50s and [18]60s, the New England tradition—of culture, religion, self-government—was brought directly or by way of New York, Pennsylvania, Illinois, Indiana, Virginia, and Kentucky. Small colleges, some of the earliest west of Mississippi, were built before the railroads were. Iowa's stately Old Capitol, the cornerstone of which was laid in 1840 (two years after the first session of the Territorial assembly), has something of symbolic value today as administrative headquarters of the University of Iowa.

The early settlers brought also a tradition of tolerance, intensified in the new land by the common dependence on the soil. Later immigrants came from adjacent states, from Canada, and from many countries in Europe—Germans, Scandinavians, Hollanders, Bohemians, English, Irish, Russians, Italians—bringing new and vital elements of culture. All of these adjusted themselves to the prevalent agricultural pattern, but the desire for cultural development remained a pronounced characteristic.

The farmer was willing to pay high taxes for the maintenance of educational institutions and to go into debt to send his children to college. But this was not enough. The younger generation showed a definite reaction from farm life, and many of those who left Iowa did so to find a more congenial field for artistic expression and what they believed could be richer human life. But memory of the prairie soil and skyline was reflected in their work, and the lives of the rural people furnished the theme for novel, poem, and picture.

Those who remained at home began to appraise critically the culture of which they were a part; literary, art, and music societies were organized; little magazines were established; and discussion groups stimulated thought in political, economic, and social fields. The depression years brought to many a more sensitive consciousness of the pattern of their society and of national conditions that were beginning to affect it. A few citizens "on the county" had always been accepted as inescapable, but the presence of many farmless farmers and great numbers of unemployed men and women in the cities required a new analysis of the state's economic conditions. The interrelationship between farming and industry had to be realized before any deliberate modification of the earlier pattern might be tried.

All these forces may have combined to bring about the centripetal movement now apparent among Iowans. The reverse swing of the pendulum seems to have begun and the general tendency among the college-trained is to remain and work in Iowa. Higher education is adjusting itself to meet modern necessities and, while the State College at Ames [Iowa State University] maintains its high rank as an agricultural school, emphasis is being laid more and more upon science, engineering, economics, and the professions. The State University [University of Iowa] sponsors schools of music, art, and drama. At the same time there is a distinctive development in the cities in the field of art. The Grandview Music Pavilion at Sioux City (the design for which was made by Henry Kamphoefner, Iowa architect, and submitted for the Paris prize of the Society of Beaux Arts), and the Davenport, Sioux City, and Cedar Rapids Art Galleries are evidences of the new direction.

The humanistic emphasis, so clearly to be seen in cultural activities, is present also in the state's approach to its economic problems. The increase of farm tenancy, particularly in the badly eroded southern counties, is being met with soil conservation programs, the forestation of land unsuited to agriculture, and other scientific measures; but not without provision for the future of the present tenants in some more prosperous area. Long-term leases are encouraged in order not only that the renter may have time to plan his crops and conserve the fertility of the soil but also that he may develop a sense of ownership and eventually become a farmer on his own property.

Careful study is being given to the development of industry and the planning for life in urban centers. Mechanization of the workers' lives, congested traffic, and slum districts are no longer unknown in the larger cities. Investigation of the possibilities of part-time farming, the provision for state and county parks within reach of everyone, traffic surveys, and the work of business bureaus indicate recognition of the problems, and something of the means by which they are being met.

A successful experiment in living, based on the fusion of agricultural and industrial forces, may possibly be carried out here, in this fertile middle ground between the congested districts of the East and the more sparsely settled West. Iowa has the opportunity—rich land, remarkably uniform diffusion of the population, traditions of culture and tolerance.

It may be that a new spirit of humility is abroad in America and that Iowans reflect a national attitude. At least they have passed beyond the self-conscious and boastful stage, once so commonly attributed to them. Aware that, in any economic pattern, their state is part of the "breadbasket of the world," they are trying to make their own adjustment to the new order—to accept the inevitable industrialization but to preserve the serenity and stability of a farm community.

RACIAL ELEMENTS AND FOLKWAYS

Iowa's population (estimated at 2,534,000 in 1935) is a blending of many elements, American and European. The first settlers were from the states to the east, as far away as New England, and to a lesser degree from the South. Thousands of Europeans forced to emigrate because of political unrest and hard times were drawn to the Midwest by persuasive advertising.

The Irish who were among the first to arrive, driven from home by the famines of the 1840s, have settled mainly in the larger towns. Scotch immigrants spread throughout the territory, but moved in large numbers to the mining towns when coal was opened up in southern Iowa. Norwegians first settled at Sugar Creek, Lee County, in 1840. The colony did not thrive, chiefly because the Norwegians were not adapted to the warm climate at the southernmost end of the state. A colony of American Fourierites, French in origin, also made an unsuccessful attempt at settlement on 320 acres of land near the present site of Oskaloosa in Mahaska County in 1843. Both Norwegian and French elements took root, however, in the late 1850s. Scandinavians—Norwegians and Swedes—settled in the western and central parts of the state, and in Jefferson County; a French group, called Icarians, came from Nauvoo, Illinois, and established the community of Icaria in Adams County. A large host of Mormons had come from Nauvoo ten years earlier, in 1846, seeking new homes. Driven first from Missouri to Nauvoo and later to Salt Lake by the antagonism of their neighbors, they established camps in the southern part of the territory. The most important of these was Kanesville, on the Missouri River, now Council Bluffs.

German immigrants arrived in great numbers after the European revolutions of 1848 and settled chiefly along the Mississippi River. A German religious communal group, the Amana Society, set up homes in Iowa County along the Iowa River, and founded the village of Amana in 1855.

Immigrants from other European countries found hospitable welcome, spreading from county to county and adapting the customs of their native lands to meet conditions in their new home. Hollanders, led by their minister Henry P. Scholte, took root in Marion County and founded the town of Pella in 1847. Hungarians, who like the Germans fled from the European revolutions of 1848, attempted unsuccessfully to found a cooperative colony called New Buda in Decatur County in 1850. Many Jews had reached Iowa as early as 1840 and established themselves in commercial and professional fields. German Jews outnumbered those from all other countries in the early days but by 1936 most of the state's twenty thousand or so Jewish families were Russian and Polish. They, too, have gained leading places in business and the professions. The greatest concentration of Jewish population is in Des Moines.

In 1854 a small party of Danes made permanent settlement near Lucerne and later at Elkhorn. The Czechs came to Johnson and Linn Counties at about the same time and founded Spillville, in Winneshiek County. Forty years later Anton Dvorak, the composer, spent a summer in Spillville and no doubt found material here for his *Symphony from a New World*.

The peak of immigration was reached by 1890 and declined steadily thereafter. According to the United States census figures of 1930, only six percent of the total population of the state is now foreign-born. Of this, the largest number—53,901—is German. The Scandinavian countries and Denmark come next, though with much smaller numbers: 16,810 Swedes, 14,698 Danes, and 12,932 Norwegians. Iowa's foreign-born groups also include Hollanders, English, Czechs, Irish, Canadians, Russians, and Italians—their numbers descending in the order named from 10,135 Hollanders to 3,834 Italians. More than a dozen other countries are listed in the census as the birthplaces of foreign-born Iowans. Approximately a third of the foreign-born population lives in the larger cities and groups of from five to ten thousand are concentrated in each of the three cities—Des Moines, Davenport, and Sioux City.

In general, racial lines are tending to grow less distinct as the population merges into a unified whole. Enriching the culture of Iowa, many groups have retained their identity and the customs they brought with them from the Old World.

Chief among these are the Germans. Throughout the state the small German communities are held together by the Lutheran and Evangelical Churches, and the German Catholics, though associated with other racial groups in their church, tend to have their own rural and small town centers. German food, festive wedding parties, and family reunions are the rule, and in some villages and country districts German is the prevailing language. Well-defined German communities are found in Clinton and Bremer Counties and in Davenport and Dubuque. In the cities and larger towns the Germans have their *Turn Vereine* (gymnastic clubs) and their musical societies. Members of the Amana Society, particularly the older people, still cling to the old forms of dress and to German as their home tongue.

The Scandinavians, like the Protestant Germans, remain close to their Lutheran churches, and in many small communities Swedish, Norwegian, and Danish customs are common. The clean white town buildings of Pella and the well-kept farms of this district are characteristic of the Hollanders, who keep to the traditions of their fathers in these and other ways. In the Bohemian (Czech) sections of Cedar Rapids and parts of Linn County, the customs and language of the old country have also endured. The Czechs have their own banks, newspapers, doctors, lawyers, and business institutions. In the rural sections surrounding Protivin, St. Ansgar, and Calmar the observance of old customs is promoted by the Bohemian societies which provide social halls for the young people and encourage Czech folk games and music.

The Welsh, who originally settled in the coalmining camps and are now found chiefly in Mahaska County, remain a unique group clinging to their *eisteddfods* (singing schools) and *cymanfa* (church conventions). They are naturally musical people, and many of the musical instructors in the schools throughout the state are descendants of the early Welsh settlers. There are groups of Italians and Greeks in the larger cities. In Des Moines particularly, the Italians have their own community and preserve their Old World customs. The Mexicans—a new element coming into the state—are spread through Polk, Cerro Gordo, Lee, and Des Moines Counties, with concentrated groups in Fort Madison, Mason City, and Bettendorf. Many of them work in the sugar beet fields in the northern part of the state.

Some negroes came to Iowa in the first years after the Civil War, but the main migration of negroes was from the South at the turn of the century. Imported by the Consolidated Coal Company to break a miners' strike near the present site of Oskaloosa, they gradually developed into a complete negro mining settlement— the largest and best coal-producing camp in Iowa. During the World War negroes came from the East as well as the South in search of higher wages and for military training at Fort Des Moines and at Camp Dodge. Approximately one-third of Iowa's 17,000 negroes live in Des Moines, where they have their own churches, restaurants, amusement centers and religious associations, and publish their own newspaper, the *Iowa Bystander*. Both in Des Moines and Sioux City, the negroes have played a creditable part in civic development. Here and elsewhere in the state they are found not only in the labor field but in business and the professions. A. A. Alexander, of Des Moines, received the degree of civil engineer from the University of Iowa in 1925, and was granted one of the two William E. Harmon Awards for Distinguished Achievement in industry in 1926—the first year these awards were made. In many towns the negroes maintain their own churches and hotels, and take active part in the educational, religious, and political activities of the community.

Many of the existing folkways had their beginning in the house-raising, husking, hog-killing, rag-sewing (for carpets), quilting, and wood-chopping bees, which filled a need for social intercourse while serving their primary purpose of cooperation in some of the undertakings of pioneer farm life. Other customs are outgrowths of the singing schools and "spelldowns" common to all rural pioneer communities.

Farmers in Iowa assemble for many gatherings—family picnics, community celebrations, fairs in their small-town centers, and Saturday afternoon shopping. Much of the social activity is centered in the churches, and church suppers, "aids," meetings, and sociables of all kinds are festive events in any small town. The 4-H Clubs, farm bureau groups, and similar organizations foster social life.

It is in the round of farming activities, in the cooperation among neighbors, that the real Iowa folkways appear. As in most agricultural states, threshing is a celebration as well as a cooperative venture. While the men work together in the fields getting the oats, wheat, barley, or rye to the threshing machine, the women gather to cook the threshing dinner. The community is likely to rate its cooks on the basis of their threshing dinners.

Community corn-picking, silo-filling, and plowing have become well established through the friendly spirit of mutual help handed down from the past. Iowa makes much of its corn-husking contests held each fall. The state contest, a picturesque event in which the county winners participate, is started by the report of a gun fired by the governor. Crowds estimated at 20,000 follow the wagons as the huskers, bareheaded and shirtless, work down the rows of corn and send the ears flying through the air to strike against the "bangboards." Hog-calling has been developed into another annual contest. At the state fair each year contenders for the state title take their turn at "whoee-ing" the hogs, and the one with the most "reach" and volume to his voice wins.

The spirit that prompted the pioneer get-togethers survives today in various annual celebrations. These generally commemorate some event or tradition characteristic of the racial heritage of the locality. Thus Germans fondly remember the past when they take part in the annual celebration of Sauerkraut Day in Ackley. The festival was first established in the late 1890s, and in 1909 the Germans of Lisbon established a similar event. Sometimes as much as 300 gallons of kraut and 600 pounds of wieners are eaten at these celebrations. During the annual Tulip Festival at Pella each May, the town is transformed into a bit of Holland. People wear their cherished Dutch costumes and clop down the streets in wooden shoes; they dance old folk dances, sing folk songs, and feast on native Dutch dishes. Everywhere in Pella bloom the thousands of tulips imported from Holland. Other local events that are racial in origin are: Orangeman's Day at Deep River, held on July 12 when the North Irish assemble; and the Bohemian Fall Festival at St. Ansgar in October where many of the activities are carried on in the native tongue.

Annually in September hundreds of negroes meet on the site of the town of Buxton in Bluff Creek Township in Monroe County. In 1910 Buxton was one of the largest coalmining towns west of the Mississippi with about 6,000 inhabitants, 5,500 of them being negroes. It is now abandoned, and the sites of the town's stores, churches, and schoolhouses are marked only by stakes. The negroes in Sioux City have developed the pleasant custom of the "poor man's party" to which all the negroes in the neighborhood come. Before the festivities are over, the "poor man" who has wares to sell has received for them cash enough to pay his rent and other bills.

The Sac and Fox Indians hold carnival with a powwow at Tama in August each year. The wikiups, tents of skins and burlap, appear on the powwow grounds, but each year the gathering is becoming more like the white man's county fair. The Indian farmers exhibit their prize ears of corn, their largest squash, and their best handicraft.

An easterner traveling through Iowa might notice the over-prominent "yah" for "yes," and other words not pronounced as they are in the East, but for the most part the speech is similar to that in other regions. Slang expressions from the cities to the East, words in the negro dialect, and words characteristically New England are heard. "Crick" for creek, "finicky" for fastidious, "catty-cornered" for cater-cornered, "nubbins" for the small deformed ears of corn, and "lickety-split" for fast are common here.

Before radios, automobiles, and paved roads brought the farmer in close contact with the city, his human newspaper was the traveler. In common with other rural regions, much of the Iowa farm lore concerns the coming of company. When the rooster crows in the doorway, or the cat licks his fur, company is on the way. The farmer knows, if he does not believe, the weather lore; and some continue to plant their potatoes, or other root vegetables, in the "dark of the moon."

Most of the folktales dealing with the Indians are lurid and romantic. The story of the Indian lovers who were refused permission to wed and committed suicide is common to many places. Local residents point out cliffs where Indian maidens leaped to their death until it would seem that the first duty of all Indian girls was to jump off cliffs. Maquoketa, for whom the river is named, is supposed to have jumped to her death, though the cliff cannot be identified. A tale, with its setting near Onawa, deals with an Indian lover who would not accept the decision of his Indian sweetheart to marry a white man. Taking the girl in his arms, he leaped into the river and each year, on the anniversary of their death, the screams of the girl are heard. In the legend of Wapsi and Pinicon, for whom the Wapsipinicon River is named, the two lovers were gliding down the river in their canoe under the eyes of a rival. When Wapsi put her fingers to Pinicon's lips, the jealous lover shot an arrow into Pinicon's heart. Wapsi, rising to help him, upset the canoe and both were drowned.

Some of the legends are history retold...with trimmings. The stories of the naming of the *Tetes des Morts* (Heads of the Dead) River Valley are many. According to one, a battle between Indians and traders left the river filled with severed heads. Another tells of a battle between two Indian tribes in which one was forced over the bow (head) of the cliff into the river. In this version of the story, the trouble began when a young Winnebago chief fell in love with Nita, daughter of a Fox chief. Finding her with a member of her own tribe, he spat in his competitor's face; the Fox tribe wiped out the entire Winnebago group in retaliation.

The yarns of the pioneers, handed down from father to son, are tall tales such as men have always made of the adventures of earlier days. One group centers around Old Man Schoonover, who told stories to his men as they gathered at the mine shafts in southern Iowa. But no one knows Schoonover's real history and the stories of his great prowess run into endless variations. In northeastern Iowa the hunting and fishing stories spun by Old Marsh Hatfield are still repeated.

Quite different in character is the story about Sarah Bernhardt. Ever since she played in Iowa City the tale persisted that she was born in the nearby little town of Rochester, and that Mary King, buried in the local cemetery, was her mother. The divine Sarah came (so they say) in a curtained carriage to place flowers on her mother's grave.

FROM **THREE MILES SQUARE (1939)**

PAUL COREY

From a big Shelby County farm family of seven, Paul Corey knew a thing or two about interrelationships, a heritage that served him well as a writer. Corey's education began in a one-room schoolhouse in Atlantic, where the family moved after the death of his father. From there, Corey gravitated, as did other writers of his generation, to the University of Iowa, where he came into contact with John T. Frederick and Corey's future wife, the poet Ruth Lechlitner. After their marriage, Paul and Ruth would live an experiment in self-sufficiency, settling down in New York in a stone house they built—a decision that informed a series of Corey's 1940s nonfiction books with titles like Buy an Acre *(1944),* Build a Home *(1946) and others. Back home in Iowa, Corey was best known for his farm life trilogy, a series that began with* Three Miles Square *(1939), the novel from which this excerpt appears. When completed by* The Road Returns *(1940) and* County Seat *(1941), the trilogy told the story of the Mantzes during the years 1910 to 1930, an Iowa farm family, who, like the Coreys, suffered unexpected tragedy and success. Note that the Battle of Vera Cruz referred to below references the April 1914 skirmish with Mexico, not the earlier battle of the same name in 1847 in the Mexican-American War. The selection below wonderfully captures two Iowa institutions of the early 1900s—the traveling, tent-show evangelism of the kind popularized by Iowa's Billy Sunday, and, of course, the good, old-fashioned agrarian prank of watermelon-stealing.*

The Revival which Widow Mantz and the good ladies of the community had sponsored was in its second week. Night after night and three times on Sunday, the swart Reverend Harper harangued the crowd in his tent behind Moss Church. He shook his fists, tore his hair, rent at his vest until the buttons popped, preaching everlasting burning and endless caroling to the Lamb. And at the end of each sermon, while the choir sang, "Shall We Gather At The River," he intoned over and over: "Come to God! Come to God!"

Folks from miles around closed in on the canvas tabernacle. When the Reverend Harper called, they shambled penitently down the sawdust-sprinkled aisles to kneel at the rough plank rostrum and pray to the god of John Wesley as interpreted by soul-seeker David Harper.

Maude Haas was the first to be "saved."

When that happened, the farmers grinned. Jack Brody said: "I see John Haas's got a new car."

"Guess Joe Bojer paid for that," put in Charlie Parsens.

"I heard that he had to pay John fifteen hundred dollars damages and John's paid off the mortgage on his stock."

"Anyhow, Brother Harper's saved her soul."

"Well, now, I don't think Brother Harper's worth any fifteen hundred dollars," drawled Brody.

The men chuckled broadly and were silent; then they broke out chuckling again.

But the evangelist finally touched their hearts. These were troubled times: war thundered in Europe; war thundered on our own southern border.

Farmer Wallace expressed the consensus: "I think the country ought to send the Army down and knock the stuffin' out of Mexico. None of this 'watchful waitin' business. Take over them Mexicans, I say, and show 'em how a country ought to be run."

Then there was the battle of Vera Cruz. And the Reverend Harper thundered: "There shall be wars and rumors of wars before the final judgment day! Sinners, repent I Repent ye, I say!"

He got Charley Parsens, that old reprobate, and the whole Parsens family; Jack Brody saw the light, and all the Carters. Dan O'Toole forsook his gin, and a halo circled his fat head with his blue-plum nose like a handle to it. The Pete Thornes brought their little girl, Eva, who was frightened and dumb on her new crutches. The Reverend Harper laid his hands on her shriveled limb and prayed. And the neighbors pleaded with God to give brother Harper a miracle.

Mrs. Mantz longed with all her heart for the healing of the little girl; Mrs. Curtis shouted "Amen" almost in hysteria as the evangelist prayed; Mrs. Wallace hoped for results because a miracle would make the community world-famous. Eva Thorne hobbled back to her parents unhealed, but that didn't dampen the religious zeal of the community.

The September full moon rode high, molding the ridges and hollows, farmyards and field-stretches with silver. The north side of Moss Church yard was parked three and more deep with automobiles. Rigs of all kinds, from lumber wagons to bright new auto-seat buggies, lined the hitching rack. The graveyard looked like a giant prairie dog town, gravestones standing rodent-erect among the mounds.

The lights inside Doctor Harper's tent glowed through the canvas. Beyond the barbwire fence, at the rear, the breeze rustled the drying corn leaves, a sound that was hardly more than a whisper because the Reverend Harper was praying. The ears of the horses lay at a backward slant, not listening.

Young Melvin Wallace, Cecil and Roy Tyler, and a couple of wedge-faced fellows from up Buffalohorn way sat in the back of the tent and whispered to each other. They made sly quips about the girls in the choir—Effie Baumgarten, Verney Mantz, and a new girl, whose family had just started coming to Moss Church, Bernodette Farrel. They snickered and squirmed on their creaky folding chairs.

The evangelist finished his prayer with a flourish; then flashing erect, he shouted: "Sons of the devil, get hence! Spawn of Satan, if you can't silence your tongues in the presence of the Almighty, leave his abode!"

His long finger shot out, pointing at the young men. Heads turned to see, mouths tightened, and faces darkened with frowns. The boys got up with a clatter of chairs and ducked under the skirt of the tent.

The Reverend turned to his sermon: "The Day of Judgment is at hand!"

Outside among the cars, young Wallace said: "The old fart!" But he hoped his folks hadn't seen him.

The five climbed into an automobile and smoked. One of the boys from Buffalohorn way growled: "I've been kicked outten better places than that."

But no matter what they said, they were outcasts. They laughed deeply and manfully, but their rural, superstition-rife consciences troubled them. They had to do something to forget.

Roy Tyler said: "I know where there's a good watermelon patch."

That's the checker, agreed the others: was it near the church?

"We want to get back in time to get ourselves some janes [girls]," said Melvin Wallace then he added: "Jingo, I'd like to get Verney Mantz in my buggy."

But the others couldn't see much in her: she was tied to her old lady's apron strings. The whole Mantz family had got religion.

The five young fellows started on foot down the road.

The melon patch, Roy Tyler said, was in the Olsen's garden. They tried to sing: "We've got a new pig in the parlor." Their voices were off key and raucous.

After passing the Jepsen place they confined themselves to talk. That was a good joke about old man Olsen's hired man. What was that? You know, that good-lookin' guy who worked for him—started working for him last spring. Oh yeah, he came from back East. Sure, well he got his soul saved the second night in the tent; then I guess he thought it was about time he married Hannah Olsen. They got hooked up two days ago. Ho! Ho! Shut up! We're gettin' near the place. There ain't nobody home anyhow. What was that guy's name? Oh, Claude Fallow, or something like that.

The young men climbed the fence, skirted a bank of fernlike asparagus, and were in the Olsen's garden. The dog barked up at the house, but the house was dark. About them the melons lay thick and silver pale on the ground. They took all they could carry and retraced their steps to the culvert in the hollow, split them open on the tile end and ate, throwing the rinds into the road. The dark seeds lay sprinkled about their feet shining like coins in the moonlight.

"I'd like to get even with that old bastard in the tent," remarked one of the boys from up Buffalohorn way.

In the revivalist's tent, the crowd was soaring with the Reverend Harper's sermon. Tears streamed on many a farmer's weather-beaten face. What would their old mothers think of their sinful lives? Had they kept their promises made to mother?

The canvas walls seemed to swell with the volume of the preaching and the tense, stark eyes of the farmer folks followed the preacher's every gesture, their glances driven by fear of the evil thoughts they had suckled when alone in their fields, their barns and their houses. When the time came for the call: "Come to God!" half the congregation left their seats and straggled down to the plank platform and, kneeling, prayed.

When they returned to their seats, the blond cherubic young man, the choir master, and the sexton of the church passed around the collection plates before the purses, sin-softened, had time to be dried by the devil's hot breath. Then it was announced that the tent-meeting would come to an end on Sunday night.

The crowd streamed out of the canvas tabernacle, slipping under its raised skirts. Car lights flashed; motors spluttered; the horses pricked up their ears as family groups straggled to their rigs. Children were called, screamed at, slapped. There was serious talk: a fine sermon; one of the best. Soon be corn-picking; yes, there's a little stack-threshing left.

Young couples paired off.

The five boys were back from their watermelon-stealing. They stood by the porch of the church watching the crowd pass, taunting the girls with catcalls. What a reputation they'd have for being rowdies! Other young men stopped and joshed with them.

Then young Wallace whispered hoarsely: "Looket! Andy Mantz is takin' Bernodette Farrel home. Andy's got himself a girl."

All of them were silent as Andrew, walking stiffly and very much embarrassed, strode by escorting the pretty Farrel girl. And Melvin Wallace's eyes searched deeper into the crowd and his mouth became suddenly dry as Verney Mantz and her mother went past together toward Star and the buggy down the rack. He was all primed to step out and ask to take her home but his courage failed him.

The crowd was thinning; the noise and confusion of conveyances in movement spread out along the road; occasionally, the general bustle was punctuated by the sound of an air horn honking or the squalk of "one of them new klaxons [car horns]."

Roy Tyler stepped out when Mildred Wheeler came along with her family and she lagged back giggling. The other boys yelled after them: "Be sure you go straight home now, Roy." "Oh, Roy. Oh, Ro—eee."

The two fellows from up Buffalohorn way stalked out to their car. This had been a poor show after all but they'd like to get even with that word-slinger for bawling them out. They took Cecil Tyler along with them. Melvin Wallace drove north in his buggy alone, feeling miserable: his folks would give him blazes when he got home.

Soon the church ground was silent. The gravestones still stood rodent-like, listening. The moon was slanting westward and the whisper had died out of the corn.

Reverend Harper and his blond choir leader retired to their cots in the church basement and there by the small oil lamp they counted the collection. "This is a rather wealthy community," brother Harper remarked.

And before they went to bed, the two knelt in their flowing nightshirts and offered up a prayer of thanksgiving.

When Sunday morning came, the last day of the meeting, terrible news passed like lightning over the community: all the tent ropes had been cut during the night. What Godless demonstration was this? The devil was surely yet in the neighborhood!

The severed guy ropes were hastily knotted for morning service. The news spread far and fast and by afternoon a greater crowd than ever before had assembled. The Reverend Harper lamented the work of the devil against him. It would cost a great deal to repair the damage done to the tent.

He shouted: "There are still sinful people in the community! Am I to retire like a coward in the very face of the Devil? No! A thousand times no! I have prayed for direction, and the Almighty God has urged me to stay on. I will continue the meetings for another two weeks to bring light to those lost souls among you and drive Satan from the land!"

Old Charley Parsens and old man Olsen and Brody, Wallace, Jepsen and others—leaders in the neighborhood—offered to help raise the money for the repair. They offered a reward for the discovery of the culprits.

Mrs. Mantz was stunned: how could anybody be so low? Mrs. Curtis flamed: it was those young scamps brother Harper ordered out of the tent last Thursday night! And sister Maude Haas wept bitterly.

But the Reverend Harper bore up well, answering the sympathy of his congregation with: "The Lord is by my side; He looks after my interests; I leave all my troubles with God."

That evening, after counting the bumper collection of the day, he dug out the insurance policy buried deep in his trunk and read the instructions about collecting for damage done to his canvas tabernacle.

FROM **NO HOUR OF HISTORY (1940)**

ELIZABETH FORD

A graduate of Cornell College in Mount Vernon, Elizabeth Ford takes on an especially interesting project in her novel No Hour of History, *which she aims to cover three hundred years of history (1630-1927) as it relates to the fictional town of Hillview, Iowa, and Crollon College—almost certainly based on Mount Vernon and Cornell College respectively. Like many fame-seeking Iowa writers before her, Ford made an attempt at New York City, where she attended Columbia University for a Masters, before returning to Iowa to work for the* Cedar Rapids Republican. *Eventually, she would earn her way back to the Big Apple and a position on the New York* Evening Telegram.

Tod Sloane won the Futurity. Berry Wall and others rode in hansom cabs. But even on Iowa roads, which Hamlin Garland described as "either bitter and burning dust" or "foul and trampled slush," a few horseless buggies with dashboards and whip sockets defied death and public opinion. "Get a horse!" the small boys taunted when there were breakdowns. Farmers swore because of the runaways they caused and promised profanely that they would see laws passed in the statehouse at Des Moines that would keep such menaces to life and limb and property off the public highways. The new contraptions chugged and wheezed on their uncertain ways, however, while rural schools were dismissed to watch their passing. Even in Hillview, mild-mannered Mr. Buser, the photographer, revealed hitherto unsuspected tendencies and startled the town by driving an electric.

And Hillview had telephones! A local company had been formed and stock to the amount of $500 subscribed. The "central" building was insured for $400 and the equipment for $1,150. For the twenty-five wall telephones, there were two operators who received $40 a month. For this they were expected also to make all repairs and extensions. The switchboard was operated only from 6 A.M. to 10 P.M. on weekdays, and on Sundays from 7 to 10 A.M. and 2 to 6 P.M. No one needed to telephone at any other time, since all were supposed to be at church. Landis always had difficulty in recalling numbers, but long years afterward when she had talked casually from London to New York and New York to California, she could still remember that the number of the Hillview meat market was 60, and the grocery store was 95

Hillview had kept abreast of the times in other ways. Cement walks began to replace the old wooden ones through whose cracks pennies and nickels and dimes and quarters and half dollars (and sometimes even a big round silver dollar) found their way. Current for the electric lights installed recently in many of the houses was available every night until midnight, and in winter was obligingly turned on again at five o'clock in the morning. Mains had been laid for the city water. There were other new bathrooms besides the one in the Ash house, and Halloween was never again so much fun for the boys. There was no sewerage system for many years to come, however, and typhoid continued to take its yearly toll. Main Street had a new restaurant on whose window was the legend "Merchants' Cafe" and the initiated had a great time laughing when the uninitiated called it the "Merchants' Calf." There was even a new kind of doctor called an osteopath who had his office in his own house instead of over one of the stores. There was a new church, which held services in the parlors of various members. "Mamma, what are Christian Scientists?" asked Landis, who had imagined hitherto that all persons were either Methodists, Presbyterians, Quakers, Catholics, or heathen on India's coral strand.

Most incredible of all was the breathless whispered confidence of the little Sonabockers that their father had locked himself from prying eyes in the library and actually smoked an experimental Sweet Caporal. Landis feared for her playmates, since who could tell but what John Sonabocker might turn into a cigarette fiend, and everyone knew what that meant.

In spite of all these innovations, neither love nor money could have bought a bottle of vintage champagne nearer than Chicago, although it was no trick at all for a farmer doing his Saturday night trading on Main Street to buy a cowbell, a twenty-gallon wash kettle, or a calf weaner.

Springtime in a prairie town did not mean bock beer. It meant sulfur and molasses, pie plant sauce, and a good mess of dandelion greens. In winter the little kiss-me-quick vestibules were put up outside the front doors, and the long-legged underwear came out of the mothballs.

It is needless to add that in all seasons in Hillview and elsewhere ladies' stockings were displayed only once a week, on Monday mornings, on the clothesline. This was no loss to the Casanovas, since they were generally shapeless black cotton articles of apparel guaranteed to obscure the perfect right and equally perfect left of a Frankie Bailey. Tights were a different matter. Ask Junior to take Grandma to a nightclub and then get Grandpa to tell you about Della Fox.

In 1900 even ladies in Hillview had their moments, however. The town had its Mrs. Lessing. Apparently Mrs. Lessing was an attractive but perfectly respectable widow who had moved there recently with her two children whom she planned to send to college. From appearances it would have been difficult to imagine anyone who smacked less of the demimonde. That went to show that you never can tell. Jezebel's first cousin can hide behind widow's weeds as well as the next gal.

Landis was sitting on the floor of the back parlor looking at the pictures in the big books of art which Elizabeth had bought at the World's Fair. She had pored over them many times and longed for a change. Perhaps her mother would let her go over to Mrs. Stone's. She wanted to look at Niagara Falls and Pike's Peak and other wonders of town and country through the stereoscope on Mrs. Stone's parlor table. Privately, Landis considered the Stone parlor much more elegant than her mother's. Beside the stereoscope was an impressively bound volume of Meredith's *Lucile* made richly puffy by stuffing under the leather. Also on the table was a large pink shell with beautiful pink insides. If you held it to your ear, you could hear what the wild waves were saying. There was a fascinating gilded love seat shaped like the letter S, and in front of it was a white bear rug. In the window a sword fern trailed its greenery over a fearfully and wonderfully made bamboo stand. The crowning glory of the room, however, was the curtain which hung in the doorway opening onto the dining room. It was made of pieces of reed strung together with intervening beads. When it tinkled in the prairie breezes the listener was transported to all the witchery of lush tropical moons, palm trees, and dusky, grass-skirted beauties.*

In the year that followed Landis knew that not only the house had changed but the whole world. In Iowa, the response to a country's call to arms was so overwhelming that entire counties avoided the draft. One-fourth of the Forty-second, or Rainbow, Division was made up of Iowa men and other Iowa troops were scattered in other organizations. When news came of the first three Americans to die in the war, one was Private Merle Hay of Glidden, Iowa. The German colony at the Amanas, a sect somewhat similar to the Amish and who did not believe in war, responded generously just as they had been among the first to send a thousand-dollar contribution to the Union in [18]61. A later demand of patriotism which entailed the visit of a Prohibition officer who confiscated their homemade wine by dumping it into the creek was not so well received.

The Battle Cry of Freedom was also the Battle Cry of Feed 'Em, and Iowa as never before was nature's storehouse of plenty. The farmers saw such crops as they had never known. Land changed hands for as high as $300 an acre, although it was generally sold with a large mortgage attached. Men threshed their grain on Sundays and some ministers approved their patriotic action from the pulpit. Not only Mother Goose's cow jumped over the moon, but also hogs and their price at the packing houses. The war, including the money lent to the Allies, was costing $36,000,000 a day, but the farmers did not need George Creel to make them feel that it was cheap at any price. Their only objection to it all was that the newfangled daylight saving made it so they did not get to town on Saturday night until ten o'clock. "God's time is better than [Woodrow] Wilson's" was their verdict.

"There's something wrong with a country when hogs go up, and to twenty-one dollars, in dog days," Victoria commented one day to her family after a wheatless, meatless meal in the August of 1918. "This is all very well for the farmer now, but what's going to happen when it's over? He acts as though these prices were going to last forever. When he finds out they won't, how is he going to payoff the big mortgage on the new land he's bought during the war? And when he can't and the bank forecloses on him, we're going to hear a hue and cry from him for help and we're all going to have hard times. The farmers in England didn't get straightened around until thirty years after the Napoleonic Wars were over.

"The trouble with the farmer nowadays—and it was coming even before the war—is that he isn't contented to be just a farmer earning a good living. He's always railing against Wall Street, but he wants to have a Wall Street of his own. He wants to be a businessman and a speculator. He isn't thinking about just having a comfortable house and his own apples and potatoes and canned vegetables and fruits in the cellar and meat in the smokehouse and his own woodlot. He expects to buy all these things while he prays for a bonanza year when he's going to make his fortune."

"Right now he thinks he's making it," her husband remarked.

"Yes, and he's wrong," Victoria answered. "He's planting his crops on quicksand and everything is going to sink when the war is over. And let me tell you another thing, for which even the farmer himself isn't going to be to blame. You young people sing a song now, Landis, about how you gonna keep 'em down on the farm after they've seen Paree. It's not so funny a song as you think it is. Well, how are you going to keep them there? When these boys come home, life is never going to be the same for them again. Even before they went to the war and Paris they were getting tired of the farm back home. Look at Clint Hays's boy, leaving as good a farm as there is in the country for his father to work all alone in his old age, and going off to town and clerking in a cigar store where he can wear good clothes instead of overalls six days a week. He doesn't stop to figure out that owning your own place and having a job that you can't be fired from and being your own boss and keeping your self-respect means something after all in life. If a cigar store in Cedar Rapids can get a boy away from the farm, what about Paris?

"Sometimes I think this war is going to just about finish the farms in this country. And then again I know I'm wrong. There have been too many times before when too many other people have thought the same thing and had plenty of statistics to prove it, just as they're going to prove it by this and that fool statement when this war is over. Machines finished the weavers and the automobile killed off the old-fashioned horse and buggy business and these new mechanical refrigerators will put the iceman out of commission before many years have passed, but food is something the world is going to go right on wanting as long as it turns on its axis.

"The farmer will never be finished, providing he keeps his head. He'll go on having his ups and downs but time makes everything even for him in the end, if he doesn't make a fool of himself in the meantime."

"Hear! Hear!" cried Landis. "Listen to the female agriculturist."

"That's just what I'm not," retorted Victoria with spirit. "I'm contented to be a plain dirt farmer, with good horse sense."

From Pedaling to Adventure (1940)

Dorothea M. Fox

As was the case with a number of Iowa's most promising writers, Dorothea Fox worked as a librarian. Employed by the Cedar Rapids Public Library, Fox loved to travel, and took advantage of a hiatus in the summer and fall of 1938 to cycle and hike Europe with a youth group. "From this trip the author returned," according to the "Resume of the Author" as printed on the Torch Press dust jacket of Pedaling to Adventure, *"ready for a cycle and boat trip through the Middle West of the United States, especially along the Mississippi to see some of the historical sections of our own part of the country." The selection following is drawn from the chapter entitled "New Mellerary Abbey and Julien Dubuque." Though Fox's journey feels like a trip back in time, it should be noted that the New Melleray Abbey is still alive and well in Peosta, Iowa, where the monks have augmented their farming skills with a newer enterprise—casket making.*

The next day was a glorious, sunny morning! I set out on my last short jaunt with a feeling of ecstasy, swizzing over the roads as if I were carried on a pair of seven league boots. Up high bluffs and down curved ribbons of road, and finally over a rough, hilly gravel road that led to the New Melleray Abbey. Up and down this jagged and cut-up path I slowly made my way, once falling off my cycle when the thin, hard tires slid over stones in the road. Shaking the dust off myself, I picked my way more carefully. Finally reaching the driveway leading to the big limestone Gothic building, I saw the gray walls and steep, slate roof gleaming in the sun. Arched windows and supporting buttresses reminded me of old world architecture.

As I looked at the Abbey I was met by a friendly guide. Asking for a drink of water, I was taken into the building by the elderly bearded monk. Here I met others of the Order. Then Father Pius showed me the dining room where I was served a warm country meal by a kind, young, red-headed Irish monk dressed in a long brown woolen gown.

"And you came all the way from Cedar Rapids on your bicycle?" he asked.

"Yes, I am on my way to Dubuque."

"Oh! that is still a long way for you to pedal," said the young monk in a sympathetic tone. "You don't have any other clothes?" he inquired looking at my traveling attire.

"No. I could not pedal such a long distance in a skirt," I replied in an amused manner, and changing the subject I hurried on—"You see, I have heard about this retreat from friends, and I have also read about the New Melleray Abbey in Mr. Jay Sigmund's short stories."

"Oh! Mr. Sigmund was a good friend of ours. He was a frequent visitor at our Abbey, and we are glad to have you stop here for a short visit."

"Thank you," I said, feeling the kind hospitality of the monks.

"And you cycled in Europe, too?" asked a young priest who had just entered. "Yes."

"Were you in Ireland?"

I shook my head.

"No? I used to ride all over Dublin on my bicycle."

"Oh! You are from Dublin?" I asked, surprised to find a young Irish monk so far away from his native home.

"Yes," and he poured me a second glass of milk, for I was very thirsty and thoroughly enjoyed the fresh milk which came from the monks' own cows.

Then merry Father Pius came in. "You know I used to bicycle all over Tipperary."

"Oh! You are also from Ireland!" laughed I.

"Yes."

"Did you enjoy cycling when you were still in the old country of Ireland?" I inquired.

"Very much," was the quick reply, and again the merry blue eyes twinkled with amusement. We all laughed, for we seemed to be thinking of the same thing—the fun of cycling. After all we seemed to have much in common, though we were worlds apart.

Before I left the kind hospitality of the monks, I was given certain information about the history of this Trappist monastery which today still adheres to the strict principles and rules of St. Benedict, the great mystic.

It was more than one thousand three hundred years ago that St. Benedict outlined a course of discipline which his followers still pursue, for the monks rise daily at two o'clock in the morning before the sun stirs the rest of the world, and retire at eight in the evening. Twelve hours are for prayers and religious service while the remaining six hours are spent in manual labor in the monastery or on the farm. Observing complete silence except when speaking to their superiors and refraining from eating meats, the monks are able to lead a meditative life.

There are two classes of monks at New Melleray; choir brothers and lay brothers. The first are more educated, spending a great deal of their time in religious study and having less time for work, since they expect to become priests. Their gown worn at prayers is a white woolen one with full sleeves and hood, but at work they put on a black scapular with hood over their shoulders and leather girdle.

The lay brothers who do most of the work on the farm, the sewing, cooking, washing, and serving, always wear long brown woolen garments. At their daily tasks, the skirts are fastened up to their leather belts. Their hair is cut close to their heads and their beards are long, and since cool linen clothing is forbidden, the monks always wear woolen garments even in the summer months.

Women or girls may not pass the inner gate.

Only men and boys are privileged to enter the Abbey. In the building is a long narrow cloister with bare walls, where the monks walk indoors saying their prayers during rainy days. Then off the cloister is the small white chapel having two altars painted white and gold. In the chapter room the monks sit on low benches along paneled side walls. It is here that these mystics listen to the Abbot's explanation of the rules of their order, and receive from him their daily tasks. Here also they confess any violation of St. Benedict's rules.

On the second floor is the large dormitory with plain white walls. Here are the small cells where the monks sleep on hard bunks having straw ticks or thin mattresses with sheets and woolen blankets. The monks sleep never removing all of their clothes.

In the other wing of the second floor is the church of the Abbey. Here on each side are raised stalls for the choir brothers while in front of them sit the lay brothers. And in the back are a few pews for visiting men who wish to attend the services. Here in this church the monks spend many hours a day worshiping their God.

In the basement of the Abbey are kitchen and dining rooms for the monks. On benches before plain tables each monk takes his usual place to eat a simple noon meal usually consisting of soup, two kinds of vegetables, eggs or cheese, fruit, bread and butter, coffee or tea. In the evening, supper is frugal with only bread and butter relieved by honey and tea or milk to drink.

The New Melleray farm is one of the finest and largest communal organizations in eastern Iowa for the monks have a splendid herd of dairy cattle, a large chicken farm, and raise many acres of corn, hay, and wheat.

This Cistercian or Trappist order has an interesting Old World origin; first in France, then in Ireland, and finally in America, for the name, Trappist, is derived from the monastery at La Trappe, France. From French soil came this first little group to Ireland to found the Mt. Melleray monastery, which flourished and grew out of bounds. Because of overcrowded conditions in Ireland, the Abbot of Mt. Melleray decided to found a new monastery in the virile fields of America.

He was finally offered a fine tract of land in Iowa southwest of the Catholic city of Dubuque. So on July 16, 1849, the Abbot with four Trappist brothers came to America where the foundations of the new world Abbey were to be laid. After years of hard work, barns were built, land was fenced in, crops were grown, and the Abbey was finally completed.

I was glad that I had tarried awhile for I had a glimpse of another world; another world where the comforts of life were little in comparison to the spiritual welfare; a place where there were few worldly possessions—a world where family and friends meant nothing in comparison to the love of God. In this spiritual world there is no confusion, no hatred, no wars—but always there is self-denial, brotherly love, and peace—peace— peace.

So it was with a light heart that I left the wooded retreat surrounded by tall coniferous trees murmuring in the mellow autumn breeze that was tinged with the spicy sap of pungent pine.

Back again onto the highway I seemed to float on the air. I pumped—pumped—pumped. Now the hills were getting higher. Slower and slower I went. Round and round went the wheels. I shifted gears, and finally arrived at the top of the hill where I stopped to drink in the beauty of the scene. In the valleys below were nestling houses and round, white silos tucked in between protecting trees and hills. Over the distant bluffs a purple-blue haze hung over the countryside like a great canopy. There was illimitable space. A feeling of peacefulness pervaded the country atmosphere. I felt as if the Great Spirit had just passed this way and waved His arms through the eons of Time to let me feel His mighty presence. Back—back—back into limitless Time I seemed to dwell.

No more dreaming. I brought my mind back to where I now stood and hopped on the pedals. Down the hill I coasted, the breeze tearing through my hair, the sun nipping my nose. I whizzed over the old military road like the flying carpet that sailed and sailed through the skies and the wind, and approached Dubuque from the southwest.

FROM **HOLDING UP THE HILLS: THE BIOGRAPHY OF A NEIGHBORHOOD (1941)**

LEO R. WARD

A neglected work even in the field of place studies, Leo Richard Ward's memoir Holding Up the Hills *is, according to literary scholar David M. Emmons "equal to [Ruth] Suckow at her finest." While the Melrose, Iowa, native went on to become a priest in the Community of Holy Cross and a teacher of philosophy at the University of Notre Dame, Ward early on demonstrated ample gifts as a nonfictionist. In fact, Ward's associate, John T. Frederick, selected his short story "Black-purple in the Corn" for Frederick's popular 1941 anthology* Present-day Stories *and famed, Iowa-sympathetic editor Edward J. O'Brien included Ward's work in the* Best Short Stories of 1931 *and* Yearbook of the American Short Story. *Since then, Father Ward has largely focused on theological and philosophical writing, publishing such scholarly titles as* Ethics and the Social Sciences *(1959) and* Philosophy of Education *(1963). In the except following, drawn from the chapter entitled "New Neighbors in Search of the Land," Ward explores an important Iowa preoccupation—neighbors—as well as the almost mystical process by which the people come to resemble the land, and the land, the people. The action takes places in the Irish-Iowan community of Monroe County in south-central Iowa.*

In the early days, the great ambition was to get to Iowa where it was understood that the soil was strong and rich. "Iowa Territory—unsurpassed in the fertility of her soil, her resources endless." So ran a toast in honor of the governor on September 4, 1838. The custom was for people to come all summer long. Men driving ox teams hundreds of miles could hardly gauge so much as the season of their arrival, and we know that it sometimes took them the whole summer. That was the case with my mother's people and the group that drove from Ontario in the fifties. My father's father came directly from Cleveland; they worked their way, perhaps mostly by canal, downstate in Ohio, then came down the river by boat and up the Mississippi. The journey took approximately three weeks. As was then the way they settled first near the river, but after the [Civil] War they came another hundred miles to our neighborhood because the church was being built.*

Muck and Letty came, lured by the promise of cheap rent, from down along old Crooked Creek, in Illinois; they thought they would be able to buy in a couple of years. Soon after Christmas, Muck had appeared unannounced and had rented the place when it was under snow, and there was nothing to tell of its quality except the lie of the land and the word of neighbors, and a few hardy cornstalks and cockleburs reaching up out of the snow, and the tumbleweeds rolled up against the hedges. He could give credentials, but he himself did not ask any; he trusted land and weather and God and people.

Letty was, then and always, out of breath. She had sinking spells but she talked. At any instant, a person would swear she was ready to take the count and could scarcely be revived by a wink at the bottle, but she kept her feet and kept going. She could whip a mess of work out of her way. The two of them worked like horses, and turned out to be the roughest and best neighbors we ever had; at least, if the words roughest and best are taken together, no other neighbors could very well compare with them. And it is sure that we had many good neighbors, such as Big Man and Mary Ann and a dozen others, and some people would think almost any of them rough and ready.

When new neighbors came, people wanted to know one or two important things about them. Were they honest? They had better be! Were they friendly, and were they so friendly as to be pests? Sometimes people turned out to be dirty, yet surely the cleanness of people was something that could be taken for granted. Well, Muck and Letty at once qualified. They minded their business, paid as they went, and were careful not to wear out their welcome. Muck was what we call a born Catholic and Letty was a convert; in any case, we felt at home with them.

Letty had a new way of making cheese. It was not a secret process; her face as colorless as water, her body pulled down like the body of a mare with colt, she worked away; she wanted to teach everybody, and nobody could be displeased with her goodwill. Yet even a layman might suggest she had made no great discovery, and might claim that the curds were less risky than the new cheese.

Neither Muck nor Letty ever played cards, but she liked to dance, and they gave dances at which the whole neighborhood was welcome to dance, to play euchre, and to eat Letty's gooseberry and pumpkin pies.

They were wonderful to help, no matter how hard the work. It was as if that was what they came into the world to do. Before a neighbor asked at all, they would come and do any kind of work for him and with him; she would scald the churn and see after the incubator, with her soul set on what the result would be; and Muck would fix up a fence or a gate, and likely as not he would never say a word about it; the neighbor's need was chance enough for him. He was a strong, rough-bodied man, and he loved people. Whenever a neighbor threshed, Muck was there early, he opened the stacks, and he never let up until the grain was scooped into the bin and the straw-pile was covered with slough-hay and weighted down with poles or rocks.

It is true that he could get hot under the collar; everybody soon knew this and allowed for it. He broke out into living flame once in a while, but really it was nothing, it was only the spurt of a match; a moment later he was, though out of wind, gentle and kind, his voice deep and quavering and mellow, his light blue eyes soft. The worst thing about him, at least when we first knew him, was his discouraged hours, and even so he enjoyed being consoled, and the greatest good in his own day was in bringing comfort to people.

When a man fell from the fork-track of a new barn, Muck rose from a sickbed and went like a wild man across the fields on an old plug, bareback, to the man who as a matter of fact was then almost a total stranger to him. It was New Year's Eve, the ground was frozen solid, and the two of us were deputized to stay with Letty till we saw him come home at midnight and eat a gooseberry pie and drink a pot of coffee. He said, "Poor Stevie! To fall like that, there all alone in the barn, and not a soul to help him out but his one sister!" The words shook up out of Muck and he used his favorite expressions: "By gol! And Stevie is such a g-good fellah!" Before daylight the next morning, Muck and Letty were on the road to Mass and to receive Holy Communion; they weren't going to miss, least of all on New Year's Day and when the poor neighbor was not able to go.

That's what they liked, not raising a bumper crop or shipping a carload of hogs to Chicago, but helping a man who was out of luck. As they saw it, that was not only the right thing but the normal thing. Life itself was for this kind of neighborliness; the fact was clear as sun and moon and stars.

We were all poor people, on every side of town, and those who were renting and moving needed no wagons to haul their money. Muck and Letty made no pretense to wealth. They came with their pockets slack; if they had a bit of cash, they may have kept it and actually have added to it in the best times, but with the times still good or ordinary and with themselves toiling they probably began to slip a little down the hill. Like all of us poor farmers, they dealt—if they dealt at all—in third-rate canners and feeders, and not as a matter of choice. And the Lord knows every calamity comes to poor farmers; the well runs dry, they get caught with land that sours or won't drain, the hog market starts down at the wrong time, the cash rent comes around much too quickly on them.

Now it is hard to weigh what odds and ends of misfortune hit Muck and Letty from one side or another. And the signs were on them. Clothes became skimpy, the house sometimes looked as if it had been robbed, and when they had produce they were so generous and wholehearted that they did not run to sell it but to put it on the table. It was almost as if they were looking for someone on whom to bestow things. So money was gone before it came, and any tramp was welcome to a share of the food they had. Muck was always turning his pockets inside out to get half a pipe of tobacco, and Letty often had a time of it, after the middle of summer, to get enough cream together for a churning.

When they first came to us, and it's hitting around thirty-two years now, Muck and Letty seemed to us children an old man and woman. Well, they have grandchildren now this good while, but are not old people, not snowed under, not by a long way. Each of them can yet do a day's work, or a season's work. Of course, Letty is wind-broken as she always was, but she can climb a big hill if given moderate time, and though we may suppose she does not dance anymore it is safe to bet she could do a turn or two. What is known is that on a summer morning not long ago she churned at five, walked a mile and a half to church, and after Mass appeared in the sacristy with a jar of the buttermilk under her arm. Neither the work nor the jaunt was too hard on her, because for a lifetime she has loved to do such things.

Muck appears like himself of thirty years ago. It is true that his face is now without the beard and is like a plowed hillside gutted and ditched with rains, and he is stooped at the shoulders and bent at the knees, but the rest of him stands fairly straight. When we see him ride an old white horse without saddle and with a kind of rope bridle, or hear him rattle along with team and rig, what we have to say is that he is not a knocked-out man. All his life long, he has known how to sit behind the kitchen stove on a winter day, or day after day, and rest up; but he never knew what hate was or is; so perhaps he will wear much better than men who were more neatly set up, but loved man less; he says that God means that every man should have something to suffer. In short, Muck remains a strong man hard to keep in clothes; he can raise good corn if he gets rain; his teeth are worn small but he has enough of them left to manage to munch at a mouthful of Granger Twist [tobacco]. When in 1934 the lean times and the drought were combined and might be thought to be at their peak, he said that he had always had good neighbors and had no complaint to make against God or man.

Long ago, when Muck was already mature in years, I heard quite a young man tell him that no man ever need be poor: "not any more, old fellow." Muck was not tolerant of that idea, "need never be poor," and though he would be tolerant of it now, he still wouldn't believe it.

They were well met, as we used to say, the two of them, Muck and Letty. In many ways he must have seemed to most people a memorable person, and in fact a genuinely remarkable person; he had a hollow Lincolnesque jaw, a big chin, and a big mouth with the corners tipping up. Besides, he was probably boss of the farm. But there is no use saying Muck without Letty, or Letty without Muck, and none of their friends ever does say one or think of one without the other. They are a pair after all, a matched team, and if possible a person might not have said fifty years ago that they were simply born to go together, they certainly have gone well and happily together; neither one could have done much of the going alone; and it would seem strange now to any of their friends to think of them as ever having been for a week of their lives apart. At any rate, from the first day we ever knew them, they have smoothly managed their small cooperative.

Certain kinds of trees, such as running-oak and crab apple, grow, not in, but out of, our clay hills; that is the case of Big Man's rough forty, on much of the Mary Ann place, and on The Granger's poorer land. And yet it is hard to say. Maybe the hills grow out of the trees, the two are so close, so native to each other. Well, Muck and Letty have remained like that, and it is only half the truth to say that they are partners. For when a person met one, he certainly met the other, though the other might not be seen, especially by a stranger. And he wouldn't want to make up his mind too quickly which was the hill, and which the rooted running-oak or wild apple.

Muck was one person, and Letty another. But without the other, each would have been notably different, and likely would not have been at all. One of the good things of our life is to have known and still to know the two together, the two as one.

A Letter from Glenn Miller to Brigadier-General Charles D. Young (1942)

Glenn Miller

The proud product of Clarinda, Iowa, where he was born on March 1, 1904, Alton Glenn Miller, like Herbert Hoover, didn't stay long in the Hawkeye State, though his grandparents had been in Page County since the 1870s. The trombonist and bandleader formed his world-famous Glenn Miller Orchestra in March of 1938 and made it big with hits "Tuxedo Junction," reported to have sold over 100,000 copies in its first week, "In the Mood," "Pennsylvania 6-5000," and his signature piece, "Moonlight Serenade." Miller's CBS-broadcast Moonlight Serenade *radio series for Chesterfield Cigarettes brought him a nationwide audience, as did the 1941 film* Sun Valley Serenade, *which made the soon-to-be million-selling record* Chattanooga Choo-Choo *and its title song of the same name part of the American vernacular. Glenn Miller's letter to Brigadier-General Charles D. Young, reprinted below, demonstrates Miller's humility, creativity, and patriotism—three well-known Iowan virtues. After many months of trying to convince military brass to induct him, he was assigned to the Army Specialist Corps as a Captain. Once trained, he was transferred into the Army Air Corps, where he created the Glenn Miller Army Air Force Band and shipped out to England. The Glenn Miller Air Force Band is credited with giving over 800 performances, approximately 500 of which reached a total of millions by broadcast. In the autumn of 1944, in what is surely one of the nation's greatest wartime losses of a national icon, Miller's plane disappeared en route to France, where his band was scheduled to play for troops who had liberated Paris. Iowa and the nation kept, and keep, the memory of Glenn Miller alive. In 1953, the film* The Glenn Miller Story, *starring James Stewart and June Allyson, was released, though Miller's mother is reported to have said that Jimmy Stewart "wasn't as good-looking" as her son. Iowa remembers Miller with the Glenn Miller Foundation, founded in 1989 by Miller's daughter Jonnie Dee, the Glenn Miller Birthplace site in Clarinda, and that community's annual Glenn Miller Festival.*

August 12, 1942

Brigadier-General Charles D. Young
Room 5136
Interstate Commerce Building
12th Street & Constitution Avenue, N.W.,
Washington D.C.

Dear General Young:

In your recent letter to me you mentioned the desirability of "streamlining" our present day military music. This touches upon a subject which is close to my heart and about which I think I can speak with some authority.

I wish you could read some of the many, many letters that have come to me during the past months from our men in military service expressing their appreciation of our various Army camp appearances and our USO broadcasts. I wish you could also read some of the newspaper reports of interviews with our servicemen in Australia and other distant places, and their pleas that broadcasts from home include a generous share of our music. These letters and reports all show that the interest of our boys lies definitely in modern, popular music, as played by an orchestra such as ours, rather than in the music to which their fathers listened twenty-five years ago, most of which is still being played by Army bands just as it was in World War days.

The many requests for broadcasts, records, programs, dedications and arrangements are very pleasing to me but they leave me wishing that I might do something concrete in the way of setting up a plan that would enable our music to reach our servicemen here and abroad with some degree of regularity. I have a feeling that if this could be arranged it would help considerably to ease some of the difficulties of Army life.

For the past three or four years my orchestra has enjoyed phenomenal popularity until we have now reached a point where our weekly gross income ranges from $15,000 to $20,000. Needless to say, this has been and is most profitable to me personally, but I am wondering if it would not be more in order at this time for me to be bending my efforts towards the continuance of this income if it could be devoted to USO purposes, the Army Relief Fund or some other approved purchase. If, by means of a series of benefit performances or other approved methods, even some part of this income could be maintained and used for the improvement of Army morale I would be entirely willing to forego it for the duration. At the same time, by appropriate planning, programs could be regularly broadcast to the men in the service, and I have an idea that such programs might put a little more spring into the feet of our marching men and a little more joy into their hearts.

With these thoughts in mind, I should like to go into the Army if I could be placed in charge of a modernized Army band. I feel that I could really do a job for the Army in the field of modern music. I am thirty-eight years of age and am in excellent physical condition. I have, of course, registered for the draft but have not been classified. Inasmuch as I have been married for twelve years, I would suppose that under present regulations I shall ultimately be placed in Class 3A. I mention this only because I want you to know that my suggestion stems from a sincere desire to do a real job for the Army and that that desire is not actuated by any personal draft problem.

I was born in Clarinda, Iowa, and raised in Colorado. Both of my parents were also American-born. I am a grammar school and high school graduate and also attended the University of Colorado for two years. My connection with music is not of recent origin. I have been playing and arranging music ever since my high school days.

I hope you will feel that there is a job I can do for the Army. If so, I shall be grateful if you will have the proper person contact me and instruct me as to further procedure.

With kind personal regards and appreciating your interest, I am

Respectfully yours,

Glenn Miller

A Letter from Mrs. Alleta Sullivan to the Bureau of Naval Personnel and Response from Franklin D. Roosevelt (1943)

Heartbreaking in its stoical strength, this letter from Waterloo's Alleta Sullivan, mother of Albert, Francis, George, Joseph, and Madison Sullivan, to the Bureau of Navel Personnel transcends time and place in its evocation of a mother's love. Despite an unofficial Navy policy calling for the separation of enlisted siblings, the five fighting Sullivan Brothers, aged 19 to 27, insisted on living out their creed: "We stick together." They enlisted in Des Moines, citing the Pearl Harbor death of their friend, Bill Ball of Fredericksburg, Iowa, as their inspiration. When the Japanese torpedoed their battleship, the USS Juneau, on November 13, 1942 at the Naval Battle of Guadacanal, all five brothers, and all but ten of their shipmates, were lost, though never forgotten. Waterloo eventually honored its native sons with the naming of the Five Sullivan Brothers Convention Center among other municipal installations. And, as some small consolation for her unfathomable loss, Mrs. Sullivan not only christened the USS Tawasa mentioned in her letter, but sponsored the USS The Sullivans, a destroyer launched on April 4, 1943. The Sullivan tragedy inspired two films, the 1944 movie The Fighting Sullivans *and, to a lesser degree, the 1998 epic* Saving Private Ryan. *Franklin D. Roosevelt's response, though obviously not form the pen of an Iowan, is included here for historical context. Naval security forbid immediate acknowledgement of the loss of ships for fear of aiding the enemy, explaining the nearly desperate, but exceedingly polite, tone of Mrs. Sullivan's missive.*

Waterloo, Iowa
January 1943

Bureau of Naval Personnel

Dear Sirs:

I am writing you in regards to a rumor going around that my five sons were killed in action in November. A mother from here came and told me she got a letter from her son and he heard my five sons were killed.

It is all over town now, and I am so worried. My five sons joined the Navy together a year ago, Jan. 3, 1942. They are on the Cruiser, *USS Juneau*. The last heard from them was Nov. 8th. That is, it was dated Nov. 8th, U.S. Navy.

Their names are, George T., Francis, Henry, Joseph, E., Madison A., and Albert L. If it is so, please let me know the truth. I am to christen the USS *Tawasa*, Feb. 12th, at Portland, Oregon. It anything has happened to my five sons, I will christen the ship as it was their wish that I do so. I hated to bother you, but it has worried me so that I wanted to know if it was true. So please tell me. It was hard to give five sons all at once to the Navy, but I am proud of my boys that they can serve and help protect their country. George and Francis served four years on the USS *Hovey*, and I had the pleasure to go aboard their ship in 1937.

I am so happy the Navy has bestowed the honor on me to christen the USS *Tawasa*. My husband and daughter are going to Portland with me. I remain,

Sincerely,

Mrs. Alleta Sullivan
98 Adams Street
Waterloo, Iowa

Prepared 13 Jan. 43

My dear Mr. and Mrs. Sullivan:

The knowledge that your five gallant sons are missing in action against the enemy inspires me to write you this personal message. I realize full well there is little I can say to assuage your grief.

As Commander-in-Chief of the Army and Navy, I want you to know that the entire nation shares in your sorrow. I offer you the condolences, and gratitude of our country. We who remain to carry on the fight must maintain spirit, in the knowledge that such sacrifice is not in vain.

The Navy Department has informed me of the expressed desire of your sons, George Thomas, Francis Henry, Joseph Eugene, Madison Abel, and Albert Leo, to serve in the same ship. I am sure that we all take heart in the knowledge that they fought side by side. As one of your sons wrote, "We will make a team together that can't be beat." It is this spirit which in the end must triumph.

Last March you, Mrs. Sullivan, were designated to sponsor a ship of the Navy, in recognition of your patriotism and that of your sons. I understand that you are now even more determined to carry on as sponsor. This evidence of unselfishness and of courage serves as a real inspiration for me, as I am sure it will for all Americans. Such acts of faith and fortitude in the face of tragedy convince me of the indomitable spirit and will of our people.

I send you my deepest sympathy in your hour of trial and pray that in Almighty God you will find the comfort and help that only He can bring.

Very Sincerely Yours,
Franklin D. Roosevelt

Mr. and Mrs. T. F. Sullivan
98 Adams Street
Waterloo, Iowa

"THE RISE AND FALL OF BUXTON" (1945)

J. A. SWISHER

Jacob Armstrong Swisher wrote countless books and articles for the Iowa State Historical Society in Iowa City, the two most popular of which were Iowa Pioneer Foundations *(1940) and* Iowa in Times of War *(1943). Here, Swisher applies his consummate knowledge of Iowa history to Buxton, the ghost Monroe County coal town that once boasted a thriving population of more than five-thousand mostly African American residents known by some as a "Black Utopia." The unusual racial harmony in this southern Iowa village, where the union dictated that blacks be paid the same as whites, encouraged the rise of a distinguished African American professional class, including Dr. E. A. Carter, the first of his race to graduate from the University of Iowa Medical School, and attorney George H. Woodson, who cofounded the Niagara Movement, which would become the National Association for the Advancement of Colored People (NAACP) in 1909. Woodson and fellow Buxton resident Samuel Joe Brown would go on to found, with the help of several others, the National Bar Association in 1925. J. A. Swisher's view of the unincorporated Buxton, as expressed in the article that follows, is an ambivalent one, but considering its publication date, 1945, even its understated acknowledgement of the town's accomplishments rekindled popular and scholarly interest in the community.*

In the decade of the eighties the town of Muchakinock, five miles south of Oskaloosa, in Mahaska County, was a flourishing coalmining community. About that time the Consolidation Coal Company, a subsidiary of the Chicago and North Western Railway Company, became interested in Iowa coal, and sent its agent J. E. Buxton to Muchakinock to purchase coal. Eventually, he was succeeded by his son, Ben C. Buxton.

When laborers at these mines became scarce because of strikes and increased demands for labor, H. A. "Hobe" Armstrong, a resident of Muchakinock, and other agents of the company went to Virginia to induce negroes to come and work in the Iowa mines. Negro miners came also from Kentucky and Tennessee, and presently Muchakinock had a large colored population.

For the transportation of coal from this area, the Chicago and North Western Railway had run a branch from its main line at Belle Plaine, southwestward to What Cheer, thence to Muchakinock and Lakonta. When the mines at Muchakinock ceased to be profitable, the railroad extended its tracks farther southward just over the line into Monroe County, and Ben Buxton and his miners, both white and colored, moved by train in a body, and founded the town of Buxton, about twelve miles north of Albia.

During the first decade of the twentieth century Buxton became one of the largest coalmining towns west of the Mississippi River. Its population of approximately five thousand was about half white and half colored. In 1906 the Regal Coal Company, the Ackers Coal Company, and mines Nos. 10, 11, 12, 13, and 14 of the Consolidation Coal Company were located near Buxton. The output from these mines that year was 1,183,143 tons of coal. This made Monroe County the largest coal-producing county in Iowa.

At that time and in the years immediately following, Buxton was reputed to be the largest unincorporated town in the United States. There was no city government—no mayor, no council, no police force. Order was maintained, insofar as order prevailed, by township and county officers, chiefly constables and deputy sheriffs.

Rowdyism and violence prevailed throughout the town. Murders were not rare. Holdups and robberies were common, and assaults were frequent. A former resident refers to the town as a modern Sodom and adds: "People think I am telling a cock and bull story when I tell them what I saw in Buxton. But it's the truth."

But Buxton was not wholly bad even in those days. There were churches of various denominations—one maintained by colored Methodists, one supported by white Methodists, a Swedish Lutheran Church, and a church for colored folk of the Baptist faith. Schools were maintained for both white and colored pupils. Usually they were not segregated. At one time Buxton had a thoroughly mixed high school, with a negro superintendent and a negro principal, with teachers of both races, and with both white and black pupils attending.

When Buxton was at its height, no other town in Iowa could boast of so many professional and business people of the colored race. Mrs. Minnie B. London, for many years a teacher in the Buxton schools, writes: "Doctors, lawyers, teachers, druggists, pharmacists, undertakers, clerks, the postmaster, justice of the peace, constable, members of the school board, and what have you" were of negro blood. There were, of course, physicians, ministers, lawyers, teachers, merchants, mechanics, and miners of the white race, too, for Buxton was a thoroughly mixed community. There, too, as in other towns, good and evil influences existed side by side. No one race or group was responsible for all the evil influences, nor was anyone race or group to be credited with all the good. Rather the good and the evil, like the white and colored population, was scattered throughout the town.

Various parts of the town or "camp," as it was commonly called, were given characteristic names. "East Swede Town" and "West Swede Town" designated areas in which Swedish immigrants predominated. Another section of town was called "Gobblers Nob"—just why, no one seemed to know. "Sharp End" applied to the "sudden termination of the town to the south." In that area was Ike Hutchinson's drugstore where Mrs. Hattie Hutchinson, said to be the only colored woman registered pharmacist in Iowa, filled prescriptions. Coopertown, named in honor of B. F. Cooper, another negro druggist, was located to the north on the Mahaska County line. But these areas were all parts of the Buxton community.

News of local interest appeared in the *Gazette*, the *Advocate*, and the *Bulletin*, which were published weekly in Buxton at different times. When Mrs. London wrote her reminiscences for the Howard Newspaper Syndicate in 1940, her descriptions of the unique community were as circumstantial as the items that might have been read during the decade from 1906 to 1916 in the columns of these papers. For example: "Manie Lobbins had a livery barn in the Sharp End, and since this was in the horse and buggy days no one was required to take Hobson's choice."

"If you wanted coffee like your mother made, you would go to the Rising Sun Restaurant in Coopertown, operated by Mrs. Anna Lobbins. She would serve you a hot lunch or a complete dinner at reasonable prices."

"Peter Carey's barber shop was also in this section, located across from Cooper's store. He was always in whenever one wanted a haircut or shave."

"The hair dressing, manicuring, face massage, and chiropody were all done by Madam Ella Yancy. She was an honor graduate of the New York College of Hairdressing. Madam Yancy was Buxton's best specialist in scalp treatment. 'If your hair won't grow, won't straighten, all you have to do is to see Madam Yancy and find out the reason and get a remedy'; and 'If your wrinkles won't leave and your cheeks won't fill out, see Madam Yancy'; and 'If your corns bother you and just won't stop hurting, see Madam Yancy.'"

"Near the depot Anderson Perkins and Son operated a hotel and confectionary. They advertised good meals and first class service. Hotel rates $1 and $1.50."

"If you desired an old-fashioned meal and did not wish to go home or bother to cook on a hot day, all you had to do was to stop in the Jeffers Restaurant, run by Andy Jeffers and his wife Maggie."

"Peter Abington, the caterer, kept his wagon on the street all day long selling ice cream, pies, bread, butter and eggs."

"Lewis Reasby had a hamburger stand in front of the Y. M. C. A. His comical manner of crying his wares would attract passers-by who would stop to listen to him, then find themselves thrusting their hands into their pockets and saying, 'A hot dog please.'"

The Y. M. C. A. was a large three-story building built expressly for the colored miners by the coal company. Though slow to be accepted, it eventually became a popular center of recreation. At one time this was reputed to be "the largest negro Y. M. C. A. in the country" with a membership of about three hundred. The third floor was occupied by the rooms of many secret societies, for nearly every adult belonged to one or more, "When a member died his lodge would turn out in full regalia. The funeral procession would be headed by the band playing a funeral dirge all the way to the cemetery." The Buxton Negro Concert Band was famous throughout southern Iowa. Under the leadership of F. E. Goggins, it had frequent engagements in surrounding towns, playing at fairs and on other occasions.

The second floor of the Y. M. C. A. was occupied by a spacious auditorium, with a stage and dressing rooms. There the Langois sisters, better known as the "French women," displayed motion pictures every night, which afforded enjoyable recreation for the miners and their families. Road shows as well as motion pictures were featured in the auditorium—among them *East Lynne* and the *Count of Monte Cristo*. Among the negro characters who entertained packed houses were Booker T. Washington, Hallie I. Brown, Blind Boone, and Roscoe Conklin Simmons.

The homes of the miners at Buxton were owned by the coal company. They were usually five- or six-room frame structures, "each built on about a quarter acre of land so that the miners could have a cow, chickens, pigs, and small gardens." The streets were irregular, "following the lay of the land." There were "no sidewalks to speak of," and of course no city treasury and no city engineer. There were, however, a few electric lights, and a telephone office. Three company doctors took care of the sick and injured, but they had no hospital facilities. Under the auspices of the company, an association was organized whereby single men for seventy-five cents a month and married men for $1.50 could have medical attention.

Ben C. Buxton was social-minded, though rather paternalistic. "He would offer prizes for the best kept yards and gardens. At each Christmas season for a time he would give a turkey and a basket of groceries to each family—white and colored—and some years a gallon of fine syrup from his father's estate in Vermont." He also tried to prevent trouble by forbidding saloons on company property. Although saloons were not permitted in the town of Buxton or in Monroe County, liquor could be obtained at the drugstores. Moreover, saloons flourished just north of Buxton, over the Mahaska County line.

A big general company store was operated by W. A. Wells, a brother-in-law of Ben Buxton, and the company meat market was under the direction of "Hobe" Armstrong. For both the store and the meat market there was a credit plan and "a check-off system" whereby charge accounts were deducted from the miner's pay. No cash was needed. As goods were ordered, the clerks punched the amount on the customer's credit card. The total sum was then withheld on the next payday. The miners, however, were not compelled to buy at the company store. "Everything is kept there from wedding garments to coffins," commented a reporter in 1910. "They have a system that takes every penny to the cashier's desk like in the biggest houses in Chicago."

On the night of February 21, 1911, a fire of unknown origin destroyed the "big store" and its contents, causing a loss estimated at from $100,000 to $150,000. Food supplies were shipped in carload lots from Oskaloosa to meet immediate demands. Although the store was soon rebuilt and stocked with new goods, it never was as prominent in the life of the community as the old store had been. At night, after the miners had cleaned up and eaten supper, they used to gather at the store to smoke and visit. There was no objection to loafing. The manager preferred to have the men hang around the store instead of spending their time and money at the saloons.

In busy seasons the miners made big wages. They were paid in gold and silver. "It was a common thing to see a man with a twenty-dollar gold coin on his watch chain." As a rule the young men were well-dressed. Many of them wore tailor-made clothes and some had high silk hats for special occasions. They spent freely. A former resident observed that as soon as they had a few dollars in the bank, they would "go to Albia and buy out the town."

In 1913 mine No. 18 was opened a few miles south of Buxton. It was believed that it would last for twenty years. The equipment was extensive, modern, and powerful. "Eight boilers were necessary to furnish steam, and an engine room filled with dynamos, steam turbines and hoisting engines occupied almost a half block." At this new mine "Billy Llewellyn hung up his hoisting record of 3,774 tons of coal in eight hours."

Meanwhile, the Chicago and North Western Railway Company had extended its tracks southwestward to Bucknell and Haydock and these towns attracted business that had formerly gone to Buxton. Then came the first World War. The railroad company not only abandoned its plans for further extension, but removed its equipment from Haydock, closed the mines at Bucknell, and stopped the train several miles short of the terminal.

During the war, however, the demand for coal was so great that the Consolidation Coal Company was forced to sacrifice everything for production. Accordingly, the big mine, No. 18, worked overtime. The peak of coal production in Iowa was reached in 1917 when over nine million tons were mined, nearly a fourth of it in Monroe County. After the war, however, the business depression, increased competition with Illinois and Kentucky coal, and the decline of railroad transportation severely reduced production. Labor trouble developed. On March 15, 1927, No. 18 closed, six years before its estimated time. Fifteen days later, No. 19, a 1950-ton mine, shut down with the declaration of a strike. Two years later more than a hundred cars of coal were still waiting at the bottom to be hoisted.

Meanwhile, the Consolidation Coal Company was disposing of its Buxton property estimated in value at $2,000,000. Company-owned miners' homes were being sold for fifty dollars each, while "junk men" were "awaiting the results of their bids on the remains at the Buxton No. 18—once the largest mine in Iowa."

In October, 1929, the *Oskaloosa Times*, commenting on conditions in Buxton reported: "The four winds called to the population and last year it literally melted away. The banking and business houses began closing. School opened in the fine high school this year with only a few pupils and one school building entirely unused…Like some ancient village in the jungle, the weeds and undergrowth are creeping in on Bucknell and Haydock. Today they are standing in the lobby of the movie theater; six months from now nature will reclaim its own, and only a few foundations, a ramshackle store or two, will mark the glory which was once only Buxton's."

Alas, how true the prophecy!

As a precaution of safety in June, 1944, the Hercules Powder Company of Chicago used twelve pounds of dynamite, set at the base of the 155-foot stack at Buxton mine No. 18 to level it to earth. Erected in 1918 at a cost of $10,000, the giant stack had served its day. Made of concrete and steel, the stack fell gracefully to the ground "and shattered within inches of the opening of the shaft." The debris was used to fill the shaft of what had been one of Iowa's greatest mines.

With the closing of the mines, Buxton became a deserted village. For the most part the area is now a cornfield. Cement foundations of the old store remain. An eroding embankment marks what was once a busy railroad. The large stone warehouse with its red tile roof still stands, but it too is now badly weathered. Yonder in the low lands are the remains of the old vault—a once substantial brick structure where great quantities of gold and silver were stored, and from which the miners received their biweekly pay. This brick and stone structure, like old Buxton itself, is all but gone.

Perhaps the most significant landmark in all this area is one that is not made of brick, or stone, or steel. Rather it is a work of art. Upon the highlands of what was once East Swede Town, the Swedish Lutheran Church, a substantial frame structure, still stands. But it is now a typical rural church with little of outward appearance to attract the attention of passers-by. Inside the church, however, just over the altar, and facing the congregation as they sit in the wooden pews, is a beautiful painting, seven by eleven feet in dimensions, with a background of blue, representing Christ in Gethsemane. It was painted by Birger Sandzen in 1904, when Buxton was a flourishing mining town. Today Buxton is gone. Only the church with its beautiful painting remains.

No, Buxton is not entirely gone. Ancient Rome fell, but it still lives in history. Buxton, as a town, with its boasted material wealth and prosperity is gone. Yet there is a hint of immortality even in a deserted mining camp. In history and in memory Buxton still lives.

Look backward across the years to the time when Muchakinock was a flourishing mining town, before Buxton was founded. A colored lad, E. A. Carter, was the son of a coalminer, and he himself worked in the mines. Young Carter was resolved to get an education. He attended the State University of Iowa, graduating in Liberal Arts and Medicine. For the practice of his profession, he located at Buxton where he became assistant and then chief surgeon for the North Western Railway Company and the Consolidation Coal Company in that community. Now he is a prominent physician and surgeon in Detroit, Michigan.

Another outstanding negro citizen of Buxton was Attorney George H. Woodson, who practiced law there for twenty years, and served his people so well that he was nominated by the Republicans for the office of state representative, the only negro ever so honored by a major party in Iowa. Other prominent residents of Buxton, both colored and white, might be mentioned, but these will suffice to show that memories of Buxton still live.

Many people throughout Iowa and neighboring states recall mining interests and activities at Buxton. Indeed, in recent years, it has been the custom to hold an annual reunion at the site of this once flourishing mining town. Former residents of Buxton come from Sioux City, Council Bluffs, Des Moines, and other cities, and, indeed, from other states to observe the annual festivities and to recall the days of prosperity and adversity—the rise and fall of Buxton.

FROM STUART'S HILL (1945)

ELEANOR SALTZMAN

Born in the country outside Mt. Ayr in south-central Iowa's Ringgold County, Kathryn Eleanor Saltzman contracted polio as a child in the early 1900s; the disease left her partially crippled, though more determined than ever. She graduated from Drake University before heading to the University of Iowa for a Masters of Arts. Her novel Stuart Hill, *excerpted here, tells the tale of an embattled rural church in a Scotch-Iowa community, and, in do doing, addresses what John T. Frederick called a "significant theme in Iowa rural life"—the rise and fall of the country church. Beautiful as well as timeless in its evocation of the secular baptism offered by a rural swimming hole, this passage lyrically traces the moment—the epiphany—of an Iowa manhood and the peace and sudden weight it brings young George Grierson. Sadly, Saltzman passed away just a year after the publication of* Stuart Hill *by the New York City press Bernard Ackerman.*

Each June, Stuart's Hill held a basket dinner in the grove behind the church. The members planned it for weeks before preparing a program to follow the dinner. The women talked of it among themselves, and Rachel Grayson promised the children she would bring a marble cake. Even Mel would come, for Rachel and Amos wished Elizabeth to be with them, lest someone should be offended if she were absent.

The people came gratefully, for the spring and early summer work was well underway and the day broke pleasantly into the heavy round of summer farming. The Griersons were at the Hill by ten, and George walked across the field to find Jim.

The hitch-racks were full by noon, and deep in the grove the cloths were laid and the food stood ready. The children gathered from their games along the hillside, and their fathers waited in groups under the oaks and hickories. When they had ranged themselves around that which was prepared for them, they stood with heads bowed while Brother Holburn thanked the Lord and called a blessing upon them. Then, stirring, the people returned slowly to their laughing and speaking among themselves, and the children crowded close for plates of chicken, salad, and cake. At the edge of the group, two babies slept or rolled to stare into the trees, while their mothers ate nearby, watching them. There was much laughter and calling to each other among the men and women, and the warm June sun was far above, shut away by the thick green of the trees on Stuart's Hill.

After they were finished, the fathers and mothers sat heavy with food and weariness from their morning labors, and some lay in the grass and slept. The boys drifted again to the woods to play, carrying their pieces of cake with them, but Margaret called Evelyn to rest near her for a little when she would have followed. So the little girls came back and only Eulah Craig and two of them older followed, seeking to play ball with the boys. But Young Dave had reached the age when he could not endure to play with girls, and so, under his leadership, the boys drove them back to the table linens still spread under the trees. The girls were eager to respond, if only by defying the boys, and so they went off alone, a small group, along the road to the creek bridge at the foot of Stuart's Hill.

The boys climbed the fence into the high timber south of the chapel and wandered into its depths. They were sluggish from much eating, so that they did not want to run in their play but sat on the deep grass of a small clearing, throwing their pocketknives in a game of mumblety-peg. They played intently, with eager words and angry quarrelling over their differences. And Jim thrust his small body forward in his place, his eyes alight with the joy of contest, the knife quick under his fingers.

But he wearied of the game before the others, his cramped feet anxious to be free. When he stood up, George Grierson lay back, his face turned into his arm, and Young Dave and Benny Murdoch rolled at their ease, the sound of their talking low in the others' ears. But Jim grew restive and was not content with the clearing, and Victor Clark followed him through the buckbrush and scrub oaks.

When they had eased themselves, they went on through the trees to the creek-banks, and Jim swung his small body into a tree to reach a grapevine. Feeling his way, he swung himself along its heavy rope to the far bank and Victor followed, his towhead scarcely visible among the branches. They had small need to talk, these two, nor did they desire words. And all the freedom of the woodland treetops, of the creek waters far below them, was theirs.

At the bend of the creek, where the stream entered David McEwen's farm, the water was cool and deep, excellent to feel against the body. Jim and Victor stepped from their clothing and the water closed over them with only a small sound of protest, for the stillness was over them and they had little desire for splashing. They dived noiselessly into the stirring brown depths till the mud from the banks was washed from their bare feet, and they came to the surface, their eyes bright with content. Their bodies were alive, rejoicing in the feel of the water against their flesh.

The urge for achievement stirred Jim, and his arms moved easily through the slow flow of the creek, carrying him cleanly forward. He left Victor and swam with all his power against the current, so that, quiescent, he might float with it back to the boy playing in the waters behind him. He swam bravely, and the sound of his body in the water was small, as if he were in truth one with the woods about him.

The woodland was deep where he heard them, and he tread water silently, his throat startled into listening. He could not see them where they lay above the banks, but the sound of their voices came to him, heavy and low as if cautious, yet somehow harsh with a passion the boy in the water did not know or understand. Something along his body responded, prickling, even as he longed to escape from listening.

Nor could he know why they spoke, and answered, as if crying to each other. "Not again. You know I do, but Mel, Mel."

"Yes, but God in Heaven—"

Their not speaking was worse than the blindness of their voices. Noiseless as a small mink seeking escape, Jim turned in the water and let himself go with the current. His throat was closed, suffocating, against the sound of what he had heard, and a deep knowledge stirred in him, an unspoken knowledge against which his consciousness struggled, yet which somehow he sought.

When he came again to Victor, he said only that they should return to Stuart's Hill. They left the creek silently, for Jim had little desire to speak. So with their clothes still damp against their bodies, they climbed the Hill quickly, driving forward against the lassitude creeping through them from their too-long tarrying in the water.

They came through the brush and flung themselves over William Stuart's fence into the grove of Stuart's Hill. When they reached the picnic ground, they saw that the people had gone into the chapel for the afternoon meeting. The boys crept to the door and looked through the listening church to find their parents.

All the people sat with quiet hands to hear what the minister was saying. He besought them earnestly to let the evangelist come into their chapel, for their souls were in need of renewing and a revival would stir again their zeal in Christ. While David McEwen stood, as the elder in charge, to seek their support in this matter, Jim went noiselessly along the aisle seeking his father, for the questioning in his throat sought the security of William, quiet, beside him.

Yes, the people responded, let us call Brother Kemp for this meeting. Let the congregation at Stuart's Hill renew faith in the work of the Lord. And they charged Brother Holburn to arrange for a revival in the autumn, even as the officials had already expressed their willingness in the plan.

Jim Stuart waited beside William while the people sang *Blessed Be the Tie That Binds*, and presently he saw his father's brown eyes upon him, deepening to see him. He knew they deepened and warmed because of the trouble still in his own, and his young heart lifted, for he knew that when his questioning came, finally, to his tongue, his father would listen quietly to answer, with his eyes softened so to understanding.

From **The Furrow and Us (1946)**

Walter Thomas Jack

The name Walter Thomas Jack has been forgotten by most Iowans, though his book of soil conservation and sentiment, The Furrow and Us, has been selected by scholars for inclusion in the premier agricultural collection in the United States, the Core Historical Literature of Agriculture at Cornell University. Raised in West Branch, Iowa, less than a mile from Herbert Hoover's boyhood home, Jack's adopted parents, Quakers John and Margaret Jack, knew the Hoovers and mourned their losses. After graduating high school, Walter taught for a short time in a rural country school near his home, as did his sister Mae, but soon opted for a career in conservation farming after marrying Amber Pickert in Lisbon, Iowa, in 1917. From that point forward, Jack would farm the Pickert family ground, originally settled in 1855 and now an Iowa Heritage Farm, until his death in 1965. The reading that follows, collaged from his only published book, consists of excerpts from chapters entitled "The Force of Circumstances," and "Soil and Sentiment"; together they bookend the period 1917 to 1946—nearly thirty years of Iowa farming. On the occasion of the sixtieth anniversary reprinting of The Furrow and Us, *Robert T. Rhode of the University of Northern Kentucky wrote, "Poisoned water, infertile land, unhealthy food. Sixty years ago, a Quaker farmer predicted these results of big farming. It's not too late to heed his warning."*

Back in 1917 I embarked on an agricultural career as a life's work and, on a fertile Iowa farm, soon found that the farm was the battleground between man and nature.

The going was good during the lush war years, and the few succeeding years put no tax on personal ingenuity, for prices were good, and if yields faltered and fluctuated somewhat, the gap between actual yields and maximum yields was spanned by high prices. There seemed to be no need for worry; old methods of doing things seemed quite adequate, and the complications of the chemical nature of the soil seemed to be of no immediate concern. The soil had always responded to our call.

When the war clouds of World War I finally cleared, I, like many other young farmers, was not ready to meet the challenge of diminished soil and falling prices. Soon the black clouds of economic disparity loomed up on every horizon, stealthily boring in, gaining momentum, until hard times peeled the shirts from our backs and swallowed up our savings. Many farmers who had purchased a farm by using up their lush-time savings as a downpayment were forced to relinquish their safety net. Some of us held on through pride and an unwillingness to accept defeat, and we did the only thing we could to meet a fixed expense—increase production. This, of course, was the wrong thing to do, as agricultural surpluses were already plaguing Washington.

This natural head-above-water mentality had its own repercussions, and with a greater percent of farmland under cultivation, it became evident that the soil was being burned out. That is, the organic matter was being consumed by the crops more rapidly than it was being replaced, resulting in a sharp decline in yields. This, in fact, was the last straw. Low price and poor yields are conjunct factors that spell ruin to any farmer. I reasoned, as did many, that while we could not raise prices with surpluses, we could cut down operating expenses by producing our requirements on fewer acres. After serious thought, I decided I had inadvertently expected too much of mother earth, and instead of mining her resources, I would study her way of doing things, listen to her hunger signs, and appreciate the fact that she mothers us all. No one can enjoy the feeling of pride and thanksgiving that has blessed his effort as he looks over a lush meadow, billowing fields of grain, and verdant pasture. This is a heritage, not to everyone, but to those who feel themselves subordinate to mother nature and are willing to follow her teachings rather than direct her thoughts.*

Because a man owns a farm does not mean that he owns the land to do with as he pleases, for, in reality, he is only the tenant, so to speak. He has use of the land for his lifetime, at the end of which he should leave the land to future generations in as good or even better condition than he found it. We may not waste that which is not ours.

Every farmer has a divine obligation, a sacred trust, to preserve the productivity of the soil, and we must not deprive future generations of good soil or understanding of the earth's goodness.

The pride one feels as he walks through the fields on a spring day is truly rooted deeply in nature. The smell of spring awakens new interests in the tasks that lie ahead. The lilt of the meadowlark sets the music to the lyrics of the denizens of fields and woods.

It is spring, Easter time—fragrance, color, music, hope. While one stands there amidst all, the emotional upsurge becomes an attribute that can be carried through old age. Many things thought important at the time are swallowed up by the swiftly moving events and changing conditions, but there is always something—perhaps a single incident or a particularly pleasant day, or maybe a song—that will cling to us throughout our lives.

I have felt this many times, and my emotions seem to center on a particular Easter Sunday many years ago. A pleasant south wind was awakening new life under the winter-whipped stems of the last season's vegetation. My daughter Helen emerged from the house bedecked in her Easter finery, humming that grand old song, "Easter Parade." This to me seemed singularly appropriate, for in it was the spirit of Easter, as far as her juvenile mind could reckon. As she backed the car from the garage and turned toward town to join the Easter parade, I did not realize, at the time, that this day embodied life's force and its greatest attribute.

Neither time nor eternity can take away the particularity of this day, and, as time passes, the charm of it all remains radiant, immortal, even inanimate. Emotions do not of themselves arise, but must have some stimulating force. To me the greatest force is the music of spring and the planting season.

For every person there is a spot, a place they pledge themselves to return some day, because they were happy and contented there. It, no doubt, is the old home, the haunts of their childhood. These places are of the earth—only things of the earth have that magnetic power. Some get back after many years and are greeted by the same landscape, just as they left it—the same old hills and streams and shrubs untouched by anything save the changing seasons.

My place is under the Iowa skies, floored with the world's best soil and walled in by the emerald skyline of native oaks. I have planted and harvested these fertile fields for many years and have learned from old mother nature that she holds no grudge. She has healed the wounds and scars I thoughtlessly made on her contour and patiently replaced the fertility I so lavishly spent. No, this is not agricultural science, but it does have to do with the story of the soil I have set out to tell, for the lack of sentiment in our associations with nature means the lack of interest in the business of farming.

This sentiment does not draw its substance from my imagination; I have lived it; it is real and everlasting.

And still today, the same reverie comes each spring; the scenes are the same— everything, in fact, save for the little girl. She has grown up now and has gone, but imagination keeps her on the set, and her role will always be that of the leading lady in the drama of spring.

Greed has shut our eyes to the really good things in life and hardened our hearts to the many little things that would add up to a more pleasant and useful life.

As I struggle to collect my thoughts and equilibrium in the morning, after a fitful night, what a lift it gives me to be greeted at the back door by Simon, my dog. He goes through with his antics; he is relaxed (only animals know how to relax), and is ready to follow at my heels wherever I go. This demonstration of affection does more for a man than the morning coffee.

Good old Simon! He has no need for tobacco or liquor to enjoy life and be congenial. If I tell him to wait for me—he waits, ignoring personal comfort—all that matters is my return. A real poet could do well with the following thought:

If I should die in some lonely place
Where friends they never knew
I'll bet a buck against your ace
Old Sime would die there too.

When the going is difficult, the weather drab, and you can but look out over the fields resting under their thick blanket of snow, time moves slowly. But in lighter moments you are heartened by the assurance that spring is coming; there will always be spring; there will always be Easter with its new life and promises.

FROM STRIKEOUT STORY (1947)

BOB FELLER

Nicknamed the "Van Meter Heater" and "Rapid Robert," Van Meter, Iowa's, Hall of Famer Bob Feller is arguably the best baseball player the state has ever produced. At the time he published Strikeout Story *in 1947, Feller had just established a single-season strikeout record of 348, an E.R.A. just above 2.00, and a record of 26-15—this after returning to the game after forty-four months in the Navy. Feller's secret was his fastball, which was clocked late in his career at over 98 miles per hour, though his reliance on the heat resulted in a more dubious record—he held the record for most career walks and hit batters upon his retirement in 1956. The first Major League ballplayer to volunteer after Pearl Harbor, Feller compiled a distinguished record at sea, too, earning many campaign ribbons and eight battle stars for his service aboard the* U.S.S. Alabama. *Few Iowans today appreciate the size of Feller's celebrity. In a short biography, "Bob Feller—Legends of the Ball," posted by the Bob Feller Museum, Dennis Hoffman writes, "Time put Feller on its April 19, 1937, cover. NBC radio jumped on the Feller bandwagon, covering the young player's graduation from Van Meter High School 'live' on its national radio network. His fastball starred in newsreels, racing against a speeding motorcycle." The pitcher of three professional no-hitters, Feller was selected as the "Greatest Living Right-Hand Pitcher" as part of Professional Baseball's Centennial Celebration in July of 1969. The magical story he tells below, truly an Iowa classic, reads as if it comes directly from* The Natural *or from* Field of Dreams.

I was born in our nine-room, frame farmhouse on November 3, 1918. I was a first child, and I represented a substantial addition to the community. Van Meter, Iowa, is a town of only five hundred people.

There was a time when it was much larger and pretentious. Until the turn of the century, a coalmine and a brickyard helped to support a population of 1500. The coal and clay ran out then, however, and Van Meter slipped back into its original identity. It again became what it is today, a farming community.

The people, I suppose, are little different from those in any small American town. Small-town people live simple lives on the surface, but their economic and personal problems are just as intense as those of people anywhere in America.

The pulse of the town beats strongest, of course, around the public square. Here is the barbershop run by Fred Fritz, O. V. White's hardware store, Jack England's grocery, the telephone office presided over by Marie Smith and the bank at which Clarence Dunn is cashier. There are other one and two-storied buildings...a garage, the post office—several other stores. It is a typical town square filled with typical Americans.

Off to the north a couple of blocks is the railroad station. Van Meter is on the main line of the Rock Island railroad. That means there is a double track curving in and out of town. It makes the people feel important to see the *Denver Rocket* and other crack trains flash through. Nothing but local trains stop, though, at Bill Freeburn's small station.

South of the square is the school. This is where I learned my three R's and this is where I played in my first baseball games.

Our home was, and is, northeast of the town, about three and one half miles. When we built a new brick home in 1940, the old farmhouse was moved a short distance. It's still there, the place where I was born. The land is still rich, like most Iowa land. It still yields good crops of wheat and corn.

From the age of nine years, the land had been my father's life. His father died at that time and there was nothing for him except work following that. I know now, though, that he dreamed with some kind of sixth sense beyond the fences of our 320 acres. Unlike many fathers, he didn't want me to follow his footsteps. It was too late for him, but it wasn't for me.

Baseball must have been in my nature from the earliest days, and he performed the wisest of fatherly duties. He recognized my bent and he encouraged it with a spirit and faith that were almost fanatical.

I suppose there had been other signs of my interest in baseball before I reached the age of seven, but my mother still saves the first strong sign. It was a composition, written in typical boyish scrawl, and titled "My Life."

"When I was a tree," it ran, "and my brothers and sisters, there were many of us there but there is not many of us now. Many of us have been cut down and made into lumber and it came my turn and they cut me down and made me into a big bo[a]rd. And Mister Stucke's manual training boys got me and made me into a home plate for the baseball di[a]mond. And that's the end."

My mother recalls that it wasn't long after that they sat on the porch and watched me bounce a rubber ball against the side of the house. On every trip into town, I insisted on the purchase of a rubber ball.

"I think I know what I want that youngster to become," my father said quietly.

She had her own ideas, but she merely waited.

"I want him to play baseball," he went on. "I don't want him to be a farmer. Baseball is a good life."

She didn't protest although there must have been a stab of dismay. Her father had been a baseball pitcher when he wasn't farming his land, which also was near

Van Meter. I remember her telling, with a mixture of pride and shame, that he was considered the best pitcher in Iowa between 1870 and 1880. He was faithful to his fields during the week, but on Sundays he pitched baseball, and the game on that day wasn't accepted as it is now. My grandmother had the same fondness for baseball that she had for a corn borer.

My mother confesses now that she felt the future would take care of itself. That the baseball idea would fade with time. She wanted a life for me among the people and things that I knew. One that would be secure, respected, and happy. She wanted an education for me and no other special talent than the ability to play the trumpet in the Van Meter Methodist Church. It was a typical maternal ambition, and there have been times when I have thought she was right. Particularly one miserable day in Chicago.

It was Mother's Day and she was in Comiskey Park with my father and my sister, Marguerite, who is ten years younger than myself. They had grandstand seats between home and first base to watch me pitch against the White Sox. Marvin Owen, the Sox third baseman, was at bat when it happened.

Owen fouled several harmless balls into the seats between first and home. Then there was one that wasn't harmless. My follow through turned me that way, and I saw the ball hit my mother in the face. I felt sick, but I saw that she was conscious. I saw them leading her out, and I had to put down the impulse to run to the stands. Instead, I kept on pitching. I felt giddy and I became wild. I know the Sox scored three runs and I'm not sure how.

I was told the injury was painful but not serious. There wasn't anything I could do, so I went on and finished the game and won. Then I hurried to the hospital.

She looked up from the hospital bed, her face bruised and swollen she smiled reassuringly.

"My head aches, Robert," she said, "but I'm all right. Now don't go blaming yourself. It wasn't your fault."

She has always been like that, so there were no complaints from her when my father came home in the spring of 1928 with an assortment of packages. They contained two baseball gloves, one a Rogers Hornsby fielding mitt and the other a Ray Schalk catching mitt. There was a striped uniform and striped stockings, a pair of baseball spikes and a green bat. They were good baseballs, not the nickel rocket kind.

Babe Ruth was still in his prime, Lefty Grove was being compared with the fastest pitchers in history, and Rogers Hornsby was the batting idol of the nation and of our home the day I wore my uniform to school for the first time.

"Change into your spikes after school," my father called after me with a smile. "Don't get tangled up in them."

I was ten years old. My mother tells me I wasn't very big for my age. I was to grow like a stalk of corn between the ages of 14 and 16.

I owned the equipment, so it was natural that I became magnate, manager, and infielder for my grade school team. I played third base and shortstop most of the time, and I fancied myself as a slugger. Like most pitchers who hit infrequently, I still do. It's too late now, though, for me to hit like Hornsby did.

Miss Wycoff was my fourth grade teacher, and I must award her an assist in my baseball career. She didn't know much about baseball, but she knew a great deal about a kid's heart and ambition.

"You'll never grow baseballs on your farm, Bobby," she told me. "They're not good to eat, you know," she smiled. "But if the game makes you happy and you don't fall down in your studies, go right ahead." Miss Wycoff was a major leaguer.

I never got enough baseball after school, so my father and I continued it at home. We played catch behind the house, we listened to broadcasts of major league games and we studied a book on the science of the game. All this, however, after the chores were done. Intense as his baseball ambition for me had become, my father never excused me from farm work. I helped with the plowing, the cultivating, and the harvest. I milked our small herd and I carried water for it. Sometimes, when I have been asked how I developed my fastball, I have been tempted to answer: "Carrying water for cattle from the Raccoon River."

The Raccoon is a narrow stream which flows through the bottom half of our farm. We couldn't get a truck closer to it than 200 yards without getting mired. I carried water from the bank to the truck in two pails, each containing about seven gallons. One day we figured we transported about 2000 gallons. That evening we did not play catch.

"Off-day on the baseball schedule," father said wearily. "Doubleheader tomorrow," he added, smiling.

I like to think that we were among the first to play night baseball, my father and I, and we must have been close to it, at that. Des Moines, in the Western League, played the first game under lights in 1930, and it was just about that time that my father turned on two arc lamps in the backyard, powered by a home plant.

In the dim light he would throw me grounders. There still was little thought about pitching. Hornsby still was our hero, and I continued to play infield that spring.

It was later in the summer of 1930, however, when I started to pitch. More exactly, to throw as hard as I could from the box.

For lack of competition, Van Meter High's team scheduled several games with our grade school team. I was eleven years old, but I could throw harder than anyone else. School baseball in Iowa isn't much different, in that respect, than it is in the big leagues. When you haven't got much hitting, you've got to have pitching. We won a majority of these games, even though our opponents were several years older.

I entered what might be called organized baseball in 1913. I joined the Adel, Iowa, American Legion team. At twelve I was about five feet, two inches tall and weighed about 140. Adel was a town close by Van Meter and approximately three times as large.

I still hadn't decided to concentrate on pitching. The Hornsby ideal was fading, but I still thought I could hit and field.

As the summer wore on and the Adel team won just ordinary success, I could see that my father was wrestling with a problem that had nothing to do with crops. We didn't play catch any more under our backyard lights, but we talked more baseball than ever before. Now it was about pitchers like Tommy Bridges, Mel Harder, Lefty Grove, and Wes Ferrell. One night he unloaded his mind.

"Bob," he began, "what do you think about pitching?"

I told him I liked it. I told him it was just about as much fun to strike somebody out as it was to hit a home run.

"Now, don't get me wrong, son," he continued. "I think you're a great batter. And a mighty fine fielder. But, you know, I think you might pitch better than you do any of those things."

Looking back, I must have sensed that this was a big moment as we sat there in the dark on the porch, listening to the cattle in the barn and the crickets in the field.

"Maybe you're right, dad," I finally told him. "I guess I do strike out more fellows than I hit home runs. Only, later on, that would mean I would get into a game only once in a while."

"In the big leagues," he said, "a pitcher is mighty important even if he comes out of his hole just once every four days. Now, you tend to your pitching."

It's still amazing to me how firmly my father believed that I couldn't miss becoming a big leaguer. He wasn't a braggart, but it was one subject upon which he was always outspoken in town. Everybody knew Bill Feller and his dream. They kidded him about it in an affectionate way.

"Just you fellows manage to hang onto earth long enough," he would tell them, "and we'll get you the best seats for a World Series." It embarrassed me, but not him. Having delivered this parting shot, his face would curl up in a tight kind of smile and we would walk out, leaving behind a chorus of chuckles.

We decided several things during the winter of 1931–32 when the farm was snowbound and our baseball was the hot stove league brand. The main thing was that I was to become a pitcher, nothing else.

"Why, you can throw hard enough to knock a bull down," he told me. "In a couple of years you'll throw faster than any one of those big leaguers."

Another thing he decided was that we would go into the baseball business. That we would build a baseball field on the farm, overlooking the Raccoon River. Some day I hope to own my own team, and I think that's another thought he planted in my mind.

"We'll lay it out up there on the hill, right above the river," he said excitedly. "We'll clear the pasture, roll the field, put in seats, sell cold drinks and sandwiches. We'll call it Oakview Park on account of that grove down by the river. We'll organize teams made up from boys in Van Meter, Adel, and the farms around here."

The spring of 1932 was a busy one. When people tell me now that I work too hard in spring training, I laugh and remember that time. We cleared the land and leveled it. We cut down saplings along the river to support chicken wire in front of our circus seats. We got real baseball bags from Des Moines and put up a scoreboard. We decided that 35 cents wasn't too much for the baseball and view.

Folks will come all the way from Des Moines to see you pitch, and hold picnics," he said. "Mostly to see you pitch," he added hastily. "Why, we've got a park here that Yankee Stadium can't touch. Maybe their infield is better, but the scenery isn't."

So we opened Oakview Park, and it was to be a happy, exciting place for several years. We never made any money, although the neighbors were sure we did. Our Sunday mornings were spent on the road, transporting players to the field. My mother cooked for our stars after the games. We drew crowds as large as one thousand people. Most important to my father, I got a chance to pitch and develop.

I am reminded of Oakview Park each spring we come north on our annual exhibition tour with the New York Giants. Many times on these tours we play games in small towns which can boast of nothing but skinned diamonds. Our field was like that. The infield was completely bare, and it didn't take long for a sudden rain to turn it into slippery mud.

Nobody ever was seriously hurt by bad hops, however. This was as much of a tribute to luck as it was to my groundskeeping. Luck and the constant wariness of the infielders.

Oakview Park was my incubator. I developed physically and I grew more confident. When 1933 rolled around, I was ready to leave the home environment and test my ability on what could be called foreign fields. In this case, they were the fields of Des Moines.

Des Moines was the big city in our parts, and when a person got his picture in the newspaper there, he was important. I got my picture in the paper after I joined the American Legion team in that city. The Van Meter merchants listened more respectfully now. I was a big boy and my father and I laughed at the size of the uniform he had brought home five years before.

The competition was much stronger in Des Moines, and I was not as successful as I had hoped to be, but the improvement in my pitching was satisfactory. I watched other pitchers, and I imitated them in what I thought were sound practices. I got the benefit of coaching from men who were interested in what the Legion was trying to do for the youngsters of the country.

I will always be grateful, like many other major leaguers, for the opportunity to play American Legion baseball. The Legion is a powerful organization which is occupied with more serious affairs, but the equipment it buys for kid players is money well spent.

By 1934 I wasn't quite ready to meet the challenge of adult competition, but I was getting close. I agreed to play with another Legion team, this one representing West Des Moines. My strikeout average was a matter of great interest to the newspapers and a never-ending topic with my father. He knew and I sensed that this was to be my last season of adolescent baseball. My apprenticeship was just about over.

We won the state championship in the annual Legion tournament that year, only to be disqualified because we used an over-age player. The disappointment was lost in plans for the future.

I was big enough and strong enough to compete against men in 1935. I played basketball in high school that winter, although not very skillfully, and I was in fine condition in the spring. As we started to plow, the offers started to come in. Not from major or minor league teams, but from strong semiprofessional teams in and around Des Moines. I was 16, but I was almost ready for anything.

My father finally decided that the Farmers' Union Insurance team of Des Moines would be the one for me in 1935. Secretly, I believe he was deeply disappointed that big league scouts hadn't been around knocking on our farmhouse door.

I don't think he knew then that my name was being brought up in the offices of major league teams. I don't think he knew that a Des Moines umpire would soon be writing a letter to the Cleveland Baseball Company, advising that I was worth inspection. If he did, he kept it from me until July 21, 1935.

We were in the fields that day, combining wheat, and I was driving the tractor. As the tractor climbed a slight rise, I could see the figure of a man coming toward us, threading his way through the wheat. Like my father, he was tall and thin. As he came closer, I decided that they looked a great deal alike.

"Howdy," he said, and my father nodded.

"I'm Cyril Slapnicka," he continued, "of the Cleveland Indians. That the boy they tell me is quite a pitcher?"

As I remember it now, I don't believe my father thought Slapnicka's reference to me was respectful enough.

"That's Bob, all right," he answered. "I've heard of you, Mr. Slapnicka. You're an Iowa man yourself, aren't you?"

"Cedar Rapids. Mr. Feller, I'd like to see your boy pitch. When will he pitch again and where?"

"He'll pitch in Des Moines for the Farmers' Union day after tomorrow, Mr. Slapnicka. Figure to be there?"

"Believe I will. Fellow named Claude Passeau pitching in Des Moines, too. Want to look at him." Slapnicka turned to me and gave me the kind of uneasy smile adults use on precocious kids.

"Do you like baseball, son?" he asked.

I nodded. It was too big a moment for talking. Slapnicka's uneasiness seemed to grow.

"Well, see you in Des Moines," he said, and started back.

I felt numb after he had gone. I hadn't dreamed it would happen like that. It always was a big league scout coming up after I had pitched a no-hit game and offering me a fabulous contract. Instead, a man came through the wheatfield, caught me in my overalls, and talked casually about seeing me pitch. I suddenly became aware that my father was speaking.

"Let's get on with this combining," he said.

I was the starting pitcher for that day in Des Moines. Naturally, I kept sneaking glances at the crowd around the diamond, trying to pick out Slapnicka. I felt sure he was there, but I couldn't locate him. Afterward, he confessed that he watched the first few innings from under a tree in leftfield. Then he moved around the backstop to get a better view of my pitches. He must have liked what he saw because he drove out to our farm that night.

When he left, my father had agreed that I would play with Fargo-Moorehead of the Northern League the following season. Fargo-Moorehead, in North Dakota, was part of the Cleveland minor league chain. I was on my way to the Indians, although I hadn't reached 17.

It was still too great an event for me to grasp completely, and my father didn't do much explaining. My father and Slapnicka understood each other, however, as I was to find out. Whether it was because they were Iowans or whether their natures were perfectly suited, I'm not sure. All I know is that they trusted each other completely, and I have always been glad of it.

That season I averaged 19 strikeouts per game for Farmers' Union. They were full games now, of course, rather than the seven-inning contests we played in the American Legion. I still didn't have much of a curveball. I just threw hard and I was wild enough so that the batters gave me plenty of room at the plate. That helped, as it was to help long into my major league career.

From **Stand Up and Be Counted (1947)**

Henry A. Wallace

Named the most influential Iowan of the twentieth century by the Des Moines Register, *Adair County's Henry A. Wallace achieved a legacy that, in many ways, eclipses Herbert Hoover's. The grandson of* Wallaces' Farmer *founder "Uncle Henry" Wallace, Henry A., raised on a farm outside Orient, Iowa, followed in his father's, Henry C.'s, footsteps, becoming Secretary of Agriculture in the Franklin D. Roosevelt administration just as his father had been in the Warren G. Harding years. While Henry A. Wallace enjoyed strong support from Democratic rank and file, he was not the most popular vice-president; many insiders viewed him as too much of an idealist and faulted him for his political pedigree (his father and grandfather had been prominent Republicans). That, and the charge that he was too much like Roosevelt to balance the ticket in 1944, caused him to be passed over for a second term as V.P. By 1947— the year Wallace announced his third-party candidacy for President in the short pamphlet excerpted below and published by* The New Republic, *where Wallace was then editor—he had come to believe that a Truman presidency would only deepen the Cold War and lead to a "century of fear." Hampered by insinuations that he was a communist, Wallace and his independent campaign failed to garner much support—around three percent—but it did shake-up the two-party system. Regardless of the outcome, Iowans could be proud of Wallace's Progressive Party platform, which called for an end to segregation, full voting rights for African Americans, and universal health insurance. Iowans are far from alone in their high regard for Wallace's legacy. Economist John Kenneth Galbraith once ranked Wallace "second only to Roosevelt as the most important figure of the New Deal," and Roosevelt himself said of his Vice President "no man was more of the American soil than Wallace." Of course, Iowans also appreciate Henry A. Wallace as a groundbreaking geneticist, and founder of Pioneer Hi-Bred seed corn, still headquartered in Johnston, Iowa.*

I am convinced that time has come for an independent presidential candidacy. I believe in the hope for world democracy. I believe that this hope can be realized, for Americans and for all peoples, in our time. But I see this hope endangered by present trends.

I have been saddened by the sight of the richest, most powerful, and, to me, most beautiful nation in the world being haunted by fear. Today, we alone of the peoples of the world speak as though Doomsday were just around the corner. We fear war. We expect depression. We await the destruction of the United Nations and the breakup of One World into two worlds. To those who admit the truth of all this and add: This is a time for waiting, I reply: We cannot wait; the welfare of Americans demands that we act now.

Our workers fear instability of present employment. As their real wages fall with rising prices, they suffer a steadily declining standard of living, and they also feel the burden of new debts.

Our mothers fear the instability of present employment. As their real wages fall with rising prices, they suffer a steadily declining standard of living, and they also feel the burden of new debts.

Our mothers and their sons in school fear the onrushing program of compulsory military training which will take a year out of the lives of millions of American boys for no useful purpose.

Our businessmen fear the instability of their markets. Thousands upon thousands of small independent producers are feeling, as never before, the squeeze of giant monopolies.

Our farmers fear their prosperity will soon end.

Millions upon millions of Americans fear to speak out against policies they know are dangerous and potentially ruinous. If they speak frankly, the know they may suffer loss of jobs and social standing. They have been intimidated by the current campaign which brands every progressive idea "communistic."

In the lifetime of my generation we have seen two world wars and a half a dozen depressions and recessions of varying length. But there is no sound historic reason for assuming that a major catastrophe must be inevitable. I know that man has the resources and the knowledge with which to prevent both depression and war. To accept the inevitability of war and depression is to deny democracy. The companion notion that personal insecurity is a necessary part of our life is outrageous.

I believe in the old-fashioned American doctrine of standing up, speaking your mind, and letting the chips all where they may. I am determined that the American people shall have a chance to speak their minds, free of intimidation.*

THE COMMUNIST ISSUE

Many of the friends who have supported my decision argued in advance that it was dangerous, because the Communists want it. But I have never believed in turning from a principled position because it happened to win the support of others with whom you have important disagreements. I have been told in times past that I shouldn't fight the poll tax because the Communists wanted its abolition. I continued to fight it. The argument is no good.

During the past year I have been urging a foreign policy based on understanding with Russia. I was told that that this was dangerous because the Communists wanted it. The alternatives were support of the present militaristic bipartisan policy or a retreat to isolationism. This would be a particularly dangerous time to leave the advocacy of peace and understanding with Russia solely to a handful of Communists. If we are to build a significant progressive movement, we shall only succeed by taking leadership and fighting for the things we seek.

I welcome the support of all people who sincerely believe you get peace by preparing for peace rather than for war. I want to mobilize all the sentiment there is for planning peace. I want the peoples of the world to know that there is another America than that which attempts to dominate their politics and dictate their economics. I want them to know that American workers, farmers, small businessmen, and professional people are their brothers, not would-be masters. I want to kill off the Universal Military training program which is entering the wedge of military fascism in the United States.

Those who call us "Russian tools" and "Communists" as we fight for the peace, security, and welfare of our country and the world are using the weapons of Adolf Hitler. They are demonstrating that they prefer war with Russia to settlement of differences in a peaceful way. We are fighting for peace with Russia—yes. But we are fighting with confidence that we can make our system work. We are not for Russia and we are not for communism, but we are for peace and for bringing real Americanism back again to the United States.

OUR FUTURE

There is talk that an independent candidacy is doomed to failure because of financing. It is said that many millions of dollars will be required for such a campaign. As sure as I am that two major parties are controlled by big-money interests, and as realistic as I am about the opposition of the big-money press, I still have confidence in democracy. I have confidence that a people's campaign can be waged in 1948.

If money for political campaigns is to come only from the "big boys," then America has become what Russia says it is. I repudiate this idea. I think the people can still make the democratic system work. I am not worried about money because I know that we shall get millions of dollars donated by housewives, stenographers, professional people, workers and shop stewards, and others who will work with a devotion big money can't buy.

We shall need money and I think we shall have it. We shall not need the Wall Street military backing because we shall build on fundamental principles rather than expediency. We expect abuse and we shall weather it, with a remembrance of the abuse accorded Jefferson, Jackson, Lincoln, and their followers. We shall not let the House Un-American Activities Committee and other smear-artists distract us. We shall keep our eyes on the future and remain confident that in November the American people will stand up and be counted. Then the whole world will know how strong is the sentiment in the United States for peace and security.

FROM **OLD ORCHARD FARM (1952)**

PAUL ORCHARD

From Des Moines County, not far from Burlington, Hugh Orchard grew up when America, and Iowa, were both still thoroughly agricultural. A minister and a lecturer on the Chautauqua circuit, Orchard eventually left the farm, but never did find its equal. In his preface to Old Orchard Farm, *Paul F. Sharp writes, "Here is revealed, with unusual clarity, the work of the real builders of modern Iowa—their years of toil; their dreams of better things for their sons." In his first chapter, "In the beginning," Orchard describes the farm as any good rural Iowan would—by the numbers—as "a jolly good one or two hundred acres in section 29, township 74, range 4 west of the 5th principle meridian in Washington Township, Des Moines County." The selection that follows consists of two of Orchard's unforgettable chapters rendered here as discrete subheadings, "The Passing of the Prairie Chicken" and "A Yarmouth Saturday Night." In them, Orchard recollects two rural Iowa institutions—hunting with family and hamming it up Saturday nights in town.*

PASSING OF THE PRAIRIE CHICKEN

In my time back on Old Orchard Farm there used to be more wild prairie chickens than chickens of tame breeds. Nowadays I know a lot of people who have never seen a prairie chicken, for they have been gone from Iowa for many years.

But they used to be plentiful. It was one of the commonest things in the world to run onto a prairie chicken nest full of eggs. Like snipes, and many other birds, the mother hen tries to fool us to prevent us from finding her nest. Many times as I walked along in the grass, a prairie chicken hen would flutter right from under my feet with all the noise she could make, and fall on her side and squabble around in the grass just like she was crippled and could barely fly at all. I would run over intending to capture her alive, and just before I got my hands on her she would give a flounce and light fifteen or twenty feet away.

I would be right after her, expecting this time to make the capture. But she would be too quick for me, and away she would flutter—maybe hitting the ground several times before she came down to stay. Then I was sure she was tuckered out, and would run with all my might to pick her up. But when I was about three steps from her she would give two or three awkward flops and rise, maybe four or five feet from the ground, and fall forty or fifty yards away. By this means she would fool along with me for a good long way, and then fly off as fine as any prairie chicken you ever saw. It was a way they had of getting a person coaxed from their nests so that you never could find them again.

A prairie chicken hatches out a covey of fifteen or so young ones, and they are the cutest little things you ever saw, except young quails. Prairie chickens were used to the out of doors, and had good luck raising their young, so they multiplied to beat anything. Every grain field of forty acres in the country had a drove or two of chickens in it. All summer long you didn't see much of them, only by chance, for they lived mostly in the cornfields and weed patches. But after the small grain had been cut and shocked, they had a habit of coming out there to feed in the cool of the evening.

By August they were half grown, and the men used to go out after supper and hunt them. Two men would generally hunt together to cover more ground. Those chickens were mighty sly, and without a good hunting dog to find them you might just as well have stayed at home. During my first experience on this kind of a hunt I was too young to shoot a gun, so I just went along to carry the game.

John Cappes came over to our house and joined my big brother Joe and me for the hunt. John had borrowed a fine setter from a German named Henry Rawhert who had lived in this country only a short time and could just scarcely talk our language. But his dog seemed to understand everything the boys said to her.

Joe had a double-barreled breech loader he had bought from Rawhert, who had set up a gunsmith shop on his farm down the lane. The left barrel was choke-bored and was made to get the game if you missed with the right barrel. That choke-bored barrel shot mighty close, and we had to be careful not to use it first or we might blow the game to pieces. Joe got a set of tools for reloading the brass shells, and these shells, when they were empty, had a smell about them that I liked better than almost any other smell. I used to help him reload on rainy days, by passing him the powder jar, or the shot sack, or the box of caps. I fully expected that some day he would let me shoot that wonderful gun. He did, too.

Early that evening of my first hunt we went out to the back oats field. The boys spread out about fifty feet apart, a short distance from the edge of the corn. The oats stubble was about eight inches high but many weeds had grown up since harvest and stuck up about a foot above the stubble in places. The dog was turned loose and went on ahead and away off to each side, and I trailed along behind.

We sauntered along that way for as much as a hundred yards or so, without finding anything to shoot. John Cappes allowed maybe it was a little too early in the evening. Joe was just starting to tell about a fine flock of young chickens he had seen in that very field earlier in the season when the setter stopped running, crouched down pretty low, and went crawling forward at a snail's pace.

I thought maybe she was getting tired or something. But the boys cocked their guns and got ready, for they said the dog was "setting game." It was all Greek to me. I had supposed that hunting dogs were used to catch game by running it down, like our blue dog did rabbits.

The setter stopped dead still, kind of crouched down, with her tail sticking out straight as a ramrod and one front foot lifted up. The boys walked a few steps closer. Then the setter went a little farther ahead, just creeping along. Then she came to a dead stop and wouldn't move a peg. We all slipped up to within a half dozen steps of her, and still she stood like she was paralyzed.

Then Joe gave her the word to "put it up." That meant, I soon saw, to scare the chicken out of the stubble so he could shoot. When he said this, that setter gave a forward spring, and out flew a fine young chicken. It flew up on John Cappes's side, so he shot, missing with the first barrel but bringing the chicken down with the second. I supposed that the hunt was all over, as no other birds flew up—and if there were any more there, I thought the crack of that gun would stampede them. But the dog stood like she was tied.

Joe motioned for the dog to go ahead, and she crept a few steps forward, while we all stood still and watched. Within ten seconds she came to another dead stop, and Joe again gave her the word. She sprang in and another chicken flew up. Joe downed it with his right barrel. Just then two other chickens came out of the stubble at the same time and the boys had a shot together. Joe missed with his right barrel, and then, taking plenty of time, he let that choke-bored barrel loose. The chicken fell seventy yards away.

That blessed setter dog worked back and forth all over that stubble, and one by one scared up about sixteen prairie chickens. It was a covey of an old hen and her brood. I don't remember how many the boys shot, but at least ten or eleven.

My first thought after four or five had been killed was what a job it was going to be to find all those dead chickens scattered all over the place of a hundred yards around. But to my surprise the dog did the work. As soon as the shooting was all over, Joe sent the setter out to bring in the game. The boys called this "retrieving." What surprised me was that the setter never stirred to go until she was told. She would go surging off, fast as she could run. I wouldn't think she could find anything at that pace, but all at once she would stick her nose down and bring up a chicken. Laying it down at our feet, she would go at it again, till she had the last one of those chickens piled up. I thought that the German who had trained the dog must be a pretty smart fellow.

Some August evenings—especially if the weather was a little drizzly—we could hear guns booming in all directions, as the farmers brought down young prairie chickens by the hundreds. They never killed more than they wanted to eat, and we never could see that there were any fewer chickens than the next year. Businessmen from Burlington, Mediapolis, and Morning Sun used to come out to hunt, for every farmer allowed hunting on his farm. There seemed to be no end of chickens.

But it was in the fall of the year that we saw real flocks of prairie chickens. When frost came the fodder was shocked, with winter just around the corner, many coveys of prairie chickens joined forces. I have seen as many as a thousand in one flock. They sometimes came early in the morning and alighted on our barn, in the apple trees, and even on our house. A big walnut tree down in the field used to be a wonderful place for the chickens to light. I have seen that big tree so full of chickens that I couldn't see through it, and hundreds more would be on the ground.

Sometimes when we were shucking corn a great flock would come flying over and we could hear the whistling of their wings and see the stripes on their necks. They usually flew about fifteen or twenty feet above the ground and always in a straight line. It was a pretty sight in the dead of winter to happen onto a great flock of prairie chickens sitting on the snow and talking to one another in chicken language. I have seen whole hillsides literally covered with them.

Early in the spring they disbanded as great flocks and simmered down to little bunches, sometimes only two or three. During this season we heard them sing, as if that is what to call it. It wasn't really much of a song, but sounded a whole lot like "Bum, bum, boo." Along between sundown and dark, in April or early May, we could hear them out in the pasture somewhere, "Bum, bum, boo; bum, bum boo." And they would keep that up until after dark. Once I happened to be near enough a covey to discover that it was the roosters who sang. They seemed to swell up around the neck, put their heads back and do their "bum-booing" much like a tame rooster crows.

Several things contributed to wiping out the prairie chicken from the country fields. One thing was the passing of wild prairie grass, which was their natural home. Another was the improvement in guns. As long as the farmers had to load their guns by hand—from the muzzle—right out in the field, there wasn't a great deal of danger to the chickens. But when the time came that everybody had a breech loader or two, it was just too bad for all game birds.

The telegraph and telephone wires killed thousands. These wires were strung on poles about exactly the height that prairie chickens flew, and the poor things would fly right into them and break their necks. We boys found this out once when we went with Pap to a sale over in the Dode Miner neighborhood. Dode's boy took us out along the railroad and we found three or four dead prairie chickens lying right under the telegraph wires. Mother never would cook any of them for us, for she said you couldn't tell how long they had been dead. But we liked to find them anyhow.

Boys are not as particular about a lot of things as grown-up people are. I remember once when a passel of us were exploring a marshy place that we found five or six big green frogs, about six inches long, sitting right on the edge of a pool. The water wasn't over a couple of inches deep, so we took after those frogs and caught them. Then one of the boys suggested that we kill them and skin them like they were Indians.

It was a pretty easy job to skin them. The meat was the whitest, prettiest looking meat you ever saw—looked good enough to eat. So we sent one of the boys back to his house to steal some matches and salt, built a fire, cooked those frogs' hind legs, and ate them. We all agreed frog legs were some of the finest meat we had ever tasted. We felt mighty guilty about it at the time and wouldn't have let the folks know about it for the world. But the time came when the same kind of frog legs would bring a quarter apiece in any good hotel.

We fried two ground squirrels once, on an old iron clock face fixed over some rocks, and they weren't so bad. One time Allen Lee shot a great big hawk over by his apple orchard, and we got it and cooked it. The meat was good enough, what there was of it, but awfully stringy and tough. Maybe we didn't get it cooked as much as it should have been, but it was nearly black when we ate it.

Once when we were coming home from school past Allen Lee's place we saw a rabbit sitting in a little brush heap at the lower end of his apple orchard. We sidled off, so as not to scare it, and ran back and told Allan about it. He got out his shotgun and came long with us, walking hunched away over with his knees bent forward long before we got near the rabbit. He crept to within two feet of the little brush pile, stuck the muzzle of that gun into it, and whanged away.

When the smoke had cleared away, we dug into the brush for our game, but all we could find of that rabbit was his ears, two paws, and some fur. That big charge, at so close range, had blown the poor bunny into the next township, I reckon—maybe clear over as far as the insane asylum at Mount Pleasant.

That old asylum stood over across the prairie fifteen miles away. It spread out over several acres of ground and we could see the black smoke rolling out of its brick chimney when we looked over that way. People claimed it was full of crazy folks, and warned that if any of them ever got loose, it would be a sorry day for us. With that great big solemn-looking asylum looming up to the southwest, we never lacked something to tone us down if we ever got too gay.

When Pap took us over there to the asylum one Sunday, we found out that it wasn't such a bad place after all. The yard covered ten acres and was mowed as level as a floor. There was a pipe spouting up water in the middle of a little pond, and five or six geese jabbering around it. There were several benches out under the tall trees, and people were resting in them.

There were big rooms inside, and offices, and desks, and a place to register your name. A stairway six-feet wide wound up and around to the upstairs, where I suppose the bedrooms were. After that I had a different feeling about the asylum.

At Fort Madison, another town only about forty miles from our house, there was a penitentiary. I could never muster up any notion of going down there, though. We never understood why our part of the state had both of these institutions so close together. Maybe we were more wicked and crazier than the rest of the state, but I doubt it.

The Mississippi River was only eighteen miles east of us, and in wet times, got to be several miles wide. It was one of the grandest sights you ever saw. When some smart aleck came along and got to bragging about the wonders of his part of the country, we used to be comforted by our Fort Madison penitentiary, the Mount Pleasant insane asylum, and the Mississippi River.

A Yarmouth Saturday Night

The little town of Yarmouth—where we traded, got our mail and had our blacksmithing done—was a mighty interesting place. After working all alone in the fields, and not seeing anybody but our own folks for several days at a stretch, it was quite a treat to go to Yarmouth and see some new faces.

Yarmouth wasn't much of a town—only three stores and a few houses. But it was a big improvement over what we had before the narrow gauge railroad was built through. Before that it was ten miles to a railroad track. We got our mail at a post office called La Vega, which was kept by the Lotspiech family in their own farmhouse, nearly four miles away.

But Yarmouth built right up, with a boom, as soon as the depot was finished, and in a year or two was big as it ever got. Since then it has gotten smaller, if anything.

A good many boys in our neighborhood went to Yarmouth about every Saturday afternoon and had a regular picnic of a time all afternoon. They would go back home to do the night chores and eat supper, and then go right back to town to spend the evening. Pap never let us go in the daytime, unless it was too wet to work in the fields—and even then he generally could find weeds for us to cut, or hedge to trim, or fence to fix. But we always got to go on Saturday nights, and we were mighty glad of that.

As many as forty or fifty teams would be tied in rows all along the hitch-racks, and the streets would be just swarming with folks. Nearly everybody would be there, and sometimes people came from as far off as six or seven miles. In every store people would be sitting around on sugar sacks, nail kegs, and right on the counters—talking about the weather, and the crops, and other interesting things. Dave Michaels always had a lot of funny stories to tell, and some of them were pretty nippy for a young person to hear. At the end nearly everybody would break out in a hearty laugh, and nod at one another and wink.

In Andy Cline's store, back toward the stove, there would be two fellows bent over a checkerboard and six or eight others standing around looking on. Every little bit one of the spectators would ask why the players didn't move this man and take two, or something like that. Andy was one of the best checker players in the county, I reckon, and his two boys had to do the waiting on customers whenever anybody bantered him for a game. John Conkling was stiff competition, and James Robert Hale had to be watched pretty close, for he had a checker book and studied it till he knew nearly every move on the board. All the good players kind of went in "cahoots" against James Robert, and would move so as not to let him get the men in the shape he wanted them, or it was bound to be his game. Every Saturday night, and all day long when there was a big rain, they were right at it, tooth and nail.

We would go over to Ben Ward's shack, where he had lemonade, peanuts, candy, and ice cream for sale. He also had a little pool table, and cigars, tobacco, and a cigar box full of pipe tobacco on the counter, free to all. It was a good smelling place—pleasant to be in whether you bought anything or not, and Old Ben generally had a new story or two to tell. It was the general opinion that he held it over Dave Michaels a little when it came to stories.

For the most part we boys had our good times out of doors, even at Yarmouth. We played every kind of a game you ever heard of. We wrestled, jumped, ran foot races, pulled square holts, chinned, boxed hats, threw the fifty-pound test weight, and worked ourselves up into a regular lather. If we had been forced to work half that hard on the farm, we would have nearly died, I'm sure. We kept it up as late as ten o'clock sometimes, and we were always sorry when the stores closed and we had to go home.

Over at the Henry County Fair at Mt. Pleasant, I got to see two real cowboys from the "wild and woolly West." They were all dressed up in leather britches, red flannel shirts, and broad brimmed hats. They rode into the ring on sure enough broncos, their saddles had double cinches, big stirrups, and a horn a foot high, spurs dangled from high-top boots, and strings of buckskin hung down from their horses' bits. The sight nearly set me wild.

The cowboys took after a little herd of wild horses that had been brought there from the West. After a good deal of galloping and circling around, they roped one of them and threw him down so hard we thought it surely had broken his neck. The two got off, blindfolded the horse and let him up, strapped a saddle on his back, and forced a riding bridle on him. Then one cowboy got on and away went the wild pony, bucking, pitching, sunfishing, and twisting this way and that—and that wonderful cowboy just sat there in the saddle as comfortable as though it was a rocking chair. After a while the pony got winded and stopped cavorting around. The cowboy jumped off and bowed at the crowd, and everybody waved handkerchiefs and yelled and clapped for five minutes. Right then I decided to be a cowboy.

On the way home I thought up what I was going to do. And the first idle time I had, I brought a three-year-old mule out of the pasture. It had never had even a halter on. I locked him behind a rail in a box stall in the barn, then strapped a sheepskin on his back, put a blind bridle on him, and got aboard. I kicked the rail loose and that big colt went out of the barn sidewise in the biggest kind of a hurry. He knocked several boards off. He backed right through a high picket fence. Then he commenced to buck and pitch something awful, but I stuck on by holding the strap that held the sheepskin. Next he ran under an apple tree and nearly scraped the top of my head off, as I scootched down trying my best to miss the limb. He went through a hedge and into the potato patch and was going through the wickedest kind of maneuvers when I dropped off. It took some time to pick all the dirt out of my right ear, my neck was all twisted around to one side, and I was as dizzy as could be for a day or so.

I never tried being a cowboy again. I know now that being tuckered out that easy was a sure sign that I wasn't ever cut out for a cowboy anyhow.

Then I got a notion that I wanted to be a clown. I had seen some good ones at a circus, noticed how everybody laughed at their antics, and just itched to have them laugh at me in the same way. It was a tedious business to work up to, but I set to work as soon as I found time. I rigged up a springboard by using a bridge plank stuck under the water trough, and held up by a chunk of wood. I got so I could jump off of this and turn a somersault and light on a straw tick and keep my feet. Then I trained two old tame cows we had to stand side by side in front of my springboard while I made the leap and somersaulted over their backs. It took a long time to train them to stand still, but at last they gave in, and generally stayed right there till I lit on the tick.

One Saturday afternoon I decided to give a matinee performance and invited my sister to see my act. I got hold of a Mother Hubbard dress belonging to one of the girls, painted my face with flour, and wore a paper hat running up to a high peak. The hat had been used in one of the schoolhouse plays the winter before. When I had everything ready, I opened the back barn door and my sisters stood up there while I climbed my springboard to show off.

I came down the board as fast as I could run—that Mother Hubbard flapping in the breeze—and made a try at a somersault. But the old cows were not used to the suit I had on and started to run away. Being upside down in the air at the time, I didn't know they were moving, and I came down astraddle of one's neck, right over its horns. They were gentle enough cows and of course wouldn't hook anybody, but in scrambling off those horns, I lost a big piece out of the Mother Hubbard dress. One old cow carried it around several days.

When I lit, the girls busted out laughing, and then came running down to see if I had been killed. They put linament on me several places, and Pap took several stitches with a rowel, sewing up a gash in my leg. A day or two later I had a high fever, and thought I was going to die before I got over it. I guess I must have been a quitter, because I never tried the clown business after that, and I made a pretty good hand in the field for a long time. Just settled right down, Pap said.

Another time I got the prizefighting craze. The *Police Gazette* was covered with colored pictures of John L. Sullivan and Jake Kilrain, and an article about their seventy-round fight at New Orleans covered three or four pages. I had never read anything that stirred me up like that did, and went to work right away to learn to be a prizefighter. I pulled wool off the fences, where the sheep had scraped under, and sewed it on the back of Pap's mittens for stuffing. It made tolerably good boxing gloves, too. I got a good many boys to practice with me, and since I was bigger than most of them, I got along fine.

One day I put the gloves on with a big fellow from New London who was out our way with his father, a cattle buyer, and that ended all the notion I ever had to be a prizefighter. He was one of the most discouraging fellows I ever knew. He thumped me right on the head, the mouth, and the nose just as many times as he liked. There wasn't any way I could find to prevent it. Pretty soon my nose was bleeding, one eye was about swollen shut, and I had a kind of sick feeling inside.

At the end of the third round, my seconds threw a towel in the air, which was the signal that the fight was over as far as I was concerned. I don't mind saying that I was glad they did. I could see more stars than you can see on a clear night in the dark of the moon, and had some queer feeling inside that I can't describe. Just like all my other ventures, this crazy notion I had about being a gladiator bogged down—like a cow in the mud—right there. I never tried it again and gave my sheepskin boxing gloves to a couple of girls that lived neighbors to us. They made a chair cushion out of them for their grandpa, so they were put to some good use after all.

I grew to be a good deal interested in girls, and finally the hankering broke out on me thick as chicken pox. All the things I had learned helped out more than you would think in getting along with girls. There wasn't a boy in our neighborhood who could hold a candle to me at writing a fine hand. I made a good many drawings of birds sitting on nests, all surrounded with the finest kind of scroll work, with maybe down below a pennant dangling with a girl's name printed on it. I never saw a girl who didn't take to that kind of present.

Then I had it over most of the boys in things to talk about. Riding around nights, I could pick out different stars and tell the girls their names, and how far off they were. I knew how to figure how many turns a buggy wheel made in going a mile. I knew a good deal about wild plants, and specific gravity, and induction, and could recite poetry from several books.

It got Belle Johnson's papa more interested in me than Belle was. He was a smart man, well-read, and liked to talk to me so well that when I went there to see his pretty daughter, he took up most of the time himself talking things over with me. Belle was a luscious, red-lipped, beautiful girl, and I fell in love with her just the worst way. But I never got very far with it. She wasn't any older, but she seemed older than I was, and she got interested in an older fellow who had a top buggy of his own, so she kind of drifted away from me.

When the time came just right, it was all settled for me in a few minutes. When I met my Lucy at choir practice, she looked just like I had always wanted my best girl to look. When we were introduced, we shook hands across the top of the organ, and Ellen Hale was playing a church tune about, "Happy Day That Fixed My Choice." In the light of what happened afterwards, it seemed almost like a good omen. Organ notes never joined in making any better melody than we did right from the start, and it has always been that way.

Pap's trying to bust up that match a year or two later just fastened it down tighter, and the time came when I stopped riding horseback fifteen miles every Sunday to see her, and just went down and got her, and have had her ever since.

But back of it all stand a lot of wonderful experiences—experience that nobody can get unless he is lucky enough to be born and brought up in the open country. Most of those experiences are as clear as though they happened only a year or so ago. I like to call them up and enjoy them over again.

One of the brightest and sweetest recollections is the picture of Mother, the busy little woman who never thought of herself in her life, but just put her time in being lovely to everybody she ever met. And there is Pap, too—hard to understand and impossible to manage, but when you came to find him out, a likable, heroic, clean, and wonderful man that any boy ought to be proud to have for a father.

"IOWA" (1956)

PAUL ENGLE

Devoted to his home state, poet, novelist, and teacher Paul Engle made Iowa his lifetime home after the fashion of his friends and fellow writers James Hearst and Jay G. Sigmund. A Cedar Rapids boy, Engle stayed put for college, attending nearby Coe, and went for a Master's just up the road in Iowa City. A Rhodes Scholar, Engle temporarily indulged his wanderlust, doing two years at Merton College, Oxford, before returning to the University of Iowa as a lecturer. In the late 1930s, he began building perhaps his greatest legacy, the world-famous Iowa Writers' Workshop, directing that venerable institution for more than twenty-five years. After his directorship ended in 1965, he cofounded the International Writers' Workshop with Chinese writer and scholar Hualing Neih who would become Engle's second wife. In August of 2008, Hualing Engle earned entry in the Iowa Women's Hall of Fame for helping to bring the world to Iowa's doorstep. While Paul Engle authored more than twenty books of poems, his greatest influence may have been as a teacher, inspiring and nurturing writers just as John T. Frederick. No less a writer than Flannery O'Connor dedicated her MFA thesis at the University of Iowa to her teacher-mentor. Though his reach was international, Engle wrote frequent prose about Iowa in books such as Portraits of Iowa, *and* The World Comes to Iowa. *In the essay below, reprinted from* Holiday, *Engle captures the Hawkeye State as only a native son and lifelong resident could. Interestingly, Engle, who refers to Soviet agricultural experts traveling to Iowa to study-up on Hawkeye methods, published his essay three years before the famous visit by Soviet Premier Nikita Sergeyevich Khrushchev to the Roswell Garst Farm in 1959.*

IOWA IS THE HEARTLAND OF THE HEARTLAND.
Its greatest single force is dirt—fat dirt; out of its soil each year more wealth is produced than in all the gold mines of the world. Gently the land rises and falls, not flat, not broken into steep hills, but always tilting its fertile face to the sun.

When a military highway was needed from Dubuque to the Missouri border in the early days of the mounted dragoons, a farmer was hired. He yoked up ten oxen to a long sod-breaking plow and headed south. Day after day they moved, ahead of them the untouched grass and grove, behind them a lengthening furrow of black dirt. No sound but the man's yell to his animals, and the silken, tearing rip of the plow splitting that sod for the first time ever. It was natural for Iowa to use for its military road only the peaceful oxen and the plow. For this is an abundant land.

And when last year the Soviet Union sent agricultural experts to America to find out what free men working on their own land could raise, it was natural that the Russians should come first to Iowa. And when the Red farmers arrived they were given, in once "isolationist" Iowa, a wealthy welcome, told everything they wanted to know, shown all the methods and secrets of production. They went to the First Presbyterian Church in Jefferson and held hymnbooks, probably for the first time in their lives, watched 4-H boys demonstrate how to kill corn borers, and 4-H girls bake sweet rolls. They lifted their arms at the right time in the Iowa song for the line "That's where the tall corn grows," and they saw their first real drugstore with a soda fountain and ate "Tummy Busters. Eat Two and Get a Free One—49 cents plus one cent tax." For this is an abundant land.

Iowa is the middlest of the Middle West. Its life and people are balanced and solid. It is a country of the small town, the average comfortable life. There are no great fortunes and there is no poverty. But it has the highest standard of living for its area in the world and it has a quarter of all the best land in America.

Look at the map of Iowa, the Missouri wavering down the west side and the Mississippi down the east. Jutting eastward is a fine round potbelly, the broad Mississippi bending around it like a belt. For this is an abundant land.

Iowa carries nothing to excess save its virtues and its weather. It has been the place of the sensible medium, and of the peace that goes with it. The only Quaker President, Herbert Hoover, came from a little Iowa town. There has never been a war on Iowa soil, or a battle of any consequence. One massacre by the Sioux of a few white settlers. John Brown trained his men at a Quaker settlement, where they did strange calisthenics and drilled with wooden swords. One of his men was censured for hugging girls, which was as violent an act as any of the group committed in Iowa. When the time for fighting came, Brown left his peaceful settlement, where the Quakers had assisted him without knowing his wicked purpose, and went oft to bloody Harpers Ferry. Iowa men marched off to Vicksburg, but the Civil War never came to their state.

When my grandfather rode with the Fifth Iowa Cavalry in the [18]60s, he chased the Sioux in Dakota Territory but never caught up with him. Inkpadutah, the leader of the Sioux who massacred thirty-two men, women, and children at Spirit Lake, realized that Iowa was too peaceful for such wild goings-on, and fled west.

Kentucky was the Dark and Bloody Ground, but Iowa has always been the Bright and Bloodless Ground.

Of the Missouri River the old saying is: too thick to drink, too thin to plow. But Iowa is just right to plow, no waste land, no swamps, no mountains, no large forests. Glaciers scoured off the soil from other states and dumped it on this lucky land, giving Iowa its long reaches of loam. After grass had grown and died for centuries, sinking its roots so deep that prairie fires couldn't burn them out, the soil became as rich as the side of a fat hog.

Then the settlers came, and the sod-breaking plows, with their great oak beams to hold the point of the plow down against the tough buck of the roots, and the great crops began to spring up. France had its Field of the Cloth of Gold, but Iowa still has its Fields of the Cloth of Green.

The common shape of Iowa landscape is the little valley, with tiny streams everywhere like veins meshing a marvelous body. And along all of the streams, wooded slopes with willow, elm, maple, hickory, black walnut. The streams are everywhere, the dark rivers with the silt of fields: Raccoon, Coon, Wolf, Catfish, Mosquito, Polecat, Opossum, Pike, Turkey, Skunk, Cedar, Crabapple, Squaw, and Five Barrel Creek, so called because dragoons found five barrels of whisky buried near it. And most lyrical of all, in the high hills of northeastern Iowa, the Tête de Mort (call it *Teddymore*), proof that the French once were here, and that a band of Dakotahs was killed by Sac Indians and scalped and thrown over a cliff.

There is no soft nonsense about the seasons in Iowa. Winter is a savage season; blizzards out of the west rattle the teeth in your skull. Frost goes deep in the fallow ground; snow piles up and when the ice comes, impenetrable, squirrels scamper over it hungrily. But then will come the incredible May morning when the sun drips a gold life on the land, seeds jump in delight under the plowed fields, the sprouted corn turns the countryside into tufted quilts, and the pigs squirm out into the light of day ("Sows opened weak on the Chicago market" says the radio report) and calves jump stiff-legged around the barn. The air itself has the quality of food and breathing is nourishment. The pastures glitter with green.

Then summer overwhelms us. We can hear the crops growing, the corn up an inch a day, the pigs grunting their growth as they crunch their food— more elaborately planned and mixed than that of any child (buttermilk, yeast, fish, soybeans, sugar, corn, limestone, cobalt, acetate, zinc carbonate, linseed oil, rolled oats, fish liver, manganese sulfate, vitamins, antibiotics, riboflavin, and many others). The porkers have had their "one-shot wormer" and are busy hanging bacon on their slick sides. The whole state turns into a skillet, frying human, animal, and plant life. Midnight differs a few degrees from intense noon. Corn grows tall and men grow limp. People droop by night and drop by day. But everything flourishes.

Autumn is the Iowa season. All of the winter's frozen rest, the spring plowing, the summer cultivating, move toward the final act of harvest. The land browns, oats ripen, corn begins to dent, hay is cut, the alfalfa for the third time. As the long corn leaves turn brittle, the air itself turns crisp and tree leaves burn the branches for a while before falling. It is a season truly called "the fall." Things come to earth, the crops to barn, the kids to school. The delirious activity of summer slows down, as the urgency of jobs to get done before it's too late falls away.

Between summer and autumn come the county fairs, with their rows of Jerseys, Guernseys (with the highest butterfat content in their milk), of Holsteins (the largest producers of milk in bulk), the mouse-colored Brown Swiss with their calves looking like heavy-boned fawns, the glistening flanks of Black Angus beef steers, polished and combed, or the ruddy Herefords with their white faces. And there is usually a single hog litter totaling a ton. The wildly carved running horses on the merry-go-round carry children to the same sweet and brassy tunes. The exhibits of farm machinery are fantastic, the prize squash, pumpkin, corn, startle the eye with their size. And of course there are the formidable yet delicate and fluffy cakes with blue and red prize ribbons on them, the prize pickles, canned beans, enough to shatter the stablest stomach. Along the racetrack where the horses are jogging with their light sulkies and the old-time horsemen with their legs straddling the shafts, families are engaged in that most typical, most delightful Iowa activity—consuming food.

What people come? Farmers with their families, faces tanned but a sharp white line around the neck where the shin collar kept off the sun, with the deliberate walk of men accustomed to plowed fields and bumpy pastures. They watch the fat-steer judging and the heavy draft horse judging, look at the machinery, take a suspicious glance at the Kewpie doll stands and the jaded girlie shows, but mostly they talk, talk to other farmers they haven't seen in a coon's age. (What is the age of a coon?) Everywhere clusters of men arguing weather, crops, prices (today's prices are mentioned in the tone of voice one uses coming home from a funeral), politics, the government (in the tone one uses for a difficult uncle you don't really want around but whose wealth might be needed later on).

The women are here, too, and the kids; it's a family affair, something for everybody, the home-convenience exhibits for the ladies and the ferris wheel for the screaming kids. But town people are here too, especially the ones who grew up on farms and moved away. They've changed some, they walk a little faster and gesture more abruptly, but they still like the smells of the barns and the bawl of the calves and the leathery tang of harness being soaped for the afternoon's first trotting heat. You can take the boy out of the farm but you can't take the farm out of the boy.

Across the top of the Great Seal of Iowa is the motto: Our Liberties We Prize and Our Rights We Will Maintain. And to prove that those rights will be maintained, a soldier with rifle stands in the foreground, a plow and a great swirling flag behind him. To a surprising extent, they are maintained, although now and then there is a little uncertainty as to just whose rights are meant. A few years ago the body of a GI was refused burial at a Sioux City cemetery, although he had died protecting his country's liberties, because he was too much a 100 percent American, a real Indian. But this is rare. It is a matter of pride that the first case to come before the Supreme Court of Iowa territory gave freedom to a negro slave. And this same regard for human liberty came up a century later when a negro Army officer stationed at a radar base near Waverly could not find housing for his family, although an apartment was available. When the other tenants heard about it, they petitioned to have him as a neighbor and welcomed his family with a celebration.

There has always been a sense of the just in Iowa. More than a hundred years ago when the defiant Sac Chief Black Hawk was presented to Andy Jackson in Washington he looked him in the eye and said simply, "I am a man and you are another."

Even obscenity gets a fair hearing. A few years ago the ladies of Dubuque were frightened by the appearance of comics, reprints, pocket books near schools. Hearings were held and the naughty evidence was introduced, such fiction as that of Erskine Caldwell, Richard Bissell (Dubuque's own, author of *A Stretch on the River* and *The Pajama Game*), and the usual popular novels, along with some gruesome comics and a history of art which charmingly proved that the female nude had interested more artists than had bowls of fruit or happy children. But in the end, the decision taken was the moderate, middle one to be expected of Iowa people: the chance of censorship was worse than the chance of indiscriminate novels being read. One argument of real power in a state essentially rural-minded was that the corset sections of mail order catalogs contained more photographs of undressed models than any of the books being questioned.

When the Russians came to Iowa they expected to find the fields full of people. As they were driven along the roads between the luxuriant corn and oats and alfalfa, with the yards and pastures full of hogs and cattle, they kept asking, "But where are the workers?" Usually they were told that a man and his wife and children, with an occasional hired man, farmed the place. One of them exclaimed, "By you one man—by us a hundred." What he did not realize was that this staggering production of food by a few people was done by the same class of farmers the Soviet had murdered in the early '30s. They had never seen a husking hook fastened to a glove. They kept asking at the agricultural college at Ames who was their *boss* in Washington, and could not believe that the college operated independently of the federal government. When they asked Guy Stover, Jr., a farmer near Reinbeck, who told him what to plant, he replied: "Nobody tells me what to plant. Nobody. I can let the whole farm grow up in weeds if I want to and nobody can say a thing."

They ate meals of roast beef, vegetables, ice cream, angel food cake, salad, milk, all of which came from the same farm. They discovered that small-town newspapers in Iowa were thicker than Russia's national dailies. They had their first experience of motels, a dime store, golf, a country club. They discovered, as the Charles City *Press* put it, every reason under the sun why the Iowa farmer produced twenty times as much food as the Russian farmer, except the main one, the freedom under which the Iowa farmer operates.

The Russians came in the hope of learning how to feed their people. That was natural, for men and women have always come to Iowa with hope. In the 1850s came a group of Germans calling itself The Community of True Inspiration, who believed that God still spoke directly to man. They settled between Iowa City and Grinnell and built seven little Amana villages in the medieval manner, the families living close together in the communities and going out to work in the fields. They had the wisdom to realize that the Lord could best be served with good land rather than poor, and took up 26,000 acres of rich bottom soil and wooded hills along the Iowa River. They ate in communal houses (five times a day, in leisure and abundance, with excellent grape and dandelion wine brought out to those working in the fields at noon). All property save clothing and furniture was held in common. Each adult received a tiny sum known as "year-money" for odd expenses, the least skilled worker in the hog house receiving the same housing and maintenance as the most responsible farm head. God was worshiped not in churches but in houses without cross or decoration, and no music save the unaccompanied human voice grandly ringing out the hymns written by their own brilliant prophet Christian Metz.

They flourished in their isolated, abundant, and devout life until the wicked world came to them by newspaper, paved road, car, radio, and the young people began to yearn for the things they saw others having, like bicycles and Sunday baseball. They voted to dissolve the old communal-property idea and to form a corporation in which everyone worked for a salary. Each adult was given one share of Class A voting stock; when issued in 1932 a share was worth fifty-four dollars—today it is worth $3400. Houses are painted, cars are everywhere, television aerials rise as high as the native hickory and oak trees.

Again Iowa released the energies of people who came to her. Working with odd items from local shops, George Foerstner and others created a little freezer. And now in the cornfields at Middle Amana, where oxen loafed not long ago and daily prayers out of the early 18th Century were uttered in praise of God and in disparagement of weak man, there is a bright new factory from which more home freezers are sold than from any other plant in the world. And where the name *Amana* used to mean a shy young girl under a black sunbonnet, now it means movie star Laraine Day opening an Amana freezer wide, as she widely smiles, on television.

Iowa has always believed in bringing together the holy and the useful. Dutch who would not conform to the established church in Holland came in 1847 to found the town of Pella, where every May the old Dutch clothes and the wooden shoes come out, and there is dancing in the street. Why shouldn't they dance? They're in Iowa raising tulips, and raising the hem of their long dresses, oh so slightly.

And the French came to start their own idealistic community at Icaria on the Nodaway. Property was held in common, but alas, not the zeal for work. A dance hall was built, however, with plenty of zeal and native wood, but soon there were only individual men and women working their own lives.

The Hungarians came after the failure of the 1848 revolt against Austria. But they were aristocrats full of zeal to build a New Buda in northwestern Iowa, and what the land needed was a sharp plow, not an edged sword.

The Norwegians came to northeastern Iowa, in the handsome hill country, to settle the town of Decorah and found Luther College. Some crossed the frozen Mississippi in the depth of winter, proving the stern devotion of a faith that could build log cabins in a wilderness and a hundred years later produce blond, unbeaten football teams with Viking names.

Naturally, the Mennonites came here to build their fine farms, with that same combination of hard work and solid faith. Around Kalona they wrestled with some hard questions: Was it right to drive an automobile? (Most drive buggies; a few, cars with the chrome painted out.) Was it proper to use a tractor with metal tires but not with rubber tires? Would pickles tied to the feet cure a child of convulsions? Should the preachers forbid turkey roasts, ice cream suppers, imposing weddings, laces, corsets, Christmas trees? The men in their beards, the women and children in their black bonnets and high shoes, come into Iowa City to shop, and to peer quietly at the naughty world. And then go home to work their rich farms with their old simplicity.

The Czechs came to Spillville in the northeastern country, where Antonin Dvořák came to write his music in the peaceful valley where his native language was still spoken. And signs across part of Cedar Rapids today are in Czech, and the Sokols do their fine gymnastics and the kolaches are made with prunes or poppy seeds. Once a Czech girl named Jaroslava Holobulova graduated from Coe College at the top of her class.

But most amusing of all the peoples who came to Iowa were the English younger sons who settled in Le Mars in the northwest to learn farming in the 1880s. They brought to Iowa their own sporting ways; cricket practice was held on Broken Kettle Creek, and the Le Mars cricket team beat St. Paul. Polo was played against Cherokee and Council Bluffs. But the polo ball proved more attractive than the humble pumpkin, and the younger sons left the plow in the furrow and rode into town to "paint the place a rip, staring red."

But the purpose of these gay British boys, since the place was Iowa, was to learn how to raise food. A visiting newspaperman wrote about them: "The young men who make up this community are…graduates of Oxford or Cambridge. On one farm I met two tall and handsome young farmers whose uncle had been a distinguished member of Parliament. The last time I had seen them was in a London drawing room. This time they tramped me through the mud and manure of the barnyard to show me some newly bought stock. They were boarding with a Dutch farmer at three dollars a week in order to learn practical farming.… Another young farmer had been an admiral in the Royal Navy, another had been connected with a Shanghai bank. There was a brother to Lord Ducie, not to speak of future baronets, viscounts, and honorables…."

But real liberty had its price. One of the Englishmen wrote that he could no longer stand the Iowa attitude: "The other evening on the closing of the House of Lords (as they had named a saloon), I was standing with four or five friends talking when the deputy marshal comes up and requests me in his usually suave manner to 'cheese this racket.' Liberty is constantly jammed down your throat here, but it seems to me an exploded theory, when an officer can do what he likes with your right of speech." Discouraged by equal parts of being told to cheese it and of hard work, the younger sons gave up their western ghosts and left.

The English were the gayest of all the Iowa settlers. More solid were the "Hook-and-Eye Dutch" who refused to put up the tops of their buggies because the sun was no harder on them than on the horse.

But no matter what their origins, Iowa people believed in education. With the lowest rate of illiteracy in the United States, it is natural that one of the country's largest manufacturers of fountain pens should be the W. A. Sheaffer Pen plant, at Fort Madison, and that one of the finest statewide newspapers should be the *Des Moines Register*, unique today in having an editorial page with generous convictions and the courage to express them. It opposed Senator McCarthy long before more timid papers did so; it began the protest which resulted in [Wolf] Ladejinsky being cleared; it invited the Russians to visit Iowa; it approved Dr. Robert J. Oppenheimer being invited to speak at Iowa State College when many colleges refused to have him. In all this, it remains staunchly Republican, believing, with the mixture of idealism and practicality which has always distinguished the people of Iowa, that personal freedom is nothing but old-fashioned right, and every man's due.

The Cowles family is a solid example of what human character can mean to a state, through its many gifts to colleges, the foundation it has endowed, and through dramatizing in the pages of the *Register* the fact that a nation's security lies as much in its ideals as in its bombs, and that liberties must be prized, even at the risk of offending subscribers.

Even in liquor, Iowa has chosen the medium way. Knowing the strong temperance feeling among the people, and yet suspecting that, since it was mentioned in the Old Testament, drinking might be here to stay, the state compromised. Under the fancy that a man would remain soberer if he took a bottle home, where there was no one to observe but the kiddies, all bars (save for beer) were outlawed. State liquor stores were set up without advertising or decoration. Some dramatic things have happened as a result.

Because of a fear that liquor purchases might be criticized by their neighbors, many people in the first year drove to the next town to buy where they might be unrecognized. On the way, they would pass the cars of those from the next town hurrying over to *their* liquor store to buy in secret. One enterprising newspaper, the Eagle Grove *Eagle*, discovered that, on the basis of gross liquor sales, Eagle Grove and nearby Clarion had exchanged populations. Any action connected with the naughty word "liquor" is news. The Iowa attorney general, willing to have his name honorably connected with the role of a white knight crusading against the dark dragon booze, obtained a plane and went off in what the Anamosa *Journal* lyrically described as an "aerial sashay," raiding thirty places across the state. Liquor was found in only three. But the attorney general is going to make Iowa "cracker-dry" he says. He'll need a big box of crackers.

The demon rum even lurks behind innocent beef cattle, causing Governor Hoegh (a firm "dry") embarrassment. At last year's Iowa State Fair, the governor accepted the grand-champion baby beef, only to discover that it was owned by the Storz Brewing Company of Omaha. He gave it away for charity. And at the Waterloo Cattle Congress, he agreed to pose with the grand-champion bull, a colossal animal, and then found that it belonged to a Milwaukee brewer named Pabst. It's a delicate thing when the governor of the state producing the finest fat cattle can't be photographed with a baby beef or giant bull without first sniffing them for fumes of alcohol.

But in the long run, Iowa's system works out for the average best. It returns an annual profit to the state of several million dollars, so that drinking might be called patriotic. At the same time that those who loathe the spectacle of public bars are spared that hideous sight, their neighbors who like a nip are allowed to buy all they wish.

Realizing that the surest way to produce a balanced people was to educate them, the first General Assembly to meet in Iowa founded a university. Later came the first law school west of the Mississippi. And since the state believes that fertility in the arts should try to equal fertility in the soil, it was only natural that the University of Iowa should have been the first in America to bring all the creative arts to the campus, boldly and with honor to the artist. Students were encouraged to write plays, novels, poetry, short stories, compose a string quartet or a symphony, to paint in oil or gouache or water colors, to carve in wood or stone or metal, or to act in plays.

At Iowa, the creative artist is equal to the scholar: Philip Bezanson of the University Music Department composed a piano concerto which was conducted by Dimitri Mitropoulos with the New York Philharmonic Orchestra, and the soloist was John Sims of the music department; and in the same field house where the Iowa basketball team won the Big Ten championship in 1955 and 1956, Mitropoulos conducted the Berlioz *Requiem*. University of Iowa painters and sculptors exhibit in the finest shows in the country; more poets from the University of Iowa were represented in the 1955 *New Campus Writing* than from any other institution. Tennessee Williams wrote some of his first plays at the superb university theater. Some thirty novels have been published out of the Fiction Workshop.

This congenial attitude toward the arts has had some remarkable effects on the personality of the state. In Des Moines the state capitol is so extreme an example of ornate decoration that it has the complex beauty of the grotesque (the people, however, seem to love it). Across town, out Grand Avenue, with its 19th Century big houses covered with gingerbread, is the new municipal Art Center, designed by Eliel Saarinen, the 20th Century architect from Finland. On the walls may be an exhibit of modern art; its variety and abundance will amaze you.

Go to one of the most congenial cities for art in America, Cedar Rapids. In the home of Owen Elliott, president of the board of trustees of Coe College (Presbyterian), you will find Renoir, Braque, Bonnard, Matisse. At Coe College itself there has been a long-term exhibit of the most advanced art from the Solomon R. Guggenheim Museum in New York. For fifty years Cedar Rapids has had its own art association and for many years its own symphony orchestra. It was not chance that Grant Wood painted his first oils here; dozens were bought locally long before he became famous. (I remember the time he painted on a canvas—for a startled eighth-grade art class I belonged to—the sound of a piece of music, following the sound over the curves and whirls with his brush.) It was in the country around Cedar Rapids that he found the neat and formal landscape for his paintings. Here were the artificial-looking trees, which he had seen first on his mother's china, trees rounded by the steady wind before Wood rounded them on his own imagined hills. Here he saw the patterned corn, the young sprouts lined across the fields like knots tied on a guilt. Wood painted the birthplace of Herbert Hoover at nearby West Branch (settled by the same Quakers who had befriended John Brown in the bloody days). With his instinct for order, which he found in the cultivated and controlled Iowa landscape, he cleaned up the field beyond the little white house. When a resident of West Branch saw the painting, he remarked gratefully, "Well, Grant, that's the house all right, and we sure thank you for mowing them weeds."

So it is natural that in Cedar Rapids there should live Marvin Cone, the country's leading painter of all the shapes and richness and variety of wooden barns, and all the intricate, many-doored interiors of haunted houses. For he, too, has found in the Iowa scene a pattern and a pride.

Every summer at the county fairs one sees the letters "4-H" everywhere. They stand for Head, Heart, Hands, Health, and are an effort not only to make better farmers out of the young people but to give them better lives, to improve the style of clothes worn by the girls and the style of public speaking used by the boys. Some of the finest baby-beef steers in the world are owned by 4-H boys and girls, who feed them, brush them, keep records of costs and diet, tend them like pets, and then compete at the fairs, selling them for the fanciest prices, often over a thousand dollars for one animal. Girls compete in the same ring with boys and sometimes beat them. It's a fine sight to see a young girl leading a Black Angus curried to glossy brilliance or a Hereford to a glowing ruddiness; and at times a tearful sight when a creature which has been pampered and worked over for a year is sold for slaughter.

When the 4-H members take part in a contest, there is no public posturing in bathing suits. The *healthiest* boy and girl from each county are chosen, and compete in a statewide and then a national contest. For the girls, there is no mere beauty contest, but one for the best groomed—in clothes each has made—but many of these girls would brighten a bathing suit too.

The Iowa farmer has come a long way since the frontier grace at meals: *Mush is rough, Mush is tough, Thank Thee Lord, We've got enough.* His problem is no longer getting enough mush, but producing too much beef, pork, corn, wheat. When nearly everybody else in America has been increasing his income, the farmer's has dropped by 30 percent. He was urged to raise as much food as possible, and the wars exaggerated this. But suddenly, just when the farmer had bought more machines to produce more food, there is too much food. Corn is sealed in round metal bins outside every town in Iowa. Too many hogs go to market (you can't let a hog wait, and you can't tell it to stop eating; when it's ready for market it's got to go), and the price is down to half what it was not long ago.

Now the farmer is traditionally "agin the guvment," but of late years he has turned, kicking and screaming most of the time, to that same government which he has cussed out with such pleasure. He doesn't want controls. The old phrase "independent as a hog on ice" is a wonderfully and miserably accurate description of the farmer's position. A fat hog sliding across the ice is the least independent thing in the world. The farmer wants to be his own boss, he doesn't want anyone telling *him* what to do, but he finds the market a mighty slippery place. He looks at his corn-fattened beef cattle, or his hogs, and knows he will get barely his cost back, and maybe not that. So he looks toward that suspicious and remote city called Washington. He wants to remain individualistic, but he doesn't want to go bankrupt. When the same situation rose in the early thirties, the farmers overturned milk trucks, brought guns to auctions, and forced the sale of foreclosed farms for a dollar. These people were called "sons of wild jackasses."

The result is a mild schizophrenia on the farms. Leave me alone but help me. The younger farmers accept the curious combination of the individual going his own way (my father, born on a farm, used to say that a real country was one where a man could go to hell the way he wanted to) and the government stretching out a long, helping arm from Washington. In maybe ten years our population will have increased so fast all farm produce will be eaten. But can the farmer wait? To a man with a rope around his neck, hanging from a tree, it doesn't matter if his feet are sixteen feet off the ground or one sixteenth of an inch. Will that old wild jackass blood come out at this autumn's election?

The state grows with the times, too, for in 1956 industrial production surpassed agricultural. New factories are coming in, many small and specialized ones to the smaller towns. The big cereal plants, the agricultural machinery factories, the Quaker Oats in Cedar Rapids where entire boxcars of grain are picked up and rolled over on their sides, an aluminum factory on the Mississippi, all expand the state's income and alter its rural character.

Even in fighting, Iowa men have struck a balance. In 1870 two men fought until they were, as the old account says, a mangled mass. Both were arrested, whereupon each said that it had all been for fun, just to see whether a man from Kentucky could beat a man from Maine. The loser even argued that the winner should not be fined because, after all, he had won.

The famous Iowa 34th Division of World War II fought from North Africa to Sicily to Italy to Germany, still looking after those plain rights. Yet Buffalo Bill, born down at Le Claire on the Mississippi, had to leave Iowa for a more violent life.

Iowa balances a furious physical climate with a congenial human climate, for the hearts of the people are as abundant as the land around them. Graced from the beginning with a fullness of food, they have made abundance and creativeness an integral part or their rights and liberties. If there is hope anywhere in this wicked world or in these many states, it is certainly here, exploding like popcorn in a pan. (Of course Iowa raises more popcorn than any other state.) When a farmer falls sick at harvest time, neighbors move in with fifteen cornpickers and gather his crop in a day. When the young writers, musicians, painters, sculptors of the United States want a sympathetic community as an alternative to New York, here is a university welcoming them not merely as students but as artists. When Marvin Cone needed a year away from teaching so that he could paint without distraction, businessmen (those same maligned businessmen of whose stony hearts we read) put together a purse of money and told him to spend it anywhere he wished. And he painted more in one year than in any other five.

Suddenly, those outrageous seasons no longer matter in the face of the life, the people, the hope. They become rather a source of pride that one survives them, a source of that very abundant fertility which hard work meets halfway, between heaven and earth, between the two great rivers.

From **The Wild Jackasses (1956)**

Dale Kramer

A Batavia, Iowa, native, Dale Kramer grew up in Sigourney in Keokuk County and went on to attend the University of Iowa. Kramer saw the state up close and personal as a newspaper reporter in Elkader, Sigourney, Iowa City, Cedar Rapids, and Des Moines. He also edited the Holiday Farm News for Milo Reno, a tenure that informs The Wild Jackasses and which led to a position as national secretary of the Farm Holiday Association. During World War II, he was a staff correspondent for Yank, the Army magazine, and in that capacity traveled to New Guinea, the Phillipines, and Japan. After the war, he returned to New York City, where he served on the staff of the The New Yorker before coming back to Iowa City for a professorship in journalism. Fittingly, he ended his life in the small town where he began it: Sigourney. The reading that follows, including three separate excerpts from chapter eighteen and chapter nineteen of Kramer's book-length work of literary journalism, The Wild Jackasses, tells a true story stranger than fiction. Known for their passivity and sometimes docility, Iowa's farmers turned violent in the early 1930s, most notably in Cedar County, where, in the famous "Cow Wars," proud yeoman took up arms to prevent state veterinarians from testing their cattle for tuberculosis, and, later, in western Iowa, blocked roads to prevent milk from reaching market. While the farmers' methods weren't always lawful, they were remarkable. Kramer points out that Iowa's Cow Wars marked the first time since 1787 that government troops had to be called out to en masse to quell farmer unrest. Kramer drops many names in this short excerpt, first and foremost Milo Reno, who was the president of the National Farmers' Holiday association, a native of Wapello County (the Reno farm was between Batavia and Agency City) and a graduate of William Penn in Oskaloosa. Dan Turner is remembered as the Iowa governor who famously declared martial law when Cedar County farmers revolted, sending thirty-one National Guard units to Tipton according to the Des Moines Register. Jake Lenker was the ringleader on the ground in Iowa, who, arrested and convicted of criminal conspiracy for his role in the violent demonstrations, was sentenced to two three-year terms at the state pen in Fort Madison.

In the autumn of 1929, after hearing so much of "Coolidge prosperity," Mr. Hoover's "two cars in every garage," and the rich killings being made in the stock market, farmers were bound to derive some amusement from the Wall Street Panic that was developing. As they were somewhat less familiar with panics than the Grangers of 1873 and the Populists of 1893 had been, and as they had contended that the nation could not remain prosperous with agriculture depressed, they believed that now the money lords would awaken to the error of their ways. Certainly the Wall Street bankers, after righting the market, would, they felt, see to it that agriculture got its fair share of the national wealth.

President Hoover and his advisers concluded, if, albeit reluctantly, that the government was obliged to take some steps to relieve agriculture. He established the Farm Board to purchase surplus grain and dispose of it abroad. But, owing to high tariff walls, few markets were available. The surpluses piled higher. As though to guarantee the Farm Board's failure, the Republican Congress enacted the Smoot-Hawley bill, raising the industry-protecting tariffs even higher.

By 1931 nearly 60 percent of all Iowa farms carried mortgages. The figure would have been higher except for the fact that during the last few years one farmer out of every seven had either been foreclosed on or else had surrendered his land in the face of the sheriff's descent.

Now, as farm prices fell lower and lower, the country banks, as if to punctuate the crisis, began to explode. It was as though the dust of worthless notes had been too much for their vaults.

Enormous crowds were turning out to hear Milo Reno, and his enemies were charging that he exploited hard times and was agitating merely to bring more dues into the Farmers Union coffers. They were in error not only in the analysis of his character but in failing to understand that in hard times farm organizations have great difficulty in collecting any dues at all.

And so, even though farmers were turning by the tens of thousands to Milo Reno's leadership, and old Farmers Union members considered themselves stauncher Union men than ever, the money was not flowing in.

During Hoover's 1928 campaign for the Presidency, his publicity managers had created a rustic idyll. The air had been filled with sweet music as they pointed to his Iowa birthplace, a vine-covered cottage in the village of West Branch in Cedar County, which lies in the eastern part of the state.

The idyll lay shattered in the slush of a March day of 1931. Half a thousand angry farmers milling in a barnyard, embattled against the duly constituted authorities of the state, were not unaware of the irony of their identification with the man billed as the Great Humanitarian. The reasons for their presence in the barnyard lay deep, but that identification may have snapped the farmers' nerves in Cedar County a little quicker than elsewhere.*

Rural telephone lines in Cedar County were humming on the morning of September 1, 1931. All eastern Iowa crackled with rumors. Caravans of farmers were said to be on their way from many counties. Newspapermen heard of dim figures on horseback moving cow herds in the rain, as if to hide them.

A crowd of "Milo Reno men" were in Jake Lenker's barnyard when Joe Newell marched his little army through the gate, and other farmers closed in behind. When Newell's men tried to clear a space for testing the herd, five hundred farmers hemmed them in. Now tear-gas guns were leveled, and this time they were fired.

For the embattled farmers this was not a signal for dispersal but for attack. Veternarians and law agents were nothing to them now. They battled as though venting their long-pent-up fury against oppressors. They attacked with clubs and bricks and bare hands. They locked in hand-to-hand battle with officers and rolled in the din. The assistant attorney general who had been threatened with a ducking in the horse tank on an earlier occasion now suffered it.

Newell's army beat a hasty—and not very strategic—retreat. Conveyances were abandoned, and the crowd, its fury not yet spent, punctured tires and smashed windows.

Dan Turner called out the National Guard. "Where men are organized against government," he said in Washington where he had been arguing with Mr. Hoover about the price of corn, "there is only one thing to do, and that is to put down the insurrection. That is exactly what I propose to do in Cedar County."

If insurrection it really was, then it was the first by American farmers since Shays's Rebellion a century and a half earlier. Not since that time had soldiers been sent to bend the yeomanry to a government's will.

Dan Turner was convinced that he had no other choice. Yet he knew—everybody knew—that the rebellion was neither against the Iowa government nor the United States government; it was against the national administration's failure to alleviate the acute distress of the nation's agricultural population.

In Cedar County the troops pitched camp at the Tipton fairgrounds and then seized Jake Lenker and locked him in a horse stall. Jake wasn't much daunted. "I believe that Dan Turner sent the guard up here for an outing," he told reporters. "I wouldn't believe anything he said anyhow, for I don't think he knows what he's talking about, and then there's Hoover. He took prosperity away from us and hid it around a corner."

Farmers good-naturedly distributed a truckload of watermelons among the soldiers. Tipton citizens were shocked to discover the militia in their town, but the businessmen found a silver lining. They said all the commotion boosted trade.

Finally, all the Cedar County herds and all the Iowa herds were tested. Jake Lenker and Paul Moore were sentenced to three years in prison for their part in the Cow War but were paroled after four months. Lenker emerged a broken man, and when he died his friends said his ordeal had killed him.

The tuberculin tests were eventually proved to be scientifically valid. But that was a minor point. Everybody knew that the agitation over them had merely ignited the explosive resentments that had accumulated during a decade and a half of farm depression.*

Then on August 11 the Sioux City Milk Producers' Association ordered a milk strike. Here was a chance to pinpoint a target. Just as striking labor often sought to close factories, so the Association farmers now tried to halt the flow of nonstrikers' milk into Sioux City. They began to picket the highways, and scores of Holiday farmers arrived from surrounding counties to help them.

Men felt, as trucks were flagged down and the drivers obligingly turned around, that something concrete was being done. There was an atmosphere of hope in the roadside picket camps. Men sipped coffee brewed over little fires and told each other that, after all, only the distributors were being hurt, for the Association had established free milk depots for consumers. Very soon they would win this strike and then all over the nation the farmers would follow their lead.

Gradually the mood in the picket camps changed. Blockade runners had made their appearance. Some were nonstriking farmers, others the employees of distributors, and a few may have been hired provocateurs. Farmer bands grew larger, up to a hundred men. Obstacles were placed on the highways to halt the trucks, and milk was dumped. Whereas normally scores of trucks carrying milk and other farm produce entered Sioux City daily, now only a few got through.

When farmers saw the August 16 papers they laughed, but with tight lips. It appeared that, in line with Mr. Hoover's pleas, they had created jobs. The sheriff of the county in which Sioux City lay had openings for a hundred deputies, and the federal unemployment director for Iowa was busily recruiting them.

The deputies were sent to the highways with orders to smash up the barricades. The pickets had developed systems. They had fastened ropes around railroad ties and spiked planks, and, when a truck approached, they would draw them over the highway. The deputies flashed their new badges and they ordered and threatened. But the pickets continued to barricade the roads.

Some progress in the negotiations with the distributors was being made. A price increase on fluid milk sold at retail was agreed upon. But it was still far below cost of production.

Besides, the "Milo Reno men" had no intention of ending the picketing. The price of their butterfat and eggs, set in the Eastern markets, had not risen. Even in the slow livestock marketing season there was always some traffic into the

Sioux City stockyards, and the strikers wanted to set an example by closing the city tight.

South Dakota Holiday farmers were cooperating by blockading the Sioux City roads on their side. When a sheriff threatened a crowd of four hundred with a shotgun, it was taken away from him and thrown into a patch of weeds.

Meanwhile some Iowa farmers, answering the deputies, tried a blockade of American flags. When a truck was sighted, a picket would stand in the road and wave a flag. Such barricades proved ineffectual, however, so the pickets went back to their railroad ties and spiked planks. Once half a dozen livestock trucks got through, and farmers pursued them to the stockyards. City police and deputies finally drove the farmers off.

As if to prove their determination, strikers halted a couple of freight trains that were carrying milk and livestock. At the same time farmers got a lesson in economics, if they needed any. Even though few hogs were reaching the Sioux City market, hog prices at the market dropped lower, for the basic price was established in Chicago. If for some reason no hogs were to reach Chicago, then the figure would be set according to the flow and demand in other markets.

The big livestock market at Omaha, on the Iowa-Nebraska line a hundred miles south of Sioux City, was the next target. To cut off access from Iowa, farmers had also to blockade Council Bluffs, on the Iowa side of the line. The Council Bluffs' sheriff was of a far more belligerent disposition than Sioux City's.

"I'm going to keep the highways open if I have to deputize a regiment," he promised.

Unemployment being what it was, he had no difficulty in recruiting his army. But his soldiers were at best raw. One of them, while demonstrating a riot gun, killed another.

A troop of fifty deputies attacked a roadside camp, using tear gas and—so the farmers claimed—lead bullets. A terrible report spread over the countryside: women and children had been in the camp and the deputies had fired without warning. It was true that women and children had been present, although none was hurt. The tear gas had had the same effect as in Cedar County: the farmers had attacked. They had smashed the windows of one of the deputies' cars before the army retreated.

Another troop of deputies seized a dozen strikers who refused to break up a picket camp and hustled them to jail in Council Bluffs. That night—it was August 25—the jail filled to overflowing as the deputies continued to raid along the highways. By morning forty-three Holiday men were behind bars.

All over western Iowa the farm telephones were ringing.

Milo Reno was in Des Moines, meeting with the Holiday leaders of other states, when newspapermen inquired about the Council Bluffs trouble. He answered that it was news to him. As usual the reporters didn't believe him, and as usual he was telling the truth.

Reno called up Dan Turner and told him he ought to get the farmers out of jail, and moreover the time was at hand for calling Middle West governors to a conference to put some pressure on Washington. Dan said nothing doing to both suggestions. The expensive Cow War had hurt him politically. Now he had buses standing by for moving troops into the troubled areas. Dan was still between the devil and the deep blue sea, and the storm was whipping the waters and the devil was laughing.

By now the western Iowa sheriffs were frantically telephoning to Des Moines. They reported truck caravans of farmers moving toward Council Bluffs. They had seen Holiday men pull their cars onto the main highways, and, grim-faced, settle themselves for swift drives.

The sheriff at Council Bluffs drew his forces around the jail as if for a siege. Detectives from Omaha arrived to stiffen his raw troops. Machine guns were mounted.

The farmers arrived by twos and half dozens and dozens until 3,000 men in overalls were standing around the county jail contemplating the citizens, men exactly like themselves, who were now behind the bars. They muttered of deputies firing on women and children and spoke of America and freedom. The word "revolution" was heard. They saw themselves as Minute Men pushed beyond endurance, as King George had pushed the Colonists. If a revolution were to come, they saw it as a revolution in defense of the Constitution rather than against it.

The sheriff was acquainted with the temper of the crowd. It would attack, he realized, and very soon. Tear gas would not be enough. Machine guns would halt the attack, but the slaughter was certain to be terrible.

Dan Turner hadn't ordered the troops into the buses, so the blood of the farmers would be on the sheriff's head.

In this moment of crisis a farmer asked to pass through the deputies' lines, saying that he had a solution. The sheriff hastily granted permission. The farmer explained that he owned some unencumbered property and if bail for the prisoners was set within his means he would furnish it.

The sheriff grasped at the offer. A bond was signed, the doors were unlocked, and the prisoners filed out. After a little while the crowds melted away.

"The Old Printing Shop" (1962)

Frank Luther Mott

Another native Iowan to win the Pulitzer Prize, Frank Luther Mott's first calling was journalism, though he was also an accomplished creative writer. Born on a farm in Keokuk County, Mott was moved by his father, a restless Quaker newspaper editor, first to What Cheer, where he edited the weekly What Cheer Patriot, *and then to Tipton, Audubon, and Marengo. Mott attended Simpson College in Indianola and assumed his first editorship, much to his father's delight, at Boone County's Grand Junction* Globe. *In 1917, he left Iowa to earn an MA and PhD from Columbia University, parlaying those credentials into a teaching gig at the University of Iowa upon his return. In 1927, he was appointed the director of the U of I School of Journalism, a post he would hold for fifteen years. The Pulitzer came for his four-volume work* A History of the American Magazine, *though more of Mott's heart and soul is revealed in his intimate book of essays* Time Enough *(1962). This excerpt, which originally appeared in the* Palimpsest, *also appeared in* Time Enough. *In it, Mott sheds light on one of Iowa's calling cards—the spirited, independent weekly newspaper.*

We called it a "country" printing office, because its chief output was a "country" newspaper. Nowadays we talk of the "community" newspaper. The word "country" is now applied mainly to hillbilly music and a curious kind of fellow known as a "bumpkin" or a "hayseed." Like the words "villain," "boor," and "churl," all of which originally meant countryman or farmer, the word "country" itself seems to have descended in the scale of respectability. The philological standing of this word-symbol appears to have followed the downward curve of the countryman's economic status.

My father was not ashamed to call himself a "country" editor: he was proud of the designation and the vocation. He hoped I might follow in his footsteps; and in recommending such a career to me when I was a boy, he said that it had been his observation that, except for an occasional rascal or drunkard, the editor was always looked up to in his small community. It might not be a big puddle, Father said, but the editor was always one of the big frogs in it. I think that was true. Whatever hierarchy of leadership the country town possessed held assured places for the editors—or at least one of the editors of the two or three local papers. The editor was usually a political oracle; and he was sometimes sent to the legislature or appointed to state office. He was actually a liaison bringing the outside world of events and situations together with the life of the home community. He was supposed to be the best-informed man in town on questions of the day. "They expect the editor to know everything," said my father, and added, "You must get a good college education."

The plant from which he issued his weekly newspaper and in which he conducted a job-printing business consisted of a "front office" and a "back office." The former was much the smaller and was devoted to editorial and management activities, and the latter contained the mechanical department. In most midwestern towns in the Eighteen-nineties, the printing office was all in one room; and that was chiefly because the editor and manager was himself a printer and carried his editorial sanctum with him while he worked at the case or the press. Entering the front door of such an office, one walked directly into a fascinating confusion of characteristic smells, sounds, litter, and orderliness within disorder. But in our shops there was always a "front office," because Father had never learned the printer's trade; and besides he liked privacy for conferences with visitors, for business transactions, and for writing.

I set my first type in the office of my father's Tipton *Advertiser* in 1896, when I was ten years old. My first copy was a piece of reprint credited to "Ex." to indicate that it had been taken from some paper obtained by "exchange"; and it probably had bounced around among many papers before Father had clipped it from one of his own "exchanges." It was a bit of verse with "run-in" instead of broken lines, dealing with a man's troubles in the spring, from housecleaning, wet feet and colds, too much gardening, and so on, in which every stanza (paragraph) ended with the plaintive plea: "Listen to my tale of wo!" It took me three or four evenings, working after school, to get this masterpiece of wit into pica type. I had almost finished the second stickful when, in my awkwardness, I dropped the whole thing on the floor. The printers laughed, thinking that now the boy was getting his first experience with pi; but when I scrambled down off the high stool to pick up the remains, I found the type intact in the stick! I had not learned to justify my lines properly, but had forced thin spaces in so that every line was very tight; indeed they were so tight that the type could scarcely be removed from the stick when it was ready for dumping on the galley.

I had plenty of experience with pi [printer's type] after that, however. Some years later, helping out in a rush hour when we were late getting to press, I removed my case, which was "poor" in type by that time, from the stand in order to shake it (a method of getting the remaining type out of the corners of the boxes and making it easier to pick up); but in my clumsy hurry, I dropped the entire case. There it was, pied all over the floor. I turned in dismay toward the foreman—and knocked a full galley of type ready for the forms off a galley rack. If I had not been the editor's son, I should have been booted out of the back door.

But usually setting type was, if not fun, at least mildly pleasurable. Monotonous it was, indeed, but there were always the twin challenges of speed and accuracy. On a Saturday, when cases were full and the office was clean and comparatively quiet after the hurly-burly of a Thursday press-day, followed by the "throwing-in" of Friday, when the type was returned to the cases—then it was that setting type was peculiarly satisfying. Beginning with a new case, the boxes rounded up full, and the type cool and damp from fresh distribution, was a little like sitting down before a generously loaded table—just as working from an almost empty case, with dust at the bottom of the boxes, had been like starvation diet.

Sometimes the copy itself was interesting and instructive. I enjoyed setting up my father's editorial in bourgeois [a popular typeface] (pronounced *berjoice*); and I was always pleased when I found an excerpt from the current *McClure's* or *Harper's*, sent out by the magazine as promotion, on my hook. But how inexpressibly boresome was the monthly job of setting the patent medicine notices in nonpareil!

My father called his group of employees "the force." It consisted of a foreman, two all-round printers, two lady compositors, and a "devil" who worked after school and on Saturdays.

At least, such was the personnel when my brother and I took turns "dwelling" on the Tipton *Advertiser* in the mid-nineties. Our duties ranged from sweeping the floor and burning trash in the back yard to setting type and learning to feed the small jobber. Cleaning up after press-day was no easy task, for wastepaper, rags grimy with grease from the press, and dabs of sticky printer's ink seemed to be everywhere. Moreover, our job was complicated by the printers' habit of chewing tobacco. It was commonly said that printers were subject to lead-poisoning because they were constantly handling type, which contains a considerable proportion of lead in its composition, and that the best antidote was chewing tobacco. This was probably a medical fable invented as an alibi by nicotine users; however, most printers chewed plug tobacco, and the "devil" had to cope with their expectoration. We improvised spittoons from the heavy, small boxes in which we had received shipments of type and plates, filling them with sawdust and placing them conveniently near the type-stands, stones, and presses; but the chewer's aim was often imperfect.

Father was always particular about his foremen, and I remember them all as men of good character and some skill in "the art preservative of arts. " Three papers that Father owned at various times he eventually sold to his foremen. For the other printers, he often had to take what he could get, and they sometimes drank too much; indeed, I remember that we were often late with the first issues following the Fourth of July and Christmas because of trouble getting reorganized after the sprees that many printers regarded as their right on those holidays. I do not wish to wrong the average printer of those days: many of them were men of industrious habit and excellent character. My Uncle Artie worked in Father's printing office for several years; he was a fine, spruce young man who excited my unbounded admiration by dressing up in approved bicycle costume—sweater, tight pants, and black stockings—in the evenings and riding a highwheeler along the wooden sidewalks and dusty streets of What Cheer.

Itinerant printers appeared once in a while, and sometimes, when job-work was plentiful, they were welcomed and put immediately to work. They came unannounced from nowhere, and they disappeared without warning into limbo. They had rainbows 'round their shoulders that lured them always to the next town, or into the next state. "Tourist typos" my father called them. They usually brought some curious craft secrets with them—a new ingredient for our homemade blocking glue, a secret for a paste for "single wraps," a formula for an ink to imitate embossing.

Usually these wanderers would stay with us no more than three or four weeks at the most, but I remember one man in his thirties who declared his intention to settle down, and who stuck with us for over a year. He was the son of parents who were circus performers and he had been trained as a child aerialist; but a fall from a trapeze had injured his feet and turned him from the big tops to the printing office. He was tattooed all over the upper part of his body; and when he worked near the big window of the shop in the summertime with his shirt off for coolness, he drew such a crowd on the sidewalk and made such a scandal that a sleeveless undershirt had to be prescribed minimum clothing. Whether this offended him, or what it was, one morning he simply did not show up. He left no debts behind him; indeed he had a couple of days' pay due him and he had paid his landlady ahead for board and room. Apparently the old wanderlust had carried him off between days. We never heard of him again.

The climax of the week in the printing office was the Thursday press-day. The stress and strain, hustle and hurry of the weekly effort to "get out" on time brought the whole office to a high pitch of activity. Putting the last paragraphs of news in type picked from nearly empty cases, setting the last heads, correcting the galley proofs with swift care, marking and placing the corrected galleys for the make-up man—all these things were parts of the planned urgency of press-day. What a welcome sound was the rat-tat-tat of mallet on planer which announced that the front-page form was ready to lock up in its chase! While the heavy form was being transferred to the bed of the press, we were laying clean papers on the stones and tables in readiness for the operation of hand-folding the edition. Also someone was preparing the patent mailer which, when it worked, addressed the folded papers; and another was laying out the wrappers for the single-list of papers to be dispatched to a distance. To help with the folding, the editor often recruited his whole family. My own mother, when her family was small, used to help fold papers on press-day. Some editors' wives worked so much in the office that they became practical printers, and occasionally one of these small plants was operated entirely by the editor's family. But on any paper, the tensions of press-day were bound to affect all the editor's family, and everyone helped as he or she could—with the news, the mechanical work, the folding, wrapping, and mailing, and the final carting of the papers to the post office.

My father was a controversialist in his editorial columns, especially on party matters; but he was never violent.... Occasionally [he] would with some effort strike a lighter note. The most famous piece he ever wrote was about a prayer he had heard a country preacher offer one Sunday. This was in the midst of the drought of 1898, and also in the time of the Spanish-American War. Here is the prayer as Father set it down on his arrival at home, and as he published it in his paper the following week:

> And O Lord, we ask for rain. Thou has taught us to come to Thee to ask for what we need, and we need rain. Thy servants of old prayed for rain, and their prayers were heard. Elijah prayed for rain, and his prayer was answered. The ground is parched, the grass is dying, the heat oppresses us so we can hardly breathe. O Lord, give us refreshing rain!
>
> We prayed for rain last week, and it has not come yet. Perhaps we did not need it as badly as we thought. Now the farmers say we will not have half a crop unless we have rain soon, but then some would say that anyway. But we know we need rain! O Lord, we need money to carry on this righteous war for humanity, and we need crops to get the money with; so, Lord, give us rain that we may have the crops.
>
> Thou hast tempered the winds to our battleships. The typhoons and the hurricanes of the Tropics have not molested them. Thou hast given us the victory, and we praise Thy name...

The story ended simply by telling how, as the editor drove home that afternoon, he noticed a cloud in the northwest "as small as a man's hand," and how that night the whole countryside received a generous downpour.

My father never thought his work trivial or of little consequence. We all looked upon our paper as the historian of many lives. We know that we put the town and country down in black and white—joys and sorrows, good and ill, peace and war, prosperity and failure. We watched the growth and development of the community, the decay of some institutions, the setting of new patterns. Our paper recorded all these things, bringing our people and the little episodes of their lives and the town's events together within the compass of a few columns weekly. Thus any country paper welds together all the elements of its social group in a continuing history.

The country paper of the nineties and the first decade of the new century seems to me to have performed three services—in some instances badly, indeed, but in many very well. It was the contemporary historian of local events; it offered an editorial column that was often thoughtful and sometimes influential; it contributed to the economic welfare of its community by affording an advertising medium and by acting as a leader in progressive movements.

For many years now, everything in America has been irresistibly swept up into the prodigious heaps of the great cities and their sprawling suburbs. But hometown papers remain to serve many small towns throughout the nation. The weekly of today, however, is not the same country paper I knew as a boy; it has a linotype, it is illustrated by local pictures, it is smarter, it serves its advertisers better. Nor is the town it serves the same; it is no longer a semi-isolated hamlet, undisturbed by the blare of automobile horns, unstirred by the incursion into its midst of the strange phantasmagoria of "show business" on electronic screens in every home.

But in spite of changing patterns, the home paper of today has the same spirit of neighborliness and service that it has always had, and continues to integrate the life of its community.

Two Letters from an Iowan in Vietnam (1968)

Frederick O. Phelps

While many young Iowans protested the Vietnam War at colleges and universities throughout Iowa in 1968, Colesburg, Iowa, native Fred Phelps documented the daily horrors and triumphs of the conflict from the central highlands of Vietnam, where he served as an Army Nurse Corps officer. Dedicated to nursing and the armed services, Phelps retired with the rank of Colonel in 1989, returning to his Delaware County hometown shortly thereafter. The author's timeless lament in this 1968 letter to the editor ("Despite sporadic demonstrations, both pro and con, about this war, it seems apparent that complacency and a spirit of procrastination still prevail") reads as if it might have been written today. The second letter, dated May 5, 1968, Phelps addresses to his friends Merle and Kay, a married couple then living in Quincy, Illinois. Ellen, Phelp's wife's name, also appears at the top of the letter in longhand (not transcribed here). The author also hand-writes, "I'll answer your tape as soon as it comes. I hope!!" in reference to audio recordings exchanged back and forth.

"Army Nurse Writes to the *Herald Whig*"

After seven months in Vietnam, I wonder if each of your readers are as aware of this "war" that is going on over here as I am? As a registered nurse and a member of the Army Nurse Corps, I have to see the worst aspects of it. I am referring to those of severe physical injury, mental anxiety and disturbance, prolonged suffering and more often than I like to admit—Death. I wish that I did not have to witness these things. I would prefer the insulation of seeing and hearing only statistical reports and newspaper headlines about offensives, skirmishes, assaults, and body counts. Instead, for me and many more thousands like me, the war is now a long and terrible list of individual tragedies. The impact of the situation we are in cannot escape me, and I sincerely hope that a personal communication from me will make a lasting impression of the gravity of the situation on each of you at home.

As the economists reassure us, it may be fiscally possible to cope with a war on poverty, race problems, continued urban development and crime, and others along with the "real war" that is going on, but I assure you that it is not emotionally possible for those who are here fighting it. With continuing outbreaks such as we are witnessing, it won't be long before an impact of terribleness, futility, and personal involvement will hit each and every American citizen, no matter how oblivious of the present situation he may now be. Despite sporadic demonstrations, both pro and con, about this war, it seems apparent that complacency and a spirit of procrastination still prevail.

I can assure the reader that one day at our hospital would make a true believer out of anyone. Please give Vietnam your undivided attention and make a conscious effort to support and encourage all reasonable approaches for people at home to terminate this situation we are in. It is a very small sacrifice that each of you can make.

Frederick O. Phelps

5 May 1968
An Khe, Vietnam

Dear Merle and Kay:

It is just a few minutes past three in the morning and things are very quiet around the hospital, so I thought that I would take advantage of the lack of activity and start this letter to you. I have just finished with my regular ward rounds, have redone the emergency drug cart on the intensive care unit and just prior to beginning this letter, helped with the feeding of the twins. They have now had their diapers changed, their bottoms powdered, and their stomachs refilled so they had ought to be comfortable for the next three or four hours.

The twins that I am referring to are the boy and girl that were delivered here a little over a week ago now. They are really precious little Dickens and are the best natured little things. I guess they know that they had better be with nine more children at home. And, what a place to have to grow up in. I guess it is a blessing that they don't know what lies ahead of them. Their mother is getting along fairly well now. She had some physical problems both before and following surgery, but I think that she is considered quite well on the mend at the present time.

Tonight is certainly a much quieter night than we had last night. Just as we came on duty last evening they were isolating a Vietnamese soldier who they thought had meningitis, so he is now out of isolation and back on the Vietnamese ward. We also admitted a G.I. just as we came on duty who had sort of raised havoc in his company and then had a "spell" of some kind. We finally got him in bed and quieted down and then he slept the remainder of the night. But, the thing that kept us really busy during the entire night was the young fellow that we had admitted to the hospital six days ago when a rocket had landed in his company area. He was severely injured at the time and had had a five and a half hour operation. He was in pretty bad shape all along but he seemed to be doing satisfactorily considering all the things that were wrong with him. Well, at about 2:30 in the morning he went bad and we worked diligently and feverishly over the remainder of the shift until we went off duty at 7:00 A.M. We had him on the respirator with 100% oxygen going, more I.V.s, whole blood, and were taking his vital signs every fifteen minutes. There was about a five-minute interval about 3:15 when he did not breathe on his own at all. But, we got him to going again after some rather fast and furious work. We knew, however, that it was just a matter of time. Finally, he expired at 9:20 A.M. It was sort of hard for all of us to take. Such a healthy-appearing, robust, and strapping young man who had lots of spunk, but the odds were against him and they finally won out after a valiant struggle of nearly one week. He had so many injuries that it is a wonder that he even lived until they got him here to our emergency room and then through surgery. After making it through all of that procedure, you sort of have higher hopes of them making it even though they do have extensive and very major wounds.

Well, I just had an interruption. As I was sitting here I thought that I heard the helicopter at the helipad starting up. Sure enough it was. There had just been a call received through the shortwave radio that there two wounded individuals at "L-Z John." This is just outside our perimeter a little over a stone's throw away. When the helicopter returned in about five minutes roundtrip (so you know how close it was), there were two older sergeants who were just new in country and were spending the night in that area as a part of their jungle school orientation. They had received fragment wounds which were not serious. They were very lucky as one of them had a rather large laceration above his right eye and just a half inch or so back it would have hit his temple. Miracles never seem to cease, it seems. Those are the first two casualties that we have received here in quite a while. These two men brought with them the word that there has been a rather "sizable" number of N.V.A. [North Vietnamese Army] spotted near our post. I hope they do more than just spot them!!!

I am typing in our empty operating room where there is an air-conditioner going. It is just terribly sultry and humid tonight. Usually it cools off in the evening, but tonight seems to be an exception to this generality.

Well, I have had quite a lapse in trying to finish this letter. It is now a quarter past eight in the evening. Just as I was in the midst of typing the above paragraph, I heard the helicopter take off again. So, I went to the Admissions and Dispositions office to inquire what the reason was. I learned that one of the checkpoints just outside of our perimeter had been overrun by NVA, or VC [Viet Cong]. And, that we were to be getting several casualties. Well, we got them alright. Two were dead on arrival, and then there were about eight others. Oh, how terribly injured they were. One had both legs gone at the area of the mid-thigh. Also one side of his face was gone, and the other side there would be air bubbling out of the side of his face near the eye every time he would breath. He was in such terrible condition that it is amazing that he was still living. He continued to live and then they finally decided that they had better make arrangement to evacuate him to the 67th Eva[caution] Hospital in Quin Non. We learned that he lived for about two hours after getting there. All the rest had multiple fragment wounds in various places. One of the fellows had lost his foot and had abdominal injuries. And, so it goes. I will not go into any greater detail simply because of the fact that I have described these things before and they are not very pleasant. One patient died on the operating room table just as they finished surgery. So, it has been a real mess again. So, from three o'clock this morning until 7:30 A.M. I spent all my time in the emergency room starting intracatheters for the administration of blood and I.U. fluids, taking vital signs, preparing patients for surgery, reassuring casualties, etc. It is a big job and a very tiring one. This is the second morning in a row now that my feet and legs have just ached miserably from being so tired. And, it is so difficult to sleep in the daytime because of the fact that is has been so terribly hot. But, I cannot be any other way than thankful, as I still have my feet and legs, and I still have a bed to sleep in, and I am well. What more could a person ever ask for?

We also received several patients during the day today who were admitted with heat exhaustion. This is getting to be quite a problem because of the extreme hot weather during the day and the lack of the temperature to fall in the evening hours.

I had a wonderful letter the day before yesterday from a friend of mine who is a nurse and is in Korea. He and his family will be stationed at Fort Dix, New Jersey, when we both returns to the States—he the latter part of this month. We are looking forward to some weekend when we will be able to spend a couple of days together sharing experiences that the two of us have had in this side of the world this past year. I also had a very nice letter from a nursing school classmate of mine who is still working at the Finley hospital in Dubuque. It was good to hear from her and she brought me up to date on the activities of many of the other classmates whom I had not heard from or about in quite a while.

Well, I think that I had better bring this to a close for now. It will not be too long until I have to prepare to go to work, and there are reports that we might be expecting more difficulty tonight. So, I thought that I had better rather abruptly finish this letter to you rather than take the chances of delaying getting it mailed any longer. I will be writing again, and I am hoping to hear more from you.

Sincerely,

Fred

Two Letters from Iowa Social Activists (1968, 1972)

Ralph and Ruth Scharnau

Classics in the making, these letters by Dubuque's Ralph and Ruth Scharnau were only recently donated to the Iowa State Historical Society and made available to scholars. The couple embodies the Iowa spirit of civic engagement; Ralph holds membership in the NAACP, the Sierra Club, ACLU, and Amnesty International, while writing monthly op-ed columns for the Dubuque Telegraph Herald *and teaching U.S. history at Northeast Community College in Peosta. A member of the ACLU since 1966 and a long-time teacher of special needs students, Ruth has been a lifetime member of the NAACP, a member of Amnesty International, and, at the time of her letter, a Sierra Club member alarmed by the potential environmental impact of the trans-Alaska pipeline. Though forty years old, the letters could not be more timely—one calling for racial reconciliation and brotherhood in public life; the other urging restraint in our relentless, sometimes rapacious pursuit of fossil fuels.*

April 9, 1968

Dear Mrs. King,

We are deeply grieved by the assassination of the Rev. Dr. Martin Luther King, Jr. He committed his life to humanity, making religious dogma a living truth. The life he gave will, we pray, have the redemptive result he would wish.

Dr. King has a special significance to us personally. It was during his leadership of the civil rights movement that we became aroused to the negro's struggle for justice and equality. It was, indeed, the historic March on Washington of August 28, 1963 that marked the beginning of our active involvement in the crusade for black liberation.

But we hold the memory and teachings of Dr. King dear for another reason. As members of the Religious Society of Friends, we regard Dr. King as not only a great man but a great Quaker. It was his concern to make Christianity not merely a spiritual exercise but a program of social action. This union of faith and practice is fundamental among Friends. And his dedication to the power of nonviolence gives new meaning and dimension to the heritage of Quaker pacifism.

Although unknown to you personally, we are moved to express our feeling about the greatness incarnate in your husband. In this hour of trial and sorrow, we would have you know that the spirit and love of Martin Luther King are penetrating the darkness cast by the ghettos in American cities and the war-scarred terrain in Vietnam.

Love and Peace,

Ralph and Ruth Schnarau

1810 N. Grandview
Dubuque, Iowa 52001
April 22, 1972

President Richard M. Nixon
The White House
Washington, D.C.

Dear Mr. Nixon:

It was with distress that I read the statement made by Mr. William T. Pecora, Undersecretary of the Interior (March 20, 1972) in which he said that the Department of the Interior does not feel that another public hearing at this time is necessary in regard to the trans-Alaska pipeline. His implication in his statement is that the public hearings are not particularly or rational.

I appeal to you, Mr. President, to grant at least 90 days for a full review of the nine-volume environmental impact statement on the proposed pipeline. Following this, there needs to be a full public hearing. Your responsibility, as well as that of every citizen of this country, is not only to those of us who live now, but to future generations. To buckle under the pressure of a few profit-hungry oil companies, and in the process sacrifice the well-being of untold numbers of wildlife as well as the unspoiled beauty of the land through soil erosion, etc. would be unforgivable.

Please, Mr. Nixon, give us the time for this most crucial issue!

Sincerely,

Mrs. Ruth Scharnau

"We All Worked Together: A Memory of Drought and Depression" (1978)

James Hearst

Born on his grandfather's farm outside Cedar Falls in Black Hawk County, James Heart is strongly associated with the University of Northern Iowa, where he taught for over thirty years, and where, today, the handsome Hearst Center for the Arts serves as a lasting monument to his legacy. Considered by Paul Engle to be the best farm poet in America and praised by Robert Frost, Hearst wrote what he knew, having helped work Maplehearst Farm with his brother Charles until 1941. Like many of the Iowans in this collection, the author lived an all-American childhood, attending a one-room schoolhouse, perfecting a fastball that would earn him a spot in semi-pro baseball, and yearly harvesting the fruit of the land. At the age of nineteen, Heart broke his neck while diving into the Cedar River, an accident that left him wheelchair-bound for the rest of his life. Best known for his thirteen books of poems, Hearst is here represented by one of a handful of essays he wrote about Iowa life collected in the State Historical Society publication Time Like a Furrow *(1981). First published in the Palimpsest in 1978, "We All Worked Together" conveys firsthand the Great Depression as Iowans experienced it— drought, grasshopper plagues, "Wild Jackasses" in the farmers' protest movement, farm foreclosures, and, ultimately, redemption.*

I think it was the family spirit that carried us through, we did all work together. Everyone suffered from the drought and Depression, but our troubles also concerned illness and death. And this is where people suffer the most and are the most vulnerable. But the drought by itself caused enough anxiety. It came right after the worst of the Depression and piled another burden on the bent shoulders of all of us farmers. A description of it, though, lacks the abrasive wearing down of the experience as a mirror image lacks the presence of the person.

The worst of it began for us in 1934. I remember how the dust settled so thickly on the pastures that the cattle would not eat, and cows, calves, and steers wandered about, bawling their hunger. We found it hard to believe. We all knew about dust storms in the dry plains of the Southwest, but for drought and wind and dust to sweep, like a plague, over the fertile fields of Black Hawk County seemed a bad dream, not real. But it was real, all right.

We endured it for three years. I think it was the dust that gave Mother the shivers. She stuck paper strips along the windowsills, rolled rugs against the doors, but still it sifted in, dry and fine as talcum powder, but gritty to taste and touch. The dust left a film on dishes in the cupboard, on sheets folded in drawers, on woodwork and chairs, on people's faces and hair. Outside, if the wind blew, visibility would be cut to a few yards. Autos ran at midday with their headlights turned on. Drifts of dust piled against fences like snow, sometimes two and three feet high. Years later, after the ground had been plowed and planted many times, the stain could still be seen where the drifts had been.

Spring came with no rain. That was the first sign. The winter snow melted and ran off during a sudden thaw in March. The water could not soak into frozen ground, so it ran off down gullies and creeks. Even then, on the bare and frozen ground, the wind chiseled furrows and filled the air with dust. In April and May the ground baked in summer temperatures. Farmers stirred the ground as little as possible, and the damp patches dried almost before they turned up. But we sowed the oats, harrowed in the clover, and planted corn when the time came. This is what farmers do.

An old farmer once said: the time to plant corn is at corn-planting time. Crops are planted in their season. This wisdom lies deep in the farmer's blood. When spring comes he rises early, looks at the sky, tests for wind and temperature, and impregnates the earth with seed. He is his own almanac.

In the spring of 1934 we came in at the end of the day exhausted from the heat and flying dirt, and feeling there was no sense in what we were doing. In some places in the field where the dust devils came whirling, seeds were pulled right out of the ground. In other places the seeds lay dormant in dry earth. It takes moisture for any roots to grow, but my brother Charles did not dare set the corn planter deep enough to reach the damp earth because the seeds would smother. So we hoped for rain and plowed and disked and harrowed and planted just like our neighbors, without knowing what else to do.

Late in May a few showers fell and some of the kernels sprouted. But in July, when the corn needs an inch of rain every week, even the clouds burned off. The sun fired the stalks that had grown and left them waving dead, white tassels with no live pollen. The ears turned out to be stubby cobs with a few kernels on them. That fall, we chopped one hundred and twenty acres of corn to fill the silo, when eight acres should have done it.

The corn had to contend with more than the drought. Hordes of chinch bugs marched out of chinch bug country to attack it. Think of a voracious appetite surrounded by legs and equipped with a mouth and you have a chinch bug. It feeds on corn in its tender, succulent stage and leaves the corn rows in tatters, flapping like rows of scarecrows. I saw them as barbarians swarming over the field in cultivation. We tried to defend our fields. We took posthole augers and dug holes along the edges of the fields, holes a foot deep and about a rod apart. We half filled them with creosote. We trapped a lot of the bugs, and only the first half dozen rows of corn suffered. Once the plant became mature—stalks tough, leaves hard and shiny—the chinch bugs went away.

But more mischief came. Grasshoppers, like the locusts of the Bible, clouded the skies and settled on our oat fields. Grasshoppers have a nasty habit of eating just the small stem that fastens the oat kernel to the stalk. We were left with a field where empty heads of straw waved in the wind and the ground was covered with kernels. Chuck said, "We ought to have a flock of turkeys and let them clean up the fields."

Alfalfa was the one crop we had that did not wither. Apparently its roots dug deep enough to find moisture. It stayed green, bloomed, made two cuttings of hay. The grasshoppers did not harm it, I don't know why. But when we cut the last few rounds in the center of the field, grasshoppers hung from the alfalfa plants in bunches, a strange yield for a hayfield.

July was the worst month. Day after day the temperature rose above one hundred degrees. When we came out to the fields after dinner, the machines were almost too hot to touch. We wound the iron steering wheels with tape to protect our hands. One day at noon as we quit for dinner, one of the men jumped on my tractor fender to ride to the house. He jumped off faster than he jumped on. "Hell's bells!" he yipped. "It's like sitting on a hot stove."

In September rain came, rain that should have fallen during the summer. It had been a starved, withered, dried-up crop season. People just did without, and we all tried to hold together our livestock and machinery. A worn-out feeling slowed steps and lowered voices. No one died of despair, but we were glad when the year became history. We harvested what crops we had, feeling that we had done all we could.

The drought had followed the Great Depression. That was really a time that tried men's souls. One of our neighbors once said, "When you break a horse's spirit, he's no good anymore." I wondered if it was the same with men. I thought about it one night, sitting at the desk in my study. All of us—father, mother, brother, sister, and myself—involved in sweat, worry, debt, trying to keep the farm going. It seemed to me like a law of diminishing returns; the harder you worked, the less you received. I saw no way out.

Depressed prices for farm products existed years before the stock market break. Most city folk did not realize that since the end of World War I farmers had been ground between the millstones of high overhead and low prices. Many farmers blamed Herbert Hoover for pulling the rug out from under them when he withdrew support for the prices he had guaranteed. When the war was over, Hoover no longer needed hogs, corn, butter, eggs, sugar to feed the troops and our allies. So prices fell and stayed low all during the Twenties.

By 1930 our family reached out all its hands to stay alive. We knew we had the muscle, and we proved it. Father's paycheck from his job with the Iowa Farm Bureau helped bolster the bank balance. My sister, Louise, taught school and her check, when she got one—during the Depression schoolteachers were not paid regularly—went to the same place. Mother made cottage cheese, and she sold it and eggs to the Blue Bird Restaurant in town. I had a small check from my army insurance. Chuck ran the farm, tried to keep worn machinery in action, the pigs healthy, the hired men paid. Farm families suffered from the Depression in a way that was different from town families. When a factory worker lost his job and paycheck, he knew where he stood—probably in the bread line. A banker knew where he stood, too, and when his bank closed its doors, unable to meet its obligations, he jumped out of a ten-story window, or shot himself, or just went home and shriveled into a sick old man.

But on the farm the situation was not as clear. Farmers knew about debt. Most farms had a mortgage on them, the machines were not paid for, the livestock had been bought on loans. In normal times these obligations were paid off with money from the sale of crops and livestock. Now, with such low prices, the money failed to appear when loans, bills, and interest came due. We ate what we produced—no one went hungry on farms. But the effort to hold together all the things they had worked for sometimes marked a man and his family for life.

One day Chuck and I received a phone call from a man who had once worked for us. He had been working in the John Deere factory in Waterloo. John Deere paid better wages than a farmer paid. Now he felt the abrasive touch of unemployment. "Come and get me," he said over the phone. "I'll work just for my food. I ain't going on relief."

Already our two hired men worked on pretty slim wages, but they each had a house to live in and food to eat. Chuck said, "What will we do? We haven't work enough for another man."

But we cranked up our Model T Ford and drove to Waterloo. I will never forget the sight of empty parking lots, taverns closed, the factory dirty and silent. No smoke from the forges, no hurrying men, no railroad cars shuttling in the yards, no clatter of machines, nothing but emptiness and the stale, brassy smell of poverty.

We found Herman standing in line at the Salvation Army headquarters. "I knew you'd come," he said, "but I thought maybe I'd get a bowl of soup."

We took him home, fed him, and turned him over to Mother. She needed help in the garden-trash cleaned up, spading done, lawn mowed. "Do you want to stay with us?" she asked.

"No," he said, "I'll walk. It ain't but four miles. I'll come every day. Why, Mrs. Hearst, I don't know when I've eaten a piece of meat."

"What about your wife and children?" Mother asked.

"My wife, she works at a little cafe and eats there. The kids get a free meal at school. She brings home scraps for the kids' supper."

That's the way it was. Herman walked out in the morning and back at night. Mother's cooking filled out the hollows in his cheeks, and the sun soon changed his factory pallor. We had plenty for him to do—on a farm, work has a habit of appearing whenever there is a spare pair of hands to do it. He kept the lawn mowed, the garden weeded, the chicken house repaired, and he chopped down a couple of dead trees. He screwed new hinges on sagging barn doors, shored up loose windowpanes with putty, and reshingled a spot on a shed roof where a tree limb had fallen during a thunderstorm.

When summer came, he worked in the fields loading hay bales and shoveling oats from the combine. Late in the fall, Chuck found him a job with a farm machinery dealer, and he walked four blocks to work instead of four miles. He earned enough to feed his family. Perhaps President Roosevelt did not lead the country into the promised land, but he pulled the economy out of its rut, dusted it off, and began to make it run again.

The terrible days of Depression put marks on people never to be erased. Families found themselves penniless when the banks closed. These were good, hardworking people whose entire savings disappeared like smoke. Retired farmers begged for jobs as janitors in schools and churches, as night watchmen in factories. One morning I heard on the radio that one of our neighbors had gone out in the field with a shotgun and killed himself so his wife and children could have his insurance. The mortgage on his farm had been foreclosed. He had nowhere to go.

"What's the good of foreclosing a mortgage?" Mother asked.

"The bank or insurance company can't sell the farm, can't even rent it and expect to get the rent."

"But that's the way things are done," Chuck said. "It's an old custom to kick a man when he's down."

The Farmers' Holiday movement spread like an epidemic. When a farm was foreclosed and the farmer's goods and livestock sold at auction, the neighbors made it a "penny sale." Everything the auctioneer offered for sale brought the bid of one cent. When the sale ended, the livestock, grain, machinery, and household goods were returned to the owner for pennies. And one look at the hard, determined faces of the men surrounding the auctioneer discouraged any outsider from raising the bid. In western Iowa a judge tried to stop such a sale with a legal writ and found a rope around his neck and the other end over a tree limb, and there were plenty of hands to pull it tight if it had come to that.

Creameries were picketed, cans of milk and cream dumped into ditches, tons of butter destroyed. It was violence born of desperation in an attempt to call attention to the farmer's troubles.

One July morning I drove two miles north to the Benson Creamery to see with my own eyes what was going on. About a half mile from the creamery a truck slowly moved across the road and blocked me. Two men with rifles got out, and I was shocked to see old Einer Clausson and Jake Miller.

I said, "What in hell do you guys think you're doing?"

Old Einer looked me right in the eye. "You ain't going any further, Jim. No one but us members can go down to the creamery. What are you doing over here anyway, you boys don't milk?"

"I just came over to see if what we heard is true."

"If you heard we was dumping milk and cream, you heard right. Right now that creamery is a dead horse."

I shook my head. "You, Einer, and you, Jake, with guns for god's sake. Are you really dumping the trucks?"

"You're damn right. Just look down that road. See that big new truck upside down in the ditch? You think the fairies did it?"

The truck lay on its side, and you could smell the milky suds that filled the ditch. I looked down the road past the creamery and there was another group of men with guns. I said, "Do you really think this kind of monkey business will raise prices?"

"We can sure raise hell, and maybe some of the big bugs will get it through their thick heads that we're hurting out here."

I thought about it. "I suppose the papers are sending out reporters and photo men?"

"You bet," Jake said, "and more are coming. Now, Jim, you get out of here before you get in trouble. This ain't any business of yours, no skin off your nose."

It seemed ridiculous, but I didn't want to laugh. I said, "Go to hell, Jake. You're going to shoot me?" These men were my neighbors.

For the first time Jake grinned. "I might have to if you get fractious."

"Well," I said, "I'm all for you if this will help. But I think you have things bass ackward."

"Listen, boy," Jake said, "you go get you forty cows to milk night and morning, seven days of the week, and find the milk isn't even worth the feed. You can get damned tired of pulling tits."

I shifted into reverse. "OK, I guess I'm in the wrong pew. Good luck."

The Farmers' Holiday movement did startle the newspapers into headlines, even the staid *New York Times*. The farmer's predicament began to haunt the public—and Congress. It helped elect Franklin D. Roosevelt.

When I drove in the yard, Chuck had started for the house to wash for dinner. At the table he asked, "Are they really doing it?"

"They're doing it, and they mean business, too."

"Crazy as coots," Chuck said.

"That may be, but our friends Einer and Jake are on patrol with guns and they aren't kidding."

Mother asked, "Do you suppose the National Guard will be called out?"

Chuck said, "Probably some jackass will blast away and kill somebody. Then they'll run for cover."

I didn't think so. "Not these boys, they aim to stay until the whole affair gets national publicity. That's what they're after. They know dumping a few trucks of cream won't bring up prices."

"They give you a bad time?"

"They thought I was nosy. We aren't dairymen, they made a point of it."

Mother said, "You should have told them what you boys got for the last load of hogs you shipped to Chicago."

"After freight, commission, and trucking, just about enough to wad a shotgun," Chuck said in harsh tones.

"I never thought of it," I said. "I doubt if they'd listen. They're all hepped up over the dairy situation."

We ate slowly, thinking about our neighbors out on the roads with guns. Mother said there was strawberry shortcake for dessert. It lifted our spirits a little.

Chuck poured cream on his shortcake. "Those bastards in Washington can't get the sleep out of their eyes."

Mother said in a choked voice, "We have been through this before."

I didn't need to be reminded. A little over ten years before, just after World War I, farm prices took a nosedive while city folk whooped it up on the stock market. Even our own banker said, "If farmers would stay at home and tend to business and stop complaining, they'd be all right."

Our memories ran back over the years. It had been late in May 1923, the corn was planted, the oats up, the cows out to pasture. But the taxes had not been paid for over a year. How could they be paid? There was no money. Robert was now slowly dying of cancer, and I was just home from a two-year stay in the hospital after my diving accident. Imagine the money it took to pay hospital and doctor bills. How could a farmer already in debt for his farm stand so much expense? And farm prices had dropped in a well once the war was over, when no longer "Food Will Win The War." One son dying, one on crutches, both in their early twenties. How could Father and Mother rally from crushing blows like that? It must have hurt Father to walk into the bank knowing he owed so much money and could borrow no more. And so the taxes were not paid.

During World War I the government had urged farmers to plow up every acre of land they could find, raise all the hogs they could, and it would guarantee prices. When the war ended the government forgot prices, forgot the huge food factory that now had no buyers for its products. Fertile Iowa land went begging. No one wanted to buy it. In the city, people bought stocks on the feverish stock exchange, all hoping to be rich.

A family is not always crushed under the weight of misfortune.

The family ties grow closer, ties of courage and strength. Louise and Charles assumed duties they knew must be carried no matter how young and untested they were. The family did not sink into the quicksand of despair. Louise brought her friends home, and they filled the house with music and talk, jazz, cheese on rye, and spiked near-beer. Chuck dropped out of college to run the farm and help look after his two invalid brothers. Family life pulled itself up by its bootstraps.

One day, we received notice that the Sheriff would serve papers for nonpayment of taxes and offer part of the farm for sale. This seemed a humiliation that Mother and Father need not suffer, so on the day the Sheriff was to come Uncle George took time off from his busy medical practice to take them out to lunch. The Sheriff, who was a friend of Uncle George, agreed to come while they were gone. The three brothers offered to act as a reception committee.

That day the weather seemed ordinary. Neither the cattle nor the hogs behaved in an unusual way. Leaves moved in a light wind. The windmill wheel turned slowly. The sun shone with the same light it gave to the battles of the Somme and Gettysburg. Peas and carrots in the garden grew in the straight or crooked rows in which they were planted. But it was a portentous day for us as we three brothers sat at the dining-room table and ate our lunch.

The dog barked as a car drove in the yard. A tall, lean man without a hat stepped out, picked up his briefcase, walked briskly to the front door. Chuck opened it. "I'm Cap Wagner, the sheriff," he said. "This isn't my idea of a good time, but I wish you young men would listen while I read this summons to you."

He opened his briefcase, took out some papers, put on a pair of spectacles with silver rims, and in a dull, low voice read the summons. He folded the papers, put them in an envelope, and tossed it toward the center of the table. "OK," he said, "that's it. Give the papers to your dad when he comes back."

He went over to Bob and put his arm over his shoulder. "How are you getting along, young man?" he asked. "You're having a tough time and I admire your guts."

Bob's voice trembled, "Will the farm really be sold?"

The Sheriff shook his head. "You have a year to redeem it. Don't worry, Bob, your dad will get the taxes paid. It's just that the law says we have to do it this way. Remember me to your folks. So long." And he was gone.

It was a day burned in our memories. To lose part of the farm would be more than the family should have to bear. The farm was home. It was part of our life, like our own flesh and blood. I remember when a man we knew who lived in town called up Father and asked him if he was going to pay the taxes or would the 80 be for sale. We young folks took an instant dislike to the poor man and always treated him coldly after that.

Years later, when Bob was gone and anxiety and grief had dulled, we thought of this as the low point in our lives. Eventually, the taxes were paid and the land redeemed. We just dug in and faced what had to be faced and survived. But no one who weathered the Depression ever escaped without a kind of obsession for security.

A couple of good crop years and we were on the way up. We had discovered that working together made all the difference as we faced illness, death, felt the abrasive touch of despair. It was the working that kept us going. President Roosevelt once said, "There is nothing to fear but fear itself." That may have been just a political ploy, but after he said it, there was hope.

One morning, a couple of years after the worst of the Depression, I was out in the field disking in oats in a field along the road. Einer Clausson drove by with his milk truck and we waved to each other like the neighbors we were.

"THREE WORLDS" (1978)

WINIFRED M. VAN ETTEN

A product of the Palo Alto County town of Emmetsburg and Mount Vernon's Cornell College, Winifred Mayne Van Etten settled down in Mount Vernon, marrying contractor Bernard Van Etten, apprenticing under legendary Cornell professors Clyde and Jewell Tull, and, ultimately, joining them as colleagues after an MA from Columbia University. Her 1936 novel I Am the Fox *shocked the literary world by winning $10,000 in the Atlantic Monthly Press and Little, Brown, and Company novel competition. Because of the author's aversion to public attention, many of her early shorts were published under the nom de plume Janet McBroom, and, after the hubbub created by her prize-winning novel, she never published another. And what a loss. In the essay that follows, Van Etten relays beautifully, and with the full tonal range of a virtuoso writer, the innermost feelings of a young Iowa feminist circumscribed by a prairie so unending it sometimes evoked a sense of nihilism. As the author contemplates the challenges of modern Iowa, she calls us to greater and more transcendent responsibility, and to reverie in the face of hardship.*

Someplace in the family archives there is a large mounted photograph. It shows my father standing in the midst of his field of corn. He was a tall man, six feet two or more, and he was stretching as far as he could above his head to hang his derby hat on the highest ear of corn he could reach. There were higher ears, but this one was the best he could do. We lived on the edge of town and just beyond the town limits he had seven acres of land that he treated as a garden. No weed dared intrude. In the days when forty or forty-five bushels an acre was usual he in some years produced one hundred. As a child I assumed that a hundred bushels was normal. Sometimes I was allowed to help with the plowing. I drove the team; my father walked behind guiding the plow. When I reached the point at which, coming to the end of a row, I could turn the team, reverse the direction, and start back the other way without tearing up any corn hills, I regarded myself as an expert.

These were the days of the tall corn in Ioway.

Years later my husband and I picked up a hitchhiker from Connecticut. We noticed him staring at the crops along the highway. Finally, he spoke. "I don't think it's so very tall," he said. Obviously the only thing he had ever heard about Ioway (at least he did not confuse it with Ohio or Idaho) was that it is the place where the tall corn grows.

We tried to explain to him that tallness was no longer an object. No more did farmers cut their tallest stalks and take them to town where rival, mast-high specimens stood in a row in front of the bank. The cornpicker had put an end to the tall corn. Uniformity was now the goal, and Ioway was the place where the tall corn grew once—but now conformed to the demands of machines. Uniformity—that was the criterion of excellence. In Iowa. Ioway was gone.

The first world: the prairie

Ioway was my first world, the world of my very early childhood. No buffalo roamed there, but it was still pretty close to true prairie. We took long excursions across it. Rover trotted along in front, tail waving as debonairly as though he had not already covered many miles. Trinket stepped it off lightly, five people and a surrey apparently nothing to her flying slender legs. We had been on the way since before dawn on our annual trip to visit an uncle who lived fifty miles north of us near the Minnesota border. We had shivered at first in the morning chill, but now it was getting warm and there were many miles still to go. Fifty miles in a day for one horse pulling a carriage and five people was a long journey, but the trip could be made no other way. There was no railroad, hardly anything that could even be called a road, only a sometimes barely discernible trace through the tall prairie grass, and as we got farther north, skirting the edges of a big slough, there was water standing along or on what passed for a road. Now and then a fox eyed us suspiciously, and once an animal my father said was a wolf sent delicious chills through us as we recalled those stories of Russians tossing first one passenger then another from their vehicle to delay the ravening wolves.

But this wolf, if it was a wolf, seemed of a mind to tend to its own business or else it was of a peaceful disposition. Everything was peace: a soft June morning, banks of wild roses, the tall grasses, the reeds and cattails. The bobwhites whistled, the meadowlarks sang. Even my father sang, He couldn't carry a tune, but there were two lines of one ditty that he droned over and over in his monotone as we rode along. I never heard him sing more than the two lines and never except on the occasion of one of these family safaris:

> Oh, green was the grass on the road, on the way
> And bright was the dew on the blossoms of May.

Sometimes we all sang, mostly hymns, since those were the songs we all knew. We did the Crusaders' Hymn over and over. It seemed to fit this lovely, lonely world through which we were passing.

> Fair is the meadow
> Fairer still the woodlands
> Robed in the blooming garb of spring.

Jesus is fairer, Jesus is purer
Who makes the woeful heart to sing.

I was never a religious child in any conventional way, but somehow I sensed a connection between the woodlands, the meadow, and that purity we were taught to call Jesus at Sunday school. The son of God and man was a concept beyond me, the Holy Ghost complete befuddlement, but fairest Lord Jesus, the fair meadow, the fair woodlands, these gave me an intuition of oneness that, without owning the capacity to think about it, I felt included me.

Dark would be falling by the time we reached my uncle's farm, all of us hungry, all so dead tired that even the mattresses stuffed with corn husks felt and smelt good and whispered and rustled soothingly. In the morning there would be prayers in the neat little living room with its center table bearing a ten-pound Bible with Doré illustrations, a tall kerosene lamp, its double globes hand-painted with flowers, perhaps a big rosy shell on the lower shelf. Of course there was the cottage organ. If the decor was what every housewife felt it should be, there would be on the organ shelves some small ornaments; a china boot; a fancy box or two; and crowning glory of home decorations, a tall vase of peacock feathers. Such proofs of culture could only be surpassed by a stereopticon set by means of which we acquainted ourselves with far climes and countries while gaudy Japanese wind chimes tinkled in the open window. It never occurred to us that we might actually sometime see these places ourselves.

Our world was bounded by what amounted to a slightly modified frontier to the north of us and to the south the little town from which we had come. The town, a sort of rough excrescence on the smoothness of the prairie, had mud streets and electric light only in the stores except for a few affluent residences and those who had their own Delco systems. But it had the county courthouse and the jail, and once in a while an automobile was to be seen, usually driven by some young blade viewed with as much disapproval as one of Hell's Angels would be a half century later. Such a monster, if my mother was driving, would set Trinket prancing on her hind legs until some gallant from the sidewalk came out and held her head until the horror had passed.

The town had eight churches: six Protestant, two Catholic, plus a Catholic grade school and the quarters for the nuns and priests. God's Geese (the nuns), so-called by one of our family friends always admired for the rightness of her views, were seldom seen on the streets, but we were conscious of their presence just as we were of some sinister existence in the priest's house. The town also had at one time, according to my elders, nine saloons. One story said that an Irish emigrant came out in the early days, set a jug of whiskey down on the prairie, and the town grew up around it and fell at once to fighting as though Cadmus had sown the dragon's teeth there and not in Greece. For it was a divided town, half-Irish Catholic, half-Protestant, a mixture of Scandinavians, Germans, Scots, and English, the latter two often referred to as "remittance men" because their money was remitted to them from the old country.

But for my family the most important element in the town was the existence of three weekly papers, two Catholic and Democrat (they were considered one and the same thing), one Protestant and Republican of which my father was the owner and editor. No issue was too small for a Battle of the Boyne and my father was always in the midst of the fray. He used to try to prevent our seeing the other two papers, but somehow we always found out what he was being accused of that week. Sometimes he was said to have been found lying drunk in the gutter (he who was a teetotaler) surrounded by dead soldiers. At other times, in fact at all times, he was up to some political skullduggery designed to keep Catholics and Democrats out of their rights. Nearly every week there was recorded some new villainy on his part, and my view of my native town was colored for years by these bitter battles. For bitter they were. What goes on in Ulster today seems more comprehensible to me because of the tenacious feuding imported to this peaceful prairie from the Old World. Even the dogs were Catholic or Protestant. On a Saturday my brother would take Rover, cross the tracks to the south side, and there take on all comers, whether curs or Catholics, in epic battle. Few of us, however, were really personal enemies.

One of my most abhorred duties as a young girl was "to meet the trains." There were trains in those days, two of them, the Milwaukee and the Rock Island, two each way, each day. When everyone else in the office was too busy, I had to do this chore. "Meeting the train" meant walking to the depot, going up to each person who bought a ticket and inquiring who he was, where he was going, and why. An ally and helper, a great icebreaker, was Rover's successor, Old Shep. He was a stray that had learned to be a station beggar until he adopted us. But he still met the trains, spotted everyone who appeared to be carrying a lunch and, though a big dog, sat up on his hind legs before his victims and tried to look underfed. He usually got something and so did I—many a handout I would not otherwise have had the courage to ask for.

Another ally, truly unexpected, was the train meeter of the rival paper, a middle-aged man, who out of pure pity for my shyness often handed over gratis some of his own garnerings. After that I was never able really to believe that all Democrats and Catholics, one and the same thing of course, were children of mischief. Still, any exception to the rule was rare and change came to Ioway very slowly. After I had become a schoolteacher, I overheard at a club meeting one middle-aged woman whisper to another behind her hand in the tone of one relating a shocking scandal about another person present, "You know, she's a Democrat."

On the other hand, one of my Ulsterite father's best friends was a priest, who for years on their wedding anniversary, sent my parents a gift of silver, a spoon, a cold meat fork, a ladle. I do not remember him, but his name was that of a friend in our house for years.

Later I came to see that probably my father hadn't minded as much as the rest of the family did, For he was Irish too, an Orangeman, and though he wanted to be sure he was on the right, the moral, side of a controversy, the fact remained that he loved a fight for its own sake. It was not so nice for his daughters. In spite of an occasional détente, there were many times when we hated to go out in public or to be seen on the streets. We yearned for the day when we could go to college and become teachers, somewhere, anywhere except at home. It never occurred to us or to anyone else that we could do anything except teach. What else could a nice girl do? She filled in the time between high school or college and marriage by teaching—for pin money, for funds for filling a hope chest, or simply for something to do. One difference for us was no hope chests. In our family it was not expected that we would marry, for only one man in the world was fit to marry, our mother had married him, and it followed logically that we would do nothing so morally equivocal as to marry at all. The teaching itself with a few notable exceptions was not really very important to anyone, the students, the teacher herself, the community. About all that was required of her was "to keep order in the classroom."

I remember vividly some of the women who toured the state campaigning for women's suffrage. Strange creatures, they seemed to me. Normally a woman's public appearances were confined to reading in mincing, ladylike tones a "paper" to her social club. But these women stood up and talked straight out as though they didn't even realize they were women. Since my parents were strong believers in votes for women, one or two of these campaigners were our houseguests, and we heard many anecdotes of their adventures that we would not have heard in a public meeting. They laughed about them, but they were bruised; the obscene remarks made to them on the streets; the filthy places in which they sometimes had to stay, collapsing country hotels patronized chiefly by bedbugs, hamlets with no hotel at all where they stayed in some private home and got revolting food to eat. One told of having to swallow for breakfast eggs boiled (it was washday) in the same boiler in which the family's clothes were simmering; the stern disapproval of most of the men and the timid reluctance of most of the women to say what they really felt. How proud I was when my mother stood up at a meeting in the county courthouse and spoke for five minutes on the issue. Of course, she was a university graduate and had been a teacher. What could you expect from such ruined females?

The day my mother went to the polls and cast her first ballot was a prideful occasion. She voted, no protest, exactly as my father "suggested" to her. And when I cast my first vote as a college senior, my father saw to it that I received an absentee ballot and a list of "suggestions" about various candidates. It never occurred to me or my father that there was anything out of the way about this manner of exercising one's citizenship. After all, what did I know about politics? I had been taking courses in history and government, but all that was theory. The thing was to know the candidates. This sort of thing occurred long after my fundamental attitudes had been fixed in childhood.

For us, young females, the world was a place governed by taboos. The stern Calvinist morality we inherited from one side amalgamated with a late Victorian gentility in a way that produced some pretty potent forbiddings. The taboo was usually related to sex, of course. Anything a girl did that in any way resembled what a boy or man did was taboo. Looking back, I can understand some of these forbiddings; others seem totally incomprehensible.

Taboo: A girl must not part her hair on the side. Boys wore theirs that way.

Taboo: Everybody knew about the bad end to which whistling girls came. In some quarters, it was no joke.

Taboo: Legs didn't even get mentioned. Before leaving for church on a Sunday morning, each of us was stood up in front of the east door through which the summer sun sent stabbings of light. If there was the slightest sign of a shadow, back we went to put on another petticoat. I have worn as many as five. I used to entertain myself in church by imagining all those buttons simultaneously bursting off and all those petticoats descending in starched white heaps to the floor. They were fun to iron, too, with "sadirons" (no object was ever more accurately named) heated on a coal-burning range. Shirts for three men. Petticoats for four women—each petticoat with a flounce, each flounce with a ruffle, each ruffle with embroidered or lace trimming consisting of two or three rows of "insertion" and a final lace frill.

Summer or winter, females wore hats in the house of God; St. Paul said they had to. My hair was tied with a ribbon at the top of my head. The stiff crown of the hat pressed hard on the ribbon knot, held by an elastic under the chin, well-chewed in an effort to loosen it a little. The result was that I spent nearly every Sunday afternoon lying in the hammock nauseated with headache and making occasional dashes for the porch railing.

Taboo: Card playing. Whenever cards were mentioned my mother saw the Devil, horns, hooves, and tail complete.

Taboo: Dancing. There were whispered tales of dissolute girls who checked their corsets in the cloakrooms at the public dance halls in order to "enjoy as much sensual pleasure from the dancing as possible."

Taboo: Looking into the open doors of a blacksmith shop as you went by.

Taboo: Walking on any street where there was a saloon.

Taboo: Walking by the horse doctor's office or the livery stable.

Taboo: Scraping your feet on the sidewalk. I got mud on my shoes one day, and when I tried to scrape it off on the sidewalk the elders with me fairly snarled reproof.

Taboo: Walking close to a business place in basement quarters. You were to take to the outer edge of the sidewalk lest some lascivious male might look up and be filled with glee to discover that you had legs.

Taboo: Owning a dog. No nice girl had a dog of her own. The family dog was all right, but as a piece of personal property the dog was taboo, especially if it was a female. The owner might as well advertise her profession.

The sheer irrationality of most of these notions not surprisingly led before too many years had passed to the so-called revolt of youth.

Actually, there was little for any young person to do, even those not reared in so austere a regime as ours. There was a lake, weedy, muddy, and scummy, but it had several small islands, one, our favorite, about the size of a haystack, good for picnicking. Later the lower end of the lake was dredged and became a favorite playground for many. Naturally no fastidious person would go into the water. After all, who knew what was going on down there under the surface? It couldn't be for nothing that those prickly wool swimsuits sold in the stores carried the label, "Urine rots wool." We could go in far up the lake, the undredged part, where some of our farming friends had houses close to shore. But the first time I tried it I came out covered with leeches. I nearly screamed myself into spasms while my country friend matter-of-factly plucked them off one by one, leaving me streaming a pale mixture of blood and water. Eventually the town made a park, its trees still baby-sized, and put in a tennis court and some swings. The park was little used for a while. Tennis, like that other foreign game, golf, or pasture pool as we called it, was for effete foreigners like the remittance men. We had the true bumpkin mentality. Whatever was outside our limited experience was bound to be either wicked or ludicrous.

The high school had a football team, but athletics were certainly not overemphasized in the schools. I never saw a gymnasium until I went to college. Once in a while we were made to stand between the rows of classroom desks and wave our arms and bend our knees and feel silly. This was called calisthenics and happened only occasionally. What we did get was a core of required courses and a very few electives: four years of English, four of history or civics, four of mathematics, and a language, Latin or German (until the First World War when French patriotically replaced German). I had a remarkable Latin teacher as a result of whose influence I studied Latin for four years and went on to another four in college. I had another reason to be grateful to her. Girls were required to take domestic science (no one called it home economics) in the seventh, eighth, and ninth grades. I loathed it so much that in the seventh and eighth grades I never would have passed if my teacher, who roomed next door to us, had not taken pity on me and finished my aprons and nighties herself. Now as I entered high school I swallowed my fear of the formidable Latin teacher-principal and begged off the domestic science requirement. There was sympathy in her soul someplace, for she let me take courses in physiology and "physical geography" instead. Perhaps she, like me, was a feminist in the cradle. It did not take me long to observe that taboos applied to girls more frequently and more firmly than to boys. The son was able to escape. His sisters could not. We were in effect incarcerated. Therefore I hated being a girl.

Before I had ever seen or heard of a penis, I envied boys. Freud, I knew when I read him years later, was wrong altogether about the envy of the female for the male. I envied males because their very existence conditioned and controlled mine. Femaleness was a condition of innate inferiority. When I once confided to our family doctor that I, too, would like to become a doctor when I grew up, he laughed his booming laugh. "Ha, ha. A hen Medic!" Clearly, an obviously absurd idea. I gave it up on the spot.

What it came down to was this. A female was both inferior and for some unknown reason obscene. The best thing a girl could do was to pretend she didn't exist. Her best strategy was silence and a poker face.

Even girls reared in a more lenient pattern than ours had no greater freedom of choice. Teach. Be a stenographer. Be a nurse. Even nursing was suspect. I heard a mother telling her daughter just what kind of duties she as a nurse would be expected to perform for male patients. "And nine times out of ten the man for whom she does these things will insult her." A sexual insult then was something only slightly less appalling than rape is now.

My first theatrical experience was a heady trip to the local nickelodeon. What was offered there (fare five cents) was ordinarily deemed trash but this time *The Odyssey* and *The Last Days of Pompeii* were to be shown. These two were considered educational. They proved at least unforgettable; the smoke belching from the upside down ice cream cone of Vesuvius, Scylla thrusting out head one and snatching a Greek, then head two and nabbing another, then, at precise mechanical intervals head three, and the rest. I saw her in dreams for years.

Thirty years later when audiovisual aids were the modish thing in educational circles, my English department, feeling the obligation to be up-to-date, ordered a catalogue, examined it, found there a film of *The Odyssey* (which our classes were at the time reading), sent for the film, showed it. Lo, it was the precise film I had seen as a child at the nickelodeon. I collapsed in mirth and so did all the students. Onward and upward with the arts. The majesty of *The Odyssey* must have stayed with that group forever.

But there were better things in that town.

The town did have aspirations to culture. The women's clubs worked hard and intelligently on worthwhile studies and projects. The men had a weekly debating club characterized by furious differences of opinion. There was an adequate opera house. Maude Adams played there. Schumann-Heink sang. We heard, oh wonder, a major symphony orchestra. There was a lyceum course and, inevitably in a self-respecting town, a chautauqua where we swallowed huge gobbets of culture and were rewarded at the end with a play (always a farce or a melodrama) or a "humorous lecturer." It was William Jennings Bryan and [his speech] "A Cross of Gold" to Strickland Gilliland and "Bibbety, Bob."

The town had two or three highly trained musicians. They shook their heads over the introduction of the phonograph, "canned," machine-made music. They were seers. The opera house soon became a motion picture theater, and no more road companies visited the town. Mothers need worry no longer about their sons hanging around stage doors. Instead they could wonder what they were up to in those Tin Lizzies.

What does growing up mean? I thought at one time that it meant that one had arrived at an immutable view of life and the world. The grown-ups I knew never seemed to change. They had all the answers, the same yesterday, today, and forever. But such a definition of growing up did not apply to a child of the twentieth century. I grew up all over again in each of my three worlds.

That first world of my early childhood was bucolic, idyllic, and, I believed at the time, everlasting. We knew, naturally, that there had been wars and torturers in the past. But those things were relics of ancient evil. They could never happen again. It was still to us, just emerging from childhood, a world of peace.

THE SECOND WORLD: GOPHER PRAIRIE

That child's world abruptly ended with the outbreak of World War I. It almost destroyed those innocent, provincial conceptions of my childhood. But not quite. We still had our faith in our American rightness. Even if the President was a Democrat, we were making the world safe for democracy. Our kind of world would prevail. We were putting a stop forever to that evil anachronism, war.

The war had its compensations, too. Though remote, it was exciting, a kind of melodrama itself with a satanic villain to hate, and dozens of nice songs, sweet or jolly, and grown-up girls marrying soldiers and weeping on the railroad platform as they left.

I remember the end of the war. In the middle of the night a truck manned by loud-voiced citizens with megaphones toured the streets shouting, "Germany has signed the armistice terms. Germany has signed the armistice terms." My father put his head out the window and roared. Then he sped to town to join the dancing, shouting celebration in the streets. We stayed at home. Girls, you know. I still relive my white rage as I lay that night in bed and listened to the revelry afar. Bed in my opinion was no place to spend a night like this one. The next night there was a proper, organized celebration with many speeches and all moral things of that kind. To that we went. And learned again that justice, goodness, and Americanism had triumphed. Our faith had been vindicated. Before too long, however, there would begin an erosion of that faith. Some not too much older than we were already thinking of the world as a place where war was inevitable, and each new war sadder and uglier than the last.

I was, in years, no child by now. Though still in high school, I was aware of fierce controversies and undercurrents of feuds on an international scale that seemed a sad magnification of the feuds and little wars of my hometown. Inside ourselves, little had changed. Therefore war. But external changes came furiously. We found them delightful. The car was the great emancipator of youth. Those brothels on wheels drove our elders crazy though they were as mad about them as their offspring who, if they considered themselves of the intelligentsia, left the prairie behind with all possible speed to live in Greenwich Village. Paris would have been better but next best was the Village where Ioway origins, Iowa itself, could be forgotten or concealed, and the frenzied world of Fitzgerald was the model, with his "gold-hatted, high-bouncing lovers."

But those of us who attended small, midwestern colleges scarcely knew we were living in the Jazz Age. Nor did we know that we belonged to the Lost Generation.

Of the writers of the period, Sinclair Lewis gave us the hardest jolt. There wasn't much resemblance between the way he presented Gopher Prairie and the prairie we thought we knew. That anyone should describe it as a place where "dullness was deified, dullness was God" was at first unthinkable. But the thinking ones thought and many ended by repudiating their childhood, the American past, and America itself. They had grown to a new stage. They were in revolt against war, against the "back to normalcy" of Harding, proud product of the Middle West. Even those of us who stayed in the Middle West didn't want to go back.

We didn't want normalcy, which we now interpreted as Babbittry, and viewed the ordinary American as "Boobus Americanus." For [H. L.] Mencken was our guru. He revealed normalcy to us as an abomination. We went about carrying copies of the *American Mercury* to prove how sophisticated we were though far from Paris where all the sad young men held forth, and Hemingway's Parisian expatriates and roving alcoholics were in reality as alien to us as Fitzgerald's frenetic youth. Actually, Fitzgerald was not as alien as we thought him to be if we had read him right. He blinded us by his glitter. We did not discern that he was writing of the death of the American Dream, that prairie land of innocence from which he too had originally come.

But Boobus Americanus we knew. He lived next door. He was Babbitt, Elmer Gantry, the Rotarian, the booster, the flapper, the campus sheik with his coonskin coat and unbuckled galoshes. Above all, he was a Methodist as were most of us. To Mencken there was something very, very funny about a Methodist. It was startling to learn that we were boobs. Perhaps we were so ready to accept Mencken because we already were feeling that this was not necessarily the best of all possible worlds. In 1931 the tomb of the Unknown Soldier was completed and inscribed.

> Here rests in
> Honored glory
> An American Soldier
> Known but to God.

But the glory and the honor had somehow faded. The war had then been fought for nothing. Prohibition increased lawlessness, the presence of women at the polls failed to produce the purification of politics expected of it. The government was corrupt. You could take your choice: since the dream was gone, you might as well have fun—bounce, bounce, bounce. Or settle down, make a living, make if possible more than a living, get rich. Be a Babbitt.

But that didn't work out either. Our elders had been telling us all along: "Come boom, come bust." And "bust" came. The period between the wars was almost two different eras, boom and bust queerly combined.

In midwestern colleges there had never been much boom. Nor had the mores changed much. Maybe the boys found a jazz age off campus someplace. On campus girls still had to be in at eight o'clock. The doors were locked. One minute's tardiness drew penalties. When it was discovered that fire escapes could provide exit from or to things other than fires, the screens on the escapes were nailed shut. "Better to burn here than hereafter," quipped one faculty member in a committee set up to survey safety conditions on campus.

Many students lived in conditions of incredible poverty. When the banks closed, we thought the end of the world had come. And we could see another war in the making, Instead of an anachronism, war was turning into a chronic condition. Four Freedoms [FDR proposed "Four Freedoms" for all countries in 1941—freedom of speech, freedom of religion, freedom from want, freedom from fear] tried hard to take the place of making the world safe for democracy, but it was a sad war hated even by those who conceded it had to be fought. And if war were a chronic disease, it must be that it proceeded from something in ourselves. Like the creeping horrors I now knew existed under the fair meadow where a praying mantis could teach men lessons in ingenious cruelty, it must be that there was some horror in ourselves. Boobus Americanus was admirable compared to what we now saw ourselves to be.

The night World War II came to an end I happened to be spending in a berth in a sleeping car. I did not sleep. At every station stop, I raised the blind a few inches and peeked out at the sorry little knots of trying-to-celebrate citizens. Before I left home there had been an impromptu gathering to take note of the end of war. It couldn't be called a celebration. It was more like a prayer meeting. I did not go. I felt it just as well not to call God's attention to what we had been up to on this planet if by some good fortune his attention had been fixed on some other part of the universe at the time. The bomb put an end forever to any good I had hoped might come from the war. Not for one moment did I believe those who were saying that this was the ultimate weapon, so hideous that war could never be used again lest we prove T. S. Eliot wrong and end the world with a bang, not a whimper. Sooner or later the bomb would be used. Whenever had men invented some fascinating, lethal toy and refrained from using it? I said a word I wouldn't even have heard in my childhood. The bomb would be used just because we had it.

This was my last growing up. I no longer expected any sort of change that involved a change in persons. I couldn't foresee all the uses of nuclear energy in addition to the bomb. All I saw was Hiroshima.

Now it was not Lewis, not Fitzgerald, not Mencken who came to mind. It was Hemingway. I had thought I hated him for seeing what he thought he saw in bullfights. Now I believed he was right. A bullfight was simply something in us coming out.

He was right, too, about our loneliness. We were not merely a lost generation but a lost humanity. A few "clean, well-lighted places" were to be found where chronic loneliness became more bearable. But loneliness was palpable. Every celebrator on the station platforms looked lonely. In every crowd each looked separate, alone.

486

I recalled the celebrating at the end of the first war. Then we were "we" or had thought so. But this time was different. There was fear and dread and something else. Hemingway had named it. *Nada.* "Some lived in it and never felt it but he [Hemingway's Spanish waiter] knew it was all *nada y pues nada y nada y pues nada y nada.*" Hail nothing. All the lives, all the money, all the destruction. And all for nothing. Hail nothing, the nothing that would always be. A sleeping car is a fine place for not sleeping. "After all," Hemingway's waiter said to himself as he hunted for a bodega, open all night, to take the place of the clean, well-lighted cafe which insisted on closing up, "it is probably only insomnia. Many must have it."

THE THIRD WORLD: TO MAKE A PRAIRIE

My third world is still in the making. It is a world of marvel, of scientific miracles. It still has its moments of glory. When America put a man on the moon, I wanted to live forever in order to see what those mighty machines and mighty men of science would discover as they started gadding about the universe. "One giant leap for mankind." Except for one thing. Something science could not provide. We are all insomniacs. And worse than insomnia is *nada.* Old people complain of loneliness. Young ones say, "I can't find myself. I just can't, you know, get my head together, you know. What's the use of it all, you know?" Hail nothing. Such feelings set many to rummaging about in old religions or new cults. But perhaps for the old, the best that could be hoped was a clean, well-lighted place that stayed open all night and an always available game of bingo. And for the young a commune, a gang, a new monasticism, a gulping materialism.

The earth, too, suffered. Polluted air, polluted water, whole species of animals disappearing forever. In their place emptiness. Ioway was gone, Iowa going, the black earth disappearing under concrete, a whole farm swallowed by every cloverleaf on a new four-lane highway.

Now every bit of the prairie that had seemed so endless to Trinket, Rover, and three children in the back seat of a surrey was something to cherish. Old bits of surviving prairie were hunted out, restored, and new ones made.

Perhaps it was recoverable after all—that feeling I had had in childhood that I, the meadow, the woodlands, were all one. But from now on, I knew, we would have to make our own prairie.

Prairie

> To make a prairie it
> takes a clover and one bee,
> One clover and a bee

And revery.
The revery alone will do
If bees are few.
        —Emily Dickinson

Insomnia must give way to revery. But we must understand Emily. The revery alone will do only if it restores what I had thought as a child that the prairie was: a fair meadow of peace inside and outside ourselves. To have peace within oneself—that would be to be grown-up. To have it outside ourselves—there may be a chance if the world can learn the meaning of revery of Emily's sort. If it can, the revery alone will do. But the revery we must have.

From Prairie City, Iowa: Three Seasons at Home (1979)

Douglas Bauer

Douglas Bauer has made a reputation for himself as one of the most successful contemporary Iowa writers. Born and raised on a farm near Prairie City in Jasper County, he was educated at Drake University and, once graduated, worked as an editor at Playboy *magazine and has since been a contributor to the* New York Times Magazine, Sports Illustrated, Esquire, *and* Harper's, *among others. Bauer excels when writing about Iowa, as his novel* The Book of Famous Iowans *(1997) and his book-length work of creative nonfiction,* Prairie City, Iowa, *attest. Forever caught between the mobile world of the writer and the down-to-earth confines of the farmer's son, a topic he addresses in the anthology* Black Earth and Ivory Tower, *Bauer writes here of his ambivalence at leaving the farm for college and of his complicated feelings upon his return to the farm as a successful editor and writer in the late 1970s. The passage following is composed of two discrete clips from* Prairie City *separated by an extra line space. The first comes from the prologue, "Leaving"; the second from the section entitled "Autumn."*

I left Prairie City in the fall of 1963, dressed in tie and sports jacket, sweltering in a full September heat, for the beckoning uncertainty of higher education. I was tremulous with fear, sensing as I rode with my parents away from the farm, chauffeured like a mourner in the back seat, that all my days in Prairie City had prepared me for nothing more than the narrow continuation of life as I'd known it on this remote piece of earth. Throughout my final year of high school, I'd considered colleges, but even at the beginning of the term, with the reality of leaving still months distant, I could not imagine a campus more than a hundred miles away. The University of Iowa was out there, to the east, but its size suggested a swarming, impenetrable population, and I dismissed it. Leaving the state for school was an alternative I did not consider even in passing.

My cowardice was aided by Prairie City's location in the smooth center of Iowa. For 150 miles in every direction, there was nothing but more of Iowa. No nearby borders afforded quick trips into another state. No matter that Iowa's neighbors only duplicated its inexorable prairie; at the state line, there would have been at least a crossing into a place with another name, provably different.

Not so in Prairie City, where everyone endured a geographic quarantine. I did not leave Iowa at all until I was sixteen years old, when, with fellow Young Methodists, I rode a chartered bus east to view the vistas and tombstones of Washington. In a tightly scheduled week, our group paid ten minutes of homage to every conceivable spot of patriotic interest. And what impressed me most were those spectrally lighted pedestrian tunnels that transported us magically from one side of the Pennsylvania Turnpike—traffic whispering violently overhead as we scurried through—to a Howard Johnson's restaurant on the other, where one could order sandwiches filled with something other than beef, costing nearly a dollar.

So the world was vague and dangerous and I instinctively reduced its radius. Drake University, where I finally enrolled, was in Des Moines, twenty miles away, at the edge of the earth. As I rode that day toward college, my parents chatting aimlessly to try to ease my silent gloom in the back seat, there rose in me a seizing desire to stay; stay forever in the strong grip of this clean and certain life, asking no more from the rest of my days than its unelaborated demands.

My father's farm expresses well the essence of him. It's some of the state's best land, on a flat, narrow ridge that the topographer would represent with a southeast line between the parallel meanderings of the Des Moines and the Skunk Rivers, safe from floods and perfectly sloped for draining rains. (He loves the story of an old man in town, gullible to the wildest story, who was told that the highway bordering the south end of our farm was flooded after a hard rain. The old man repeated it, eyes wild with catastrophe, to everyone he met on the streets. "If that road was flooded," my father laughs, "all central Iowa would be under water.") He inherited its advantages, but has immaculately maintained them, taking no risks with the way he's used his land. His machinery has been adequate for the work and well cared for, perhaps a size smaller than would have been convenient, and a couple of sizes smaller than the latest models.

I have recognized his need for security only since I've been back and have seen the adventurous drive of other farmers. I'm not ashamed of his unfashionable timidity, his hesitant ambition, his rejection of conventional greed.

He's reached an enormously difficult time. Nearing sixty, he knows that the farm will soon be hard on him; on the longest days, it already is. Since Grandma's death, the farm is his and his sister's, my Aunt B. They equally divided its 140 acres, and in order to own 80, the historical denominator, he must buy land from her. "If I had just an eighty," he's said, almost wistfully, "I could really take care of it, work it right, by myself, and come out about as good as I am now." Yet the idea of taking on debt at his age touches Depression-raised fears.

From the small back porch, my father and I survey the fields and soundlessly share his preoccupation. Finally, he gives words to it. "I could just sell the whole thing, too," he says. "A fella could live pretty well off the interest. I tell ya, you see what they're getting for land, it makes you stop and think." Temptation has come as close as a neighboring farm. From where we sit, looking straight south and across the highway that was flooded in the lie, we can see 70 acres generally considered nearly as rich as my father's; they were sold a few weeks ago for $2340 an acre.

"Man!" Dad says, and exhales loudly, as if to relieve himself of the pressure from all that money across the road. As when anyone else speaks of local land prices, his voice fills with an almost fearful wonder. He recites a litany of purchases that the town apparently regarded as unsurpassable foolishness when they occurred. "Everybody thought T was crazy when he paid five hundred an acre for the Lamson place, and that was only ten years or so ago. And then everybody said S was completely out of his mind when he paid fifteen hundred for the Carter place, and that was just a few years back. I said then, I just didn't see how a man could farm that back out of a place. I still don't. Now it's up to twenty-three forty, and they say it's not a corporation, either, just some guy down around Monroe with a lot of land and wanting more."

We sit for several minutes, thinking of this major decision that has come at a point in his life when he assumed all his hardest choices would have been made long before. He turns and says to me, "What do *you* think I should do?" With that sentence, he has laid himself open and vulnerable to me, has drawn me past all parental guises into the intimacy of one man exposing his humanness to another. Immediately, in some defense, I suppose, I move the moment back an entire generation, to him and his father. By the time I was old enough to share any of the work, my father was clearly making the daily decisions regarding fields that should be tilled, with what instruments, and by whom; and Grandpa easily followed them. In my mind, I've drawn their life lines many times and have imagined that seismic moment when they crossed, when authority passed from father to son; and I've only guessed at the measureless ambivalence of feeling that must have been involved. Now, fully unprepared, I'm sitting with my father and he's asked me into his hardest problem, and I begin to understand that the exchange comes gradually, in delicate steps, and that we've taken one.

But it's surprised me. I want to remind him that I'm here to claim my own feelings about the farm, and so I'm carrying some very selfish notions that wish the place left undisturbed. I want to say that I've seen some rootlessness in the past few years, and felt some also, and while there may be a lot of money just waiting for him, if he wants that, he now has something else—a piece of the planet with a consistent and unfinished history.

And when I try all that out on myself, it sounds easy and lofty, the sort of thing a spectator to a problem would say.

"I don't know, Dad…it's up to you and Mom. I don't want to tell you what to do." I look at him, expecting to see my failure on his face.

"I know," he says softly, but he makes no effort to free me from our new equality. "I was just wondering what you thought. It's hard. All I know for sure is, this is the last year I'll farm Byrdie's place. It's too much for me, by myself. I said the same thing last year, but a fella gets a little greedy, I guess. All the years.…I get a statement from the bank every year that shows what I'm worth. And for years it was in the red. And then you see it go a little bit in the black, and now, in the last few years, it's been way in the black, and you just hate to give any of it up."

"Sure," I say, and find something easy: "But if you're too tired from making it to enjoy any of it…" I'm still trying to get back to that safe place beneath his fatherhood, and I conjure us together on the tractor when I was quite young. I was driving, the steering wheel big as a tire in my hands, and he was standing behind me on the hitch, but seemed all around me, body and arms, blocking the sun, and I felt tucked into him. I was fighting the tractor, and losing, as it hopped up out of the furrow again and again, and in a sharp turn jumped completely free, like a derailed train. At last he gave up on me and, without warning, angrily jerked the wheel with my hands still squeezing it, jerked me, also, and I felt in his takeover the strength required to keep the tractor in.

"Did you ever think what would have happened if I'd been interested in farming, and any good at it?" I ask. He looks at me quizzically.

"I mean, it would have changed your life, too. You might have felt like you had to get more land, get bigger."

He understands now, and says, "That's right. And it would have been a problem. I see it happening all over. I was talkin' just the other day with Harley Lammons. He asked me if I wanted to sell some ground. His boy wants to farm, and he's looking for some to get him started. He said, 'I've tried to talk him out of it. I told him, it ain't great, ya know. But it's all he wants to do.'"

"No, I never really minded that you weren't interested, 'cause I never really loved farming, myself. My problem with farming is I've never been able to just settle in and accept the conditions. Always wanted things ideal. A wet spring'd drive me crazy. I'd worry I'd never get in the fields. A dry spring would drive me crazy, too. 'Why plant, if it's gonna be a drought?'

"But farming was the safest thing to do, and it's worked out for the best, financially. Otherwise, I'd just be workin' for a wage somewhere and I couldn't stand that."

I try to see him in that way, a man whose working life was beholden to something smaller than nature, and can't. I've already seen his subservience to his part-time factory job—worrying about some extra minutes that spilled over from a half-hour lunch break—and can imagine that anxiety magnified by forty years.

Mother joins us from the kitchen. I realize that I have less to learn from her than from Dad. She and I have an almost extrasensory kinship, picking up each other on a wordless spiritual register. And yet, we've talked more than Dad and I have, often disagreeing. But such confrontations leave an inimitable closeness.

"You guys ready for dinner?" she asks, and then sits with us, while her marvelous cooking steams inside the house. She specializes in what I call "Iowa soul food": creamed chicken over baking-powder biscuits, ham and soup beans with corn bread, beef stew, and fried chicken served with the Western world's definitive potato salad, rich with eggs and mustard and mayonnaise. I've often told her that if she would move that menu, with her fruit pies, to Chicago, find a North Side storefront and do it over in a kind of early Willa Cather, she'd have the beautiful people lining the sidewalks of Clark Street.

Her presence on the porch completes us, a circle coming closed, and activates a soothing, almost mirthful warmth in me. This is the deep, effortless pull I've not felt from the town, and perhaps I should not have expected to. This is my center, and I find it now, as always, in this big white house. I sit very still, so as not to disturb it, and wonder if the ease with which I've been able to find it throughout my life has in some way ill-served me. I've been content with the center and paid no attention to what feeds it—the farm, the business of it and the way it works, the people in town on whom the farm and my parents depend.

"You never know how many's going to show up over there," Dad says of the factory's transient workforce. "There were four guys there today. Makes a fella curious to go to work, just to see who left town during the night."

"If they'd pay decent wages, they'd get some people in there who might work and stay," Mom says.

I agree, and am pleased within the wholesome inanity of a family sharing its day. I feel the adhesion in the act, and a comfort that stays through most of the meal. Then it begins to fade as a small and dreadful hallucination I've fought off a few times works its way in. It is the premonition that something tragic is going to occur while I'm in Prairie City. And, more than that, it's the fear that, after being away for a dozen years and coming back now expressly to put the coming months on paper, my parents will oblige me in the most unfathomable way; that one of them will die while I'm home. From behind my fear, I watch their mouths moving.

From **Broken Heartland: The Rise of America's Rural Ghetto (1990)**

Osha Gray Davidson

Journalist and author Osha Gray Davidson grew up in Iowa and lived for many years in Iowa City, but his subject here is Mechanicsville, in Cedar County, a good forty-five-minute drive north and east of the University of Iowa. With a population historically hovering around 1000, McVille, as its residents sometime call it, is a little town with big import. A key player in Iowa's famous Cow Wars of the Great Depression and the subject of a 2004 feature in The Iowan *magazine entitled "Above Main: Iowa's New Urbanist Inroads," the town has often been viewed as a litmus test for the condition of agrarian Iowa in particular, and rural America in general. Mechanicsville, as its name suggests, is also important for another reason—cars; Main Street runs directly atop what was once called "America's Main Street", a U.S. Highway 30 that became the nation's first transcontinental highway. In this excerpt, a reprinting of chapter one from* Broken Heartland, *"Decline and Denial," Davidson turns to his journalistic skills and reporterly sensitivity to troubled times suffered in a proud town. In fact, two of the businesses mentioned prominently in the article that follows—Jim Cook's hardware store and the restaurant Village Inn—have long since closed their doors.*

Mechanicsville, Iowa—This handsome town is much like any of the thousands of rural communities dotting the gently rolling hills of the midwestern prairie. Built along a narrow, mile-long ridge rising out of open land in eastern Iowa, the town of slightly over 1,000 residents stands above unbroken fields of corn and soybeans like a ship at sea. The old-fashioned water tower at the center of town together with the augers and grain silos clustered around the nearby Farm Service Center reach into the midwestern sky like masts and rigging. The fields surrounding Mechanicsville do, in fact, resemble an ocean—especially in the summer when the wind blows hard from the south, stirring the corn into waves that race to the horizon.

While there is no mistaking the fact that Mechanicsville is essentially a farm community, with its roots deep into the land, few people living within the town limits actually farm. Residents work at a variety of jobs, mostly low-skill, low-wage jobs in Mechanicsville or in one of the surrounding communities.

At 10:30 on a chilly Monday morning in spring, the town's business district, a two-block area of turn-of-the-century red brick buildings, is nearly deserted. A solitary car sits outside the post office, its motor running while the owner is inside picking up his mail. Across the street, a trio of beat-up pickup trucks are

494

parked in front of the Village Inn, the downtown's one remaining cafe. Inside, four elderly men in seed-corn hats play pinochle at the bar while another group of men sit around a table drinking black coffee and telling me about their town.

Jim Cook, owner of the local hardware store, is the obvious leader of this last group. Cook is a World War II veteran with a shaggy mane of gray hair, a salt-and-pepper, pencil-thin mustache, and a handshake you're not meant to forget. He is a diehard conservative, a supporter of President Ronald Reagan from back when Reagan was still governor of California—that is, when it really meant something to be a Reagan man.

Over the next two hours Cook dominates the discussion, talking up the town's school system, volunteer fire department, and the principles that made Mechanicsville great: hard work, thrift, simple living, and, most of all, community pride.

"We want to show everybody else that we can do it better than they can," he says with a smile that shows he has no doubts about Mechanicsville's ability to always come out on top.

In the same firm tones, Cook ticks off the major evils of the day: greedy farmers, back-stabbing politicians, welfare mothers who "keep right on having kids," and people who don't shop locally. The two other men at the table exchange a quick glance over their coffee cups when Cook mentions this last ill. The issue of "buying local" is one of the town's sore points, especially with Cook, a topic that can escalate from hard words to threats of a fist fight in seconds.

The issue surfaced recently after Cook asked a local farmer why he made all his large hardware purchases 30 miles away in the city of Cedar Rapids instead of buying local at Cook's store.

"I'm really sorry," the man told Cook, "but they sell cheaper over there. I can't afford to shop at your store."

Cook said nothing. He just stared the man down and walked away. A week later the same farmer came into Cook's hardware store to buy two bolts—a purchase of about a dollar.

"Sorry," Cook told the man without a smile when the farmer laid the bolts on the counter at the cash register. "You'll have to drive over to Cedar Rapids for them. You can't buy them here."

The farmer thought Cook was joking. He wasn't. The man left the store threatening to pop Cook one in the nose and later sent his son in to buy the bolts.

"'Course, I wouldn't sell them to him either," says Cook mildly, and takes a sip of coffee.

Cook demands even more of himself. He once wanted to buy a bed but found nothing at the local furniture store that quite suited him, so he drove over to Cedar Rapids, found the bed he wanted, and went back to order it locally. The owner of the store said he wasn't interested in ordering anything other than what he had in stock. Cook tried everything he could think of to get the man to order the bed, but he wouldn't do it. But Jim Cook does not give in that easily. He called the company that distributed the bed, pretending to be the owner of the furniture store across the street from his own business. When the bed was delivered there, Cook went over and paid for it, including a healthy retail mark-up.

Throughout our conversation, Cook jumps at any suggestion that his town is anything other than a vital, thriving village. When one of the other men at the table recalls the time when every building in town had a business going and observes that "it was a very prosperous place back then," Cook leans forward in his chair and directs his words with cold precision at the man who has just spoken: "It is still."

The other man, an ex-farmer now in his seventies, blushes and fumbles for words. "Oh, sure…that's right. She still is. She's a prosperous place."

The most that Cook will allow is that there have been some problems lately.

"Sure, we may be seeing some troubles due to the downturn in the farm economy," he says, "but nothing different from anywhere else. Look, we've been through this before, during the Great Depression. We've been here for 150 years and we've always gotten through. And we'll get through now."

With that, the interview ends. Cook has to get back to his store, and I have other interviews. We shake hands and I promise to stop by his hardware store on my way out of town.

A few hours later, interviews completed, I go to say good-bye to Cook. His store turns out to be a combination hardware–kitchen appliance–gun shop. Back behind the crock pots and hammers is a long glass case packed with guns and ammunition. Blue steel pistols and chrome-plated six-shooters lie behind the glass; dozens of rifles line the walls. The store is modern on the inside, which is surprising because of the building's saloon-style brick and wood front, the kind you rarely see except in Hollywood westerns.

"Oh, I remodel every now and then," explains Cook. "You have to if you want to stay in business for 110 years like we have. My dad bought the place in the summer of 1926, but it's been a hardware store since 1876. 'Course, a lot of new places in cities are remodeling to make them look like they're 110 years old. That's 'in' now. But I get sick and tired of that old-fashioned look. You've got to keep moving forward."

We're standing by the cash register still talking when an old man walks slowly in, nods to Cook, and heads for the greeting-card section.

"You should talk to Everett Ferguson," Cook says, nodding in the direction of the old man. "He's 90-something, still lives in the house he was born in. Hey, Everett," Cook calls out. "Talk to this guy. He wants to know about Mechanicsville."

I walk over and introduce myself. Ferguson is a small man, dressed in a plain green shirt that is buttoned to the top and a gray sports coat. His narrow face is surprisingly smooth, as if he has outlasted even his wrinkles, but his hands look as if they were made of wax paper that had been crumpled into a ball and then smoothed out, leaving a fine network of sharp creases.

"Everett," calls Cook, "tell him what's happening to Mechanicsville."

Ferguson doesn't say anything for some time. He stares at me through thick-lensed glasses that make his eyes appear large and liquid. I begin to wonder if he heard Cook, or, if he did, if he's capable of answering coherently.

Finally, just as I've decided that Everett Ferguson is lost in the mists of age, he answers in a voice that is slow and surprisingly deep. "What's happening to Mechanicsville?" he asks with a scorn reserved for those who ask the obvious. "It's dying."

The words seem to hang in the air. I hear Cook suck in his breath as if about to say something, and I turn to face him. Cook is standing silently at the cash register, one hand on the counter, the other in his sweater pocket. He looks out the store's large front window to where the late-afternoon sunlight cascades down the facade of an empty building across the street. His face is empty, too; suddenly gone is the mask of belligerent optimism, replaced by a new face—or a new mask—this one of studied indifference. It is as if he hadn't heard Ferguson, as if he were alone, waiting out the last few minutes until closing time in the store his father bought back in the summer of 1926.

The similarity of the prairie to an ocean (which is something of a paradox, since the Midwest is about as far as you can get from an ocean in this country) was noted immediately by the earliest white explorers and settlers who christened the region the Inland Sea. Judging from their diaries and letters, it was not so much the wave-like motion of the prairie grasses that inspired the name, but rather the emotions stirred in the settlers when confronted by something so vast it hinted at the infinite.

"I had the feeling that the world was left behind, that we had got over the edge of it, and were outside man's jurisdiction," wrote novelist Willa Cather. "This was the complete dome of heaven, all there was. Between that earth and that sky I felt erased, blotted out.... That is happiness, to be dissolved into something complete and great."

Many of the early Europeans didn't find the experience of dissolution quite so idyllic. Some, in fact, were terrified by the dimensions of the open land—a quarter of a billion acres of shimmering, chest-high grasses stretching from Illinois west to what is now Kansas, and from the Dakotas south through Oklahoma and into Texas.

"Wherever a man stands he is surrounded by the sky," wrote the stunned diarist of the conquistador Coronado in 1541, as the party of Spanish explorers huddled around the campfire on the Kansas prairie. Bewildered by the scale of the land, the group stayed only long enough to satisfy themselves that there were no "cities of gold" to be found and then hurried back to New Spain, where the vistas were more manageable.

Mechanicsville's first residents were neither as enamored by the prairie as Cather nor as frightened by it as Coronado's group. They were a hard-headed, pragmatic, nose-to-the-grindstone conglomeration of German, Scandinavian, and Scotch-Irish pioneers who drifted into the territory west of the Mississippi River in the mid-1800s. They came from both the Yankee East and the deep South to form a new society of farmers and shopkeepers whose values, culture, and even dialect showed the influence of the two strains.

The Southerners brought with them a high regard for generosity and liberty combined with an almost visceral distrust of authority. That last trait has always been particularly strong in this area. In 1931, when the government began testing all dairy cows in Iowa for tuberculosis, scores of armed area farmers vowed to shoot the first son-of-a-bitch to touch a Cedar County cow. The National Guard had to be called in to protect the veterinarians.

"Not that we thought it was a bad idea to test for TB," recalled a local farmer who was a teenager during the Cow War. "In fact, most everybody thought it was a good idea. We just didn't like being told we had to do it."

Mechanicsville's residents could be as ornery with private officials as they were with public authorities. The town once had a railroad depot on the south edge of town that serviced 12 trains a day—one every two hours around the clock. In November of 1867, a spark from a passing train landed on the wooden-shingled depot roof, setting it on fire. Because many townspeople felt the railroad hadn't been very helpful hauling firewood a few winters before, they decided to pay the railroad back. People rushed down to the depot and instead of helping to put the fire out, they stood happily by, watching the building burn to the ground.

But these attributes have always been tempered by a Southern respect for hospitality and good manners—attributes that are characterized in Iowans by a tendency to politeness that often borders on the absurd. When 1988 Democratic vice-presidential candidate Lloyd Bentsen received a few scattered boos from the crowd at the Iowa State Fair, a campaign spokesperson noticed that the catcalls were more subdued than at other stops. "In Iowa, even the hecklers are pretty polite," he observed.

The Yankees added respect for education, dedication to hard work, and a stern puritanical morality. A foreign visitor dubbed the resulting Midwestern amalgam "the most American part of America." That observation was echoed during the 1988 presidential caucus when a visiting Italian journalist called the small-town Iowans he encountered "the original Americans, as if preserved in amber."

A visitor traveling through Mechanicsville today would probably agree with that assessment. From the straight, tree-shaded streets, with their large old houses and sprawling wraparound porches, down to the neatly trimmed front lawns edged with rows of petunias, the town looks as if it belongs to an earlier era. For generations, Mechanicsville has remained the knot tying together the lives of the farm families who till the rich black earth in this small piece of America's Heartland. They went to school here and shopped in the modest downtown. They socialized here, attending dances at the American Legion Hall and softball games at the dusty field by the railroad tracks. They were married here at one of the three churches (Catholic, Presbyterian, and Methodist), and on anniversaries they feasted on steak and potatoes at the restaurant Our Place. When the nearby farm couples grew old, they passed their farms down to their children and moved to town. And when at last they died, usually at home among family and friends, they returned to the earth here, buried beneath the prairie grasses in the Rose Hill Cemetery on the west edge of town.

Like most small towns, Mechanicsville always had trouble holding onto its young. Many felt stifled here, their possibilities too limited, the pace of life too slow. And so every year one or two of these ambitious young men and women left for the bright lights of Des Moines or the even brighter ones of Chicago, Minneapolis, St. Louis, or beyond. But many remained, settled into small-town life, and raised families. In fact, over one-quarter of Mechanicsville's residents have lived in the area for more than forty years; nearly 80% have lived there for at least a decade.

Jim Cook was one of those who stayed. "When I got out of the service," he recalls, "people said, 'What the hell you come back here for?' I looked them right in the eye and said, 'I've been every place I could be, and Mechanicsville is no different from the rest of them. It's just as good as Carmel, California, or Timbuktu. Everyone of them has their faults, and if I'm going to have faults, it's going to be with the people I know. That's why I came home: because it's home.'"

That longing for a community that is "home," the need to feel part of a group that is larger than a family but more embraceable than a nation, is a familiar theme throughout American social history. Since the earliest days of settlement, rural communities have satisfied that desire by playing a wide variety of roles. "It is the community that cushions pain, the community that provides a context for intimacy, the community that represents morality and serves as the repository for old traditions," observes sociologist Kai Erikson.

Life in the tightly knit rural community of Mechanicsville has always been profoundly different from that found just thirty miles away in Cedar Rapids, with a population of around 100,000. The main difference between the two is that while most Mechanicsville residents have always been essentially united— whatever factors happened to divide them—in Cedar Rapids, residents have always been essentially divided—whatever factors happened to unite them.

Eleanor Anstey, a professor of social work at the University of Iowa, recalls an incident from her high school days on an Iowa farm that for her sums up this experience of life in a rural community: "I telephoned the local flower store for lilies, but they said they were sold out. Suddenly, a voice on the party line said, 'Oh, I've got some nice ones you can have, Eleanor.' It wouldn't have occurred to you to feel that your privacy was violated."

Of course, it is easy to idealize small towns such as Mechanicsville, to forget the schisms, economic and social, that *do* exist there. It's easy, too, to ignore the currents of racism and anti-Semitism that run just below the surface, currents that appear in crude but relatively harmless jokes—or in far uglier ways in hard times. And one needn't be African-American or Jewish to feel shunned in a small town; the Yankee inheritance of puritanism allows for little deviation of any kind. For example, a woman who chooses to pursue a career while her husband stays home to raise their children can expect little support from the community for such a decision.

Besides, not everyone appreciates the kind of intimacy a small town provides. A 1981 survey revealed that almost half of Mechanicsville residents felt their neighbors interfered in their business too often. But 90% of respondents also believed their neighbors would help out in an emergency, and for most, the trade-off was worth it. For all the drawbacks to small-town life, that sense of belonging to a caring community is what Heartland towns like Mechanicsville have always provided their residents.

But today that is changing. Small towns are in trouble. Strictly speaking, Mechanicsville and the thousands of rural communities like it are not dying, as Everett Ferguson put it. To use the term "dying" in this way at once overstates and understates the problem faced by small-town residents.

It overstates the problem, in literal terms, because most rural communities will survive—at least they will have residents and so will remain on the map for decades. But in many ways, the situation would be less dire if the towns simply folded up and the residents moved away. Instead, formerly healthy, mostly middle-class communities throughout the Midwest, the small towns that have given the area its distinctive character since its settlement, are being transformed into rural ghettos—pockets of poverty, unemployment, violence, and despair that are becoming more and more isolated from the rest of the country. As the coastal economies have boomed, the Heartland has collapsed. "The most American part of America" is fast becoming "America's Third World."

The dimensions of the problem are sobering. Between 54 and 60 million rural Americans, one-quarter of the country's population, are touched by the decline. Over 9 million people now live in poverty in America's rural areas. In Iowa, the hardest hit of all midwestern states, one out of six individuals falls below the federal poverty line, and in some counties the poverty rate approaches 30%. With an irony that is especially bitter in this region, the nation's breadbasket, hunger has become a common problem.

"We've seen a steady and continuing increase in the need for food in the past five years," says Karen Ford, director of Food Bank of Iowa, which supplies donated food to two hundred food pantries and nonprofit agencies throughout the state.

As the economy stagnates, manufacturers layoff workers or shut down completely. Hospitals, banks, and businesses close. Depression, suicides, and child-abuse rates grow. The need for foster care rises to an unmanageable level as families break up under the pressure of poverty. Towns compete for factories paying poverty-level wages. Mass migrations become commonplace. Local governments cannot afford the most basic services.

"People talk about the middle class being in jeopardy in Iowa, but that's inaccurate," says University of Iowa economist David Swenson. "A significant portion of the state is already out of the middle class. The notion of upward mobility in Iowa is gone."

It is ironic that the victims of this blight, the inhabitants of the new rural ghettos, have always been the most blindly patriotic of Americans, the keepers of the American dream. Their response to any criticism of America was summed up in the bumper sticker that was once common around here: AMERICA, LOVE IT OR LEAVE IT. That patriotic decal can still be seen on pickup trucks throughout the Heartland, but today it competes with another bumper sticker that reads: SHIT HAPPENS.

The speed with which the recent decline hit rural America has made the problem even more difficult for Midwesterners to deal with. Iowans, especially rural Iowans, are well known for their resistance to quick changes of any kind. A retired farmer once told me that his father was the first person in the area to try raising soybeans back in the early part of this century, when corn was the undisputed king.

"It probably took quite a while to catch on," I remarked.

"Oh, no," he assured me. "Why, some of the neighbors were giving the new crop a try just six or seven years later."

And so the reaction to the decline over the last few years has been, as usual, to wait it out—to endure. But this catastrophe is not like a period of drought that can be outlasted. Whatever recoveries may temporarily come this way, short of more structural changes in our economy and government, the rural problem is here to stay. According to a study prepared for the U.S. Congress's Joint Economic Committee, "Iowa could become the State that the Nation leaves behind."

Despite the magnitude of the problem, the disintegration of rural America is largely an invisible crisis. Driving along Interstate 80—the way most outsiders see the state—you would never guess anything is wrong. From that narrow corridor you drive for hours passing fields of corn and beans that cover the horizon in lines as straight as a table's edge. Giant tractors or combines crisscross the land, planting in the spring, cultivating or spraying in the summer, harvesting in the fall. Everything you see speaks of abundance and prosperity.

Even for those few adventuresome souls who pull off the interstate and head into small farm towns like Mechanicsville, appearances are deceiving. The disaster that is sweeping through the Midwest is not like a tornado or a flood that leaves a trail of rubble and twisted-up cars in its path. (For this reason the rural crisis makes for poor film footage and so doesn't rate a spot on the nightly news.)

But if you look carefully at downtown Mechanicsville, you will notice that although the buildings still stand, a majority of them stand empty. At one time the town had as many as thirty Main Street businesses. There were two feed stores, two farm implement dealers, two hotels, two clothing stores. Also a pharmacy, a jewelry store, a soda fountain, a shoe store, an opera house, a pool hall, a bakery, a butcher shop, and a produce market. Today none of these remain.

Kathy Lehrman and her husband Kelvin bought the local paper, the *Pioneer Herald*, in 1979. In the spring of 1986 she stood outside her downtown office looking across the street at a row of empty storefronts.

"I don't know what's going to happen here," she confided. "In the past six months we've lost ten businesses in the three towns we cover. Maybe somebody ought to come in, buy the whole downtown, and just tear it all down."

One month later, the *Pioneer Herald* office was also dark. The Lehrmans had sold the paper to a chain and were looking to try their luck somewhere else.

"People are hoping for things to get better," says 49-year-old Steve Seehusen, who runs a combination real estate firm and insurance agency from an office in what used to be a bank (until it closed in the Great Depression). "These are hard times. We used to sell houses as fast as they came on the market. Right now I've got seven houses listed, and they're just sitting there."

Even with homes that sold for $45,000 just a few years ago now selling for $25,000, there are no takers. "So many things are out of our control," says Seehusen dolefully.

The creation of rural ghettos is a complex process, and despite the rapid changes of the last decade it has been evolving over several generations for reasons that are less than obvious. To understand the decline in America's Heartland we have to start, with the well-known but little-understood event associated with it: the farm crisis.

"What Is a Weed?" (1991)

Aldo Leopold

Born and raised in Burlington, Iowa, Aldo Leopold is regarded by many as the most influential conservationist of the twentieth century—a claim supported by the more than two million copies sold to date of his classic book, A Sand-County Almanac (1949). Leopold absorbed his famous land ethic in the timeless way of many Iowa boys and girls—romping around the home state's woods, prairies, and backwaters. That thoroughly Iowan experience led Leopold to pursue a degree in forestry at Yale University, and upon graduation, to accept a position in the newly created U.S. Forest Service in Arizona and New Mexico. Leopold would ultimately be transferred back to his native Midwest, where his experience restoring and reforesting a worn-out farm would lead to A Sand-County Almanac. The essay that follows, "What is a Weed?" was drafted in 1943, but published only in 1991, hence its chronological positioning here. The author first penned the article primarily as a review of a book on weeds then published by the Iowa Geological Society, but turned it into a persuasive piece, rife with satire, exposing our ecological scapegoating. The essay, likely withheld from publication out of respect for the environmentalist's more conservative agricultural colleagues according to Eric Freyfogle and J. Baird Callicott—the editors of For the Health of the Land (1999), wherein this article previously appeared—contains a blank space of several lines that Leopold never completed.

To live in harmony with plants is, or should be, the ideal of good agriculture. To call every plant a weed which cannot be fed to livestock or people is, I fear, the actual practice of agricultural colleges. I am led to this baleful conclusion by a recent perusal of *The Weed Flora of Iowa*, [*The Weed Flora of Iowa*, Bulletin No. 4, Iowa Geological Survey, 1926] one of the authoritative works on the identification and control of weed pests.

"Weeds do an enormous damage to the crops of Iowa" is the opening sentence of the book. Granted. "The need of a volume dealing with weeds...has long been felt by the public schools." I hope this is true. But among the weeds with which the public schools feel need of dealing are the following:

Black-eyed Susan (*Rudbeckia hirta*) "succumbs readily to cultivation."

A model weed!

Partridge pea (*Cassia chamaecrista*) "grows on clay banks and sandy fields," where it may be "readily destroyed by cutting."

504

The inference is that even clay banks must be kept clean of useless blooms. Nothing is said of the outstanding value of this plant as a wildlife food, or of its nitrogen-fixing function.

> Flowering spurge (*Euphorbia corollata*) is "common in gravelly soils" and "difficult to exterminate. To eradicate this plant the ground should be given a shallow plowing and the root-stocks exposed to the sun."

Nothing is said of the wisdom of plowing gravelly soils at all, or of the fact that this spurge belonged to the prairie flora, and is one of the few common relics of Iowa's prairie years. Presumably the public schools are not interested in this.

> Prairie goldenrod (*Solidago rigida*), which "though often a very troublesome weed in pastures, is easily killed by cultivation."

The locality troubled this uncommon and lovely goldenrod is indeed exceptional. The University of Wisconsin Arboretum, in order to provide its botany classes with a few specimens to look at, had to propagate this relic of the prairie flora in a nursery. On my own farm it was extinct, so I hand-planted two specimens, and take pride in the fact that they have reproduced half a dozen new clumps.

> Horsemint (*Monarda mollis*). "This weed is easily exterminated by cultivation," and "should not be allowed to produce seeds."

During an Iowa July, human courage, likewise, might easily be exterminated but for the heartening color-masses and fragrance of this common (and as far as I know) harmless survivor of the prairie days.

> Ironweed (*Veronia baldwinii*) is "frequently a troublesome weed, but it is usually not difficult to exterminate in cultivated fields."

It would be difficult to exterminate from my mind the August landscape in which I took my first hunting trip, trailing after my father. The dried-up cowtracks in the black muck of an Iowa bottomland looked to me like small chasms, and the purple-topped ironweeds like tall trees. Presumably there are still schoolchildren who might have the same impressions, despite indoctrination by the agricultural authority.

> Peppermint (*Mentha piperita*). "This plant is frequently found along brooks. The effectual means of killing is to clear the ground of the root-stocks by digging."

One is moved to ask whether, in Iowa, nothing useless has the right to grow along brooks. Indeed why not abolish the brook, which wastes many acres of otherwise useful farm land.

Water pepper (*Polygonum hydropiper*) is "not very troublesome…
except in low places. Fields that are badly infested should be
plowed and drained."

No one can deny that this is a weed, albeit a pretty one. But even after drainage, would not some annual, and perhaps a more troublesome one, follow every plowing? Has Iowa repealed the plant succession? It is also of interest to note that the Iowa wildlife research unit finds *Polygonum hydropiper* to be [Several notes of blank space appear here in the manuscript, Ed.]

Wild rose (*Rosa pratincola*). "This weed often persists," as a relic
of the original prairie flora, "in grain fields of northern Iowa.
Thorough cultivation for a few seasons will, however, usually
destroy the weed."

No comment.

Blue vervain (*Verbena hastate*) and hoary vervain (*V. stricta*). The
vervains, admittedly weedy, are "easily destroyed by cultivation"
and are "frequent in pastures," but nothing is said about why
they are frequent.

The obvious reasons are soil depletion and overgrazing. To tell this plain ecological fact to farmers and schoolchildren would seem proper in an authoritative volume on weed control.

Chicory (*Cichorium intybus*) "is not often seen in good farming
districts except as a wayside weed. Individual plants may be
destroyed by close cutting and applying salt to the root in hot
dry weather.

Schoolchildren might also be reminded that during the hot dry weather this tough immigrant is the only member of the botanical melting pot courageous enough to decorate with ethereal blue the worst mistakes of realtors and engineers.

If the spirit and attitude of *The Weed Flora of Iowa* were peculiar to one book or one state, I would hardly feel impelled to challenge it. This publication is, however, only one sample of a powerful propaganda, conducted by many farming states, often with the aid of federal subsidy, and including not only publications but also weed laws and specialized extension workers. That such a propaganda is necessary to protect agriculture is, I think, obvious to all who have ever contended with a serious plant pest. What I challenge is not the propaganda, but the false premises which seem to be common to this and all other efforts to combat plant or animal pests.

The first false premise is that every wild species occasionally harmful to agriculture is, by reason of that fact, to be blacklisted for general persecution. It is ironic that agricultural science is now finding that some of the "worst" weed species perform useful or even indispensable functions. Thus the hated ragweed and the seemingly worthless horseweed are found to prepare the soil, by some still mysterious alchemy, for high-quality, high-yield tobacco crops. Preliminary fallowing with these weeds is now recommended to farmers. [Here Leopold footnotes the article titled "Tobacco Following Bare and Natural Weed Fallow and Pure Stand of Certain Weeds" by Lunn, Brown, and McMurtrey, Jr. as it appeared in the *Journal of Agricultural Research* 59, No. 11 (1939), pp. 829-846, Ed.]

The second false premise is the emphasis on weed control, as against weed prevention. It is obvious that most weed problems arise from overgrazing, soil exhaustion, and needless disturbance of more advanced successional stages, and that prevention of these misuses is the core of the problem. Yet they are seldom mentioned in weed literature.

These same false premises characterize public predator control. Because too many cougars or wolves were incompatible with livestock, it was assumed that no wolves our cougars would be ideal for livestock. But the scourge of deer and elk which followed their removal on many ranges has simply transferred the role of pest from carnivore to herbivore. Thus we forget that no species is inherently a pest, and any species may become one.

The same false premises characterize rodent control. Overgrazing is probably the basic cause of some or most outbreaks of range rodents, the rodents thriving on the weeds which replace the weakened grasses. This relationship is still conjectural, and it is significant that no rodent-control agency has, to my knowledge, started any research to verify or refute it. Still if it is true, we may poison rodents till doomsday without effecting a cure. The only cure is range-restoration.

The same false premises beset the hawk and owl question. Originally rated as all "bad," their early defenders sought to remedy the situation by reclassifying part of them as "good." Hawk-haters, and gunners with a trigger-itch, have had lots of fun throwing this fallacy back in our faces. We should have been better off to assert, in the first place, that good and bad are attributes of numbers, not of species; that hawks and owls are members of the native fauna, and as such are entitled to share the land with us; that no man has the moral right to kill them except when sustaining injury.

It seems to me that both agriculture and conservation are in the process of inner conflict. Each has an ecological school of land-use, and what I may call an "iron heel" school. If it be a fact that the former is the truer, then both have a common problem of constructing an ecological land-practice. Thus, and not otherwise, will one cease to contradict the other. Thus, and not otherwise, will either prosper in the long run.

FROM OUT OF THIS WORLD: A WOMAN'S LIFE AMONG THE AMISH (1995)

MARY SWANDER

A Distinguished Professor of Liberal Arts and Sciences at Iowa State University, Mary Swander is as Iowa as they come, her roots in the state dating back to Irish great-grandparents who homesteaded her native Carroll County. In a 1994 interview with Iowa Woman, *Swander commented, echoing many Iowa writers before her, "When I came back to Iowa, I think I finally realized that my subject matter was here right now." As a writer, she has lived out that maxim, reflecting on the Hawkeye State in several volumes of poetry, including her most recent,* The Girls on the Roof *(2009) and in previous prose publications and productions, including her cowritten musical* Dear Iowa *(1991), her coedited nonfiction collection* The Land of Fragile Giants *(1994), and in several individual essays in collections of place, including* A Place of Sense *(1988),* Townships *(1992) and* Iowa: A Celebration of Land, People, and Purpose *(1995). Swander's most popular book about Iowa, recently reissued by the University of Iowa Press, is* Out of This World, *which carried the subtitle "A Woman's Life Among the Amish" when first released in hardcover in 1995. The revised subtitle: "A Journey of Healing" is perhaps a better encapsulation of its gist, as the book traces the path by which Swander moved to Kalona, Iowa, to a converted old schoolhouse (Fairview School) among the Amish to battle Environmental Illness through renewed self-sufficiency and purity of living. The passage that follows, the chapter entitled "To Plant from Branches," finds the author both attracted and repulsed by the demands of the new life awaiting her. In it, she praises Iowa for its healing power and chastens the state for its sometime high-handedness in accommodating illness and disability.*

The spring when I was thirty-three, I paid Johnny the neighbor boy a quarter for every frog he could catch. The amphibians arrived on my porch in coffee cans, Kermits squiggling, croaking, and hopping against the round metal sides. Inside my house, quickly and as painlessly as I knew how, I smashed the frog's head with a hammer, cut off its legs, and broiled them for dinner. Johnny laughed when I wrapped my hand around the frog's neck and readied it for execution.

"Ooh, look at its eyes bug out!"

I trembled and gripped the hammer hard. Johnny thought this all great fun and more profitable than a paper route. I found it repulsive but cheaper than spending twelve dollars every week on the delicacy.

Why so much trouble for frog legs? I desperately needed them, not for gourmet pleasure but for survival, as they were one of the few safe foods I could tolerate in the early days of my Environmental Illness. Since I'd also become sensitive to chemicals, most of that first year was spent in my house isolated from people with their cigars and cigarettes, their scented, formaldehyde-based lotions, their hair sprays and colognes, which gave me raging headaches and crippling, double-over stomach pains. I avoided going anywhere where I might come into contact with moldy basements, new carpet and its glue fumes, fresh varnish or paint, fresh tar, gasoline or diesel exhaust, insect or yard sprays with their 2-4D, office machines with their inks and alcohols.

After a long confining winter, a spring frog gig became one of my first ventures into the outside world. Before I struck my deal with Johnny, I tried to catch the amphibians myself.

"No big deal," a fisherman had told me. "You just dangle a little piece of red cloth over their heads on the end of a pole. They jump for it and you've got 'em."

Seemed easy enough, so one cool, wet evening, pole and flashlight in my backseat, I ventured out of my house and drove to my friend Peggy's farm. We waded toward the squishy edge of her pond, pushing away the shoulder-high weeds, our sneakers, covered with stick-tights, sinking into the mud. Frogs sang and jumped through the reeds. Slowly, deliberately, I inched toward them with my pole, a tiny piece of a bandanna stuck to the fishhook. But just when I got in position, the crunch of a bur oak sapling gave me away, and the frogs fell mute, diving down into the depths of the algae-filmed water, fanning out for safer ground.

"Hey, they're over here now." Peggy waved on the other side of the pond. I trudged in her direction, the sun fading, the mosquitoes buzzing and bombing my ears. I tried again, crouching in the weeds, my pole shooting out over the bank. Peggy stood ready with the flashlight in hopes of stunning the frogs into submission with its glow. But the creatures only fell silent and eluded us. I moved again and again, until the darkness engulfed us and my line became bound up, tangled in a willow branch, and we finally had to cut off the hook to free it from the leaves. At last, we groped our way back to Peggy's farmhouse, laughing and croaking our own frog imitations.

"Rivet, rivet," we called, giggling at our failure, joking and telling fish stories until I found my way to my car.

"Well, no frogs for you tonight. You'll just have to eat lobster," Peggy cracked.

I pulled out of the lane and headed home, leaving Peggy on her front porch still with tears in her eyes from the fun, then nosed through the dark night, tears streaming down my face in frustration and rage. Suddenly, nothing was funny.

Emotionally that spring, I became both predator and prey.

While "on the hunt," I felt like one of those frogs, operating at some base level, completely on instinct, displaying raw, gut reactions. If something poked me one place, my whole being retracted, drew in. If something poked me another place, I'd gather up all my strength and leap away. My days were spent hopping from one task to another, searching out, preserving, and cooking my organic foods, fighting my insurance company, trying to keep my therapeutic massage practice going to make enough money to pay for air, water, and furnace filters, drops, drugs, and vitamins, special clothes, bedding, and soaps. I felt the constant presence of a human inching toward me, a creature who might lift me out of the pond and gobble me up. I stroked through the water, trying to keep just a few inches ahead of my descent into the great beyond.

I plunged through the stages of grief, swimming from one to another in a matter of weeks. At first, I was stunned by what had happened to me and couldn't visualize my future life without Christmas dinner, or ever again tasting a single bite of bread. I raged against smokers, who kept almost every public building, site, or private home inaccessible to me. I sank into despair when I opened my closet door and realized I'd have to give away most of my clothes and rid my house of any synthetics. I made a bargain with God to keep me alive long enough to complete my new book of poems. I was ashamed my affliction was so big and such an inconvenience to others.

"I'm sorry to have to ask," I said, "but when you come to my house, could you not wear perfume?"

I was ashamed my affliction was so small. How could I complain when I still had a roof over my head and could get up and down the stairs alone? Finally, I accepted my problem and buckled down to gig frogs. What I never did was deny my illness nor its seriousness. I didn't have to. Everyone else did that for me.

Most disabled people fight to let the able-bodied world know that they are not their disability, that they are capable of normal activities and functioning. I wanted the able-bodied to grasp that I was different, very different, and couldn't "function normally," couldn't eat, sleep, dress, work, or socialize the same way they did. I tried to get my point across, but couldn't. Even most traditional M.D.s deny Environmental Illness exists, and explain it away as "depression." So, how was the layperson going to understand? I was locked inside myself, and grew to resent even the majority, the supportive people who tried to understand.

When my hands became crippled and I had to close my therapeutic massage business, friends and even other disabled urged me to go underground with my condition. "Don't tell them you're ill," they said as I set off for job interviews. "Just sign the contract." The advice, as wise as it may have been at the time, made me crazy. Even if I had wanted to pass as able-bodied, I couldn't. I couldn't work in an air-tight building. I couldn't attend smoke-filled meetings seated next to perfumed colleagues. I couldn't travel to conferences. I couldn't "do lunch."

I couldn't get anybody to get it. I applied for disability compensation and was turned down because they didn't have a code number for Environmental Illness in their books. I went to Social Services for help to pay for my prescription drugs and was advised to emigrate to a country with socialized medicine. I joined support groups, but no one had ever heard of a situation like mine. I read through women's health literature, and even in books like *Our Bodies, Ourselves* couldn't find one line on EI—an illness whose population is 90 percent female. I subscribed to magazines for the disabled, but never saw a single article addressing autoimmune diseases. I took my accessibility problem to my city's Disability Rights Commission, and was waved away with a laugh and shrug.

I went on TV to fight my insurance company to pay my hospital bill. I sued the doctor who had given me the vaccine overdose, and couldn't get my own lawyer to understand I couldn't fly a thousand miles on a smoky plane to a highly polluted city for a deposition. I contacted my San Francisco specialist, the man who had analyzed the contents of my vaccine and told me I was lucky to be alive, but couldn't get him to testify on my behalf. Then, a month before my trial, I couldn't go on any longer.

I cried for two weeks. Every day, I worked and functioned for three to four hours at a time, then put my head down on my desk and wept. I dug organic carrots out of my garden, washed and juiced them, then ranted at anyone, anything around—the plumber, the dog, the petunia planter—collapsing into bed in a heap. Night after night, I dreamed of chocolate cake, a luscious piece of dessert, deep, rich, and swirled with frosting, on the end of a fork, just about to glide onto my tongue. My watering mouth hung open, the cake approaching ever so closely. I wanted to eat it, how I wanted to jump at the bait, take just one bite of that cake, but knew I didn't dare close my lips around it. I woke wild and weepy. Psychically, I was leveled, back on Peggy's bank on my hands and knees, hunting for sustenance, my fishing line hopelessly wound up in the willow tree. Something had to change. I needed to set myself free from the tangle.

One night, cake poised in front of my face, I said to myself, "This is only a dream. You can forget the frog legs for now and go ahead and eat the dessert." The fork rose to my lips. I hesitated, staring at the chocolate. "That's right, go ahead. This is only a dream. You have permission." My teeth parted. "You'll be all right, really." My mouth closed, encircling the tines. Oh, the sponginess, the delicate texture, sweet taste of the cake against my tongue! I savored the first bite, then taking my time and enormous pleasure in the sight and smell of the dessert, the way it was arranged on the china plate, the gleam of light bouncing off the silver fork drifting down into the frosting, I ate the entire slice.

I woke up smiling, understanding that my life was reality—not a dream—and even if others denied it, I could find a way to live with its consequences more peacefully. After that, in my nighttime fantasies, I gobbled up elegant entrees at the best French restaurants, toured the globe to sample full-course Indian, Bulgarian, and Moroccan dinners with wine, candlelight, linen tablecloths, with violinists serenading, cadres of dancers swirling and twirling past in long, flowing black dresses, clicking castanets. In the morning, my cravings were satisfied, my stomach full.

Then I discovered ways to find satisfaction in my waking state. First, I found my meditative eating method, with yucca. Then within my isolation, I found I had the time and space to read hundreds of books—poetry books, novels, travelogues, natural history narratives about deserts and wetlands, about yucca and frogs. I wrote three more books of my own and learned to build glass-enclosed cases to shelve my books away from dust. Within the confines of my diet, I developed extensive gardening skills, not only branching out into heirloom varieties but experimenting with designs, shapes, and configurations, adding fruit trees, prairie grasses, and flowers to my yard. I learned to distinguish between a black Samson and a prairie coneflower, between a pipevine and an eastern tiger swallowtail butterfly, delighting in the insects' paths as they glide and dip over the wild cherry tree. My world was small but well explored.

And the exploration turned inward.

"What can we list as losses?" my lawyer had asked me before we filed the suit. "You didn't have much income to begin with. You had no spouse, so we can't sue for loss of affection. See, if you could no longer have relations with your husband, we could get money out of that for him."

Once again, I tried to explain to him my circumstances.

"You're condemned to a life of loneliness," he said at last.

"Yes."

"Going to be hard to pitch. You don't have any burn marks or a missing leg. That's what a jury wants to see. There's where you get the big awards."

The big awards, or rewards, I finally discovered were going to come from turning my life sentence around into a life passion. The Bird Man from Alcatraz. The Frog Woman from Iowa. Why not? Loneliness became solitude, with time to sort through the chain of events that had let me to Fairview School. Solitude gave me time away from the noise of the world, the constant croaking of other people's needs and desires, to mourn my losses—even though I had no missing limbs. Then, as if I'd spread myself in a dissecting tray in a high school biology class, I probed and poked at my soul to try to better understand the strengths and weaknesses of my character, the intricacies of my relationships to others, and my connection with my spirituality.

The country roads became my nerve fibers, and up and down the hills, over the gravel, through the old railroad beds I bicycled, building up my strength, observing the exotic environs of my own neighborhood. I raced Amish buggies and whizzed by farmsteads with rag dolls, white and faceless, pinned to the clothesline, tumbling and turning in the wind. Their small owners, barefoot and aproned, tumbled their own turns on the trampoline in their yard, flipping over in somersaults in midair. While my friends showed me slides of their latest trip to Tahiti, their grass hotel hut crammed full of tropical fruit, I showed them slides of Esther Chupp's root cellar, her fifty canning jars of peaches lining the far wall.

When things weren't peachy keen, I learned to confront the gigglers, the eyebrow raisers. "You've never *heard* of Environmental Illness?" I asked. Little by little, I became a more assertive, more political animal, recognizing the ripples that emanate from the plop of my illness in the pond. I had a problem that was part of a much bigger pattern of disregard for our environment, for the invisibly disabled, for women. I began to write letters, editorials, become involved in environmental causes larger than myself.

Within my circle, my individual case became educational.

I've read that frogs are very sensitive to polluted water, and will die from chemical contaminants long before fish in the same pond. Dozens of people have told me that they would never have given a thought to problems like pesticides in the food chain nor indoor air pollution if they hadn't known me. Sure, they understood things on an abstract level, and although they still weren't real certain about the validity of my illness, they began to entertain the thought that there might, just might, be a link between their sudden headache and their new carpet glue fumes.

Daily, my health is improving, the environmental and disability rights movements gaining momentum. Women's physical problems are at least beginning to be discussed. But losing my health has made me question not only the goodness of doctors, but every principle, every custom and mode of behavior I once took for granted. It has made me critical of the whole American way of life, and thrown me back to a more primitive existence. I have enough foods in my diet now that I don't have to eat frog legs, but it would be nice to go down to the local cafe once in a while for pancakes, sausage, and a cup of coffee.

Instead, every spring when the leaves unfurl with their sudden burst of energy, and when tadpoles transform themselves to full-grown adults in just a few short days, I take my breakfast to the pond and eat on the picnic table. Chewing slowly,

I remember the anniversary of my illness, thankful I've seen another year. Above me, the sun shines down, beginning to warm the surfaces of things—my skin, the ground, the ripples in the pond. Next to me, the frogs burrow out of the deep mud where they've hibernated for the winter, hop from log to lily pad, singing out over the water one of their first tunes of the season.

FROM **LOCAL WONDERS: SEASONS IN THE BOHEMIAN ALPS (2002)**

TED KOOSER

Something of a surprise pick for U.S. Poet Laureate in 2004, Ted Kooser, another Iowa Pulitzer Prize-winner, did folks in the home state proud in a tenure marked by greater public exposure to accessible, down-to-earth verse. Born and raised in Ames, Iowa, Kooser's mother's parents hailed from the Mississippi River town of Guttenberg in Clayton County. Kooser writes often of Iowa, both in poetry and prose, most recently in Local Wonders: Seasons in the Bohemian Alps, *which was named* ForeWord *magazine's book of the year and earned the Friends of American Writers Literary Award. Of* Local Wonders, *the publication* Booklist *wrote, "Through his eyes we learn to see, then appreciate, the beauty and grace in everyday miracles, the comfort and sanctity in local wonders." Two parts Nebraska and one part Iowa, the book crosses state lines with ease, as in the excerpts below, collaged from several sections of the book, and including Kooser's inimitable reflections on Iowa's Lincoln Highway, Iowa's rumored role in the Manhattan Project, and Iowa's status as a place called home.*

These late-fall, early-winter days are sometimes so still and sunny that they look like painted backdrops. And this morning, against such a backdrop, sitting in my uncle's recliner, I have been remembering being a little boy during World War II.

I was born in the spring of 1939, when, far beyond the serrated cornfield horizons of Iowa, Eastern Europe was tooth and claw at war. Ames was a peaceable, elm-shaded town, dead center in the continent, and though it would eventually be proven that our fifteen thousand citizens had always been safe from the Axis Powers, we weren't to relax until peace was declared. Though we were never to hear the searing whistles of V-2 rockets or feel the ground-shuddering thumps of falling blockbusters or smell any smoke other than that of our own leaf fires on peaceful October evenings, we had been warned that there was always the possibility we might be attacked from the air by long-range German bombers, and we watched the skies, ready to huddle under the basement stairs when we heard the roar of the Luftwaffe and the blitz came hurtling down.

As the war grew and took America in, I began to grow up among adults descended from immigrants. Although I was much too young to understand it as a boy, this pioneer background influenced the way the older generation behaved. My parents and their neighbors had learned from their forebears to prepare for the worst. A Nazi air attack was just one of many horrible things that might happen to a family along the long, hard, Calvinistic trail to life's end. But years before, in the dark forests of Europe, our ancestors had developed a charm against ill fortune such as we now faced. It was what today's therapists refer to as magical thinking.

For example, when my family prepared to embark upon an excursion, my mother, like her mother and, I suppose, her grandmother and great-grandmother before her, would pause on the front stoop while the rest of us waited in the idling car. Gripping her purse in both hands and blankly staring into the middle distance, she would silently go over all of the awful things that might befall us: (1) we might have a flat tire, and if we did, (2) you never knew who might come along and try to take advantage of you there by the side of the road, or (3) a truck might come along and blow the car off the jack and hurt one of us, and (4) where could medical help be found for someone badly injured, perhaps bleeding to death, there by the road. And so on, down the long bitter litany of potential misfortunes. By listing all those possible horrors, you somehow kept them from happening. "You never know" became a kind of motto, and it could be tailored to the fear of bombing raids.

So the people of Ames, locked in common dread of the possible, stood frozen on their front stoops, staring into space, silently preparing for an attack by the Germans from one direction or the Japanese from the other. You never knew if the camouflaged bombers might be approaching, hidden from view amidst the shining cottonwood fluff that spiraled high over the fields on summer thermals. Though it was reported that German and Japanese submarines had been sighted off the coasts, the danger never came any closer than that. A childhood friend told me recently that he always felt secure during those years because he was certain President Roosevelt lived just up the street from our house, at Roosevelt Elementary School. In fact, he said, he had been told that Sir Winston Churchill has visited the president there.*

Now that we've set aside daylight saving time, it gets dark very early. The world beyond the windows is black by six o'clock.

We had frequent blackouts during the war years, and as my family sat in our darkened bungalow, we could hear the stealthy tread of our fat, moon-faced neighbor, Mr. Posey, as he passed. He was our neighborhood's civil defense observer, and it was his duty to see if any light showed beneath drawn blinds. If he saw any, he would rap sharply on the glass with a short black stick, and the lights inside the chastened house would immediately snap out, as if by magic.

Sometimes I hid behind the Mezvinskys' honeysuckle hedge and watched Mr. Posey waddle past, wearing his Frank Buck white pith helmet that glowed like a lampshade. That spot of white must have presented the only visible bombing target in the darkened town. He was one of those fat men who could move as gracefully as a ballerina, as if he were on silent rollers, and he would emerge from the darkness, float past, and vanish, his Old Spice aftershave perfuming the darkness.

My uncle Tubby was a civil air observer. It was his responsibility to identify the silhouettes of incoming bombers against the sky. The Civil Air Patrol had assigned him a set of hard rubber models of enemy aircraft, wonderfully detailed, to hold over his head and study. I was not permitted to play with them, but I coveted them from a distance. For years I have searched flea markets and antique shops hoping to find just one of these magnificent models, but they have all been rolled into the dark deep hangar of the past.

The Atomic Energy Commission had a laboratory at Iowa State College in Ames, including a mysterious cyclotron that whirled round and round in a low brick building behind a chainlink fence in the woods. I have since learned that the blackouts were intended in part to protect that building and the secret work being done there. Something the engineers and physicists were doing there was connected with the Manhattan Project. When I was a little older, after the war, my friends and I used to hang on the fence trying to see what was going on, absorbing all manner of radiation, I suppose (That, in addition to the radiation I got by sticking my feet in the x-ray machine in the shoe department of my father's store.)*

It's a rainy morning, and I've forsaken the Bohemian Alps to take care of a family errand in Iowa. I'm driving east along a section of the old Lincoln Highway across Marshall County. You know this road, or one just like it—a narrow winding ribbon of concrete, broken up like river ice by some fifty-odd winters of heaving frost and patched in a thousand places by velvety black asphalt that turns so soft in July and August you can pinch up a wad and chew it like Blackjack gum. The tires slap along over the mended seams with the same easy rhythm set up by the wiper blades. A yellow maple leaf the size of a child's hand presses itself to a corner of the windshield.

What used to be U.S. Highway 30 is now, officially, an unnumbered road in the care of the county. Highway 30 is now a new divided four lane a couple miles south. The highway is like a dry wash left by a river that's changed its channel, like a bullsnake skin, spotted black and gray, cast off in the woods to dry up and blow away. Once a week, a county maintenance man drives a yellow pickup slowly along its length, gazing into the ditch as if he were checking his trotlines and hoping that nothing was on them.

Things close in on an old road, but it still knows its way out. Pressing against it and reaching out over it are groves of oak and maple and hickory and box elder. Buckbrush and burrs move up out of the ditches. Grasses bend over it, blurring its edges. But the Lincoln Highway pushes on, like a silver streamliner out of the forties, racing past clusters of fading signs that lean this way and that, reminiscing about long-lost motels and forgotten brands of motor oil.

I pass through State Center, "The Rose Capitol of Iowa." The red of the roses is gone with the summer. Today is a day for a particular yellow, the yellow of a washtub of marigolds in front of a bungalow; the yellow of a school bus—parked and ticking under a dripping tree—its hood still warm beneath red leaves that have just now fallen there; the yellow of SLOW CHILDREN signs. (Inside the school, at their little desks, sit the slow children.)

Taped to the windows of the schoolrooms and to the windows of little clapboard houses along the highway are orange paper jack-o'-lanterns, black cats with raised tails and fiery orange eyes, white skeletons with little silver rivets joining their awkward bones. In front of one old house is a shock of corn, sagging in the rain as if it were made of papier-mâché. A fat pumpkin nestles into its weary skirts.

The windows of many of these houses are warm with the sort of yellow light that fills small kitchens with wooden cupboards that have been painted a hundred times, kitchens with old linoleum turning up along the baseboards, kitchens in which the coffee is on, in which the white porcelain sink is never completely dry to the touch, in which a woman of indefinite age is wiping her hands on her apron or pushing her hair back from her face with her fingertips or holding her hands out before her and looking down upon their veiny backs with mild wonder, as if they were old newspapers she'd just found lying under the honeysuckle bushes. Daydream believer, homecoming queen.

This is the life I have chosen, one in which I can pass by on the outside, looking back in—into a world in static diorama, the world that Edward Hopper seemed to see. Driving east, the globe spins beneath me, the marigold yellow centerline on the old Lincoln Highway like a stripe on a whistling top. State Center rushes into the past, bright yellow leaves flying behind.

"A Great Many Iowans" (2007)

Robert Leonard

Robert Leonard was born in Des Moines in 1954, graduated from Johnston high school in 1972, and earned his undergraduate degree from the University of Northern Iowa (where he was a member of the wrestling squad) in 1977. After an MA and PhD in anthropology from the University of Washington, Seattle, Leonard gave up a promising academic job in New Mexico to return to rural Knoxville, Iowa, with his family. The author of a highly regarded work of creative nonfiction and participatory journalism, Yellow Cab, *as well as dozens of anthropological papers and monographs, Leonard now serves as news director of KNIA/KRLS radio serving Knoxville and Pella, where he hosts the popular radio program "In Depth with Dr. Bob Leonard." During the 2007–2008 presidential primary and caucus season, Leonard kept his listeners well-informed, earning for his small station unlikely interviews with nearly all the major candidates. The essay below, adapted from a piece written for the anthology* Letters to a Young Iowan: Good Sense from the Good Folks of Iowa for Young People Everywhere, *first appeared in 2007. For its length, it is as powerful a distillation of contemporary Iowa as can be found anywhere, and serves as fitting note on which to end.*

I have known a great many Iowans in my day. They include a man who built great sailing ships over a century ago, a homecoming queen with a beautiful smile and polio, a sculptor who uses butter as her medium, a hooker who works the streets of Des Moines because she doesn't believe in welfare, a reformed drunk and truck driver who found God and became Governor and might have been President, a 20-year-old friend who I wish had talked to me before he hung himself in 1974, a 65-year-old woman from Pleasantville who seems 16 when I look into her eyes, a retired merchant marine who changes the world one letter to the editor at a time, an old man in an engineer's cap who makes ropes at county fairs so children can learn the old ways, a man who washes chicken heads down a drain in Waterloo, enough Olympic medalists and All-Americans in wrestling to fill a bus, a cattleman from Oskaloosa who believes that cows belong in green pastures and not feedlots, a mayor who lays awake at night trying to figure out how to bring an ethanol or switchgrass plant to his town, a single mom who home-schools nine kids in a trailer with the guidance of God, a gentle man who loved appaloosas and blew his brains out when his wife left him, a book-loving doctor with four unpublished novels in a drawer at home who will write forever, a woman who teaches children of all ages how to ride bicycles at the state hospital in Woodward, a woman who buys organic produce for HyVee who believes going organic is liberal nonsense, a boy in Ritalin chains, a man on TV with a dog puppet, a philosopher from Sioux City who believes that you and I exist only to serve as background to his own existence, a professor who teaches the world about Neanderthals from Iowa City, a man who chose to study criminology and social work in college after his little sister was murdered when he was 14, a sniper in Vietnam burdened with images that flip through his mind day and night like a slide show, a former wrestler at UNI who teaches cowboy poetry at a university in Arizona, a couple who danced the night away at the Surf Ballroom in Clear Lake the night Buddy Holly, Ritchie Valens, and the Big Bopper crashed and died, that same couple who cried together the next morning, changed forever, a farmer who knew the world had gone to hell when hay bales got too big for one man to lift, a 60ish woman who played half-court girls basketball on the guard side of the court who could still cover Kobe better than half the NBA, a car thief from Keokuk, a concrete salesmen whose face beams when he's told his adopted daughter looks just like him, a girl who pours beer in a small town bar who thinks we don't know that she has a meth problem, a heating and cooling man who collects Corvettes and ex-wives, a young man who chooses to build an elaborate and successful existence for himself on MySpace rather than in the real world, an old carpenter with big knuckles, a gruff demeanor, and a huge heart, a fallen lawyer who picked himself up and found success on the sales floor at the Home Depot in Ames, a young man fighting in Iraq, a gentle and forgiving Lutheran minister who wrote beautiful poetry for us all, and another who took lascivious pleasure in looking down from the pulpit and scolding generations of us for being sinners, a time traveler from the 60s still drinking Boone's Farm wine and smoking ditchweed, a television newswoman so focused on work she lives in a dumpy hotel in Urbandale, a successful restaurateur whose parents came from Mexico fifty years ago to pick sugar beets near Mason City, a successful restaurateur whose parents came from Italy a century ago to mine coal in West Des Moines, a man I suspect murdered his brother, the first black president of a national bar association, five cops who beat a man down with nightsticks in an alley, a man who cheats at cribbage, a trumpeter in the Navy band, and a former priest still saving souls and fighting for you and me and our way of life even as they toss him in jail for protesting, as well as thousands of other Iowans who take what life gives them and then make choices.

Those are some of the thousands of Iowans I have known. I hope that I will know many more. Maybe even you.

Look for love, and when you find it, hold its warm and tender hand in your own, gently.

ACKNOWLEDGEMENTS—

Selection by Clara Hinton is reprinted from "Clara Hinton Dairy" by Clara Hinton (1907). Used with permission of the State Historical Society of Iowa.

"Iowa" by Ruth Suckow is reprinted from *The American Mercury*, 9 (September 1926), 39-45. Used with permission of Barbara Camamo.

Iowa Federation Home Pamphlet by the Iowa Federation Home (1929). Used with permission of the Iowa Women's Archives of the University of Iowa Libraries and the State Historical Society of Iowa.

"A Boyhood in Iowa" copyright © Herbert Hoover (1931). Used with permission of the Herbert Hoover Presidential Library Association.

"Blueboy" by Phil Stong is reprinted from *State Fair*. Copyright © 1932 by Phil Stong. Reprinted with permission of Harold Matson, Inc.

Remembering Laughter by Wallace Stegner. Copyright © 1937 by Wallace Stegner. Copyright renewed © 1965 by Wallace Stegner. Reprinted by permission of Brandt and Hochman Literary Agents, Inc.

"Iowans: The Social Pattern" and "Racial Elements and Folkways" are reprinted from *The WPA Guide to 1930s Iowa by the Federal Writers' Project*. Copyright © 1938 by the State Historical of Iowa. Used with permission of the publisher.

"A Letter from Glenn Miller to Brigadier-General Charles D. Young (1942)" is used with the permission of Steven D. Miller and Jonnie Dee Miller.

"A Letter from Mrs. Alleta Sullivan to the Bureau of Naval Personnel and Response from Franklin D. Roosevelt" (1943) appears from the National Archives and Records Administration <http://www.archives.gov/exhibits/a_people_at_war/war_in_the_pacific/articles_war_in_the_pacific/sullivan_letter.html> <http://www.archives.gov/exhibits/a_people_at_war/war_in_the_pacific/articles_war_in_the_pacific/letter_sullivan_brothers.html>

Selection by J. A. Swisher is reprinted from "The Rise and Fall of Buxton," by J. A. Swisher, *Palimpsest* 26 (June 1945), 179-92. Copyright © 1945. State Historical Society of Iowa. Used with permission of the publisher.

"The Passing of the Prairie Chicken" and "A Yarmouth Saturday Night" is reprinted from *Old Orchard Farm* by Hugh Orchard (1952) with the permission of the University of Iowa Press.

"Iowa" by Paul Engle is reprinted from *Holiday* magazine (1956). Used with permission of Hauling Engle.

Selection by Frank Luther Mott is reprinted from "The Old Printing Office" by Frank Luther Mott, *Palimpsest* 43 (January 1962), 41-61. Copyright © 1962 State Historical Society of Iowa. Used with permission of the publisher.

"Two Letters from an Iowan in Vietnam" (1968) by Frederick O. Phelps. Used with permission of the author and the State Historical Society of Iowa.

"Two Letters from Iowa Social Activists" (1968, 1972) by Ralph and Ruth Scharnau. Used with permission of the authors and the State Historical Society of Iowa.

Selection from James Hearst is reprinted from "We All Worked Together: A Memory of Drought and Depression" by James Hearst, *Palimpsest* 59 (May/June 1978), 66-76. Copyright © 1978 State Historical Society of Iowa. Used with permission of the publisher.

"Three Worlds" by Winifred Van Etten is reprinted from *Growing Up in Iowa*. Copyright © 1978 The Iowa State University Press. Used with permission of Blackwell Publishing (formerly Iowa State University Press).

Selection by Douglas Bauer is adapted and reprinted from *Prairie City, Iowa: Three Seasons at Home*. Copyright © 1979 by Douglas Bauer. Used with the permission of the author and the University of Iowa Press.

Selection by Osha Gray Davidson is reprinted from *Broken Heartland: The Rise of America's Rural Ghetto*. Copyright © 1990 by Osha Gray Davidson. Used with the permission of the author.

Selection by Mary Swander is reprinted from *Out of This World: A Journey of Healing*. Copyright © 1995 by Mary Swander. Used with permission of the author and the University of Iowa Press.

"What Is A Weed?" by Aldo Leopold is reprinted from *For the Health of the Land: Previously Unpublished Essays and Other Writings* (1999). Copyright © 1991. Used with permission of the Aldo Leopold Foundation.

Selection by Ted Kooser is adapted by permission of the author and is reprinted from *Local Wonders: Seasons in the Bohemian Alps* by Ted Kooser and by permission of the University of Nebraska Press. Copyright © 2002 by the University of Nebraska Press.

Selection by Robert Leonard is reprinted under alternate title from *Letters to a Young Iowan: Good Sense from the Good Folks of Iowa for Young People Everywhere*. Copyright © 2007 by Ice Cube Press. Used and adapted with permission of Ice Cube Press and the author.

About the Editor

Zachary Michael Jack is the author or editor of many books, and several on Iowa and featuring Iowans, including *Letters to a Young Iowan: Good Sense from the Good Folks of Iowa for Young People Everywhere* (2007) and, most recently, *Uncle Henry Wallace: Letters to Farm Families* (2008). Zachary was raised on the Mechanicsville, Iowa, Heritage Farm his family settled before the Civil War. A graduate of both Iowa City High School and Iowa State University, he writes often about the intersection of education and place, a topic taken up in his first book, *Black Earth and Ivory Tower: New American Essays from Farm and Classroom* (2005). Prior to his years as a college English professor, he served as a section editor for the Tipton *Conservative* and worked as a children's librarian and bookmobile driver at the Ames Public Library. Zachary has been the keynote or feature speaker at events in celebration of Iowa across the state, from the Iowa Studies Forum in Des Moines, to the Herbert Hoover Presidential Library in West Branch, to the Hearst Center for the Arts in Cedar Falls, and to the Irving B. Weber Chautauqua Series in Iowa City. A regular columnist for the *Iowa Source* and a frequent reviewer for the *Annals of Iowa*, his state-based writing, education and outreach efforts have been featured in the *Des Moines Register*, the *Cedar Rapids Gazette*, the *Iowa City Press-Citizen*, the *Waterloo-Cedar Falls Courier*, and the *Quad City Times*, among others. Zachary teaches courses in writing, rural and urban history, and place studies at North Central College and continues to call home an eastern Iowa farm.

 Ice Cube Books began publishing in 1993 to focus on how to live with the natural world and to better understand how people can best live together in the communities they share and inhabit. Since this time, we've been recognized by a number of well-known writers, including Gary Snyder, Gene Logsdon, Wes Jackson, Patricia Hampl, Greg Brown, Jim Harrison, Annie Dillard, Ken Burns, Kathleen Norris, Janisse Ray, Alison Deming, Richard Rhodes, Michael Pollan, and Barry Lopez. We've published a number of well-known authors as well, including Mary Swander, Jim Heynen, Mary Pipher, Bill Holm, Connie Mutel, John T. Price, Carol Bly, Marvin Bell, Debra Marquart, Ted Kooser, Stephanie Mills, Bill McKibben, and Paul Gruchow. As well, we have won several publishing awards over almost twenty years. Check out our books at our web site, with booksellers, or at museum shops, then discover why we strive to "hear the other side."

Ice Cube Press (est. 1993)
205 N Front Street
North Liberty, Iowa 52317-9302
steve@icecubepress.com
www.icecubepress.com

from high and low, near and far
thanks, hugs, kisses and cheers to
Fenna Marie & Laura Lee

CPSIA information can be obtained at www.ICGtesting.com
Printed in the USA
BVOW08s1216170713

PP5273700001B/1/P